Visible Unity
and the
Ministry of Oversight

Visible Unity and the Ministry of Oversight

The Second Theological Conference
held under the Meissen Agreement
between the Church of England
and the Evangelical Church in Germany

West Wickham, March 1996

CHURCH HOUSE
PUBLISHING

BV
670.2
.V57
1997

Church House Publishing,
Church House,
Great Smith Street,
London SW1P 3NZ

ISBN 0 7151 5755 8

Published in 1997 by Church House Publishing for the Council for Christian Unity of the General Synod of the Church of England

Cover design by Sarah Hopper

Printed in England at the University Printing House, Cambridge

Contents

Contents

Foreword

by the Co-Chairmen of the Meissen Commission

The Meissen Declaration, signed in 1991, was the first agreement ever made between the Church of England and the German Protestant churches. The Common Statement on which it was based recorded an agreement on the goal of unity and ten points of 'agreement in faith', but registered a 'remaining difference' over episcopal succession.

Instead of waiting for agreement on this outstanding issue, the Common Statement recommended that the churches make a Declaration committing them to take all the steps to closer fellowship which were already possible, with a view to advancing 'on the way to full, visible unity'. Within the context of this committed relationship, conferences would be held 'to encourage the reception of the theological consensus and convergence already achieved and to work to resolve the outstanding differences between us'.

Since 1991 the Meissen Commission, which oversees relations between the Church of England and the Evangelical Church in Germany, has sponsored two theological conferences. The first, held in 1995, examined issues raised during the process of approval of the Meissen Declaration by the German churches, in particular concerning the Eucharist. It confirmed that 'there is sufficient agreement among us... to endorse the Meissen decision to enter eucharistic *koinonia*'. This cleared the way for the second conference, held in 1996, to begin work on the outstanding difference over episcopal succession. The Meissen Commission is grateful to the Co-Chairmen of the first two theological conferences, Prof. Dr Ingolf Dalferth and the Rt Revd Dr Rupert Hoare, Bishop of Dudley, for planning and chairing them.

At the second conference, a series of important papers was given by expert speakers on *episkope* (oversight) and episcopacy in the history of our churches and in their current practice, as reflected in their liturgies, their ecclesiastical law and the experience of their bishops. The papers formed the basis of the Conference Report, which maps out an agenda for future discussion. In publishing the papers together with the Report, the Meissen Commission hopes to stimulate discussion within our churches and among our ecumenical partners. We would welcome suggestions that might lead to the achievement of consensus on these issues.

As the papers present and evaluate information about each church's tradition and practice which is often not readily accessible to members of the other church (or even to non-specialists within the church concerned), publication of these papers will, we hope, also perform a service to the academic community and to the wider Church.

Because few people in England are able to read German easily, we are publishing the papers which were delivered in German in English translation as well as in the original language. They were translated by the Commission's Anglican Co-Secretary, Dr Colin Podmore. It has been found most convenient to collect the German-language material together at the end of the volume. By gathering the conference material in a single volume we wish to make these papers accessible to as many readers as possible world-wide.

The Commission commends this book to the members of our churches and to our fellow Christians in other churches for study. It would welcome comments on the Report of the Conference, in the light of the papers delivered. These can be sent to either of our Co-Secretaries – OKR Paul Oppenheim (Kirchenamt der EKD, Postfach 21 02 20, D-30402 Hannover) and Dr Colin Podmore (CCU, Church House, Great Smith Street, London SW1P 3NZ).

HANS CHRISTIAN KNUTH   ✠ MICHAEL WULFRUN:
Bischof Dr Hans Christian Knuth   The Rt Revd Michael Bourke
Bishop for Schleswig   Bishop of Wolverhampton

List of Participants

Church of England

The Rt Revd Dr Rupert Hoare (Bishop of Dudley), *Co-Chairman*

The Revd Prebendary Dr Paul Avis

The Revd Dr Timothy Bradshaw

The Rt Revd Colin Buchanan (now Bishop of Woolwich)

The Revd Dr John Findon

The Very Revd Dr John Moses (Provost of Chelmsford; now Dean of St Paul's)

Augur Pearce, Esq.

The Rt Revd Dr Gordon Roe (Bishop of Huntingdon; now retired)

The Rt Revd Stephen Sykes (Bishop of Ely)

Dr Mary Tanner

The Revd Canon Dr Joy Tetley

Dr Colin Podmore (Secretary)

Evangelical Church in Germany

Prof. Dr Ingolf Dalferth, *Co-Chairman*

Prof. Dr Axel von Campenhausen

Prof. Dr Reinhard Frieling

Prof. Dr Eilert Herms

Prof. Dr Jan Rohls

Bischof Dr Hans Christian Knuth (Bischof für Schleswig)

Prof. Dr Dorothea Wendebourg

OKR Paul Oppenheim (Secretary)

Observers

Mrs Tonie Smith

The Revd Peter Townley

On the Way to Visible Unity: *Episkope* in the History, Theology and Practice of our Churches, and in the Future we Share

The Second Theological Conference held under the Meissen Agreement between the Church of England and the Evangelical Church in Germany

The Emmaus Centre, West Wickham, 17–22 March 1996

REPORT OF THE CONFERENCE

I

1.　The second Meissen Theological Conference of the new series met in the Emmaus Centre, West Wickham, from 17 to 22 March 1996 to study the theme: 'On the Way to Visible Unity: *Episkope* in the History, Theology and Practice of our Churches, and in the Future we Share'. Our particular task was to explore the question whether there are ways of overcoming the unresolved questions relating to the interchangeability of ordained ministries (Meissen, para. 17B (vi)).

2.　It was important that our work was set in the context of regular prayer together, morning and evening, the sharing of the Eucharist according to rites of both our churches, and Bible study every morning.

3.　The following papers were presented to the conference: Ingolf Dalferth, 'Amt und Bischofsamt nach Meissen und Porvoo. Anmerkungen zu einigen ungeklärten Fragen aus evangelischer Sicht'; Dorothea Wendebourg, 'Die Reformation in Deutschland und das Bischofsamt'; John Findon, 'Developments in the Understanding and Practice of Episcopacy in the Church of England'; Jan Rohls, 'Apostolizität, *Episkope* und Sukzession. Die lutherische, reformierte und unierte Tradition'; Mary Tanner, 'The Anglican Position on Apostolic Continuity and Apostolic Succession in the Porvoo Common Statement'; Colin Buchanan, 'Anglican Ordination Rites. A Review'; Ulrich Kühn, 'Das Amt des Bischofs in liturgischen Formularen der Kirchen der EKD'; Augur Pearce, 'The Expression of the Anglican Understanding of *Episkope* in the Law of the Church of

1

England'; Eilert Herms, 'Ausübung und Verständnis der Episkope im Recht der EKD und ihrer Gliedkirchen'; Hans Christian Knuth, 'Die öffentliche Rolle eines nordelbischen Bischofs als Repräsentant der Kirche und in Entscheidungsprozessen. Eine Beschreibung'; Gordon Roe, 'The Public Roles of those exercising Episcopacy in the Church of England'; Axel von Campenhausen, 'Historische Aspekte des evangelischen Bischofsamts vor und nach dem Ende des landesherrlichen Kirchenregiments'; John Moses, 'The Current Exercise of Episcopacy within the Church of England, reflecting on the respective Relations of Church and State'.

4. Although the theme was a very large one, and although it became clear that there were no short or easy answers to the questions surrounding the specific issue of interchangeability, the Conference wishes to record its view that real progress was made in the understanding of each other's history, and in appreciation of the respective positions relating to *episkope*, both in theory and practice, which it hopes may with more work lead to a solution.

5. Of particular significance to our task were the differences set out in Meissen, para. 16, regarding the particular role of the 'historic episcopate' in the matter of the interchangeability of ministers. We started from the agreements set out in The Meissen Common Statement:

   (a) para. 15 (ix): 'that a ministry of pastoral oversight (*episkope*), exercised in personal, collegial and communal ways, is necessary to witness to and safeguard the unity and apostolicity of the Church';

   (b) para. 17A (iv): 'that personal and collegial oversight (*episkope*) is embodied and exercised in our churches in a variety of forms, episcopal and non-episcopal, as a visible sign of the Church's unity and continuity in apostolic life, mission and ministry';[1]

   (c) para. 17A (iii) and 17B (iv): that in each of our churches ministers are lawfully ordained (*rite/legitime vocatus*).[2]

6. In the course of our discussions we found ourselves in agreement on the following points.

7. With regard to the continuity, apostolicity and unity of the Church, the continuity of the Gospel always takes priority. This obliges every Christian to participate in the mission of the Church, within which it is the task of the ordained ministry 'to serve the ministry of the whole people of God'

---

1. Meissen omits 'communal' in this paragraph.
2. *Confessio Augustana 14*; Article XXIII.

(Meissen, para. 15 (viii)), in the public proclamation of the Gospel through word and sacrament. In both our churches there is unbroken continuity of authorized ordination of ministers. While in the Church of England the continuity of the historic episcopate, in terms of the personal succession of bishops, served as a focus of unity, uninterrupted by the changes of the Reformation, the continental reformers found themselves having to choose between the continuity of the Gospel and the existing episcopate, and therefore reformed the exercise of *episkope* in ways which sought to safeguard the priority of the Gospel over any particular form of ministry and *episkope*. In doing this, they referred back to the early patristic model, whereby the *episcopus* was the pastor of the local Christian community.

8. We found that in the actual exercise of *episkope* there are great similarities. *Episkope* is not the task of bishops only, but involves lay people and other synodical structures of the Church. This became especially clear to us when we considered the legal provisions our respective churches have made. But within these structures the personal exercise of *episkope* is an important element in both our churches, and plays a significant role in the presentation of our churches to the general public and to the secular world.

9. We recognized that the Church of England is part of the Anglican Communion and is also committed to the Porvoo Agreement (between the British and Irish Anglican churches and the Nordic and Baltic Lutheran churches) as the Evangelical Church in Germany (EKD) is bound by the Leuenberg Concord. These relationships need to be taken into account, if we want to make progress on the way to visible unity upon which we set out in the Meissen Declaration.

10. We also agreed that in any future theological conference we have to address questions of theological method, as we work at the particular substantial issues.

II

11. In the Meissen Common Statement our churches have committed themselves to 'strive for the "full, visible unity" of the body of Christ on earth' and 'to work for the manifestation of unity at every level' (para. 7).

12. According to the Meissen Common Statement the characteristics of full, visible unity include 'the service of a reconciled, common ministry' and 'bonds of communion', which possess 'personal, collegial, and communal aspects' and which serve as 'outward and visible signs of ... communion' (para. 8).

13.   Having already agreed that together, we now need to clarify what we mean by 'full, visible unity' and how it goes beyond the present relationship between us, in particular:

–   what concrete personal, collegial, and communal forms full, visible unity would require;

–   what the implications of our other ecumenical engagements (e.g. Leuenberg, Porvoo, talks with the Methodist, Orthodox, Roman Catholic churches) for this task are;

–   to what extent diversity of theological interpretation is compatible with common practice, especially regarding a possible future common ministry.

III

14.   We shall also need to discuss further the historical actualities of the apostolicity and continuity both of *episkop*e and of the episcopate in our two churches.

(a)   With reference to *episkope* we shall need to delineate:

(i)   how the necessary functions of *episkope* are carried out, and

(ii)   how each function has its own sign character.

(b)   With reference to *episkope*, we shall need to distinguish appropriate requirements and forms (including personal, collegial and communal), from inappropriate (for example, separation from the whole people of God).

(c)   This discussion of history will provide us with the opportunity to delineate a concrete future hope inspired by memory, and all that holds good for *episkope* will be the ground and criterion for a discussion of the episcopate.

(d)   Again, with reference to the episcopate we shall need to delineate the change and varieties of its historical forms in both our churches, and to what extent the differences are appropriate and healthy and which examples offer us positive models.

(e)   On the basis of the evidence provided in the legal annex it appears that, while the recognition of academic qualifications provides a practical challenge, there are probably no objections of principle on the German side to the unrestricted interchange of ministries. On the English side, however, there are a number of obstacles.

So on the English side it will have to be clarified what further steps would need to be taken (including consideration of the relevant liturgical material and the existing legal obstacles) to accord such recognition to the episcopate of the churches of the EKD as to make possible the unrestricted interchange of ministries.

On the other side, the churches of the EKD should clarify why and in what sense they are ready to regard the Anglican episcopate as an appropriate model. In this way they would make explicit the substantial grounds for their readiness for ministerial interchange.

(f) In the process of this study it would become clearer what structure of unity would be adequate to the unity of the universal Church on earth.

LEGAL ANNEX

INTERCHANGEABILITY OF MINISTERS BETWEEN THE CHURCH OF ENGLAND AND THE MEMBER CHURCHES OF THE EKD – THE PRESENT LEGAL POSITION

We have considered the question of interchangeability both as regards 'altar and pulpit hospitality' to visiting clergy, and as regards the possibility of permanent appointment of the minister of one tradition to a post in the other.

1. In Germany

Following the Meissen Agreement there is presently no legal obstacle to a priest of the Church of England being invited as a visitor to preach or celebrate the sacraments in any of the member churches of the EKD.

The appointment of such a priest, while remaining an Anglican, to a benefice (*Pfarrstelle*) in a member church would require the priest to be recognized as eligible for appointment (*anstellungsfähig*) under the terms of the applicable *Pfarrerdienstgesetz*. The *Pfarrerdienstgesetz* of the *Evangelische Kirche der Union* was available to us at the Conference and the comments below are accordingly based on EKU law. The *Pfarrerdienstgesetze* of the EKU and of the *Vereinigte Evangelisch-Lutherische Kirche Deutschlands* may (on this point) be taken as typical of EKD member churches' law generally.

The *Pfarrerdienstgesetz der EKU (in der Fassung vom 31.5.1991)* provides in relation to those who have not studied in Germany:

> '*Akademisch ausgebildete Theologen aus anderen evangelischen Kirchen und Kirchengemeinschaften können nach angemessener Zurüstung und aufgrund eines Kolloquiums die Anstellungsfähigkeit als Pfarrer erhalten.*' (§5 Abs. 1 Satz 1)

That the Anglican priest needs to be 'suitably equipped' (*angemessen zugerüstet*), presumably in terms of competence in German, understanding of Lutheran/Reformed tradition and structures, etc., is self-evident; also that the appointment should follow an interview (*Kolloquium*) to establish his suitability for appointment in Germany.

More restrictive is the requirement that the priest be an '*akademisch ausgebildete/r Theologe/in*'. This is a matter for assessment by the competent *Kirchenleitung* (§ 2 Abs. 2), and requires German recognition of the sufficiency of English theological training for the ministry of the word. Should recognition be withheld, the priest would have to pass the *Zweite Theologische Prüfung* (§5 Abs. 1 Satz 2).

The applicability of §5 Abs. 1 to Anglican priests also depends on the recognition of the Church of England as an '*andere evangelische Kirche*' for the purposes of the *PfDG*. The term '*evangelisch*' is not defined in the *PfDG*, and certain other legal sources offer definitions (e.g. by specific reference to continental confessional documents) which would not apply to Anglicans. However, there has been at least one judicial decision in the church taxation field suggesting that Anglicans may be taken for legal purposes as *evangelisch*, and particularly after Meissen the likelihood is that this requirement would be taken as satisfied. (If this were not so, amendment of the *PfDG* would be necessary to give full practical effect to the Meissen Agreement.)

Finally, a question may be raised by the existence of 'church treaties' with the German *Länder* under which many EKD member churches have undertaken to appoint to *Pfarrstellen* only persons who have completed three years of study at a German university. Exceptions to such provisions in *Kirchenverträge* have been admitted in the past; the member churches would need to investigate whether a general exception could be allowed that allowed for the full interchangeability envisaged as the goal of the Meissen process.

Axel Freiherr von Campenhausen

C.C. Augur Pearce

2. In England

Most of the legislation and judicial decisions bearing on the subject of the exercise of ministry and on eligibility for preferment in the Church of England date from a period in which section 10 of the Act of Uniformity 1662 confined both preferment and the celebration of the Eucharist to those episcopally ordained. The former restriction is still in force today, the latter was repealed as a statutory provision by the Church of England (Worship and Doctrine) Measure 1976 but remains in Canon B 12 and probably as a common law provision. There is a strong argument that, in the context of the time, 'episcopally ordained' meant 'ordained by a bishop in the historic succession'.

The Overseas and Other Clergy (Ministry and Ordination) Measure 1967 place restrictions on ministry as a priest or deacon in the Church of England by those ordained by 'overseas bishops'. These in turn are defined by being in communion with the Church of England, or at least by consecration in a church having 'recognised and accepted' orders (of which the two Archbishops are to be the judge). At present the bishops, *Präsides* and other ministers of ordination in the EKD are not considered to fall in this category, and the clergy ordained by them cannot therefore be authorized under the Measure to officiate as priests or deacons in England. If they could so officiate apart from the Measure, this would place them in a better position than Old Catholic or American Episcopalian clergy, which could not have been the intention of the legislators in 1967.

The conclusion must be that they cannot officiate as priests or deacons at all, and that the words 'priest', 'deacon', 'ordained', 'holy orders', where appearing in the relevant authorities, must still be taken to imply episcopal ordination in the historic succession. Consequently a German Protestant minister without re-ordination ('GPM') is not a 'clerk in holy orders', cannot satisfy the requirements of, for example, Canon C 10.2 or Canon C 12.2, and can neither be instituted to a benefice nor licensed to exercise a priestly or diaconal ministry in an Anglican parish.

The ministry of a GPM in the Church of England therefore continues to be seen as the ministry (by invitation) of a minister from another denomination. He/she would not be numbered among the clergy for the purposes of parochial church council or synodical membership or representation. He/she could share pastoral care in a team ministry as a 'member of the team', but not the cure of souls as a member of the 'team chapter' (i.e. a team vicar) – Pastoral Measure 1983, s. 20 (1).

As a visiting minister, his/her liturgical ministry may now extend *inter alia* to officiating at Morning and Evening Prayer, preaching and the conduct of funerals. (The approval of the parochial church council, and of the bishop for a long-term arrangement, is required – Canon B 43.1.)

7

The GPM may only baptise or preside at the Eucharist in an Anglican building if Canon B 43.9 is invoked, which covers invitations to members of the other churches (i.e. here, German Protestants) to use the building for *their* worship. If this were done, the service would not be seen as an Anglican one, even though the congregation might attend.

The position is different in a local ecumenical project in three respects:

(1) The bishop may authorize the GPM to baptise, so that such baptisms would then be seen as having taken place in the Church of England – Canon B 44.1(c).

(2) The bishop may authorize regular communion services in the Anglican building, presided over by the GPM, which the Anglican (or mixed) congregation would attend. But the fact of his/her presidency must be published in advance, and the service may not be held out to be an Anglican eucharist – Canon B 44.4(1)(f), 4(3).

(3) The specifically Anglican provision in the area of the local ecumenical project may be reduced, even to the extent that the GPM's services become the congregation's staple diet. But a Eucharist celebrated by an episcopally ordained priest must still be provided at least on the five main festivals – Canon B 44.5.

There is no legal provision under which a bishop (or any other minister) of an EKD member church can confirm or ordain in the Church of England.

C.C. Augur Pearce

West Wickham, March 1996

Ministry and the Office of Bishop According to Meissen and Porvoo: Protestant Remarks about Several Unclarified Questions

Ingolf Dalferth

1. Starting Point and Task

On 29 January 1991 the Meissen Declaration was signed. This not only put the relationship between the Church of England and the Protestant (i.e. Lutheran, Reformed and United) churches of Germany on a new basis, but it was also one of the rare ecumenical events in which the results of theological discussions between churches were received in an orderly process and put into effect in a binding manner. The *Meissen Common Statement* is more than the common statement of a theological commission: it is binding for the churches of both sides and is therefore fundamentally of a different weight than texts such as – to name only a few examples – the Lima report *Baptism, Eucharist and Ministry*, the documents *Lehrverurteilungen – kirchentrennend?* on the Protestant side or *Episcopal Ministry* and *Apostolicity and Succession* on the Anglican side. And that is true – for the time being anyway – also of the Lutheran-Anglican report *'Toward Full Communion' and 'Concordat of Agreement'* and the Porvoo Common Statement *Together in Mission and Ministry**. This difference must be taken note of theologically and hermeneutically during our work. Hermeneutically this means – and I expressly take up this point from our conversations last year in Berlin and the consultation on the Liebfrauenberg deliberately at the beginning – that we may not read or interpret the *Common Statement* in such a way as to contradict or place a question mark against what was expressly declared and signed on 29 January 1991. What was established there is rather the basis which we no longer have to discuss, but from which we have to depart. Included in this in particular are the following points (para. 17 A):[1]

(i)   that both sides are true churches, 'belonging to the One, Holy, Catholic and Apostolic Church of Jesus Christ and truly participating in the apostolic mission of the whole people of God';

(ii)   that 'in our churches the Word of God is authentically preached and the sacraments of baptism and eucharist are duly administered';

(iii)   that our ordained ministries are 'given by God and instruments of his grace'; and

(iv)   that 'personal and collegial oversight (*episkope*) is embodied and exercised in our churches in a variety of forms, episcopal and non-episcopal, as a visible sign of the Church's unity and continuity in apostolic life, mission and ministry'.

That all that is the case in our churches is clearly and unmistakeably mutually acknowledged. It should also not be made into a problem by pointing out that in the English text the passages quoted have only the relatively weak 'acknowledge' and not the strong and legally binding 'recognize'. The German text is quite clear here and, in view of the expressly mentioned rule 'that the English and German texts are equally authentic' (Foreword, footnote), also formally binding. Moreover, the English text speaks in other equally important places expressly about the 'recognition... of churches and ministries' (para. 19) and 'our mutual recognition of one another's ministries' (para. 16). Our conversations must therefore take this recognition as their starting point and everything which we still have to clarify and discuss is subordinate to this fundamental point.

There still remain several things to clarify and discuss, however, since the signing of the Meissen Declaration by no means removed all theological differences. Rather, both sides expressly committed themselves 'to continue official theological conversations between our churches... and to work to resolve the outstanding differences between us' (para. 17 B (i)). Meissen, then, was understood from the outset not as a conclusion, but rather as a significant step on the way to visible unity. Thus the *Common Statement* soberly notes, along with the fundamental agreements achieved, also the points still remaining open, at which within the achieved consensus – i.e. in not fundamental but theologically subordinate questions – differences remained. To work to overcome them is the task of our discussions.

The remaining open points and questions are theologically subordinate – that must indeed now also be stated – because the *'consentire de doctrina evangelii et de administratione sacramentorum'* (CA 7) established in the Meissen Declaration is sufficient for our Protestant side to enter into full church fellowship unreservedly and without qualifications. With the recognition 'that in our churches the Word of God is authentically preached and the sacraments of baptism and eucharist are duly administered' (para. 17 A (iii)) we have established that which according to CA 7 *'ad veram unitatem ecclesiae satis est'*. That is not to say that there must be theological agreement (which can or should be expected in no church) or that all questions touched upon by this must fall among the *'traditiones humanas seu ritus aut ceremonias ab hominibus institutas'* of which it is said that it is not necessary that they '*ubique simile esse*'. Nor does it mean that questions such as those about the Church or the '*ministerium docendi evangelii et porrigendi sacramenta*' are theologically unimportant. It does, however, mean that these questions can only be dealt with correctly in their functional subordination to (and thereby also their differences from) the fundamental features which are church-constituting and thereby also decisive for the completion of church fellowship – the proclamation of the gospel through word and sacrament. Not by chance does Ephesians 4. 4f, which is expressly quoted in CA 7, speak about *one* body, *one* spirit, *one* hope, *one* Lord, *one* faith, *one* baptism and *one* God, but *not* about *one ministry*. To make the completion of full church communion – and concretely that means unreserved communion at the table of our Lord – dependent on this, 'until we have a reconciled, common ministry' (para. 17 B (vii)), is therefore a proviso which from the Protestant point of view is theologically meaningless. Meissen lets there be no doubt that this reservation is on the Anglican not the Protestant side (paras 16, 17 B (vii)). We shall therefore have to clarify why and on what grounds it exists on one side and not on the other, if we want to overcome it together. Since there would be no reservation however, if it did not exist on the Anglican side, I shall above all do my best in what follows to track down the reasons for the Anglican attitude. This will lend a certain one sidedness to my questions and considerations, and I apologize for this in advance, in case I should miss the decisive points or give them insufficient weight. I am counting on your corrections and help, since this is the reason why we have come together for this theological conference.

2. Open Questions in Meissen

That we still do not have a 'reconciled, common ministry' (para. 17 B (vii)) is probably the most important open question in Meissen. At least both sides agree:

–   that 'all members of the Church are called to participate in its apostolic mission', so that one must speak of 'the ministry of the whole people of God', that is demonstrated in the manifold ministries which are 'given by the Holy Spirit' to individuals (para. 15 (viii));

–   that 'within the community of the Church... the ordained ministry of word and sacrament' exists 'to serve the ministry of the whole people';

–   that 'a ministry of pastoral oversight (*episkope*), exercised in personal, collegial and communal ways, is necessary to witness to and safeguard the unity and apostolicity of the Church' (para. 15 (ix)); and therefore also

–   the ordained ministries are acknowledged as 'given by God and instruments of grace' (para. 17 A (iii)).

Thus there is agreement on the following points:

–   that all Christians participate in the apostolic ministry of the Church as a whole,

–   that the ordained ministry is given by God to serve this fundamental ministry of the whole people of God, and

–   that the ministry of pastoral oversight (*episkope*) 'is necessary' to witness to and safeguard the unity and apostolicity of the Church, but without therefore being singled out as a special ministry of divine institution alongside the ordained ministry.

But how exactly are *priesthood of all believers, the ordained ministry* and *episkope* related to each other? Here many questions remain open. Only the following is clear:

–   The *priesthood of all believers is grounded in baptism*. 'The vocation of all the baptised is to live as a corporate priesthood offering praise to God, sharing the good news and engaging in mission and service to humankind' (para. 4).

–   The *ordained ministry is an 'office of divine institution'* which is different from 'ministry of the whole people', but which serves and is subordinated to it (para. 15 (viii)).

–   Everyone participates in the *priesthood of all believers* by reason of baptism, whereas to exercise the *ordained ministry* a special *ordination* is needed (cf. paras 17 A (iii) and 17 B (iv), (vi) and (vii)).

–   While there is agreement with regard to *baptism* (and thereby to the calling to the priesthood of all believers) (para. 15 (iv)), there remain differences which have yet to be removed with regard to *ordination* (and thereby the vocation to the ordained ministry) (paras 17 B (vi) and (vii)).

–   These differences are not spelled out in detail. But the text of the *Common Statement* gives various indications, which may be grouped into three questions.

1.   *Understanding of Ordination*: Is ordination to be understood as a sacramental action like baptism and the eucharist? The sequence of 'baptism, eucharist and ordination' used in various places could indicate this (paras 17 B (iii), 8).[2] Conversely, the opposite is implied by the fact that in para. 17 A the acknowledgement of the due administration of the sacraments of baptism and the eucharist on the one side is clearly distinguished from the acknowledgement of the ordained ministries on the other side. In the first case the acknowledgement is without reservation, whereas in the second case it is linked with the reservation that 'our

churches' are not yet reconciled (para. 17 A (iii)). Baptism and eucharist are thereby clearly reckoned as belonging to what Christians have in common, ordination on the other hand to what is particular to different churches.

This is also appropriate. According to Protestant understanding ordination, which commissions and authorizes for the service of public proclamation and administration of the sacraments, is not a sacrament (means of salvation), but rather the orderly calling to the church's ministry, which as a public service of word and sacrament stands on a different level from these. Sacraments are actions in which we use words to include people in the salvation event in Christ and to keep them in fellowship with Christ and with one another. They distinguish between Christians and non-Christians but never between Christians: it is impossible to have a difference between Christians founded on the sacraments. Rather, through the sacraments all are incorporated equally into the one body of Christ and upheld by him. Sacraments therefore never bring about inequality within the body of Christ, but exactly the opposite, namely the fundamental equality of all Christians, through which all natural, social, cultural, religious, economic, political or other differences between Jews and Greeks, slaves and masters, men and women, rich and poor, powerful and dependent within the Christian community become theologically invalid (cf. Galatians 3. 28). Sacraments are therefore also different from charisms: they lay the foundation for the equality of all Christians, on which their individual gifts can first develop and unfold at all, for the building up of the whole.

The alternative is therefore clear:

• Either ordination is a sacramental action, in which case it can only lay the foundation for the equality of all Christians, and is useless for commissioning and authorizing for the particular ministry of the Church and of use at most for the priesthood of all the baptized in which case it would, however, compete with baptism and would undermine the very distinction between the priesthood of all the baptized and the Church's ministry to which it is directed.

• Or ordination is understood as empowering and giving responsibility for the particular service of public proclamation and administration of the sacraments, but then it cannot be a sacramental action.

2. *Form and Area of Responsibility of Ordination*: Is ordination a church action whose form the churches may decide for themselves and which can therefore be ordered in various ways, or is the orderly calling to the ordained ministry tied to a certain form, which the Church is not free to alter? The text of the *Common Statement* similarly offers only hints as to the answer to this question. What is undisputed is that the ordained ministry is not at the discretion of the

Church, but as a 'gift of God to his Church' (para. 15 (viii)) is one of the basic components and thereby the continuing elements of the Church; and it is also undisputed that there are in each of our churches 'authorized ministers' and therefore there is an ordered calling to the ministry (para. 17 B (iv)).

What is unclear, on the other hand, is whether ordination as a calling to the public 'ministry of word and sacrament' (para. 15 (viii)) is the ecclesially-regulated introduction into *the* ministry of *the* Church or the *ordained ministry* of a *particular* church. Can one speak in the same breath of the common participation 'in one baptism, one eucharist and one ministry' (para. 8), or must one distinguish – as must be emphasized on the Protestant side – between the *obligation* of the Church, resulting from the gift of God's word, and the *commission* given her, which to this extent is changeless, to order the preaching ministry of public proclamation of the gospel in word and sacrament, and the *concrete way* in which this obligation is fulfilled in a church and justice done to this commission? In the first case it would not be sensible to expect from one of the priests ordained in the Anglican (or Roman or Greek and so on) Church, to be ordained again, if he was seeking to enter the preaching ministry in a Protestant church – or the other way round.[3] But in the second case it would be thoroughly appropriate, because ordination is always introduction into the ordered preaching ministry of a *particular* church and only thus into the ministry of proclamation of the Church.

The distinction has a series of far-reaching consequences. *The* Church does not exist other than in the form of *particular churches*. She is not an entity alongside or in addition to the particular churches, but rather the one Body of Christ, in which all Christians participate *each in their own church*. Membership in one church is membership of the Body of Christ, and membership of the Body of Christ is available to us in this life only on the grounds of membership (however remotely it may be made use of) *of a particular* church. Unlike the churches the Body of Christ knows no ministries, but only the one ministry, which Christ himself exercises. For this ministry, however, there is no ordination and no-one can be ordained into this ministry. One can only be ordained for the *ecclesial* ministry, and that is always the ministry of particular churches. Thus in the public enjoyment of fellowship this ministry performs those tasks which every Christian is capable of performing and obliged to perform. For through baptism everyone participates in the one ministry of Jesus Christ and in his priestly immediate access to God. Participation in the one ministry of Christ is therefore given by baptism, not by ordination. Ordination only authorizes and obliges someone to exercise *publicly* the competence and obligation to proclaim the gospel through word and sacrament, which have been given to all Christians. But *publicly* always means in the *publicity of a particular church*, and therefore ordination can in principle only be understood as authorization for the public ministry in a particular church.

Accordingly, the uniqueness and unrepeatability of ordination must be understood in a different way from that in the case of baptism. In 'baptism with water in the name of the Triune God' all the baptized are united 'with the death and resurrection of Jesus Christ' (para. 15 (iv)). In ordination, on the other hand, individually baptized persons are entitled 'to the exercise of ordained ministries as given by God and instruments of his grace' (para. 12) in a particular church. Anyone who is baptized therefore always remains baptized and cannot be baptized again. On the other hand anyone who is ordained, is called to the – lifelong – public preaching ministry of a particular church and cannot be called to it again.[4] He is not, however, thereby called to the public preaching ministry of every other church. For this reason although a second baptism is unthinkable, a *further ordination* to the preaching ministry of *another church* is conceivable – a *further* ordination, it should be noted, not a *re*-ordination – because the authority, validity and effectiveness of the earlier ordination does not have to be called into question by this in any way.

3.   *Ordained Ministry and Episkope*: What is the relationship between the ordained ministry and the 'ministry of pastoral oversight (*episkope*)'? Here also the *Common Statement* makes only indirect statements. There is no talk of *episkope* being a ministry of divine institution: that is only said of the ordained ministry. *Episkope* is also not described as a (functional) differentiation of the ordained ministry[5] and thereby specified as a particular form or as a part of the particular 'gift of God to his church' (para. 15 (viii)). On the other hand it is not held to be optional or dispensable but is declared to be necessary 'to witness to and safeguard the unity and apostolicity of the Church' (para. 15 (ix)). How then is this 'necessity' of *episkope* to be understood? Various possibilities can be put forward.

- Is the ministry of pastoral oversight – which differs from the ordained ministry of proclamation – *functionally necessary*, in order to preserve the unity and apostolicity of the Church in the multitude of congregations? Or is it constitutive for there being an ordained ministry in the Church at all, or for orderly appointment to it? Is this ministry then – in other words – *pragmatically necessary* (i.e. helpful and useful for overcoming specific problems of church life) or is it objectively constitutive for there being a church life at all?

- Is a *particular form* necessary for this ministry, so that it can fulfill the task ascribed to it, or is it only necessary that it is *exercised* in a personal collegial and communal manner, in whatever concrete form this may happen? To what – in other words – does the admitted necessity of *episkope* extend: to the *form* or the *fact* of its exercise?

• Is this special ministry, which differs from the ordained preaching ministry, necessary to lead the Church and particularly to ensure an orderly calling to the ordained preaching ministry? According to Protestant understanding it is not one of the specific tasks of the ordained ministry to take care of the *order* of this ministry or to order the orderly calling to this ministry. Its sole task is the proclamation of the gospel in word and sacrament. To take care of the *order* of this ministry and the calling to this ministry is the task of the *whole* Church and therefore of *all* Christians, not only those occupying the ordained ministry. For that is one – if not the – central task of *church leadership*, and the leadership of the Church like the ordering of church life is the responsibility of all Christians, not only those occupying the ordained ministry. A church may delegate this task to those who hold the preaching ministry or create a special ministry for this purpose. But this ministry too remains a ministry of the whole Church, which must in principle remain open to all, including those laity who are competent in leadership, and not only ordained minsters. It can therefore in principle always be exercised by the whole Church and 'in case of necessity must be exercised by it again'.[6] This is the sense in which the episcopal office is exercised in many Protestant territorial churches. In this case it is only necessary for the church to be led and church life to be ordered, but it is not necessary for this to happen by means of an episcopal office with its own independent tradition.

One can hardly dispute that in all these points differences exist between Anglican and Protestant interpretations. They are, however, not laid out in the *Common Statement*. The only thing which is categorically stated is that the Protestant side, although it honours 'episcopal succession "as a sign of the apostolicity of the life of the whole Church"', is nevertheless convinced that 'this particular form of *episkope* should not become a necessary condition for "full, visible unity"', while on the other side 'the Anglican understanding of full, visible unity... includes the historic episcopate and full interchangeability of ministers' (para. 16).

One must read carefully, in order to grasp the point of the difference described above. Both sides honour episcopal succession as a sign of the apostolicity of the whole Church, or are at least increasingly prepared to do so. Neither side, however, describes it as a necessary condition for full, visible unity. It is expressly rejected as such by the Protestant side. But neither is this view attributed to the Anglicans. Rather, it is said, more cautiously, that their understanding of full visible unity includes the historic episcopate and the full interchangeability of ministers. This not only leaves open what this 'include' means, but also what further relationship exists between episcopal succession and historic episcopate beyond that, so that the former is connected in a particular way with apostolicity, the latter on the other hand with the unity of the Church. What is clear, by contrast, is that the difference noted has to do with a different understanding of what full, visible unity means and what role within it is ascribed to the historic episcopate. And also one cannot overlook the conclusions drawn from this difference:

–   a full interchangeability of the clergy or ministers is regarded as impossible (para. 16, 17 A (iii));

–   the 'eucharistic fellowship' which is expressly encouraged (para. 17 B (v)) may only be practised in such a way as to 'reflect the presence of two or more churches' (para. 17 B (vi)), i.e. 'concelebration, in the sense of co-consecration, by word or gesture is not envisaged' (footnote).

–   while acceptance of 'an invitation to take part in an ordination of another church' is urged, it is impressed upon us that at ordinations in Protestant churches 'a participating bishop or priest' of the Church of England 'may not by the laying on of hands or otherwise do any act which is a sign of the conferring of Holy Orders' (para. 17 B (vii)).

In the German text the words 'Holy Orders' are translated as *'das anglikanische Priesteramt'* [the Anglican priesthood]. This phrase does not occur in the English text. But the question is, whether that is what is meant and whether the talk here is really of ordination as an act which is primarily to be understood in terms of ecclesiastical law. According to the Anglican understanding *conferring of Holy Orders* is not to be understood as the calling to an office in the Anglican Church (though this is its factual consequence), but as the ordination to the ministry of word and sacrament instituted by God, as Bishop Stephen Sykes has pointed out.[7] But this not only represents the threefold ministry of bishop, priest and deacon – for that is what 'Holy Orders' means in this context – as the unchanging ministry of the one, holy, apostolic and catholic Church, which can hardly be justified theologically; other problems present themselves too. That the ministry of word and sacrament, instituted by God – as distinct from an 'Anglican priesthood' in its tripartite structure – is also present in the Protestant churches is just as expressly recognized (para. 17 A (iii)) as is the fact that here too there is 'a fidelity... to the exercise of ordained ministries as given by God and instruments of his grace' (para. 12) and here too 'authorized ministers' exercise these ministries (para. 17 B (iv)).[8]

But if the ordained ministry exists in both churches and if in both churches clergy are duly called to this ministry, where does the *theological* difference between Protestant and Anglican ordination lie, which hinders us from speaking not only of mutual recognition, but also of full reconciliation of ministries? What *theological* quality does the Anglican *conferring of Holy Orders* possess, which is missing from the Protestant calling to the ordained ministry?

17

The question remains open in the *Meissen Common Statement*. The answer to it apparently has to do with two questions, namely

–   what theological meaning the Anglican side apportions to the structure of the threefold ministry of bishop, priest and deacon as an appropriate form of ordained ministry, and

–   what role in ordination the Anglican side ascribes to the episcopal office in the form of the historic episcopate.

As things stand, there is every suggestion that according to Anglican understanding there can be *no common ministry without the threefold ministry*,[9] *no full interchangeability of ministers without episcopal ordination – that is to say without ordination by a bishop in historic succession – and no 'visible unity of the Church' without a 'single episcopate'*.[10] In accordance with this it was stated as long ago as 1973 in the Anglican-Lutheran International Conversations: 'The Anglican participants cannot foresee full integration of ministries (full communion) apart from the historic episcopate' (para. 89). And with regard to this nothing has changed right up until the most recent official statements.[11]

The fundamental question with which we must engage is therefore not, whether in our churches there is an ordained ministry or whether in them a 'ministry of pastoral oversight (*episkope*)' (para. 15 (ix)) is necessary, but only whether it is necessary for the *full, visible unity* of our churches for this ministry to have the form of the *threefold ministry* and of the *historic episcopate*. **Is the full, visible unity of our churches possible without the threefold ministry, the historic episcopate and episcopal succession or not?** If it is possible, on what is the reservation that we do not yet have 'a reconciled, common ministry' (para. 17 B (vii)) based, with all the consequences which are drawn from that? If it is on the other hand not possible, how then can it be recognized that both churches have an ordained ministry and are duly administered? And in this case, what is added by the structured form of the threefold ministry and the exercise of *episkope* by bishops in historic succession which is lacking in the – differently ordered – form of ministry and exercise of *episkope* in the Protestant churches?

3.   The Background to the Problem[12]

1.   In order to be able to assess the problem and its consequences properly, one must go back to the fundamental text for Anglican ecumenical work, the Chicago-Lambeth Quadrilateral of 1888, and its pre-history. The specifically Anglican term 'historic episcopate' was introduced into the discussion by the American Anglican William Reed Huntingdon (1838-1909) in his book *The Church Idea.*

An Essay toward Unity (1870). By this term is meant the historic succession of episcopal ordinations to the threefold ministry through which the Anglican Church claims to stand in unbroken continuity with the pre-Reformation Church and through it with the apostolic beginnings of the Church. This claim is complex and encompasses several elements which must be distinguished from each other, namely

–   the *historical* and *institutional claim* that the Church of England stands in its teaching and order in the tradition of the early Church, notwithstanding the re-orderings of the sixteenth century;

–   the *theological claim* that it thereby preserves the apostolic tradition and succession, i.e. 'that the Church of England traces its ecclesiastical formation back to the early Church';[13]

–   the *ecclesiological claim* that this is symbolized in the structure of its ordained ministry. Although the threefold ministry of bishop, presbyter and deacon could 'not claim to be the only one authorized in Scripture', it was nevertheless the standard manifestation of the genuine tradition of the early Church, insofar as 'the threefold pattern eventually prevailed and was generally adopted by the Church';[14]

–   the *soteriological claim* that the episcopal succession, although it does not guarantee the presence of the apostolic tradition and thereby the valid and effective mediation of salvation (as is said today, but was not always said), certainly symbolizes it visibly.

2.   This last point at least is also very much disputed within Anglicanism, since it goes too far for some but not far enough for others. 'Anglicans have no single, common, official explanation of *why* the historic episcopate is important; but we overwhelmingly concur in the consensus that it is.'[15] This consensus is expressed in the four Anglican fundamental pre-requisites for church unions in the Chicago-Lambeth Quadrilateral by the fact that alongside the Scriptures of the Old and New Testaments, the Apostles' Creed and the Nicene Creed and the sacraments of baptism and the eucharist the 'Historic Episcopate' is additionally expressly mentioned in fourth place, 'locally adapted in the methods of its administration to the varying needs of the nations and peoples called of God into the Unity of His Church'.[16] It is noticeable that *Succession* is not mentioned in this formulation or in the repetition of these conditions for unity in the *Appeal to all Christian people* of the 1920 Lambeth Conference.[17][18] In view of the emphasis on the idea of succession in the Anglo-Catholic Oxford Movement, this is at least worthy of notice, although John Henry Newman had already pointed out in 1840 that the unity of the Church could only lie in the visible legal organization of the Church, and not

in the apostolic succession of its ministers, because the Church after all lived in schism despite the claim of such an unbroken derivation from the Apostles.[19] Episcopacy in apostolic succession cannot guarantee the unity of the Church. It was not least of all for this reason that Newman felt obliged to convert in 1845. And it is not least of all for this reason that in more recent texts the unity and apostolicity of the Church is no longer said to be guaranteed by episcopacy and historic succession.

3.   The element of apostolic succession in the concept of the historic episcopate was, by contrast, expressly emphasized by Bishop Palmer in Lausanne in 1927,[20] and on this point there was and is agreement with the Orthodox churches: 'The apostolic doctrine and tradition, with the apostolic succession, are the elements in which the apostolicity of the Church consists'.[21] It was precisely for this reason, however, that the uncompromising rejection of the validity of Anglican orders by Leo XIII in his encyclical *apostolicae curae et caritatis* of 13 September 1896 had such traumatic effect for many Anglicans: 'auctoritate Nostra, motu proprio, certa scientia pronuntiamus et declaramus, ordinationes ritu Anglicano actas irritas prorsus fuisse et esse omninoque nullas' (DH 3319, p. 903). This said nothing new, but merely repeated and underlined the judgement which the Holy Office had already made in 1685, 1704 and 1875 on the Ordinal of Edward VI, which was introduced in the Church of England for the first time in 1550 and came finally into force in 1559 after having been abolished by Mary.

4.   This, however, brought to a fundamental crisis the Anglo-Catholic efforts to prove the full validity of the ministry of the Church of England by their theory about the transmission of grace through an unbroken chain of the laying of hands from the Apostles down to the present. Back in 1841, in the dispute about the ecumenical experiment of a protestant bishopric in the apostolic succession at Jerusalem, which had been initiated by Frederick William IV of Prussia and supported by the Church of England, to the horror of the Tractarians, Newman had protested against the 'recognition' of the 'heresies' of Lutheranism and Calvinism, and it was not least of all for that reason that he had left the Church of England.[22] In his view, the Church of England could only be linked to churches which had preserved episcopacy in apostolic succession or submitted themselves to it, renouncing their previous errors. The traditional Anglican position had thereby been sharpened in a direction which, if it had been maintained, would have made the ecumenical initiatives of the twentieth century impossible.[23] According to this view, only those who are linked with the Apostles by the historic episcopate can belong to the visible Church, only priests ordained in apostolic succession can celebrate the eucharist validly, and the historic episcopate therefore belongs to the *esse* of the Church.

5.   This was not always the Anglican view. The Caroline Divines of the seventeenth century distinguished between 'the essence of a Church', which they conceded also to the reformed churches, and 'the integrity or perfection of a Church', which there could not be without the episcopate. In this view, even churches with so-called presbyteral ordination are true churches, and their ministries, although irregular, are effectual,[24] so that protestant pastors could take over parishes in England without being re-ordained.[25] The underlying view was, therefore, that the Church could exist without the episcopate, but that this was the 'God-given focus of unity and seat of authority in the Church'.[26]

At the outset, this did no more than to give expression to the existing situation in the Church of England. In removing the Church of England from papal jurisdiction and placing it under his own supreme authority, Henry VIII did not alter the internal structures of the Church in any way. The traditional hierarchical form of the ordained ministry of bishop, priest and deacon were continued unbroken, and under Edward VI and Elizabeth I two bishops were consecrated according to the traditional order. Theologically, however, the function of the bishops was focussed on their spiritual and pastoral tasks, in line with the Reformation view that bishops should not be secular rulers but spiritual leaders and teachers of the Church. Since this meant little change in the actual role of the bishop, Calvinistic Puritan criticism was increasingly directed not only against the political and secular misuse of the episcopal office, but against that office itself. One side emphasized 'that between a Presbyter and a Bishop the Word of God alloweth not any inequality or difference to be made',[27] while the other side insisted that 'A Bishop is a Minister of God, unto whom with permanent continuance, there is given not onely power of administring the Word and Sacraments, which power other presbyters have; but also a further power to ordain Ecclesiastical persons, and a power of Cheifty in Government over Presbyters as well as Lay men, a power to be by way of jurisdiction a Pastor even to Pastors themselves'.[28] The decisive difference between bishops and other priests was therefore seen as lying in the right to ordain: both are priests, but the function and authority of priests depends on their ordination by bishops in *apostolic succession*.[29]

6.   The term *apostolic succession* was coined in the sixteenth century in connection with this debate and was introduced into the discussion by Thomas Bilson in his work *The Perpetual Government of Christ's Church*, which was published in 1593. (A new edition appeared in 1842.) In this Bilson distinguishes between the 'succession of function', the orderly transmission of the apostolic commission by the laying on of hands, and the 'orderly succession of place'. Apostolic succession meant the passing on of the apostolic function, not – as he emphasized against Rome – the continuation of a 'perpetual chair of succession' or even the functional equivalence of bishop and Apostle. Bishops continued only part of the

complex of functions which made up the ministry of the Apostles. The Apostles could have no successors as witnesses of the incarnation and as founders of the Church directly commissioned by Christ, as Hooker also emphasized. As servants of God's word and sacrament their ministry was continued by the priests. Only their function of *episkope* and jurisdiction had passed to the bishops, and the succession of bishops was only concerned with the passing of this function.[30] The apostolicity of the Church was, therefore, not seen as lying in the office of bishop alone. Nevertheless, that part of the functions given to the ministry of the Apostles which the bishops continued was important for the Church, and they were therefore a visible sign of the continuity of the Church with its apostolic origins.

Hooker left open whether 'the apostles themselves left the bishops invested with power above other pastors' or whether after the death of the Apostles 'Churches did agree among themselves... to make one Presbyter in each city chief over the rest'.[31] This historical uncertainty did not reduce the certainty that as a matter of fact bishops have this particular function and authority in the Church. Article 23 of the Thirty-nine Articles may only say that the ministry of public preaching and administration of the sacraments might only be exercised by persons 'which be chosen and called to this work by men who have public authority given unto them in the Congregation, to call and send Ministers', without expressly mentioning bishops, but in practice it is precisely the bishops who are meant by this. Although in the course of time it became ever more apparent that the historical origins of this practice are obscure, that it is not clearly founded on Scripture and that it cannot be traced back to a clear institution by Christ or the Apostles, towards the end of the seventeenth century Edward Stillingfleet could insist that 'there is as great Reason to believe, the *apostolical succession* to be of *Divine Institution*, as the *Canon of Scripture*, or the *Observation of the Lord's Day*'.[32] In this way, the development of the Canon of Scripture, the creeds and the episcopate were seen theologically as parallel and their position and function in the Church were legitimized in comparable ways. Even in our present century the particular position of the episcopate is justified in this way, despite the lack of biblical legitimation. In this view, the gradual historical development of the episcopate in the early Church 'would be no evidence that it lacked divine authority, but rather that the life of the Spirit within the Church had found it to be the most appropriate organ for the functions it discharged'.[33]

7.   The motivation for Stillingfleet's arguments was, however, not solely theological. The *Act of Uniformity* of 1662, passed in connection with the restoration of Charles II, had created a new situation with far-reaching consequences, in that a *de facto*, but not exclusive, practice of the Church of England had legally been raised to a theological norm out of church-political considerations but without biblical or theological justification. The statement in the Prayer Book of Edward VI

'that no man (not being at this present Bishop, Priest or Deacon) shall execute any of them [i.e. one of these offices] except he be called, tried, examined, and admitted, according to the form hereafter following', was sharpened after the confusion of the Civil War period in the following way: 'no man shall be accounted or taken to be a lawful Bishop, Priest or Deacon in the Church of England, or suffered to execute any of the said Functions, except he be called tried, examined, and admitted thereunto, according to the Form hereafter following, or hath had formerly Episcopal Consecration, or Ordination.'[34]

This rule still applies today. Since that time, only episcopally ordained priests may minister in the Church of England – and in the other Anglican churches – and only the threefold ministry of Bishop, Priest and Deacon counts as ministry in the Church. These decisions *made the Church of England into an episcopalian confessional church* and thereby destroyed its traditional claim to be *the Christian Church* in England.[35] For while '[T]he Church of England had always been episcopal, it now became episcopalian, that is, what had been a matter of practical policy became the requirement of religious principle'.[36] The *Anglicana ecclesia*, the Christian Church in England, thereby turned into the *Church of England*, the English episcopal church, and thereby too ordination became legally an action of this particular church. This transformation into a particular confessional church alongside others (not seen as such at all initially), not only put an end to the appointment of protestant pastors to ministries in the Church of England without re-ordination, which was at least occasionally practised before 1662, but theological and confessional demarcations were made as they had not been in the sixteenth century. Many of the protestant, puritan-minded clergy in England could not or would not allow themselves to be re-ordained and refused to accept the Book of Common Prayer, which had been revised in a catholic direction, or to give up their Reformation principles. On 24 August 1662 over 2000 Puritan clergy were therefore driven out of their offices, and as a result of the *Conventicle Acts* (1664/1670), which forbad participation in non-Anglican acts of worship, over 8,000 dissenters were imprisoned (among them, for twelve years, the Baptist John Bunyan) and more than 60,000 were punished in other ways.

8.   The decisions of 1662 began a development which fundamentally changed the Church of England in at least two respects. On the one hand, it was transformed for political reasons and at the behest of Parliament from a comprehensive national church to a privileged state church among or alongside other religious bodies in England. On the other hand, within the Church protest against the political influence of Parliament on the leadership of the Church expressed itself by an important minority developing the legal requirement of episcopal ordination after 1662 into a theological and ecclesiological fundamental principle.

8.1. In 1672 Charles II issued the *Declaration of Indulgence* which permitted protestant nonconformists to hold public acts of worship in certain places and allowed Roman Catholics private masses at least. Parliament saw in this a hidden attempt to introduce Roman Catholicism and reacted in 1673 with the *Test Act*, which made the holding of public offices dependent on membership of the Anglican Church. The results of this increasing struggle between royal attempts at recatholicization and parliamentary Anglicanism were the revolution of 1688 and the *Toleration Act* of 1689, which gave protestant dissenters (Baptists, Quakers etc.) the right to independent exercise of religion outside the Anglican state church. For political reasons, the Roman Catholics and the Socinians (Anti-trinitarians) were excluded from this toleration. The Church of England thereby gave up its claim to be a comprehensive state church and became an *established church*, a church with state privileges. Although the *Test Act* remained in force until 1828, and schools and universities and therefore the education system also remained in Anglican hands, other churches and religious bodies played a legitimate role in the religious life of England from 1689. As a result of the *Act of Uniformity* of 1662 a state-sanctioned separation between 'conformists' and 'nonconformists' had come about, and the idea of a comprehensive, inclusive state church had been given up.

8.2 Right from the beginning there was resistance within the Church to this development and to the influence of politics and Parliament on the leadership of the Church. After the legally problematic 'abdication' of James II and the parliamentary appointment of William III as King, a not unimportant group of bishops had refused to take the oath of allegiance to the new, in their view illegitimate, King and therefore lost their positions. Among these *Non-Jurors*, as they were called, the 1662 legal requirement of episcopal ordination was interpreted in a high-church way as a rejection of all secular, political influence on the leadership of the Church and as basing church leadership on the legitimate ministry of the Church alone. The Church, it was emphasized, was an independent body with its own legitimation independent of all social factors. Only the Church itself had the right to call people to offices in the Church, and it had this right only insofar as there was within it an unbroken succession of authorized persons since the time of Christ: 'If there be no *Uninterrupted succession*, then there are no Authorized Ministers from Christ; if no such Ministers, then no Christian Sacraments; if no Christian Sacraments, then no Christian Covenant, whereof the Sacraments are the Stated and Visible Seals.'[37] It was this view which the Tractarians were able to take up in the nineteenth century with their theory of the unbroken chain of the laying on of hands as the physical transmission of grace and thereby as the only authoritive legitimation of the validity of ministries in the Church. The *de facto* practice of the Church of England had thereby, having been made the legal norm in 1662, become a fundamental theological principle, which made the identity of the Church and the fact that it was the Church dependent on the historic succession of the ministers: where there is no bishop in apostolic succession, there is also no Church.

9.   That was and is only *one* view in the Church of England and at present it is not the dominant view. But this view makes it particularly clear that with the historic episcopate it is not only the question of the theological legitimacy of ministries in the Church and the question of the ecumenical unity of the churches which is under discussion, but also the *independence of the Church* and the independence of the Church's leadership from state and society. To put it bluntly, one could say that the driving forces in the development of the Anglican theology of episcopacy were not primarily or exclusively theological, but always also (church) political considerations.

4.   Theological Assessment

A theological assessment of the Anglican emphasis on the historic episcopate will therefore have to distinguish between

–   the *de facto* church practice before 1662,

–   the legal situation after 1662, and

–   theological theories used to explain and justify this legally sanctioned practice, such as the high-church Anglo-Catholic succession theory of a transmission of the grace of orders through an unbroken chain of physical laying-on of hands (which can be understood as a theological justification of the regulation of 1662 to maintain the independent identity of the Church and its independence from state and society) or the theology of sign which takes over this function in Porvoo and seems to have replaced the Anglo-Catholic theory in more recent Anglican theology.

That the practice of the Church of England is theologically legitimate is indisputable from a protestant point of view. Bishops are consecrated in continuance of pre-Reformation practice, priests ordained by the laying on of hands by a bishop, baptized people confirmed by the bishop. Bishops therefore stand in the continuity of the 'historic episcopate' and priests in 'apostolic succession', and baptized persons are made full members of the Church of England by episcopal confirmation. This is the *de facto* practice and order of the Church of England, which is in agreement with the practice and order of some but not all other churches.

Following the regulation of 1662 this practice is binding for the Church of England, but it is not yet therefore and as such binding for other churches.[38] It could be so because of its theological justification. But wherein does this lie? Varying answers are given to that question by Anglicans.

The Anglo-Catholic justification, which sees in the unbroken chain of the physical laying on of hands since the Apostles a necessary condition for the transmission of grace and therefore for a church being a true church, is disputed even amongst Anglicans. Not only does it rest on historical theses about the origin and the uninterrupted continuity of the historic episcopate which can hardly be maintained,[39] but it is also theologically inadequate. On the one hand, it does not achieve what it is supposed to achieve, because there is 'no support from the Bible' for the assertion that 'the apostolic succession through the laying on of hands guarantees the church', as Michael Ramsey emphasized as long ago as 1936.[40] On the other hand, the idea of the 'transmission of grace through the linear chain of episcopal laying on of hands assumes a material, immanent and "possessive" understanding of grace which is at the same time linked juridically to the ministry', which makes the 'apostolic succession [become] an extension of the incarnate and risen Lord in time and space'.[41] And finally, it is ecumenically useless, because it inevitably denies that non-episcopal churches are churches and asserts the deficiency of their ministries. It is not by chance that the Chicago-Lambeth Quadrilateral therefore does not speak of apostolic succession but of the *historic episcopate*, and it is not by chance that from the beginning of this century Anglicans have emphasized in ecumenical conversations that their demand for the taking on of the historic episcopate should not be confused with the taking on of a certain – namely the Anglo-Catholic – doctrine of the apostolic succession.[42]

The Anglo-Catholic doctrine of succession has also been rejected within Anglicanism by the dominant theological movement in our century, without this meaning that one was theologically indifferent to the historic episcopate. Its importance is seen, however, in its function not for the *esse* of the Church but for its *visible unity*. According to this view, the episcopal office is an effective sign and instrument of the unity of the Church. This justification – that is its advantage – is not tied to questionable historical theories about the origin of the episcopal office, but is a theological statement about its *true function*. It can therefore also not be refuted by pointing to the historical failure of the episcopal office. Moreover, it does not claim that the succession of this ministry alone constitutes the continuity of the Church. Rather, it is the proclamation through word and sacrament which is fundamental to the continuity of the Church, and ministry in succession can only witness to and preserve this continuity.[43] Therefore, it cannot be denied that churches which do not have this sign are also churches, without this meaning that they are equivalent to the Church of England as far as the visibility of unity is concerned. It was in line with this view that the Lambeth Conference of 1948 said that for Anglicans it was equally impossible 'to declare the sacraments of non-episcopal bodies null and void', and 'to treat non-episcopal ministries as identical in status and authority with the episcopal ministry'.[44]

This leaves open the question, however, of wherein the lesser status and authority of non-episcopal ministries is supposed to consist, if the Anglo-Catholic justification for their deficiency is untenable. What do the ministries of a church which does not possess the historic episcopate and the threefold ministry lack, or what would be gained if such a church took on the historic episcopate and the separated structure of ministry, as is suggested or envisaged in *'Toward Full Communion' and 'Concordat of Agreement'* and in the Porvoo Common Statement *Together in Mission and Ministry*? If there is no fundamental difference in both cases with regard to the carrying out of ordained ministry, there is then no theological reason (as distinct from a legal one) to demand the re-ordination of non-episcopally ordained ministers. It is therefore right that this demand is now no longer made in *'Toward Full Communion' and 'Concordat of Agreement'* and in *Together in Mission and Ministry*. That can only mean, however, that the demand that other churches take over the historic episcopate and episcopal ordination as a *condition and pre-condition* for the establishment of unlimited eucharistic fellowship with other churches is dropped, as J.A.T. Robinson and other Anglican theologians demanded as long ago as the early 1960s and as is now to be practised.[45] Why then is the claim held to that the historic episcopate and the threefold ministry 'in historic succession' which is linked to it must be the 'future pattern of the one ordained ministry of Word and Sacrament'[46]? Is not a legal situation in the Church of England here given an ecclesiological weight which, theologically speaking, it does not deserve? For an Anglican has also admitted that 'historic episcopate or apostolic succession as a condition of a true church is certainly incompatible with a genuine Reformation ecclesiology, according to which word and sacrament suffice for the full integrity of ecclesial life since through their means Christ has promised to be present with his people'.[47] Does this not then also apply to the understanding of *church* which stands behind it, insofar as the relationship between the one, holy, apostolic and catholic Church which is believed in as the universal body of Christ and the particular historical institution of the Church of England (or any other church) is not clearly defined? And should there not then be in the understanding of *ordination* a distancing from a parallelizing of baptism and ordination, with ordination being understood more strictly as commissioning and entitling to the exercise of the ordained ministry in a *particular* church, without making the concrete form in which this is undertaken in one church also binding for others? And can such weight still be given to an historically contingent form of the ministry in some churches, such as the threefold ministry in historic succession, that unlimited visible church fellowship is made dependent on this being taken over?

That all of this produces ecumenical difficulties is clear. They are hardly apparent where relations between Anglican churches and churches which have the historic episcopate, such as the Old Catholic Churches of the Union of Utrecht or the Church of Sweden are concerned, or relations with churches, like the Philippine Independent Church, which took on the historic episcopate when they established full communion with the Anglicans. But already in the case of the Church of South India, in which for a transitional period non-episcopally ordained ministers functioned alongside episcopally ordained ministers, there were reservations on the part of some Anglicans churches.[48] And in Meissen the last step to unlimited communion was not taken, because the differences of opinion over the importance of the historic episcopate for the visible unity of the Church could not be overcome.

But why does the Church of England insist on this condition? The Anglo-Catholic position had a clear answer to this, even if it proved not to be sustainable. The criticism of this answer among Anglicans overturns the Anglo-Catholic justification, but holds fast to that which is justified. It must therefore give another reason why there cannot be 'a reconciled, common ministry' (Meissen, para. 17b (vii)) without the historic episcopate and the threefold ordering of the ministry. Nothing is said about this in the *Common Statement*. In *Apostolicity and Succession*, by contrast, a justification is hinted at, as follows. Since the New Testament beginnings of the Church there has been a 'ministry of oversight' which consolidated itself 'in the patristic centuries' in the context of a 'relatively settled and consistent system of threefold ministry, the central task of this ministry being [to] serve the unity of the community' (para. 44). Since this unity of the Church is no longer present today, an ecumenical demand is made, that it is 'necessary to bring into being a single ministry of oversight, for only then will the churches renew the ministry of oversight and be able to take common decisions for the whole Church, teach together with conviction and engage in common service and mission' (para. 51).

But why should the activities listed only be possible if there is a 'single ministry of oversight'? Does not an unstated 'ministerial church' understanding of unity come into play here, which does not only declare that it is necessary that the task of *episkope* be ordered in every church, but that in all churches it should be ordered in *the same way*? Can that be a realistic goal of ecumenical endeavour? Is there not rather everything to be said for the view that we will not achieve common decision-making by Christian churches in their diversity in doctrine, ministry and mission if this is made a precondition? Is it not the case that precisely those Christian churches world-wide are fast-growing which have long since set out on quite different paths? And even if it were the case that 'the visible unity of the Church served by a single episcopate' were necessary for the performance of the activities listed (para. 69), this would not at all be to say that this 'single episcopate' would have to take on the form of the historic episcopate. Even if one is of the opinion that 'the continuity with the Church of the Apostles finds profound expression in the successive laying on of hands by bishops' (para. 50), it does not follow from this that this continuity would have to be expressed in this way or that it would be better, more visibly, more effectively or more convincingly expressed in this way than through the faith-inspiring proclamation of the Gospel by word and sacrament in a church which continually orientates its proclamation to and examines it against the apostolic norm of Scripture afresh.

That is not the way which *Apostolicity and Succession, 'Toward Full Communion' and 'Concordat of Agreement'* or *The Porvoo Common Statement* have gone. Following on from and continuing manifold preparatory work by Anglican theologians in the last fifty years[49] a different solution is sought here. I shall confine myself to what is set before us in Porvoo.

5. The Solution attempted by Porvoo

The differentiated treatment of the areas of *succession*, *apostolicity* and *episcopacy* of which there was already an intimation in the *Meissen Common Statement* is developed in Porvoo in such a way that the problem of historic episcopate is approached indirectly rather than directly. The method is that the thinking progresses from the *Church* via the *ministry* to the *episcopal ministry* and the *historic succession*. The argumentation which is built up in this way can be summarized as follows.

- *Apostolicity* is primarily, fundamentally and comprehensively a characteristic of the Church as a whole. The Church is apostolic insofar as it fulfils in the totality of its liturgical, missionary and diaconic activitiy, and thereby in all its actions of *leitourgia, marturia, koinonia* and *diakonia* its apostolic commission to be sign, instrument and foretaste of the Kingdom of God (paras 32f, 36–39).

- Within this 'apostolic tradition of the Church as a whole' (para. 39) the *ordained ministry* – which is instituted by Christ and passed on by the Apostles – has the particular task 'to assemble and build up the body of Christ by proclaiming and teaching the Word of God, by celebrating the sacraments and by guiding the life of the community in its worship, its mission and its caring ministry' (para. 41).

- This ministry is given to individual *persons* for the whole of their lifetime by ordination and the laying on of hands.

- The *one* ministry has *different tasks*, which find their expression in the *structure* of the ordained ministry. Since the early Church the threefold *ministry* of bishops, priests and deacons has gained general acceptance, although it has experienced considerable changes in the course of history and is still changing today (para. 41).

- A distinction is made, also in the case of the episcopal office, between the *ministry* (*episkope*) and the person who exercises that ministry (bishop). The differentiation and diversity of the gifts of God and of the tasks of the Church requires a 'ministry of co-ordination' or 'ministry of oversight, *episkope*' (para. 42). This ministry 'is the particular responsibility of the bishop' (para. 43) and is exercised by the bishops personally, collegially and communally (para. 44).

- The concept of the *apostolic succession* is applied to the continuity of the *ministry* and the succession of the *holders* of this office. This succession manifests itself primarily in the apostolic tradition of the Church as a whole (para. 39), to which the 'continuity of the ministry of oversight' also belongs (para. 46).

- To be distinguished from this is the '[a]postolic succession in the episcopal office', which is described as 'a visible and personal way of focusing the apostolicity of the whole Church' (para. 46). This is expressed in 'the ordination or consecration of a bishop' by 'the laying on of hands by the ordaining bishop' (para. 47).

- This laying on of hands at the consecration of a bishop is an action which serves as a sign which is effective in four respects. It bears witness to the trust of the Church in God's faithfulness; it expresses the intention of the Church to maintain God's gift faithfully; through the participation of other bishops it demonstrates the acceptance of the new bishop and the catholicity of the Church; and it transmits the episcopal office of leadership and its authority 'in accordance with God's will and institution' (para. 48).

- The 'Historic Episcopal Succession' is therefore altogether to be understood 'as Sign', and this at three levels: (1) 'The whole Church is a sign of the Kingdom of God'; (2) 'the act of ordination is a sign of God's faithfulness to his Church'; and (3) the ordination of a bishop 'in historic succession (that is, in intended continuity from the apostles themselves)' is also a sign – a sign of the concern of the Church 'for continuity in the whole of its life and mission' (para. 50).

- 'The use of the sign of historic episcopal succession' as such guarantees neither 'the fidelity of a church to every aspect of the apostolic faith, life and mission' nor 'the personal faithfulness of the bishop'. But the retention of this sign 'remains a permanent challenge to fidelity and to unity' and to a more complete realization of the 'permanent characteristics of the Church of the apostles' (para. 51).

- A church 'which has preserved the sign of historic episcopal succession is free to acknowledge an authentic episcopal ministry in a church which has preserved continuity in the episcopal office by an occasional priestly/presbyteral ordination at the time of the Reformation'. And in turn such a church can 'enter a relationship of mutual participation in episcopal ordinations with a church which has retained the historical episcopal succession, and... embrace this sign, without denying its past apostolic continuity' (para. 52). For taking up again 'the use of the sign of the laying on of hands in the historic succession' does not imply a negative judgement on the ministries of a church which has hitherto not used this sign, but is 'a means of making more visible the unity and continuity of the Church at all times and in all places' (para. 53).

A series of *methodological* and *theological aspects* of this argumentation are particularly worthy of note.

- *Methodologically* significant is the attempt

   – to 'contextualize' the problem of the historic episcopate ecclesiologically and to look at it not in isolation but in the whole context of the Church; and

   – to distinguish clearly between *ecclesial ministry* and *ministers*,[50] and thereby also between the *continuity of the ministry* and the *succession of the ministers*, and this with regard not only to the ordained ministry in general (para. 41) but also with regard to the episcopate in particular (paras 42ff).

- *Theologically* noteworthy on the other hand is

   – that the threefold ministry is explained functionally through the different tasks of the one ordained ministry (and not as instituted by the Apostles or by Jesus Christ) and is legitimized not theologically but pragmatically, as the result of an historical development;

   – that *episkope* as 'requirement of the whole Church' (para. 42) is distinguished from the 'bishop's office' (para. 43) or 'episcopal office' (para. 46), so that – although this does not occur – non-episcopal structures of the 'ministry of oversight' could be spoken of and the personal, collegial and communal exercise of *episkope* need not be

> understood only – as actually occurs (paras 44f) – as functional dimen-
> sions of the episcopal office;
>
> – that the episcopal office, unlike the threefold ministry, is justified *not*
> functionally, pragmatically or historically but *theologically*, in that the
> consecration of the bishop is characterized as the transmission of the
> 'ministerial office and its authority in accordance with God's will and
> institution' (para. 48) and is thereby derived (this remains unclear)
> either directly from the institution of the ordained ministry by Christ
> (para. 41) or from a different institution by God;
>
> – that an attempt is made to justify the significance which is ascribed to
> the apostolic succession in the episcopal office and the historic epis-
> copate as a whole with the help of a 'theology of sign' which is set out
> ecclesiologically in a comprehensive manner.

It cannot be overlooked that the unclarities in the theological argumentation
increase with every step and culminate in the theology of sign.

- While the ordained ministry in the Church is justified theologically as
  'instituted by our Lord and transmitted through the apostles', its development into the threefold ministry is justified functionally and pragmatically
  (para. 41).

- In the case of *episkope*, on the other hand, the argumentation is precisely
  the opposite: the necessity of a 'ministry of co-ordination' is justified functionally by 'this diversity and multiplicity of tasks' in the service of the
  unity of the Church (para. 42), consecration to the episcopal office by contrast theologically as the transmission of office and authority according to
  'God's will and institution' (para. 48).

But if the *existence* of the ordained ministries is theologically necessary but not its
contingent structuring as *threefold ministry*, how then, by contrast, can the episcopal office be theologically necessary in the context of the threefold ministry?
Should this not – if at all – be said of *episkope*, the necessity of which is justified
functionally? Are not statements about the *office* (*episkope*) and about the historically contingent *exercise of the office* by bishops in historic succession being
mixed up? And is not an importance being ascribed to bishops which at best
belongs to the ministry of *episkope*, but not to the ministers? And is it not only
through this that the succession of ministers is raised to the status of a sign of ministerial continuity, whereas in fact this is established with the Church and
continually given with it, because it arises functionally from the tasks of the
ordained ministry?

The unclarities increase when one turns to the theology of sign, with the help of which Porvoo seeks to justify the particular importance of the historical episcopal succession in the Church's life. At first sight it seems that the claims traditionally made for the historic episcopate are withdrawn to a considerable degree, but the appearance is deceptive. After all, it is not said that the Church is *only a sign* of the Kingdom of God, the act of ordination *only a sign* of the faithfulness of God, the ordination of a bishop in historic succession *only a sign* of the apostolic continuity of the Church (para. 50). Rather, the Church *is* a sign of the Kingdom of God, the act of ordination *is* a sign of the faithfulness of God and consecration to the historic episcopate *is* a sign of apostolic continuity. None of these signs can be dispensed with without thereby losing or obscuring the thing which is signified. For these signs *effect* what they signify; they are – as is said with sacramental language and detailed in four ways in the case of the consecration of bishops – 'effective' (para. 48). If, however, these signs effect what they signify, that means that not having or using them or not doing so correctly means being in – at least – an irregular situation. That is why churches which have preserved 'continuity in the episcopal office by an occasional priestly/presbyteral ordination' but not 'the sign of historic episcopal succession' (para. 52) should at all costs embrace this sign again, in order to make the unity and continuity of the universal Church *more visible* (paras 52f). It seems possible, then, to *increase* the visibility of the unity and continuity of the Church by means of effective signs, and among these particularly the historic episcopate. But the whole argumentation gives no theological justification for this assertion, but merely says *that* it is so. But is it so? Is the historic episcopate an effective sign of a greater visibility of the one Church of Jesus Christ? That is expressly asserted despite the self-critical admission that the use of this sign has often not achieved the effects attributed to it and also cannot guarantee them. It is said that the sign does not achieve unity, and possessing it also does not guarantee unity, but it is nevertheless 'a means of making more visible the unity and continuity of the Church at all times and in all places' (para. 53). For this reason, it is said, 'the retention of the sign' is important, for it represents at least 'a permanent challenge to fidelity and to unity' (para. 51). It is hardly possible to withdraw further from the thesis of the supposed effectiveness of this sign for the making visible of unity, but it is nevertheless held fast to.

This is indicative of the problem of the whole argumentation. Behind Porvoo's theology of sign lie elements of an undeclared and unelaborated *sacramental theology*. In justifying the outstanding importance of the 'Episcopal Office in the Service of the Apostolic Succession' (Chapter IV, Section C) and the 'Historic Episcopal Succession as Sign' (Chapter IV, Section D) for the full visible unity of the Church with a concept of sign from the realms of sacramental theology, *a sacramental understanding of ordination to the ministry of the Church* and of *con-*

secration to the episcopal office is supported, without the consequences of this in view of the historical realities being drawn. The argumentation dazzles because the concept of sign is not clarified. The theology of sign which operates with it has the opposite of a clarifying function. It describes something dark with the help of something darker and thus precisely does not perform the task which it is supposed to – that of making reasonable the significance which is ascribed ecclesiologically and ecumenically to the historic episcopate. And it does not in the slightest represent a retraction of the traditional assertion of the indispensable necessity of historic episcopate for the Church, but on the contrary represents a theological heightening of this claim, arguing that ordination and ministry or consecration and episcopal office are to be understood sacramentally and to that extent are indispensable *as signs* for the visible unity of the Church.[51] The Anglo-Catholic thesis that the historic episcopate is indispensable for the *esse* of the *Church* is thus replaced by the new Anglican thesis that it is indispensable for the *visibility* of the *unity* of the Church.

I regard this theology of sign with its sacramental under- and overtones as the wrong path to take. It operates with an unclear concept of sign; it does not describe precisely what is used as sign, for what reasons, by whom and for whom; it does not say what theological advantage the use of certain signs (for example 'the sign of the laying on of hands in the historic succession' (para. 53)) has over the use of other signs (for example the laying on of hands without historic succession); it leaves unexplained what the 'whole Church', which is said to be 'a sign of the Kingdom of God' (para. 50) is; it oscillates in an unclear way between understanding the *ministry* (the ministry of preaching or the episcopal ministry) or the *act of appointment to a ministry* (ordination or consecration) or the *minister* and *holder* of the office as sign; and thus altogether it does not lead forward theologically, but leads into a cul-de-sac. In order to clarify the concept of sign which is used – and that would be necessary as a matter of urgency – one would have to examine problems such as the representational structure, the effectiveness, the function of describing and making clear, the reference, the involvement in systems etc. of signs, as well as their effect on the understanding of the objects which are understood as signs such as Church, ministry, ordination, historic episcopacy etc. That opens up a wide field of theological research, but would hardly be able to clarify the questions left open in Meissen in such a way that they could be brought to solutions. For one would then have to discuss a theological theory which is most unlikely to meet with general approval. In its status and function Porvoo's theology of sign is on the same level as the Anglo-Catholic pipeline theory, except that the latter has one advantage of the former – it is clearer.

In my view it is not Porvoo's theology of sign, but the process adopted in Porvoo which can bring us further. Here there are points which could usefully be developed in conversation. In conclusion, I shall give some indication of this.

6. From Understanding of the Church to Understanding of the Ministry of the Church

Approaching dark and controversial questions from clear and uncontroversial ones is an old and well-founded way of proceeding. It is therefore also methodically right to approach the controversial question of the historic episcopate and the whole complex of problems of threefold ministry, ordination and consecration which are linked with it from the non-controversial understanding of the Church as whole. That there is agreement in essentials on this point is expressly stated in the *Common Statement* (paras 15 (vii)-(ix) , and 17 A (i) and (ii)). Both sides confirm that they are true churches, 'truly participating in the apostolic mission of the whole people of God', and that in them 'the Word of God is authentically preached and the sacraments of baptism and eucharist are duly administered'.

If one takes this seriously, it has a series of consequences.

1.   First of all, this *confirms with regard to content*, in an agreed manner, what is meant by the *apostolicity* of the Church. The *apostolicity* of the Church is essentially seen in the *mission of the whole people*, which in turn manifests itself centrally in the *authentic preaching of the Gospel and right administration of the sacraments*. This *mission*, in which *all* the baptized (the whole people) participate equally, is thereby characterized by a *particular commission*, the content of which is determined by the apostolic *Gospel*, to which the canonical scriptures bear witness. The commission consists of bearing witness to this Gospel to the whole world in word and deed. The apostolic mission therefore consists of commissioning and authorization for a particular *ministry – diakonia* (which is to be understood comprehensively) to the world.

2.   It is emphasized in all the ecumenical dialogues of recent years that the characteristic of apostolicity applies fundamentally and primarily to the Church as a whole. This underlines the fact that all Christians are equally empowered for, and obliged to, participation in the apostolic mission by their common baptism. This is the Reformation principle of the priesthood of all believers which flows from this understanding of apostolicity. Because the Church as a whole is apostolic, every Christian equally has the task of participating in its mission in the service of reconciliation in the world.

3.   This apostolic commission given to the whole Church and thereby to all Christians is in no way limited or removed by the particular ordained ministry, but rather confirmed and strengthened by it. For the ordained ministry has no other apostolic commission and no other task than the priesthood of all believers has, but is a functional making specific of some of its duties for a particular area – the ministry of *public proclamation*. So in the Reformation understanding the ordained ministry is not *sacerdotium*, but *ministerium*, more precisely *ministerium verbi divini*, and as such 'the exercising of the ministry which is entrusted to and laid upon the whole congregation'.[52] Its special character lies in the fact that it carries out this ministry which is entrusted to and laid upon the whole Church on the one hand with a view to certain functions, namely the *proclamation of the Gospel through word and sacrament*, and on the other hand in a particular way, namely *publicly*. Thus it exercises the tasks of proclamation belonging to this ministry on behalf of and in the name of the whole Church, in order thus 'to serve the ministry of the whole people of God' (para. 15 (viii)). However, no-one can speak in the name of the whole Church of his own accord; rather, the right and the authority to do this must be conferred by the whole Church. This is why the exercise of this particular ministry in the Church requires *ordination*, the orderly commissioning and authorization for the ministry of *public* proclamation.

4.   The public exercising of the ministry entrusted to and laid upon the whole Church is not left to its discretion. The Church cannot not exercise it. To this extent the ordained ministry as 'a gift of God to his Church' (para. 15 (viii)) is essential to the Church being the Church. It is not an institution of the Church such that the Church may have it or not have it, but an institution without which it could not exercise its apostolic mission in the service of reconciliation. For this service is accomplished essentially in the proclamation of the Gospel through word and sacrament, for the sake of which alone there is the *'ministerium docendi et porrigendi sacramenta'* as a divine institution in the Church (CA V), and both proclamation of the Word in the congregation and celebration of the sacraments of baptism and the eucharist are by their very nature *public proceedings*. As such they need ordering, and taking care of this is a task of the Church as a whole, to which it is entitled and committed because of its apostolic mission.

5.   The fact that the ordained ministry is not an institution of the Church which can be dispensed with but a gift of God to the Church does not mean that it stands alongside word and sacrament. Rather, it is clearly distinguished from them because it is functionally subordinated to them. The ministry is not a means of salvation like word and sacrament, which build up the Body of Christ and constitute the Church, but it is given to the Church for the sake of the proclamation of the Gospel in word and sacrament. It belongs to the Church as Church because the Church is only what it is if the acts which constitute it are indeed carried out. And

the ministry is that indispensable concretion-form of the Church, in which the Church, fulfilling its commission in the form of an institutional self-commitment, takes care actually to fulfil its commitment to the public carrying out of the basic acts of word and sacrament which constitute it, and takes care that it is able to fulfil that commitment at every time. Unlike word and sacrament, the ministry of the Church is therefore not objectively prior to the Church, but is given with it, but not as an institution of the Church which would be dispensable in certain circumstances, but as an institutional implication of the basic tasks given to it and the basic acts which constitute it – tasks and acts of proclamation of the Gospel.

6.   As an institutional implication of the basic acts of proclamation of the Gospel in word and sacrament which constitute the Church, the office which serves this function is not only an expression of the apostolicity but also of the *unity* of the Church. The Church is one, in so far as it proclaims 'the one Word of God which we must hear and which we must trust and obey in life and in death'.[53] It is thereby that community 'in which Jesus Christ presently acts in word and sacrament through the Holy Spirit'.[54] The unity of the Church is the one Lord who unites members of the Church by his action. This uniting action occurs in proclamation of the Gospel through word and sacrament. The congregation gathered around the word and sacrament is therefore the Church in the full, universal sense of the term. For through unification with Christ the Church is not only united in itself, but placed in the context of the universal Church with the *communio sanctorum* of all who are united with it and thereby with each other through Christ at other times and in other places. In serving the proclamation of the Gospel, with the aid of which that occurs, the ministry at the same time also serves the unity of the Church. As an institutional self-commitment of the Church to this proclamation it is at the same time the self-commitment of the Church to unity – admittedly, the unity which is effected through Christ himself alone and not through the Church, because the Church itself always remains the receiver of this unity. This ministry of the Church can neither create nor represent this unity, but only make visible through it that it points unmistakeably away from itself and towards that which it serves – the present action of Christ in the proclamation of the Gospel through word and sacrament. The more clearly this occurs, the better the ministry makes visible the unity which characterizes the Church of all times and places.

7.   Precisely because the Church is not responsible for the institution and existence of the ministry, it has the inescapable duty to see to the *ordering of this ministry*. As the result of church action the ordering of the ordained ministry is therefore, unlike its existence in the Church, historically changeable and variable. The fact that the ordained ministry is 'an office of divine institution' (para. 8 (viii)) does not imply that this could also be said of any ordering of this ministry. The *Common Statement* rightly says nothing to the effect that the ordained min-

istry must have the structure of the threefold ministry. For every structure and ordering of this ministry is the historical result of church activity in ordering and as such only to be measured by whether the way this ministry is formed, structured and ordered suffices for the unchangeable *task* of this ministry, which is 'to serve the ministry of the whole people of God' (para. 18 (viii)) in the best possible way given the particular historical circumstances which apply. It is part of the apostolic commission of the Church to order the ministry of the public carrying out of this commission. However, a church is not apostolic through a particular ordering of this ministry, but only through the fact that it exercises this ministry. A fundamental distinction must therefore be made between the *existence of the ordained ministry in the Church* and the *structuring of the ordained ministry in a church* – an insight which has borne its first fruits in Porvoo.

8.   The same also applies to *episkope*. This too is not an optional or dispensable structure of ordering of the Church, but nor is it constitutive for the Church in a way different from the ordained ministry or the expression of a particular sacramental hierarchy of clerical ranks in the Church. Where the Church is, there is the ministry of the Church and thereby also *episkope*. If *episkope* becomes apparent institutionally in a particular way, this is only as the functional shaping of an area of tasks in the Church, which is strictly to be understood in the light of the fundamental tasks, rites and duties of the Church as a whole and thereby from the starting point of the priesthood of all believers. Viewed in this way, *episkope* is, however, characterized by two factors.

On the one hand, as 'a ministry of pastoral oversight' (para. 15 (ix)) it is a functional making specific of the ordained ministry for the exercising of the tasks which are assigned in Porvoo to the 'ministry of co-ordination' (para. 42). It marks out a particular field of pastoral tasks within the ordained ministry, and is therefore the expression of a grouping of the tasks, but not of the spiritual competences of those who have them. As a rule, among these tasks is especially the responsibility to see that no local church separates itself from its connection with the *communio sanctorum* of other times and places and that the duty which is laid upon the ordained ministry to pay attention to and protect the universal church context is also fulfilled.

On the other hand, however, it is also a functional particularizing of tasks which belong not only to the ordained ministry but also to every Christian – the tasks of ordering and leadership of the Church. Through baptism every Christian is entitled and obliged to carry out all tasks and functions which are given by the apostolic mission of the whole Church. Among these, alongside the proclamation through word and deed, is also the ordering and leadership of the Church. In their public exercise these tasks have to be ordered by the Church. The ordained ministry is the functionally specific manifestation of the general obligation of proclamation for the area of public teaching and leadership of worship, and *episkope*, as an ordained ministry of proclamation, shares in this. But the ordered ministry is not at the same time the ordering ministry; rather, it remains embedded in the context of the Church as a whole. The task of ordering and leading the Church is and remains the task of all Christians and not only of the ordained ministers. But this ordering and leadership task of all Christians needs ordering in its public exercise, and this is the second component of *episkope*. In this regard, however, it is never only the concern of the holders of the ordained ministry of proclamation, but also of other Christians. Therefore, in the Protestant view the exercise of *episkope* can *never be limited to ordained clergy*, but is in a quite decisive regard the concern of *congregations and synods*. It is not by chance but on material grounds that it is exercised 'in our churches in a variety of forms, *episcopal and non-episcopal*' (para. 17 A (iv) – my emphasis). The fact that *episkope* is practised in personal, collegial and communal ways (para. 15 (ix)) cannot therefore according to the Protestant understanding be applied from the outset and exclusively to the clergy who are active in the office of bishop. It would be better to speak of a *synodical episcopate*, the authority of which rests on the authority given to all Christians through baptism and therefore to the Church as a whole, and not on particular lines of tradition of the transmission of the episcopal office in the succession of the historic episcopate.

Precisely for this reason, the distinction between *episkope* and *episcopal office* which is opened up in Porvoo but not consistently followed through is important and can take us further. *If the office of bishop is understood as a differentiation within the ordained ministry, it cannot completely take on the tasks of* episkope. *If it is to be able to take these tasks on completely, it must be an 'office of bishop' which in principle is also open to Christians who are not ordained to the ministry.* This proviso must also be made if in a church *episkope* was, would be or is as a matter of fact only exercised by ordained ministers. The continuity of *episkope* in a church cannot be identified with or reduced to a succession of ordained ministers in the exercise of this function. But the historic episcopate could function as a sign only for *this* succession, and therefore it is only a sign which means something in a church in which the whole church makes the exercise of *episkope* the responsibility of specially called ministers. For the Protestant churches this can only be a possible and not a theologically binding arrangement, because in consequence of the priesthood of all the baptized they understand the task of leading and ordering the Church, as a matter of principle, as the task of the whole Church and not only of a part of the Church. Here too therefore it is the case that a church is not free to practise or not to practise *episkope*, but is committed to do so because of its apostolic mission. A church is, however, very much free to shape the *ordering and exercising of episkope*, the only condition being that this shaping may not contradict the mission given to the whole Church, and the specific remit of *episkope* must so further the ministry of the whole Church that this ministry can be exercised in the best possible way in the given historical circumstances.

9.   Every true church is therefore apostolic as a whole, not only by a specific legally describable ordering of its offices of ministry. The Church of England and the Protestant churches of Germany confirmed expressly in the Meissen Declaration that in this sense they are apostolic. But if every church as a whole participates in the way described in 'the One, Holy, Catholic and Apostolic Church of Jesus Christ' (para. 17 A (i)), and if the ordained ministry is constitutive and essential for the Church (para. 15 (viii)), then this participation extends also to the ordained ministry of the church concerned. For if it was not the case with the ministry, it could also not be the case for the church as a whole, if the ordained ministry as 'an office of divine institution' (para. 15 (viii)) is constitutive for the church as a whole. But if both sides are true churches with an ordained ministry, then the ordained ministries of both the Anglican and the Protestant churches must be appropriate for their apostolic commission – and they are indeed, if they promote the right proclamation of the Gospel in word and sacrament, which is their apostolic duty and task and is mutually confirmed as a fact in Meissen. It follows from this, however, that neither of the two churches has any advantage over the other in their ministries with regard to the fulfilment of their apostolic commission. Both perform precisely what they should and must perform. And both do this in a way and in a form which reflect their specific history and the experiences which have shaped them.

10.   I have already pointed out that the legal and theological emphasis on the historic episcopate on the Anglican side reflects quite materially the religious and (church-) political experiences which the Church of England had in the course of its history. The same also applies to the Protestant churches. The ordering of their ministries may have begun in the sixteenth century as an irregular emergency ordering, but only to understand it in this way would be to overlook the fact that from the beginning and with good reasons it was also an ordering of Reformation renewal. It was such because the form of the ordering of the ministry which was regular at that time had proved to be incapable of ensuring that it was carried out responsibly. Bishops gave 'through their hardness reason... for division and schism which they should clearly have helped to prevent' (CA 28, BSLK, p. 133, 4–7). They ask, Melanchthon complained, 'nothing at all about how one teaches or preaches, they do not ask how the Christian usage of the sacrament is kept up, they ordain silly asses; Christian teaching is undermined by the fact that the churches are not provided with capable preachers'.[55] They drew the consequence from this that no ordering of the ministry deserves to be called regular which leads to a situation where necessary reforms in the Church which are in accordance with

the Gospel can be hindered by the holders of offices of ministry. For this reason they insisted that ministry and ministers must allow themselves to be measured against the Gospel and not the other way round, and that the ordering of the ministry and of all other structures and activities of the Church is and must be *semper reformanda* in the life of the Gospel. In holding to this principle, they remained faithful to the apostolic commission of the whole Church and in regulating and ordering ordination to the public ministry of preaching and the fulfilling of the necessary tasks of *episkope* differently, following this principle in view of the failure of the holders of the office of bishop, they carried out in practice the apostolic duty of the Church as a whole to care for the right proclamation of the Gospel, administering of the sacraments and leadership of the Church. This means, however, that *the Protestant churches did not only remain apostolic as a whole, but they have never left or given up the apostolic succession with regard to the ordained ministry, but precisely the opposite – they have preserved and applied it.*

11.   It is therefore theologically false to speak of a *'defectus ordinis'* with regard to their ministries (as occurs on the part of the Roman Catholic Church), and it is theologically problematic to concede 'apostolic continuity' to them,[56] but to insist on their reincorporation into the succession of the historic episcopate in order to achieve a visible representation of the unity of the Church and the establishment of full communion (as occurs from the Anglican side). Both views are only plausible if one evaluates them not as theological arguments but as arguments of ecclesiastical law. The ordained ministry in the Protestant church is not the same as that in the Roman or Anglican churches, even if it fulfills the same apostolic functions in the Protestant church, which the Roman or Anglican ministries fulfill. But why should the regulations of the *Codex iuris canonici* or of the Anglican Ordinal of 1662 have to apply in the Protestant churches or their regulations in the Roman or Anglican Church?

12.   The only argument recognizable in the debate since Meissen is that of the *better or greater visibility of the Church* – without the 'service of a reconciled, common ministry'[57] the – existing and not at all contested – unity of both churches in Jesus Christ and their (expressly confessed) unity in faith cannot be made sufficiently visible.[58] But whatever that means, it cannot mean the mutual taking over of regulations of ecclesiastical law. It can only be meant that *both sides bear witness each in their own way* to the unity and apostolicity *not only of their but also of the other church.* And they can do that no more visibly and convincingly than by proclaiming the same Gospel celebrating the same sacraments expressing the same faith, emphasizing and recognizing the same capabilities and duties of every Christian resulting from baptism, fulfilling the same task of ordering the public ministry in the Church, and attempting in the same way to fulfil their commission to *diakonia* to the world.

This cannot mean, however, that they must also realize in the same way their equal essential and original task of ordering the ministry, or that the same shaping of the ordained ministry is therefore necessary for the full, visible unity of the Church. The goal of the movement towards visible unity is, after all, not a uniform Church but 'the reconciliation of churches and ministries within the wider fellowship of the universal Church'.[59] The universal Church, however, is not a particular institutional organization alongside the Anglican and Protestant churches, but that which makes these churches churches and must itself become manifest in them, if they really want to be churches and to be visible and effective as churches. The universal Church also has no ministries, but only the one ministry of Jesus Christ, in which all of the baptized participate in the same way. There are only ministries in the historical life of the Church, where the ministry of Jesus Christ comes into play visibly, perceptibly and effectively in the proclamation of the Gospel through word and sacrament in space and time and forms a particular ecclesial community. And these ministries exist not as visible signs, images or representations of the ministry of Jesus Christ, but only as *ministeria verbi divini*, that is to say as *offices of service* of the actions in which and through which the ministry of Jesus Christ is accomplished in historical churches. The *unity* of these ministries is therefore only shown in the identity of their functions and thereby in the *one common service* which they perform, not in an identical form, historical origin or theological legitimation. Accordingly, the 'wider fellowship of the universal Church' in which the ministries are to be brought to 'reconciliation' can only be found *in* each church, not alongside or outside it, and in it it can only be found in that which makes not only it but also every other church a church – the proclamation of the Gospel in word and sacrament, which is the only thing which the ministry has to serve.

Notes

* Since this paper was written, the Porvoo Common Statement has officially been accepted by all the Anglican and Lutheran churches involved, except for the Churches of Denmark and Latvia.

1. Paragraph numbers refer to The Meissen Common Statement in *The Meissen Agreement: Texts* (CCU Occasional Paper No. 2, 1993).

2. It is above all L.W. Countryman who on the Anglican side has recently spoken in favour of a sacramental understanding of ordination, in *The Language of Ordination. Ministry in an Ecumenical Context* (Philadelphia, 1992), ch. 3.

3. In this case, moreover, it is also not sensible in the case of 'full communion' between different churches to contest or limit the transitivity of this matter and, as in *'Toward Full Communion' and 'Concordat of Agreement'. Lutheran-Episcopal Dialogue, Series 3* (ed. W.A. Norgren and W.G. Rusch, Minneapolis/Augsburg, 1991), to make the proviso that '[t]his Concordat of

Agreement with the Evangelical Lutheran Church in America does not imply or inaugurate any automatic communion between the Evangelical Lutheran Church in America and the other provinces of the Anglican Communion or any other churches with whom the Episcopal Church is in full communion' (para. 12, p. 103). This proviso only makes sense if one takes as the basis for one's thinking the ministry and ministerial acts of *particular* churches, and thus precisely does not have the *one* ministry of the *one* Church in view.

4.   On the basis of this understanding too, the regulations of *'Toward Full Communion' and 'Concordat of Agreement'*, para. 7 only partially make sense theologically. Why should the conclusion be drawn from the lifelong commission to the ministry of a church that those also who have left their office through 'retirement, resignation, or conclusion of term' (*ibid.*, p. 101) should – as is said here in the case of bishops – continue to 'be regular members of the Conference of Bishops' (*ibid.*, p. 101)? All church offices are given for a time, even if people are given a life-long commission for them: leaving the office does not end the commission, but participation in the exercising of it. This rule seems not to apply in the case of bishops.

5.   Unlike in *'Toward Full Communion'* and *'Concordat of Agreement'*, 'the distinct ministry of bishop within the one ministry of Word and Sacrament' (para. 3, cf. *ibid.*, pp. 99, 101) is not expressly mentioned.

6.   Cf. E. Herms, 'Stellungnahme zum dritten Teil des Lima-Dokuments "Amt"', *KuD*, 31 (1985), 65–96, 71f.

7.   S.W. Sykes, 'The Laying on of Hands in Succession' in H. Meyer (ed.), *Gemeinsamer Glaube und Strukturen der Gemeinschaft* (Frankfurt/Main, 1991), 185–97, 191f. Bishop Palmer had declared, in line with this, in Lausanne in 1927 that churches which had retained 'the traditional form of the ministry of Holy Orders' assumed that 'In ordination Christ ordains': 'It is Christ who consecrates or ordains, and in consecration or ordination He, using the bishop as His mouthpiece, makes a man a bishop, or a priest, or a deacon' ('The Church's Ministry', in H.N. Bate (ed.), *Faith and Order. Proceedings of the World Conference, Lausanne, August 3–21*, 1927 (London, 1927), 233–48, 236f. And Archbishop William Temple confirmed this view in 1943 in an address to the Convocation of Canterbury, as follows: 'When I consecrate a godly and well learned man to the office and work of a Bishop in the Church of God, I do not act as a representative of the Church, if by that is meant the whole number of contemporary Christians; but I do act as the min-isterial instrument of Christ in His Body the Church.... This authority to consecrate and to ordain is itself witness to the continuity of the life of the Church in its unceasing dependence on its Head, Jesus Christ.... (W. Temple, *Christian Unity and Church Reunion. The Presidential Address delivered in full synod to the Convocation of Canterbury, Tuesday, May 25th* (London, 1943), pp. 18f, bound with *The Chronicle of the Convocation of Canterbury* (London, 1943).

8.   What 'authorized' precisely includes is, admittedly, the open question. The *rite vocatus* of CA 14 had been expounded expressly in *Apologie* 14 as not being identical with canonical ordination: because 'the bishops do not wish to tolerate our people', we must 'let the bishops go their own way and be more obedient to God', for we know 'that the Christian Church is present where

God's word is rightly taught' (BSLK, 297, 11–20). In practice, someone who is called according to the *orders of the church concerned* is described as *rite vocatus*. In the Thirteen Articles of 1538, which were closely based on the *Confessio Augustana*, it was expressly said of the right to ordain, in accordance with this, that it lay with 'those in the church into whose hands the laws and customs of each region, in keeping with the Word of God, have placed the right of calling and admitting people into the ministry' (quoted by S.W. Sykes, 'The Ministry and the Episcopal Office: An Anglican Approach to the *Confessio Augustana*' in H. Meyer (ed.), *The Augsburg Confession in Ecumenical Perspective* (Stuttgart, 1980), 29-59, 45). This phrase was dropped when the Forty-two Articles of 1553 were composed. In Article 23 of the Thirty-nine Articles *rite vocatus* is translated 'lawfully called' (*legitime*), and in Article 36 this is made concrete with a reference to the Ordinal of Edward VI. In the Preface to the Ordinal a practice is claimed as being traceable back to Scripture and 'ancient Authors', without any special theological, let alone sacramental, claims being made for it. Only in 1662 was this practice specified as being 'Episcopal Consecration, or Ordination' and made a requirement in ecclesiastical law. On this problem, see R.H. Fuller, 'Sukzession oder Ordination? Zum anglikanisch-lutherischen Gespräch' in K. Fröhlich (ed.), *Ökumene: Möglichkeiten und Grenzen heute* (Tübingen, 1982), 24–31; B.M.G. Reardon, 'The Thirty-nine Articles and the Augsburg Confession', *LuthQ*, 3 (1989), 91-106, 102.

9.   This is formulated unmistakeably in para. 4 of *'Toward Full Communion'* and *'Concordat of Agreement'*: 'the threefold ministry of bishops, presbyters, and deacons in historic succession will be the future pattern of the one ordained ministry of Word and Sacrament in both churches as they begin to live in full communion' (loc. cit. note 3, p. 99).

10.   *Apostolicity and Succession. House of Bishops Occasional Paper* (GS Misc 432, 1994), para. 69, 28.

11.   The Porvoo Common Statement, *Together in Mission and Ministry* (London, 1993) evidences this just as unmistakeably as the document *'Toward Full Communion'* and *'Concordat of Agreement'* (cf. note 3).

12.   Among the extensive literature I mention N. Sykes, *Old Priest and New Presbyter* (Cambridge, 1956); W. Telfer, *The Office of a Bishop* (London, 1962); P. Avis, *The Church in the Theology of the Reformers* (London, 1981); *ibid., Anglicanism and the Christian Church. Theological Resources in Historical Perspective* (Minneapolis, 1989); S.W. Sykes / J. Booty (eds), *The Study of Anglicanism* (London, 1988). For the more recent ecumenical discussion from an Anglican point of view, see R.H. Roberts, 'Der Stellenwert des kirchlichen Amtes im ökumenischen Gespräch aus anglikanischer Sicht unter Berücksichtigung der Leuenberger Konkordie und der Lima-Erklärung', *ZThK*, 83 (1986), 370–403.

13.   W.S.F. Pickering, *Sociology of Anglicanism* in Sykes/Booty (cf. note 12), 364-75, 367.

14.   *God's Reign and Our Unity*, para. 91.

15.   L.W. Countryman (cf. note 2), 10.

16. Quoted by *ibid.*, p. 9.

17. Cf. G.K.A. Bell, *Documents on Christian Unity* (London, 1924), 1ff.

18. Resolution 6 of the 1920 Lambeth Conference does not even speak of the historic episcopate, but of '[a] ministry acknowledged by every part of the Church as possessing not only the inward call of the Spirit, but also the commission of Christ and the authority of the whole body' (*The Lambeth Conferences, 1867-1930* (London, 1948), 39).

19. J.H. Newman, 'The Catholicity of the Anglican Church' (1840) in *Essays Critical and Historical* (London, 1871), ii, 1-75.

20. 'The bishop has inherited the authority of the Apostles, and he, like them, speaks for Christ in ordination'. That 'involves the apostolic succession', whatever historical objections may be made against it, for the practical experience in mission areas taught that this 'is exactly how the authority of the Apostles passed into that of the bishops' (Palmer, in H.N. Bate (cf. note 7), 247ff).

21. Archbishop Chrisostomos, 'The Nature of the Church' in H. N. Bate (*loc. cit.*), 106–15. Cf. also the reservations on the part of the Orthodox churches against the final document of Section V (The Ministry of the Church) in Lausanne, expressed in a minority report: 'The Orthodox Church, regarding the ministry as instituted in the Church by Christ Himself, and as the body which by a special *charisma* is the organ through which the Church spreads its means of grace such as the sacraments, and believing that the ministry in its threefold form of bishops, presbyters and deacons can only be based on the unbroken apostolic succession, regrets that it is unable to come in regard to the ministry into some measure of agreement with many of the Churches represented at this Conference...' (H.N. Bate, *loc. cit.*, 470f).

22. J.H. Newman, *Apologia pro vita sua* (London, 1948); cf. E. Benz, *Bischofsamt und apostolische Sukzession im deutschen Protestantismus* (Stuttgart, 1953), 183ff.

23. Not for nothing is it repeatedly emphasized by Anglicans that – as Lausanne formulated it – 'the acceptance of any special form of ordination as the regular and orderly method of introduction into the ministry of the Church for the future should not be interpreted to imply the acceptance of any one particular theory of the origin, character or function of any office in the Church' (H.N. Bates, *loc. cit.*, 469).

24. Thus Cosin, for example, emphasized, following John Overall, 'though we are not to lessen the *jus divinum* of episcopacy, where it is established and may be had, yet we must take heed that we do not, for want of episcopacy where it cannot be had, cry down and destroy all the Reformed churches abroad, both in Germany and France and other places, and say they have neither ministers nor sacraments, but all is void and null that they do' (*Works*, iv (Oxford, 1850), 449, quoted by S.W. Sykes, 'The Ministry and the Episcopal Office' (cf. note 8), 56).

25. Cf. A.J. Mason, *The Church of England and Episcopacy* (Cambridge, 1914), 223ff.

26. Quoted by H. Werner (cf. note 7), 601.

27. Richard Hooker, *Of the Laws of Ecclesiastical Polity* (1661), VII, x, 1, ed. P.G. Stanwood (The Folger Library Edition of the Works of Richard Hooker, Cambridge (Massachusetts) / London, 1981), iii, 202.

28. VII, ii, 3: *loc. cit.*, p. 152.

29. In practice, *'Toward Full Communion' and 'Concordat of Agreement'* (cf. note 3) takes up precisely this regulation. In para. 7 it is said that Lutheran bishops 'like other pastors' are ordained 'for life service of the gospel in the pastoral ministry of the historic episcopate', while in para. 8 it is urged that care should be taken 'that only bishops shall ordain all clergy' (p. 101).

30. R. Hooker, VII, iv, 1-4: *loc. cit.*, pp. 155-8.

31. VII, xi, 8: *loc. cit.*, p. 208.

32. *Fifty Sermons* (London, 1710), 374.

33. Thus the Lambeth Conference of 1930 (cf. note 18), 218. How problematic this excessive theological elevation of actual historical developments is becomes clear when one sees that, for example, the universal primacy of the Bishop of Rome can thereby be accepted as God's will for his Church. Cf. ARCIC I: *The Final Report of the Anglican–Roman Catholic International Commission* (London, 1982), 83ff.

34. Preface to the Ordinal, appended to the Book of Common Prayer (Cambridge/London, 1992), 534.

35. Ordination too thereby becomes no longer simply commissioning for *the* ministry of *the* Church, but commissioning for the ministry *of one church among others*.

36. H.H. Henson, *The Church of England* (Cambridge, 1939), 123.

37. W. Law, *Works, Three Letters to the Bishop of Bangor* (London, 1762; 1892 reprint, Hildesheim/New York, 1974), i, 9.

38. It is theologically not convincing to think that it would be sufficient to reject the Anglo-Catholic theory of succession in order to be able to meet ecumenically on the basis of the legal regulations of 1662. This was the path taken in the case of the Church of South India. This seems also to be the path taken in *'Toward Full Communion' and 'Concordat of Agreement'* (cf. note 3), when a 'temporary suspension' of the 1662 rule is spoken of, in order to make possible the 'full interchangeability and reciprocity of all Evangelical Lutheran Church in America pastors as priests or presbyters and all Evangelical Lutheran Church in America deacons as deacons in the Episcopal Church without any further ordination or re-ordination or supplemental ordination whatsoever' (para. 5, p. 100). This rule is then to apply to both churches without restriction: 'the threefold ministry of bishops, presbyters, and deacons in historic succession will be the future pattern of the one ordained ministry of Word and Sacrament in both churches' (para. 4, p. 99). A theological justification for the taking over of the '17th century restriction... of the Ordinal of 1662' (para. 5, p. 100) is not given.

39. The assertion of the 1662 Ordinal that it is 'evident unto all men diligently reading holy Scripture and ancient Authors, that from the Apostles' time there have been these Orders in Christ's Church; Bishops, Priests, and Deacons' (*loc. cit.*) is certainly false as stated, but does not rest on a problematic theory of succession. Neither the alleged historical situation nor the theological theory offered for it can be justified patristically. The reference to Irenaeus only indicates that Irenaeus was aware of a list of bishops and gave this theological significance. It does not prove that the Apostles appointed bishops and that there is an unbroken chain of such appointments. That the Roman bishop Linus (the second after Peter) is probably a fiction and arose from the misunderstanding of a Greek adjective is well known and only one of the problematic cases. Cf. R.L. Fox, *Pagans and Christians* (London, 1986), 498f; see also G. Gassmann, 'Apostolische Sukzession und Einheit der Kirche in der anglikanischen Theologie', *KuD*, 10 (1964), 257–83, 269f.

40. *The Gospel and the Catholic Church* (1936), quoted by H. Werner (cf. note 7), 602.

41. G. Gassmann (cf. note 39), 269f.

42. Cf., as early as 1922, 'Church Unity' in G.K.A. Bell (cf. note 17), 46. Exactly the same must apply today with regard to the theology of sign set out in the Porvoo Common Statement: the demand that the historic episcopal office be taken on cannot mean that one has to take it on. Without this demand, however, there is no theological reason to take on the historic episcopate.

43. Cf. *The Fullness of Christ. The Church's Growth into Catholicity being a report presented to His Grace the Archbishop of Canterbury* (London, 1960), 81f.

44. *The Lambeth Conferences, 1867-1948*, part II, p. 50.

45. J.A.T. Robinson, *On Being the Church in the World* (London, 1961), 101ff; *Intercommunion – An Open Letter to the Archbishop of Canterbury and the Archbishop of York* (London, 1961).

46. *'Toward Full Communion' and 'Concordat of Agreement'*, para. 4 (cf. note 3), 99.

47. P. Avis, 'What is Anglicanism?' in Sykes/Booty (cf. note 12), 405-24, 419.

48. Cf. L.W. Countryman (cf. note 2), 11. Similar problems may be expected in the case of the solutions sought with the Scandinavian and American Lutherans.

49. This is fully documented and set out in G. Gassmann, *Das historische Bischofsamt und die Einheit der Kirche in der neueren anglikanischen Theologie* (Göttingen, 1964).

50. Making this distinction reacts to a difficulty which Hermann Sasse pointed out as long ago as 1929 in translating the Lausanne documents in *Die Weltkonferenz für Glauben und Kirchenverfassung. Deutscher amtlicher Bericht über die Weltkirchenkonferenz zu Lausanne 3–21. August 1927* (Berlin, 1929), 297f, n. 2: 'The English word "ministry" has a double meaning. It means either "the spiritual office" or "its holders as a whole, the clergy".... In German we do not have a word which precisely corresponds with the English "ministry".... The word *Amt* in its full sense, which Luther used, in accordance with its fundamental meaning, for the Greek

diakonia, and which was used in the middle ages to translate *ministerium*, is the only possible way of translating "ministry". Unfortunately, we also have to use this word to translate the English "office", where it cannot be translated as *Stelle*. As a result, the contrast between "ministry" and "office" cannot be represented precisely in German. The word "order" is untranslatable. Where it is emphasized, we translate it as *Stand*, but otherwise we speak of the *Stufen/Graden des Amtes*, e.g. in a phrase like "the three holy orders of ministry [episcopate, presbyterate, diaconate]".

51. That Anglican theology thinks in precisely this sacramental direction is clearly evidenced by L.W. Countryman (cf. note 2) and *ibid.*, 'The Gospel and the Institutions of the Church with Particular Reference to the Historic Episcopate', *ATHR*, 66 (1984), 402–15.

52. Barmen Theological Declaration, Thesis IV, in *Die Barmer Theologische Erklärung. Einführung und Dokumentation*, ed. A. Burgsmüller and R. Werth (3rd edn, Neukirchen-Vluyn, 1984), 37.

53. Thesis I (*ibid.*), p. 34.

54. Thesis III (*ibid.*), p. 36.

55. *Apologie* 28, BSLK 397, 23ff.

56. *The Porvoo Common Statement*, para. 52 (cf. note 11).

57. *The Meissen Common Statement*, para. 8 (cf. note 1).

58. Cf. G. Evans, '*Episcope* and Episcopacy: The Niagara Report', *One in Christ*, 25 (1989), 281-6, 284ff.

59. *The Meissen Common Statement* (cf. note 1), para. 19.

The Reformation in Germany and the Episcopal Office

Dorothea Wendebourg

The development of the episcopal office in the protestant churches of Germany[1] was determined by two factors: by the theological principles laid down by the Reformation, and above all the Wittenberg Reformation, and by the political circumstances of the Holy Roman Empire of the German Nation as they had developed in the course of the Middle Ages, which remained determinative for the Empire until its end. Let us begin with the second point.

I.   The Church in the Holy Roman Empire

In all the kingdoms of the mediaeval West the Church, and above all the bishops, were integrated into the political system. This reflected the understanding of the unity of Christian society in its secular and spiritual dimensions which was taken as read in the Middle Ages despite all the disputes about the concrete relationship of the one to the other. Within this general framework the Holy Roman Empire of the German Nation was distinguished by a particular legal structure, the spiritual and political being bound up much more closely together through the spiritual principalities, which by around 1500 made up a good fifteen per cent of the territory of the Empire.[2] According to this legal structure, which had its roots[3] in the Ottonian and early Salian Imperial Church of the tenth and eleventh centuries,[4] archbishops and bishops – as well as other spiritual dignitaries – were at the same time princes, ranking indeed above the secular princes. As such they constituted estates subject only to the Emperor. Their representatives were voting members of the Imperial Diet, and their number included three of the seven Electors, who elected the Emperor, and the holders of the most important imperial offices, above all that of Arch-Chancellor, which belonged to the Archbishop and Elector of Mainz.[5] In the Imperial Diet they outnumbered the secular princes – in 1521 by about fifty to twenty.[6] In short, the bishops were cornerstones of the Empire, their political role as territorial rulers an indispensable element of the Imperial Constitution.

However, the opposite was also the case: the Empire was the context for the Church. In the Empire, the Church did not have any inter-diocesan structures such as synods. The only body in which the bishops came together was the Imperial

Diet, and here they met as princes. What is more, even within the Church, their practical power had its basis and its limits in their power as princes. That can be seen in what happened within their dioceses. These included, because of the constitutional position which has been sketched above, areas of two sorts: the territory in which the bishop was also the prince – the *Hochstift* – and territories and cities which had their own, usually secular, authorities. The possibilities for enforcing episcopal jurisdiction were very different in these two types of area. Their jurisdiction could be enforced in the *Hochstift*, where there was no competing secular ruler and their ecclesiastical jurisdiction was linked with political power, whereas in the secular territories and cities the government of the Church lay to a considerable extent in the hands of the secular authorities, i.e. the princes and the city councils. Visitations, ecclesiastical patronage, monastic reforms and many other activities were carried out here to a considerable extent by the secular authorities and not – or only nominally or in the context of initiatives by the secular prince – by the bishop.[7] The Church of the Empire was *de facto* a church run by the princes. That was true of the secular territories, but was also true in a specific and in some ways heightened manner in the ecclesiastical territories, insofar as the bishops were only able to enforce their authority here because of their position as territorial rulers.

II. The Wittenberg Reformers' Understanding of the Episcopal Office

Martin Luther's understanding of the episcopal office is expressed very clearly as early as 1520 in his tract 'To the Christian nobility of the German Nation'. He says:

> According to the will of Christ and the Apostles every city should have a pastor or bishop, as Paul clearly writes in Titus 1, ... For a bishop and a pastor are one and the same thing for St Paul, as St Jerome also proves. But the bishops we have now are unknown to Scripture, but have been installed by a Christian congregation, so that one pastor should rule over many.

Nonetheless, according to the Apostle the pastor or bishop should 'have several priests and deacons alongside him..., who help him to rule the flock and the congregation with preaching and sacraments'.[8]

This quotation contains and implies a series of statements, to which Luther continued to hold and which came to be included in the confessional documents of the churches reformed from Wittenberg.[9] According to this view, 'episcopal office' is the term for the fundamental apostolic ministry of the church, which was instituted by Christ. The task of this ministry is that of leading the congregation through preaching the word of God and administration of the sacraments, which is consti-

50

tutive for the Church. Where does such activity take place? In the local congregation gathered around one pulpit, one font and one table. That is to say, the episcopal office is none other than the office of pastor. Luther takes the identity of the office of pastor and the office of bishop as the fundamental apostolic ministry in the Church from the Pastoral Letters, according to which the *episkopos* is the leader of a single congregation. In addition, he adduces Jerome's exegesis of these letters.[10] He also liked to refer to the situation in the early Church: 'Every city had a bishop, just as they now have pastors, and St Augustine, who was consecrated or ordained by his pastor or bishop Valerius and after the latter's death became bishop in his place, had no larger parish than our parish of Wittenberg, if it was indeed as large at all.'[11]

However, for Luther the real reason for this identification lies not in one biblical or patristic quotation or another, but in the nature of the office itself: in the fact that the office by definition is the ministry of preaching and administration of the sacraments, and is therefore primarily realized in ministry to the individual congregation. Against this background, how the office is named is of secondary importance.[12] Since the New Testament and the early Church use the word 'bishop' in this context, it is, however, appropriate to follow their usage and thereby at the same time bring the original meaning of the word in the Christian context back into currency. Indeed, it is even useful to do so, since going back to this original terminology also – as will become apparent – offers the opportunity to bring to the fore once again the essence of this office in the face of a good deal of obfuscation.

All of this is not to say that in the Church there are no ministers ranking above the pastor – 'bishops' in the sense of the word which has developed in the course of church history, i.e. leaders of whole dioceses. But not only this use of the term, but even this grading of ministry itself is secondary in comparison with the office of pastor, having arisen 'by decision of the Christian congregation'.[13] Nor do the passages quoted above intend to deny that the pastor-bishop has other ministers around him – presbyters ('priests'), and deacons, as they are known in the pastoral letters. But these are subordinated to him, and integrated into his ministry to the congregation – appointed to 'help' him in this.[14]

In regarding not an office above the parish level but the apostolic ministry (*ministerium*)[15] in the congregation as the fundamental ministry instituted by Christ, Luther does not only stand in continuity with the early Church, but also perpetuates the dominant line in the mediaeval theology of ministry.[16] Admittedly, the inter-parochial diocesan structure had long since developed – in the West outside Italy, moreover, with large territorial dioceses – and the term '*episcopus*' had 'migrated up' to this level. Nonetheless, it was not the leader of an area encompassing many parishes, now called 'bishop', in whom the fundamental apostolic ministry of the Church was now seen as being realized. The order of ministry in its fullness was, rather, in the view of most mediaeval theologians, given in the presbyterate.[17] Peter Lombard wrote in his Sentences, and thereby shaped the later thinking of the Middle Ages, that according to his sources there were only two sacred orders (*sacri ordines*), the diaconate and the presbyterate.[18] The episcopate therefore did not represent a separate order, but only a specific dignity and function (*dignitas et officium*).[19]

This development was consistent with the fact that the presbyters had gradually taken over most of the tasks of the bishops in the congregations and had themselves become congregational leaders. However, it also went along with a substantive change in the understanding and practice of the ministry. The ministry was more and more shaped by its function in relation to the eucharist understood as sacrifice. That is to say, the presbyter was regarded in the first place as a priest, and also as the minister of absolution. At the centre of his ordination, therefore, stood the transfer of sacrificing power with the gift of the sacrificial instruments (*porrectio instrumentorum*).[20]

The rehabilitation of the term '*episcopus*' in its New Testament and early church meaning by Luther and the other Wittenberg theologians was a protest against this understanding and represented a substantive redefinition of this office – or rather the recovery of its original meaning. However much he joined with the mediaeval theologians in seeing the apostolic ministry at the local level as the fundamental, full ministerial office of the Church, he did not at all start from the mediaeval office of priest in defining its tasks, but rather emphasized that its tasks were those of the bishop in the Pastoral Letters and the first centuries.[21] The holder of this office is to proclaim the Gospel, as the letters to Timothy and Titus prescribe for the *episkopos*, he is to preach and to administer the sacraments, as described by the sources of the first centuries.[22] In this way the meaning of the ministry of the Church which is true to the Gospel was regained, and at the same time the term 'bishop' was once again filled with genuine spiritual meaning.

Luther's taking up the understanding and practice of the episcopal office which was current in the New Testament and early church periods could be demonstrated in a variety of contexts. I shall refer only to two. For the *Formula Missae*, the reformed liturgy of 1523, the leader of worship is *episcopus*[23] – as in the church orders and liturgies of the early Church, such as the Apostolic Tradition, the *Didaskalia* or the Apostolic Constitutions. And in the Wittenberg Ordinal of 1535[24] the ordination of pastors follows the form of an episcopal consecration. The readings are 1 Timothy 3. 1–7 and Acts 20. 28–31; the admonition which follows addresses the ordinands as future 'bishops';[25] and in accordance with the information given in the Pastoral Letters about the ordination of a bishop and with the usage of the early Church, it is the laying on of hands with prayer which forms the ritual climax – there is no giving of instruments. The ministers of ordination are to be the pastors of neighbouring cities, i.e. neighbouring bishops, as prescribed for episcopal consecrations by Canon 4 of the Council of Nicaea,[26] to which explicit reference is made.[27] The fact that in Wittenberg and elsewhere pastors performed these ordinations is part of this line of tradition. They did it as the holders of the one, full, episcopal office, to which – as the sources from the early Church show – belongs also the power to pass this office on. The person ordained thereby entered into an episcopal line of succession.[28] However, this thought plays no part in the thinking of those involved, just as the concept of the apostolic succession in the episcopal office was of significance – on all sides – only at the margins.[29] For the Wittenberg theologians, what was important was faithfulness in the transmission of proclamation in accordance with the Gospel – 'succession in teaching'; it was this succession that ordination from bishop to bishop had to serve.[30]

Now the identification of the pastoral office and the episcopal office in Luther's writings and in the church which was reformed from Wittenberg was only one side of the coin, for at the same time the episcopate understood as an office above the parish level was also affirmed here. The quotation from the tract *To the Christian Nobility* does not plead for the abolition of diocesan episcopacy and neither do the Wittenberg theologians elsewhere, despite all their criticism of the existing bishops. And as early as the following years, Luther often[31] made positive suggestions for the form which a legitimate episcopal office above the parish level which was true to the Gospel should take. In 1523, in the short tract *De instituendis ministris Ecclesiae*, he advised the Bohemians,[32] to whom it was addressed, that they should not be content with pastors, but should also have bishops above the pastors leading the Church, who would have the oversight over the pastors. That is to say, if one were to be faithful terminologically to the identity of the pastoral office and the episcopal office – to which Luther remains faithful here – there should, as in the early Church, be metropolitans or archbishops for whole regions, above the bishops in the individual cities.[33]

Before following this line of thought further, however, it is necessary to emphasize that the affirmation and eventually also the deliberate formation of episcopal structures above the parish level does not in the slightest alter the principle that the apostolic office of ministry in the Church is the pastoral office. Indeed, the higher-level offices rest entirely on the pastoral office. In them certain functions are set apart which in essence are implied in the tasks of the pastor, namely preaching and administering the sacraments.[34] The bishop above the parish level is therefore in essence a pastor, a bishop in the original sense of the word – the proclamation of the Gospel is his fundamental task too. Nonetheless, he is a pastor whose peculiar duty it is to undertake certain functions of the ministry. The fact that he does so as the special minister commissioned for that purpose is – unlike the essence and existence of the ministry of the Church itself[35] – a matter for decision by the Church,[36] it is not *iure divino*, but *iure positivo*,[37] *humana auctoritate*.[38]

Is it also for the Church to decide, whether connections are made and oversight undertaken above the parish level at all? Luther's preface to Melanchthon's *Instruction for Visitors*,[39] the first church order in Saxony, gives a clear answer to this question: the undertaking of the *Besuchsdienst* ['ministry or service of visiting'], as he calls the task of visitation or *episkope* in German, is 'beneficial and necessary' for Christendom.[40] How, in which institutional form, it occurs is variable – although the Wittenberg theologians generally envisage it as taking place in personal rather than synodical form.[41] But that it should happen cannot be open to discussion, for in it a dimension of the Church is expressed which belongs to its essence: its catholicity, that is to say its unity in the truth through space and time. This dimension of catholicity is given with the Gospel itself and therefore with the ministry of proclamation in preaching and sacrament in itself. But its maintenance is served when ministers especially commissioned for this task expressly and continually devote themselves to it in regulated forms. For this purpose they have to be superior to the parish pastors in certain fields:

> So that the Church should be one and of one accord, God has always propagated the same Gospel, through the partriarchs and the prophets and thereafter through Christ and the Apostles, and Christ instituted the ministry (*ministerium*), which will remain to the end of the world.... For he maintains the Gospel and intended that after the Apostles shepherds should be called in all congregations to undertake the task of proclamation of the Gospel. These he stirs up, though their gifts differ, nevertheless as holders of the same office of ministry. The unity of the Church therefore consists in this being linked together under one head through the same Gospel and the same ministry.... But so that everything should happen in an orderly fashion in the Church according to the rule of Paul, and the shepherds should be more strongly bound together..., and that the one should take on a duty of care for the other and divisions or schisms should be avoided, the useful rule came about, that out of many presbyters one bishop was elected, who should lead the Church through the teaching of the Gospel and the upholding of discipline, and should preside over the presbyters.... This ordering of the Church, if those who preside carry out their duty, is beneficial for the upholding of the unity of the Church.[42]

The concrete tasks of the 'presiding' bishops are teaching and judging questions of doctrine, ordination, including the examination of ordinands, visitation, legislation and administration of the law in the Church, and where necessary the calling of synods.[43] For all these tasks the same applies as to the ministry of proclamation from which they are derived: they serve the word of God, that is they are ecclesial and spiritual tasks. They may not be enforced by political means or linked with political goals.[44] For the existing church situation that meant that a legal structure such as that of the ecclesiastical principalities is not, as a matter of principle, compatible with it.[45]

III. The Attempt to Develop Episcopal Structures above the Parish Level in the Context of the Mediaeval Diocesan System

In principle, there were ministers whose task it was to undertake the episcopal functions sketched above – the diocesan bishops with their well-defined dioceses and their traditional episcopal sees.[46] For the Wittenberg Reformation no course of action was more obvious than to hold on to this state of affairs. The precondition for this, however, was that these bishops should in practice prove themselves to be episcopal holders of the apostolic ministry. But that was precisely what the reformers denied about the serving bishops of the Empire, and that with two arguments. First, they do not serve the Gospel, but they represent and cover up false doctrines and practices and are therefore those who bear chief responsibility for the ruinous condition in which the Church finds itself;[47] nothing shows that more clearly than the fact that they persecute the adherents of the Reformation.[48] Secondly, they are only nominally bishops,[49] but in reality princes, their whole interests and behaviour politically determined.[50] In other words, the serving bishops should repent and become true Christian bishops.[51] Then the Reformation could and would recognize them as the holders of *episkope* over their parishes.[52] That is to say, they should return to pure preaching of the Gospel and to due administration of the sacraments. And they should really do that which is the task of a bishop: proclaiming and teaching, visiting, ordaining etc.

Luther sketched a picture of the converted, reformed diocesan bishop who was therefore to be recognized by the parishes of the Reformation as early as 1522, the year in which the necessity of a certain institutional consolidation of the Reformation movement became apparent for the first time. The tract *Against the falsely named Spiritual Estate of the Pope and the Bishops*,[53] which – as the title makes clear – represents a biting settling of accounts with the serving bishops of the Empire, was attempting at the same time to shake these bishops up and bring them to their senses with regard to the Gospel and the true meaning of their office.[54] Had this attempt been successful, the German Lutheran churches – and most of the United ones – would today have a similar appearance to those of Scandinavia. They would display the pre-Reformation dioceses with bishops who could look back to a chain of predecessors into the Middle Ages and in some cases even into antiquity. These bishops, however, would be committed to proclaiming the Gospel according to the teaching of the Wittenberg Reformation and to undertaking their specific duties in accordance with it. And their office itself would be so defined as to correspond with the Reformation understanding of episcopacy above the parish level, as a particular expression of the one ministry of proclamation in the Church, which is primarily realized in the office of parish pastor.

Idle though such speculations are, it must be admitted that the hope which Luther expressed for a reformation of the existing episcopate and with the existing episcopate was not entirely unrealistic. Three years later, in 1525, the first cases occurred. In Prussia, which had just become a protestant duchy, two bishops joined the Reformation – Georg von Polentz (1478–1550), Bishop of the Samland since 1519 with his see in Königsberg, and Erhard von Queiß (1490–1529), whose election as Bishop of Pomesania in 1523 had, however, not yet been confirmed by the Pope, with the result that he had not been consecrated. They transferred their territories to the Duke. Luther watched this development with approval and offered advice.[55]

Prussia was not part of the Holy Roman Empire. This highlights the decisive problem which prevented a similar step by representatives of the episcopate within the Empire. The Prussian bishops were not princes of the Empire, and their positions lacked the constitutional significance which the ecclesiastical principalities within the Empire possessed. If their understanding of their office and the way they carried it out changed, that may not have been without political consequences, but its impact was limited. Such action by the bishops of the Empire, by contrast, would have shaken an important element of the whole political edifice. The institutional linkage between the Empire and the Emperor on the one hand and the Roman Church on the other hand, which the position of these men in the Imperial Diet and the Electoral College provided, would have been at stake. And the character of a large number of states within the Empire would have been fundamentally altered if, as in Prussia, the consequences of the Reformation demand for a genuinely ecclesial episcopal office and its criticism of the ecclesiastical principalities had been drawn and these had been turned into secular territories.[56]

The Prussian developments were therefore not imitated within the Empire.[57] However, in order to achieve some movement amongst the bishops here as well, the Wittenberg theologians came round to doing without full realization of their ideal of a protestant bishop and to suggest compromises. If conversions could not be expected among the serving bishops, they should at least allow protestant preaching to take its course, not persecute its adherents and ordain protestant pastors; if they did so, the Reformation parishes would recognize their jurisdiction.[58] Furthermore, the Wittenberg theologians were prepared not to insist on their demand that the ecclesiastical principalities should be abolished. This concession was, in any case, implied by the recognition of bishops who did not go over to the Reformation but were prepared to tolerate it; the pre-condition of this, though, would be that the ecclesiastical princes would have to distinguish strictly between their ecclesiastical and their political offices and not mix up the aims and means of the one with those of the other – a programme which was laid before the Emperor by the twenty-eighth article of the Augsburg Confession.[59] However, the Wittenberg theologians were also ready, where necessary, to allow bishops who went over to the Reformation to retain their princely rule, a concession which was intended to make it easier for them to join the Reformation and which left the constitutional system unaffected.[60] All the attempts which were actually made to achieve a protestant episcopate within the context of the mediaeval diocesan structure of the Empire[61] were based on this status quo. Nevertheless, even if this status quo was respected, should prince bishops go over to the Reformation then this threatened a profound alteration, in that the protestant estates within the Imperial Diet and the Electoral College would gain the majority. On every occasion, the Emperor made clear with all means at his disposal that he was not minded to accept such a shift, and in this he was successful.[62]

As a result, no bishop of the Empire was won for the Reformation together with his episcopal see. There were various moves in this direction, for example in the 1540s with the Archbishop and Elector of Cologne, Hermann von Wied (1477–1552), one of the highest ecclesiastical princes of the Empire, or with the Bishop of Minden, Münster and Osnabrück, Franz von Waldeck (1491–1553). Cologne was kept in line by the Emperor himself by military means (1547), the Archbishop being forced to abdicate and dying as an excommunicated protestant.[63] His Osnabrück colleague escaped a similar fate by turning his back on protestantism.[64] There was one exception which, however, proves the rule. The Bishop of Brandenburg, Matthias von Jagow (c.1480-1544), in office since 1516, joined the Reformation in 1539/40 and worked for its implementation in the Electorate of Brandenburg.[65] But his *Hochstift* – the territory which was under his secular rule – was no longer immediate to the Emperor.[66] No legal or political complications therefore arose for the Empire here, and there were no enduring protests.[67]

The suggested compromises led no further, and Matthias' case remained unique. The Wittenberg theologians therefore made yet another attempt to realize their project of 'mediaeval episcopal office in accordance with the Gospel'. If nothing was to be expected from the serving bishops, one must make use of vacancies in sees and place protestant candidates on vacant episcopal thrones from the outset. On the face of it, the same difficulties stood in the way of such attempts as impeded a bishop of the Empire from joining the Reformation. For that reason they could only succeed, if at all, where a bishop's independence within the Empire was restricted and he was protected by – but also dependent on – a protestant prince. This was the case in the three instances in which in the first half of the sixteenth century protestant men were appointed to vacant episcopal sees: in the Saxon dioceses of Naumburg-Zeitz (1542) and Merseburg (1544) and in Pomeranian Kammin (1545).

We shall now look briefly at the developments in Naumburg and Merseburg regarding Bishops Nikolaus von Amsdorff (1483–1565)[68] and Georg von Anhalt (1507–33),[69] because they are highly informative about how those involved understood the episcopal office and its bestowal. The rite used for their institution[70] corresponded to a considerable extent with the ordinal of Wittenberg, with some additional elements, partly stemming from the rite of episcopal consecration in the mediaeval pontificals, which were related to the particular tasks of the new bishop.[71] These differences are slight – the liturgical expression of the conviction discussed above that the regional episcopate now being conferred was no other ministry than that of the office of proclamation which is primarily realized in the congregational pastoral office. Is this office now bestowed for a second time here, i.e. is the ordination – which all of the candidates concerned had already received – simply repeated? Strikingly, there was no discussion of this question. All of those involved regarded the fact that the ordination which had once been received was not to be repeated as being just as obvious as the essential identity of pastoral office and episcopal office. Clearly, for them the installation of a bishop represented the actualizing of the ordination for the specific episcopal duties.[72]

The choice of the consecrators speaks the same language. In the case of the Saxon dioceses it was Luther together with the Superintendents and clergy from neighbouring cities, while in the case of Kammin it was the Superintendents of the neighbouring duchies.[73] This corresponded with the rule already made for ordination, that the bishop or pastor was to be ordained if possible by several neighbouring bishops, following the practice of the early Church.[74] It is noteworthy that the candidate from Merseburg had initially attempted to get a bishop – naturally one who supported the Reformation – to consecrate him. Three bishops came into question – the Archbishop of Cologne, one of the Prussian bishops and Matthias, Bishop of Brandenburg, although reasons of distance meant that in practice only the latter was a realistic possibility. Georg therefore made contact with him. Matthias agreed, but died before his planned journey, so that the whole plan came to nothing and Martin Luther conducted the laying on of hands.[75] It was suspected that Georg had engaged in these negotiations in order to enter into the apostolic succession of bishops through Matthias.[76] That is not impossible, but it cannot be proved from the sources. It is true that in those years the concept of the apostolic succession in the episcopal office, understood as the office of diocesan bishop,

was discussed once again in certain circles, the linkage of ordination and consecration to the bishop having been regarded as a firm rule for centuries – without,
however, having been made the subject of theological discussion. We shall come
back to this. But there is no statement of Georg in which he bases his wish for
episcopal laying on of hands on this argument,[77] and the speed with which he
turned to Luther after Bishop Matthias' death[78] tends to speak against the supposition that he was interested in such an episcopal laying on of hands for the sake
of an apostolic succession given by it. It can certainly not have been a case of
obtaining a succession of consecration to episcopal orders, since Matthias of
Brandenburg was unconsecrated.[79] The interest of the Merseburg episcopal candidate, who was known for his conservative attitude and concern for the
conservation of as many traditions as possible, was surely more in the maintenance of a good order, and in addition the recognition of his office within the
Empire, which, if at all, could only be achieved by his being installed by a
bishop.[80]

In these cases too, the fact that the bishops were also princes was an unfortunate
burden. One would think that now that the bishop was protestant it would have
been possible to bring about the separation of the ecclesial office of oversight
from the bishop's political position for which the reformers had campaigned. In
Merseburg (but not in Naumburg or Kammin) this indeed happened – but at a
price. The final consequence had to be drawn from the concept of the political
bishop of the Empire. The title of bishop went to the person who held the political power, a (now protestant) prince. The princely and the spiritual tasks of the
Bishop of Merseburg were separated, the former being taken over by a Saxon
duke, who thereby gained a territory for himself,[81] the latter by Georg.[82] The pre-
condition for this, however, was that the title of bishop with all its political
implications was attached to the territory and its (now purely secular) prince.[83]
This was the only solution consistent with the constitutional system of the
Empire – a solution which anticipated the development after the Peace of Augsburg
and the decisions of the Peace of Westphalia with regard to the ecclesiastical
territories of central and northern Germany.[84] The real bishop was officially only
allowed to call himself 'Coadjutor'.[85]

Georg nevertheless sincerely attempted to undertake all the duties which belonged
to a protestant bishop.[86] Here too, however, he soon found his possibilities for
action limited. As a bishop without an area in which he possessed political power,
he lacked the finances which were necessary for the carrying out of his episcopal
tasks, because the *Hochstift* represented a bishop's most important financial base.
He was therefore financially dependent on the Saxon dukes, to whom he was in
any case bound by his precarious legal position. In other words, it was precisely
the attempt to detach episcopal from political power which in another way

destroyed the possibility of episcopal independence from political power. The Merseburg episcopal experiment therefore had feet of clay despite and indeed because of its theological purity. Within the context of the Empire's constitutional system, such purity was not otherwise to be had.

The Emperor's victory in the war of Schmalkalden put an end to all of this in any case and therefore marked the conclusion of the experiments east of the Elbe as well as that in Cologne on the Rhein. In Merseburg the Emperor forced the separation of spiritual and secular power to be given up, and on his orders a bishop loyal to Rome, chosen by Charles himself, took over the see, once again holding also the territorial lordship and the status of a prince of the Empire.[87] A Counter-Reformation candidate was also appointed in Naumburg, where the link between spiritual and secular power and the status of the bishop as a prince of the Empire was confirmed.[88] The same was the case with the new Bishop of Kammin, who was acceptable to the Emperor as to the Pope.[89] But this situation too was not to last for long. In the 1550s the political support for the prince bishops disappeared with the decline in imperial power. After the Peace of Augsburg, therefore, the solution which had already been tried out in Merseburg won through: protestant princes took over the episcopal sees as Administrators.[90] They no longer had Coadjutors for the spiritual side of the bishop's responsibilities. By that time other authorities existed for that purpose.

Before this section is concluded, the question should be asked, why the Wittenberg reformers attempted so energetically to retain the episcopate in the traditional form. The persistence and the degree of readiness to compromise with which they sought to achieve this end is indeed striking. On the one hand, no doubt, political motivation was behind this attempt. They did not want to place themselves outside the constitutional structure of the Empire. But the constitutional question arises, whether there were not also other reasons, possibly including theological ones.

The first thing to say about this is that at any rate the reformers did not attempt to retain the existing episcopate because they held it to be necessary, to be commanded by the Gospel (*iure divino*). That can be seen from what has been said above, but it also became very clear when they had to develop other solutions and regarded these as just as legitimate theologically, indeed as the only legitimate solutions in the given circumstances. Neither did the concept of apostolic succession in the sense of succession in the office of diocesan bishop have any binding force for them. As already indicated, in the discussions of the Reformation era this idea only played a role at the margins, as it had hardly played a role in the mediaeval period. It was in the theological discussions at Worms and Regensburg that, having been rediscovered shortly before,[91] it came onto the agenda.[92] The Wittenberg reformers rejected it sharply, saying that the theory of apostolic succession in the episcopate made the Church dependent upon the episcopal succession. For according to that theory, the true, apostolic preaching would be guaranteed by the chain of succession and bound to it.[93] Such an idea stood in contradiction to the experiences which one had had with the bishops. And it contradicted the Reformation understanding of the Gospel, the Church and its ministry.

Nonetheless, the reformers would have been glad to retain the existing episcopate, had this been possible. This was because it was thought to be an age-old institution which had proved its worth over long periods, and which was in principle capable of reform and deserved to be reformed: 'We have often affirmed that we very much wish to conserve the structure and orders of the Church, even if they have been created by human authority. For we know that the structure of the Church was established by the Fathers in the form described by the Canons with good and beneficial intentions'.[94] This expresses the conservative attitude of the Wittenberg Reformation – sometimes praised and sometimes criticized – which was intent on continuity even in points which were not held to be defined by God's word. The order and reliability given by such continuity was valued, and traditional structures were only changed when this was necessary, i.e. when they could not be reconciled with obedience to the word of God[95] – then, though, to be sure with passion and a clear theological conscience.

In the case of the episcopate, there was another special consideration. The Wittenberg reformers were well aware that their criticism of the bishops was music to the ears of the secular princes, whose own interests made them eager for the bishops to be deprived of their power. For in that criticism the princes saw not only the legitimation for their attempts to gain power over the episcopal territories and thus round off their own, but also the justification for their efforts to consolidate their influence on the life of the Church and indeed to extend it beyond the government of the Church by the territorial princes which had already existed in pre-Reformation times. The Wittenberg reformers certainly saw through that.[96] They may themselves, because of the lack of figures in the church hierarchy who were willing to undertake the task of reformation, have made use of the princes and been able to describe the prince as an 'emergency bishop' who in the given circumstances had to do what the actual bishops failed to do,[97] but for them the provisional character of this solution was beyond question. They believed that in the reformed part of Christendom the government of the Church should be exercised as soon as possible by non-political church authorities, and for the Wittenberg reformers that meant first and foremost by bishops. One could not fail to notice that there was little interest among the secular princes for such a prospect and that in most cases[98] they wished to hold on to the provisional arrangements as a permanent solution. Luther saw this danger, as did Melanchthon. Their wish for protestant bishops, or at least bishops who would tolerate the Reformation, was not least of all aimed at preventing it.

The question was, admittedly, from whence a protestant bishop should secure the material infrastructure which would enable him to act independently – the problem which showed itself so clearly during Bishop Georg of Merseburg's period in office. It was above all the bishops' own territories which had provided this infrastructure for them hitherto; indeed, it was on the territories and the political role given with them that their episcopal authority and their power to enforce it had to a considerable extent been based. Because they had to admit this, the Wittenberg reformers came round not only to admitting the territorial power of bishops as a compromise,[99] but also even to conceding a positive function to it in the given circumstances – it was only on such a basis that the bishops would be able in the long term to stand up to the princes and to protect the Church from their attempts to gain power:

> [It will] be necessary for the churches in time..., that they should be visited by impressive persons. For the secular princes will not pay great attention to the Church as time goes on.... It would now be beneficial if a number of prelates would devote themselves faithfully to the Church, since they have the wealth and could keep up visitation....[100]

This statement, however, amounts to no less than an admission that what the reformers had actually sought to achieve – a genuine ecclesial episcopate in the reformed part of Christendom – could not be achieved in the present circumstances. Episcopal independence was not possible without the ecclesiastical principalities, or to put it another way, it was for its own part only possible as political, territorial independence and not as ecclesiastical independence. As such it had a function in the Empire which was strongly tied, both politically and constitutionally, to the Roman Catholic Church, as the events which have been sketched above show. This situation was to be enshrined in the Peace of Augsburg.[101] Untying this confessional link meant the loss of the bishops' politically and legally based independence and, since this was the only independence they had, that of episcopal independence itself. That means that there was no possibility of a protestant episcopate, since it would not be anchored in the constitution of the Empire, and that the assumption of episcopal power by the princes, in the long term and not just temporarily, was unavoidable. The form of the government of the Church by princes which was thus established in the protestant territories represented the opposite, mirror image of the political episcopate of the Empire[102] and thereby reflected the same linkage of political and ecclesiastical order which it was only possible to overcome after the end of the Empire.[103]

IV. The Office of Superintendent as a Distinct Type of Episcopate

Hitherto we have concerned ourselves with the efforts of the Wittenberg reformers to achieve an office of bishop above the parish level in the form of the (purified) mediaeval episcopate. These attempts to achieve continuity are not the only thing which can be mentioned under the heading 'Reformation and Episcopal Office'. Alongside it, indeed at the forefront as far as actual church life was concerned, stood the exercise of oversight on individual initiative and the development of a special episcopal office – that of Superintendent. The fact that this new approach came about was due to the failure of the existing bishops. The fact that it was possible to make a new approach had its basis in Reformation theology. That it looked the way it did was once again the result of the historical context.

The necessity of taking episcopal measures without regard to the diocesan bishops first became apparent in the second half of the 1520s, when it could not be overlooked that the protestant parishes needed visitation.[104] This had consequences which were to determine all that followed. Since those whose offices included the duty of visitation failed, Luther suggested that they should set up their own protestant Visitors. Oversight in the Church was necessary, he said,[105] and if it was not provided, a remedy must be supplied. In the circumstances which obtained, only the Elector had the means and the authority to do this.[106] He did then indeed ensure that commissions of Visitors were formed. These were ad hoc bodies of theologians and lawyers, coming together on each occasion for a particular visitation, rather than permanent authorities. Nonetheless, they did precisely the thing which is one of the most important forms of episcopal activity: they exercised oversight over the parish clergy, and did so concretely, by examining their theological education, preaching and doctrine, their professional conduct, their manner of life, the financial situation in the parishes etc., and where necessary took measures to remedy abuses. It was therefore appropriate that Luther described the Visitors, of whom he was at times one himself, as 'bishops'[107] – bishops because and as long as they did that which defines that office.

Such an ad hoc exercise of episcopal functions was not regarded as a long-term solution, however. Oversight and coherence above the parish level should be provided permanently and continually, and for this reason a new episcopal office was established in the context of these visitations. This office was also called episcopal office, but in Latin rather than in Greek: the office of '*Superintendent*' or '*Superattendent*'[108] – an old translation of *episkopos* which is attested as early as the patristic period.[109] The ministers of the county towns were selected as holders of the new episcopal office[110] – an obvious option, which has its parallels in the institutional development of the early Church, when the bishops of the provincial capitals were given precedence over their brother bishops. And as in the early Church, among these protestant 'metropolitans' some gained a more extensive importance, above that of other Superintendents – generally those of the capitals of an entire territory, such as the Superintendent of Wittenberg in Electoral Saxony.[111] In some cases, these were given the title 'General Superintendent'.

The Superintendents were and remained parish clergy, and in that equal to all the other clergy of their district. This gave concrete expression to the fact that their episcopal activity was a development of the one ministry of the Church which was common to them all – an unfolding of its catholic dimension. It was not only exercised in the oversight of the clergy of the district and related functions like the examination and installation of candidates; rather, the tasks of the Superintendent included pastoral care of the clergy, binding them together through clergy chapters, and laying the basis and content of their activity before them again and again through public teaching[112] – classical episcopal activities. And what about ordination? Since the necessity to act on one's own initiative was not as urgent here as it was with visitation, it was possible to wait longer for possible co-operation on the part of the diocesan bishops without – except in individual cases – developing one's own solution. In the end, this task generally came to belong to the Superintendent or the central Superintendent.[113]

If one looks at the list of functions which the office of Superintendent and then also that of General Superintendent encompassed, there can be no doubt that this is an episcopal office – in the long term, even the most important episcopal office in the history of the Lutheran Church. This raises the question of why the holders of this office were not simply and straightforwardly called 'bishops'.[114] What was the reason for the circumlocution of the Latin translation?

The title 'bishop' was not used for holders of this office in order to keep it clear for those who did use the title, namely the existing bishops. That meant at the same time that the possibility was kept open of integrating the superintendencies into the dioceses and placing the superintendents under the authority of the bishops, should they convert or at least tolerate the Reformation. Where such a conversion or toleration occurred, this was indeed done. In Liegnitz in Silesia the protestant superintendents recognized the Bishop of Breslau, who although he had not adopted the Reformation permitted it to take place, for decades.[115] Furthermore, the superintendents of the Saxon dioceses of Naumburg and Merseburg were even placed under protestant bishops – the above-mentioned Nikolaus and Georg. But precisely here it became apparent that in the superintendencies an independent episcopate had in fact already developed. There were disputes over rights and duties which could not be satisfactorily resolved.[116]

The self-limitation which lay at the root of the use of the term 'Superintendent' instead of *episcopus* or 'bishop' had yet another dimension, however. It was also a limitation over against the territorial prince. Just as the prince caused the visitation commission to be formed and endowed it with his authority, so the new office of Superintendent was also established in his name.[117] The Superintendent had to use state power to bring to their senses refractory clergy in his district whom he could not move to see the error of their ways by amicable means,[118] and he had to work together with state officials in questions of moral discipline.[119] So in many respects he himself behaved as an official of his prince.[120] This dependence, this forming part of the overall church government context of the territory, is also expressed in the non-use of the title of bishop and the use of the non-current Latin equivalent.

In the end, admittedly, both dimensions of the self-limitation in the Reformation episcopal office tended in the same direction. The 'emergency episcopate' of the prince became a long-term institution, and the protestant territories did not receive ecclesiastical heads in the form of church ministers, and that means bishops, in this sense. And the constitution of the Empire, which had forced the adoption of this solution provisionally, also sanctioned and integrated it indefinitely in the Peace of Augsburg, negatively as well as positively. The Peace enshrined the old situation of the Church in the Empire in the new multi-confessional arrangements. It confirmed the ecclesiastical principalities in their old form and their constitutional position within the Empire and bound them to the Roman Catholic confession.[121] The title *'Bischof'* remained tied to them and was reduced still further to its political aspect, since in a large part of the Empire there were no longer dioceses extending beyond the *Hochstifter*. Officially, the rights of the bishops of the Empire in the protestant areas were held to be suspended,[122] which on the one hand maintained the fiction that the episcopate of the Empire remained the occupants of the episcopal office throughout the Empire, and on the other hand gave a constitutional framework for the exercise of episcopal rights by the protestant princes.

Thus things remained until the beginning of the nineteenth century, until the end of the Holy Roman Empire. It is significant that the demise of the Empire began with the abolition of the ecclesiastical territories in the *Reichsdeputationshauptschluß* of 1803.[123] Even at its end, the fundamental importance of this constitutional structure for the Empire was confirmed.

The collapse of a thousand-year-old order which occurred here affected the Imperial Church, that is the Roman Catholic Church, and for the latter it was therefore the starting point for a fundamental reconstruction of the episcopal office as an ecclesiastical office. On the protestant side, the disentangling of princely and episcopal power had to wait for another hundred years, until the collapse of the monarchies after the First World War, which swept away the government of the Church by princes. The protestant churches then took their organization and leadership above the parish level into non-political hands.[124] The majority of them sooner or later introduced the title of bishop, which now no longer had political connotations, for the holder of the highest ecclesiastical office, who nevertheless stands at the head of a hierarchy of other episcopal ministers – superintendents, *Landessuperintendenten* etc. – who in most cases are responsible for visitation and ordination. The flexibility in the practical exercise of *episkope* which was advocated by the Reformation thereby characterizes the form which the episcopal office takes in the protestant churches to the present day.

Notes

1. The following relevant publications on this theme, to which reference will often be made in this paper, should be listed at the outset: P. Brunner, 'Vom Amt des Bischofs' in *Pro Ecclesia. Gesammelte Aufsätze zur dogmatischen Theologie*, i (Berlin and Hamburg, 1962), 235–95; M. Brecht (ed.), *Martin Luther und das Bischofsamt* (Stuttgart, 1990); G. Kretschmar, 'Die Wiederentdeckung des Konzeptes der "Apostolischen Sukzession" im Umkreis der Reformation' in *Kirche in der Schule Luthers. FS. J. Heubach* (Erlangen, 1995), 231–279.

2. On this, see J. Ficker, *Vom Reichsfürstenstande*, i (Innsbruck, 1861), 270–376; A. Hauck, *Die Entstehung der geistlichen Territorien* (ASGW.PH 27,18, Leipzig, 1909). Summary: P. Moraw, 'Fürstentümer Geistliche, I. Mittelalter', *TRE* 11, 711–15. Moraw speaks of these territories as comprising 'about one sixth or one seventh of the narrower Empire' (p. 711).

3. This does not mean that the lines of development could not be followed back into the Franconian period or even into the late Roman Empire, but the decisive turning points came in this epoch.

4. For this, cf. L. Santifaller, *Zur Geschichte des ottonisch-salischen Reichskirchensystems* (SB Akad. Wien 229,1, 2nd edn, Vienna, 1964) ; J. Fleckenstein, *Grundlagen und Beginn der deutschen Geschichte* (2nd edn, Göttingen, 1980), 148–51; 'Zum Begriff der ottonisch-salischen Reichskirche' in E. Hassinger, J. H. Müller and H. Ott, *Geschichte – Wirtschaft–Gesellschaft. FS. Cl. Bauer* (Berlin, 1974), 61–71. For a survey of the later legal development in the middle ages, see A. Werminghoff, *Geschichte der Kirchenverfassung Deutschlands im Mittelalter*, i (Darmstadt, 1969 – reprint of 1905 edn), third section, especially § 35f, and *Verfassungsgeschichte der deutschen Kirche im Mittelalter* (2nd edn, Berlin, 1913), third section, especially § 26, 27, 31–4; H. Conrad, *Deutsche Rechtsgeschichte*, i (Karlsruhe, 1962), 287–96.

5. See R. Aulinger, *Das Bild des Reichstages im 16. Jahrhundert* (Göttingen, 1980), 103. For a picture from the inside which reflects the multi-confessional situation after the Peace of Westphalia but otherwise says much also about the earlier period, see J.J. Moser, *Grund-Riß der heutigen*

Staats-Verfassung des Teutschen Reichs (7th edn, Tübingen, 1754), especially book IV, ch. 5, § 11ff; ch.8, §1; ch. 10, § 1, 2, 4.

6. Aulinger (cf. note 5), 104.

7. Cf. M. Schulz, *Fürsten und Reformation. Geistliche Reformpolitik weltlicher Fürsten vor der Reformation* (Tübingen, 1991): Conrad (cf. note 4), 317f; for the wider European context, see J. Hashagen, *Staat und Kirche vor der Reformation. Eine Untersuchung der vorreformatorischen Bedeutung des Laieneinflusses in der Kirche* (Essen, 1931).

8. WA 6, 440, 21-35; cf. WA 10/2, 140, 9–17.

9. See the *Tractatus de potestate papae*, especially 60f, BSELK 489, 30-43.

10. From 1519 he used Jerome's statements about the original identity of the offices of bishop and presbyter (see WA 2, 227, 32ff). In 1538 he published the church father's letter to Euangelus/Evagrius (CSEL 56, 308–12) with a foreword of his own, emphasizing that identity (WA 50, 339–43). Cf. Brunner (cf. note 1), 253f and on this whole complex of issues H.-M. Stamm, 'Luthers Berufung auf die Vorstellungen des Hieronymus vom Bischofsamt' in Brecht (cf. note 1), 15–26. Moreover, Jerome's argument is also used by Erasmus in his *Instrumentum Novum* on 1 Timothy 4, which Luther used ('antiquitus nihil intererat inter presbyterum, sacerdotem, et episcopum, ut testatur et divus Hieronymus', edn Basel, 1516, 569). As the quotation from *An den christlichen Adel*, to which note 8 refers, shows, Luther is certainly able to make a distinction between bishop and presbyter in this context, but – and this is the decisive point – in accordance with the situation in the first centuries, at the level of the individual congregation: the bishop as its leader and the presbyters as his assistants (cf. the quotation to which note 13 refers).

11. WA 38, 237, 25–30.

12. The Reformers can therefore also use the word 'Presbyter' for the parish minister, when at the same time they are speaking of the minister above the parish level and call him 'bishop', following what had now become the customary language; for example, see the quotation to which note 42 below refers.

13. The quotation to which note 8 refers.

14. *Ibid.*

15. Cf. Brunner (cf. note 1), 236–43, 252.

16. See the survey in L. Ott, *Das Weihesakrament* (M. Schmaus, A. Grillmeier and L. Scheffczyk (eds), *Handbuch der Dogmengeschichte*, iv, 5, Freiburg/Br., Basel and Vienna, 1969), chs 4 and 15, especially § 10, 15, 16; also, M. Landgraf, 'Die Lehre vom Episkopat als Ordo' in *Dogmengeschichte der Frühscholastik* (Regensburg, 1955, III/2, 277-302 and R. P. Stenger, 'The Episcopacy as an Ordo', *Medieval Studies*, 28 (1967), 67-112.

17. Cf. the summary in Ott (cf. note 16), 80f: 'The overwhelming majority of scholastic theologians regard the episcopate... not as an order, but as a dignity added to the priesthood and as an office, e.g. Alexander of Hales, Albert the Great, Bonaventure, Thomas Aquinas. In line with this, they regarded episcopal consecration not as a sacrament, but only as a sacramental.'

18. Sent. IV, 24, 12, 1.

19. *Ibid.*, 14f: 'Sunt et alia quaedam, non ordinum, sed dignitatum vel officiorum nomina. Dignitatis simul et officii nomen est episcopus'. On Lombard cf. Ott (cf. note 16), 50. Kretschmar (cf. note 1), 234 points out that in the Roman-German Pontifical (10th cent.) the consecration of bishops is already 'no longer placed with the clerical ordinations at all, but with the orders for the blessing of kings and the coronation of emperors'. Landgraf (cf. note 15), 301 gives a 13th-century text, which places it on the same level as the anointing of kings and queens, the consecration of abbots and nuns, the blessing of brides and pilgrims.

20. See, for example, Thomas, S. Th. suppl. q37 a5; *Decretum pro Armenis*, DS 1326. Cf. Ott (cf. note 16), 94f.

21. Highlighting the way in which the Wittenberg theologians took up the understanding and practice of the early Church is the particular concern of the relevant contributions by G. Kretschmar, e.g. 'Das Bischofsamt als geistlicher Dienst in der Kirche anhand der altkirchlichen und reformatorischen Weihegebete' in *Der bischöfliche Dienst in der Kirche. Eine Dokumentation über die zehnte Begegnung im bilateralen Dialog zwischen der Russ.-Orth. Kirche und der EKD vom 25. – 29. Sept. 1984 in Kiew* (Beih. ÖR 53, 53–89) and 'Die Wiederentdeckung des Konzepts der "Apostolischen Sukzession" im Umkreis der Reformation' (cf. note 1). Kretschmar rightly complains that this important aspect of Luther's writings about the ministry of the Church is not highlighted in the more recent monographs on this theme (*Das Bischofsamt als geistlicher Dienst*, 69, n. 45). That is unfortunately also true of the most recent book on the subject, O. Mittermeier, *Evangelische Ordination im 16. Jahrhundert* (St Ottilien, 1994), which, although it touches on the matter (e.g. 65f, 104, 138), does not make it fruitful for its analysis.

22. E.g. WA 10/2, 143, 3f, 27f; 12, 194, 26f; 53, 253, 6–8.

23. E.g. WA 12, 211, 6; 214, 4; 215, 8, 19, 27; 216, 8; 218, 19; 219, 13f; on occasion – 215, 8 – linked with the functional term 'minister'. The Zwickau clergyman Nikolaus Hausmann, to whom the tract is addressed, is also addressed as 'episcopus' 'Bishop of the Congregation of Zwickau' ('episcopus Cygneae ecclesiae') (*ibid.*, 205, 3f). It is significant that the first German translation to be printed, the so-called 'Nuremberg' edition, which appeared already in 1523 (*Die weyse der Meß und geniessung des hochwirdigen Sakraments für die Christliche gemain verteutscht* (Wittenberg, 1523)) uses the word 'Pfarrherr' in place of 'Bischof' (see the passages which correspond with the WA references given above – A4v, B2v, B3r, B3v, B4r, Cv, C2v and even the dedication to Hausmann, who is now called 'Pfarrherr zu Zwickau') – clearly in order to avoid misunderstandings and to safeguard the sense meant in the text against the understanding of 'Bischof' which had now become common. Paul Speratus' translation (*Ein weyse Christlich*

Mess zu halten und zum Tisch Gottes zu gehen (Wittenberg, 1524)), made at Luther's request (*ibid.*, A3r) and under his oversight, says 'Bischof' throughout (see B2v, Cv, C3r, C3v, C4r, D3r, D4r, also the address to Hausmann). Speratus himself describes himself in an opening dedication to the parish of Iglau, where he had been the minister, as its bishop (A2v / WA 12, 204, 29).

24. WA 38, 423–33.

25. This applies to the German rite (I) in the *relationes* I and R and to the Latin rite (II); I.D contains no admonition after these readings, but only an address after the collect. On this ordination rite see H. Lieberg, *Amt und Ordination bei Luther und Melanchthon* (Göttingen, 1962), 191–6 and Mittermeier (cf. note 21), 102-112. Both works, however, overlook precisely the point that the ordination is here understood as and given the form of an episcopal consecration (Mittermeier touches upon this on p. 104, but without drawing the consequences) (cf. note 21 above).

26. *Die Canones der wichtigsten altkirchlichen Konzilien*, ed. Fr. Lauchert (Freiburg and Leipzig, 1896; reprint Frankfurt am Main, 1961), 38.

27. WA 53, 257, 19–21 (previous reference to this Canon in Luther WA 2, 238, 15–18, but with another – namely anti-papal – intention [see also 258, 17f; 397, 26; cf. Melanchthon's *Tractatus de potestate papae*, 13, BSELK 475, 13–15]); WABr 12, Nr.4330, 5A, 10; Nr. 4330, 16, 17f; Nr.4330, 7, 10f; Nr.4330, 8, 16f. (Letters of orders, 'at least partly composed by Melanchthon', *ibid.*, 447).

28. Against the background of this understanding of ministry, it would not be appropriate to describe ordination in the Lutheran churches as 'presbyteral ordination'.

29. See below.

30. See the admonition to the ordinands and the corresponding promise, which is followed by the laying on of hands (WA 38, 427f; 432, 27ff), and cf. also the fact that the candidates have to undergo a doctrinal examination before the ordination (see the beginning of the Wittenberg ordination rite, WA 38, 423, 6f, and the letters of orders in WABr 12, 451ff and in B. Moeller, 'Das Wittenberger Ordinationszeugnis für Bartholomaeus Wolfart vom 27. September 1544', *Lutherjb.*, 61 (1994), 117–22, 121f). This allocation of the succession of ministers to the succession in proclamation, in the service of which it stands, matches precisely the concern of the Pastoral Letters (see 2 Timothy 2. 2).

31. See, alongside the tract addressed to the Bohemians, the tract *Wider den falschgenannten geistlichen Stand des Papstes und der Bischöfe* (see below).

32. WA 12, 169–196.

33. *Ibid.*, 194, 18f.

34. Cf. Brunner (cf. note 1), 252.

35. E.g. WA 6, 440, 21 (see the quotation to which note 8 above refers); *ibid.*, 441, 24; CR 4, 367 (see the quotation to which note 42 below refers).

36. WA 6, 440, 29: 'vonn Christlicher gemeyn ordnung gesetzt' (see the quotation to which note 8 above refers); 2, 229, 39 and 230, 10: '[ex] ecclesiae consuetudine'; CR 4, 368: 'accessit utilis ordinatio' (see the quotation to which note 42 below refers).

37. WA 2, 228, 36f; *ibid.*, 229, 39–230, 2, 9–11: not *dispensationis divinae veritate*, but *ecclesiae consuetudine*.

38. Apologie 14, 1, BSELK 296, 18; *Tractatus de potestate papae*, 63; *ibid.*, 490, 29f.

39. CR 26, 49-96 / WA 26, 201-240 / Ph. Melanchthon, *Werke in Auswahl*, ed. R. Stupperich (Gütersloh, 1951), i, 220–71.

40. CR 26, 43-44 / WA 26, 196, 33 / Melanchthon, *Werke*, i (cf. note 39), 217, 32f.

41. But see ASm II 4, BSELK 430, 7-10, where Luther, linking both together, sketches the ideal of a Church held together by the co-operation of the bishops. Brunner (cf. note 1), 264 describes the understanding which is expressed here as 'synodical episcopalianism'.

42. CR 4, 367f (position paper of the Wittenberg theologians on the Regensburg Book, drafted by Melanchthon, CR 4, Nr. 2254): 'Ut sit... una Ecclesia et consentiens, semper Deus idem Evangelium propagavit per patres et Prophetas et postea per Christum et Apostolos, et instituit Christus ministerium duraturum usque ad consummationem mundi.... Conservat enim Evangelium et voluit post Apostolos vocari pastores in omnibus Ecclesiis, fungentes officio docendi Evangelii, quos excitat, quanquam dissimiles donis, tamen eodem fungentes ministerio. Consistit igitur unitas Ecclesia iuxta Pauli regulam, et ut Pastores inter se magis devincti essent... ac alii aliorum curam susciperent et dissidia seu schismata vitarentur, accessit utilis ordinatio, ut ex multis presbyteris eligeretur Episcopus qui regeret Ecclesiam docendo Evangelio et retinenda disciplina, et preaesset ipsis presbyteris.... Hae ordinationes, si hi, qui praesunt, faciant officium suum, utiles sunt ad retinendam unitatem Ecclesiae.' This passage differs from the quotations cited hitherto, in that where structures which link the parishes are spoken of, the local minister is called 'Presbyter' and the word 'Bishop' is reserved for the minister with tasks above the level of the parish. This following of the customary usage does not, however, alter in the slightest the fact that here too the apostolic ministry of the Church is seen as lying in the parish ministry.

43. CR 4, 547. 368f; 5, 601f. Cf. Brunner (cf. note 1), 271–9.

44. CA 28, 1–9, 12–17, 20f, BSELK 120, 1–122, 9, 21, 123, 9, 22–124, 5.

45. WA 10/2, 154, 25–30: It conflicts with the will of Christ. WABr 3, Nr.756, 37: Neither secular nor spiritual, it resembles an hermaphrodite.

46. Hereinafter, following the customary usage, the word 'bishop' is used for the person having oversight above the level of the parish, unless otherwise stated.

47. E.g. WA 10/2, 119, 29–120, 18; 125, 8–126, 18; 133, 14–23; 137, 34–138, 17; CA 28, 70, BSELK 131, 40–132, 3; *Apologie* 21, 38, BSELK 325, 36–42.

48. E.g. *Apologie* 14, 2, BSELK 297, 1–5; 21, 38f, BSELK 325, 36–50; ASm III, BSELK 458, 5f; *Tractatus de potestate papae*, 66, BSELK 491, 1f; WA 10/2, 143, 10–12; 158, 12f.

49. CR 4, 546f: 'Nos in Germania titulos habemus Episcoporum, Episcopos qui officium suum faciant, non habemus'.

50. E.g. WA 10/2, 135, 6f; 141, 7–9; ASm III, BSELK 458, 1–5 (cf. 411, 27 - 412, 6); CR 5, 599.

51. WA 10/2, 107, 19–21; 154, 10f; 158, 7f; 12, 240, 10–13.

52. WA 10/2, 154, 10–22; 158, 7–10; ASm III, BSELK 457, 7–11; CR 5, 599.

53. WA 10/2, 105–158; on this, see G. Krodel, 'Luther und das Bischofsamt nach seinem Buch "Wider den falsch genannten geistlichen Stand des Papstes und der Bischöfe"' in Brecht (cf. note 1), 27–65.

54. WA 10/2, 107, 19–21; 154, 10f. Krodel (cf. note 53), 33 summarizes the tract to the effect that Luther was pursuing both a negative and a positive intention: the destruction of the papal episcopal office and the construction of a genuine, protestant episcopal office; in order to achieve the latter, Krodel argues, he wanted to show what such a genuine 'episcopal office is and how a protestant bishop acts', and to move the serving bishops to repentance, so that the desired protestant episcopal office could be constructed with them.

55. For this development, cf. J. Höß, 'The Lutheran Church of the Reformation. Problems of its formation and organization in the middle and north German territories' in L.P. Buck, J.W. Zophy (eds), *The Social History of the Reformation. FS H. J. Grimm* (Columbus, Ohio, 1972), 317–39, 332–9 and 'Episcopus Evangelicus. Versuche mit dem Bischofsamt im deutschen Luthertum des 16. Jahrhunderts' in E. Iserloh (ed.), *Confessio Augustana und Confutatio* (Münster, 1980), 499–516, 512–6; P. Gabriel, *Fürst Georg von Anhalt als evangelischer Bischof von Merseburg und Thüringen 1544-1548/50 – ein Modell evangelischer Episkope in der Reformationszeit* (Frankfurt am Main, Berlin etc., 1997), 42–9.

56. WA 12, 232, 25–32; 18, 408, 17–20; 410, 5–13; WABr 3, Nr.756, 22–45. This separation of the two aspects of an ecclesiastical principality are demonstrated in the Reformation of Prussia, which was itself one of these. Its ruler, Albrecht of Brandenburg (1490–1568), cleric and spiritual prince, gives up his ecclesiastical status and retains only the secular power, by turning his territory into a secular duchy and ruling as its duke. Alongside him are bishops who, by contrast, relinquish the political power in their *Hochstift* to Albrecht and concentrate entirely on their spiritual tasks. (Cf. Bishop Georg's justification for giving up secular power: that it 'would not be fitting for him, as a prelate and bishop who ought to preach and proclaim the word of God, to rule over land and people and to own castles, land and cities' (P. Tschackert, *Urkundenbuch zur Reformations-geschichte des Herzogthums Preußen*, ii (Leipzig, 1890), no. 356).) Admittedly, this was a special case, not only because Prussia lay outside the Empire, but also because the spir-

itual prince at the head of the territory was not himself a bishop but a knight of an order, the Grand Master of the Teutonic Order.

57. Luther had hoped for precisely this, especially with a view to the Archbishop of Mainz and Elector Albrecht, the cousin of the Prussian Albrecht, who did in fact consider such a move in the mid-1520s (see WA 18, 408, 17–20; 410, 5–13; cf. M. Brecht, *Martin Luther*, ii (Stuttgart, 1986), 188).

58. CA 28, 77, BSELK 132, 33–8; Apol. 14, 1f, BSELK 296, 14–297, 7; WA 30/II 342, 3–8. Although this suggestion could hardly offer a fruitful solution for the future, in some places people acted accordingly up to a certain point. The Lutherans of Silesia recognized the jurisdiction of the Bishop of Breslau into the second half of the century and he undertook jurisdictional duties for them. Precisely what these consisted of is not clear, but they included at any rate decisions in matrimonial cases and at least occasional visitations, and although they did not include ordination, they did possibly involve the confirmation of protestant pastors presented to him (see A. Sabisch, *Beiträge zur Geschichte des Breslauer Bischofs Balthasar von Promnitz* (1539–62), part i: *Bis zum Regierungsantritt* (Breslau, 1936), 67–70, and *Die Bischöfe von Breslau und die Reformation in Schlesien* (Münster, 1975), 85, 87–9); cf. Kretschmar (cf. note 1), 245, who also refers to upper Hungary, where 'similar things' were 'possible'.

59. On this programme, cf. W. Maurer, *Historischer Kommentar zur Confessio Augustana*, i (Göttingen, 1976), §9–§14.

60. WA 10/2,154, 32f cf. on this Krodel (cf. note 53), 34; CR 5, 599f.

61. See below.

62. See below.

63. Cf. A. Franzen, *Bischof und Reformation. Erzbischof Hermann von Wied in Köln vor der Entscheidung zwischen Reform und Reformation* (2nd edn, Münster, 1971); A. Schröer, *Die Reformation in Westfalen*, ii (Münster, 1983), 72–111.

64. Cf. F. Fischer, *Die Reformationsversuche des Bischofs Franz von Waldeck im Fürstbistum Münster* (Hildesheim, 1907); Schröer (cf. note 63), 203–35; M. Kißener, *Ständemacht und Kirchenreform. Bischöfliche Wahlkapitulation im Nordwesten des Alten Reiches 1265-1803* (Paderborn, Munich, etc., 1993), 81–3, 106–9, 126–8; T. Unger, *Kirche und Konfession im Niederstift Münster. Der Reformationsversuch von 1543 und seine Folgen bis 1620* (theological dissertation, Göttingen, 1995 – to be published).

65. Cf. P. Steinmüller, *Die Einführung der Reformation in die Kurmark Brandenburg durch Joachim II* (Halle, 1903); H.-U. Delius, 'Die Reformation des Kurfürsten Joachim II von Brandenburg im Jahre 1539', *ThViat*, 5 (1953/54), 174–93, and 'Die Kirchenpolitik des Kurfürsten Joachim II von Brandenburg in den Jahren 1535–41', *JBBKG*, 40 (1965), 86–123.

66. See P.-H. Hahn, 'Kirchenschutz und Landesherrschaft in der Mark Brandenburg im späten 15. und frühen 16. Jahrhundert', *JGMOD*, 28 (1979), 179–220, 194f, 204f. As Hahn shows, this did not mean subinfeudalisation, however, as is commonly asserted.

67. For the *Stift's* transition to the Reformation see W. Schößler, 'Die Reformation im Domstift Brandenburg', in H.-U. Delius, M. O. Kunzendorf and F. Winter (eds), *'Dem Wort nicht entgegen...'. Aspekte der Reformation im Domstift Brandenburg* (Berlin, 1988), 49–62. The episcopates of the Lübeck bishops Detlev Reventlow (1535-6) and Balthasar Rantzau (1536-47) represented short-lived transitional phenomena. They turned to the Reformation and permitted it, but they did not formally introduce it and were followed by Counter-Reformation bishops. Only after the Peace of Augsburg did the *Stift* become protestant under a bishop who had joined the Reformation, Eberhard von Holle (1561–86). It remained the only protestant spiritual principality in the Empire, albeit at the price of its lords, who held the title of bishop, being non-clerical princes and the episcopal functions being transferred to a Superintendent who was not called 'bishop' (see W.D. Hauschild, *Kirchengeschichte Lübecks* (Lübeck, 1981), 225f). There were also similar transitional phenomena in Verden after 1555 (see I. Mager, 'Die drei evangelischen Bischöfe von Verden', *JGNKG*, 86 (1988), 79-91).

68. For him, see P. Brunner, *Nikolaus von Amsdorf als Bischof von Naumburg. Eine Untersuchung zur Gestalt des evangelischen Bischofsamtes in der Reformationszeit* (Gütersloh, 1961); J. Rogge, 'Amsdorff, Nikolaus von', *TRE* 2 (487–97).

69. For him, see Gabriel (cf. note 55); cf. also G. Wartenberg, *Landesherrschaft und Reformation. Moritz von Sachsen und die albertinische Kirchenpolitik bis 1546* (Gütersloh, 1988), ch. 7.

70. Naumburg: (Anon.), 'Bericht über die Wahl und Einführung des Nikolaus von Amsdorff als Bischof von Naumburg', *Neue Mitteilungen aus dem Gebiet historisch-antiquarischer Forschungen*, 2 (Halle, 1835), 180–5, reprinted in Mittermeier (cf. note 21), 119–23, compared with the Wittenberg ordinal in Brunner (cf. note 68), 67–9. Merseburg: E. Sehling, *Die evangelischen Kirchenordnungen des 16. Jahrhunderts*, (i/1ff (Leipzig, 1902ff)), ii (1904), 6f, reprinted by Mittermeier, 130–6, summary in Gabriel (cf. note 55), 149f.

71. Naumburg: acclamation by the congregation of the election of the new bishop at the beginning and enthronement at the end of the service, both corresponding with mediaeval pontificals, further references in the admonition of the candidate to his future responsibility for the whole *Stift* and diocese, as well as, in a very general form, to his distinctive tasks (cf. Brunner (cf. note 68), 69; Mittermeier (cf. note 21), 124–6). Merseburg: *scrutinium* at the beginning, as in the mediaeval pontificals, although no question specific to the office of bishop is posed and such a rite is clearly also envisaged for the ordination of pastors in Merseburg, and an express reference to the task of ordination in the candidate's vows before the laying on of hands (cf. Mittermeier, 137).
    It seems that the installation of the protestant Bishop of Kammin, Bartholomäus Suave, in 1545 was much more closely orientated to the liturgical traditions of the middle ages (see H. Waterstraat, 'Der Camminer Bistumsstreit im Reformationszeitalter', *ZKG*, 22 (1901), 586–602, 23 (1902), 223–62, 228) – this ought to be investigated more deeply at some point.

72. This act is described both as 'ordination' (e.g. WABr 10, Nr. 3728, 25; Sehling, ii (cf. note 70), 6f) and, using the mediaeval term, as 'consecration' (WA 53, 219 (title); 256, 19; 257, 14, 20); sometimes both terms are used together (WA 53, 231, 5; 232, 21) – no difference is made as to meaning. What is actually meant by these terms cannot be deduced from the terms themselves, but only from what they refer to and from the Wittenberg theologians' reflections on it. Cf. Brunner (cf. note 68), 69f.

73. For Naumburg, see Brunner (cf. note 68), 71f; for Merseburg, see Gabriel (cf. note 55), 148f; for Kammin, see J. Wächter, 'Das Verhältnis von Territorialgewalt und Kirche in Pommern nach Einführung der Reformation (1534/35)', *JGNKG*, 86 (1988), 93–107, 96.

74. Expressed by Luther with regard to the installation of the Bishop of Naumburg in WA 53, 257, 13-21.

75. Gabriel (cf. note 55), 141–6.

76. Kretschmar (cf. note 1), 275. Cf. Gabriel (cf. note 55) 141f.

77. This is shown not only by the printed sources, but also by the unprinted sources, which Gabriel (cf. note 55), 139–146 adduced for the first time. Kretschmar (cf. note 1) assumes an interest on the part of Georg in 'apostolic succession' in the episcopal office, but the circumstances which he produces (p. 275) do not lead to such a finding. It is noticeable that he relativizes his own conclusion with the little word 'offenbar' [obviously] – '[one] then... obviously took up again the newly introduced concept of the *episcoporum successio*' – and in this context he also speaks of 'speculation'. The bridges of argumentation which lead to this supposition are not very stable. Georg von Anhalt's part in producing the Brandenburg church order cannot with certainty be estimated so highly as Kretschmar does (*ibid.*, 270 – cf. R. Stupperich, 'Die Eigenart der Reformation in der Mark Brandenburg' in Delius et al. (cf. note 67), 13–30, 20), and there is no evidence that the Regensburg book or a source immediately dependent upon it was known to and important to Georg.

78. It is also significant that with regard to the laying on of hands which he received, he speaks of 'Dr Martin Luther and other pastors and real (*re vera*) bishops' (Gabriel (cf. note 55), 123), and thus locates the 'episcopal succession' not at the level of the diocesan bishops but at that of the pastors. The sentence may have been written some years after the event, but it was on the basis of the view which it expresses that Georg turned to Luther.

79. Kretschmar (cf. note 1), 270: he was not even a deacon – 'nothing unusual at that time'.

80. Not for nothing were the dukes concerned interested in proceeding in a way which would give as little offence as possible; thus, Duke August, who wanted to become the ruler of the *Hochstift*, advised Georg expressly to have himself 'consecrated by a protestant bishop' (Gabriel (cf. note 55), 140). Although Georg had already had this thought himself (*ibid.*, p. 141) and was not dependent on the Duke for it, it goes without saying that acceptance in the Empire was an important consideration to him too.

81. I.e. Duke August of Saxony. Behind him stood his brother Duke Moritz, who sought by this means to tie Merseburg, which was already his protectorate, more closely into his duchy. For the ecclesiastical policy of Moritz, who nonetheless wished to retain an episcopal church order within his territory, cf. Wartenberg (cf. note 69) and Gabriel (cf. note 55), especially pp. 156, 311–4.

82. For these events, see Gabriel, *ibid.*, 117–38.

83. To be precise, the prince called himself 'Administrator' of the See of Merseburg, a title used by bishops-designate who had not yet been consecrated (cf. P. Hinschius, *System des katholischen Kirchenrechts mit besonderer Rücksicht auf Deutschland*, ii (Berlin, 1878), 254). This arrangement had already earlier served to secure episcopal sees for princes who had no intention at all of themselves exercising the spiritual functions of a bishop (see Schulze (cf. note 7), p. 29). This continued to be the case in the Imperial Church in Germany after the Reformation (see H.E. Feine, *Die Besetzung der Reichsbistümer vom Westfälischen Frieden bis zur Säkularisation* (Stuttgart, 1921), 34f).

84. Cf. M. Heckel, *Deutschland im konfessionellen Zeitalter* (Göttingen, 1983), 71f, 191f; J. Heckel, *Die evangelischen Dom- und Kollegiatstifter Preußens, insbesondere Brandenburg, Merseburg, Naumburg, Zeitz* (Stuttgart, 1924).

85. In internal documents of *Hochstifter* and dioceses the theologically appropriate title 'Bishop' is also found. On the question of titles, see Gabriel (cf. note 55), 136–8.

86. On his episcopal activity and his relationship to the Saxon dukes, see *ibid.*, ch. V.

87. The Emperor ordered the cathedral chapter to elect the titular Bishop of Sidon and auxiliary bishop of Mainz Michael Helding, and after papal confirmation bestowed the territorial rights upon him (*ibid.*, 350f).

88. For Naumburg, where Julius Pflug, the firm opponent of the Reformation who had originally been elected by the cathedral chapter, now came into office, see Brunner (cf. note 68), 145–8, 152.

89. For the highly complex events in Kammin, which mirrored the transitions between the confessions which in some respects were still fluid, where Martin Weiher, in fact a protestant candidate, became Bishop but declared his readiness to be consecrated, and received papal confirmation and permission to be consecrated and was thereafter treated by the Emperor as a prince of the Empire, see Waterstraat (cf. note 71), 230–47.

90. Brunner (cf. note 68), 157f; Waterstraat (cf. note 71), 248–51; J. Heckel (cf. note 84), 23.

91. This is the discovery of G. Kretschmar and the theme of his essay 'Die Wiederentdeckung des Konzeptes der "Apostolischen Sukzession" im Umkreis der Reformation' (cf. note 1), p. 247ff.

92. *Ibid.*, pp. 251–67. See the nineteenth chapter of the Regensburg Book, which is based on a draft produced in Worms (in *ARCEG*, vi, 24–88), 75, 1–15.

93. Melanchthon's criticism on the relevant passage in the Regensburg Book in CR 4, 415: 'Erant et haec errata in articulo, Episcopos successisse in locum Apostolorum: quo dicto multi errores continentur. Alligatur Ecclesia ad successionem ordinariam, quasi impossibile sit, Episcopos errare, quia Apostolorum locum teneant, aut quasi hi sint Episcopi, qui sic vocantur, et necesse sit, eos tanquam Ecclesiae capita audiri (Ger. 423). Cf. also CR 3, 598f / Melanchthon, *Werke*, i (cf. note 39), 330, 16–29.

94. 'Saepe testati sumus, nos summa voluntate cupere conservare politiam ecclesiasticam et gradus in ecclesia, factos etiam humana auctoritate. Scimus enim bono et utili consilio a patribus ecclesiasticam disciplinam hoc modo, ut veteres canones describunt, constitutam esse' (Apol. 14, 1, BSELK 296, 19–297, 1).

95. Cf. the continuation of the quotation from the Apology in note 94, where the reason is given why one could nevertheless not recognize the bishops who were in office – that they forced the supporters of the Reformation to renounce the protestant confession (Apol. 14, 2, BSELK 297, 1–7).

96. E.g. WABr 10, Nr. 3930, 13–16: 'Sathan pergit esse Sathan. Sub papa miscuit ecclesiam politiae, sub nostro tempore vult miscere politiam ecclesiae. Sed nos resistemus deo favente et studebimus pro nostra virili vocationes distinctas servare. WABr 10, Nr. 4011, 9–12: 'es ist doch mit dem Hofe nichts. Ihr Regiment ist eitel Krebs und Schnecken.... Christus optime ecclesiae consuluit, quod aulae non commisit ecclesiarum administrationem'. Cf. Melanchthon CR 2, 334 with regard to the councils of the imperial cities. See also Luther's criticism of the transformation of *bona ecclesiastica* into *bona politica*, WATR 5, Nr. 5635b / 286, 3–5, which made him initially reject the Merseburg solution of a separation of government of the *Stift* and episcopal office. Cf. Brunner (cf. note 1), 268f; K. Holl, 'Luther und das landesherrliche Kirchenregiment' (in *ibid.*, *Gesammelte Aufsätze zur Kirchengeschichte*, i: Luther (4th edn., Tübingen, 1927), 326–80), especially pp. 375-7.

97. WA 53, 255, 5–8: 'Now our secular lords must be emergency bishops and protect us clergy and preachers (the Pope and his gang having not worked towards this but against it) and help us to be able to preach, and serve churches and schools. Cf. J.L. Schaaf, 'Der Landesherr also Notbischof' (in Brecht (cf. note 1), 105–8, who by the way shows that such statements are not commonly found in Luther.

98. An exception was Moritz of Saxony, who sought to achieve an episcopal church order, albeit in the context of a territorial church. Cf. note 81 above.

99. See above.

100. WABr 9, Nr. 3436, 480–7. In what follows this solution is represented as a concession: 'If now many bishops and *Stifter* wanted to accept the true doctrine and the necessary items and serve the Church, they should be allowed to retain their dignities...'. i.e. the attitude towards the political circumstances oscillates between a realism which is directly pragmatic and one which is shot through with idealism. Another pragmatic example is CR 5, 599f: 'If there are now to be bishops who have supervision over others, they must have property.... ... since government and property

are ordered, and godfearing bishops can make good use of them: we leave this order as it is, and wish that nevertheless these episcopal territories, lordships and counties should be brought to the right and saving doctrine and knowledge of Christ.'

101. See below.

102. The comparison with a mirror image does not apply in every respect, however, for while the ecclesiastical prince had the whole ecclesiastical and political power in his hands, the spiritual functions in the narrow sense, such as preaching, administration of the sacraments or ordination, did not form part of the secular prince's government of the Church.

103. Cf. Kretschmar (cf. note 1), 272f.

104. For details of these events, see Brecht (cf. note 57), 253–66.

105. See above.

106. He was made use of for this service not because of his political role, i.e. not as the secular authority, but as a member of the Christian congregation, who was obliged to perform the service of love towards the Church like all Christians, but because of his special position was obliged to do so in a particular way (see Luther's preface to the *Instruction to Visitors,* WA 26, 197, 19–29 / Melanchthon, *Werke,* i (cf. note 39), 218, 22–34; on this, Holl (cf. note 96), 366–75). On the pre-Reformation practice of visitation on the initiative of the prince due to the lack of episcopal visitation, which served as a precedent, cf. Hashagen (cf. note 7), 324–36; Schulze (cf. note 7), especially 136–8.

107. E.g. WABr 4, Nr. 1347, 5f; Nr. 1350, 14; 5, Nr. 1410, Anrede, 20; cf. Holl (cf. note 96), 376.

108. For him, see W. Elert, 'Der bischöfliche Charakter der Superintendentur-Verfassung (*Luth.*, 46 (1935), 353–367). Historically, this office has a root in the mediaeval office of archpriest (*ibid.*, 353), and here and there it was named thus ['*Archipresbyterat*'] (*ibid.*, 353 also mentioning further terms), but it gained episcopal characteristics which went beyond the mediaeval office, and this was reflected in the choice of the term 'Superintendent'.

109. Augustine, *De civitate Dei*, 19,19; cf. Jerome, Ep. 146,1.

110. Electoral Visitation Instruction of 1527 (in Sehling (cf. note 70) I/1, 142–8), 146; Melanchthon, *Unterricht der Visitatorn* (cf. note 39), CR 26, 89 / WA 26, 235, 7f / *Werke* I 264, 20f.

111. Elert (cf. note 108), 365.

112. *Ibid.*, 360-363.

113. First and foremost must naturally be mentioned here the senior Superintendent of the Saxon electoral district, the City Pastor of Wittenberg, who ordained from the time that there was a regulated practice of protestant ordination in Saxony onwards. The first holder of this position, Johannes Bugenhagen, even acted as the minister of ordination for candidates from the whole area of influence of the Wittenberg Reformation – and alongside him, other clergy from the city such as

Luther, for example. This episcopal activity extending over several regions corresponded with the particular importance of Wittenberg for the Lutheran Reformation. On ordination by the Superintendents in other territories, see for example the Braunschweig Church Order of 1543 in *Die evangelischen Kirchenordnungen des 16. Jahrhunderts*, ed. A.L. Richter (Weimar, 1846), ii, 56–64, 60 and the Württemberg Synodical Order of 1547 (*ibid.*, 93–97), 94.

114. Cf. for example the case of Denmark, where the Superintendents installed after the Reformation were very quickly called 'bishop' (P.G. Lindhart, *Skandinavische Kirchengeschichte seit dem 16. Jahrhundert* (KiG M3, Göttingen, 1982), 239).

115. Sehling (cf. note 70), iii (1909), 391, cf. Elert (cf. note 108), 363 and cf. note 58.

116. Brunner (cf. note 68), 133–6; Gabriel (cf. note 55), ch. 5.8.2.

117. Visitation Instruction of 1527 (cf. note 110), 146.

118. *Ibid.*, Melanchthon, *Unterricht der Visitatorn* (cf. note 39), CR 26, 89 / WA 26, 235, 16–25 / *Werke*, i, 264, 31–265, 7.

119. Visitation Instruction of 1527 (cf. note 110), 146.

120. This was all the more the case, as the government of the Church by princes developed more strongly, within which the Superintendent was then mostly subordinated to the Consistory, which had developed into an administrative office of the prince and therefore took on the characteristics of a state bureaucracy (cf. Elert (cf. note 108), 353f; E. Schling, 'Superintendent', *RE* (3rd edn), xix (167–72), 169). Elert, 355f shows, nonetheless, that the office of Superintendent did not become absorbed in this dimension.

121. *Augsburger Religionsfriede*, 6 (*Der Augsburger Religionsfriede vom 25. Sept. 1555*, ed K. Brandi (Munich, 1896), 23f).

122. *Ibid.*, 8 (28f).

123. For this (briefly), see K.O. von Aretin, *Vom Deutschen Reich zum Deutschen Bund* (Göttingen, 1980), 90–6.

124. For this re-ordering, cf. A. v. Campenhausen, 'Entstehung und Funktion des bischöflichen Amtes in den evangelischen Kirchen in Deutschland' in A. Campenhausen, *Gesammelte Schriften*, ed. E. Christoph, Chr. Link etc. (Tübingen, 1995), 8–26, 17–23.

Developments in the Understanding and Practice of Episcopacy in the Church of England

John Findon

The Reformation of the Church in England was not achieved by clergymen or the-ologians. In all of the years between 1527, when Henry VIII began to seek a divorce from Queen Catherine of Aragon, to 1662, when the Act of Uniformity enforced the ejection of dissenting ministers from their livings, the agents of reli-gious change in England were the successive governments of the realm. There was, of course, in England as elsewhere in Europe, heated and impassioned debate throughout this period about the truths of the Christian religion: these passions successive governments had to take into account when they made policy, as they had to take account of other relevant facts. At the two critical points in the for-mation of the Church of England – the Settlement of 1559 at the beginning of Elizabeth I's reign, and the re-settlement under King Charles II between 1660 and 1662 – the decisions were taken by the Crown in Parliament. In each case the final shape of the settlement was at least in part the result of political compromise or accident. No one, at either point, would have chosen, or indeed predicted, just the set of decisions that was actually implemented. The Church of England, in a word, has no architect: it does not reflect the mind of any one person or group. It has no Luther or Calvin, no Fox or Wesley.

Indeed, although historians differ about the extent to which the Settlement of 1559 accorded with the designs of the Queen and her Council, it is clear that the gov-ernment at that time was actively concerned, after the divisive experience of the previous twelve years, to have a religious polity which should be broad and loose enough to include as wide a spread of English religious opinion as possible. The Prayer Book and the Articles are capable, notoriously, of being interpreted in a variety of different ways. This was Thomas Fuller's meaning when he said that the Thirty-nine Articles were like children's clothes, made of a larger size so that the children might grow up into them. It is because of this that, when disputes have arisen between Anglicans (as, to take two examples, in the Arminian controver-sies of the 1620s and the Tractarian debates of the 1830s), both sides have claimed and believed that they were doing no more than stating or re-stating traditional teaching.

It is important to state these facts at the outset because they explain the nature of much of the material which we shall be considering. Anglican writing on theology of the Church does not set out *a priori* to prescribe what *ought to be*, but sets out, rather, to commend what *has been* established. Nowhere is this clearer than in the work of the greatest Anglican writer, Richard Hooker. Hooker, in the Preface to his *Lawes of Ecclesiastical Politie*, fairly makes the point that Calvin's fourfold Genevan order was constructed by him on pragmatic grounds, to suit the social and political realities of Geneva, and then afterwards given scriptural and theological support.

> Wherefore a marvaile it were if a man of so great capacitie, having such incitements to make him desirous of all kind of furtherances unto his cause, could espie in the whole Scripture of God nothing which might breed at the least a probable opinion of likelihood, that divine authoritie it selfe was the same way somewhat inclinable.[1]

It could fairly be observed that, in the same way, Hooker inherited the episcopal polity which Queen Elizabeth had judged appropriate for the monarchical society of England, and then proceeded to provide it with a philosophical and theological justification.

In these circumstances, we should not expect to have available a long list of authorized or authoritative Anglican statements. We have the Book of Common Prayer, including the Ordinal, the Thirty-nine Articles of 1562, the two Books of Homilies. From time to time other works were given a semi-official authority when it was commanded that copies of them be placed in parish churches: Jewel's *Apologie*, for example, and Erasmus's *Paraphrases*. Beyond this circle of authority, however, stretches a vast collection of Anglican writing, most of which was reprinted for partisan reasons during the disputes of the nineteenth century: the fiercely protestant volumes of the first fathers of the English Reformation issued by the Parker Society; the volumes of the *Library of Anglo-Catholic Theology* issued by supporters of the Tractarians; collected editions of the works of practically every significant divine of the sixteenth and seventeenth centuries – Hooker, Sanderson, Hall, Stillingfleet, Taylor and the rest. Every visitor to an Anglican theological library will be familiar with the dusty rows of their spines on yard upon yard of shelving. 'We have', wrote Newman in 1837,

> a vast inheritance, but no inventory of our treasures. All is given us in profusion; it remains for us to catalogue, sort, distribute, select, harmonise and complete.[2]

Nowhere is the difficulty of sorting and harmonizing more acute than in consideration of the place of episcopacy within the self-understanding of the Church of England.

The issue of episcopacy necessarily put into sharp focus the controversial battles which the Church of England had to fight, both against the claims of Rome and against the significant minority of English protestants who believed that 1559 had left reform only half achieved. But the stance taken by the opponent against whom an Anglican writer happened to be engaged would obviously influence the kind of argument that he would use: John Jewel, for example, justifying the Church of England against Roman Catholic claims of irregularity and giddy innovation, is sometimes concerned to stress the ancient, inherited credentials and succession of Anglican episcopacy:

> I answer you, I am a priest, made long sithence by the same order and ordinance and I think also by the same man and the same hands, that you, Mr Harding, were made priest by...

> I answer you, I am a bishop, and that by the free and accustomed canonical election of the whole Chapter of Sarisbury...

> Our bishops are made in form and order as they have been ever, by free election of the chapter; by consecration of the archbishop and other three bishops...[3]

On the other hand, in the 1570s and 1580s, John Whitgift, in controversy with Presbyterians who held that the Genevan order was laid down by Scripture and necessary for the Church, was concerned to prove that *no* polity was required by God, and that episcopacy was one of the options which a godly Prince might choose to impose, appropriately so, indeed, in a monarchical society like England. We need always to be aware, however, of the exigencies of theological debate, and not assume, for example, that Jewel was wedded to the principle of Apostolic Succession, or that Whitgift's view of episcopacy was merely pragmatic.

There was never any doubt that the polity established in the Church of England in the sixteenth century would be firmly episcopal. No Tudor monarch would have been willing to dispense with the services of such effective royal agents in the localities. But of course the nature of the episcopacy so established was another question. From the beginning, English protestantism, with its inheritance of anti-clericalism from the Lollards, had drawn a sharp distinction between the gospel bishop and the lordly prelate. 'God's grace is promised to a good mind, and to one that feareth God', wrote John Jewel again, 'not unto sees and successions'.[4]

The late mediaeval Church, it must be said, had very unclear notions of the office and work of a bishop. From the twelfth century in the West an understanding had emerged in which the Church was thought of as a spiritual monarchy, with the Pope as king, and all other ministers deriving their authority from him, as his subordinates in the hierarchy. On this model, the bishops were the nobility taking their place beneath the spiritual monarchy of the Pope. They had everything to do with prelacy, and very little to do with a teaching and pastoral ministry. All of the reformed churches sought to end this semi-secularized prelacy in their different ways. In England, the Reformation began as an alliance between godly prince and godly bishop.

Thus we find John Jewel, Bishop of Salisbury, writing to his friend Josiah Semler after his nomination to the episcopate:

> As to your expressing your hopes that our bishops will be consecrated without any superstitious and offensive ceremonies, you mean, I suppose, without oil, without the chrism, without the tonsure. And you are not mistaken; for the sink would indeed have been emptied to no purpose, if we had suffered those dregs to settle at the bottom. Those oil, shaven, portly hypocrites, we have sent back to Rome from whence we first imported them. For we require our bishops to be pastors, labourers, and watchmen. And that this may the more readily be brought to pass, the wealth of the bishops is now diminished and reduced to a reasonable amount, to the end that, being relieved from that royal pomp and courtly bustle, they may with greater ease and diligence employ their leisure in attending the flock of Christ.[5]

Such high hopes were not fulfilled however. Queen Elizabeth might be willing to reduce the incomes of her bishops, but that had to do not with concern for evangelical simplicity but with the needs of the royal coffers. Bishops until the nineteenth century continued to be, *willy nilly*, great magnates, with a place to keep up in county society. They were obliged to practise lavish hospitality and to maintain the 'port' of peers of the realm. Worse still, no attempt was made to reduce the size of their vast dioceses: Bishop Jewel had oversight of some 600 parishes in two counties; dioceses like Lincoln, Lichfield, Chester and York were much bigger – Lincoln stretching from the Humber to the Thames, a quarter of England. Worst of all, no effective reform was made of the canon law, and many of the episcopal functions – in particular the exercise of discipline – remained in the hands of lay ecclesiastical lawyers.

This, then, was the pattern of protestant episcopacy which was established in 1559. It was not a promising beginning, yet it can be shown that, by the reign of King James I (1603–1625), bishops were held in far greater esteem than they had been for many generations, and seriously attempted and in part succeeded in making something of Jewel's vision a reality. Their dioceses were still absurdly too big, but very many of them exercised effective teaching and preaching, and a pastoral ministry at least among their clergy in spite of the demands of attendance at Court and of course the House of Lords.[6]

In the years between 1559 and 1689, I propose in what follows to distinguish four different views of episcopacy, held by significant numbers of members of the Church of England. It goes without saying that, since then as now the clergy have tended to have more to say for themselves than other folk, the great bulk of the written evidence comes from the clergy; with the equally untypical exception of Members of Parliament, the views of the laity on these matters are almost totally hidden from us.

I: Adiaphorist

Particularly in the early years after 1559, there was widespread belief that church polity was a matter at heart indifferent. God had given no commands and it was right that local circumstances should be allowed to dictate the most appropriate pattern. The early years of Elizabeth's reign saw some quite astonishing examples of this position. Bishop James Pilkington of Durham wrote in 1564 that

> The Bishops' privileges are rather granted by man for maintaining of better order and quietness in the commonwealth than commanded by God in his word.[7]

Chancellor John Hammond of London, twice an M.P. in the 1580s, who in 1578 attended the Diet of Smalcald as a representative of the English Government, offered the following opinion to Lord Burghley in 1588:

> If it had pleased her Majesty to have assigned the imposition of hands to the Dean of every cathedral church... which in no sort were bishops... there had been no wrong done to their [the bishops] persons that I can conceive.[8]

That is an extreme case, but listen here to Archbishop John Whitgift:

> because the essential notes of the church be these only: the true preaching of the word of God, and the right administration of the sacraments,... so that, notwithstanding government, or some kind of government, may be a part of the church... yet it is not such a part of the essence and being, but that it may be the Church of Christ without this or that kind of government...[9]

> That may be profitable for the churches of Geneva and France etc., which would be most hurtful to this church of England... [10]

The same view is to be found in the Third Book of Hooker's *Lawes*.

II: Bancroftian

In 1589 Richard Bancroft preached at Paul's Cross a notable sermon from which traditionally English church historians have dated the assertion within the Church of England of the *jure divino* rights of episcopacy. The sermon in fact says nothing that had not been often said before: that episcopacy is of apostolic origin. Its significance is more in what it did *not* say: it did not couple these apostolic claims with the adiaphoristic point that no particular form of Church order was prescribed by God, although Bancroft makes this point often enough elsewhere. The implication therefore seemed to be that episcopacy existed in the Church by divine right. From the 1590s indeed a succession of Anglican writers were concerned to demonstrate the apostolic claims of episcopacy.

It is important here to note that these first two positions could be held separately, but were, in the Elizabethan period, very commonly held together. John Hammond and James Pilkington indeed would not have accepted Bancroft's position at all, but Whitgift and Hooker, for example, for all that they believed that no form of Church order was *prescribed* by Scripture, were both clear that the episcopal pattern was *commended* in Scripture. This distinction is clearly made by Hooker:

> Bishops, albeit they may avouch with conformity of truth, that their Authority hath thus descended even from the very Apostles themselves, yet the absolute and everlasting continuance of it, they cannot say that any Commandment of the Lord doth injoyn.[11]

God had not fixed any system of order as immutable necessity in the Church; the necessity for the Church was only the preaching of the word and the administration of the sacraments: but it did not therefore follow that order was a thing indifferent, or indeed that God had given his Church no guidance in the matter. Thus Whitgift:

> Although this name [Archbishop] is not expressed in the scripture, yet is the office and function as it is evidently to be seen in the example of Timothy and Titus, yea and in the apostles themselves, whose office of planting churches through the whole world is ceased, but their care for the good government of those churches... doth and must remain.[12]

> [Episcopacy] is most ancient in the church, it is confirmed by the best and noblest councils, it is allowed by the best learned fathers, it hath the pattern from the practice of the apostles.[13]

This has been called the 'Elizabethan consensus' on episcopacy;[14] it was in part a rebuttal of the Calvinist claims of Beza for the exclusive necessity of Presbyterian order, and partly the recognition of the ancient credentials of episcopacy:

A thousand five hundred years and upward the Church of Christ hath now continued under the sacred Regiment of Bishops. Neither for so long hath Christianity been ever planted in any Kingdom throughout the world but with this kind of government alone, which to have been ordained of God, I am for mine own part even as resolutely perswaded, as that any other kind of Government in the world whatsoever is of God.[15]

Indeed it continued in substance to be the mainstream Anglican position on episcopacy until well into the seventeenth century: an unashamed assertion of the divine right of the order, coupled with a refusal to insist on its necessity at all times and in all places.

The subtlety and flexibility of this position has not always been appreciated. Thus, for example, Hadrian Saravia, a Dutchman of Spanish descent who eventually settled in England, wrote in his *De diversis gradibus ministrorum evangelii* in 1590 probably the most uncompromising statement of episcopal claims to be published in Elizabethan England. Yet he can also, without any sense of inconsistency, write as follows of the Colloquy of Poissy in 1561:

> Although those who met there in Poissy... had not all received the same ordination – some had been ordained by bishops of the Roman Church, others by the Reformed Churches – no-one needed to be ashamed of his ordination. So far as I can see, they could, without danger, declare that they had been ordained and called, some by bishops of the Roman Church, others by orthodox presbyters, according to the order which has been accepted in the Christian churches, after prior examination of morals and doctrine, on the authority of the magistracy and with the people's consent.[16]

Indeed, it seems exceedingly likely that Saravia himself, although ordained in the Dutch Reformed Church, held his various livings in the Church of England without reordination.[17] This question of the admission of clergy presbyterally ordained abroad to cures of souls in England has been frequently discussed by Anglican writers; Mason and Sykes come down on different sides of the matter, unsurprisingly in view of their own strong convictions. The truth seems to be that there are a few cases of Presbyterian clergy being thus admitted in the sixteenth and early seventeenth centuries: in the nature of things at the time, such cases would not be numerous, and it does appear that there was some unease among the bishops concerned, though this may have been more to do with doubts about the standing of such orders in English law, than with doubts about their validity.[18] Certainly, there was not at this time any thought of a total denial of the validity of the orders of the foreign reformed churches. Thus in 1610, Archbishop Bancroft, although a doughty champion of episcopal claims, made his position clear on the occasion of the consecration of new bishops for Scotland:

A question in the meantime was moved by Dr Andrewes, Bishop of Ely, touching the consecration of the Scottish bishops, who, as he said, 'must first be ordained presbyters, as having received no ordination from a bishop'. The Archbishop of Canterbury, Dr Bancroft, who was by, maintained 'that thereof there was no necessity, seeing where bishops could not be had, the ordination given by the presbyters must be esteemed lawful; otherwise that it might be doubted if there were any lawful vocation in most of the reformed churches'.[19]

That indeed was a consequence which Andrewes himself was not willing to contemplate. In his correspondence with the Huguenot Pierre du Moulin in 1618 he wrote as follows:

> Nevertheless if our form be of divine right, it doth not follow from thence that there is no salvation without it, or that a church cannot consist without it. He is blind who does not see churches consisting without it; he is hard-hearted who denieth them salvation. We are none of these hard-hearted persons; we put a great difference between these things. There may be something absent in the exterior regiment, which is of divine right, and yet salvation to be had... To prefer a better, is not to condemn a thing. Nor is it to condemn your church if we recall it to another form, namely our own, which the better agrees with all antiquity.[20]

'To prefer a better is not to condemn a thing.' There could hardly be a more succinct statement of the Anglican view of foreign reformed orders at this time.

In the above extracts also we see another essential element in the Anglican position – the 'argument from necessity'. '*Where bishops could not be had*, the ordination by presbyters must be esteemed lawful' said Bancroft. The notion of distressed Protestant churches wishing that they had opportunity to embrace the blessings of episcopacy was dear to Anglican mythology at this time.[21] It goes without saying, of course, that the charity extended to the foreign reformed churches on these grounds of necessity could not be extended to the English Puritans. Archbishop Whitgift, for example, had no hesitation in refusing to institute Walter Travers to a cure of souls, since he, though born in England, had wilfully chosen to seek ordination in the Dutch Reformed Church. In this connexion, Hadrian Saravia's reasons for writing on episcopacy are interesting:

> I saw that our [Dutch emigrant] churches in England were suspected as siding with the rebels and schismatics in the English Church and of thus encouraging these to secede from their church and to hold it in contempt. In order to protect our churches against this suspicion I have surveyed the sacred ministry in the English Church and published the treatise... I was

attracted by the example of the bishops of the English Church who not only tolerated and allowed foreigners to maintain rites and ceremonies in their dioceses which differed from their own, but also kindly welcomed and aided them. They do wrong who separate from each other on account of external rites and ceremonies.[22]

III: Laudian

One of the charges brought against Laud at his trial was that he had 'traitorously endeavoured to cause division and discord between the Church of England and other reformed churches'. In fact, Laud, for all his commitment to *de jure* episcopacy, nowhere denies the validity of orders of any of the reformed churches – indeed his reticence on the subject is remarkable. On the other hand, his protégé John, Viscount Scudamore, as Ambassador in Paris in the 1630s, caused a stir by refusing to communicate with the Huguenots at Charenton as his predecessors had done, and was 'careful to publish upon all occasions... that the Church of England looked not on the Huguenots as a part of their communion'.[23] There can be no doubt that Laud's instincts were less friendly to the reformed churches abroad than those of his predecessors, though he does seem to have had some sympathy for those Lutheran churches which retained 'the thing if not the name' of episcopacy.[24] Temperamentally, he was inclined to push a question to an issue of 'either/or', and it is no surprise in his correspondence to find him questioning the 'necessity' argument.[25]

At the heart of Laud's viewpoint, however, stood a great reverence for antiquity, Scudamore wrote to him from Paris in 1637 that there was no possibility of the French or Dutch protestants being drawn to any scheme for union:

> If a man doth but speake to them any thing that comes neere Antiquitie, presently he is a Papist and subverter of religion with them.[26]

Laud's reverence for antiquity was not new within Anglicanism: that reverence is the premiss, for example, that underlies almost all the writings of John Jewel from the very beginning of the Reformation in England; but he shared in a growing tendency during the seventeenth century to believe that the mere piling up of historical precedents could settle ecclesiastical disputes. The trend is exemplified later in the century by Bull and Bossuet.[27] Add to these trends the fact that Laud had defended for his D.D. at Oxford the thesis that episcopacy was a distinct order in the Church, and not merely a degree,[28] and it is not difficult to see how during his archiepiscopate the earlier consensus began to break up.[29] His experience of Puritans at home and Presbyterians in Scotland had not made him inclined to engage in the mental gymnastics that had been necessary for earlier Anglicans who had wished both to defend episcopacy and to admit the validity of the orders of the foreign reformed churches.

Many factors contributed to the acceptance of this more exclusive Laudian understanding of the place of episcopacy in the years after 1660. The experiences of the previous two decades had undermined the credibility of Puritan divinity and polity for many Englishmen, as the debates in the Cavalier Parliament make clear. Anglican churchmen who had spent those years in poverty and exile were not inclined to make compromises. In addition, scholarly and controversial publications of the intervening years had all contributed to a hardening of the position. Jeremy Taylor, Henry Hammond, and Herbert Thorndike had produced thoroughgoing defences of episcopacy during these years, even of its necessity to the Church: Taylor indeed includes episcopal government among the *credenda* of the Church's life. In addition, in 1644 Archbishop James Ussher of Armagh had published his *Polycarpi et Ignatii Epistolae*, which demonstrated the reliability of these texts, so useful to controversialists defending episcopacy. The Church of England's Ordinal was amended at the Restoration, so as to leave no doubt that bishops were consecrated to a different order from priests ('Receive the Holy Ghost for the office and work of a Bishop in the Church of God... ', previously 'Take the Holy Ghost, and remember that thou stir up the grace of God which is in thee... '); the Preface now removed any ambiguity about the admission of ministers not episcopally ordained ('No man shall be accounted or taken to be a lawful Bishop, Priest or Deacon in the Church of England, or suffered to execute any of the said Functions, except he be called, tried, examined and admitted thereunto, according to the Form hereafter following, or hath had formerly Episcopal Consecration, or Ordination'; previously 'it is requisite, that no man (not being at this present Bishop, Priest or Deacon) shall execute any of them, except he be called, tried, examined and admitted, according to the form hereafter following)'.

IV: Dodwellian

The great weakness in the position of the Church of England in the years after 1660 was in its dependence upon the Crown. Charles II and James II, sons of Queen Henrietta Maria, were both Roman Catholics, James openly so and Charles cryptically. Both of them pursued policies of attempting to establish an alliance with Dissenters from the Church of England – both Catholic and Protestant – as a counterbalance to the Anglican monopoly. In answer to this, the leadership of the Church of England was much preoccupied with attempts at 'comprehension' – the making of such changes in the liturgy and practice of the Church as should persuade the Dissenting protestants to come in. In these circumstances, it was not surprising that some Anglicans should have been uneasy. What the Church does it must do because it believes it to be right and true, not because it is expedient, they said. On these policies, complained Archdeacon Samuel Parker, that will be the Church of England that happens to get uppermost. 'Whoever can mount Bucephalus will be your Alexander', he quipped. It was in this context that the 'High Church' party arose in the Church of England;[30] people who were not prepared to negotiate about Anglican ceremonies and liturgy simply in order to do a deal, as they saw it, with the Dissenters. 'We have our fanatics too', wrote Bishop Francis Turner of Ely; 'theirs [the Dissenters'] think our ceremonies unlawful; ours think them necessary'.[31]

The underlying issue here was precisely that of dependence on the Crown. Was Anglicanism to be commended because it was established and not unlawful, or because it was believed to be true? A significant part in these controversies of the 1670s and 80s was taken by Henry Dodwell, who was largely responsible for the articulation of another view of episcopacy within the Church of England. On the basis of the Jewish roots of Christianity, in particular the significant primacy in Jerusalem of James the Lord's brother, Dodwell argued that the nature of ministry within the new Christian '*peculium*' must be exactly parallel to the ministry of the Jewish priesthood under the Old Covenant.

There had been only one legitimate priesthood in Israel, whose sacrifices and ministrations could claim legal validity within the terms of the Old Covenant; likewise there was only one legitimate priesthood in the Church of Christ, whose ministrations had legal validity within the terms of the New Covenant. The only legitimate ministers, he claimed, were those episcopally ordained. The Christian believer could have no confidence that he would receive the benefits of sacramental grace outside the episcopal communion.[32]

Dodwell's theology of the episcopate laid huge stress on the episcopal succession as a channel of sacramental grace. While such notions had been occasionally adumbrated in the years before the Civil Wars,[33] Dodwell's was the most complete statement of that viewpoint to appear in seventeenth-century England. It was a break altogether with the Reformation principle of the succession of doctrine. Indeed, Dodwell was later to define a heresy as an opinion that caused a division in the Church,[34] small wonder that

> It was the saying of an Eminent Man concerning Mr Dodwell... that, allowing his Plea to stand, he had made Religion for the Church, not the Church for Religion.[35]

Small wonder that so many critics pointed out that, if the men of the sixteenth century had held Dodwell's principles, the Reformation could not have happened. But the attractiveness of Dodwell's views in the years after the Revolution of 1689 can hardly be over-estimated. When the Crown had deprived bishops for political crimes as Nonjurors, when the Toleration Act undermined the state monopoly of Anglicanism, what more attractive doctrine for hard-pressed churchmen than this of Dodwell's, which denied the validity of baptism or the eucharist when administered outside an episcopal communion, and faced Dissenters with the prospect of imminent damnation? Obviously, on Dodwell's principles, reformed churches overseas were in no better case than the English Dissenters.[36]

Conclusion

I have sketched four views of the place of episcopacy in the life of the Church, which were held by Anglicans in the years from 1559 to 1689. The Adiaphoristic view holds that church policy is a matter indifferent – one among a number of possible ways of organizing the life of the Church. What I have called the Bancroftian view holds that episcopacy is ancient and apostolical – even divine – but that it is not so divinely prescribed as to be necessary to the Church's life. The Laudian view, largely on historical grounds, is prepared to go higher, and to claim that episcopacy is God's unalterable will for his Church. The Dodwellian view reaches the same conclusions as the Laudian about the necessity of episcopacy, but for different reasons: the point here is not that episcopal government is God's will for his Church (though of course Dodwell would say that it is) but rather that, by an almost mechanistic logic, the episcopate is the necessary channel of sacramental grace by which we are united to God and brought to salvation.

While accepting the point made at the beginning about the deliberate latitude allowed within the Church of England, one might possibly wonder whether the Adiaphoristic and the Dodwellian positions can readily be accommodated within Anglicanism. If episcopacy were indeed a matter indifferent in the life of the Church, it would seem perverse that the Church of England should make so great an insistence on it as it does in the Preface to the Ordinal; if grace unto salvation is, in Dodwellian terms, so transmitted through a human succession, does not that undermine the whole ground of the Reformation of which the Church of England is part?

Notes

1. Hooker, Preface, 2.7.

2. *Prophetical Office of the Church*, p. 30.

3. Jewel (Parker Society), iii, 334.

4. *Ibid.*, p. 103.

5. Jewel (Parker Society), iv, 1221.

6. K. Fincham, *Prelate as Pastor* (Oxford, 1990).

7. Pilkington (Parker Society), p. 493.

8. John Strype, *Whitgift* (1822), iii, 223.

9. Whitgift (Parker Society), i, 185.

10. *Ibid.*, i, 369.

11. Hooker, *Lawes*, VII. v. 8.

12. Whitgift (Parker Society), ii, 108, 281–2.

13. *Ibid.*, ii, 281, 259, 262–3.

14. M.R. Sommerville in *Journal of Ecclesiastical History*, xxxv (1984), 177–88.

15. Hooker, *Lawes*, VII. i. 4.

16. W. Nijenhuis in Derek Baker (ed.), *Reform and Reformation* (Studies in Church History, *Subsidia*, Oxford, 1979), p. 160.

17. *Ibid.*, pp. 159–60.

18. Anthony Milton, *Catholic and Reformed, the Roman and Protestant Churches in English Protestant Thought 1600-1640* (Cambridge, 1995), 481–2, cites the two cases of Cesar Calandrini and Peter de Laune from his period as 'unequivocal'.

19. Mason, pp. 71–2.

20. *Opuscula Posthumata*, p. 191.

21. Milton, pp. 484–5.

22. Nijenhuis, pp. 157–8.

23. W.J. Tighe, 'William Laud and the Reunion of Churches', *Historical Journal*, xxx (1987), 717–27.

24. Laud, *Works*, iii, 386.

25. Laud, *Works*, vi, 572–8: letters to Joseph Hall. Tighe, p. 718.

26. Tighe, p. 726.

27. Owen Chadwick, *Bossuet to Newman*, ch. 1.

28. That bishop and priest were degrees of the same order was an important plank in Anglican defences of the orders of the reformed churches overseas. See, for example, *The Validity of the*

Ordination of the Ministers of the Reformed Churches beyond the Seas, attributed to Francis Mason (Oxford, 1641).

29. Milton, pp. 486–94.

30. George Hickes, 'Letter to the Author' in Roger Laurence's *Lay Baptism Invalid* (London, 1710).

31. Francis Turner in MS Rawl Letters 99, f. 101r, Bodleian Library.

32. Henry Dodwell, *Book of Schism* (1679); *A Discourse concerning the One Altar and the One Priesthood* (1683).

33. Notably John Yates, *A Treatise of the Honour of God's House* (1637).

34. Henry Dodwell, *A Vindication of the Deprived Bishops* (1692), pp. 26–7.

35. Francis Lee, *Life of John Kettlewell* (1718), p. 317.

36. The issue as regarding the Lutherans became specially relevant as the probable accession of George of Hanover drew near. See, for example, Thomas Brett, *A Review of the Lutheran Principles* (1714).

Apostolicity, *Episkope* and Succession: The Lutheran, Reformed and United Tradition

Jan Rohls

The commonality of the Lutheran and Reformed traditions with regard to the questions of apostolicity, *episkope* and succession results from demarcation over and against the Roman position. That does not mean, however, that the Lutheran and Reformed positions are identical. Nonetheless, there seems to have been no disagreement between Lutherans and the Reformed during the Reformation and Confessional periods with regard to apostolicity and succession. Rather, such a disagreement first arose when certain neo-Lutheran circles developed a high-church understanding of ministry in the nineteenth century, in support of which they believed they could appeal to the Lutheran Reformation. On the other hand, there was from the beginning a difference between the Lutherans and the Reformed, or more precisely the Calvinist, understanding of ministry, and this difference had its effect on the understanding of *episkope*. Moreover, since the union movement at the beginning of the nineteenth century the Calvinist understanding of *episkope* has had a decisive influence not only in the United, but also in the Lutheran churches. And in the last analysis, it was over against these new forms of *episkope*, which developed in the United and Lutheran territorial churches at the beginning of the nineteenth century, that high-church neo-Lutheranism developed its own understanding of *episkope*. The differences between Lutherans and Reformed on the question of ministry, which have been deeper since that time, break out at regular intervals, and do so, moreover, when differing ecumenical interests are at stake. Following this introduction, I shall describe the Lutheran, Reformed and United understandings of apostolicity, *episkope* and succession one after the other.

I

In none of the classical Reformers is the concept of the priesthood of all believers, which is fundamental to the demarcation over and against the Roman understanding of ministry, so developed as in Luther. According to him, all Christians are ordained as priests in baptism, so that all Christians are clergy. All Christians therefore have equally direct access to God and have the same rights and duties before God. This means the double power, the *potestas ordinis* and the *postestas iurisdisctionis*, which according to the Roman understanding are restricted to the ordained priests. Luther is therefore able to declare in the tract *De instituendis ministris ecclesiae*, which is decisive for the subject of ministry, that all baptized Christians have the power to preach, to administer Baptism and Holy Communion, to exercise the power of the keys in confession, to make intercession, to offer thank-offerings and to judge questions of doctrine. But these are functions which according to the Roman view are tied either, like the administration of Holy Communion, to the power of consecration or, like the exercise of the power of the keys, to the power of jurisdiction which belongs to the ministerial priesthood. The concept of the priesthood of all believers makes the Roman institution of a particular ministerial priesthood redundant. This does not mean, however, that there is no special ministry in Luther. It is just that because of his criticism of the sacrifice of the mass this is no longer for him the ministry of a priest who because of his ordination is alone capable of offering such a sacrifice. Luther defines it instead as the ministry of public proclamation of the word and administration of the sacraments, and that means that the special ministry is a public ministry. However, in its public nature lies the reason why a Christian can only exercise it with the approval of other Christians, that is to say of the congregation. Its exercise by a certain person requires that that person should have been properly called by the congregation, and this calling or appointment may certainly be compared with appointment to secular offices. Just as a mayor is, before his appointment, already a citizen who has the rights of a citizen, and is appointed to the office by the body of citizens because of his suitability, so the ordained minister is already a priest before his appointment, therefore enjoys priestly powers and is similarly appointed to the special office or ministry by the congregation because of his suitability. According to Luther, however, God himself ordered the public proclamation of the word of God and the administration of the sacraments, so that the special ministry which undertakes this task is something instituted by God. That also follows from the Augsburg Confession (*Confessio Augustana*), if one reads CA 5 in conjunction with CA 14. For the preaching ministry instituted by God, which consists of the public preaching of the Gospel and the administration of the sacraments, is then identical with the special ministry which is exercised by people who are duly called (*rite vocatus*).

In the Lutheran view, therefore, there is alongside the priesthood of all believers the special ministry of the public proclamation of the word and the administration of the sacraments, the exercise of which requires a call by the congregation. This call brings us now to the questions of apostolicity, *episkope* and succession, because it takes the place of the Roman sacramental ordination to the priesthood, which is performed by a bishop who stands in the apostolic succession because of his consecration. Luther and Melanchthon came to a new understanding not only of ordination, but also of the bishop and of apostolic succession. For Luther, ordination is in the last analysis identical with the act of calling or vocation, insofar as this is a matter of the conferring of a special ministry to which someone is duly called. Luther therefore also regards ordination in the actual congregation to which one is called as the ideal. According to Luther, again, such an ordination is performed by a bishop, but the difference is that Luther and Melanchthon, following Jerome, identify the bishop with the presbyter and pastor of the local congregation. They are able to do this because they are working with the concept of the one special ministry instituted by God. In actual practice there may therefore be a difference between the pastor of a local congregation and a regional bishop, but this difference cannot be derived from divine institution. It is not *iure divino*, but only *iure humano*, and there is therefore no hierarchical ministry instituted by God with the episcopal ministry at its head. The legitimacy of ordinations is therefore also not dependent on them being performed by bishops in whom, thanks to their episcopal consecration, the spiritual gift has been passed on through the laying on of hands from the Apostles to their helpers and so down to us. That such an apostolic succession in the sense of the historical continuity of the chain of the laying on of hands from the Apostles onwards has a theological significance in itself is indeed disputed by Luther as much as by Melanchthon. For it is precisely the fact, in their eyes a manifest fact, that the Roman bishops, who derive their succession from the Apostles, had not preserved the apostolic teaching which causes both to doubt the theological significance of the episcopal succession and the historic episcopate. For them, rather, it is the maintenance of the apostolic teaching which is theologically relevant for the concept of apostolicity. This is to define apostolicity not in formal terms, but in terms of content, and continuity with the apostolic teaching is neither guaranteed nor made possible by the apostolic succession in the sense of an unbroken chain of episcopal laying on of hands.

One reason why Luther and Melanchthon finally moved to presbyteral ordination and legitimated this with the original identity of bishop and local pastor of course lies in the fact that in the German situation which existed at that time no bishops were prepared to ordain protestant pastors. It is one of the distinguishing features of Lutheranism – or even more, of the system of territorial churches in Germany – that following the Diet of Spires the government of the Church, which had previously been exercised by bishops, came into the hands of the princes. Because of the lack of Reformation-minded bishops, the princes became emergency bishops, who had to see to it that word and sacrament were duly administered. The episcopal office of oversight and therefore the *episkope* were thus exercised by secular princes. Melanchthon was able to justify this government of the Church by princes by the fact that a protestant prince was the senior member of the Church (*praecipuum ecclesiae membrum*), to whom belonged in addition the care for both of the tables of the Ten Commandments (*custodia utriusque tabula*). This implied care for due worship, to which the first table pointed. It is therefore the Prince, who has taken the place of the bishop, who exercises *episkope*. However, this is not done by him directly as a secular ruler or by a secular commission established by him, but with the help of spiritual office-holders or ministers, the superintendents. In German Lutheranism the old office of bishop is therefore inherited by several authorities. Since there is no difference *iure divino* between the bishop and the local pastor, the local pastor is himself a bishop, since there is only a single ministry of public proclamation of the word and administration of the sacraments which exists *iure divino*. The local pastor is, therefore, the inheritor of the office of the bishop as a spiritual office-holder. On the other hand, it is the Prince as emergency bishop who takes over the functions in the governance of the Church which belonged to the bishop, and in the end it is to him that the superintendents are subordinated as officials. These are pastors with a special commission, who are entrusted with the visitation of the pastors of a particular region. They are the actual inheritors of the title of bishop, insofar as the term '*superintendens*' is the Latin translation of '*episcopus*'. In practice the superintendents therefore exercise the *episkope* over the work and lifestyle of the pastors of the district allocated to them, acting as church officials in visitation commissions and consistories appointed by the Prince. The visitation commissions and later the consistories are organs of the government of the Church by princes, formed from a mixture of ecclesiastical and secular office-holders. This means that the Superintendent always worked in co-operation with secular officials.

The Superintendent's tasks are sketched out for the first time in the Saxon 'Instruction for Visitors'. The underlying assumption is that the superintendents are officials of the Prince, but Luther himself attempts to counteract this by defining their tasks in the Preface to Melanchthon's 'Information for Visitors' as being purely within the Church. That Luther was interested in a genuine protestant episcopal office as an office of visitation which undertakes the task of *episkope* is evidenced not least by the installation of Nikolaus von Amsdorf as Bishop of Naumburg-Zeitz, together with the tract 'Example of Consecrating a True Christian Bishop' which was composed for this occasion. Melanchthon too pleads for the retention of the episcopal office of oversight, providing that the Gospel is truly proclaimed. The basic premise for this, however, is that this office is not an institution which exists *iure divino*, but one which is purely human and exists for the sake of order. In the context of the human church order the Lutheran bishop as the holder of the office of oversight is therefore placed above the local pastor. However, this does not alter in the slightest the fact that the episcopal office was not able to survive in the Lutheran territorial churches of Germany. It was rather the office of Superintendent, an official of the Prince as emergency bishop, which took over the function of the office of oversight. In this way, the government of the Church by princes established itself completely and pushed to one side every institutional alternative to the exercise of *episkope* by the Superintendent. In just the same way, however, this model also excluded another possibility for the exercise of *episkope*, which was similarly established by the Lutheran Reformation. Just as the traditional episcopal constitution of the Church suggests that the ecclesiastical task of *episkope* should be given to a bishop, who is placed above the pastors of his episcopal area, so the specifically Lutheran idea of the priesthood of all believers suggests that the task of *episkope* should be transferred to the congregation. For according to Luther, the congregation has the right and the duty to care for the true proclamation of the word and administration of the sacraments, just as it also has the right and the duty to call pastors. Yet this alternative of congregational *episkope* came just as little into play as did episcopal *episkope*. Rather, with the victory of the government of the Church by princes and the introduction of the office of Superintendent, the spiritual teachers and the secular defenders divided the task of *episkope* between themselves.

II

It is characteristic of the Reformed understanding of ministry that fundamental considerations about the relationship between the priesthood of all believers and the particular ministerial office are entirely absent from it. This is true not only of the individual confessions, where such considerations after all have no place in Lutheranism either, but also of Reformed theology altogether. For Bullinger as for Calvin, the ministerial office of public proclamation of the word and administration of the sacraments is instituted by God in order to gather, found, lead and maintain the Church through his servants. In this designation of the function of the pastoral office there is just as little difference between the Reformed and the Lutheran understanding of ministry as there is in the question of the apostolic succession, which is naturally seen in the Reformed world too as succession in the apostolic teaching, and in the ordination of pastors by pastors, which is justified by the identity of bishop and pastor in the early Church. The difference between the Reformed and the Lutheran understanding of ministry commences rather with the fact that Calvin speaks at the local congregational level not only of one ministry, but of three or four ministries. More must be said about this here, because this difference also has its effect on the understanding of *episkope*. Moreover, this is not a trait general to the Reformed understanding of ministry, but one which is absent in Zurich but decisive for Geneva and the churches influenced by Geneva.

In Zurich the followers of Zwingli know only the one particular ministerial office, so that there is no difference here from Lutheranism. The New Testament terms 'bishop', 'elder', 'pastor' and 'teacher' are only different descriptions of the one ministerial office of public proclamation of the word and administration of the sacraments. Now Calvin also does not doubt the central importance of the public proclamation of the word and administration of the sacraments for the Church, since for him too the Church only exists where the word is truly preached and the sacraments duly administered. But for him there are nevertheless also other functions in the Church which arise out of the embryonic ecclesiology of the New Testament. From this Calvin proceeds to the thesis that three further ministries are subordinated to the pastoral ministry – those of teacher, deacon and elder or presbyter. The fact that this is not a rigid scheme is shown by the Huguenot Confession, of which Calvin was one of the drafters, which has alongside the pastor only the offices of deacon and elder. The fundamental distinction for the Calvinist doctrine of ministry is that between deacon and presbyter, in which – in an interpretation of the New Testament which was believed to be correct – two types of presbyter are distinguished from each other. On the one hand there are the presbyters who are entrusted with the public proclamation of the word and administration of the sacraments, that is the pastors, and on the other hand there are the church elders who exercise discipline in the Church. The decisive fact is that the leadership of the local congregation does not, as in Lutheranism, lie with the individual pastor but with the consistory, comprising the pastor and the elders and sometimes also the deacons, that is to say a collective body.

Episkope in Calvinism is no longer undertaken by the secular power, unlike the position in Lutheranism and Zwinglianism, where it was admittedly exercised jointly with representatives of the ministry of the Church. Rather, *episkope* is placed in the hands of the church's collegial body. If the function of *episkope* lies in watching over the purity of the public proclamation of the word and the correctness of the administration of the sacraments, in Calvinism it is undertaken at local level by the elders as the office-holders who are represented in the consistory. The existence of the Church is after all endangered where the constitutive characteristics of the true Church – true proclamation of the word and administration of the sacraments – are no longer provided by the holder of the office of public proclamation of the word and administration of the sacraments, that is to say, the pastors. The elders are entrusted with a spiritual jurisdiction of their own, which does not only make it possible for them, but also requires them, to call to account and discipline a pastor who deviates from the true proclamation of the word and administration of the sacraments. This means that implicit in the Calvinist doctrine of ministry is the fact that *episkope* within the Church is undertaken at the local level.

Now the traditional episcopal office was a regional office of oversight, while the consistory only undertook a local *episkope*. Such a regional office of oversight is, of course, first and foremost necessary in churches which do not have a local office of oversight, and that is the case not only with the Lutherans, but also in Zwingli's area of influence. The office of Superintendent, which is also present among the Lutherans, is also to be found in the Reformed territorial churches of Germany. Thus, for example, the Herborn General Synod describes the superintendents as servants of the word, that is to say as pastors, on whom in addition to their normal duties, namely the public proclamation of the word and administration of the sacraments, the task of inspection is also conferred, and who visit the congregations and are to lead the clergy chapters and the clergy. Here, then, the Superintendent has a role which is also familiar to Bullinger in the cantonal church of Zurich. The *Antistes* or *Senior* here has the chairmanship of the church senate, following the model of Peter in the Jerusalem congregation. Among other things he has the responsibility to see that there is no disorder, although this function is not accompanied by a greater spiritual power. Rather, such an office of *episkope* above the level of the local pastoral office is seen, as it is in Lutheranism, as identical in its spiritual power with that of the local pastoral office. As has been said, however, such an office of oversight established in imitation of the old office of bishop is lacking in Calvinism. This does not mean that Calvin considered it to be unsupportable, for he himself was of the opinion that there was such an office in the early Church, and he was even able to suggest to the King of Poland a constitution which in this sense was episcopal. According to this view, the task of the bishop lies in the chairmanship of synods and ensuring unity and order in his diocese, and naturally this episcopal office is a human institution. In Calvinism, however, an office of *episkope* of this type was not developed, and what is more, this form of the exercise of *episkope* was noticeably devalued. Thus Beza distinguishes between three forms of episcopacy. The Roman view of the episcopate as a *iure divino* institution ranking higher than that of the pastor he describes as *Satanus Episcopatus*. By contrast, he tolerates the merely *iure humano* higher ranking of the bishop in the Lutheran churches and those influenced by Zwingli as *Humanus Episcopatus*. But in his eyes, only the *Divinus Episcopatus*, as laid down in the Calvinistic church orders, is in accordance with the Scriptures and therefore desirable. According to this the ministry of *episkope* at the regional level is undertaken by the synod. The synodical model of *episkope*, which was first developed by the Huguenot Church Order, subsequently established itself, via the Dutch Church and its exile congregations, in Western Germany as well. Here we have an independent model of *episkope*, which differs from the superintendent model which is found in the context of the government of the Church by princes both on the Lutheran and on the Reformed side, in that it is not a personal but a collegial office. The presbyterian-synodical church order is the product of a church which exists independently of the protection of the state authorities. According to this, the Church does not only exercise the office of *episkope* through presbyteries or consistories at the local level of the local congregation, but problems concerning the ministry of oversight which cannot be solved in the local presbyteries or which concern several congregations or indeed the whole Church must be passed up to the higher synods – the chapter of the classis, the provincial synod and finally the General Synod. In this way a system of *episkope* structured in layers ranging from the local presbytery up to the General Synod, in which the principle of subsidiarity rules, comes into existence. The link between the local presbyteries and the higher synods is arranged in such a way that the synods are composed of members of the presbyteries appointed for that purpose. This also expresses the fact that no one congregation has a pre-eminence or any authority over another. The regional office of *episkope* is thus undertaken by the synodical representatives of the local presbyteries on an equal basis.

It is important to look clearly at this presbyterian-synodical model of *episkope* as a totality. *Episkope* is exercised at every level, from the individual local congregation right up to the whole church of a territory, by institutions which belong to the Church. And at each level, it is undertaken by an institution of that same level. The oversight of the local congregation lies with the presbytery, that of the whole church with the General Synod. Unlike the Lutheran synods, these synods do not consist purely of clergy. Rather, like the presbyteries or consistories they are composed of pastors, elders and deacons. Between the presbyteries and the General Synod there are several levels of synodical bodies which meet regularly, so that a thoroughgoing oversight of the Church results. It is important to note, however, that neither the synods nor the presbyteries are representative of the members of the congregations. Rather, both presbyteries and synods are composed only of office-holders. The decisive factor, however, is that it is not only at the lowest regional level is there a collegial organ of *episkope*, namely the classis as the synod of the neighbouring congregations, but such a collegial organ of *episkope* exists already at the lowest level of all, that of the local congregation, in the form of the presbytery or consistory. The difference from Lutheranism is clear. There three powerful figures had divided the inheritance of the old episcopal office. The spiritual power of the bishop had been transferred to the pastor, the episcopal governance of the Church to the Prince, and the actual oversight to the superintendents as officials of the Prince. In Calvinism the spiritual power of the bishop may go to the pastors, which means that the old *iure divino* superiority of the bishop over the pastors disappears, but by contrast with Lutheranism, the episcopal government of the Church goes not to the Prince as emergency bishop but to the synods. And the actual *episkope* is finally exercised by collegial bodies from the presbytery right up to the General Synod.

III

Just as one cannot understand the Anglican Church of today without the changes which it experienced in the nineteenth century through the influence of Tractarianism and Ritualism, so too one cannot comprehend the German Lutheran and Reformed churches of today if one does not take into account the influence of synods in the German territorial churches in the nineteenth century. The introduction of synods in the Lutheran territorial churches did not only change their previous structure. Rather, it also brought about a significant change in the Calvinist understanding of synods and within Lutheranism prompted as a reaction the development of a specifically high-church concept of ministry. All of this was not without its consequences for the understanding of *episkope*. The introduction of the presbyterian-synodical elements in the German territorial churches was preceded by criticism of the old Lutheran understanding of ministry, above all by the Pietists. This criticism drew on Luther's concept of the priesthood of all believers, as that of Socinianism and Spiritualism had done before it. As this idea of Luther had itself been directed against the Roman priesthood, so now it was turned against the Lutheran ministerial office, which in the eyes of its critics tends to render the congregation powerless. In order to activate the life of the congregation, one could set up Calvin's presbyterian church order as a model. It was, however, only in the wake of the rationalization of the German territories caused by Napoleon's appearance on the scene that a fundamental change in the constitution of the German territorial churches came about. This rationalization produced confessionally mixed territories, which in turn led in some cases to unions between the Lutheran and Reformed churches. These unions responded both to the fact that Pietism had made doctrinal differences within protestantism a matter of indifference as well as to the enlightenment criticism of compulsory adherence to a confession. Moreover, within the context of the unification movements sponsored by the princes, demands arose for a fundamental change in the form which the government of the Church by princes took. Decisive for this were the developments in Prussia, to which the Rheinland and Westphalia were added by the Congress of Vienna, for here the presbyterian-synodical church order had already become established in the Reformed regions in the Reformation era, via the Netherlands. Schleiermacher now took up elements of this church order in his tract 'On the Synodical Constitution which should be established for the Protestant Church of the Prussian State'. His aim was to achieve by this means a greater independence for the Church over against the state. Of course, he was not in a position to abolish completely the government of the Church by princes which had existed since the Reformation, but in his eyes this should be limited to oversight over the property of the Church, while the internal administration of the Church should be carried out by independent church bodies. To this end,

Schleiermacher argued for the establishment of presbyteries at the local congregational level and of synods. Initially, he envisaged these synods as being purely clerical, and they were to lead the Church together with the bishops appointed by the King. In this way the exercise of *episkope* would have lain with a body which linked the old Lutheran personal ministry of the Superintendent, now raised to that of bishop, with the collegial ministry of the synod. However, the form of the synod does not correspond with the old Calvinistic model, being a purely clerical synod. At the same time, the introduction of a protestant episcopal office failed, as it had done in the Reformation era, because the princely government of the Church was opposed to it. Schleiermacher then modified his original proposals in the above-mentioned tract. In this, he gave up both the idea of a protestant episcopal office and that of purely clerical synods. Instead he argued for the addition of a synodical constitution to the existing consistorial constitution. Also, the synods were to be attended, in addition to the clergy, by elders as further representatives of the local presbytery.

This model of Schleiermacher, which combines the consistorial with the presbyterian-synodical model of *episkope,* was, however, only realized within Prussia in the Rhenish-Westphalian church order. Since this church order served as a model for the establishment of synods in other German territorial churches as well, its description of *episkope* should be described in somewhat more detail here. First of all, at the local level there is the presbytery, which represents the local congregation in all congregational matters and consists of elected pastors, elders and deacons. Even at this level, the elders undertake the function of *episkope* over the pastors. At the next level above is the district synod, which consists of the pastors of the district and one elder from each of the congregations of the district. Every district synod is presided over by a directory elected by the synod itself, which consists of the Superintendent, the Assessor and the Clerk. The Superintendent, who in this case is not a state official but a purely ecclesiastical office-holder elected by the synod, has the task of exercising *episkope* at the district level. It is his duty to watch over conformity with and execution of the church order and synodical decisions in all church matters, and of safeguarding the rights of the Church. He also exercises oversight over the presbyteries, over continuing study and over the candidates from the district, over how the clergy and other servants of the Church conduct their ministry and their lives in accordance with the principles of the church order. Finally, at the highest level is the provincial synod, which consists of the superintendents of the province and one pastor and one elder elected by each district synod. The provincial synod in turn elects a *präses* and an assessor, and it too has the task of *episkope* at the level of the province. It is to watch over the maintenance of the purity of protestant teaching in churches and schools and see that the church order is adhered to. This development meant that the old presbyterian-synodical church order, in which the task of *episkope* at the different levels is undertaken by presbyteries and synods, entered the western provinces of Prussia. However, the presbyterian-synodical element forms only one part of the constitution, which still includes in addition state authorities exercising oversight over the Church. Alongside the consistories and governments there is the General Superintendent. He is appointed by the Prince, and is therefore the old Superintendent of the Reformation period – that is to say an official of the Prince. It is his task to oversee the individual superintendents of the province, according to the instructions given to him by the ministry for church affairs. He also participates in the provincial synods as a state official, in order to safeguard the interests of the state. This results, as far as the exercise of *episkope* is concerned, in a peculiar hybrid. On the one side we have the office of General Superintendent, in accordance with the government of the Church by princes, on the other presbyteries and synods which organize themselves. The decisive difference from the old Calvinistic presbyterian-synodical order lies in the fact that in this case the governance of the Church does not lie with the synods, but as hitherto with the Prince. Rather, the synods stand over against the princely government of the Church as the representative of the Church and exercise a scrutiny over it, as in turn the princely government of the Church, with the help of the General Superintendent, scrutinizes the synods. Thus the *episkope* is exercised by both sides.

The presbyterian-synodical model in this watered-down form has prevailed even in German territorial churches which are not United but, like the Bavarian Church, for example, purely Lutheran. The more on one hand the presbyterian-synodical model prevailed even in the Lutheran Church, the more on the other hand Lutheran criticism of it in the shape of high-church episcopal model grew. There was, however, no difference of intention between the supporters of the presbyterian-synodical and the high-church models, for in both cases the priority was the independence of the Church from the state. High-church Lutherans wanted to take the governance of the Church from the prince, to whom it had fallen because of the emergency situation at the time of the Reformation, and give it back to the bishops, who had held it previously. Like the supporters of the presbyterian-synodical model, the advocates of the high-church episcopal model sought to demonstrate that their model was to be found in Luther and that the government of the Church by princes represented a departure from Luther's intention. The high-church neo-Lutherans like Stahl, Löhe and Vilmar begin with an institutional understanding of the Church. The Church is not considered from the perspective of the priesthood of all believers, but as an institution in which the teaching body stands over against the congregation. The members of the teaching body are, according to Stahl, the successors of the Apostles in the teaching office instituted by Christ. This independence of the ministry over against the congregation finds its expression in the increased sacramental value attached to ordination, for according to Löhe and Vilmar a special grace of orders is conferred through ordination. Ordination can therefore only be performed by ministers who are already ordained. This is to avoid the impression that ordination is a matter of conveying to the future pastors the rights of the congregation which arise from the priesthood of all believers. The idea of the apostolic succession is thereby no longer understood in the sense of the succession in the apostolic teaching, but also in the sense of the succession from the ministry of the Apostles which was instituted by Christ. Vilmar emphasizes that the Holy Spirit is given through prayer and the laying on of hands in the act of ordination in a continual succession commencing with the Apostles. Only this can guarantee the maintenance of pure doctrine and the administration of the sacraments. Moreover, the ministerial office is to be understood not only as an office of teaching and administration of the sacraments, but also as a pastoral office, to which alone the leadership of the congregation belongs. However, since the aim of this emphasis on the independence of the ministry over against the congregation is the unfolding of the independence of the Church over against the state, it is necessary for the bishop to lead the whole Church just as the pastor leads the congregation. Thus according to the high-church episcopal model the government of the Church lies with the bishop. According to this view, the bishop as the possessor of the highest power in the Church has oversight over doctrine, worship and discipline. Löhe therefore, quite in accordance with the Anglican understanding of ministry, demands an episcopal church order for the Lutheran Church too, albeit emphasizing that according to the Lutheran understanding there is no difference *iure divino* between bishop and pastor. According to this high-church episcopal model *episkope* lies with the bishop alone, and it is his task to oversee public preaching and public religious education. This model of *episkope* is opposed to the presbyterian-synodical model, because it places the exercise of *episkope* exclusively in the hands of the clergy and destroys the link between clergy and congregation.

IV

In most of the German territorial churches, be they Lutheran, Reformed or United, presbyterian-synodical institutions developed in the course of the nineteenth century. They nevertheless remained tied in to the system of the government of the Church by princes, however. To this extent, the end of the government of the Church by princes after the First World War meant also the end of the form of oversight practised up to that time. In most cases, individual clergymen became leaders of the territorial churches, often with the title of 'bishop'. They are, however, in no sense bishops in the sense of the high-church episcopal model, outlined above, which emphasizes the complete independence of the ordained ministry, and thereby naturally also that of the episcopal office, from the congregation. The form of the episcopal office may have been based on the Reformation model of a Lutheran bishop, who now no longer acts as an official of the Prince, but the bishop is elected by the synod and can if circumstances require also be dismissed by it, so that he does not only stand over against the congregations as supreme pastor. It is consequently a synodical office of bishop. The bishop is not differentiated from the pastor by divine law, and neither does he stand in the apostolic succession, if that is understood as the unbroken chain of episcopal laying on of hands since the time of the Apostles. But according to human law he is differentiated from the local pastor both by the extent of the area for which he is responsible and also by the particularities of his functions, for these concern the whole particular church which he leads and all serve the exercise of *episkope*. Among them are above all the ordination of pastors and the visitation of congregations, which then also includes responsibility for purity of doctrine, public proclamation of the word and administration of the sacraments. At a lower level, however, these functions are also undertaken by superintendents and rural deans, to whom, as to the bishop at the level of the whole territorial church, the exercise of *episkope* falls. Unlike the high-church episcopal model, in the German territorial churches the leadership of the church and thus the exercise of *episkope* does not lie in the hands of the bishop alone. Rather, these are hybrids of two different forms of *episkope*, namely that of the Lutheran episcopal office of the Reformation period and that of the Calvinistic presbyterian-synodical church order. By contrast, a pure high-church episcopal model was no more able to prevail in the German territorial churches after the collapse of the government of the Church by princes than was a pure presbyterian-synodical system. In general one can say that at the level of the particular church the structuring of *episkope* has always been a matter of a Lutheran-Reformed hybrid, and that even in non-United churches.

The question of the form of *episkope* played a central role in the German Protestant Church once again in this century in the dispute about the so-called leadership principle in the Church. The German Christians demanded a new constitution for the church, which would no longer construct the organs of church life according to the democratic electoral system. Rather, all important decisions should be the personal responsibility of a spiritual head of the German Protestant Imperial Church, the *Reichsbischof*. The *Reichsbischof* was to possess authority in the Protestant Church corresponding to his role as leader. First two Reformed declarations and then the 'Theological Declaration' of Barmen, which was supported equally by Reformed, Lutheran and United members of the Confessing Church, were made against this leadership principle. All of these declarations are influenced by the understanding of ministry of Karl Barth and the Reformed declarations also draw on Calvin's doctrine of ministry. The first of these declarations, the 'Düsseldorf Theses', starts with the kingly rule of Christ in the Church, which is accomplished through the establishment of the ministry of preachers, teachers, elders and deacons, which is instituted and ordered by Jesus Christ. According to this view, the spiritual leader, that is to say what the German Christian *Reichsbischof* claimed to be, is Jesus Christ alone, and this kingly rule of Christ does not correspond to the rule of a single congregation over the others or that of an episcopal office which is placed above the other ministries, but it corresponds rather to the service which the individual congregations owe to each other and which they seek to give each other in the form of the ministers they have called. In this way, the presbyterian-synodical church order in the sense of a representative Christian democracy is held up against the office of *Reichsbischof*, which is conceived in analogy to the State's leadership principles. The second Reformed declaration, the 'Declaration about the True Understanding of the Reformation Confessions in the German Protestant Church of Today' similarly bases the four offices which are described as 'ministries' on the commission of Christ. It is not the office of an episcopal leader but the individual congregations themselves who bear the responsibility for the proper exercise of these offices. It is precisely against the background of the discussion about the introduction of the leadership principle in the German Protestant Church and in view of the arguments deployed for this by the Lutheran theologians Elert and Althaus, namely that according to the Lutheran Confession the church order belongs to the variable church law, that the Barmen 'Theological Declaration' now insisted that the Church may not leave the form of its order to its own discretion or to the vicissitudes of the currently dominant ideological and political convictions at any particular time. Instead of only the one ordered ministry being spoken of, reference is also expressly made, following the presbyterian-synodical tradition, to different ministries in the Church. What is decisive in this, however, is that the presbyterian-synodical understanding of ministry is linked with the concept of the priesthood of all believers. This linkage is completely missing in the old Calvinistic doctrine of ministry, while the link between ordained ministry and the priesthood of all believers plays a decisive role in Luther's thinking. The Barmen Declaration emphasizes that the different offices in the Church represent the exercise of the ministry which is entrusted to and laid upon the whole congregation. Apart from this ministry, it says, there could be no special leader to whom ruling power is given. For this would contradict the affirmation which the Declaration makes, picking up what is said in the old Calvinistic church orders, that the different offices of ministry in the Church do not represent a hierarchy in the sense that one office has the rule over the others. This means, however, that the leadership of the Church and thereby also *episkope* are also seen as something which are entrusted to and laid upon the whole congregation as a ministry, even if this ministry is exercised by certain offices. Moreover, the claim to rule over the other offices may not be linked with the office of *episkope*. The Declaration thereby starts from the premise that all of the different ministerial offices are equally original.

The linkage between ordained ministry and the priesthood of all believers which the Barmen Declaration affirms has now been taken up by the Tampere Theses and the text 'The Church of Jesus Christ' of the Leuenberg Church Fellowship. Thesis 3 of the Tampere Theses is concerned with the ministry of leadership, that is to say *episkope*. The leadership of the congregation is understood as part of the ministry of the word which belongs not only to the ordained ministry but to the whole congregation. The same is also true for the leadership of the congregation or for *episkope* both at the level of the individual local congregation and also the level above that of the parish, namely that it belongs not only to the ordained ministry but also occurs through other ministries. In spite of the difference between Lutherans and Reformed in the question of the form of the ministry of oversight, the German protestant churches which have signed the Leuenberg Agreement are agreed first that they understand the ministry of *episkope* as a ministry of the word for the unity of the Church, and secondly that in all churches non-ordained members of the congregation also participate in the leadership of the Church. The differing structures of church leadership in the individual Lutheran, Reformed and United churches do not pose any obstacle for church fellowship in the sense of eucharistic fellowship and the mutual recognition of ministry and ordination. In addition it is said that no single form of church leadership which has grown up historically can be a precondition for church fellowship and the mutual recognition of churches. Seen in this light, the text 'The Church of Jesus Christ', which takes up the Tampere Theses, is able to value both the historic episcopal office and also the fourfold ministry of the presbyterian-synodical church order as a ministry of unity. It is in this mutual recognition of the differing forms of the ministry of leadership or in the maintenance of church fellowship while keeping differing forms of ministry of leadership that the fundamental difference occurs from the considerations which are proposed by the Protestant-Catholic Commission 'Lehrverurteilungen – kirchentrennend?'. For these considerations tend, as the 'Lima Text' did before them, to a one-sided support for the episcopal office and for entering into the historic succession. Broadly speaking, it can therefore be said that in the present German discussion about apostolicity, *episkope* and succession by representatives of the Leuenberg Church Fellowship the line of tradition which stretches from Schleiermacher via the presbyterian-synodical tradition up to Barmen is followed, while the representatives of the Protestant-Catholic Commission continue the high-church episcopal line of tradition which leads from Stahl and Löhe via Vilmar to the Lutheran supporters of the high-church liturgical movement in our century.

The Anglican Position
on Apostolic Continuity and
Apostolic Succession in the Porvoo Common
Statement [1]

Mary Tanner

I. Anglican Tradition

The question of apostolic continuity and apostolic succession has been a concern of Anglicans since the time of the Reformation, as Anglicans have sought to understand their own identity – often in discussions, not always eirenic, with other traditions. Continuity was understood as multi-faceted: continuity in the faith grounded in the Scriptures; continuity with the Fathers and the Councils of the early Church; continuity in the worship and sacramental life of the Church; continuity in the ministry, ordered in the threefold pattern, and continuity in the episcopate and in the collegial gatherings of the bishops – all of this expressed in the continuing life and witness of the faithful people in the parishes. Living in this continuity was what determined Anglican self-understanding rather than adherence to any confessional documents. There was discontinuity too: most obviously and sadly in the break with the papacy. Anglicans understood themselves to be part of the one, holy, catholic and apostolic Church in a particular place, living in dynamic continuity with apostolic teaching, order and mission.

Within this broader and multi-faceted view of continuity there has always been a debate focussed upon the continuity of the ordered ministry. In the face of Roman Catholic, Puritan and Reformed traditions, writers of the late sixteenth and seventeenth centuries addressed themselves to questions about the relation of the episcopal office to the apostolic office, the divine right of the episcopal office and continuity in ordination. The insistence on ordination by bishops who themselves had been ordained in traditional fashion by other bishops was a way of testifying that legitimate reception of authority – as distinct from seizure of it – presupposes both continuity in office and orderly transmission of office. One theme that exercised the minds of Church of England leaders was the precise link between the Apostles and the first bishops. Hooker was more nuanced than others in the claims he made. At one time he argued that 'after the Apostles were dead, the churches agreed amongst themselves ... to make one presbyter chief in each city over against the rest.'[2] In another place he writes: 'the Apostles themselves left bishops invested with power above other priests'. He is confident that the Apostles did in one way or another have a hand in matters.[3]

The seventeenth-century discovery of the works of Ignatius of Antioch led someone like John Pearson, Bishop of Chester (1673-86), to summarize things in this way:

> As the Father sent Christ, so Christ [sent] the Apostles, and the Apostles their successors... By this apostolic action of handing on [*traditio*], the entire power of ordination is resident in the bishops.[4]

Up until 1662 the debate was shaped largely in the attitude taken to foreign reformed churches. Anglicans demanded episcopal succession in the ordering of the Church at home. While commending it abroad, some nevertheless were inclined to recognize these churches as genuine churches with a real ministry which of *necessity* had introduced presbyterian polity, an attitude which was not extended to groups within England where no such necessity could be claimed. The elegant and generous letters of Lancelot Andrewes, Bishop of Winchester (1555-1626), and John Cosin, Bishop of Durham (1660-1672), make fascinating reading today, especially in the light of the current Church of England discussions with the French Lutheran and Reformed churches. In a letter in 1618 to Peter Du Moulin, Andrewes is anxious not to deny that a church could consist without episcopal succession:

> He is blind who does not see churches consisting without it; he is hard-hearted who denies them salvation... There may be something absent in the exterior regiment, which is of divine right, and yet salvation is to be had... To prefer a better thing is not to condemn a thing. Nor is it to condemn your church if we recall it to another form, namely our own which better agrees with all antiquity.[5]

A year later in replying to the same correspondent he writes:

> You asked me whether your churches have sinned in the matter of divine authority. I did not say that. I said only that your churches lacked something which is of divine authority...[6]

He goes on to suggest that what is lacking can nevertheless be supplied now by God's grace.

Some thirty years later the debate was continuing in equally fascinating letters between John Cosin and a Mr Cavel of Blois. Cosin writes of the 'great presumption to depart from the example of the Apostles' but still cannot bring himself to say '*factum non valet*' and pronounce them 'utterly void' – 'altogether null and invalid'. He points out that if any minister from France comes to receive a cure of souls in England ('as indeed I have known some to have done') they were not, and are not, re-ordained. To do so would be to declare their former ordination void. This generous attitude of Cosin compares with France and Geneva's own attitudes in insisting on re-ordaining 'papist priests'.

> I dare not take upon me to condemn, or determine a nullity of their own ordinations against them: though, in the interim, I take it to be utterly a fault among them, and a great presumption, deserving a great censure...[7]

In 1642 the view of the Bishop of Down and Connor in Ireland, Jeremy Taylor, was somewhat different. He was in no way persuaded by the argument of necessity. While it was not his place to condemn the action of the Reformed, he was clear that there were many archbishops, and cardinals, that joined in the Reformation who could have been employed.[8] Edward Stillingfleet, Bishop of Winchester from 1689-99, came to the view that 'there is as great reason to believe the Apostolic Succession to be of Divine Institution as the Canon of Scripture...' an idea which has re-surfaced in this century in the Lambeth Conference of 1930 and in ARCIC I's work.

All of this illustrates the Anglican interest in episcopacy and its own adherence to historic episcopal succession. The views expressed are not identical: they illustrate differing and shifting reactions to the reformed churches. However, there is no doubt that for all these writers, for the Church of England, episcopacy and historic succession were fundamental for the life of the Church. It was the Act of Uniformity in 1662 that formally excluded clergy who had not been episcopally ordained from pastoral office in the Church of England.

In the eighteenth century other events were to influence perceptions of apostolic continuity. High Church clergy who refused the oath to William III began making claims for episcopacy, this time not over against the Reformed, but over against political power. Episcopacy is a divine gift and in the apostolic office of a bishop lay the Church's authority and identity – independent of Parliament. The succession of bishops was emphasized in the continuity with the Apostolic office. The Church's constitution is independent of that of civil society and only by maintaining that constitution – ordination by persons standing in succession to the Apostles – can the Church maintain its identity. The historic episcopate comes to be seen as one of the definitions of the Church, a tradition which in the nineteenth century was re-asserted by the Tractarians.[9] The way was open for a debate between those who see the 'historic episcopate' as belonging to the *esse* of the Church, and those who see it as a matter of *bene esse* or *plene esse*. This is a debate which still rumbles on, though as Bishop John Hind pointed out in a recent lecture, Anglicans have never expressed a common mind about this: all three views have been and still are held within the Church of England and the Anglican Communion today.[10]

Whatever answer is given to this rather outdated form of the episcopal question, the Anglican position that the historic episcopate is a non-negotiable for the unity and continuity of the Church was set out in the classical Chicago-Lambeth Quadrilateral in 1888 which outlines the conditions for re-union with other churches and in doing so also makes a statement of Anglican self-understanding. These are the fourfold items of Holy Scriptures as containing all things necessary to salvation: the Apostles' Creed and the Nicene Creed as a sufficient statement of the Christian faith; the two sacraments ordained by Christ, Baptism and the Lord's Supper, and the Historic Episcopate locally adapted in the methods of its administration. In recent years there has been discussion as to whether a fifth item needs adding to this fourfold list – an item which refers to structures of authority and common decision-making.

The strength of the Quadrilateral is that in setting out requirements for unity it does not isolate one item from one another. The four items of the Quadrilateral are not separate, unconnected to one another. They are integrally bound together as what Stephen Sykes calls 'parts of a single system of communication'. Anglicans would want to hold, as the Roman Catholic Response to *Baptism, Eucharist and Ministry* does, that they are not content merely to list and juxtapose such items 'without showing how they have their own function within the totality and how they are related among themselves'.[11] To quote Jean Tillard on the items of the Quadrilateral:

> They are not a catalogue of items, the addition of which creates the presence of the Church God wills... a kind of anatomical glue. They belong within an experienced *koinonia* in discipleship, service, prayer, witness, and commitment to mission.[12]

These little vignettes of Anglican engagement with the question of the historic episcopate and apostolicity and succession are, on any reckoning, highly selective and inadequate. They will hardly satisfy rigorous historians. However, they are sufficient to illustrate that Anglicans have always had a very particular concern for continuity and apostolicity and for the place and role of the historic episcopate. They have been influenced by the changing relations to state authority, by biblical and historical research, by the temperament and sensitivities of individual theologians, by the differing outlooks of evangelical, catholic, liberal and puritan Anglicans, and, not least of all, by relations with other churches.

At best continuity has been seen within the totality of the life of the Church, bound by inter-related elements of continuity. All too often, however, historic episcopal succession has been lifted out of the context of the life of the Church and made the sole determinative element of continuity. Christopher Hill, in a shortly-to-be published essay, shows how, partly as a consequence of the publication of

Apostolicae Curae, the ecumenical agenda for Anglicans became dominated by a very narrow concentration on orders and succession. He comments that Anglicans overemphasized episcopal succession in isolation as an 'unconscious compensation for an Anglican esteem dented by *Apostolicae Curae*'.[13] In their turn, Anglicans have found it difficult to commend the historic episcopate, without seeming to be clinging arrogantly to a narrow pipe-line view of succession and in so doing denying the ministry of partners in the dialogue. This has been the rock on which many a scheme of unity has foundered.

All of this forms the background for understanding the Anglican position on apostolic continuity and apostolic succession in the *Porvoo Common Statement*.[14] To state it this way is not quite right. Before I go on I must rephrase what could be misleading in the title of this paper. It is not the Anglican position of apostolic continuity and apostolic succession that we must look for in the *Porvoo Common Statement*. It is rather a 'fresh' common Anglican-Lutheran twentieth-century statement on continuity and succession which Anglicans can recognize as a statement of the faith of the Church, the catholic faith. It is a statement which Anglicans can recognize as consonant with the faith that Anglicans have sought in their history to affirm. It is important to get hold of this distinction because in voting for Porvoo, Anglicans in Britain and Ireland were voting for a greater visibility in Northern Europe of the one, holy, catholic and apostolic Church, living in continuity with the faith of the Church through the ages.

II.   The Porvoo Common Statement

It is important to set what is said about *episkope*, apostolicity and succession in the context of the entire *Porvoo Common Statement* and within an understanding of the dynamic of the Statement.

The text begins with a description of the contemporary context, the opportunity for mission in a changing Europe. The unity of the Church is required for effective mission and for the credible proclamation of reconciliation.

A second section explores the common understanding of the nature of the Church and describes the goal of visible unity to which the partner churches are committed. The aim is to establish visible unity. Next follow twelve agreements on fundamental matters of faith. Here the document resembles, but is not identical with, *The Meissen Common Statement*. The twelve agreements include those on Scriptures, Creeds, the doctrine of God's justifying grace, the sacraments, the ministry of the whole people of God and within that an ordained ministry with a basic oneness but in threefold form. There is agreement on a ministry of pastoral oversight, *episkope*, exercised in personal, collegial and communal ways – witnessing to and safeguarding the unity and catholicity of the Church. Further, there is agreement that all the churches employ the episcopal office as a 'sign of our intention, under God, to ensure the continuity of the Church in apostolic life and witness'.

These agreements in faith draw upon the theological convergence of ecumenical dialogues: the work of the Faith and Order Commission of the World Council of Churches, Anglican-Lutheran, Anglican-Reformed, Anglican-Roman Catholic, Lutheran-Roman Catholic and Roman Catholic-Orthodox dialogues.

On the basis of explicit agreement about the goal of visible unity with a commitment to move towards that goal, and on the basis of the agreements in faith, including an extensive treatment of apostolicity and succession, the Declaration follows. The Declaration contains mutual acknowledgements and mutual commitments.

It is only within the overall dynamic of *The Porvoo Common Statement* that the agreement on apostolicity and succession can be understood. The strength of the Porvoo treatment of apostolicity and succession is that, unlike so much Anglican, and ecumenical, discussion in the past, it treats apostolicity in an holistic way, refusing to wrest the apostolic ministry apart from the apostolic life of the whole people of God. It begins with a consideration of the apostolicity of the life of the whole Church, the Church whose vocation it is to play its part in the reconciliation of all things in Christ.

> Apostolicity means that the Church is sent by Jesus to be for the world, to participate in his mission and therefore in the mission of the One who sent Jesus, to participate in the mission of the Father and the Son through the dynamic of the Holy Spirit.[15]

Here Porvoo is making its own the words of an earlier Anglican-Lutheran international text, *The Niagara Report*.[16] Porvoo is receiving the insights of this earlier ecumenical dialogue into a text which is now not simply registering convergence in words, but which is intending to change a relationship. Here is a new genre of text, one which moves us from theological convergence in words, to convergence in changed relations in the lives of the churches.

Paragraph 37 of the Porvoo text emphasizes that the apostolicity of the Church is related to participation in the relational life of the Trinity and through this participation identification with the divine mission is established. Apostolicity in Porvoo is relational: the Church lives in relation to the divine persons in whose life it participates, it lives in relation to the Apostles, and it lives in an intricate network of social relations. The apostolic character of the Church is also dynamic. Founded on the Apostles whom Jesus taught and sent, it is sent in mission through time, looking beyond history to eternity, to the eschaton. It experiences in its midst here and now both the memory of the past and the foretaste of the future.[17]

This opening insistence of Porvoo on the apostolicity of the whole Church is fundamental to the logic of the document. It restores a proper balance to some recent ecumenical texts. Apostolic tradition in the Church, according to Porvoo, means continuity in the permanent characteristics of the Church of the Apostles that is:

> witness to the apostolic faith, proclamation and fresh interpretation of the Gospel, celebration of baptism and the eucharist, the transmission of ministerial responsibilities, communion in prayer, love, joy and suffering, service to the sick and needy, unity among the local churches and sharing the gifts which the Lord has given to each.[18]

The words this time are taken straight from *Baptism, Eucharist and Ministry*, for that text was considered to sum up well the characteristic elements of the Church's apostolicity.

The description is familiar to Anglicans. It is very close indeed to the Chicago-Lambeth Quadrilateral which describes both Anglican identity and unity and the identity and unity Anglicans seek to live with others. The Anglican formula holds together the interlocking elements of a total life of faith, sacraments and ministry as part of a single, apostolic system of communication.

To borrow another analogy from Stephen Sykes, the Porvoo argument on apostolicity and succession proceeds like a series of Chinese boxes. The apostolic community lives within the divine trinitarian life. Within, and not over and above the life of the apostolic community itself, the apostolic ministry builds up and assembles the Church. The different tasks of the one ministry find expression in its structuring in the threefold ministry of bishops, priests and deacons.

And so the text moves inwards in the series of Chinese boxes, to the ministry of oversight, *episkope*. The two sections on the ministry of oversight which follow need to be taken together: one section describes the ministry of bishops. It is followed immediately by a section on the personal, collegial and communal exercise of oversight. In this way the oversight ministry itself is not seen in isolation but as essentially relational: a bishop's ministry is exercised in relation to his diocese, in relation to other bishops in collegiality and in relation to the community in synodal gatherings – communal gatherings.

This emphasis on the personal, the collegial and the communal, the threefold dimension of *episkope*, is familiar to Anglican theology and Anglican experience, though like all Christian churches Anglicans struggle with how best to express the personal, collegial and communal forms of oversight. They hope, through ecumenical dialogue, to be helped to find a creative way of developing these structures of communion. Here it is worth drawing particular attention to two lines of the final paragraph of this Porvoo section:

The personal, collegial and communal dimensions of oversight find expression at the local, regional and universal levels of the Church's life.[19]

In a quick reading of the text this section is easily passed over. It needs to be noted that this passage contains a reference to a personal ministry of oversight at the universal level. For Anglicans this dimension of apostolic life is not unfamiliar. Provinces have their presiding bishop or archbishop. And the developing role of the Archbishop of Canterbury at the world level represents a personal focus of unity for the entire Anglican Communion. The passage implicity looks forward to that conversation on a ministry of universal primacy which is asked for by the Pope in *Ut Unum Sint*.[20] Ecumenical understanding of the place of universal primacy, serving apostolic continuity and apostolic succession, would be greatly advanced by a serious ecumenical and open exploration. The Pope is surely right to identify this as a crucial issue for the future ecumenical agenda.

The Chinese boxes have been opened. The argument has arrived at a critical point: the exploration of the episcopal office in the service of apostolic succession. The text has emphasized that the continuity of the ministry of oversight is to be understood within the continuity of the apostolic life and mission of the whole Church. Apostolic succession in the episcopal office is a visible and personal way of focusing the apostolicity of the whole Church.

The concept of 'sign' is fundamental to the Porvoo argument. 'The whole Church is a sign of the Kingdom of God; the act of ordination is a sign of God's faithfulness to his Church... To ordain a bishop in historic succession (that is, in intended continuity from the Apostles themselves) is also a sign.'[21] It is a visible and personal way of focussing and signifying the apostolicity that belongs to the whole Church. The historic episcopal succession is *not* for Porvoo an optional extra – but neither is it a guarantee of the fidelity of a church to every aspect of the apostolic faith, life and mission. We must be honest; such a claim simply cannot be made in the face of history itself. Continuity in the episcopate first signifies God's promise to the Church. At the same time it signifies the Church's intention to be faithful to its apostolic calling. It gives assurance to the faithful that the Church today intends both to do and to be what it has always intended to do and to be. The laying on of hands by bishops in succession is a sign – an *effective* sign – of that intention.

It is worth pausing for a moment on the term 'guarantee'. Porvoo is clear that the historic episcopal succession is *not* a 'guarantee' of the fidelity of the Church to every aspect of the apostolic faith, life and mission. The 1994 Report of the Church of England's House of Bishops, *Apostolicity and Succession*, considered whether there is a difference between those who with Porvoo claim historic episcopal succession is neither an optional extra nor a guarantee and those who would, in some sense, wish to retain the use of the word guarantee, as does the Roman

Catholic Church's response to *Baptism, Eucharist and Ministry*.[22] The English bishops concluded that in fact there is no fundamental difference. The Roman Catholic response, while using the word guarantee:

> does not claim that the indefectibility, infallibility and apostolicity of the Church are unquestionably assured merely by an historically demonstrable laying on of hands from the time of the apostles. It follows that the word 'guarantee' should be understood in the context of a system of symbols and symbolic language. Symbols and symbolic language give and communicate meaning in complex and subtle ways. The historic episcopal succession is an expression first of Christ's faithfulness to the Church, second of the Church's intention to remain faithful to the apostles' teaching and mission. It is a means both of upholding that intention and of giving the faithful the confident assurance that the Church lives in continuity with the Lord's apostles and in anticipation of a glory yet to be fully disclosed.[23]

For Porvoo then continuity belongs to the apostolic life of the whole Church. Historic episcopal succession is not a guarantee of fidelity but neither is it an optional extra in the dynamic apostolic life. But Porvoo sees continuity as also manifested in the ordered succession in the historic episcopal sees of the catholic Church. The stress on 'bottoms on seats' as well as hands on heads is well attested in the early Church. The Porvoo contention is that succession in the Church should, therefore, be seen as a rope of several strands of continuity. If one strand, such as that of the personal tactile succession is broken, another strand, such as the historic sees, can hold it, even though the rope of succession may be weakened. This is because 'being apostolic is a many-sided reality'.

It was precisely at this point that this Anglican-Lutheran agreement was influenced by the Orthodox-Roman Catholic dialogue. The *Munich Statement* of 1982 relates apostolic continuity to the life of the local churches:

> Apostolic continuity is transmitted through local churches. It is a matter of succession of persons in the community, because the Una Sancta is a communion of local churches and not of isolated individuals... apostolic succession... is a succession in a Church which witnesses to the apostolic faith, in communion with other churches, witnesses of the same apostolic faith. The 'see' (cathedra) plays an important role in inserting the bishop into the heart of ecclesial apostolicity.[24]

This is precisely the same rich view of apostolicity and succession which Porvoo expounds when it refuses to wrest historic episcopal succession from its location within the life of the whole Church.

It is this carefully set out agreement in faith in Porvoo, with the supporting strength of many bilateral ecumenical texts, that 'frees' Anglicans to acknowledge 'an authentic episcopal ministry in a church which has preserved continuity in the episcopal office by an occasional priestly/presbyteral ordination at the Reformation'.[25] At the same time a church which, like the Church of Denmark, has preserved continuity through such a succession is free to enter a relationship of mutual participation in episcopal ordinations with a church which has retained the historical episcopal succession, and to embrace this sign, without denying its past apostolic continuity. The use of the phrase 'free to embrace' is not used in the sense of free to decide whether to embrace the sign or not. It is a strong and emphatic use of the word 'free'. As the text itself says, these churches *should* embrace the sign. The agreement liberates them and they can do no other than embrace the sign.

So the new relationship of communion established by the Porvoo Declaration is based upon an agreed goal of visible unity, agreements in fundamental matters of faith and an explicit agreement on *episkope*, apostolicity and succession. The new relationship is further based upon the intention of the churches to remain faithful in the past to the apostolic teaching and mission and also to sign that intention to be faithful *together* into the future in a single, reconciled episcopal ministry in the historic succession. While Porvoo refuses to make a negative judgement on the existing ministries of any of the participating churches, it at the same time maintains historic episcopal succession as a requirement for the visible unity of the Church.

What the *Porvoo Common Statement* says about apostolic continuity and apostolic succession is consonant with what Anglicans have sought to uphold since the sixteenth century. More than that, it is what Anglicans believe is consonant with the faith of the Church through the ages. The Porvoo statement on apostolicity and succession is a fresh common statement of the faith of the Church springing from a shared re-reading of Scripture and tradition, while at the same time taking account of the teaching and lived experience of both traditions. It is also consistent with what Anglicans have said in other bilateral dialogues – with Roman Catholics, Orthodox and Reformed partners. And, for the Church of England, it is consistent with unity conversations in England. As the House of Bishops said in its guidance on Porvoo to the General Synod:

> What we agree with Lutherans across the water cannot be different from what we seek to agree with churches in England ... The House can only imagine entering into a relationship of visible unity with another church in England if that entailed a unity in faith, sacramental life, a single presbyteral ministry with a common episcopate in the historic succession and

common structures: in short a single Church for the sake of strengthening mission and service to all.[26]

Porvoo comes from a *regional* Anglican and Lutheran dialogue. It establishes a communion of churches in Northern Europe. It is based upon what the two traditions believe to be the faith of the Church through the ages. It was formed not only from Anglican-Lutheran documents but from texts from Orthodox, Roman Catholic and Reformed bilateral dialogues. There is no ecumenical council in which to test the conclusions of Porvoo. Nevertheless, it could be asked whether, or in what way, the theology of the *Porvoo Common Statement*, and the *dynamic* of the Porvoo way, might serve as a model for a wider communion in Northern Europe – and beyond – so that together we might become a more effective and credible instrument of God's saving and reconciling purpose for the whole of humanity and creation.

Notes

1. This paper was given at a Consultation on Apostolicity and Succession at the Centro Pro Unione, Rome in November 1995. The text was revised and made appropriate for this meeting.

2. R. Norris, 'Episcopacy' in S. Sykes and J. Booty (eds), *The Study of Anglicanism* (SPCK/Fortress Press, 1988), 296 ff.

3. *Ibid.*, p. 303.

4. *Minor Theological Works* (Oxford, 1943–55), ii, 73, 75. As quoted by Norris.

5. In reply to Peter Du Moulin's Second Letter, 1618, L. Andrewes, *Opuscula quaedam Posthumata* (Library of Anglo-Catholic Theology, Oxford, 1852), p. 191.

6. In reply to Peter Du Moulin's Third Letter, 1619, L. Andrewes, *Opuscula*, p. 211.

7. Letter to Mr Cavel at Blois, in Cosin's Works, iv, 400–7.

8. J. Taylor, *Of the Sacred Order and Offices of Episcopacy*, 1642 in *Works*, ed. R. Heber, VII, 138–143.

9. J. H. Newman, *Tracts for the Times*, No. 1, p. 3.

10. J. Hind, 'The Porvoo Common Statement: Process and Contents and the Hopes of the Anglican Churches' in W. Hüffmeier and C. Podmore (eds), *Leuenberg, Meissen and Porvoo* (Leuenberg, Texte, 4, 1996).

11. *Churches Respond to BEM*, vi, ed. M. Thurian (Faith and Order Paper 144, WCC, Geneva, 1987).

12. J. Tillard, 'The Chicago-Lambeth Quadrilateral in the Service of Communion', in J. Draper (ed.), *Communion and Episcopacy* (Cuddesdon, 1988).

13. C. Hill, 'Anglican Orders: An Ecumenical Context' in R.W. Franklin (ed.), *Anglican Orders. Essays on the Centenary of Apostolicae Curae 1896-1996* (London, 1996).

14. *The Porvoo Common Statement* (CCU Occasional Paper No. 3, 1993).

15. *Ibid.*, para. 37.

16. *The Niagara Report of the Anglican-Lutheran Consultation on Episcope* (ACC/LWF, London, 1988).

17. *Ibid.*, para. 37.

18. *Ibid.*, para. 36.

19. *Ibid.*, para. 45.

20. *Ut Unum Sint*, Papal Encyclical, DO636, 25 May 1995.

21. *Porvoo*, para. 50.

22. *Churches Respond to BEM*, vi, 33.

23. *Apostolicity and Succession*, House of Bishops Occasional Paper (GS Misc. 432, 1994), para. 57.

24. *The Munich Statement*, the Report of the Anglican-Orthodox Dialogue (1982), paras 45 and 46.

25. *Porvoo*, para. 52.

26. *The Porvoo Agreement. A Report by the House of Bishops* (GS 1156, 1995).

Anglican Ordination Rites: A Review

Colin Buchanan

Anglicanism as a distinct doctrinal and institutional entity traces itself back to the Reformation. The Reformation in England functioned in two stages: first, a shaking off of the authority of the Bishop of Rome in Henry VIII's reign; and secondly, once that national independence and autonomy had been gained, the doctrinal reformation which was set in train during the reign of Edward VI (1547–53) and then, after the reign of the papist Queen Mary (1553–8), was consolidated in the reign of Queen Elizabeth (1558–1603). In terms of ordination there are two major, apparently opposed, factors to note.

Firstly, the Reformation was led 'from the top down'. This made it almost inevitable that the orders of bishop, presbyter and deacon would be retained; for the progress of the Reformation in both Henry's and Edward's reigns depended in large part upon the clergy *using the offices they already held* to promote the newly reformed liturgy and doctrine. Had the archbishops and bishops of the Church of England at any point called in question the sufficiency or propriety of their own ordination, they would, in the English idiom, have cut off the branch they were sitting on. Thus, even when individuals were reluctant to fall into line, ordinations were conducted regularly and 'according to law' (the law of England from 1534 onwards was the law of the Church, and *vice versa*). This type of Reformation was bound to function with emphasis upon 'continuity'.[1] The monarch now took full responsibility for choosing new bishops, and for commanding deans and chapters of the cathedrals of vacant dioceses to 'elect' them[2] and Archbishops and/or other bishops to consecrate them – and in the Church of England itself (though, of course, not in the rest of the Anglican Communion) diocesan bishops are still to this day appointed under the terms of Henry VIII's Act of Parliament of 1534.[3] So the orders (and offices and appointments) in the Church of England continued, from the legal aspect and in terms of their places in the Church's structures, unchanged *faut de mieux*. By the time of Elizabeth's reign there was also the force of martyrdom – five bishops had been burned for their reformed faith, and they were being celebrated in Foxe's *Book of Martyrs*, the next book after the Bible to be read in English homes till *Pilgrim's Progress* came out. In the next century or so the matter of episcopacy became so entangled with monarchy that it was crucial for all royalists to leap to the defence – indeed sometimes the assertion of the necessity – of episcopacy for the safety of the throne. This is interesting (and doctrinally it was bound up with the divine right of kings), but it has, of course, to be recognized as rather different from some of the doctrines that have been wished upon the sixteenth century retrogressively since. And if you consult the text of Article XXIII, you will find that, at the point where the Lambeth Quadrilateral of 1888, or even the presuppositions of the Meissen talks, would have made some statement about the historic episcopate, there is instead the most general statement about ministering in the congregation in a form which would probably unite us on the spot.[4] Other Articles do refer to bishops, priests and deacons,[5] but none refer to the need of them!

The way these orders were 'continued' was by means of successive revision of the ordination rites, which yet retained 'Bishops, Priests and Deacons', and ordained the candidates by the laying on of episcopal hands. The revised Ordinal (drawn indirectly from the pre-Reformation Pontifical, but more immediately from Bucer) was not ready in time to be part of the 1549 Prayer Book, but was instead a separate book of the three rites for ordaining deacons, priests and bishops (in that order) published by authority in 1550. Because the Ordinal arose separately from the rest of the Book of Common Prayer, it has traditionally not been a legal part of it (though normally bound between the same set of covers), so that the title page of the '1662 Book of Common Prayer' (the Book that is still part of the foundational documents of the Church of England) actually reads

The Book of Common Prayer
and Administration of the Sacraments and other Rites and Ceremonies of
The Church
according to the use of
The Church of England
together with
The Psalter or Psalms of David
and the Form or Manner of
Making Ordaining and Consecrating of
Bishops Priests and Deacons

The Ordinal has actually, in both its 1550 origins and in its later binding into the covers of the Book of Common Prayer as above, a slightly separable history from the rest of the Prayer Book. Indeed it was apparently overlooked in law at the beginning of Elizabeth's reign, which is why Article XXXVI retrospectively affirms its propriety for ordinations, whether or not that is sufficient for legality![6] The Ordinal is cited as a separate Book in the Canons and in the Declaration of Assent, and has become therefore a separate leg on which the Church of England – and in turn the rest of Anglicanism – rests.[7] And it will be recognized that, just as with the universal use of Latin for worship in the Church of Rome for upwards of

1000 years, many features of church life ordered by authority in the sixteenth and seventeenth centuries may still be questioned and changed; and it is frankly unclear from the mere fact of something being ordered by Act of Parliament in those centuries for universal observance whether such requirements have the same doctrinal force as credal statements about the Trinity, or whether they are merely disciplinary, contingent and open to change.[8] To that extent I would have to count myself an adiaphorist, and the highest contention I can make for the episcopal system of the Church of England is that it is of the *bene esse* (perhaps even the *optime esse*) of the Church, and certainly not of the *esse* and therefore not *de fide*. This position, which is closest of all to the reticence of the Articles on episcopacy, is always agreed to be an allowable position to be held in the Church of England as a theory, but the Church of England corporately has for a century or more been nervous of anyone acting on the theory. There is very considerable frustration in being so boxed in practice by the opposite theory, a theory which goes beyond the doctrinal position of the Reformers and their formularies.

The 1550 Ordinal, the first revision of the Sarum uses, provided the 'continuity' terminology. The actual word occurs in the Preface to the Ordinal:

> ... to the intent that these orders should be continued, and reverently used, and esteemed, in this Church of England, it is requisite, that no man... shall execute any of them, except he be called... and admitted, according to the form hereafter following.[9]

Vast edifices have been built upon the words *'that these orders should be continued'*. Yet the words may be hardly doctrinal at all, but may be (a) asserting the propriety of the orders already held by ministers, and (b) exerting a discipline – both thrusts being designed to exclude sectarian upstarts rather than express a particular – let alone a conservative – doctrine about ordination. You will perhaps know that Cranmer is ready to argue that, if in any Christian country a succession of bishops ceased through failure to appoint or through an attack of the plague, the monarch has power in himself to appoint new bishops, without the participation of existing ones – and it is even arguable to the present day that the confirmation ceremony makes a man legally bishop of his diocese (at the monarch's command) even when other episcopal hands have not yet been laid on him!

For, secondly, even whilst the orders were being 'continued', they were being so completely re-modelled as to look like an almost new start. If there is a 'continuity' in titles and appointments and in episcopal ordination, yet there is a great 'discontinuity' in the contents of the rites: and it is the discontinuities in the ordinal that I come now to examine. For this purpose I am looking at the ordination of priests, as that is the point of arrival of most ministers, and the parish priest is the normal minister most laypeople encounter.[10]

I shall now set out the changes in the ordination of presbyters from Sarum to 1552 – i.e. through the two stages of change, first from Sarum to 1550, and then from 1550 to 1552.

First, there is a totally new question of a totally reformed sort:

> Be you persuaded that the holy Scriptures contain sufficiently all doctrine, required of necessity for eternal salvation through faith in Jesus Christ...?[11]

The pre-Reformation use did not include questions to candidates for the presbyterate. So this stems from Bucer rather than from any pre-Reformation question.[12]

Secondly, the central task of the order was changed – it ceased to be 'to offer sacrifice for the living and the dead'; and it became 'to preach the word of God and to minister the holy sacraments'.[13]

Thirdly, the subsidiary laying on of hands of the Sarum rite became the central act (the 'matter') of ordination, still retaining the words from John 20. 23 – not, however, to justify, let alone to make central, the Roman practice of 'Penance', but because Cranmer saw no reason to dispense with scriptural words, and must have long since concluded (and surely rightly?) that Jesus' commissioning of his disciples in John 20 was not, and could hardly be stretched to be interpreted as, a command to go and spread a network of confessional boxes across the world. It is indeed typical of Cranmer, as you can see in many places in the eucharist, to preserve pre-Reformation biblical material and give it a better context. And it is fairly clear that he must have conceived of the John 20 passage as a highly personalized way of chartering the original disciples to proclaim a gospel of repentance (cf. Luke 24. 47, a passage which reports the same evening) throughout the world. It is often commented among scholars that Cranmer thereby lost the great ordination prayer which was the 'form' of ordination – and although there is *a* prayer preceding the laying on of hands, it is hardly comparable (and the rite for deacons includes no such prayer at all).

Fourthly, in two stages Cranmer completely changed the *porrectio instrumentorum*.[14] In the Sarum rite, the new priest received paten and chalice (with their respective elements) with the instruction to offer sacrifice for the living and the dead. In 1550 the bishop handed over the actual sacramental symbols of a cup and bread, but added a Bible as well; and in 1552 the sacramental symbols disappeared, leaving the Bible alone as the outstanding tangible indicator of the character of the reformed ministry. Gone were not only the 'instruments' of the mass, but also the vesting of candidates, the anointing of their hands, and any possibility of 'concelebration'.[15]

Nor was this all. The Preface to the Ordinal prescribed episcopal ordination for the Church of England, but it did not proscribe those, in reformation churches elsewhere, who were being ordained by other means (usually Presbyterian); and for a hundred years after the Reformation the Church of England was ready to receive them into the threefold order as presbyters as if they had been episcopally ordained.[16] Nor was it different when James I and Archbishop Bancroft insisted that the Church of Scotland become episcopal – for, although the first bishops had to be existing presbyters who came to London to be consecrated bishop in 1610, they were not at that point first episcopally ordained deacon and presbyter before being made bishop; and when they returned to Scotland they did not attempt to ordain again the existing presbyters, but recognized and accepted them as true presbyters in the Church of God.

This latter loophole ceased at the Restoration. Charles II was called (or re-called) to the throne in May 1660. The restoration of the Prayer Book took two years and it was finally imposed by Act of Uniformity from 24 August 1662. Until that point there were, as a run-on from the Commonwealth, perhaps thousands of ministers functioning as parochial clergy without benefit of episcopal ordination. The returning Royalists were Episcopalian to their last bit of ermine – not so much because episcopacy guaranteed the form of the Church, or provided an exclusive channel of grace, but because the monarchical throne of England, as they saw it, was settled upon a sub-structure of monepiscopacy. Charles I could have saved his life and his throne if he had been prepared to ditch episcopacy, but he judged the loophole not worth the price. Thus the heaviest possible re-imposition of episcopacy was basic to the Restoration Settlement, and by the terms of the 1662 Act of Uniformity the non-episcopal ministers, ordained by whatever method during the Commonwealth, were forced to leave their parishes or to submit to episcopal ordination as though they had not been ordained at all.[17] The Preface to the Ordinal was strengthened in an exclusive direction:

> ... No man shall be accounted or taken to be a lawful Bishop, Priest or Deacon in the Church of England... except he be called, tried examined and admitted thereunto, according to the Form hereafter following, *or hath had formerly Episcopal Consecration or Ordination.*[18]

I have added the emphasis to the last eight words, to indicate that they were added in 1662. The door open to Presbyterianly ordained ministers was now shut, and the episcopal framework was complete and without exceptions. The Puritan ministers who would not accept (re)ordination were chased out of their parishes, and the Church of England looked as though it were now a closed episcopal system. And so it was – but closed for what to-day we might well think were politico-religious reasons rather than purely theological ones. Curiously, in the actual changes

124

in the Ordinal made in 1662, the slightly vague opening rubric to the ordination of deacons and priests in 1552 was clarified as follows:

(i)   *... there shall be a Sermon or Exhortation, declaring the duty and office of such as come to be admitted Deacons; how necessary that Order is in the Church of Christ ...*

(ii) *... there shall be a Sermon or Exhortation, declaring the duty and office of such as come to be admitted Priests; how necessary that Order is in the Church of Christ ...*

In the consecration of bishops, whilst a sermon has been added (which was lacking in 1552), it comes in the normal place in the communion service, and without any hints as to its subject matter. Perhaps that 'Order' was not *quite* so necessary in the Church of Christ! And I put 'Order' in quotation marks because it is not even absolutely clear that the liturgical books of the Reformation period treat the episcopate as an 'order' (and therefore do not 'ordain' people to it, but instead 'consecrate' them); but it can be argued that (as with Aquinas and the mediaevals) the Church of England at the time thought of the episcopate as an 'office' somehow within the presbyterate.[19]

What I hope is clear is that the Church of England, by design or perchance, left itself still some room to negotiate as to the theological necessity of the office of a bishop, even whilst its formularies required unvarying use of episcopal ordination.

There are three subsequent trends I want to examine. They are: (a) the rise of catholicism in the Church of England; (b) controversies related to *Apostolicae Curae*; and (c) modern revisions of the Ordinal.

The first of these is well known. Keble insisted on apostolic succession in his Assize Sermon in July 1833. Newman wrote in September 1833 in Tract no. 1 '[when all else fails] There are some who rest their divine mission... upon their temporal distinctions. This last case has, perhaps, been too much our own; I fear we have neglected the real ground on which our authority is built – OUR APOSTOLICAL DESCENT'. And John Mason Neale wrote a hymn which is still to be found in *Hymns Ancient and Modern Revised*:

> His twelve apostles first he made
>   his ministers of grace:
> And they their hands on others laid
>   to fill in turn their place.
>
> So age by age and year by year
>   this grace was handed on;
> and still the holy Church is here,
>   although her Lord has gone.

It would be my contention that the theological doctrine of apostolic succession, drawing upon the rubrical uniformity of the sixteenth and seventeenth centuries, then began to engulf Anglicanism in a way previously unknown (though perhaps adumbrated in the narrow sectarianism of the Nonjurors). It produced its own concepts of ministerial authority (with its concomitant clericalism), its own insistence on episcopal confirmation for true Christian initiation (with its concomitant Anglican exclusiveness) and its own magnification of the bishop's office in all accounts of ecclesiology (and thus of terms for inter-communion and re-union). We need to note these effects – relatively new to the nineteenth century – but need not now stay on them. I submit that such insistence is neither integral to the gospel nor grounded in the Reformation settlement, but is a partisan and over-narrow view which has deeply affected and damaged our relationships with reformed churches.

Secondly, I wish to refer to the Roman Catholic condemnation of Anglican orders. This was a condemnation of the liturgical texts. It included a statement that the orders conferred were not clearly identified in 1552, but that is (a) special pleading, and (b) likely to pull out the rug from early rites also. The major objection was 'defect of intention'; and the defect was that the Edwardine Ordinal was not intended to make priests whose role was to offer the sacrifice of the mass. This argument was threefold:

(a) Orders are conferred in order to provide priests to offer the sacrifice of the mass;

(b) Cranmer's eucharistic rites had abolished all hints of the sacrifice of the mass;

(c) Cranmer's Ordinal therefore could not be said to ordain priests for that task (and the more so as it gave no hint in its own text that it did so ordain them).

Whilst *Apostolicae Curae* undoubtedly arose from English Roman Catholics manoeuvring to get the Pope to put Anglo-Catholicism out of court, it needed refuting rather than merely dismissing. A robust Anglican answer (such as Jewel would have given in Elizabeth's reign) would have been that we had never claimed that the validity of our orders rested upon any acceptance of (a) and thus it was unnecessary and even misleading to argue about (b) and (c) – points which, once (a) had been challenged, a good Anglican might well concede! It might however be argued back that what was needed was not robustness, but sensitivity – and that if any *rapprochement* were ever to happen (which was not what the Pope or the Cardinal Archbishop of Westminster in 1896 actually wanted), then the Roman Catholics would have to be convinced, on *their* terms, that Anglicans had retained a valid succession. This was how the Archbishops of Canterbury and

York went about replying – their 1897 document, whilst profoundly and satisfyingly scathing of the Pope and his scholarship on most points of both history and logic, veered a bit near him on this point of the eucharist. It virtually allowed (a), denied (b) and thus dismissed (c).[20] But I think myself that both the polemical needs of the 1890s and the Reformation formularies and a constructive laying of foundations for the future actually called for what I have called the 'robust' reply on this point which would have challenged the basis of the papal condemnation, and I do not think we ought to concede the starting point of the two Archbishops.

Thirdly, I come to revision of the ordination rites, which has happened round the world since the early 1970s. In my collection of the rites[21] I have traced their origins to the CSI rites of 1950, the Lambeth Conference document of 1958, and the Anglican-Methodist Ordinals of 1967 and 1968. Almost all of these have seen a shift from an indicative or imperative formula at the laying on of hands to a prayer or thanksgiving (indeed a 'eucharistic' prayer) within which or following which comes the laying on of hands.[22] It is a move sufficiently sharp as to raise the question as to whether we had a sufficient rite before! – and I recall Arthur Couratin telling me in the early days of my time on the Liturgical Commission 'I never assist at an ordination in Durham Cathedral without saying to myself "Invalid orders – defect of form" '. But *that* would be to open a retrospective can of worms ...

There is one other issue bearing upon Ordinals to which I think we need turn some brief attention. The Anglican world has at intervals thrown up a concept of 'unifying' or 'reconciling' episcopal and non-episcopal orders by an ordination-like mutual ritual. This arose because the Anglo-Catholic hegemony at the time of the formation of the Church of South India in 1947 opposed that form of integrating so forcefully, and compelled others into the 'unifical' pattern of rites. I observe that Paul Bradshaw in his book, *The Anglican Ordinal* (1972), gives a chapter to such ritual concepts, and thus groups them under the 'ordination' title of his whole book. I would only say at this point that, if such rites can be understood as subliminal ordination, then they are morally out of court (and I have written at some length about this elsewhere and can easily discuss it if required) – whereas if they cannot be understood as in any way open to being treated as a kind of ordination, then they are out of court for the purposes of the present paper.[23]

For the rest, I must cite myself from the Introduction to my collection of Anglican ordination rites, 'What ordination *is* and *does* remains elusive'.

Notes

1. The word 'continue' with its cognates has been a key word in this sort of discussion. It is found in the Preface to the Ordinal, to which fuller reference is made below.

2. The word 'elect' is put in quotation marks, because the dean and chapter had no choice whatsoever, and were required (under threat of appalling penalties) to 'elect' the royal nominee.

3. See my book on disestablishment, *Cut the Connection* (DLT, 1994), pp. 81–5.

4. The text of Article XXIII runs as follows:

   It is not lawful for any man to take upon himself the office of publick preaching, or ministering the Sacraments in the Congregation, before he be lawfully called and sent to execute the same. And those we ought to judge lawfully called and sent, which be chosen and called to this work by men who have publick authority given unto them in the Congregation to call and send Ministers into the Lord's vineyard.

5. Notably Article XXXVI quoted below.

6. The text of Article XXXVI runs as follows

   The Book of Consecration of Archbishops and Bishops, and Ordering of Priests and Deacons, lately set forth in the time of *Edward* the Sixth, and confirmed at the same time by authority of Parliament, doth contain all things necessary to such Consecration and Ordering: neither hath it any thing, that of itself is superstitious and ungodly. And therefore whosoever are consecrated or ordered according to the Rites of that Book, since the second year of the forenamed King *Edward* unto this time, or hereafter shall be consecrated or ordered according to the same Rites; we decree all such to be rightly, orderly, and lawfully consecrated and ordered.

   This has a slightly odd ring for those who assent to the Articles today!

7. Though the Church of England (Worship and Doctrine) Measure 1975 defines the Book of Common Prayer as containing the Ordinal, and thus makes modern ordination rites 'alternative services' within the meaning of the Measure.

8. A comparable ambiguous requirement in this category might be the wearing of the surplice, or the use of the sign of the cross in baptism – ceremonies which were not urged as of divine commandment, but were nevertheless imposed by strict church discipline.

9. The full text of the 1550/1552 Preface is appended to this essay with the 1662 text in parallel with it.

10. The word 'priest' is, of course, an unfortunate hang-over from the pre-Reformation days, and, although its etymology in English is undoubtedly that it is 'presbyter writ small', its general use as the standard English translation of the words from the *hiereus* stem in the Greek New Testament makes it inappropriate as the translation of *presbyteros*. Nowadays there is a slow but steady recovery of the English word 'presbyter' and that helps stop the doctrine of ordination

falling into unnecessary confusion. We are wise to use the word 'presbyter' ourselves. It is the word Newman used of himself at the beginning of Tract no. 1 'I am but one of yourselves – a presbyter', and it is officially into our formularies now in the modern ordination rites – the title of the relevant service being 'The Ordination of Priests (also called Presbyters)'.

11. Cf. Article VI of the Thirty-nine: 'Holy Scripture containeth all things necessary for salvation: so that whatever is not read therein, nor may be proved thereby, is not required of any man, that it should be believed as an article of the Faith, or be thought requisite or necessary to salvation...'

12. The full eight questions are appended to this essay.

13. Cf. the 'notes' of the visible Church in Article XIX of the Thirty-nine (Anglicans were criticized at the time for omitting reference to 'discipline'!). The sacraments, of course, had been reduced to two only.

14. The texts of the *'Porrectio'* at the various stages are appended to this essay.

15. For the consecration of bishops, in 1550 there was still the laying on of a Bible on the neck, and the delivery of a pastoral staff; and in 1552 this became the delivery of a Bible (as with the ordination of a presbyter).

16. Norman Sykes' book *Old Priest New Presbyter* works carefully over the evidence for this.

17. There was a very strong bias against them among the Royalists, and therefore the exclusive requirements of the Act of Uniformity are not above suspicion of a deliberate and vengeful attempt to twist the Puritans' tails.

18. The 1662 text is in parallel with the 1550/1552 one in the appendix to this essay.

19. Thus the Preface to the Ordinal only mentions 'these orders', and, whilst delineating 'Bishops, priests and deacons', does not use the enumerative 'three' anywhere; nor does the Preface say bishops are 'ordained' until 1662 (when the word must have been deliberately added – see the texts). But a more frequent view is that the Church of England was *correcting* the mediaeval pattern by making the major (indeed the only) orders bishop, presbyter and deacon, thus adjusting the pre-Reformation error of presbyter, deacon and sub-deacon.

20. The crucial sentence ran: 'Primo enim sacrificium laudis et gratiarum offerimus; tum vero *sacrificium Crucis Patri proponimus and praesentamus*, et per illud remissionem peccatorum... impetramus' (*Answer*, para. XI – emphasis mine). The question is 'What does "*Patri proponimus et praesentamus*" mean?'

21. Colin Buchanan (ed.), *Modern Anglican Ordination Rites* (Alcuin/GROW Joint Liturgical Study no. 3, 1987).

22. This had been worked into the CSI rite through the participation of Edward Ratcliff, and it was then propounded strongly as a matter of principle in the 1958 Lambeth report (through the person of Leslie Brown, who had been on the CSI Liturgy Committee in 1949–50), and Ratcliff in turn affected the Anglican-Methodist Ordinal of 1968.

23. I wrote in length about the inadequacies and improprieties of such rites in the 1960s, reaching a (successful) climax in *Growing into Union* in 1970. The appendix on such rites has never yet been answered, and the mood has swung away from them (mercifully) – cf. the 'Limuru' principle of ACC-1 and the 'Covenant' proposals in England in 1978–82.

The Preface to the Ordinal
(1550/1552)

It is euident unto all men, diligently readinge holye scripture, and auncient aucthours, that fro the Apostles tyme, there hathe bene these orders of Ministers in Christes church, Bisshoppes, Priestes, and Deacons, which Offices were euermore had in suche reuerent estimacion, that no ma by his own priuate aucthoritie, might presume to execute any of them, except he were first called, tried, examined, and knowen, to haue suche qualities, as were requisite for the same. And also by publique prayer, with imposicion of handes, approued, and admitted thereunto. And therfore to the entent these orders shoulde bee continued, and reuerentlye used, and estemed in this Church of England, it is requysite, that no man (not beynge at thys presente Bisshop, Priest, nor Deacon) shall execute anye of them, excepte he be called, tryed, examined, and admitted, accordynge to the forme hereafter folowinge.

And none shalbe admitted a Deacon, except he be xxi yeres of age at the least. And euery man, which is to be admitted a Priest, shalbe full xxiiii yeres olde. And euery man, which is to be consecrated a Bishop, shalbe fully thyrtie yeres of age.

And the Bisshop knowinge, eyther by hymself, or by sufficient testimonye, any person to be a man of vertuous conuersacion, and wythoute cryme, and after examinacion and triall, fyndynge hym learned in the Latyne tongue, and sufficiently instructed in holye Scripture, maye upon a Sondaye or Holyday, in the face of the church, admitte hym a Deacon in suche maner and fourme, as hereafter foloweth.

The Preface to the Ordinal
(1662)

It is evident unto all men diligently reading holy Scriptures and ancient Authors, that from the Apostles' time there have been these Orders of Ministers in Christ's Church: Bishops, Priests and Deacons. Which offices were evermore had in such reverend estimation, that no man might presume to execute any of them, except he were first called, tried, examined, and known to have such qualities as are requisite for the same; and also by publick Prayer, with Imposition of Hands, were approved and admitted thereunto by lawful authority. And therefore, to the intent that these Orders may be continued, and reverently used and esteemed, in the Church of England: No man shall be accounted or taken to be a lawful Bishop, Priest, or Deacon in the Church of England, or suffered to execute any of the said functions, except he be called, tried, examined, and admitted thereunto, according to the Form hereafter following, or hath had formerly Episcopal Consecration or Ordination.

And none shall be admitted a Deacon, except he be twenty-three years of age, unless he have a Faculty. And every man which is to be admitted a Priest shall be full four-and-twenty years old. And every man which is to be ordained or consecrated Bishop shall be fully thirty years of age.

And the Bishop, knowing either by himself, or by sufficient testimony, any person to be a man of virtuous conversation, and without crime; and after examination and trial finding him learned in the Latin tongue, and sufficiently instructed in holy Scripture, may at the times appointed in the Canon, or else, on urgent occasion, upon some other Sunday or Holy-day, in the face of the Church, admit him a Deacon, in such manner and form as hereafter followeth.

Interrogation of Priests (1550–1552–1662)

Do you think in your heart that you be truly called, according to the will of our Lord Jesus Christ, and the order of this Church of *England*, to the Order and Ministry of Priesthood?

Answer. I think it.

The Bishop.

Are you persuaded that the holy Scriptures contain sufficiently all doctrine required of necessity for eternal salvation through faith in Jesus Christ? And are you determined out of the said Scriptures to instruct the people committed to your charge, and to teach nothing (as required of necessity to eternal salvation) but that which you shall be persuaded may be concluded and proved by the Scripture?

Answer. I am so persuaded, and have so determined by God's grace.

The Bishop.

Will you then give your faithful diligence always so to minister the doctrine and sacraments, and the discipline of Christ, as the Lord hath commanded, and as this Church and Realm hath received the same, according to the commandments of God; so that you may teach the people committed to your cure and charge with all diligence to keep and observe the same?

Answer. I will so do, by the help of the Lord.

The Bishop.

Will you be ready, with all faithful diligence, to banish and drive away all erroneous and strange doctrines contrary to God's Word; and to use both publick and private monitions and exhortations, as well to the sick as to the whole, within your cures, as need shall require, and occasion shall be given?

Answer. I will, the Lord being my helper.

The Bishop.

Will you be diligent in prayers, and in reading of the holy Scriptures, and in such studies as help to the knowledge of the same, laying aside the study of the world and the flesh?

Answer. I will endeavour myself so to do, the Lord being my helper.

The Bishop.

Will you be diligent to frame and fashion your own selves, and your families, according to the doctrine of Christ; and to make both yourselves and them, as much as in you lieth, wholesome examples and patterns to the flock of Christ?

Answer. I will apply myself thereto, the Lord being my helper.

The Bishop.

Will you maintain and set forwards, as much as lieth in you, quietness, peace, and love, among all Christian people, and specially among them that are or shall be committed to your charge?

Answer. I will so do, the Lord being my helper.

The Bishop.

Will you reverently obey your Ordinary, and other chief Ministers, unto whom is committed the charge and government over you; following with a glad mind and will their godly admonitions, and submitting yourselves to their godly judgements?

Answer. I will so do, the Lord being my helper.

Laying On of Hands and *Porrectio* (1550)	Laying On of Hands and *Porrectio* (1552)	Laying On of Hands and *Porrectio* (1562)
¶ *When this praier is done, the Bisshope with the priestes present, shal lay theyr handes seuerally upon the head of every one that receiueth orders. The receiuers humbly knelying upon their knees, and the Bisshop saying.*	¶ *When this praier is done, the Bishoppe with the Priestes present shal lay theyr handes seuerally upon the head of euery one that receiueth orders: the receiuers humbly knelyng upon their knees, and the Bishop saying:*	¶*When this prayer is done, the Bishop with the Priests present shall lay their hands severally upon the head of every one that receiveth the Order of Priesthood; the receivers humbly kneeling upon their knees, and the Bishop saying,*
RECEIUE the holy goste, whose synnes thou doest forgeue, they are forgeuen: and whose sinnes thou doest retaine, thei are retained: and be thou a faithful despensor of the word of god, and of his holy Sacramentes. In the name of the father, and of the sonne, and of the holy gost. Amen.	RECEIUE the holy gost: whose sinnes thou doest forgeue, they are forgeuen: and whose synnes thou doest retayne, they are retayned: and bee thou a faithful dispensor of the worde of god, and of his holy Sacramentes. In the name of the father, and of the sonne, and of the holy gost. Amen.	RECEIVE the Holy Ghost for the office and work of a Priest in the Church of God, now committed unto thee by the imposition of our hands. Whose sins thou dost forgive, they are forgiven; and whose sins thou dost retain, they are retained. And be thou a faithful dispenser of the Word of God, and of his holy Sacraments; In the Name of the Father, and of the Son, and of the Holy Ghost. Amen.
¶ *The Bisshop shall deliuer to euery one of them, the Bible in the one hande, and the Chalice or cupp ewith the breade, in the other hande, and saying.*	¶ *The Bishop shal deliuer to euery one of them the Bible in his hande, saying.*	¶ *Then the Bishop shall deliver to every one of them kneeling the Bible into his hand, saying,*
TAKE thou aucthoritie to preache the word of god, and to minister the holy Sacramentes in thys congregacion, where thou shalt be so appointed.	TAKE thou aucthoritie to preache the worde of God, and to minister the holy Sacramentes in this congregacion where thou shalte be so appointed.	TAKE thou authority to preach the Word of God, and to minister the holy Sacraments in the Congregation, where thou shalt be lawfully appointed thereunto.

The Office of Bishop in the Liturgical Formularies of the Churches of the EKD

Ulrich Kühn

This paper will set out the understanding of the office of Bishop which can be seen in the liturgies for installation of bishops in the churches of the EKD. These are:

–   The order for the induction of a bishop (*Landessuperintendent, Kreisdekan, Prälat*) from Volume IV of the *Agende für evangelisch-lutherische Kirchen und Gemeinden* (Hannover, 1987) – valid for the churches of the United Evangelical-Lutheran Church of Germany (VELKD);

–   The order for induction into service above the parish level, from *Einführung. Gottesdienstordnungen für Einführung, Bevollmächtigung und Vorstellung*, published by the Arnoldshainer Konferenz (Gütersloh, 1974) – valid for the churches of the Arnoldshainer Konferenz;

–   The order for the induction of a bishop, a *Präses* or a church president, from *Agende für die Evangelische Kirche der Union*, Vol. II: *Die kirchlichen Handlungen* (Witten, 1964) – valid for the churches of the Evangelical Church of the Union.

Attention will also be given to mentions of the bishop in rites of ordination and blessings.

I

The following observations can be made about the VELKD rite (the newest among the rites currently authorized in the EKD).

1.   The induction of a bishop appears amongst the so-called 'Induction Rites', which are specifically differentiated from the ordination rites (to the pastoral ministry) and the rites of blessing (into the office of deacon, etc.). It is therefore not a case of the conferring of spiritual tasks and functions, but of the allocation of tasks and functions already conferred in ordination to a specific area of function and task. The induction of a bishop therefore corresponds, for example, with the 'induction of the pastor of a parish', which is intended to now concretely allocate the ministry fundamentally conferred on him in ordination to a specific parish.

2. The rite for the 'induction of a bishop' is also used for the induction of a *Landessuperindentent*, a *Kreisdekan* and a *Prälat*. In addition there is, for example, a rite for the induction of a pastor 'in the ministry of ecclesiastical oversight' (*Superintendent, Dekan, Propst*). This points to the variety of ministries of *episkope* above the parish level and at regional level in the Lutheran churches.

3. Nonetheless, the induction of a bishop is distinguished by the fact that the rite only envisages bishops (among them the Presiding Bishop of the VELKD) as performing the induction, whereas for the other leading ministries two non-episcopal leading clergy are envisaged, alongside the responsible *Landesbischof*. One can, therefore, speak of something like an episcopal succession.

4. As regards the textual content of the rite for induction of a bishop, the readings envisaged here are identical with those envisaged for the induction of a pastor in a parish, the induction of a pastor in a special ministry and the induction of a pastor in a ministry of ecclesiastical oversight. In each case, the passsages are the following: Luke 10. 16; Matthew 18. 18; Acts 20. 28; 2 Timothy 2. 1–3, 5. Clearly this is intended to underline the fact that in all these cases the spiritual task is the same.

5. This is also apparent in the so-called induction question and the induction prayer. The induction question expressly refers back to the ordination promise which is the basis and content of the concrete function into which the person concerned is now being inducted. The formulation of the induction prayer corresponds with this when it names as the spiritual duties 'that he/she preaches your word rightly and serves your congregation with the sacraments according to your will'. The wording is identical with the questions in the other rites for the induction of ordained ministers into the other ministries mentioned above. These prayers do not give any indication that this is a specific, special form of ordained ministry.

6. The only two places (apart from the title of the office as such and the specification of those who are to conduct the induction) which give any indication of the special nature of the ministry into which the person is being inducted are the following: (1) the question about acceptance of the person to be inducted is addressed 'to the members of the (general) synod and the clergy of this territorial church/this episcopal area' (p. 80); (2) the induction of a bishop (*Landessuperintendent, Kreisdekan, Prälat*) is distinguished from the other induction rites by the handing over of a pectoral cross.

7.   Further indication of the specific episcopal functions is given in the rites by the specifications about those who are to ordain (ordination rite, rite of blessing) or to induct (here, admittedly, the bishop is only mentioned in the case of the induction of a *Superintendent* and then, of course – as already shown – in the induction of another bishop). So it is said that an ordination is conducted by the 'bishop or one commissioned to do so and two pastors' (Ordinal, p. 17), a blessing by 'the bishop or an ordained pastor commissioned to do so by the bishop' (p. 25). The induction of a *Superintendent* is 'performed by the bishop or his commissary'. These specifications make clear that it is the bishop who is actually responsible for ordination and blessing into office, which is not apparent from the rite for the induction of a bishop itself.

II

If we compare the rite for the induction of a bishop contained in the liturgy of the VELKD with the respective rites of the EKU and the Arnoldshainer Konferenz, the following is noticeable.

1.   As in the case of the VELKD, in the EKU and the Arnoldshainer Konferenz the induction of a bishop, as the induction of someone already ordained, is clearly differentiated from the rite of ordination or that of blessing into office.

2.   The EKU has, moreover, a special rite for the induction of a bishop, *Präses* or church president. In the biblical texts, the questions and the prayers of this rite, the specific nature of the ministry of church leadership is more apparent than it is in the VELKD rite. So, for example, the task of driving away false doctrine as one of the tasks of the ministry of church leadership is expressed in the readings, through a more extensive quotation of Acts 20 and also by the reading from 2 Corinthians 4. The induction question refers not only to the earlier ordination of the person concerned, but also expressly to the regulations of the church, according to which he is to conduct his ministry. These are, of course, above all the legal regulations in which his ministry is described concretely. Finally, the commissioning sentence in the EKU rite is linked with a sort of 'admonition' (as is also customary in the ordination rites of the EKU). In this admonition the person conducting the induction says: 'I commit the parishes and all who serve in the ministry of the Church to you and you to them and admonish you to preside over the church entrusted to you in the fear of God with diligence and faithfulness... '. In these places again the specific ministry of the

office of church leadership is more clearly referred to than in the VELKD rite (where only word and sacrament are mentioned).

3. The book of induction rites of the churches of the Arnoldshainer Konferenz contains a common induction rite for all inductions of those already ordained from the induction of a religious education teacher to the induction of a bishop. This clearly integrates the episcopal ministry into the other ministries of the ordained. Additionally, the integration of this ministry into the mission of all Christians is underlined by the fact that according to this Arnoldshain rite a non-ordained assistant is to take part in performing the induction. In the readings, similarly, the episcopal ministry is taken into the variety of charisms and gifts through Romans 12, while Acts 20 and 2 Timothy 2 are not envisaged (1 Peter 5. 2ff, which speaks of the feeding of the flock, is given as an optional reading). In a specific prayer for a bishop being inducted, however, the Arnoldshain rite speaks clearly of the 'ministry of leadership' which is conferred in this induction.

Comparing the EKU and Arnoldshain rites with the Lutheran rite, one can say that on the one hand the specific nature of the ministry concerned is now expressed more clearly (especially in the EKU), while on the other side the integration into the responsibility of the whole church is underlined (Arnoldshain). So we have before us variations in which varying expressions of the protestant understanding of ministry are embodied in the liturgy of episcopal ministry.

III

The theological conception which underlies the liturgical rites for the induction of a bishop in the churches of the EKD is clear. The bishop is an ordained pastor with a concrete area of responsibility. His spiritual task is none other than that which was conferred on him through ordination to the pastoral ministry: the proclamation of the Word of God and the administration of the sacraments (expressed particularly clearly in the VELKD rite). This is also apparent in the fact that the readings envisaged for the different institutions are identical and in the parallelism in the induction questions in the Lutheran rite, which matches the altogether common induction rite of the Arnoldshainer Konferenz for the different inductions of ordained people. There is no difference between the spiritual task of a pastor and that of a bishop (or any other clergyman in a ministry of church leadership), while there is such a difference between the task given in ordination and that given in the rites of blessing (*Agende*, iv.i – cf. EKU *Agende*). If you like, the liturgical rites indicate not a threefold, but only a twofold ministry. The identity of the spiritual task of pastor and bishop matches the Reformation conviction, expressed in

Melanchthon's *Tractatus de potestate et primatu papae*, that this equality as a matter of principle arises from the witness of the New Testament and was then underlined again by Jerome (Tract. 60–65).

The problem with this conception would appear to lie in the question of whether it is able sufficiently to do justice to the special nature of the (episcopal) ministry of church leadership as it is practised in our churches and also legally defined. In the VELKD rite this special nature is more indirectly implied (e.g. through the ceremony with the pectoral cross), whereas in the other two rites, especially that of the EKU, it is named more clearly. The Lutheran Reformation too is capable of unfolding the specific nature of the regional episcopal office more clearly. The article of the Augsburg Confession about bishops (CA 28) certainly speaks fundamentally of the ministry of word and sacraments. But this is then clearly made more specific in formulations such as '... to judge doctrine and condemn doctrine that is contrary to the Gospel, and exclude from the Christian community the ungodly whose wicked conduct is manifest. All this is to be done not by human power but by God's Word alone. On this account parish ministers and churches are bound to be obedient to the bishops... ' (CA 28, 21 f.). This is the description of the tasks which bishops have *iure divino* – of these tasks nothing is said at least in the VELKD rite for the induction of a bishop. This is an indication of the weakness of a protestant theology of the episcopal office.

Behind all of this, of course, lies the controversy about what in this connection is divine and what is human law. Quite certainly the difference between pastors and bishops (in the modern sense) is one which has grown up in history. But the allocation to the ordained ministry of the task of the public proclamation of the word together with that of the administration of the sacraments is also, after all, the result of an historical development after the New Testament. Why does this allocation count as a spiritually fundamental *ius divinum* (according to CA 5 and 14), but the further differentiation not? The discussion of these problems has led to the question of whether the traditional differentiation between *ius divinum* and *ius humanum* is sufficient. Must not the development of regional ministries of church leadership with their particular spiritual tasks also be regarded as a development in which the spirit of God has his hand at work? Does it not conform with the spiritual nature of the Church that alongside the spiritual task locally there is a spiritual task at the regional level to which specific spiritual functions are attached: the particular care for apostolic truth and for the unity of the whole Church and, linked with that, the responsibility for the conduct of ordinations?

The consequence would be: the protestant churches would have to examine the relationship between their liturgical formularies and how they are divided up and the particular spiritual task which characterizes the offices of regional *episkope* and especially the episcopal office. In any case, the allocation of the liturgical rite for the conferring of the episcopal office to the 'rites of induction' represents an open problem. Theologically, it needs to be asked whether in addition to the distinction between the spiritual task given in ordination on the one hand and that given in a rite of blessing on the other hand there should also be a similar distinction between the spiritual task given in ordination at the local level and that given at the level of regional *episkope*. However, this would then *de facto* – *horribile dictu*? – be a plea which comes close to ecumenical convergence with a view to a threefold ministry. But should the protestant churches close their minds to this convergence?

The Expression of the Anglican Understanding of *Episkope* in the Law of the Church of England

Augur Pearce

Introduction

The Anglican understanding of *episkope* is a theological matter. Many in the Church of England would, I think, agree that while there is a theological basis for our church law, it is not the first place to which one would turn for a systematic presentation of theological propositions. Even when a canon contains a direct doctrinal statement, it tends to be a restatement of what has been declared elsewhere; the procedure for the making of canons is not particularly suited, and does not always follow the safeguards which the General Synod's Constitution provides,[1] for the making of new doctrinal formulations. The sort of theological statements you might find in the Roman Catholic *Codex Juris Canonici*, or in the preamble to certain *landeskirchliche Grundordnungen*, for example, will generally not be found in English legislation.

I do admit some exceptions to this generalization. The preambles to certain pieces of Reformation legislation, also Section A of the 1964 code of Canons (containing provisions largely taken from the 1604 code and by that from earlier Elizabethan sources), are undoubtedly theological in character. I will come back to the Reformation preambles at the end of my talk; so far as section A is concerned, I have to mention the statements that the services of the Ordinal and the Church's episcopal structure are not contrary to the Word of God;[2] but since these are bare statements with which one can merely agree, or (as a non-Anglican) disagree, they do not take us much further and I shall rapidly pass on.

Canon A 5, indicating the scriptural basis of Anglican doctrine and listing certain sources in which such doctrine is particularly to be found, does not mention amongst these the canons themselves. It does, however, mention the Book of Common Prayer and the Ordinal; and these are for Anglicans both doctrinal and legal sources simultaneously. Liturgy is a part of law, in that Anglican liturgical orders are approved by the Church's legislative authorities and required to be used in public worship.[3] Their texts are thus expressions of the mind of the legislature and evidence of the law's attitude, at least where they are not in conflict with more direct expressions of that mind. Very specific statements about the bishop's role may be found in the Ordinal and the Alternative Service Book; institution services tell us more about how his relationship to parishes is perceived, and so on. But despite the obvious relevance of these texts to my subject, I shall leave them to one side (to avoid re-crossing ground already covered by Bishop Buchanan or to be covered on Thursday by Provost Moses), and invite you to turn your attention to the law's practical provisions.

Because what the rest of church law has to tell us about the ministry of oversight is largely indirect and practical. It tells us what a bishop does, what duties and prerogatives he has, how bishops are chosen, and what other forms of oversight exist. By looking at such provisions, however, or the pattern which several such provisions form, one can frequently deduce theological presuppositions which lie behind the law.

The Role of the Diocesan Bishop

It will surprise no participant in this Conference at this stage to hear that Anglican church law focusses the ministry of oversight largely in the person of the diocesan bishop. As well as an assortment of provisions in Canon C 18 which express this principle, numerous other canons and statutes[4] show it in action, as do some rules of the English common law or the inherited mediaeval canon law.

A final caveat. Since the law moves slowly and often follows changes in practice, the picture that I shall be painting does not fully reflect modern thinking on such matters as the collegiality of bishops within a diocese, ecumenical consultation in matters of oversight, and the like. I have also interpreted my brief narrowly, reading 'oversight' as the oversight by one person or body in the Church of the activities of others, not widely as covering all aspects of church government. The synodical element, particularly the considerable moral and financial influence of synods in today's church, therefore comes to the fore less frequently than a wider consideration of church government would show.

Local *episkope* may be said to be expressed and symbolized in the law in five main ways. The bishop is (a) the chief minister of worship in his diocese. He is (b) its chief pastor, having besides his personal pastoral ministry the duty to provide for the cure of souls throughout his territory, and to visit the places in which this is exercised. By extension from this, he has a particular responsibility for (c) the oversight of his clergy. This incorporates a disciplinary power, but the bishop's (d) disciplinary role extends also to the one form of ecclesiastical discipline still applicable to the laity. His pastoral concern finds expression, finally, in (e) the partial oversight of the stewardship of the Church's property.

A few examples must suffice for each of these propositions.

(a) So far as *worship* is concerned, the bishop may officiate personally in any church at any time.[5] He is the sole minister of Confirmation,[6] which ensures that every active church member has at least one time in his life when he encounters a bishop face to face. The framework of the liturgy to be used in public worship is a crucial aspect of Anglicanism where *lex orandi* is *lex credendi*, and therefore a legislative matter rather than falling within the bishop's *episkope*; but he may control questions of detail, by dispensing from the duty to hold certain services,[7] providing liturgies for special occasions[8] or – significantly – by ruling on whether local variations 'depart from the doctrine of the Church of England'.[9]

(b) As *chief pastor* the bishop has a say on the territorial arrangements made for pastoral provision; he can initiate and influence reorganization proposals[10] and must consent to local ecumenical projects.[11] The clergy, and those lay office-holders whose role is primarily pastoral or liturgical, exercise their ministries in the parish with his authority, given by institution or licensing.[12] The cure of souls in a parish is not handed over, but shared by the bishop with the incumbent; and the bishop's responsibility does not end there. Since both minister and people can benefit from outside advice, encouragement and supervision, he has the right of visitation for 'the edifying and well-governing of Christ's flock, ... the supply of such things as are lacking and the correction of such things as are amiss'.[13] In practice a visitor's main concerns today are the life of the local church and the state of its property. Part of the machinery of visitation is a report to the visitor by the parish's churchwardens, laypeople locally chosen but acting as *oculi episcopi*,[14] drawing the attention of the bishop's senior staff to matters that require outside attention.[15]

(c) The bishop's personal *oversight of his clergy* is expressed firstly in his exclusive right to ordain.[16] He cannot be forced to ordain a candidate, nor (except in a very few cases) prevented from so doing. Those ordained or appointed to minister in his diocese swear to pay him 'true and canonical obedience'.[17] But his authority over individual members of the clergy is by no means absolute. The oath promises 'obedience in all things lawful and honest', binding a cleric to observe all such commands as the bishop is by law authorized to impose.[18] For example, clergy wishing to omit certain weekly services required by the canons,[19] to pursue secular occupations,[20] to live outside their parishes[21] or to minister regularly in other denominations' churches,[22] require his consent. One who violates such legal obligations, despite being warned by the bishop, thereby aggravates the seriousness of the offence. But the oath does not *extend* the range of commands which the bishop can give: it does not enable him to impose additional obligations or to restrict the clergy's lawful discretion.

143

(d) Turning to *disciplinary jurisdiction*, a minister may refuse communion to a person guilty of 'grave and open sin without repentance' on his own authority if there is an immediate risk of scandal; but otherwise this step, the only form of discipline of the laity, must be reported to the bishop and his directions followed.[23] The licence to officiate may be withdrawn from a minister without security of tenure, either as an administrative or a disciplinary measure.[24] In the case of secure office-holders and more serious offences, resort is had to a judicial procedure provided by statute, in which the bishop's court is the tribunal of first instance.[25]

(e) *Property.* Both buildings for worship, and the endowments supporting the local clergy, are important incidental aspects of the Church's local presence. Land and buildings to be used for worship or burial may be solemnly set apart by the bishop for that use; thereafter any deviations from that use, the granting of rights over the property or alterations to its fabric or contents, needs his court's permission. The endowments of benefices are in the bishop's care during vacancies; he arranges for their stewardship pending a new appointment,[26] and then directs the new incumbent to be admitted to the 'temporalities'.[27] (Statutory centralization of such endowments has, however, greatly reduced the significance of this in recent years.) In many other matters concerning the local church's property, where control now lies with parochial representative bodies, these are supervised by the statutory Diocesan Board of Finance, on which the bishop sits *ex officio.*[28]

Turning from local *episkope* to the wider picture, the bishops may also be seen coming together in three bodies which represent the Church in different ways at provincial or national level: the Convocations, the General Synod and Parliament. Insofar as Parliament still plays a part in ecclesiastical legislation, the bishops' presence there is obviously of considerable importance and provides part of the justification for that body's continuing claim to be a sort of supreme synod. In the General Synod, the bishops form a separate House and so, through the device of 'voting by Houses',[29] enjoy a potential veto over most classes of business. I would not, in fact, class this veto as itself an example of *episkope*: for one thing, other Houses enjoy it as well; and for another, the General Synod's primary task is legislative, and to my mind legislation is not a form of oversight, so much as the framework within which executive and judicial oversight is exercised. However, the fact that legislation on forms of worship or doctrinal formulae may only be finally approved by the General Synod in a form which the House of Bishops has approved[30] is, as I see it, a further expression of the bishops' role as collective guardians of the faith.

So much for the general picture: locally, a single individual at the centre of a great many areas of the Church's life, and nationally, a doctrinal oversight exercised by the same people acting collegiately. What is interesting for our purposes, though, is to ask what the law tells us about the reasons for this pattern, and also about the qualifications and exceptions to it.

Factors Uniting the Episcopate

The reason why this wide range of powers and functions is conferred upon the bishop becomes clearer when we consider four factors that unite bishops with each other. The first, tying in with the bishops' guardianship of doctrine at the national level, is profession of the faith as the Church of England has received it. On consecration, or translation to a new see, a bishop must make a Declaration of belief in the faith revealed in Scripture, set forth in the Creeds and attested in the historic Anglican formularies. The ministers whom the bishop ordains or admits to office must then make effectively the same Declaration before him.[31]

A second factor uniting the English episcopate is the chain of succession sealed by the laying on of hands. Canon C 1 presently provides that no person not consecrated a bishop according to the Anglican rite, or in some church whose orders the Church of England recognizes, shall be accounted a lawful bishop. This single point is perhaps the one which above all brings us here this week – but is noticeably not the only factor which the law takes into account.

The third factor is that of mutual recognition. Those who exercise oversight must recognize each other's authority to do so. Few legal provisions expressly state this point: as examples, however, I would point to the fact that a minister seeking preferment in a new diocese must produce his letters of orders, evidence of his former bishop's action which the new bishop will recognize,[32] and to the fact that the disqualification of a cleric from holding preferment, pronounced by one bishop's court, has automatic effect for all dioceses in England.[33]

Finally, the overseers are themselves subject to oversight: as Bishop Stephen Sykes has written, 'uncoordinated oversight is no oversight'.[34] The old pattern of episcopal appointment is that the clergy elect their bishop but the metropolitan confirms their choice of a suitable candidate. This pattern is still to be seen in the form of a legal ceremony, even though this has been emptied of practical meaning by the involvement of the Crown and by wider diocesan consultation.[35] Many episcopal executive decisions, and of course all decisions of the bishop's court, are not final but subject to appeal. The bishops of a province form a collegiate tribunal to hear disciplinary charges against one of their number.[36] The metropolitan, that is the Archbishop, may carry out a visitation of other diocesan bishops within his province;[37] and the Crown, about whose role I shall speak at the end, may itself appoint a commission to visit the Archbishops.[38]

Qualifications and Exceptions to the Pattern of Personal Oversight

(a) Exercise of oversight by others

Under modern conditions, a diocesan bishop cannot exercise his *episkope* unaided. Since the Reformation he has had the possibility to appoint suffragan bishops to whom certain of his tasks may be delegated.[39] Such delegation is also the legal basis on which the 'provincial episcopal visitors', the so-called 'flying bishops', exercise a ministry within the dioceses of those bishops who have ordained women, in relation to parishes who cannot accept this development.[40] Insofar as these officers are in law mere representatives of the diocesan bishop, they do not disturb the principle of a single personal focus of *episkope*. But the general principle that a suffragan bishop's role is limited to following his diocesan's instructions, and may be terminated at any time, knows one exception: namely in those dioceses subdivided by an 'area scheme', in which the diocesan's oversight is not merely delegated but 'shared', and the area bishop has an independent competence within his territory which the diocesan cannot unilaterally revoke.[41]

From even earlier days, the bishop has also been able to share all matters of spiritual jurisdiction with a 'Vicar-General in Spirituals';[42] an office which is today usually held by a legally qualified layperson, male or female. (In the Church of Rome this office has developed differently and is today regularly held by a senior priest.) If given full scope, the Vicar-General may visit on the bishop's behalf, institute to benefices, grant dispensations, and (when not personally in bishop's orders) commission other bishops to confirm or ordain.

In the judicial function, the bishop is represented by a diocesan judge, today called the Chancellor.[43] Economy and efficiency commonly require that the Chancellor and the Vicar-General be one and the same person; but 'separation of powers' thinking has given this person considerable independence and security of tenure in the office of Chancellor,[44] and excluded the bishop from exercising much of his judicial power in person.[45]

At an inferior level, the bishop is assisted by archdeacons, experienced priests with responsibility for oversight of part of the diocesan territory. The archdeacon exercises his/her office 'under the bishop',[46] and in regard to some duties is expressly required to follow the bishop's directions. But here again the law provides an element of independence: in the ministry of parochial visitation, which the archdeacon in practice exercises much more frequently than the bishop, the archdeacon's jurisdiction is seen as an 'ordinary' one, not derivative, and one which the bishop can only inhibit if he (or his Vicar-General) is currently visiting in person.[47]

In none of these cases do I want to suggest that autonomous rival jurisdictions are regularly claimed against the diocesan bishop. Area bishops, other suffragans and archdeacons co-operate very much as part of a leadership team; 'flying bishops', although brought in from outside the diocese, can do nothing without the diocesan bishop's goodwill. The diocesan chancellor's judicial function requires him/her to hold somewhat aloof from episcopal policy, but in practice relations between bishops and their chancellors tend to be cordial. The theory, rather than the practice, is significant to our discussion; but it is significant that the theory of the law can now envisage episcopal oversight shared between two persons, functions of oversight which (although exercised in the diocesan's name) are exercised by a layperson with considerable independence, and functions of oversight vested, as a matter of original right, in a person not in bishop's orders.

Those who exercise these functions are united by three of the four uniting factors which we have previously considered in relation to diocesan bishops themselves. The law secures the recognition of their acts, and subjects them to superior oversight; they are all, lay and ordained officers alike, required to profess a common faith in the Declaration of Assent.[48] Only the chain of episcopal succession is lacking, since the roles of chancellor, vicar-general and archdeacon do not depend upon this.

One further case is worthy of mention here. It is a rare, some may say an obscure example of oversight, but still I believe worthy of mention since it shows a collegiately exercised *episkope* which is not in any sense derived from an individual bishop, but rather an alternative solution adopted when such a bishop is lacking. I refer to the so-called 'guardianship of the spiritualities' of a vacant see.

The functions of a diocesan bishop and his vicar-general cease when the former leaves office. The other officers' functions continue, but may not be comprehensive. Coadjutor bishops with right of automatic succession are unknown to English law. Until the new diocesan takes office, therefore, the law has traditionally provided for guardians of the spiritualities to assume the whole spiritual jurisdiction of the see; and by the mediaeval *jus commune*, the chapter of the bishop's cathedral (which also elected his successor) was to assume this role.[49] In many cases, admittedly, a local English custom transferred this responsibility to the metropolitan; but those dioceses where the Dean and Chapter still act as guardians today bear witness to the older tradition, which the modern canons also recognize.[50] A Measure of 1983, allowing the Archbishop in all cases to delegate functions to another bishop during a vacancy-in-see, overlaps with the rights of the guardians but does not abolish them;[51] and indeed an earlier attempt to abolish the old rule was resisted by no less a defender of catholic orthodoxy than Bishop Eric Kemp, who described the chapter as the rightful source of authority since it represented the 'collective presbyterate of the diocese'.[52]

(b) Oversight and the synodical structure

I have already distinguished between my understanding of *episkope* as executive and judicial, and legislative functions which provide a framework within which it is exercised. I would not, therefore, normally describe the General Synod as a body exercising oversight. The same applies to the diocesan and more local representative bodies for which the law has provided since the 1920s. But there can be no doubt that such bodies have in practice influenced the way in which leadership in the Church is understood. The diocesan bishop must consult the diocesan synod on matters of general concern and importance to the diocese;[53] a parochial church council is to co-operate with the minister in promoting within the parish the whole mission of the Church.[54] All synods make decisions by majority vote; and I have already mentioned the device of voting by Houses. Regarding the diocesan bishop's veto in the diocesan synod, it is interesting to note that the law expressly requires him to use this power with restraint.[55]

Particularly at the parish level, it is clear that oversight is not the same as direction. A parochial church council controls its own funds and property (though these do not include the church building or the incumbent's residence). Its accounts are subject to scrutiny and its property transactions sometimes require diocesan approval, but it cannot be instructed how to deal with its resources. The view has even been voiced in recent years that the law tends here too far in favour of parish autonomy at the expense of unity and co-operation in the wider Church.

The Role of the Crown

I have left until last the part played in English church life by Parliament and the Supreme Governor, though I know this to be an aspect on which German textbooks describing the Church of England generally love to dwell. I should say at once that my aim is to avoid an overlap with tomorrow's topic, and in particular I am not concerned with the realities of the Church-State relationship as it is practised today. I do not even have much to say concerning Parliament, beyond stressing that this body is correctly thought of as the Queen in Parliament, and therefore much of what I say concerning the Queen alone applies to Parliament as well.

My concern is simply with the role of the Queen as overseer of the overseers, a sort of English '*summa episcopa*' and the sixteenth-century context against which that is to be understood.

The Sovereign is not a minister of word and sacraments. The Thirty-nine Articles are clear on that point, as indeed was Elizabeth I herself. Yet to her are entrusted a number of ecclesiastical functions which clearly amount to a ministry of oversight. She stands, namely, where the Papacy used to stand, at the top of both executive and judicial trees. When a bishop's court passes a disciplinary sentence upon a defaulting cleric, or indeed when a defaulting bishop is punished by his fellow bishops, the final court of appeal is one appointed and acting in Her Majesty's name.[56] The visitation of parishes by bishops' officers and of dioceses by the metropolitan, is complemented by a general right of visitation vested in the Crown, ensuring that even the Archbishops are not exempt from scrutiny.[57] As the metropolitan's representative ceremonially confirms the election of a new bishop, so a royal commission must confirm the choice of an Archbishop. The Queen does not preside at worship or ordain clergy, but the consecration of a bishop takes place by her mandate.

The relevance of this to our discussion is, I submit, to be seen in the understanding of the Church/State relationship current when the Crown assumed these rights: in short, in the ecclesiology of the 1532 Ecclesiastical Appeals Act. Put briefly, the draftsmen of that Act proceeded on the basis that English society was a body of people which, wearing its 'spiritual hat', could be called the English Church. Wearing its 'secular hat', it was the nation; but the headship of Church and nation were one because the entities themselves – and their membership – were one.[58]

When people are looking at the Church/State nexus nowadays and finding it anachronistic, the way this reasoning is normally described is to say: the King represented the nation, so identifying the nation with the Church enabled him to claim headship over the Church. But, given the single-society theory, there is no reason why we have to look at things that way round. We could just as easily say directly that the King represented the English Church, and the recognition in him of these supreme powers of oversight which I have described was a recognition that they belonged properly to the whole Church and not to any one member of the ordained hierarchy.

The fact that the single-society theory (which the law, incidentally, has by no means consistently abandoned) found no support in many theologies of the Church and became wholly unrealistic after 1689 should not prevent us using it as an aid to construction of the legislation of its time; and the fact that we might not, today, choose to entrust the whole Church's *episkope* to a hereditary monarch bound to follow political advisers need not alter our recognition of the fact that such an *episkope* exists, and has in Anglican tradition been seen as a ministry which a layperson can properly discharge.

Conclusion

To sum up, therefore: the law of the Church of England recognizes a need for a ministry of oversight. It focuses that ministry chiefly in individuals, diocesan bishops, who are linked together by a common faith, the laying on of hands, mutual recognition, and subjection to superior oversight. Most functions of oversight in the Church, both executive and judicial, are carried out by or in the name of these individuals; this is the norm, and it would be idle to pretend otherwise. But from early times there have been others entrusted in their own right with such functions, or whose functions derived from the bishop have come to be exercised with a certain degree of autonomy. These may be individual officers or collegiate bodies, ordained or lay, male or female. And the position accorded to the Queen as Overseer of the overseers, the English *summa episcopa*, is in my submission to be seen as one which subjects the ministry of all ordained office-holders to the authority of the whole Church.

Notes

1. Constitution of the General Synod, Art. 7 (Sch. 2 to the Synodical Government Measure 1969).

2. Canons A 4 and A 6.

3. Church of England (Worship and Doctrine) Measure 1974 and Canons B 1–B 5.

4. I should explain briefly for my German listeners that a Measure is a form of ecclesiastical legislation which, although passed by General Synod, has the force of an Act of Parliament and can amend earlier parliamentary legislation for the Church – Church of England Assembly (Powers) Act 1919; Synodical Government Measure 1969. I use the umbrella term 'statute' to cover both Acts and Measures. A canon, also passed by the Synod but without any form of parliamentary control, cannot do this and must indeed be consistent with the existing law as laid down in Measures and Acts – Submission of the Clergy Act 1533. A new code of canons promulged in the 1960s restates many general principles concerning the structures of the Church, and has been supplemented (as regards the ministry of oversight) by newer canons as well as some provisions in synodical Measures.

5. Canon C 18.4.

6. Canon B 27.1.

7. E.g. Canons B 11.2, B 14.1.

8. Canons B 4.3.

9. Canon B 5.4.

10. Pastoral Measure 1983.

11. Canon B 44.1.

12. E.g. Canons C 8, E 6.

13. Canon G 5.1.

14. Canon E 1.4.

15. Canon G 6.

16. Canon C 18.4.

17. Canon C 14.3.

18. *Long v. Bishop of Cape Town* (1863) 1 Moo PCC NS 411.

19. See note 6 above.

20. Canons C 28.2, Pluralities Act 1838, s. 29.

21. Canon C 25.2.

22. Canons B 43.3.

23. Canons B 16.1.

24. Canon C 12.5.

25. Ecclesiastical Jurisdiction Measure 1963.

26. See now Church of England (Miscellaneous Provisions) Measure 1992, s. 1.

27. Canon C 11.1.

28. E.g. Parochial Church Councils (Powers) Measure 1956, s. 6; Diocesan Boards of Finance Measure 1925, s. 1.

29. Constitution of the General Synod, Art. 5 (Sch. 2 to the Synodical Government Measure 1969).

30. *Ibid.*, Art. 7.

31. Canon C 15.1.

32. Canon C 10.2.

33. Ecclesiastical Jurisdiction Measure 1963, s. 49.

34. *Unashamed Anglicanism*, p. 161.

35. Appointment of Bishops Act 1533.

36. Ecclesiastical Jurisdiction Measure 1963, s. 9.

37. Canon C 17.2.

38. Act of Supremacy 1558, s. 8.

39. Suffragan Bishops Act 1534; Dioceses Measure 1978, s. 10.

40. Episcopal Ministry Act of Synod 1993.

41. Dioceses Measure 1978, s. 11.

42. Canon C 18.3.

43. Ecclesiastical Jurisdiction Measure 1963, s. 2.

44. Church of England (Miscellaneous Provisions) Measure 1992, s. 12.

45. Ecclesiastical Jurisdiction Measure 1963, s. 46(1) proviso.

46. Canon C 22.4.

47. Canons C 22.2, G 5.2.

48. As to the making of the Declaration by Chancellors see Canon G 2.3.

49. See P. Hinschius, *System des katholischen Kirchenrechts*, ii (Berlin 1878, repr. Graz, 1959), pp. 232–3.

50. Canon C 19.2–3.

51. Church of England (Miscellaneous Provisions) Measure 1983, s. 10.

52. Letter to the Secretary-General of the General Synod in January 1976, quoted in B. Till, *York versus Durham: the Dispute over the Guardianship of the Spiritualities of the See of Durham* (1985).

53. Synodical Government Measure 1969, s. 4.

54. Parochial Church Councils (Powers) Measure 1956, s. 2.

55. Church Representation Rules, rule 28.

56. Ecclesiastical Jurisdiction Measure 1963, ss. 1,11.

57. See note 38 above.

58. Ecclesiastical Appeals Act 1532, Preamble.

The Exercise and Understanding of *Episkope* in the Law of the Evangelical Church in Germany and its Member Churches

Eilert Herms

Summary

The full German text of Professor Herms' paper can be found on pp. 325–43.

The first part of the paper comprises the following sections:

1. *The basis and nature of the law of the EKD and that of its member churches;*

2. *The three main areas regulated by ecclesiastical law (doctrine, worship and organization);*

3. *The doctrinal bases for the law of the protestant churches in Germany and for the law of the EKD.*

4. Episkope *in the Law of the Individual Churches*

Professor Herms begins this section by stating that a consensus on three points underlies the church orders of all the member churches of the Evangelical Church in Germany (EKD):

(i) *that the ministerial office of proclamation of the Gospel and adminis-tration of the sacraments is given by Christ himself;*

(ii) *that the responsibility for order in all areas of the life of the commu-nity of faith, including the ministry of proclamation of the Gospel and administration of the sacraments, lies with the local community of faith (in Reformation terminology, 'the congregation');*

(iii) *that ordered* episkope *in the sense of leadership is indispensable, this leadership having the function of oversight, ensuring that order is maintained, and the power to make decisions which serve the devel-opment, correction and improvement of church order in the face of new challenges.*

He goes on to point out that the second of these points is met by the fact that the church orders declare the synods, as representatives of the whole regional church, to be responsible for the ordering of the life of the community of faith. This development was assisted by the democratic movements of the nineteenth and twentieth centuries, but is based on the insights of Reformation theology as to the understanding of the Church which is to be found in Holy Scripture.

The first point is met in all of the church orders by the fact that they order

- *the tasks and duties of the pastoral office;*

- *the conveying of the pastoral office to individuals by ordination;*

- *the qualifications for ordination.*

The third point is met in all of the church orders by the fact that the individual churches are led through the interplay of a number of organs (regulated in the individual church orders) – at least a synod, a synodical committee, a church office and a spiritual office of oversight exercised by people ordained to the ministry of the word. In many of the church orders there is also a body called the Church Leadership, which has the supreme decision-making power between meetings of the Synod, on behalf of the Synod and with accountability to it. In the majority of cases the holder of the spiritual office of oversight is a member of the Church Leadership, often as its regular chairman.[18] All of this ensures that the relationship of word and community of faith is the same (and is expressed institutionally) at the level of the individual churches as it is at the level of the individual congregations.

A translation of the remainder of Prof. Herms' paper follows.

We turn now to the organization and tasks of the spiritual office of oversight held by ordained persons, according to the church orders of the member churches of the Evangelical Church in Germany (EKD).

In the overwhelming majority of cases it is exercised collegially. Where that is not so, this is mostly because of the small size of the church concerned.[19] The collegial exercise of oversight is regularly linked with regional responsibilities. The ministers concerned may be equals,[20] or there may be a hierarchy of levels between regionally limited offices of oversight, which are equal, and one office of oversight (or several) at the level of the whole church.[21] Both systems may exist simultaneously in the same church.[22]

In all of the church orders, the holders of the office of oversight are given virtually no tasks in the areas of legislation and administration, but all of them give it the duty of watching over conformity to the church's doctrinal order and seeing that acts of worship are in conformity with the church's confession. Especially linked with this is the duty of ordaining pastors (in some cases also the right and duty to take the final decision about the suitability of candidates[23]), the right to preach from all pulpits and the right to communicate with the entire membership of the church through official statements or pastoral letters. However, all questions of church order and therefore also all questions of church legislation and administration have in the end to be decided according to criteria which are contained in the doctrinal teaching of the church. This means that official statements by the holder of the office of oversight on matters of church doctrine may have as their content the principles contained in the church's doctrine which are relevant to legislative decisions which are about to be taken, or even to administrative decisions (such as decisions about investments or budget reductions). By this means they can influence these decisions, which are taken by the synod or the church administration, and ultimately even be one of the influences on the process of the continual reformation of the Church.[24] By concentrating the office of oversight which is exercised by ordained persons on doctrinal order, the church orders make it relevant to the whole life of the Church. They shape it as an office of comprehensive *leadership of the Church by teaching*, through an explication and application of the doctrine of the Church, which applies its changeless intention to the needs of the particular time.

Admittedly, this responsibility is concentrated on watching over the doctrine *which is already in force*. The church orders do not make it possible for the office of oversight to intervene in the church's doctrinal or liturgical order by the reception of new doctrinal texts or the authorization of new liturgies. These decisions once again belong rather to the synod. They too are to be watched over by the ordained 'exercisers of *Episkope*', and their coming into force can in some cases – at least temporarily – be prevented by episcopal action. But the church orders do not give the holders of the office of oversight the possibility permanently to prevent or to enforce decisions about the church's doctrinal or liturgical order against the will of the synod.

The most thoroughgoing influence on the whole leadership of the church is given to the ordained holders of the office of oversight by those church orders which bestow on them chairmanship in the synod, the church administration and the church leadership simultaneously. This is true in particular of the church orders of the Rhenish and Westphalian churches. However, most of the church orders – especially the Lutheran ones – preserve the separation of powers between the synod and the office of oversight, by not even according membership of the synod to the holder of that office.

So much for the main tasks and responsibilities of the office of oversight in the law of the individual churches. What about the regulation of oversight in the law of the federations and communions of churches? We shall examine first the confessional federations and then the fellowship of all German protestant churches in the EKD.

5. *Episkope* in the Law of the VELKD and the EKU

5.1   The United Evangelical-Lutheran Church of Germany (VELKD) understands itself as a church, the union of confessionally identical Lutheran churches. Accordingly, its constitution provides for a certain limitation of the autonomy of its member churches in the matter of reception, which could only be regained by their withdrawal from the United Church. Also in accordance with its self-understanding as a united church, it has its own level at which there is an office of oversight with legally regulated tasks and responsibilities, above all within the interplay of the United Church's leading bodies. Partly through this and partly directly, the United Church's office of oversight also has tasks and responsibilities *vis-à-vis* the member churches.

Within the interplay of the United Church's leading bodies the office of oversight has a stonger function than is the case in all of its member churches, because of the fact that the synod's decisions can only come into force with the approval of the bishops' conference. Insofar as the laws of the United Church also apply *per se* to the member churches, the office of oversight's greater influence in legislation also applies indirectly to the member churches.

The United Church's office of oversight has direct responsibilities with regard to the member churches through the powers of the bishops' conference and the Presiding Bishop, which are regulated by the United Church's constitution. Both have the right to communicate with the entire membership of the United Church by means of official statements or pastoral letters. The Presiding Bishop has the right to preach from all of the pulpits of the United Church. The United Church has a common law concerning clergy discipline and conditions of service and a common disciplinary law regarding doctrinal matters (which also applies to the whole of the pastors' liturgical activity). This gives the Presiding Bishop – as chairman of the church leadership and the bishops' conference – a key role in inaugurating and taking forward disciplinary cases, but on the other hand also makes clear that the emphasis in the responsibilities of the office of oversight lies in watching over the *existing* doctrine. The law also does not provide for unilateral decisions about the teaching and liturgical activity of individual pastors.

The reason for the fact that a jointly exercised office of oversight is relatively strongly developed at the level of the United Church is that one of the fundamental tasks of the United Church is 'to have a care for the maintenance and deepening of the Lutheran teaching and administration of the sacraments by fostering Lutheran theology and advising the member churches on questions of Lutheran teaching, worship and congregational life, and to foster the formation of a clergy which is confessionally tied (Constitution of the VELKD, Art. 7, para. 2).

5.2   Since 1951, when the church provinces of the 'Evangelical Church of the Old Prussian Union' became independent churches with full powers to regulate their own affairs, the Evangelical Church of the Old Prussian Union has lived on, under the name 'Evangelical Church of the Union', no longer as a church but as a '*communion*' (order of the EKU, Art. 1, para. 1) of its member churches (that is, the former church provinces of the Evangelical Church of the Old Prussian Union[25]). It serves its member churches as a means of joint action in those matters and cases in which the independent churches wish to act together – without losing their independence (cf. order of the EKU, Art. 6–8). The organs of the communion – synod and council – also serve this purpose. They do not have powers of leadership which limit the member churches' power to regulate their own affairs or their autonomy in the matter of reception, but only the right to offer 'suggestions and guidelines' (Art. 7, para. 1),[26] as well as the right to make suggestions for common laws (Art. 7, para. 2).

Accordingly, the law of the EKU does not make any provision for addition to the tasks and responsibilities of the office of oversight over doctrinal and liturgical order exercised by ordained persons which are laid down in the church orders of its member churches. There is merely a common 'order of proceeding in doctrinal disciplinary cases concerning ordained ministers of the word', which, however, regulates these as proceedings which are to be carried out within and by the member churches.

6.   *Episkope* in the Law of the EKD

The EKD too is not *a church*, but only the *communion* of several independent churches. As such it has been declared and ordered by the member churches on the basis which is declared in their own teaching (and which is now publicly expounded in the Leuenberg Concord). It has been declared and ordered for the purpose of directing the actions of the member churches according to common 'principles' (Art. 6, para. 2; Art. 19, S 2) as far as is possible (i.e. insofar as their own confession does not conflict with this) and representing the churches uniformly to the 'holders of public power' (Art. 19, S 1). In addition, the member churches can pass matters on to the EKD, and leave to it decisions (Art. 13) and

157

even in certain circumstances the making of legal regulations (Art. 10(b)). The organs of the EKD can, of their own volition, only take the following initiatives *vis-à-vis* the churches which participate in the communion of the EKD:

– They can make suggestions (Art. 8);

– They can create guidelines for matters falling within precisely-defined areas (Art. 9);

– They can make announcements to the public both within the churches and beyond them (Art. 20, para. 1; Art. 29, para. 1 S 3).

In accordance with the particular character of the EKD and with its tasks, the EKD's church order does not offer a doctrinal and liturgical order of its own as a basis, but only an organizational order, which lays down the tasks and interplay of its organs.

Notes

(Footnote numbers follow the numbering in the original paper.)

18. This is true of United churches (e.g. Hessen-Nassau, Westphalia and the Rhineland) as well as of Lutheran churches (the United Lutheran Church (VELKD) and the Northelbian Church), but not of the churches of the Palatinate or Bremen.

19. E.g. Oldenburg, Lippe, Schaumburg-Lippe, Görlitz.

20. E.g. in the Church of Hessen-Nassau (the Church President is merely the chairman of the 'leading spiritual office' – the college of deans). In the Palatinate too there is a college of deans.

21. E.g. in Bavaria (regional deans and Bishop), Hannover (superintendents, *Landessuperintendenten*, Bishop), Württemberg (deans, prelates, Bishop), Rhineland and Westphalia (superintendents, *Präses*).

22. E.g. in the Northelbian Church: in the Areas: deans, Area Bishop, in the church as a whole: the College of Bishops.

23. E.g. in the Church of Kurhessen and Waldeck.

24. The most recent model example: the study of the office of church leadership of the Church of Hessen-Nassau entitled 'Task and Form. From the need to save to the improvement of the Church. Theological principles for the concentration of resources and changes in structure', 1995.

25. Together with the Church of Anhalt, which recently joined the EKU.

26. This is roughly comparable with the rights of the organs of the EKD *vis-à-vis* its member churches.

The Public Role of a Northelbian Bishop as Representative of the Church and in Decision-making: A Description

Hans Christian Knuth

It follows from the 'the structural change in public life' (*Habermas*) that in the office of a bishop – at least the office of a protestant bishop – there is often a wide gulf between public representation and actual influence. Only in a small proportion of episcopal duties does the public role entail the public exercise of power. Since the bishop exercises his ministry in church, society and in public life, I shall structure my presentation accordingly.

I.   Function of the Northelbian Bishop in the Church

I spend most of my time preparing and delivering sermons, lectures and addresses. Fulfilling the role of spiritual leadership, *sine vi sed verbo*, theological life and personal preferences combine in this to create an admittedly strenuous but generally fulfilling ministry. In this my original vocation to be a pastor and my previous experience of doctoral research, as a member of staff of the Northelbian Church headquarters, as a parish pastor, as Director of Studies of a theological college, as a senior staff member of the United Evangelical–Lutheran Church of Germany responsible for doctrinal questions, and as the pastor and rural dean in Eckernförde, complement each other and help me to fulfill my episcopal duties.

Alongside the sermons, lectures and addresses are ordination and visitation, as the classical public episcopal roles, but sadly the task of visitation often gets crowded out. Contact with the parishes has moved from the context of visitations to inductions, official openings, anniversaries, festivals, visits in cases of conflict and regular advice to pastors and rural deans in chapter and committee meetings. My role is mostly an advisory one, although occasionally it falls to me to take decisions as bishop, especially in disciplinary cases. The questions in the episcopal area where the decision rests with the bishop are ordination, parochial appointments, moving clergy where pastoral relationships have broken down and the supervision and oversight of rural deans.

In all other circumstances, both at the level of the episcopal area – of which we have three in our church – and at the level of the whole Northelbian Church, the bishop is only a voting member of committees and does not have a sole power of decision. I therefore spend a disproportionate amount of my time in committees (at the moment 38), in which I am mostly allowed to vote – but am often enough outvoted – but in some cases do not even have a vote (Church Council, Synod, Church Office, various committees – sometimes as chairman – advisory groups, boards, governing bodies, commissions, etc.). It is the bishop's task to network the committees and to seek to achieve consensus both internally and with the church at large.

For instance, in order to appoint a new director for our Northelbian Mission Centre the following steps were necessary:

a) Nominations Committee (six meetings).

b) Presentation of the candidate to the board of the Northelbian Mission Centre.

c) Presentation of the candidate in the Northelbian Church Office.

d) Presentation of the candidate to the Church Council.

e) Presentation of the candidate prior to the General Meeting of the Mission Centre.

f) Election of the candidate by the General Meeting.

In addition there were extensive discussions with the Director's future colleagues and with various individual interest groups within the bodies listed above. A similarly important election to another senior position in the Northelbian Church has just failed when the Church Council objected, after all the other bodies had already approved the candidate unanimously; now the whole process has to be started again from the beginning with a re-advertisement.

Our church is led by three different bodies: the Synod, the Church Council and the College of Bishops. All three have equal status. The Synod does not have a final decision-making power over the other two bodies. However, the College of Bishops can, if its decision is unanimous, veto decisions of the Synod which conflict with Holy Scripture and the Constitution of the Church.

II.   The Role in Society

It is also mostly by giving speeches that I represent the Northelbian Church as a bishop in society at large. Most frequently these are short speeches at receptions, for example those of the army, the chamber of commerce, the farmers' union, political parties, the country women's groups, etc. and at the anniversaries and festivals of clubs, associations, schools, etc., but longer speeches are also required, for example, about the role of the Church in Russia (to the army and the Rotary Club); about basic values (to trade guilds and to the Christian Democrats); at state and civic events for Remembrance Day; about the unity of the Baltic culture to the German minority; etc. At the opening of the newly elected parliament of Schleswig-Holstein I shall conduct the act of worship at the request of the parliamentary parties.

But contacts to the state government, to parties both within and outside parliament and to associations are just as important – often even more important – when public speeches are not given but social responsibility is to be borne together. Some time ago a conversation with the party groupings in the parliament of Schleswig-Holstein about the work of the committee investigating the Barschel affair drew public attention. Such conversations take place continually. Normally, what is thought, said, accepted or rejected in exploratory discussion is not then disseminated by deliberate indiscretion.

III. The Role of the Church in Public Life

In addition to public speeches and conversations, the Church itself performs a part of the tasks which would otherwise fall to the state and is therefore not only a partner but also part of the public apparatus.

As a result of the state requirement of subsidiarity – i.e. the preference for the general tasks of society being undertaken by voluntary bodies – on the one hand, and the church tax system on the other hand, the Church has involved itself in diaconal/social tasks to a considerable extent. Therefore, for example, the chairmanship of the governing body of the Deaconess Institution in Flensburg is one of the tasks of Schleswig's Bishop. The institution has 2,000 employees and an annual turnover of about 100 million DM. Here, of course, the church and public responsibilities are bound up together, for example in the area of medical ethics (transplants, abortion, embryo research, etc.), but above all with regard to the care of patients and as an employer. All three Northelbian bishops exercise such responsibilities, sometimes in even larger establishments. Including its diaconal/social work, the Northelbian Church employs a total of 31,000 people. This makes us the second largest employer after the state itself. The unions are our partners in pay negotiations, and as an employer we must ourselves carry out what we publicly recommend as a church to employers and employees in general.

In order to give an indication of the decisions and conflicts which arise here for the bishops, I should like to recall that the former Northelbian bishops Dr Hübner and Dr Wölber resigned from chairmanship of the Church Council when the

Northelbian Church made pay agreements with trade unions. Against the background of their experiences in the Church Struggle they regarded the possibility of such non-church bodies having an influence within the Church as incompatible with the Church's confessional basis and with exclusive obedience to Christ alone. The Synod nevertheless approved the pay agreements, since the Church had recommended this to other employers.

There may be similar conflicts tomorrow and the day after tomorrow, when our Synod is invited, against the expressed opinion of Northelbian bishops, to approve the blessing of homosexuals and unmarried couples living together in parsonage houses.

Direct confrontation with the Government has arisen as a result of the abolition of the Day of Repentance and Prayer as a public holiday. The State of Schleswig-Holstein had – following a recommendation from Bonn – abolished the Day of Repentance as a public holiday. We are seeking to overturn this with the help of a law which permits plebiscites.

The role of the media in such conflicts should not be underestimated. The media do give considerable help to the Church in its proclamation of the Gospel, for example when they publish or broadcast spiritual meditations, when information about the Church's work is given in interviews, reports and pictures or when even whole services are broadcast on the radio or on television. Publishers have already kindly taken books of prayers, Luther texts and theological studies from me as a bishop. But here it is more a case of my own personal work.

However, in the media's reporting – especially at the national level – reports about scandals and conflicts are in the majority. While the local media report in a friendly way about the bishop as the Church's representative, in the national media it is more social-political remarks which are quoted and this often results in misrepresentation. In the Barschel affair we were not understood at all by the public, in asylum cases and also in the dispute about homosexual and heterosexual cohabitation we are classified either as a political opponent or a political friend, as the case may be, and treated accordingly. The press is following the struggle about the Day of Repentance with well-meaning curiosity. Altogether one would have to say that the press's image of the bishops accords as little with reality as does its image of the Church as a whole. It has little interest in the fact that a bishop preaches, conducts visitations, chairs committees and serves as a member of them, administers, manages, conducts examinations, inducts, opens things, gives lectures, deals with conflicts in the parishes, spends many hours in one-to-one conversations as a pastor, and works diaconically, with the church at large, ecumenically and scientifically. If he says or does something eccentric, he can be certain to gain attention.

Let me give a true example of that. I spent four years of my life writing a thick book about the history of the exegesis of a single psalm by Greek and Latin church fathers, by Luther and up to modern times. The book has been read by perhaps ten or twelve people. But I had a sensational public relations success with an interview, given as I was leaving the house, about the question of whether our former Minister of Justice Leutheuser-Schnarrenberg could name her dachshund Dr Martin Luther. Three minutes before leaving for a business trip I just said, 'Is it legal for a dachshund to use the title Dr, then?' In addition I allowed myself to express doubts as to whether the name was not too long for use in keeping the dog under control, since he would have bitten someone long before one had finished calling his name to tell him to stop. This interview was broadcast from Flensburg to Konstanz. Whether it had episcopal quality I rather doubt, but in any case it did have this success as an expression of episcopal opinion.

But leaving fun on one side, according to the Lutheran confessional documents the original public task of the bishop is, of course, the *publice docere*, the public standing up for scripture and the confession of the Church. This task can usually be fulfilled by the positive unfolding of testimony in sermons and lectures. However, if conflicts arise, we have in German Lutheranism a process for dealing with discipline cases involving questions of doctrine, and should such a case arise, the chairmanship of the appropriate court, the court for doctrinal questions, within the United Evangelical-Lutheran Church of Germany would fall to me. So far this court has been convened only once since the war (Schulz case). Prosecutions in doctrinal cases usually arouse considerable public interest. If a breach of ordination promises is proved against the clergyman he has to be admonished, transferred, suspended or in the worst case dismissed.

Finally I should like to point to a serious conflict between the tasks given to the bishop and the means at his disposal to fulfill this task. Public expectation tends to match the catholic image of a bishop, whereas the reality within the Church matches more closely the image of a *pastor pastorum*, who creates consensus, leads and represents the Church by pastoral care and advice, but even more through prayer, intercession and preaching.

There is often a contradiction between disciplinary and spiritual action, or at least there is a considerable degree of tension there. But every Christian lives in that tension, because it can be traced back to the relationship between law and Gospel and for this there is no final solution.

The Public Roles of those exercising Episcopacy in the Church of England

Gordon Roe

Two influences shape the development of the public exercise of episcopacy. The first is the Bible and the tradition of the Church as One, Holy, Catholic and Apostolic. The second is the nature of the society in which it is exercised. The history of the exercise of episcopacy has been the history of the Church within society. Sometimes Church has dominated society. Sometimes the standards of a society have unduly influenced the Church. There has been a continuing process of reformation of the Church by the standards of Bible and tradition. The way in which episcopacy is exercised in the Church of England now is the result of this complex interaction.

The Nature of the Church

Episcopacy as it is at present exercised is derived from our understanding of the Church as One, Holy, Catholic and Apostolic.

The description of the Church as 'one' is notoriously difficult to keep anchored in reality, but as far as the Church of England is concerned, the bishop is the focus of unity. The local church (i.e. the diocese) is the assembly of all those who are in communion with the bishop, who owe obedience to him 'in all things lawful and honest'. All ministry in the name of the Church is under his care and authority. Even when there are deep differences of view in a diocese, for example about the rightness of women being ordained and exercising a ministry as priests, which require complicated patterns of oversight, that oversight is provided by bishops (Provincial Episcopal Visitors) who act with the authority of the diocesan bishop.

The note of 'holiness' asserts that the Church belongs to God and is his instrument. Notwithstanding that the Church is a human institution and not infallible, it and its servants the bishops strive to be obedient to God and to be open to sanctifying. This means that a bishop, as public representative of the Church, is expected to show signs of sanctified humanity: humanity which recognizably shares the frailties and ordinariness of his fellow human beings, but is sanctified by contact with the living God.

There are two related emphases in the description of the Church as 'catholic': orthodoxy and universality. It is the nature of the Church and therefore of the bishop that it receives truth from the Bible and tradition. The preface to the Declaration of Assent made at every ordination and licensing says: 'The Church of England... professes the faith uniquely revealed in the Holy Scriptures and set forth in the catholic creeds, which faith the Church is called upon to proclaim afresh in each generation'. The bishop, then, as representing the catholicity of the Church, believes and teaches the faith and proclaims it in ways which are appropriate in each generation. He probes and explores catholic truth and relates it to the situation in which the Church finds itself, not as an individual theologian but as one who is charged to represent the mind of the Church.

The nature of the Church as universal is compromised by division and disagreement. Since there is only partial agreement about what, universally, constitutes 'the Church' then there can be only partial recognition of the way in which bishops and episcopacy can serve our growing unity. The days are gone when churches existed in isolation without recognizing each other, at least in some measure. The bishop, as a representative of the universality of the Church, has a special role to play in relationships with other churches. The way in which bishops and church leaders relate to each other is both a reflection of and an encouragement to deeper Christian unity.

Similarly the Church as apostolic has two emphases: it is continuous with our Lord and the Apostles, and it is missionary, sent out to live and proclaim the truth of God. The bishop is a particular sign of that continuity. The apostolic succession is a sign, but not necessarily the guarantee, that the bishop represents the same Church which descends from Jesus and the Apostles. The fact that in any one place that faith is focused in a particular person means that for those who are willing to hear (and many are, even outside the ranks of committed Christians) his utterances are capable of bearing an authority which goes beyond the strength of personal conviction. The acceptance of that authority may be waning, but it has not yet entirely disappeared.

The role of the bishop as apostle, the one sent to be a leader of the mission of the Church, is slowly being recovered as secularism grows. It always has been an important part of the Church of England's understanding of mission in foreign lands, but it is increasingly the case that the bishop as the public representative of the Church seeks not only to defend the faith in society, but to promote its practice.

The Nature of Society

There are those who would characterize society as fragmented, secular, individualized, relativized and existential. The more one perceives society in that way, the more the Church is separated from it. But if one recognizes, as the Church of England does, that both Church and society are subject to the same influences, and that it is the task of the Church, as the divine society, to be a transforming force in society, then it is inevitable that the marks of society will exert particular pressures on the marks of the Church and thus influence the shape which the Church must take if it is to be heard. The old style of prelate, for example, corresponded well with social structures of the time. It was a style which could become worldly and corrupt (and often did). But it was also capable of transfiguration by the Gospel. Similarly, a more democratic style of episcopacy is capable both of seeming to dance to the world's tune and of revealing common humanity touched by God. Each society (and each church within it) is the product of its particular history. Episcopacy as practised in the Church of England is, in part at least, a product of our history and the pressures it has exerted upon us. Our history is evolutionary rather than revolutionary. We have preferred to preserve and reform ancient institutions rather than remake them. The fact that the majority of the world's Christians have done the same (often in circumstances much more revolutionary than ours) has confirmed us in our belief that it (or something like it) is God's way for us.

The Characteristics of Episcopacy as exercised in the Church of England

All recent ecumenical documents have recognized episcopacy as having three essential characteristics: personal, collegial and communal. These three characteristics inform the way the Bishop exercises his public role.

The life of the local Church (the diocese) is focussed in the person of the bishop. It is he who chooses (after advice) those to be ordained, and then ordains them. No-one may be ordained without being sponsored by a bishop. It is he who institutes or licences those who serve in the ordained ministry in his diocese. At their licensing he says 'Receive your cure and mine'. In his diocese he is the ordinary minister of the sacraments of baptism and the eucharist, although in his absence these are delegated to priests. He is the *pastor pastorum* and the invariable minister of confirmation. He is constantly visiting the parishes in his diocese, as a public sign that although the Church in each place is a full expression of the Church of God, it is in communion with all the other parishes and the wider Church. Although there may be many bodies in the diocese which enable a wide

166

number of people to share in God's work, most of the diocesan bodies are advisory and their recommendations need the bishop's approval. So he puts his personal stamp on what the diocese is doing.

Visitors from non-episcopal churches are sometimes surprised at, and suspicious of, the respect shown to the bishop. It is not always easy to see that the representative nature of his public role is essential to an understanding of the Church itself. It would be neither realistic nor theologically sound to expect this representative nature to be divorced from human characteristics, interests or weaknesses. So it is that a diocese is inevitably coloured by the character of its bishop. But it does not undermine his representative function.

Inevitably this makes a lot of work for one man. The practice has therefore arisen of consecrating suffragan bishops to share the diocesan bishop's responsibilities, and in his absence to be the bishop. Together, they exercise a corporate episcopate. Sometimes the diocesan delegates the oversight of a geographical area in the diocese to his suffragan (this usually happens when there is more than one suffragan), and sometimes, especially when there is only one suffragan, the two bishops share tasks with the ultimate responsibility remaining with the diocesan. Both are consecrated as bishops with the identical liturgy. Suffragans are part of the whole episcopate of the Church of England. In most respects, their public role is identical with that of diocesans.

In the personal exercise of his episcopate, the bishop is required to act collegially, that is in concert with his fellow bishops. The House of Bishops (all diocesan bishops and certain elected suffragans) meets regularly to review legislation in the General Synod, and to come to a mind on issues before the Church. All bishops receive all the papers of these meetings. In addition, there is an annual meeting of the whole college of bishops and there are regular regional meetings of all bishops. Matters of liturgy and doctrine receive special attention from the House of Bishops. In these ways, all bishops may take their part in the government and guidance of the Church. For example, in the debate about homosexuality, the bishops consulted carefully together about homosexuality and its practice. The resulting statement *Issues in Human Sexuality* commits each bishop to act and speak according to its provisions.

The result of this collegial responsibility is that individual bishops can represent the rest of the Church of England as spokesmen in all matters of concern to Church and society.

The Bishop is also required to act communally, that is, synodically. Although he has a wide freedom of guidance and leadership in his diocese, it is the diocesan synod which votes the money. In practice, most episcopal guidance (given after consultation) is accepted, but in the end it is the responsibility of the whole diocesan synod of bishops, clergy and lay people to decide whether or not any particular policy can be paid for.

Decisions for the Church of England as a whole are made by the General Synod. It is the duty of all bishops in the public exercise of their office to abide by decisions of the General Synod. Most decisions leave some room for flexibility of interpretation, but in the interests of cohesiveness it is necessarily limited. Bishops, for example, differed in their views of the ordination of women to the priesthood, but they are all committed to a common view that such ordinations are now the practice of the Church and that ensuring appropriate pastoral care for those who are opposed is equally a part of their oversight.

The Exercise of Episcopacy in the Wider Community

Often it is in the public exercising of episcopacy in the wider community which attracts the most attention and often criticism. The history and nature of the Church give it a particular if not always favoured position in society. As we noted earlier, there has been a gradual development of the Church of England from the time when the bishops had large temporal responsibilities to the present time when, although there is a lingering awareness of former history, usually illustrated by the presence of twenty-six bishops as members of the upper house of Parliament, the House of Lords, the Church of England in general and the bishops in particular have an ill-defined role in public consciousness. The Church, while trying to witness to Gospel truth, still speaks to the nation as a whole as well as specifically to itself. The reports *Faith in the City* and *Faith in the Countryside*, for example, were addressed equally to nation and Church. It still has some claim to represent the conscience of the nation.

This view of the history of the Church of England is supported by its understanding of membership. Membership is by baptism, not necessarily by conscious commitment. The result is that many regard themselves as members of the Church who have no obvious allegiance to it. This view of things provides a wide base for the public role of the bishop. He will, for example, be as concerned for secular institutions, and usually welcomed by them, as for religious ones. These will be not only those bodies which have traditional connections with the Church, like universities, schools, hospitals and prisons, but also research institutes, centres of business, commerce and industry, agriculture, government at all levels, social services, broadcasting and leisure. In planning his diary, the bishop usually tries to see that these are well represented.

Difficulties arise, however, when the bishop espouses causes which are socially divisive. The fact that he, as a conscientious Christian, campaigns against home-lessness, or the National Lottery, or for disarmament and animal welfare, does not mean that his views are representative of the Church as a whole. He has to be aware that by taking a strong line on a social or political issue (which he must do if it is a Christian view in which he believes), he is not making a statement repre-sentative of the Church as a whole, but a contribution to the Christian picture. In the early 1980s I associated myself with peace protesters, partly because I believed that the policy of nuclear deterrence was wrong, and partly because in the very Conservative Diocese of Ely, peace protesters were an oppressed minority. On one occasion I was preaching at a church in a small parish and as I left the church the churchwardens stood and shook their fists at me, saying, 'You don't represent us'. There are many occasions like this when Christians are reminded of the complex and sometimes painful nature of the Gospel they believe in. And by 'Christians', I do not necessarily mean only those who go to church.

In general, though, in the exercise of episcopacy in the wider community, the bishop will be called upon to give the Church's interpretation of something sig-nificant in the world. This may vary from the Archbishop of Canterbury's New Year message to the nation about the significance of time and its sanctification, through moral issues, like abortion or relationships in the Royal Family, to 'fun' questions like the nature of Association Football. Because of the world's continu-ing interest in the Church as a strange institution within society, he will need to address issues that are of significance in the Church and which arouse curiosity in the world. He will often be challenged to relate them to secular understanding of the world. These may range from the Church's doctrine of hell, through the behav-iour of charismatic churches, to the sale of episcopal palaces.

All these issues relate to bishops only to the extent that they are representatives of the Church. It is the representative nature of their office in a fallible, sinful, human institution, charged to proclaim divine truth, which is both a problem and an opportunity.

The Declaration of Assent

(As required by Measure and by canon law from 1st September 1975)

PREFACE (*to be read by the person requiring the Declaration*)

The Church of England is part of the One, Holy, Catholic and Apostolic Church worshipping the one true God, Father, Son and Holy Spirit. It professes the faith uniquely revealed in the Holy Scriptures and set forth in the catholic creeds, which faith the Church is called upon to proclaim afresh in each generation. Led by the Holy Spirit, it has borne witness to Christian truth in its historic formularies, the Thirty-nine Articles of Religion, the Book of Common Prayer and the Ordering of Bishops, Priests and Deacons. In the declaration you are about to make will you affirm your loyalty to this inheritance of faith as your inspiration and guidance under God in bringing the grace and truth of Christ to this generation and making Him known to those in your care?

DECLARATION OF ASSENT

I, A.B., do so affirm and accordingly declare my belief in the faith which is revealed in the Holy Scriptures and set forth in the catholic creeds and to which the historic formularies of the Church of England bear witness; and in public prayer and administration of the sacraments, I will use only the forms of service which are authorized or allowed by Canon.

I, A.B., swear by Almighty God that I will be faithful and bear true allegiance to her Majesty, Queen Elizabeth II, her heirs and successors, according to law. So help me God.

I, A.B., swear by Almighty God that I will render true and canonical obedience to the Lord Bishop of Ely and his successors in all things lawful and honest. So help me God.

The Episcopal Office of Oversight in the German Churches, its Public Status and its Involvement in Church Decisions in History and in the Present

Axel Freiherr von Campenhausen

I

The protestant bishop is a pastor who is called to the office of church leadership for the area of a territorial church. He shares the one ecclesial ministry, which exists in the Church according to its institution (and which can therefore be called *iuris divini*), with all pastors. The office of oversight, visitation and ordination, which is an institution of human church law (therefore *iuris humani*), he shares with further holders of episcopal offices of oversight, who are called *Superintendent, Landessuperintent, Dekan, Kreisdekan, Prälat* or *Propst*. The particularity of the office of a protestant bishop lies in the fact that he exercises the episcopal functions in the whole territorial church, that he represents his part of the Church externally and internally, that he leads the territorial church jointly with other (differently named) leading bodies and in particular stands over against the territorial synod.

The German protestant bishops stand, as ordained pastors, in the succession of the ministry of proclamation. Through their ordination they also stand in the succession of the laying on of hands which has been customary since apostolic times. Whether this is a matter of the laying on of hands by bishops or presbyters or even of a physically unbroken chain of the laying on of hands since the Apostles is not of principal interest, because this is only a matter of the spiritual identity of the Church.[1]

This understanding of the protestant office of bishop enjoys general recognition today. This can be confirmed by glancing at the church constitutions[2] and at the literature of ecclesiastical law.[3] The path to this position, in which jurisprudence and practice meet, was not without obstacles.

The Reformers provided no basis for it. Rather, it was the development of the external life of the church after the religious Peace of Augsburg (1555), which was shaped by the superimposition of state law, which did so.

Taking up biblical language afresh, the Reformers and confessional documents understand the episcopal office in two ways. First, according to the protestant understanding, the 'right episcopal and visitation office' (WA 26, 197, 12ff) is identical with the office of the proclamation of the Word and administration of the Sacraments. There is only one ministry *iuris divini*. Luther uses the terms *'episcopi, ministri seu pastores'* synonymously (WA 12, 194, 1f); the Augsburg Confession followed him in this (CA 28). Alongside this, the episcopal office is an office of human church law for the leadership of the Church. The Reformation and the confessional documents (CA, Smalcald Articles) sought to preserve the traditional office of bishop, so far as this is defensible in the light of the Gospel, that is as the office to which the visitation, examination and ordination of pastors is entrusted.[4]

With its functions limited in this way, the Reformers were prepared to recognize episcopal government as a useful, praiseworthy, but nevertheless human ordering, and to submit themselves to it for the sake of peace, but also because it would be dangerous to change legitimate ordering arbitrarily.[5]

The power of the Church (spiritual force) is, according to this understanding, the force of the Word. It is the basis for the one ministry of the Church. The functions of this ministry are the proclamation of the Word, including the burden of doctrinal assessment and condemnation of false doctrine, the administration of the Sacraments and the power of the keys. It is through these functions that the Church is led.[6] In the present context the breakthrough of the Reformation can therefore be said to have occurred in two points. First, the church leadership dispenses with any support by external force. It must achieve its ends by its intrinsic authority, *non vi sed verbo*. Secondly, this church power, which CA 28 does not hesitate to call *jurisdictio*, is entrusted to all holders of the one ministry of the Church equally. The Reformers and the confessional documents do not only use the terms *episcopus, minister, presbyter* and *pastor* synonymously, but they all start from the premise of the unity of the ministry. That means that all servants of the Church participate to the same extent in the divinely instituted ministry.

Moreover, it was precisely the transfer of the secular functions of the episcopal office to the princes and its limitation to spiritual functions which the bishops of the Reformation era in Germany rejected, with few exceptions. The resignations of individuals and the ordination and installation of some protestant bishops in Saxony, Prussia and Brandenburg were the exception. They remained mere episodes.[7]

The function of the former episcopal office lived on in the protestant superintendents. If Germany before the Reformation had people with the title of bishops who did not exercise episcopal functions or did not do so rightly,[8] so after the

Reformation it at first had clergymen who carried out the functions of the episcopal office, but used other titles.[9]

With the word *Superintendent* (also *Superattendens*), the Reformers did not only take over a Latin translation of the Greek *episkopos*; they also thereby held fast to the episcopal office itself.[10]

So far as it seemed defensible in the light of the Gospel, the traditional office of bishop was to remain. But even under the name *Superintendent* the protestant office of bishop could not develop freely. Already in the *Instructions for Visitors*, it is not only the characteristic tasks of the ecclesial office of oversight which are assigned to the Superintendents; here already their co-option in the service of the authorities' concern for moral discipline begins.[11]

And the more the government of the church by princes with its characteristic consistorial bureaucracy developed, the more the specific approach of the protestant office of oversight within the uniform ministry of the church was covered over by secular law and its development hindered. The awareness of the problem remained, however; that can be seen from the theoretical attempts to limit the influence of the prince over the spiritual leadership of the Church.[12]

The decisive steps towards an independent office of bishop came in the nineteenth century.

It was the conscientiousness of the Prussian King as *Summus Episcopus* which gave a new push to the development that was to culminate in the establishment of an independent protestant office of bishop. The roots from which it grew were the office of *Superintendent* and that of *Generalsuperintendent*.[13]

In 1828 the office of General Superintendent was newly created by Friedrich Wilhelm III, its particular powers being listed in an Instruction for Prussia's eastern provinces of 14 May 1829. This Instruction was extended to the western provinces on 31 May 1836.[14]

According to this Instruction, the General Superintendents were clergymen on whom the oversight over several Superintendents' areas was conferred alongside the provincial consistories (1). They were to 'inform themselves of the condition of protestant church life..., particularly through personal contact, although correspondence for the completion and facilitation of this personal activity should not be completely excluded' (2). They were 'to encourage, to assist, and to mediate' (5). In particular, they were given oversight over the 'manner of teaching' of the clergy, the family and official life of church officials, and care for 'the maintenance and the establishment of the purity, order and dignity of public worship' (6). They were to encourage, nourish and support the continuing education of the clergy (6) and have an eye on the preparation of candidates (6). They could participate as members of the Consistory in the examinations of the latter, in order to 'be placed in a position to obtain a precise knowledge of the depth and breadth of their education and the character of their theological tendency' (20). Their primary task was 'the business of church visitation' at the seats of the Superintendents (7ff). Alongside this regularly recurring business of visitation, which was to be linked with inspection of the registers and archives, they could take part in the Superintendents' visitations (13) and not least, from time to time undertake extraordinary and unexpected examinations on the spot...'(14). 'Among their duties is the personal introduction of newly appointed Superintendents' (15) and 'moreover, the matter of ordination' (22). They were involved in the oversight of schools (6, 13) and examined the 'annual conduct lists about clergy and schoolmasters' which the Superintendents submitted (23). The General Superintendents were to act as 'paternal carers' (5). They formed 'no intermediate instance' of authority (3). In their liturgical acts, such as the 'ceremony' of the introduction of a Superintendent, they were to 'knit the bonds of fraternal fellowship amongst the diocesan clergy tighter together by the introduction of a new mediator...' (16).

Despite the bureaucratic style of this Instruction it is unmistakeable that in the office of General Superintendent the church's office of oversight and visitation achieved independence once more.

In fact, this Instruction of the Prussian King as *Summus Episcopus* served as an example to all the German territorial churches. The catalogue of tasks of territorial bishops in the church constitutions of the twentieth century has remained to a substantial extent the same.[15]

The strange thing in all of this is that the initiative for the establishment of the office of Superintendent represented the efforts of the pious King for a spirit-filled strengthening of the government of the church by princes. He hoped to find in the General Superintendents people who enjoyed both the confidence of the King on the one hand and that of the pastors on the other.

Admittedly, the General Superintendent still clearly displayed the characteristics of a high royal official. The fact that his office was derived from royal authority was also shown when the title of bishop or even archbishop was bestowed by royal grace and favour, rather like an Order, and by the fact that this did not prevent the General Superintendents from being described as royal commissaries in para. 52b of the Rhenish-Westphalian Church Order, even in the version of 1908.

The other root of the protestant episcopal office was the office of Superintendent. After the Reformation, as we have seen, this was soon integrated into the system of government of the church by princes. The Superintendent was not the holder of a state office of oversight, but the agent of the lowest ('district') synodical association, the synod and standing committee of which he chaired.[16] He was therefore precisely not a state agent of oversight and a clergyman at the same time, but rather he was always a clergyman who as Superintendent was the exponent and representative of the district synod. Because of the government of the church by princes, the state may have played a role in the appointment of a clergyman as Superintendent, but as Superintendent he was nevertheless the holder of a spiritual office which derived from the Synod, and the latter was a spiritual institution.[17]

The office of Superintendent thereby contributed an element to the development which the office of General Superintendent still lacked. The latter was truly set up in an episcopal manner, but the General Superintendent nevertheless exercised his office because of the royal will and because of his royal office stood over against the Synods which were church institutions. The office of Superintendent, by contrast, was not furnished with episcopal powers in the sense in which the Reformers and the modern church constitutions understand the office of territorial bishop. The Superintendent is, rather, the chairman and agent of the Synod.[18]

II

The outward occasion for the restoration of the protestant episcopal office in Germany was the abolition of the role of the prince as *Summus Episcopus* in 1918. The fact that this transition took place without great outward upheavals is linked with the fact that the protestant churches had already received a complete church constitution with their own church institutions in the course of the nineteenth century. In establishing these, use had been made of older theories of ecclesiastical law, according to which the King embodied two legal persons – on the one hand the ruler of the state and on the other hand the emergency bishop of the protestant church. In this character, he had, in the course of the nineteenth century, gradually extracted the churches from the immediate administration of the state and, by establishing a body called the *Evangelischer Oberkirchenrat*, had ended direct control by the state authorities. In 1919, therefore, it was only a question of deciding who should now fill the vacant position which had previously been occupied by the *Summus Episcopus*. The episcopal question was soon the subject of lively discussion. 'In almost all German protestant territorial churches the question of whether, alongside the synodical and the consistorial elements, the episcopal element should not also be incorporated in the constitutional structure had been occasioned by the need to revise their constitutions. It was not, however, proposed that the supreme episcopacy of the prince, which had collapsed because of the upheaval in the state, should be re-established in some modernized form, but rather a case of including the ministry in the constitutional life of the church and, in a manner appropriate to its nature, involving it in the leadership of the church.'[19]

175

Initially, both the function and the title of the office were disputed.[20] A distinction must therefore be made here between the introduction of the episcopal office in the new church constitutions on the one hand, and the title '*Bischof*' or '*Landesbischof*', on the other hand, which is not necessarily linked with it. The importance of this is shown by the fact that the Bavarian Church Constitution, which created 'the most powerful and weighty office of bishop in German protestantism', gave the holder of this office the title 'Church President'.[21]

In the old Prussian Territorial Church too, the position of General Superintendent was so constructed that it was clear from the beginning that 'they will be bishops with the title General Superintendent'.[22]

A survey of the church constitutions after 1919 shows that the bishops or holders of the episcopal office had the following responsibilities:[23]

–   gathering together and caring for all elements in the church, fostering and watching over them;

–   watching over and fostering the training and continuing education of the clergy;

–   pastoral counselling of the clergy;

–   leading theological examinations and responsibility for the theological colleges;

–   the right of ordination, as a rule competing with the occupants of regional episcopal offices;

–   nomination rights for clergy appointments;

–   the installation of Superintendents, Provosts, Deans, General Superintendents, Rural Deans;

–   regular discussions with the Superintendents, Deans, General Superintendents;

–   the right of visitation, in part competing with the Superintendents;

–   watching over and fostering youth work, pursuing church interests in schools, watching over the work of church voluntary organizations, home and overseas missions, etc. Ordering services of repentance and celebration, etc.;

–   consecration of churches and worship centres;

–   the right to address pastoral letters to the clergy and parishes of the territorial church, which are to be read in public worship and published in the official church gazette;

– the right to preach during public worship in all parishes.

The view prevails throughout that the bishop must be in touch continually with the central authorities of the church. As a rule, he is also the legal head of the territorial church.

This involves the following responsibilities:

– representation of the territorial church externally;

– the appointment of clergy and church officials;

– the signature and execution of laws and regulations.

In addition to this there is the bishop's involvement in the central authorities of the church, often as chairman. Because of his pastoral duties, the holder of the episcopal office is only rarely given disciplinary powers. The bishop is (like the other members of the governing and administrative bodies) as a rule excluded from membership of the territorial synod, but has the right, sometimes even the duty, to take part in and speak during sittings of the synod.[24] It is above all in Bavaria that the bishop has an independent position over against the territorial synod (right to delay decisions, right to dissolve the territorial synod – Art. 36, 37). The territorial bishop is appointed for life, i.e. until the normal retirement age. Several territorial churches have gone over to appointing the bishop for a term of years.[25]

III

Everywhere in Germany the territorial bishop or leading clergyman is entrusted with the representation of the church externally, not least therefore representing the church to the state.

The relationship between state and church was regulated comprehensively at the time of the end of the monarchies, in a way which was able to build on centuries-old arrangements. The Christian character of the state and the preference for the Christian creed over against others were removed in the process. The provisions of the Imperial Constitution of 1919 were taken over word for word into the basic law of the Federal Republic of Germany in 1949. This set the context, the detail being supplied by the *Länder*, with which the main responsibility for matters relevant to the church traditionally lies.

The guarantee of religious freedom (Art. 4 GG) is fundamental. It is underlined by the organizational separation of state and church, which is described by the strange sentence 'There is no state church' (Art. 140 GG, together with Art. 137 (I) WRV). What is important for Germany is that this separation follows the laws of the German Constitution and cannot therefore be compared with the separation of state and church in the USA, in France or in the Eastern bloc which corresponds with it only verbally. Here it was not a case of combatting the church. It was also not to be disturbed in its external circumstances by state manipulation. It was above all a case of untying the traditional institutional bond between throne and altar which had existed throughout Europe since Constantine the Great. The state dispensed with its confessional link. The church lost its preferential treatment, but won for the first time in its history complete freedom and responsibility, also for its external form. A mood such as that expressed by the slogan 'cut the connection' was not determinative.[26] The purpose of the German Constitution was to secure freedom for all citizens equally. This had the consequence for the church that the centuries-old state supervision of the church stopped. The involvement of the state in the appointment of the leading clergy lost its original meaning and was continued at most in the form of an oath to the Constitution on the part of the Roman Catholic bishops or polite enquiries whether there were any reservations. This, however, is an expression of courtesy and not of sovereign power on the part of the state.

Since the state and the church have the same people as members and are active in many of the same fields of work (school, nursery school, hospital, old people's home) and since citizens have the right to exercise their religious freedom within the confines of state institutions (hospital, army, prison), consultation is needed so that state and church authorities do not come into conflict and the state, maybe without wishing to do so, does not infringe religious and church freedom. While the state exercised oversight over the church, many things could be sorted out through internal official channels. Contrary to what one might at first sight suspect, the legal independence of both institutions makes discussions necessary to a much greater degree than they were before. This is the reason why countless agreements with the Roman Catholic Church and the protestant churches, and later also with small religious bodies, have been made in Germany since 1924. Here it is a case not least of regulating co-operation in areas which are of interest to both sides. For some such questions the Constitution itself envisaged and made provision for co-operation. This applies to religious education, which, under Art. 7 GG, is to be given as part of the teaching provided by the state in all state schools (with certain exceptions) according to the principles of the respective religious bodies. For the theological faculties there are regulations in the Constitution of the *Länder*, but above all in the agreements between church and state, as to how the state involves the churches in the appointment of theology professors, who of course perform both church and state functions. Finally, there are agreements about army, prison and hospital chaplaincies. It is important to note that all these rights can of course be exercised especially by the churches to whom a large part of the population belongs, but that legally other religious bodies also have the same possibilities. The fact that Muslims have so far not made use of the right to levy church tax and provide religious education is connected with their internal problems. They have difficulties in organizing themselves, because at home they were not organized in membership institutions. The state, on the other hand, can understandably not dispense with discovering who belongs to the religious body which is claiming rights for itself.

For our context, the German system is characterized by the fact that it links in the best way possible legal independence with readiness for co-operation between the institutions of state and church in many areas, and in some cases regulates this. State and church work on the basis that religious freedom and separation of state and church necessitates both distance and co-operation in equal measure.

It is in these contexts that the bishops come to the fore once more. They are the natural spokesmen of the church, and the authority of the episcopal office makes possible the establishment of some contacts which would otherwise be more difficult. Within the church, however, bishops are in the protestant understanding in no sense autocrats, but form one of a number of agents of leadership in the territorial church, such as the synod, synodical standing committee, the church administration, and a body (often called the Church Leadership) which brings the other bodies together. The territorial bishop speaks for them all. Agreements under state ecclesiastical law often envisaged that the state and the church should be ready to solve any problems which arise together in a friendly spirit. For this purpose, provision is made for regular contact and discussions, as well as for official visits by new office-holders.

It is not least the public image of the churches which indicates that although the churches often behave like large associations they are not submerged by this role. Unlike associations, their position is regulated by the Constitution itself, not, as was earlier the case, in the interest of Christian truth, but today in the interest of the freedom which is enjoyed by all citizens. In the process, significant possibilities for action in secular society result for the churches.

What remains above all from the upheavals of the Church Struggle is the widespread recognition of the episcopal office as one of the factors of the protestant churches' life and constitution. This is reflected in the adoption of the title of Bishop in Württemberg and Bavaria[27] and in the literature on the episcopal office since the war.[28] What now occurred was – from the point of view of ecclesiastical law – essentially the development of the legal position which had been won and the systematic determination of the relationship of the episcopal office to other offices of leadership.

Notes

1. For the understanding of the ordination (or consecration) of Amsdorff as Bishop of Naumburg by
    Luther cf. P. Brunner, *Nikolaus von Amsdorff als Bischof von Naumburg*, p. 60ff. Amsdorff him-
    self expressed the same view: 'For title, name and office have no effect, therefore the Church
    does not descend to their successors, unless this voice of our dear Lord and Shepherd Jesus Christ
    comes with it. For that reason it is of no help to the mass-priests that they glory in the apostolic
    succession, because they do not have the succcession of the word and teaching of Christ. If, how-
    ever, they could glory in the succession of the word, we should be glad to regard them as part and
    parcel of the Christian Church.' (*Antwort Glaub und Bekenntnis auff das schöne und liebliche
    INTERIM, Niclasen Amsdorffs des verjagten Bischoffs zur Naumburgk*, in *Nikolaus von
    Amsdorff, Ausgewählte Schriften*, ed. O. Lerche (1938), p. 50.)

    The theological basis for the ministry and therefore for ordination in the Reformation period have
    not yet been studied exhaustively. The following studies are of value: W. Brunotte, *Das geistliche
    Amt bei Luther* (1959), E. Kinder, *Der evangelische Glaube und die Kirche* (2nd edn, 1960), H.
    Lieberg, *Amt und Ordination bei Luther und Melanchthon* (1962). Also S. Grundmann,
    Sacerdotium – Ministerium – Ecclesia particularis (1959) and *Kirche, allgemeines Priestertum
    und kirchliches Amt* (1962), now in *Abhandlungen zum Kirchenrecht* (1959), p. 156ff, 454ff.
    Although these studies address our problem, they treat the questions predominantly in terms of
    the history of doctrine, rather than adopting a truly historical approach. For this, see G.
    Kretschmar, *Die Ordination im frühen Christentum* and a further promised work about the
    Reformation understanding of ordination.

2. Cf. among the church orders: *Grundordnung der Ev. Landeskirche in Baden*, § 120 Abs. 1: '(1)
    The *Landesbischof* is the holder of the preaching office who is called to service in the leadership
    of the church, who calls the congregations and ministers of the territorial church under God's
    word. As the clergy lead the local congregations, so the *Landesbischof* leads the territorial church
    through God's word. He can hold services and other gatherings in all congregations of the terri-
    torial church.' *Verfassung der Ev.-Luth Kirche in Bayern*, Art. 59, Abs. 1: '(1) The *Landesbischof*
    is a clergyman, who is called to the ministry of church leadership for the area of the Evangelical-
    Lutheran Church in Bavaria'.

3. What follows is based on v. Campenhausen, *Entstehung und Funktionen des bischöflichen Amtes
    in den evangelischen Kirchen in Deutschland* (1975), now in *Gesammelte Abhandlungen* (1995),
    p. 8ff.

4. 'For bishop means an overseer or visitor and archbishop one who is overseer and visitor over the
    bishops, so that every clergyman should visit his parishioners (*pfarkinder*), wait and oversee how
    they teach and live. And the archbishop should visit bishops, wait and oversee how they teach.'
    (WA 26, 196, 5ff); cf. *Tractatus de potestate et primatu papae*, paras 61ff, in *Die
    Bekenntnisschriften der evangelisch-lutherischen Kirche* (5th edn, 1963), p. 489ff; Apol. XIX;
    Schmalk. Art. 1, part III, Art. X.

Here the Reformation went back to the practice of the early Church, where every congregation was led by an ordained bishop. Whether in fact bishops in the early Church undertook the tasks of the parish minister of today cannot be answered uniformly. In areas where even smaller towns had a bishop, we can assume that this was so, but in Antioch it can hardly have been the case. H. Dörries, 'Erneuerung des kirchlichen Amts im vierten Jahrhundert', in Moeller and Ruhbach (eds), *Bleibendes im Wandel der Kirchengeschichte* (1973), pp. 1ff, 4.

5. All the arguments in the *Bedenken der Wittenberger Theologen* (1530), composed by Melanchthon, Corp. Ref. T. II, Sp. 280ff. (283, 284) and in the contemporary *Gutachten, ibid.*, T. II, Sp. 373ff, 376. On this (with extensive quotations) L. Richter, *Geschichte der evangelischen Kirchenverfassung in Deutschland* (1851, reprinted 1970), pp. 62ff, 67ff; fundamentally: P. Brunner, 'Vom Amt des Bischofs. Pro Ecclesia', *Gesammelte Aufsätze*, I (1962), p. 235f.

6. If the protestant church orders of the sixteenth century take this meaning of church leadership – that is government of the Church through God's word alone – over into protestant church law, they take up the language of the pre-Reformation Church in doing so. There too *regere ecclesiam* was used to refer to the spiritual leadership of the congregation. That also is why the parish minister was called *ecclesiae rector*. Cf. Richter, Dove and Kahl, *Lehrbuch des katholischen und evangelischen Kirchenrechts* (8th edn, 1886), p. 526, n. 7 and p. 465ff.

7. Cf. A. Nicolovius, *Die bischöfliche Würde in Preussens evangelischer Kirche* (1834); E. Benz, *Bischofsamt und apostolische Sukzession im deutschen Protestantismus (1953); P. Brunner, Nikolaus von Amsdorf als Bischof von Naumburg* (1961).

8. Cf. Melanchthon, *De abusibus Ecclesiarum emendandis* (1541), Corp. Ref. T. IV, Sp. 542ff. The decisive passage is cited in Richter, *Geschichte der Kirchenverfassung*, p. 69.

9. Elert strongly emphasizes the 'episcopal character' of the superintendency constitution in an essay of the same name in *Luthertum*, 46 (1935), p. 353.

10. The bishops in Sweden, Denmark, Norway and Schleswig used the title Superintendent for a time. P. Brunner, *Amsdorf*, p. 12, emphasizes that it was in the office of Superintendent that the unity of *pastor* and *episcopus* was best maintained, thereby matching best the office of bishop in the early Church.

11. WA 26, 235, 21ff; Sehling, vol. 1, p. 149ff (171).

12. Those who advocated the episcopal system, like the early collegialists, developed their theories of state ecclesiastical law with a view to binding the prince into the church organism, explaining his functions in the Church ecclesiastically, but also limiting them.

Martin Heckel, *Staat und Kirche nach den Lehren der evangelischen Juristen Deutschlands in der ersten Hälfte des 17. Jahrhunderts* (1968); Klaus Schlaich, *Kollegialtheorie. Kirche, Recht und Staat in der Aufklärung* (1969) and 'Kirchenrecht und Vernunftrecht. Kirche und Staat in der Sicht der Kollegialtheorie', *ZevKR*, 14 (1968/69), p. 1ff. On Johann Gerhard and his helpful distinction between spiritual leadership and the power of the sovereign, cf. Wilhelm Maurer,

'Geistliche Leitung und Leitung der Kirche' in Frör and Maurer, *Hirtenamt und mündige Gemeinde* (1966), pp. 51ff, 57ff; Martin Honecker, *Cura religionis Magistratus Christiani. Studien zum Kirchenrecht im Luthertum des 17. Jahrhunderts, insbesondere bei Johann Gerhard* (1968).

13. On the following see especially, in addition to the literature listed above, W. Maurer, *Das synodale evangelische Bischofsamt*, p. 8ff.

14. For the text, see Hinschius, *Das Preußische Kirchenrecht im Gebiete des Allgemeinen Landrechts. Abdruck von Theil II Titel 11 aus der achten Auflage von C.F. Kochs Kommentar zum Allgemeinen Landrecht* (1884), p. 161ff. In what follows, the numbers in brackets represent the section numbers of the *Instruktion*.

15. This is pointed out by W. Maurer, *Das synodale evangelische Bischofsamt*, p.8.

16. P. Schoen, *loc. cit.*, p. 264. This was the legal position in the West from the coming into force of the *Rheinisch-Westfälische Kirchenordnung* in 1835, in the East from the *Kirchengemeinde- und Synodalordnung* of 1873.

17. This is not affected by the fact that the synod was often seen as paralleling secular parliaments. That they were comparable neither with corporations of the estates or with parliaments, but were ecclesiastical bodies, was clear from the beginning. The parliamentary misunderstanding seems ineradicable, as the modern democratization in the churches shows.

    On the understanding and self-understanding of the synod cf. from the flood of literature S. Grundmann, *Abhandlungen zum Kirchenrecht*, pp. 99ff, 139ff, 476ff; A. v. Campenhausen, 'Synoden in der evangelischen Kirche', in *Synode. Amtliche Mitteilungen der Synode der Bistümer in der Bundesrepublik Deutschland*, no. 4 (1971), p. 4ff; G. Heinemann, 'Das Verhältnis von Synode und Parlament', in E. Lomberg (ed.), *Emder Synode 1571-1971* (1973), p. 285ff. Against this repeated demand for a parliamentary understanding of synods in R. v. Thadden, 'Kirche ohne Demokratie?' in Böll, Gollwitzer and Carlo Schmid, *Anstoß und Ermutigung. Gustav W. Heinemann, Bundespräsident 1969-1974* (1974), p. 111ff.

18. It has remained thus in Westphalia and the Rhineland to this day, and this is how the office of *Präses* of these churches is explained. 'The Präses of the territorial synod is chairman of the church leadership and of the church office' (Art. 200 *Kirchenordnung der Ev. Kirche im Rheinland*; derived from this, Art. 148, Abs. 1 *Kirchenordnung der Ev. Kirche von Westfalen*).

19. P. Schoen, 'Der deutsche evangelische Bischof nach den neuen evangelischen Kirchenverfassungen', *Verw Arch*, 30 (1925), pp. 403ff.

20. *Die Religion in Geschichte und Gegenwart* reflected this controversial situation in 1927 when it did not include an article about the episcopal office, but only one about the 'question of episcopacy': cf. *RGG* (2nd edn), i (1927), col. 1131.

21. P. Schoen, 'Der deutsche evangelische Bischof', *loc. cit.*, p. 406 and R. Oeschey, *Verfassung der ev.-luth. Kirche in Bayern r. d. Rhs.* (1921), p. lv, already point to this.

22. Thus Frhr. von Soden in the *auserordentliche Kirchenversammlung zur Feststellung der Verfassung für die Evangelische Landeskirche der älteren Provinzen Preußens. Erster Teil, Sitzungsverhandlungen* (Berlin, 1923), p. 122. The Prussian Church Constitution itself justified this view, when it saw the bestowal of the name of bishop on the General Superintendents as solely involving a change in the title of the office, to which which Art. 111 (2) 6 refers as a possibility. Quoted by P. Schoen, *loc. cit.*, p. 405.

23. P. Schoen, *loc. cit.*, p. 414ff, and *Das neue Verfassungsrecht der evangelischen Landeskirchen in Preussen* (1929), p. 165ff; W. Maurer, *Das synodale evangelische Bischofsamt seit 1918*, p. 17ff, Irmtraut Tempel, *Bischofsamt und Kirchenleitung* (1966).

24. In Nassau, Bavaria, Brunswick and Lübeck the Bishop has no duty to give information to the Synod; in Hanover and Nassau the Bishop is responsible to the Synod.

25. Martin Heckel, 'Kirchenreformfragen im Verfassungssystem. Zur Befristung von Leitungsämtern in einer lutherischen Landeskirche', *ZevKR*, 40 (1995), p. 180ff.

26. Colin Buchanan, *Cut the Connection. Disestablishment and the Church of England* (London, 1994).

27. *Württembergisches Vorläufiges kirchliches Gesetz zur Ermächtigung des Kirchenpräsidenten* of 15.5.1933 (ABl., vol. 26, p. 54; AKBl., p. 164); proclamation of the *Evangelischer Oberkirchenrat* about the title of office of the Church President of 8.7.1933 (ABl., vol. 26, p. 128).

28. Cf. from the literature on ecclesiastical law the publications listed in the articles 'Bischof' III and IV (Tröger), *TRE*, vi (1980).

The Current Exercise of Episcopacy within the Church of England, reflecting on the Respective Relations of Church and State[1]

John Moses

Canon law declares that the Church of England, which is established according to the laws of the realm, belongs to the true and apostolic Church of Christ.[2] This statement affirms the wider community of faith and order to which the Church of England belongs, but recognizes the historical process by which it has evolved. Establishment provides the legal framework within which the Church of England offers public ministry to the whole community. Establishment does not determine the fundamentals of faith and order – the scriptures, the sacraments, the credal statements, the orders of ministry – but it has unquestionably influenced the Church of England's self-awareness and the wider perceptions which have facilitated or inhibited the exercise of ministry. Establishment does not determine the nature and function of the episcopate in the Church, but it has shaped to some degree the expectations that surround the office of a bishop.

The authority of a bishop in the Church of England derives from his ordination and from his office in the Church as a guardian of the word and of the sacraments. But he is inevitably caught up in a web of expectations which are inseparable from the position of the Church of England as the established church whose distinctive task is to offer public ministry to the community in its entirety.

A bishop is required to embody a variety of roles and responsibilities which belong to the Church as a whole. He is the focus of the Church's unity. He is the chief pastor and teacher. He lives out so far as he is able the Church's apostolic calling. Establishment has importance for our purposes only in so far as the bishop has been entrusted with the guardianship of the Church and its doctrine and, therefore, of an institution which possesses a philosophy of history, a set of values and a way of looking at life which are judged by Christian people to be essential to the health of the Church and of the wider community.

The ordinals of the Church of England reflect the special insights of their respective periods. The Book of Common Prayer was concerned to restore to the offices of bishop and priest the emphasis upon the teaching ministry that had been lost. The Alternative Service Book reflects the substantial changes that have taken place in thinking concerning the nature of the Church and the relation of the bishop to its mission.

The Form of Ordaining or Consecrating of an Archbishop or Bishop in the Book of Common Prayer places its primary emphasis on the teaching office of the bishop, but there is strong emphasis also on the discipline of the bishop's office and on the life of holiness to which the bishop is called.

The Ordination or Consecration of a Bishop in the Alternative Service Book makes reference to all the priorities that are to be found in the Book of Common Prayer, but it fails to give a special emphasis to any one of them. The declaration that is read by the Archbishop sets out the multiplicity of tasks that are laid upon a bishop and reflects the contemporary understanding of episcopacy and the contemporary expectations surrounding the episcopal office.

But the primary emphasis in the service is on leadership. The opening words of the declaration remind the congregation that 'A bishop is called to lead in serving and caring for the people of God and to work with them in the oversight of the church'. The final question that is asked of the bishop-designate concerns his willingness to 'lead your people to obey our Saviour's command to make disciples of all nations'. The prayer that follows immediately upon the laying on of hands asks for grace and power that the bishop 'may lead those committed to his charge in proclaiming the gospel of salvation'. The post-communion collect has at its heart the petition that the bishop 'may lead the people committed to his charge'.

The Book of Common Prayer and the Alternative Service Book both take much for granted. The duties and functions of a bishop are set out in broad terms. There are, however, six areas where the bishop is required to exercise his ministry.

First, *leadership*. The bishop is required to exercise leadership in the Church and in society at large. He is a symbol and an enabler of the unity of the Church in its mission. He presides over its liturgy. He is the ordinary – the original or primary expositor of the word and minister of the sacraments. It is by his authority that the ministry of word and sacraments is exercised. He is the head of the family of the Church in its wholeness, the centre of its life and love. He represents the Church to itself and to the wider community in a way that is impossible for any other person. He is a public representative.

Secondly, *teaching*. The bishop is the guardian of the Church's apostolic faith. He is required to teach and to interpret that faith. His teaching ministry will require an informed awareness of what is happening in the world, a working knowledge of contemporary concerns. His office gives him the freedom to speak with an independent mind and a questioning and critical voice. Indeed, his responsibility to teach and defend the faith will demand at times that he shall also be a voice of conscience within society – locally and nationally – proclaiming the justice of God in the context of the gospel of loving redemption.

Thirdly, *pastoral care*. It is expected that the bishop will be a pastor to his clergy, to the people of his diocese. Many of these expectations will be unrealistic, but it is required that he will 'know his people and be known by them'.[3] There will be many occasions when the bishop is required to be a pastor, but for much of the time it will be sufficient for him to provide a framework of support, supervision, assessment and pastoral care. It is necessary that he is known to be a man who will find time for people, a man who has empathy, a practical commonsense and a quiet godliness.

Fourthly, *administration*. The bishop of a diocese is required to administer his diocese, to exercise the jurisdiction that belongs to his office, even though the administration and the jurisdiction will often be exercised by others acting on his behalf and with his authority. A combination of factors – and especially the evolution of synodical government and the expansion of the administrative apparatus of diocesan life – have led to a massive increase in the administrative load that is carried by all bishops.

Fifthly, *authority*. There are constraints upon the authority of the bishop which derive in large measure from the checks and balances within the life of the Church of England, but there are three distinct ways in which the bishop exercises authority. First, the bishop of a diocese is the chief minister and it is in this capacity that he gives authority to others – to candidates at their ordination; to incumbents at their institution; to all who hold his licence for public ministry. Secondly, the bishop has responsibility for the integrity of the Church's life and circumstances may arise in which he is required to exercise discipline. Thirdly, there is an affirmation – a formal or informal validation – which he gives by virtue of his involvement in the life of the parish or of an institution within the community which is inseparable from the authority of his office. He is required to endorse by his presence what is happening around him.

Sixthly, *collegiality*. There is an ancient tradition of collegiality in the episcopal office. Indeed, it is a part of the wider responsibility that a bishop has for the integrity and coherence of the Church that he shall hold, together with his brother bishops, corporate responsibility for these things at diocesan, provincial, national and international levels. Collegiality takes on a new interpretation in the contemporary Church through the work of synodical government. A bishop's collegiality is expressed not merely through membership of the House of Bishops in Diocesan and General Synods but through his participation with clergy and laypeople in the governmental life of the Church.

I suspect that all observers of the English scene would speak about the work of the bishop in words that are not dissimilar to the ones that I have used, but the overall title of this morning's session requires us to consider the public status, roles and place in decision-making of those exercising episcopacy in the Church of England *in today's world*. The question must therefore be asked, what are the peculiarities of the English situation which shape the context, the contemporary framework, in which episcopacy is exercised?

By contrast with most other churches in Western Europe, the Church of England has retained to a significant degree its constitutional relationship with the state, its historic privileges, and a vital place within the network of expectations and opportunities that are part and parcel of the life of the local community. Churchmen might disagree about the appropriateness of a continuing establishment of religion, but what cannot be denied is the extent to which the Church as an institution remains embedded within the structures, the fabric, the expectations and the opportunities of community life.

It may well be the case that there are many for whom establishment provides a recognition of the place of religion – of the Christian religion – within English society; but any analysis of today's world – of the contemporary scene – is bound to take serious account of the precarious situation in which the Church finds itself.

The Church of England – in common with all churches of the Reformation – embodied amongst other things the principle of nationality, of locality. There are large questions concerning the meaning of a nation state in an international world order; concerning the meaning of an established church in a multi-racial, multi-faith society; concerning the meaning of the establishment of the Christian religion in a secular society.

The state has long since acknowledged the religious diversity, the religious neutrality, of the nation. The culture of the modern world has become profoundly secular, and societies such as England which are nominally Christian are for all practical purposes secular in thought and feeling and action. There is a long-standing tradition of indifference, of conscious or unselfconscious secularism. There is an increasingly large body of people who are unconnected in faith or practice with the institutional life of the Church. Indeed, there appears to be a fundamental change throughout the western world where the validity of religion and the credibility of religious institutions are concerned.

One English Roman Catholic historian, reflecting upon the English scene, observes that 'huge areas of our common life are de-Christianised; [that] growing numbers of people [are] cut off from real contact with Christian values; [that we are becoming] a society increasingly anchorless and bereft of shared ideals; [that] the Christian contours of society and the humane values they perpetuated can no longer be taken for granted, and are daily eroded'.[4]

It is also true, however, that there remains 'a general, diffused, inarticulate assent to Christianity as an ideal in the body of the nation'. Something of what this means is still encapsulated for me in T.S. Eliot's book, *The Idea of a Christian Society*.[5] He distinguished between the Christian State, and the Christian Community, and the community of Christians. The Christian State refers to the traditions of public life and the framework within which laws are made and administered. The Christian Community speaks of the values that are embedded in society and which find expression in largely unconscious behaviour. The community of Christians relates to those who are consciously attempting to live according to the insights and the disciplines of the Christian faith.

Eliot published this book in 1939, but he is describing a situation that still exists, albeit in a seriously attenuated form. It is not merely the fact that the Christian churches constitute the largest voluntary association in the country, maintaining a tentative connection with significant outer constituencies of faith and feeling. It is far more the fact that there is still an implicit Christian faith in large numbers of people.

When I attempted to do some thinking and writing two or three years ago on the whole question of what it means for the Church of England to retain its status as the established church, I found myself asking a series of questions as the criteria by which in my judgement the appropriateness of establishment might be considered. The questions can be put very simply. Is the Church of England serviceable? Is it accessible? Is it evocative? Is it worthy of respect? Is it tolerant? These are questions that might properly be asked in any exploration of the public ministry that is offered by the Church of England – indeed, by any one of our churches – but the questions might also serve to indicate areas of the nation's life where there is a foothold for appropriate patterns of ministry.

Questions concerning the rightness or otherwise of the Church of England's establishment in law can be left on one side; but there still remains a church-state or a church-society or a church-community connection which provides something of the framework within which episcopacy is exercised. It is this connection which can be usefully examined in the light of these questions.

Is it serviceable? There remains a significant moral element in the traditions of public and political life which derive from the Jewish-Christian faith. The churches are still able to provide a framework for morality within which there is an acknowledgement of values, priorities, obligations, responsibilities.

Is it accessible? There is a demand in many places for the active involvement of people in a voluntary capacity who have a representative role within the wider life of the community and who can be trusted to be informed, sensitive, compassionate and objective. It is one of the more intriguing aspects of the contemporary scene that the fact of having status without power actually enables the churches, and not least of all the Church of England, to represent something that is still judged to be important in the life of the nation or of the local community.

Is it evocative? There is a continuing place for all that is understood by civic or civil religion. It provides a public recognition and public hallowing of institutions and relationships. Its forms of expression are dignified and uncontroversial, but they draw freely upon the traditions, the associations, the symbolism of the Church's and the nation's heritage.

Is it worthy of respect? The benign pragmatism that all too often informs public debate cannot adequately respond to the sensitive and complex questions which society is bound to address. The churches have secured the necessary degree of detachment from vested interests within society. Establishment – either in law or in the minds and hearts of people – does not inevitably mean compliance or collusion. The churches are well able to ask critical questions, to be the conscience of the nation, to speak the prophetic word.

Is it tolerant? Church and state are both concerned with human life lived in community. The churches have been concerned to articulate the anxieties of minority groups which can so easily be marginalized. There is a proper role for the churches – and not least of all for an established church where such a church already exists – in representing the legitimate concerns of *all* communities of faith within society.

If these questions do indeed serve to indicate areas of the nation's life where there is a foothold for appropriate patterns of ministry, then they might serve also to throw some light upon the reasons why bishops are still able to exercise authority not merely in the Church but in the life of the wider community.

England, in common with all the nations of Western Europe, is a country where the Church has been a primary institution for over fifteen hundred years. It has shaped the institutions, the law, the language, the values of national life. There is still in many places an expectation that the Church is able to provide for those who seek it some over-arching vision or philosophy or approach. The bishop embodies all that the Church represents. There are certain situations in which he is still required to articulate and to inform the values, the aspirations, the priorities and the disciplines of community life.

It is in fact as a community figure that the bishop takes his place alongside other community figures within society. The community in question might be local or regional or national, but there is a good deal of openness about community life. Nothing can be taken for granted, but those who have the mind and the will to do so are able to take their place alongside others and make their own distinctive contribution.

It is this aspect of the bishop's office that was expressed so succinctly by Lord Habgood in a recent letter to the *Church Times*.[6] I quote: 'A bishop's job differs from that of other clergy in scope and scale. All share the same central ministry of prayer, public worship, pastoral care, preaching, teaching, leadership and good works. It is the bishop's unique responsibility to fulfil this role at regional and national level, rather than in the face-to-face encounters of parish life'.

The letter went on to say that the bishop 'will, of course, meet many people in parish contexts, and must be able to relate to them. But his primary focus must be on those issues which have diocesan, regional or national applications, and with people who, like him, operate on a similar scale. This is not because such issues and people are necessarily more important than local and personal ones, but because the Church needs to have a public face at various levels and this level is his particular responsibility.'

It needs to be said also that the bishop in his role as a community figure enjoys certain advantages which are not necessarily shared by other community figures. He will often hold office for a longer period than the incumbents of other public offices. He enjoys a position of political neutrality. He stands outside the political arena and yet he has a place within it. The church which he represents is a community of faith *and* a voluntary society *and* an established institution. The expectations that surround the bishop are inevitably related to these ways of being and of seeing the Church.

The bishop – and I speak specifically of a bishop in the Church of England – is not alone in these respects. I have already said that there is a good deal of openness about community life. And I have referred also to the part that can be played by those who have the mind and the will to do so. It is worthy of note that in recent years the Cardinal Archbishop of Westminster and the Chief Rabbi have both enjoyed a significant public profile and have exercised an influence in public debate. It is not, perhaps, too fanciful to suggest that what is being demonstrated in a society that is both secular and pluralist is the continuing public place of religion and the continuing public role of the primary representatives of religion.

It is, of course, self-evident that the Church of England no longer has an exclusive concern for the spiritual well-being of the nation. All that I have attempted is to indicate some of the factors that shape so far as I can see the context in which bishops in the Church of England exercise their episcopacy not only in the Church but in the community at large. But the fact remains that the Church of England is still the established church. It functions day by day with a degree of independence which means that it can be properly described as the most significant voluntary agency in the country. It possesses vast resources in plant, manpower, financial reserves, traditions of involvement, and personal and public expectations.

The Church of England is primarily a community church. It exists – in Archbishop William Temple's notable words – for the sake of those who do not belong. It continues to provide a framework within which the religious aspirations of non-churchgoing people might find expression from time to time. Ties that are legal and historical, public and personal, local and sentimental, ensure that the Church of England continues to have a special place in English society.

Six areas were identified earlier in this paper where bishops are required to exercise their episcopacy – leadership, teaching, pastoral care, administration, authority (in the sense of giving authorization or validation to others) and collegiality. It is easy to describe what these things mean within the domestic life of the Church. It is relatively easy to indicate what these things mean in practice within the wider life of the community. What has seemed to me to be of far greater importance is to reflect upon some of the circumstances – some of the dynamics – of the contemporary situation which facilitate the exercise of episcopacy in society at large, and which can never be totally dissociated from the Church of England's continuing relationship with the state as the established church.

Notes

1. The writing of this paper has drawn in part upon John Moses, *A Broad and Living Way* (Canterbury Press, 1995).

2. The Canons of the Church of England, Canon A 1.

3. Alternative Service Book (1980): The Ordination and Consecration of a Bishop.

4. Eamon Duffy, article in *The Tablet*, 22 February 1994.

5. T.S. Eliot, *The Idea of a Christian Society* (Faber and Faber, 1939).

6. John Habgood, letter to the *Church Times*, 1 March 1996.

Scripture and the Orders of Ministry

Stephen Sykes

The intention of this statement[1] is to meet the request for contemporary reasons why the Anglican churches still use the historic episcopate as a criterion of recognition of ministry, on the clear understanding that it is bound to be a subordinate criterion.

1. Anglican sources make clear that the ordained ministry cannot be separated from the gospel of salvation, which is the point of there being the Holy Scriptures (as primary witness to that salvation) and the Church (as the agent under the Holy Spirit to that salvation). We can readily distinguish, however, the gospel as the power of God unto salvation from the historic and fallible form of the Church. Indeed, the Thirty-nine Articles insist on it!

   a. According to the preface to the 1662 Ordinal, there have been three orders of ministry 'from the Apostles' time'.

   b. The 1662 Ordinal makes the point that these orders are of divine appointment. The Collect for the Ordination Service begins, 'Almighty God, who by thy Divine Providence hast appointed divers Orders of Ministers in thy Church'.

   c. The Ordinal prescribes 1 Timothy 3. 8ff and Acts 6. 2ff to demonstrate the dignity of the deacon's order; Ephesians 4.7ff in the case of a priest; and 1 Timothy 3. 1ff and Acts 20. 17ff for a bishop.

   d. The ministration of Word and Sacrament is carried out in Christ's name, and with his commission and authority. Article XXVI of the Thirty-nine Articles states that ministers 'do not the same in their own name, but in Christ's, and do minister by his commission and authority'. In the Ordinal the priest pledges assent to the following form of words: 'Will you then give your fruitful diligence always so to minister the Doctrine and Sacraments, and the Discipline of Christ, as the Lord hath commanded?'

   e. The work of ministry is the salvation of humanity. Therefore, the study of Scripture is essential to it. The Bishop's charge contains the following phrase: 'And seeing that you cannot by any other means compass the doing of so weighty a work, pertaining to the salvation of man, but with doctrine and exhortation taken out of the holy Scriptures'.

f.   The authority of the ministry is discharged under the Scriptures. The 1662 Ordinal abolished the mediaeval *porrectio instrumentorum* and substituted the delivery of the Bible with the following words: 'Take thou Authority to preach the Word of God, and to minister the holy Sacraments in the Congregation, where thou shalt be lawfully appointed thereunto'.

g.   The Chicago-Lambeth Quadrilateral of 1886–8 defined the place of the Scriptures in the following way: the Holy Scriptures of the Old and New Testaments 'contain all things necessary to salvation' and are 'the rule and ultimate standard of faith'.

h.   *Saepius Officio*, which contained the official reply of the Archbishops of Canterbury and York to the papal condemnation of Anglican orders *Apostolicae Curae* (1896), states: 'The intention of our Fathers was to keep and continue these offices which come down from the earliest times, and "reverently to use and esteem them"' (ch. 17). This is followed by the paragraph (ch. 18), 'But all this and other things of the same kind are called by Pope Leo "names without the reality instituted by Christ". But, on the contrary, our Fathers' fundamental principle was to refer everything to the authority of the Lord, revealed in the Holy Scriptures.

The first Anglican–Roman Catholic International Commission (ARCIC I) described Scripture as 'a narrative record of the authentic foundation of the faith' (Authority in the Church, I, para. 2). It further affirmed that 'the person and work of Jesus Christ... are the primary norm for Christian faith and life' and emphasized that 'the Scriptures are the uniquely inspired witness to divine revelation'.

2.   'From the Apostles' time' has been subjected to thorough scrutiny since the days of historical biblical criticism, notably by J.B. Lightfoot, R.C. Moberly and C. Gore. Sources accept the relevance of historical criticism, and the reconstructions of the evidence are various and disputed. But it should be noted that we are not obliged to argue that the orders are 'founded by Christ'. The fluidity of the leadership in the early churches is not disputed. The New Testament writings reflect a variety of situations, and the churches they reflect pass through the ordinary stages of institution building (or routinization, Weber).

3. The appeal to origins in the 'apostles' time' has two interrelated features to it.

    a. It relates to the substance of what the apostles preached. To intend to continue those orders means that they should witness to and embody the apostolic gospel.

    b. It relates to the provision they made to continue that witness after their death. They chose people, prayed and laid hands on them.

4. Fundamental to the orders which eventually came to characterize the Church is that service of the unity of the Church, itself a sign, instrument and foretaste of the eschatological unity of all things in Christ.

    a. The Anglican use of the idea of tradition is not intended either to conform to the First Vatican Council's *partim ... partim*, or to be a guaranteed reason for resisting the arguments of biblical scholars. Anglicans were as shocked as anyone by the official Roman defence of the 'Johannine comma', and ARCIC I accepted a scholarly consensus on the origins of the ministerial office (to the irritation of the official Roman response). But the relatively uncontroversial reception of episcopacy as a development of the early Church from the dynamic of its own life produces a certain presumption in favour of reading the evidence on this way. This is not, of course, to deny that Anactetus or Cletus in the early episcopal lists may be an invention based on the adjective *anencletus* in Titus 1: 6. The arguments for the episcopate do not stand or fall by mere uncertainty.

    b. Anglicans are not obliged to defend the phrase 'successors of the apostles' or the literal foundation of the hierarchical structure of the Church by Jesus Christ, as set out in Vatican II. But there are two things to say. The apostles were unique, as people who personally knew our Lord and witnessed his death and resurrection. They were not exclusive witnesses, but the number 12 is designed to be an inclusive representativeness. There is a proper following of the apostles in a Church built upon their witness. The life of the Church is eschatological, and its structures should be consistent with its inclusive representative calling. It is no bad thing if the bishop himself or herself has the same goal.

5. It can be accepted that the idea of 'office' is far from clear in the biblical documents. There are no stable titles designating separate and specific spiritual endowments or even functions. But the concept of office, that is a stable ministry whose function is to secure the permanence of the apostolic

witness and service, is not foreign to the biblical writings. The negative criterion is important, because the developments begun in the churches of the New Testament had plainly not reached their term. Exigencies in the life of the Church required new initiatives. It is relevant that the developments should be both:

a. *consistent* with the apostles' preaching and actions;

b. *not contradictory* to the forms of ministry in the New Testament.

There are those who argue that office is opposed to charismatic ministry. Anglicans disagree. There may be a tension between charisma and office, but there is no contradiction in principle. The Church is not forbidden to provide for continuity by an office. An office may be held by a person in such a way as to serve the gospel.

6. Specific to episcopal office is responsibility with and for other clergy and congregations within a region, and responsibility with other bishops. These responsibilities include guardianship of the deposit of faith (that is for the authenticity of preaching and sacraments, including the responsibility of discipline); and care for the unity of the Church. The responsibilities are the same as those of other clergy, except that responsibility for ordination is reserved to the bishop, as part of his guardianship of the deposit of faith.

7. Episcopal office grows in importance with the growth of the Church, because size makes radical differences to the mission undertaking. To attempt to run a Pauline-scale church in a population of 50 million is to invite disaster. Episcopal office is:

a. consistent with the apostles' preaching and actions, especially as described in Acts and the Pastoral Epistles. There is no inherent contradiction between the content of the gospel and the concept of rule in holy things. (An important caveat must be entered here about the abuse of power; see next paragraph.) It is possible to live and preach the gospel, and to rule in the Church, on the example of Jesus, and in accordance with his explicit instructions to the disciples.

b. The idea of an episcopal office is not contradictory to the forms of ministry alluded to in the New Testament. Indeed in the case of the Anglican ordinal so greatly influenced by Martin Bucer, there is a conscious reformulation of the office on the pattern outlined in the pastoral epistles.

8. On the issue of the abuse of power I want briefly to say the following. The Scriptures require us to take seriously the danger of misusing the powers of eldership (1 Peter 5: 1–5). The historic exaltation of powers in the Church has usually occurred at moments of threat. But power is not simply exercised by those who have the capacity to coerce. After Foucault we have to take seriously the power of knowledge and of literate elites. We cannot now innocently use Pauline appeals to so-called 'powerlessness' in contrast to the power of office or of hierarchs.

Note

1. The statement was drafted during the meeting.

Bible Studies

I: Hebrews 13. 7-21

Joy Tetley

Remember your leaders, those who spoke to you the word of God; consider the outcome of their life, and imitate their faith. Jesus Christ is the same yesterday and today and for ever. Do not be led away by diverse and strange teachings; for it is well that the heart be strengthened by grace, not by foods, which have not benefited their adherents. We have an altar from which those who serve the tent have no right to eat. For the bodies of those animals whose blood is brought into the sanctuary by the high priest as a sacrifice for sin are burned outside the camp. So Jesus also suffered outside the gate in order to sanctify the people through his own blood. Therefore let us go forth to him outside the camp, and bear the abuse he endured. For here we have no lasting city, but we seek the city which is to come. Through him then let us continually offer up a sacrifice of praise to God, that is, the fruit of lips that acknowledge his name. Do not neglect to do good and to share what you have, for such sacrifices are pleasing to God.

The first recipients of *Hebrews* were clearly in a parlous state. Disheartened, confused, afraid, ready to give up, this Christian community had assembled to hear an urgent communication from someone who knew them well; someone who had authority over them but who, for some reason, could not be with them in person. He has sent them a sermon, born out of his passionate concern for their deepest welfare; his passionate concern to keep them on the way of Christ. We do not know who he was, nor the precise identity and location of those who first heard his sermon. But its call to persevering faith, even in the most dire of circumstances, speaks powerfully across the centuries. It speaks not of an impossible ideal, but of a faithful God, who stays with the needy through the bleakest of experiences and, in the strongest possible sense, takes their distress to heart. So we can all draw near in faith because we have a God whose commitment to us is absolute at all times and in all places.

If the discouraged are to rediscover that truth and find fresh strength and confidence, urges *Hebrews*, they must look to Jesus – and make in his direction. But where is that? Heaven certainly; but there is another, distinctly earthly dimension. Movement towards Jesus will not always seem like a heavenly experience. 'The bodies of those animals whose blood is brought into the sanctuary by the high priest as a sacrifice for sin are burned outside the camp,' the preacher reminds his Jewish Christian congregation. 'Therefore Jesus also suffered outside the gate in order to sanctify the people through his own blood.' That is the theology. But true theology always has searching consequences for human life. The preacher continues: 'Let us then go to him outside the camp and bear the abuse he endured' (Hebrews 13. 10–13). 'Outside the camp' – the place for those who were polluted and defiled, the place for things of no further use, the place where rubbish was dumped and criminals executed. Looking to Jesus, following Jesus, means that earthly security and respectability have to be abandoned as priorities. For Christ's sake, Christ's followers have to be prepared to be treated as rubbish – and worse. Yet at the same time, they are called to offer up continually a sacrifice of praise to God. Praise from the refuse tip; praise from a locus of marginalization, rejection, uselessness and contempt; praise from a place of danger, exclusion and loneliness.

What is this strange praise, this costly sacrifice? 'The fruit of lips that confess God's name.' Faithfulness. Obedient discipleship. Persevering worship. Speaking out boldly for God. All this, not just occasionally but continually. Not to satisfy God's vanity or to twist God's arm, but to identify with God in his mission of love; to respond with the will if not the feelings to the extremity of God's grace; to become party to the opening up of opportunities for God.

It is in this context that *Hebrews*, right at the end of his sermon, addresses the character of Christian leadership.

Three times in chapter 13, *Hebrews* highlights the community's leaders (vv. 7, 17, 24). Interestingly, these are the only occasions in the whole Epistle where leaders are specifically mentioned. Even then, the preacher does not address them directly (contrast 1 Timothy 6. 11–21; 1 Peter 5. 1–4). In fact, at verse 24, the people are exhorted to greet their leaders on behalf of the preacher. That raises the question as to whether their leaders are even present at their gathering. If not, why was this assembly taking place without them? Has there been some kind of breakdown in relationships? Or are the leaders, though contactable, prevented by their circumstance from being present (in detention, perhaps, because of hostile secular authorities?).

Certainly, it has to be noted that in the sermon as a whole, the people of God are in much stronger focus than their leaders. And whatever the particularities of the context, such a focus is closely associated with the preacher's theological message.

It is the Christian *laos* of God who are addressed directly by the preacher. He sees them as being in real continuity with the old covenant people of God. From God's people of old, they can learn both what to avoid like the plague (disobedience and lack of endurance) and what to imitate with all their strength (perseverance and steadfast faith, even in situations of extreme testing; the willingness to move forward as pilgrims). And *Hebrews* is in no doubt that the new covenant people of God bear the prime responsibility for their own pilgrimage. They are directly accountable to God. They must make their own decisions. They must take on the consequences of their faith (or lack of it). Whatever leaders are for, they are not there to lead people's lives for them. This theme of the responsibility (and privilege) of the people of God permeates the whole of *Hebrews'* sermon.

It flows from the people's status as beneficiaries of the new covenant. As such they are God's children; brothers and sisters of Jesus (2. 10ff), members of God's household (3. 5–6; 10. 21). They are a worshipping community (12. 22–24, 28) looking to Jesus, the very self-expression of God (1. 1–4; 12. 2), who is both ahead of them (2. 10) and right in the middle of them (2. 12). Jesus joins in their worship and teaches them of God. Through Jesus, they all have direct and confident access to the presence of God. They need no intermediaries. They still have sacrifices to offer, but now they are sacrifices of praise and generosity (13. 15–16), the surrender to God of a life of dedicated faithfulness (e.g. 10. 19–39; 12. 14–29).

They are to listen for God's voice in the present ('today', as *Hebrews* is fond of saying, 3. 12–4: 11), for they are living in the end-time before the final coming of God (1. 2; 9. 28). This means paying close attention to Jesus (3. 1), in whose life they are called to share (3. 4). So they must be a pilgrim people, characterized by steadfast endurance and a willingness to leave the past behind. They are moving towards God's rest, their rich reward (10. 35, 36). Yet paradoxically, they can already experience it through prayer and worship (4. 16; 10. 19–22; 12. 22–24).

With all this they should be a growing and maturing people, developing the capacity to teach the things of God (5. 11–6. 2). They should hold together as God's family (10. 25), encouraging and exhorting one another to love, good works and steadfast faith, taking responsibility for one another's spiritual welfare (12. 15). Together they must be prepared for hard struggle, abuse and suffering, seeing this as part of their training to be like Jesus. Through their commitment, and the working of God within them (13. 21), they will discover eternal joy, they will come into their own, they will share the life and ministry of the God who created them for glory (2. 5-10). They could not wish for a more fulfilling destiny. But they are free to throw it all away.

If the people of God have such a comprehensive vocation and responsibility, what place is left for leaders? From the references in chapter 13, it would seem that, for *Hebrews*, their task is committed oversight, setting an example and giving faithful and authoritative guidance. They are not endued with 'titles', like elder, bishop or deacon. The word used to refer to them is, quite simply, a description of function: 'those who lead'. Here there is no suggestion of hierarchy, of different 'orders' of leadership. And there is certainly no hint that these leaders are to be regarded as having special access to God. It is of no little significance that *Hebrews* does not describe 'those who lead' as priests. As he has made very clear in his sermon, this preacher sees the priesthood of Jesus as the priesthood to end all priesthoods. It is the expression of God's own priestliness. It can never be repeated, nor anywhere near effectively imitated. The only priest now needed to bring us to God is the one who lives for ever with God – Jesus. God's priestly life can be shared, certainly; but shared by everyone who looks to Jesus, not just a separated few. (*Hebrews* does not speak of Christians as 'a royal priesthood', as does *1 Peter*. Perhaps he wants to avoid that term, feeling it might lead to misunderstanding. But he would agree that God's priesthood is shared by all believers.) Neither the old priesthood, nor a new form of specialist priesthood is required. Both would be superfluous – not to say misleading.

So, according to *Hebrews*, what is the role of church leaders? It is clear, first of all, that they are not to operate alone. In common with other New Testament writers, *Hebrews* speaks of a corporate leadership (all his references to leaders are plural). No individual has all the authority – nor all the responsibility. That is healthy. It guards against tyranny of various kinds, whether it be expressed in overwork, delusions of deity, abuse of power or the devaluing of others. The only person in whom leadership can be absolutely and safely vested is God, the one who leads those who will follow into glory. To God alone the people of God owe their allegiance. And so do the people's leaders.

Nonetheless, human leaders are not to be despised but honoured and heeded. At 13. 7, *Hebrews* bids his community 'remember' their past leaders, those who spoke the word of God to them. They are to learn from these worthies and imitate them, for they were messengers of God in what they proclaimed and in the way that they lived. Their preaching was backed up by exemplary and faithful lives. The fruit of such lives must be carefully looked at again and again. It should bring out a similar faithfulness in God's people.

Leaders, then, are those who communicate God's message in word and life; and in such a way as to call out faith in others. They are to be good and encouraging examples. Verse 17 of chapter 13 gives us a further dimension. Leaders are those who keep watch over those entrusted to them as people who will have to render account. The word used for keeping watch means, literally, going without sleep and staying alert (Mark 13. 33; Luke 21. 36; Ephesians 6. 18). Those with oversight must be prepared to lose sleep over those for whom they are responsible! They also have to 'give an account' – that is, to God. They should be able to do this with joy rather than groaning (στεναζοντες). The latter is a strong word. It is used by Mark, for example, to describe the powerful spiritual and emotional activity going on within Jesus before he heals a deaf and dumb man ('he looked up to heaven and groaned', 7. 34). It is also used by Paul to describe the creation groaning in travail (Romans 8. 22) and the groaning of this earthly body as it longs for its heavenly destiny (2 Corinthians 5. 2). For leaders to render account with groaning would involve inner suffering at a deep level before God.

But such a state of affairs would not let the community off the hook. Leaders might be accountable but they are not vicariously responsible. If an unhappy account were to be rendered, that would be of 'no advantage' to the people. They, too, would have to face the consequences. *Hebrews'* sermon will have left them in no doubt of that. They cannot shift the whole burden of responsibility onto their leaders. They must answer to God for themselves. They must also obey and submit to those who lead them. Though such 'authority figures' are most certainly not God, they have been given (by a means *Hebrews* does not specify) the task of overseeing and guiding God's people. They must be respected.

It may be that *Hebrews'* community had a particular problem in this area. They seem to be meeting without their leaders. And they were in danger of drifting away from full-blooded faith. Perhaps in the light of their less than wholehearted spiritual condition, leaders were for them an irksome pressure to whom they were inclined to pay little heed. It is interesting to speculate how *Hebrews* himself may have fitted into the picture. He speaks with authority as one who expects to be heard. He is well known to the community. He has an urgent passionate concern for them. But he is clearly not one of their local leaders. Was he perhaps, like Paul, a travelling missionary, who had a special connection with this group of Christians? Whatever the truth of the matter, *Hebrews* is concerned that the group's leaders should receive that obedience which can move the community forward together.

According to *Hebrews*, those who lead have a crucial role in furthering the faithful pilgrimage of the people of God. They do so as fellow pilgrims.

II: 2 Corinthians 4. 1–12

Joy Tetley

Thefore, having this ministry by the mercy of God, we do not lose heart. We have renounced disgraceful, underhanded ways; we refuse to practise cunning or to tamper with God's word, but by the open statement of the truth we would commend ourselves to every man's conscience in the sight of God. And even if our gospel is veiled, it is veiled only to those who are perishing. In their case the god of this world has blinded the minds of the unbelievers, to keep them from seeing the light of the gospel of the glory of Christ, who is the likeness of God. For what we preach is not ourselves, but Jesus Christ as Lord, with ourselves as your servants for Jesus' sake. For it is the God who said, "Let light shine out of darkness", who has shone in our hearts to give the light of the knowledge of the glory of God in the face of Christ.

But we have this treasure in earthen vessels, to show that the transcendent power belongs to God and not to us. We are afflicted in every way, but not crushed; perplexed, but not driven to despair; persecuted, but not forsaken; struck down, but not destroyed; always carrying in the body the death of Jesus, so that the life of Jesus may also be manifested in our bodies. For while we live we are always being given up to death for Jesus' sake, so that the life of Jesus may be manifested in our mortal flesh. So death is at work in us, but life in you.

Our passage begins by referring to what has gone before: 'Therefore, since it is by God's mercy that we are engaged in this ministry... '. What is this ministry? In 3. 4 Paul has spoken of God making 'us competent to be ministers of a new covenant'. According to 3. 7–9, this new covenant ministry is a ministry of glory rather than a ministry of death, a ministry of justification rather than of condemnation. It is a ministry that calls out bold action. Above all, it is a ministry which has transforming effect (3. 18).

4. 1 affirms that this ministry is exercised in God's name and by God's mercy. That is its motivation and its empowering. It is marked by truth, for all that is deceitful or contradictory to what is known of God's word is rejected. It is exercised openly and honestly. As Paul had already stressed earlier, 'we are not peddlers of God's word like so many, but in Christ we speak as persons of sincerity, as persons sent from God, and standing in his presence' (2. 17). Those who

fail to see the truth, says Paul, have been overcome by worldly concerns. It is as though a curtain has fallen between the open proclamation of God's glory as it was perceived in Christ and the minds that belong to those who are set on an ungodly course, whose vision is taken up by that which refuses to admit of Christ.

Paul himself had once been in the position of refusing to recognize the truth of Jesus. He was acutely aware that his own exercise of Christian ministry owed everything to the mercy of God. As he acknowledges in not a few places in his letters, he had been an active and violent opponent of Christ. God's mercy runs very deep.

Which is more than can be said for the attitude of some of the Christians in Corinth. In this church, as elsewhere, Paul's ministry was not universally appreciated. For certain Corinthian Christians (influential ones, it seems), Paul did not cut a very impressive figure. As he himself records later in 2 Corinthians (10. 10): 'They say, "His letters are weighty and strong, but his bodily presence is weak, and his speech contemptible"'. Compared with others on the scene (perhaps, notably, Apollos), Paul evidently came across as an unsophisticated simpleton. The strong nature of Paul's response to this critical and dismissive judgement suggests that, in personal terms, it hurt him a great deal. Wounds inflicted by brothers and sisters in Christ are hard to bear. But, for him, this was not the key issue. What mattered above everything was the transforming message of God in Christ. Where that was being undermined, firm action needed to be taken.

For Paul, the medium is most definitely not the message. The messenger is not to be the centre of attraction. That honour belongs solely to Christ Jesus – crucified, risen and exalted. The message entrusted to Christ's ministers is that Jesus is Lord. This proclamation is their primary function and privilege. Being a minister, a messenger, is not about high-profile personal status. In fact, in worldly terms, it is a lowly occupation. 'We proclaim Jesus Christ as Lord and ourselves as your slaves for Jesus' sake' (4. 5). We may note here something very challenging about ministry, according to Paul. It is not simply that ministers are God's servants (or slaves); they are also slaves of those to whom they proclaim the truth of God, those to whom they bring the good news of Christ. Being enslaved for the sake of the gospel has more than one reference point. This is a tall order. Can anyone successfully serve two masters? Perhaps Paul's pervasive perception of Christians as being 'in Christ' has light to shed here. Serving the Christian community is serving Christ – but such service must be consistent. Anything within the community that is clearly not of Christ cannot command allegiance. To serve that would be tantamount to being enslaved by the forces that are arrayed against Christ. Little wonder, then, that Paul puts such a strong emphasis on the discerning of the Spirit. Those who minister as Christ's slaves need the Spirit's gift of discernment in large measure.

The Creator God, so Paul goes on to argue, has in Christ effected a new creation. As God said in the beginning, 'Let there be light', so in the life, death and resurrection of Jesus God has confronted and transfigured the darkness in a world gone astray, the darkness in human hearts. As Paul puts it a little later in the epistle, 'If anyone is in Christ, there is a new creation' (5. 17). This is evidenced by hearts and lives that reflect what has been seen in Jesus, 'the light of the knowledge of the glory of God' (4. 6). The messengers, the ministers, are light-bearers. But, as the Fourth Evangelist might have put it, they are not that light. And they need to recognize that fact if they are not to be deluded into adopting the wrong kind of self-projection. They are pointers, witnesses to the light of God, shining in Christ.

Their condition (as clay jars, earthen vessels, 4. 7) makes it clear that the proclamation, the uncovering of the light of Christ, comes not from themselves but from God. Their human condition leads them into all kinds of suffering. But the fact that they carry within themselves the death of Christ paradoxically manifests the life of Christ, for those who have eyes to see.

The whole section (vv. 7–12) is shot through with what, at first sight, appear to be irreconcilable contradictions.

Treasure in the most unlikely containers: utilitarian clay jars, readily expendable, destined to be broken, to be thrown away, on the sort of rubbish tip we were thinking of yesterday. In Paul's case, his Corinthian detractors thought him a pathetic specimen indeed. Who wants to look at Paul? What has he got to offer? Paul himself was not reticent about acknowledging his human frailty and shortcomings. In his first letter to the Corinthians he admitted that he came to them 'in weakness and in fear and in much trembling' (1 Corinthians 2. 3). Later he tells them of his struggle with a 'thorn in the flesh' (2 Corinthians 12. 7). His prayer to God to remove it eventually brings the response, 'My grace is sufficient for you, for my power is made perfect in weakness' (12. 9). Again and again, Paul stresses that effective power belongs to God. Moreover, it is a power expressed focally in Christ crucified. 'We proclaim Christ crucified,' said Paul in his first Corinthian letter, 'a stumbling block to Jews and foolishness to Gentiles, but to those who are being called, both Jews and Greeks, Christ the power of God and the wisdom of God' (1 Corinthians 1. 23–4). Ministers of Christ must seek no other power. And this power will be both the death of them and the making of them.

They must carry in their bodies the death (literally the dying, the killing) of Jesus. In the experience of Paul and his companions this was not just a theological concept. It was a painful reality. 'Afflicted in every way, perplexed, persecuted, struck down' (v. 8). Elsewhere, he expands and elaborates on that list (6. 3–30; 7. 14–16; 11. 22–9; 12. 1–10). On one occasion he is provoked by those who deride him into a pained rehearsal of his παθημετα, his suffering (11. 21b–30). As with

Christ, so Paul's ministry cost him dearly. Yet at the same time, and in a way that brought life and hope to others, he lived the reality of Easter. The earthen vessel was bursting with the treasure of Christ.

In the prophecy of the new covenant, God had said, 'they shall all know me, from the least of them to the greatest of them' (Jeremiah 31. 34). We get to the heart of the matter in relation to Paul's ministry when we recall his heartfelt sharing with the Philippians: 'All I want is to know Christ, and the power of his resurrection, and the fellowship of his sufferings' (Philippians 3. 10). 'For me, to live is Christ' (Philippians 1. 21). Being in such intimate relationship with Christ means more than everything and gives meaning to everything. It transfigures the whole of life. It brings life to others. It is the priority of ministry, the source and substance of proclamation.

For Paul, theology is not static propositions, but exploration in relationship – and it always carries a mission imperative. And it is in this deep and dynamic relationship that the tensions and contradictions of ministry are held together – not explained or removed, but held together; in a God for whom the tension and contradiction of Good Friday and Easter constitute one great enterprise of redemptive love.

III: Mark 10. 32-45

Reinhard Frieling

And they were on the road, going up to Jerusalem, and Jesus was walking ahead of them; and they were amazed, and those who followed were afraid. And taking the twelve again, he began to tell them what was to happen to him, saying, 'Behold, we are going up to Jerusalem; and the Son of man will be delivered to the chief priests and the scribes, and they will condemn him to death, and deliver him to the Gentiles; and they will mock him, and spit upon him, and scourge him, and kill him; and after three days he will rise.'

And James and John, the sons of Zebedee, came forward to him, and said to him, 'Teacher, we want you to do for us whatever we ask of you.' And he said to them, 'What do you want me to do for you?' And they said to him, 'Grant us to sit, one at your right hand and one at your left, in your glory.' But Jesus said to them, 'You do not know what you are asking. Are you able to drink the cup that I drink, or to be baptized with the baptism with which I am baptized?' And they said to him, 'We are able.' And Jesus said to them, 'The cup that I drink you will drink; and with the baptism with which I am baptized, you will be baptized; but to sit at my right hand or at my left is not mine to grant, but it is for those for whom it has been prepared.' And when the ten heard it, they began to be indignant at James and John. And Jesus called them to him and said to them, 'You know that those who are supposed to rule over the Gentiles lord it over them, and their great men exercise authority over them. But it shall not be so among you; but whoever would be great among you must be your servant, and whoever would be first among you must be slave of all. For the Son of man also came not to be served but to serve, and to give his life as a ransom for many.'

The suggestion of making Mark 10. 32–45 the basis for today's Bible study is one which I gladly accepted. The text consists of what appear at first sight to be two independent conversations and events, which, however, when one thinks about it further have important aspects in common: the third prediction of the suffering and resurrection of Jesus, and then on the basis of the questions of the sons of Zebedee the problem of ruling and serving.

206

In the context of our conference about the historic episcopate and church leadership it might seem appropriate to proceed with our questions straight to a meditation on the text. I regard that as legitimate in principle. But the text only becomes helpful if we first of all analyze these two texts with historical-critical exegesis.

Verse 32

Going up to Jerusalem indicates to Jesus' followers that something decisive is about to happen. Jesus' teaching about the coming of the Kingdom of God comes into its decisive phase. The attitude amongst Jesus' followers is described drastically. 'They were amazed' $\varepsilon\theta\alpha\mu\beta o\hat{v}v\tau o$ and 'they were afraid' $\varepsilon\phi o\beta o\hat{v}v\tau o$. A reason is not given. Was it an indefinite apocalyptic fear? Was it fear of violent conflicts which would threaten their own lives, because Jesus' followers had clearly not prepared themselves for violence. We do not know.

Who were these $\alpha\kappa o\lambda ov\theta o\hat{v}v\tau\varepsilon\varsigma$, followers of Jesus? The talk here must be of a larger group of followers which included both people who had flocked of their own accord to the well-known Jesus of Nazareth and also people whom Jesus had himself called to follow him. Of these, Jesus demanded considerable renunciation in an unstable, wandering life – e.g. giving up their previous profession, leaving family and property. But this was, nevertheless, not a classical teacher-pupil relationship, as was otherwise customary with the scribes. The pupils of rabbis were trained in order to become rabbis themselves one day. Those who were called to follow Jesus, by contrast, remained disciples of their rabbi for the rest of their lives. Jesus' band of disciples must have been more like the prophetic-charismatic movements which had already played a part in the Old Testament (1 Kings 19. 19–21: Elijah) and achieved a new blossoming in the time of Jesus.

What was different about Jesus and his followers was that Jesus called them to take part in the task which had been given to him by God: to call people to repentance and to announce the coming of the reign of God. And now on the way up to Jerusalem it meant participating in Jesus' path to suffering, dying and rising again. That goes much further than a teacher-pupil relationship.

Verses 33–4

Before discussing the particular role of the Twelve, I should like first to say something briefly about the prediction of suffering in verses 33–4. After Mark 8. 27– 9. 1 and Mark 9. 31–50 it is Jesus' third prediction of suffering. The small differences of accent do not need to interest us now.

What is important is that Jesus does not see his going up to Jerusalem as the triumphal procession of a powerful earthly reign of God, but as 'delivery' to the 'high priests' and to 'the Gentiles', the heathen. 'Deliver' represents παραδώσουσιν in the Greek text. This could prompt a meditation about *'paradosis/traditio'* and about 'tradition and succession' in this deeper theological sense. I shall come back to this later, when we discuss the connection between 'serving' and 'participation in Jesus' way of the cross'.

Jesus predicts his death here in verses 33–4 and interprets it as the way to resurrection. In verse 45, Jesus additionally interprets his own death as salvation, as λύτρον ('ransom') for many. The exegetes are agreed that verse 45 in this form represents something formed by the later Christian Church in the Semitic-Palestinian area. Λύτρον means deliveration of a prisoner or slave, whose guilt makes him liable to a death penalty. To interpret Jesus's death soteriologically in this way certainly does not contradict Jesus' teaching, which understood the whole suffering, death and resurrection as the eschatological event of the incipient reign of God. The imitation of Isaiah 53 with the Song of the Suffering Servant of God is unmistakable.

These references to what happened in Jerusalem must suffice. I must now come back to the fact that according to the Gospel of Mark Jesus did not unfold this prediction of suffering at large in front of the whole body of his followers, but only in the circle of the Twelve.

In Roman Catholic as in Greek Orthodox tradition, interpreters have been inclined to see in the circle of the Twelve a group which stood out from the rest of the circle of Jesus' followers by reason of their rank or function. Here in this text Jesus has indeed, as often elsewhere, taken the Twelve on one side and explained something to them separately. Jesus also clearly only invited 'the Twelve' to the Passover meal (Mark 14. 17ff.) – οἱ δώδεκα without any substantive like 'disciples' or 'apostles'.

But does it necessarily follow that Jesus in calling the Twelve gave the Church an hierarchical ministry, whereby a particular group of Christians is raised above other Christians like the clergy? There is no talk of a particular act of consecration by Jesus of the Twelve; the call of Jesus was alone constitutive. So at least in Mark and the other synoptic Gospels there is no talk of a special consecration.

If no grade of consecration is to be assumed, the next question would be, whether Jesus does not by choosing the Twelve lay down a clear structure of order within the Jesus movement and then in the later Church. Does Jesus not here from the outset provide for something like church leadership and *episkope*?

The choice of Matthias as the successor to Judas Iscariot (Acts 1. 15ff.) could suggest that the group of the Twelve should be seen as having been intended by Jesus

Christ as a permanent basic structure of the Church. But this conclusion reaches its limits, when we see that already in the continuing original Church the principle of the Twelve is not held to. The circle of the Twelve ends with the martyrdom of James, the Son of Zebedee (Acts 12. 2), which is believed to have occurred in 44 A.D. Another replacement by election does not take place. And already when Paul made his first visit to Jerusalem (see 35–7) he no longer found the Twelve in position as a collective leadership (Galatians 1. 18 and ff.), while other witnesses of the resurrection already enjoyed the title 'apostle' and alongside Peter it was above all James, the brother of Jesus, who played a leading role.

I, therefore, identify with the general protestant exegesis which I find, which is that the calling of the Twelve represented a symbolic action which serves to demonstrate Jesus' teaching for Israel. The number 12 is the symbol for the totality of the people of God in its twelve tribes, and for Jesus the choice of the Twelve was a symbol for the eschatological restitution of the people of God in His activity. To the extent to which the original Church later became a Jewish heresy and developed its own forms of life in separation from the temple and the synagogue, it needed its own organization structure, for which the symbol of the Twelve was no longer constitutive.

Alongside these observations about the particular status of the Twelve in the whole witness of the New Testament, it is precisely our text Mark 10 which sets another particular accent. I will express it sharply: it was not a particular form of organization – be it hierarchical or tied to a consecration or perhaps limited to men – which was newly or permanently constitutive in Jesus' organization nor principle. No, newly and permanently constitutive is the principle of serving!

Verses 35–45

The text Mark 10. 35–45 illustrates this strikingly. The focal point is clearly verse 43: earthly structures of domination are not adequate and certainly not constitutive for the Church. Whoever wants to be 'great' μεγα must be a servant διακονος and whoever wants to be 'first' πρῶτος must be δοῦλος of all, servant. The proper translation for this is '*Knecht*' or '*Sklave*' in German; the English Bible says 'slave'.

In Jesus' mouth these are stronger words than, for example, 'minister', which, of course, originally also means 'servant'. But in the political world 'minister' is a title for the exercise of state power and in English it is a technical term in the Church. This language makes it clear how ambiguous it is when again and again in society and in the Church power is exercised in the name of serving and when, by contrast, those who enjoy power emphasize – certainly in good conscience – that they only serve. How many kings and absolute rulers have liked to call themselves 'the first servant of the State' and have ruled and oppressed their subjects in the name of service for reasons of state – doing exactly what Jesus had in mind in verse 42!

In the Church we must pose precisely the same question. The pretty title 'servant of the servants of God' was chosen with rhetorical cunning by Pope Gregory the Great as the title of papal sovereignty, in order to counter the Patriarch of Constantinople, who had given himself the title 'Ecumenical Patriarch'. Referring to Mark 10. 43 the Pope presented himself as the servant of all – and thereby of course as the 'first'. I regard this playing with words as a fateful story of the influence of our text.

We must now link up again in Mark 10 to the first part with the prediction of the Passion and consider Jesus' answer to James and John. Spiritually and theologically, 'serving' means participating in Jesus' service, as it unfolds in his path to suffering, dying and resurrection.

Verse 38: 'Are you able to drink the cup that I drink?' Jesus asks and James and John say: 'We are able' (verse 39). Martyrdom is meant, which is attested in the case of James (Acts 12. 2), but not John.

Already in the Old Testament (in the Septuagint) ποτήριον is the cup which God gives and which is filled with the wine of the grapes of wrath. It means calamity, suffering and death. Later, as in Mark 10, ποτήριον became a picture for the suffering and death of a martyr.

In this passage the parallel picture of baptism is synonymous with 'cup' and martyrdom. We do not meet this meaning of baptism elsewhere in the New Testament. In Romans 6 Paul links baptism with the death of Jesus, but that has a different meaning than physical martyrdom: it is baptism as the death of the old Adam by submersion and cleansing from every sin. The common point of reference of 'cup' and 'baptism' is the participation in Jesus' journey through death to resurrection.

Several commentators say that there were therefore two means of privileged participation in the way of Jesus: on the one hand, Christian martyrdom, and on the other sacramental communion in baptism and in the eucharist through the cup and the bread.

Now comes the particular punchline of our text – that even martyrdom does not bestow special rank in the Kingdom of Christ (in Jesus' 'Glory', verse 37 calls it). To whom it is granted to sit at Jesus' right hand or his left hand is left completely open in verse 40.

The indignation of the other ten disciples is then answered by Jesus with radical service. Verse 45 expresses what is important: serving like Jesus means radically being there for others, even to the extent of giving up one's own life. Anyone who wants to be or is supposed to be the 'first' or the 'greatest' in the Church as the Communion of Christ has to behave like the slave who serves the guests at table and takes nothing for himself, but is there entirely for the guests.

After these exegetical remarks, I return to the opening question of whether this text contributes anything to our conference theme *'Episkope* and church leadership'. I think the answer is both 'No' and 'Yes'.

1.   'No' if we are asking whether the calling of the twelve disciples and their special position close to Jesus offers anything which is permanently valid for our church constitutions and structures of ministry. The priesthood or the episcopate as necessary structures cannot be derived directly from the choosing of the Twelve. If we consider pastors and bishops to be important or essential, we must justify them in another way.

The idea that people who participate in a particular manner in the mission of Jesus need a sacramental consecration for this and then have something like a special ontological status as it is expressed for example in talk of a particular charism of ministry and a *character indelebilis* which are given through the act of ordination can similarly not be derived from our text. A theology which teaches that cannot base that on the Synoptic Gospels at least. How it might otherwise be based on scripture and tradition, I cannot discuss here. I wish only to indicate that I personally, in common with the tradition of the Reformation, see the ministry of proclamation and church leadership as being justified only functionally as participation in the mission of Jesus Christ, not ontologically through special consecrations which give a new quality to the person of the minister.

2.   I say 'Yes' to our text having a significance for the exercise of every ministry in the Church, however it may be justified or structured. The dimension of service which is demanded by Jesus here admittedly does not apply only to the ordained ministers of the Church, but is a basic category of Christian existence.

This may and should, admittedly, be recognizable in a particular way in the case of those who represent the followers of Jesus Christ. It is here that our text challenges all our officers and ministries in the Church.

Whom do we serve, when in the ecumenical movement we often devote ourselves less to the struggle against guilt and sin than to questions of church order and full mutual recognition and reconciliation? The best service which I hope for from this conference on the basis of Mark 10 is that we should all as Anglican and Protestant Christians, as clergy and as bishops, indeed as the Church altogether understand ourselves as διακονοι and δοῦλοι 'acknowledged and reconciled' by Christ and by each other as churches.

IV: John 13. 1–17

Joy Tetley

Now before the feast of the Passover, when Jesus knew that his hour had come to depart out of this world to the Father, having loved his own who were in the world, he loved them to the end. And during supper, when the devil had already put it into the heart of Judas Iscariot, Simon's son, to betray him, Jesus, knowing that the Father had given all things into his hands, and that he had come from God and was going to God, rose from supper, laid aside his garments, and girded himself with a towel. Then he poured water into a basin, and began to wash the disciples' feet, and to wipe them with the towel with which he was girded. He came to Simon Peter; and Peter said to him, 'Lord, do you wash my feet?' Jesus answered him, 'What I am doing you do not know now, but afterward you will understand.' Peter said to him, 'You shall never wash my feet,' Jesus answered him, 'If I do not wash you, you have no part in me.' Simon Peter said to him, 'Lord, not my feet only but also my hands and my head!' Jesus said to him, 'He who has bathed does not need to wash, except for his feet, but he is clean all over; and you are clean, but not every one of you.' For he knew who was to betray him; that was why he said, 'You are not all clean.'

When he had washed their feet, and taken his garments, and resumed his place, he said to them, 'Do you know what I have done to you? You call me Teacher and Lord; and you are right, for so I am. If I then, your Lord and Teacher, have washed your feet, you also ought to wash one another's feet. For I have given you an example, that you also should do as I have done to you. Truly, truly, I say to you, a servant is not greater than his master; nor is he who is sent greater than he who sent him. If you know these things, blessed are you if you do them.'

In this passage, John stresses the comprehensive authority and divine significance of Jesus. Yet here, in this passage, is a Jesus who, on the night that he was betrayed, eschewed 'godlike' qualities and behaviour, putting himself at the mercy of those he could so easily have controlled. Those who wash feet risk being kicked in the teeth. And, effectively, that is what happened. Jesus having humbled himself at the feet of Judas, the erstwhile disciple goes out into the night to betray him. Having attended to the needs of his friends, they desert and deny him when he needs them most. Through it all, the slave, paradoxically, remains lord. His sovereignty is that of a love that refuses to be turned into bitterness and vengeance, whatever the provocation. His sovereignty is characterized by the integration of authority and humility. Notable by its absence is any concern to protect or emphasize status or dignity. The whole purpose of the sovereignty of Jesus is to open up the extremity of the sacrificial love of God. This Lord kneels riskily in the hard and heartbreaking places of life. And where the Lord is, there his servants must be also.

As John 13 opens, it is clear that the momentous hour is imminent, that hour to which the whole Gospel has been leading, the decisive moment in God's great enterprise of incarnation. It is a time of crisis, a time of judgement and opportunity, a time of crucial revelation.

The Evangelist sets the scene quite carefully in what is effectively a kind of mini-Prologue to the last great section of his work. It was just before the festival of Passover. And we recall that in the Fourth Gospel the timing of the crucifixion is such that Jesus dies at the same time as the Passover lambs are being slaughtered in the Temple. We remember, too, that near the beginning of this Gospel John the Baptist points to Jesus as the Lamb of God. God's new, and greater, act of deliverance, God's new Passover, is imminent.

Jesus knew that his hour was approaching. The Johannine Jesus is very knowing in the biblical sense of that verb, a verb which invariably carries connotations of inner, experiential awareness. As becomes apparent, Jesus was aware that treachery was at hand; betrayal by one of his specially chosen ones, one now sharing supper with him. And yet, even in this context, what is stressed is his love. 'Having loved his own who were in the world, he loved them to the end': εἰς Τελος, to perfection, into maturity. But this love has to be willingly accepted. Forced acquiescence would deny its very meaning. So Judas is lovingly ministered to, and then allowed to go out and do what he has to do. This love, this Lord, is totally open to hurt and rejection.

Yet there is no disputing that he is lord, leader. At verse 13 he himself confirms that fact: 'You call me Teacher and Lord and you are right, for that is what I am.' Verse 3 sets that truth in a divine context: 'Jesus, knowing that the Father had given all things into his hands, and that he had come from God and was going to God...'. Then come verses 4 and 5, which must constitute one of the most powerful non-sequiturs in all literature: 'he got up from the table, took off his outer robe, and tied a towel around himself. Then he poured water into a basin and began to wash the disciples' feet and to wipe them with the towel that was tied around him.' He does something entirely inappropriate to his status. He does the job of a slave; a job, moreover, that where possible was assigned to a Gentile slave. And his action is quite deliberate: 'I have set you an example,' he says in verse 15, 'that you also should do as I have done to you.'

He is teaching his disciples a lesson, these ones whom he had chosen as disciple leaders. And at this critical moment he teaches them not by lecture, not by diktat, not by words, but by a memorable and bewildering action, something that would stay with them, something they would reflect on until they came to the place of understanding, something that would reach into their hearts with radical challenge, something that would touch them for ever. Here is a leader, a teacher, who demonstrates rather than pontificates. For the recipients of such ministry this is not always easy to take, as Simon Peter illustrates. He wanted his Jesus on a proper pedestal – 'you will never wash my feet' (v. 8); and then at a word from Jesus, he moves quickly to the other extreme – 'Lord, not my feet only but also my hands and my head!' (v. 9). Jesus does not capitulate to either of Peter's perceptions as to what is fitting. Just as Jesus does not control his servants, so he will not be controlled by them.

Nor in human terms is his ministry completely effective. The ministry of Jesus to Judas did not make Judas clean. Or, if it did, Judas was able to soil it, to foul it up. The results of Jesus' ministry were in some sense out of his hands, though held within the determined purpose of God. Ministry cannot always be assessed by reference to evident results. This ministry to the disciples was hidden. And it came at a time when Jesus himself was under enormous pressure. Not many hours later, all seemed lost. Yet as things turned out, the consequences of this hidden domestic act reverberated across the centuries, and continue to issue their challenge, 'You also should do as I have done to you.' What Jesus has done is to risk ridicule, not to say injury. He has led by example, overturning accepted convention.

'Servants are not greater than their master.' Jesus takes a commonplace truth and infuses it with new and shocking meaning. To be servants of this master, slaves must be prepared to receive ministry from their lord. And they have to be prepared to minister humbly to one another. So those entrusted with teaching and leading roles must be ready to exercise that ministry in a way that seems out of character with their expectations, their perceived status, or even their wishes. If there is hierarchy, it's a topsy-turvy one. For Christian leaders, as for Christ, exaltation is to do with the lifting up of the Cross. Jesus does not do away with the concept of comparative positions. What he does, according to the Fourth Gospel, is to redefine radically the balance between such comparative positions. Normal expectations lose all sense of normality. Those who send can expect to be sent. Those who give orders can expect to be subject to those they naturally think of as owing them obedience.

Ministry based on the Jesus of John 13 is urgent (because time is short), time-consuming (because people argue about it and find it difficult to receive), outrageous (because conventions are flouted), not entirely effective (because the constituency is bound to include Judas-like spirits), risky (because you can get badly hurt), and apparently unnecessary (because it was someone else's job in the first place). But it also has an element of surprise, which carries with it the possibility of change. And the ministry of Jesus is very much to do with effecting change (often painfully). Those who claim his authority for their ministry could do worse than consider what John 13 has to say to them. 'Servants are not greater than their master.'

'If you know these things, blessed are you if you do them' (13: 17).

Bibliography

English publications

C. J. Podmore, *The German Evangelical Churches: An Introduction following the Meissen Agreement* (CCU Occasional Paper No. 1, 1992)

The Meissen Agreement: Texts (CCU Occasional Paper No. 2, 1993)

The Porvoo Common Statement (CCU Occasional Paper No. 3, 1993)

Together in Mission and Ministry. The Porvoo Common Statement with Essays on Church and in Ministry in Northern Europe (GS 1083, London, 1993)

Apostolicity and Succession. House of Bishops Occasional Paper (GS Misc. 432, 1994)

The Porvoo Agreement: A Report by the House of Bishops (GS 1156, 1995)

W. Hüffmeier and C.J. Podmore (eds), *Leuenberg, Meissen and Porvoo. Consultation between the Churches of the Leuenberg Church Fellowship and the Churches involved in the Meissen Agreement and the Porvoo Agreement* (Leuenberger Texte, 4, 1996)

The Report of the Meissen Commission, 1991-1996 (GS Misc. 490, 1997)

May They All Be One. A Response of the House of Bishops of the Church of England to Ut Unum Sint. House of Bishops Occasional Paper (GS Misc. 495, 1997)

[The above are all available from CCU, Church House, Great Smith Street, London SW1P 3NZ.]

Episcopal Ministry. The Report of the Archbishops' Group on The Episcopate (GS 944, London, 1990)

German publications

Christus allein – allein das Christentum: Vorträge der vierten theologischen Konferenz zwischen Vertretern der EKD und der Kirche von England (Beiheft zur Ökumenischen Rundschau 36), Frankfurt 1979

Das religiöse Bewußtsein und der Heilige Geist in der Kirche: Beiträge zur fünften theologischen Konferenz zwischen Vertretern der EKD und der Kirche von England (Beiheft zur Ökumenischen Rundschau 4), Frankfurt 1980

Christlicher Glaube und soziale Verantwortung: Beiträge zur siebten theologischen Konferenz zwischen Vertretern der EKD und der Kirche von England (Beiheft zur Ökumenischen Rundschau 52), Frankfurt 1986

Pluralität und Einheit der Kirche in der heutigen Gesellschaft, Achte theologische Konferenz zwischen der EKD und der Kirche von England (Beiheft zur Ökumenischen Rundschau 58), Frankfurt 1988

K. Kremkau, *Die Meissener Erklärung. Eine Dokumentation* (EKD-Texte 47)

Die Erklärungen von Meißen und Porvoo. Apostolizität und Sukzession (epd-Dokumentation Nr. 23/1995)

Das "Meissener Modell" hat sich bewährt: Gemeinsamer Bericht der Meissen Kommission 1991–1996 (epd-Dokumentation 5/1997)

Porvooer Gemeinsame Feststellung. Stellungnahme der VELKD (Texte aus der VELKD Nr.73/1996)

Die Kirche Jesu Christi: Der reformatorische Beitrag zum ökumenischen Dialog über die kirchliche Einheit (Leuenberger Texte 1), Frankfurt 1995

H. Meyer, *Ökumenische Zielvorstellungen: Ökumenische Studienhefte 4* (Bensheimer Hefte 78), Göttingen 1996

C.P. Thiede, *Religion in England: Darstellung und Daten zu Geschichte und Gegenwart* (GTB 635), Gütersloh 1994

German text of the report
and of the papers
given in German

Ergebnisprotokoll der 2. Theologischen Konferenz der neuen Reihe zwischen der Evangelischen Kirche in Deutschland und der Kirche von England vom 17. bis 22. März 1996 in West Wickham, England

I

1. Die zweite Theologische Konferenz der neuen Reihe fand unter dem Thema "Auf dem Weg zu sichtbarer Einheit: Episkope in der Geschichte, Theologie und Praxis sowie in der gemeinsamen Zukunft unserer Kirchen" vom 17. bis 22. März 1996 im Emmaus Centre, West-Wickham statt. Unsre Aufgabe war es vor allem, danach zu fragen, ob es Möglichkeiten gibt, die noch bestehenden Unterschiede im Zusammenhang mit der Austauschbarkeit ordinierter Geistlicher zu überwinden (vgl. Meissen 17 B(6)).

2. Es war wichtig, daß das regelmäßige gemeinsame Morgen- und Abendgebet, die gemeinsame Teilnahme am Abendmahl nach den Ordnungen unserer jeweiligen Kirchen sowie die tägliche Bibelarbeit den Rahmen für unsere Arbeit boten.

3. Auf der Tagung wurden die folgenden Vorträge gehalten und diskutiert:

    1. Ingolf Dalferth, Amt und Bischofsamt nach Meissen und Porvoo. Anmerkungen zu einigen ungeklärten Fragen aus evangelischer Sicht

    2. *Dorothea Wendebourg*, Die Reformation in Deutschland und das Bischofsamt

    3. *John Findon*, Developments in the Understanding and Practice of Episcopacy in the Church of England

    4. *Jan Rohls*, Apostolizität, Episkope und Sukzession. Die lutherische, reformierte und unierte Tradition

    5. *Mary Tanner*, The Anglican Position on Apostolic Continuity and Apostolic Succession in the Porvoo Common Statement

    6. *Colin Buchanan*, Anglican Ordination Rites. A Review

7. *Ulrich Kühn*, Das Amt des Bischofs in liturgischen Formularen der Kirchen der EKD

8. *Augur Pearce*, The Expression of the Anglican Understanding of Episkope in the Law of the Church of England

9. *Eilert Herms*, Ausübung und Verständnis der Episkope im Recht der EKD und ihrer Gliedkirchen

10. *Hans Christian Knuth*, Die öffentliche Rolle eines nordelbischen Bischofs als Repräsentant der Kirche und in Entscheidungsprozessen. Eine Beschreibung

11. *Gordon Roe*, The Public Roles of those exercising Episcopacy in the Church of England

12. *Axel von Campenhausen*, Historische Aspekte des evangelischen Bischofsamts vor und nach dem Ende des landesherrlichen Kirchenregiments

13. *John Moses*, The Current Exercise of Episcopacy within the Church of England, reflecting on the Relations between Church and State

4. Obwohl es sich um ein sehr breit angelegtes Thema handelt und obwohl uns deutlich wurde, daß es keine kurzen oder einfachen Antworten auf die mit der Austauschbarkeit der Ämter zusammenhängenden Fragen geben kann, möchte die Konferenz festhalten, daß im gegenseitigen Verständnis der jeweiligen Geschichte und der jeweiligen theoretischen wie praktischen Positionen bezüglich der Episkope wirkliche Fortschritte erzielt wurden, die ihrer Ansicht nach, die Hoffnung begründet sein lassen, eine Lösung könnte durch Fortsetzung der Arbeit gefunden werden.

5. Die in Abschnitt 16 der Meissener Gemeinsamen Feststellung beschriebenen Unterschiede im Verständnis des "historischen Episkopats" und seiner Bedeutung für die Austauschbarkeit der Pfarrer hat für unsere Aufgabe eine besondere Rolle gespielt. Unser Ausgangspunkt waren folgende in der Meissener Gemeinsamen Feststellung aufgeführten Übereinstimmungen:

a. Abschnitt 15 (9): "... daß ein in personaler, kollegialer und gemeinschaftlicher Weise ausgeübtes Amt pastoraler Aufsicht (Epikope) nötig ist, um die Einheit und Apostolizität der Kirche zu bezeugen und zu schützen";

b. Abschnitt 17A (4): "... daß personale und kollegiale geistliche Aufsicht (Episkope) in unseren Kirchen in einer Vielfalt von bischöflichen und nichtbischöflichen Formen als ein sichtbares Zeichen der Einheit der Kirche und der Kontinuität des apostolischen Lebens, der apostolischen Sendung und des apostolischen Amtes verkörpert und ausgeübt wird";[1]

c Abschnitt 17A (3) und 17B (4): daß in unseren jeweiligen Kirchen die Pfarrer ordnungsgemäß ordiniert sind (rite / legitime vocatus).[2]

6. Im Verlauf unserer Gespräche konnten wir in folgenden Punkten Übereinstimmung erzielen:

7. Im Blick auf die Kontinuität, Apostolizität und Einheit der Kirche hat die Kontinuität des Evangeliums immer Vorrang. Dies verpflichtet jeden Christen, an der Mission der Kirche mitzuwirken, innerhalb derer das ordinierte Amt dazu da ist, durch die öffentliche Verkündigung des Evangeliums in Wort und Sakrament "dem Amt des ganzen Volkes Gottes zu dienen" (Meissen 15 (8)). In unseren jeweiligen Kirchen besteht eine ununterbrochene Kontinuität in der ordnungsgemäßen Ordination der Pfarrer. Während die Kirche von England in der Kontinuität des historischen Episkopats in der Form der persönlichen Sukzession von Bischöfen den Ausdruck ihrer Einheit ohne Unterbrechung durch die Umwälzungen der Reformationszeit sehen konnte, sahen sich die Reformatoren auf dem europäischen Kontinent gezwungen, zwischen der Kontinuität des Evangeliums und der Beibehaltung des Episkopats wählen zu müssen, und reformierten daher die Ausübung von Episkope in einer Weise, die die Priorität des Evangeliums vor einer bestimmten Ausformung des Amtes und der Episkope gewährleisten sollte. Hierbei bezogen sie sich auf das frühkirchliche Model, demzufolge der *episcopus* der Pastor der christlichen Stadtgemeinde war.

8. Wir konnten feststellen, daß es in der tatsächlichen Ausübung von Episkope große Ähnlichkeiten gibt. Episkope ist nicht die alleinige Aufgabe der Bischöfe, vielmehr sind Laien und synodale Strukturen der Kirche daran beteiligt. Dies wurde uns besonders deutlich, als wir uns mit der rechtlichen Bestimmungen in unseren jeweiligen Kirchen zuwandten. In unseren Kirchen stellt die personale Ausübung von Episkope ein wichtiges Strukturelement dar, das in der öffentlichen Darstellung unserer Kirchen eine bedeutende Rolle spielt.

9. Wir haben uns bewußt gemacht, daß die Kirche von England zur Anglikanischen Gemeinschaft gehört und sich der Vereinbarung von Porvoo (zwischen den britischen und irischen anglikanischen Kirchen und den nordischen und baltischen lutherischen Kirchen) ebenso verpflichtet weiß, wie die Evangelische Kirche in Deutschland (EKD) durch die Leuenberger Konkordie gebunden ist. Diese Beziehungen müssen berücksichtigt werden, wenn wir auf dem Weg zur sichtbaren Einheit, auf den wir uns mit der Meissener Erklärung begeben haben, fortschreiten wollen.

10. Wir haben uns auch darauf verständigt, daß bei jeder künftigen Theologischen Konferenz theologische Methodenfragen bei der Bearbeitung der einzelnen inhaltlichen Fragen angesprochen werden müssen.

II

11. In der Meissener Gemeinsamen Feststellung haben sich unsere Kirchen dazu verpflichtet, "nach der 'vollen, sichtbaren Einheit' des Leibes Christi auf Erden zu streben" und "für die Darstellung der Einheit auf allen Ebenen" zu arbeiten (Abschnitt 7).

12. Nach der Meissener Gemeinsamen Feststellung gehören "der Dienst eines versöhnten, gemeinsamen Amtes" und "Bande der Gemeinschaft", die "personale und kollegiale Aspekte wie Aspekte der Gemeinde besitzen" und die als "äußere und sichtbare Zeichen der Gemeinschaft" dienen, zu den Merkmalen für volle, sichtbare Einheit (Abschnitt 8).

13. Von dieser Übereinstimmung ausgehend, müssen wir klären, was wir mit "voller, sichtbarer Einheit" meinen, und in welcher Weise das über unsere derzeitige Beziehung hinausgeht, insbesondere:

welche personalen, kollegialen und gemeinschaftlichen Formen für die volle, sichtbare Einheit konkret erforderlich sind;

welche Auswirkungen unsere anderen ökumenischen Verpflichtungen (z.B. Leuenberg, Porvoo, Gespräche mit Methodistischen, Orthodoxen und Römisch-Katholischen Kirchen) diesbezüglich haben;

inwiefern unterschiedliche theologische Deutungen mit einer gemeinsamen Praxis -besonders hinsichtlich der Möglichkeit eines gemeinsamen Amtes in der Zukunft - kompatibel sind.

III

14. Wir werden außerdem die historischen Fakten bezüglich der Apostolizität und Kontinuität sowohl der Episkope wie des bischöflichen Amtes in unseren jeweiligen Kirchen näher zu erörtern haben.

a. Hinsichtlich der Episkope werden wir zu beschreiben haben,

1. wie die notwendigen Funktionen von Epikope ausgeübt werden,

2. wie jede dieser Funktionen ihren eigenen Zeichencharakter hat.

b. Hinsichtlich der Episkope werden wir zwischen angemessenen (einschließlich personaler, kollegialer und gemeinschaftlicher Formen) und unangemessenen (z.B. Trennung vom ganzen Volk Gottes) Erfordernissen und Formen von Episkope zu unterscheiden haben.

c. Diese Diskussion der Geschichte wird uns Gelegenheit geben, eine konkrete Hoffnung für die Zukunft zu beschreiben, die sich aus der Erinnerung nährt, so daß alles, was für die Episkope Gültigkeit hat, als Grundlage und Kriterium für eine Erörterung des bischöflichen Amtes dienen kann.

d. Hinsichtlich des bischöflichen Amtes müssen weiterhin die Veränderung und die Verschiedenheit seiner historischen Ausprägungen in unseren jeweiligen Kirchen beschrieben sowie die Frage erörtert werden, inwieweit bestehende Unterschiede angemessen und gesund sind und einzelne Beispiele als positive Modelle gelten können

e. Auf der Grundlage der geltenden Rechtslage (siehe Anlage) scheint es wohl - abgesehen von der praktischen Frage der Anerkennung akademischer Qualifikationen - keine grundsätzlichen Einwände von deutscher Seite gegen einen unbeschränkten Pfarreraustausch zu geben. Auf englischer Seite bestehen hingegen eine Anzahl von Hindernissen.

f. Auf englischer Seite wird geklärt werden müssen, welche Schritte zu erfolgen hätten (einschließlich einer Überprüfung der relevanten liturgischen Texte sowie geltender rechtlicher Hindernisse) damit das bischöfliche Amt in den Gliedkirchen der EKD in solcher Weise anerkannt werden kann, daß der uneingeschränkte Austausch der Ämter ermöglicht würde.

g. Die Gliedkirchen der EKD hätten ihrerseits zu klären, ob, bzw. weshalb und in welchem Sinne sie bereit sind die englische Form des Bischofsamtes als ein angemessenes Modell zu betrachten. Auf diese Weise könnten sie dei Sachgründe für ihre Bereitschaft zum pastoralen Austausch deutlich machen.

h. Im Verlauf einer solchen Untersuchung käme auch deutlicher zum Vorschein, welche Struktur für die Einheit der universalen Kirche auf Erden die angemessene wäre.

Anhang
zum Ergebnisprotokoll der Zweiten Theologischen Konferenz

Austauschbarkeit von Geistlichen zwischen der Kirche von England und den Gliedkirchen der EKD - die gegenwärtige Rechtslage

Wir haben uns mit der Frage der Austauschbarkeit der Geistlichen sowohl hinsichtlich einer zeitweisen Gastfreundschaft an Kanzel und Altar als auch hinsichtlich der unbefristeten Berufung von Geistlichen aus der einen Kirche auf eine Stelle in der anderen Kirche.

1. In Deutschland

Axel Freiherr von Campenhausen

Infolge der Meißener Vereinbarung spricht aus rechtlicher Sicht gegenwärtig nichts dagegen, daß ein Priester der Kirche von England eingeladen wird, als Gast in einer Gliedkirche der EKD zu predigen oder die Sakramente zu verwalten.

Die Berufung eines solchen Priesters auf eine Pfarrstelle in einer Gliedkirche der EKD unter Beibehaltung seiner anglikanischen Konfession würde die Anerkennung seiner Anstellungsfähigkeit nach Maßgabe des jeweiligen Pfarrerdienstgesetzes voraussetzen. Weil das Pfarrerdienstgesetz (PfDG) der Evangelischen Kirche der Union uns während der Konferenz zugänglich war, beziehen sich die folgenden Bemerkungen auf die rechtlichen Bestimmungen der EKU. Es kann davon ausgegangen werden, daß die dienstrechtlichen Bestimmungen der Gliedkirchen der EKD - bezüglich der anstehenden Frage - mit den Pfarrerdienstgesetzen der EKU und der VELKD übereinstimmen.

Das Pfarrerdienstgesetz der EKU in der Fassung vom 31.5.1991 sieht bezüglich derjenigen, die nicht in Deutschland studiert haben, folgendes vor:

"Akademisch ausgebildete Theologen aus anderen evangelischen Kirchen und Kirchengemeinschaften können nach angemessener Zurüstung und aufgrund eines

Kolloquiums die Anstellungsfähigkeit als Pfarrer erhalten." (PfDG §5 Abs. 1 Satz 1)

Es ist selbstverständlich, daß anglikanische Priester vermutlich in Bezug auf ihre deutschen Sprachkenntnisse sowie bezüglich ihrer Kenntnisse der lutherischen bzw. reformierten Traditionen und Strukturen usw. einer "angemessenen Zurüstung" bedürfen; es ist ebenfalls selbstverständlich, daß ein Kolloquium zur Feststellung ihrer Eignung für den Dienst in Deutschland einer Berufung vorausgehen sollte.

Das Erfordernis, er/sie müsse ein/e "akademisch ausgebildete/r Theologe/in" sein, ist hingegen restriktiver. Dies ist eine Angelegenheit, die im Ermessen der zuständigen Kirchenleitung (PfDG § 2 Abs. 2) liegt und die beinhaltet, daß die englische theologische Ausbildung von deutscher Seite als ausreichend anerkannt wird. Sollte eine solche Anerkennung ausbleiben, müßte der anglikanische Priester die Zweite Theologische Prüfung bestehen (PfDG § 5 Abs. 1 Satz 2).

Die Anwendbarkeit von PfDG § 5 Abs.1 auf anglikanische Priester hängt davon ab, ob die Kirche von England als eine "andere evangelische Kirche" im Sinne des PfDG anerkannt wird. Die Bezeichnung "evangelisch" wird im PfDG nicht näher definiert. Einige andere Rechtsquellen enthalten Definitionen (zB. Bezug auf bestimmte Bekenntnisschriften), die auf Anglikaner nicht anwendbar wären. Es liegt jedoch in einer kirchensteuerrechtlichen Angelegenheit mindestens ein Gerichtsurteil vor, das es nahelegt, Anglikaner hätten in rechtlicher Hinsicht als "evangelisch" zu gelten. Besonders nach Meißen würde man wahrscheinlich davon ausgehen, daß dem so ist, andernfalls müßte das PfDG an dieser Stelle ergänzt werden, um eine volle praktische Ausführung der Meissener Vereinbarung zu ermöglichen.

Schließlich könnte sich aus den Staatskirchenverträge mit den Bundesländern ein Problem ergeben, da sich viele Gliedkirchen der EKD darin verpflichten, nur solche Personen auf Pfarrstellen zu berufen, die mindestens drei Jahre an einer deutschen Universität studiert haben. Ausnahmen von solchen Bestimmungen in den Staatskirchenverträgen wurden in der Vergangenheit zugelassen; die Gliedkirchen müßten prüfen, ob eine allgemeine Ausnahmeregelung getroffen werden könnte, um die in der Meissener Vereinbarung als Ziel genannte volle Austauschbarkeit der Geistlichen zu ermöglichen.

2. In England

C. C. Augur Pearce

Rechtliche Bestimmungen und gerichtliche Entscheidungen bezüglich der Ausübung des Amtes und der Voraussetzungen für die Berufung in bestimmte Ämter der Kirche von England stammen zum größten Teil aus einer Zeit, da der *Act of Uniformity* von 1662 sowohl die Berufung in solche Ämter als auch die Sakramentsverwaltung auf jene beschränkte, die bischöflich ordiniert (*"episcopally ordained"*) waren. Die erste Einschränkung gilt noch heute, während die zweite zwar durch die *Church of England (Worship and Doctrine) Measure 1976* aufgehoben wurde, aber im Canon B 12 noch enthalten ist und wahrscheinlich auch noch im Gewohnheitsrecht (*"common law provision"*) fortbesteht. Es spricht viel dafür, daß in damaliger Zeit "bischöflich ordiniert" gleichbedeutend war mit "ordiniert durch einen Bischof in historischer Sukzession" (*"ordained by a bishop in the historic succession"*)

Die *Overseas and Other Clergy (Ministry and Ordination) Measure 1967* legt jenen gewisse Beschränkungen bei der Ausübung des Priester- oder Diakonenamtes in der Kirche von England auf, die durch überseeische Bischöfe (*"overseas bishops"*) ordiniert wurden. Diese Bischöfe werden als solche definiert, die mit der Kirche von England in Kirchengemeinschaft (*"in communion"*) stehen oder die ihre Weihe (*"consecration"*) in einer Kirche erhalten haben, welche (nach dem Urteil beider Erzbischöfe) eine anerkannte Ämterordnung (*"recognised and accepted orders"*) vorzuweisen hat. Gegenwärtig werden Bischöfe, Präsides und andere ordinierende Amtsträger in der EKD dieser Kategorie nicht zugerechnet, so daß die von ihnen ordinierten Geistlichen gemäß dem genannten Gesetz zur Ausübung des Priester- oder Diakonenamtes in England nicht zugelassen werden dürfen. Wäre ihnen - ungeachtet dieses Gesetzes - eine solche Amtsausübung gestattet, wären sie gegenüber den Geistlichen der Alt Katholischen Kirche oder der Episkopalen Kirche der Vereinigten Staaten von Amerika bevorzugt, was gewiß nicht der Intention des Gesetzgebers von 1967 entsprechen würde.

Daraus muß gefolgert werden, daß sie überhaupt nicht als Priester oder Diakone dienen können und daß mit den Begriffen "Priester", "Diakon", "ordiniert", "geistlicher Stand" (*holy orders*) in den einschlägigen Rechtsquellen, nach wie vor eine bischöfliche Ordination in historischer Sukzession (*"episcopal ordination in the historic succession"* vorausgesetzt wird. Demnach ist ein deutscher evangelischer Pfarrer ohne Re-Ordination kein Geistlicher (*"clerk in holy orders"*); er kann den Erfordernissen zB. des Canon C 10 §2 oder des Canon C 12 §2 nicht genügen und es kann ihm daher weder eine Pfarrstelle übertragen noch die Genehmigung zur Ausübung des Priester- oder Diakonenamtes in einer anglikanischen Gemeinde erteilt werden.

Der Dienst eines deutschen evangelischen Pfarrers in der Kirche von England wird deswegen noch immer als gastweiser Dienst (*"ministry by invitation"*) eines Pfarrers anderer Denomination betrachtet. Er/sie würde im Hinblick auf den Gemeindekirchenrat (*"parochial church council"*) oder der Mitgliedschaft, bzw. Vertretung in Synoden nicht zur Pfarrerschaft (*"clergy"*) gezählt werden. Er/sie könnte an den pastoralen Aufgaben in einem *"team ministry"* als Mitglied des Teams teilhaben, ihm/ihr könnte jedoch nicht die Verantwortung für die Seelorge als einem Mitglied eines Teampfarramtes ("team chapter") übertragen werden (vgl. Pastoral Measure 1983, s.20).

Als Gastpfarrer kann sich jetzt sein liturgisches Handeln unter anderem auf die Leitung des Morgen- und Abendgebetes, auf den Predigtdienst und die Durchführung von Trauerfeiern erstrecken. Gemäß Canon B 43 §1 ist die Zustimmung des Gemeindekirchenrates und, bei längerfristigen Einsätzen, die des Bischofs erforderlich.

Der deutsche evangelische Pfarrer darf nur unter Berufung auf Canon B 43 §9 - wonach Angehörige anderer Kirchen (dh. hier: Deutsche Protestanten) eingeladen werden können, ein Kirchengebäude für *ihre* Gottesdienste zu nutzen - in einem anglikanischen Kirchengebäude taufen oder einer Eucharistiefeier vorstehen. In einem solchen Fall würde der Gottesdienst nicht als anglikanischer Gottesdienst gelten, auch wenn die Gemeinde daran teilnähme.

Die rechtliche Lage ist in dreifacher Hinsicht anders, wenn es sich um ein "local ecumenical project" handelt:

1. Der Bischof kann einem deutschen evangelischen Pfarrer die Genehmigung zum Taufen erteilen, so daß diese Taufen als solche anzusehen wären, die in der Kirche von England vollzogen wurden - Canon B 44 §4(1)(c).

2. Der Bischof kann regelmäßige Abendmahlsgottesdienste, an denen die anglikanische, bzw. eine gemischte Gemeinde teilnehmen, in einem anglikanischen Kirchengebäude unter Leitung des deutschen evangelischen Pfarrers zulassen. Die Tatsache, daß ein deutscher evangelischer Pfarrer die Eucharistiefeier leitet muß vorher bekannt gemacht werden und der Gottesdienst darf nicht als anglikanische Eucharistiefeier ausgegeben werden - Canon B 44 §§ 4(1), 4(3).

3. Die spezifisch anglikanischen Gottesdienstangebote im Rahmen eines "*local ecumenical project*" können auch soweit reduziert werden, daß die vom deutschen evangelischen Pfarrer gehaltenen Gottesdienste zum Normalfall in der

Gemeinde werden. Allerdings muß wenigstens an den fünf Hauptfesten des Kirchenjahres eine Eucharistiefeier angeboten werden, der ein bischöflich ordinierter Priester vorsteht. - Canon B 44 §5.

Es gibt keine rechtliche Bestimmung, aufgrund derer ein Bischof (oder ein anderer Pfarrer) aus einer Gliedkirche der EKD in der Kirche von England konfirmieren oder ordinieren dürfte.

---

[1] In diesem Abschnitt hat Meissen das Adjektiv "gemeinschaftlich" ausgelassen

[2] Confessio Augustana 14, bzw. Art. XXIII der 39 Artikel

Amt und Bischofsamt nach Meissen und Porvoo

Evangelische Anmerkungen zu einigen ungeklärten Fragen

Ingolf Dalferth

1. Ausgangspunkt und Auftrag

Am 29. Januar 1991 wurde die *Meissener Erklärung* unterzeichnet. Damit wurden nicht nur die Beziehungen zwischen der Kirche von England und den evangelischen (d.h. lutherischen, reformierten und unierten) Kirchen Deutschlands auf eine neue Basis gestellt. Es war auch eines der seltenen ökumenischen Ereignisse, in dem die Resultate theologischer Lehrgespräche zwischen Kirchen in einem ordentlichen Verfahren rezipiert und verbindlich in Geltung gesetzt wurden. Die *Meissener Gemeinsame Feststellung* ist mehr als das Konsenspapier einer theologischen Kommission: Sie ist für die Kirchen beider Seiten verbindlich, und sie ist deshalb von grundsätzlich anderem Gewicht als Texte wie - um nur einige Beispiele zu nennen - das Lima-Dokument *Taufe, Eucharistie und Amt*, die Dokumente *Lehrverurteilungen - kirchentrennend?* auf evangelischer oder *Episcopal Ministry* und *Apostolicity and Succession* auf anglikanischer Seite. Und das gilt - vorläufig jedenfalls - auch für das lutherisch-anglikanische Dialogpapier *"Toward Full Communion" and "Concordat of Agreement"* und das Porvoo Common Statement *Together in Mission and Ministry*. Dieser Unterschied ist bei unserer Arbeit theologisch und hermeneutisch zu beachten.

Hermeneutisch heißt das, - und ich greife diesen Punkt im Anschluß an unsere letztjährigen Gespräche in Berlin und die Konsultation auf dem Liebfrauenberg mit Bedacht gleich zu Beginn ausdrücklich auf -, daß wir die *Gemeinsame Feststellung* nicht so lesen und auslegen dürfen, daß dem widersprochen oder daß das problematisiert wird, was am 29. Januar 1991 ausdrücklich erklärt und unterzeichnet wurde. Das dort Festgestellte ist vielmehr die Basis, die wir nicht mehr zu diskutieren, sondern von der wir auszugehen haben. Dazu gehört insbesondere (Nr. 17 A, S. 47-49)[1],

- daß beide Seiten wahre Kirchen sind, "die zu der Einen, Heiligen, Katholischen und Apostolischen Kirche Jesu Christi gehören und an der apostolischen Sendung des ganzen Volkes Gottes wahrhaft teilhaben" (Nr. 17 A (1));

- daß "in unseren Kirchen das Wort Gottes authentisch gepredigt wird und die Sakramente der Taufe und des Herrenmahls recht verwaltet werden" (Nr. 17 A (2));

- daß unsere ordinierten Ämter ... von Gott gegeben und ... Werkzeuge seiner Gnade" sind (Nr. 17 A (3)); und

- daß "personale und kollegiale geistliche Aufsicht (Episkope) in unseren Kirchen in einer Vielfalt von bischöflichen und nichtbischöflichen Formen als ein sichtbares Zeichen der Einheit der Kirche und der Kontinuität des apostolischen Lebens, der apostolischen Sendung und des apostolischen Amtes verkörpert und ausgeübt wird" (Nr. 17 A (4)).

Daß all das in unseren Kirchen der Fall ist, ist klar und unmißverständlich gegenseitig anerkannt. Es sollte auch nicht mit dem Hinweis problematisiert werden, im englischen Text stehe in den zitierten Passagen nur das relativ schwache 'acknowledge' und nicht das starke und rechtsverbindliche 'recognize'. Der deutsche Text ist hier eindeutig und angesichts der ausdrücklich genannten Regel "Der englische und der deutsche Wortlaut dieser Erklärung sind in gleicher Weise maßgebend" (S. 75) auch sachlich verbindlich. Im übrigen spricht auch der englische Text an anderen, sachlich gleichgewichtigen Stellen ausdrücklich von der "recognition ... of churches and ministries" (Nr. 19, S. 54) bzw. von "our mutual recognition of one another's ministries" (Nr. 16, S. 44). Von dieser Anerkennung ist bei unseren Gesprächen daher auszugehen, und alles, was wir noch zu klären und zu erörtern haben, ist diesem grundlegenden Sachverhalt gegenüber nachgeordnet.

Zu klären und zu erörtern gibt es aber noch einiges, denn mit der Unterzeichnung der *Meissener Erklärung* sind keineswegs alle theologischen Differenzen behoben. Beide Seiten verpflichteten sich vielmehr ausdrücklich, "offizielle theologische Gespräche zwischen unseren Kirchen fortzusetzen ... und an der Überwindung der zwischen uns noch bestehenden Unterschiede zu arbeiten" (Nr. 17 B (1), S. 49). Meissen wurde also von Anfang an nicht als Abschluß, sondern als wesentlicher Schritt auf dem Weg zu sichtbarer Einheit verstanden. So notiert die *Gemeinsame Feststellung* neben den erreichten grundlegenden Übereinstimmungen nüchtern auch noch offene Punkte, an denen innerhalb des erreichten Konsenses - also in nicht fundamentalen, sondern theologisch nachgeordneten Fragen - Differenzen bestehen blieben. An ihrer Überwindung zu arbeiten, ist der Auftrag unserer Gespräche.

Theologisch nachgeordnet sind die noch offenen Punkte und Fragen - das muß nun freilich auch gesagt werden -, weil das in der Meissener Erklärung konstatierte "consentire de doctrina evangelii et de administratione sacramentorum" (CA 7, BSLK, S. 60,4-6) für unsere evangelische Seite hinreichend ist, vorbehaltlos und ohne Einschränkungen in volle Kirchengemeinschaft einzutreten. Mit der Anerkennung, "daß in unseren Kirchen das Wort Gottes authentisch gepredigt wird und die Sakramente der Taufe und des Herrenmahls recht verwaltet werden" (Nr. 17 A (2), S. 47), ist das festgestellt, was nach CA 7 "ad veram unitatem ecclesiae satis est" (BSLK, S. 60,3f). Das heißt nicht, daß in allen Fragen theologische Übereinstimmung bestehen muß (was in keiner Kirche erwartet werden kann und soll) oder daß alle damit nicht berührten Fragen unter die "traditiones humanas seu ritus aut ceremonias ab hominibus institutas" (BSLK, S. 60,7-9) fallen müßten, von denen gesagt wird, daß es nicht notwendig sei, daß sie "ubique similes esse" (BSLK, S. 60,6f). Es heißt auch nicht, daß Fragen wie die nach der Kirche (CA 8) oder dem "ministerium docendi evangelii et porrigendi sacramenta" (CA 5, BSLK, S. 57,3f) theologisch nicht wichtig wären. Es heißt aber sehr wohl, daß diese Fragen nur in ihrer funktionalen Zuordnung zu (und damit auch Unterscheidung von) den kirchenkonstituierenden und damit auch für den Vollzug von Kirchengemeinschaft maßgeblichen Grundvollzügen der Evangeliumsverkündigung durch Wort und Sakrament recht behandelt werden können. Nicht von ungefähr ist in Eph 4,4f, das CA 7 ausdrücklich zitiert, von *einem* Leib, *einem* Geist, *einer* Hoffnung, *einem* Herrn, *einem* Glauben, *einer* Taufe und *einem* Gott die Rede, aber *nicht* von *einem Amt.* Den Vollzug voller Kirchengemeinschaft - und das heißt konkret: uneingeschränkte Gemeinschaft am Tisch des Herrn - davon abhängig zu machen, "[b]is wir ein gemeinsames, in vollem Einklang befindliches Amt haben" (Nr. 17 B (7), S. 53), ist deshalb ein Vorbehalt, der aus evangelischer Sicht theologisch keinen Sinn ergibt. Meissen läßt auch keinen Zweifel daran aufkommen, daß dieser Vorbehalt auf anglikanischer, nicht auf evangelischer Seite besteht (Nr. 16; Nr. 17 B (7), S. 45; 53). Wir werden deshalb klären müssen, warum und mit welchen Gründen er dort besteht und hier nicht, wenn wir ihn gemeinsam überwinden wollen. Da es aber keinen Vorbehalt gäbe, wenn er auf anglikanischer Seite nicht bestünde, werde ich mich im folgenden vor allem bemühen, den Gründen für die anglikanische Haltung auf die Spur zu kommen. Das wird eine gewisse Einseitigkeit meiner Fragen und Überlegungen zur Folge haben, und ich bitte schon jetzt um Entschuldigung dafür, wenn ich die entscheidenden Punkte verfehlen oder unzureichend würdigen sollte: Ich rechne auf Ihre Korrektur und Klärung, denn dazu sind wir zu dieser theologischen Konferenz zusammen gekommen.

2. Offene Fragen in Meissen

Daß wir noch kein "gemeinsames, in vollem Einklang befindliches Amt haben" (Nr. 17 B (7), S. 53), ist die wohl wichtigste offene Frage von Meissen. Zwar sind sich beide Seiten einig,

- daß "alle Glieder der Kirche zur Teilnahme an ihrer apostolischen Sendung berufen sind", so daß von "dem Amt des ganzen Volkes Gottes" gesprochen werden muß, das sich in den "vielfältige[n] Ämter[n]" konkretisiert, die den einzelnen "vom Heiligen Geist ... gegeben" sind (Nr. 15 (8), S. 45);

- daß "[i]nnerhalb der Gemeinschaft der Kirche ... das ordinierte Amt des Wortes und Sakramentes" als "eine Gabe Gottes an seine Kirche und daher ein Amt göttlicher Einsetzung" besteht, "um dem Amt des ganzen Volkes zu dienen" (Nr. 15 (8), S. 45);

- daß "ein in personaler, kollegialer und gemeinschaftlicher Weise ausgeübtes Amt pastoraler Aufsicht (Episkope) nötig ist, um die Einheit und Aposto-lizität der Kirche zu bezeugen und zu schützen" (Nr. 15 (9), S. 45), und es werden deshalb auch

- die "ordinierten Ämter gegenseitig als von Gott gegeben und als Werkzeuge seiner Gnade" anerkannt (17 A (3), S. 47).

Es besteht also Übereinstimmung darin,

- daß alle Christen am apostolischen Amt der Kirche als ganzer teilnehmen,

- daß das ordinierte Amt von Gott dazu gegeben ist, diesem grundlegenden Amt des ganzen Volkes Gottes zu dienen, und

- daß das Amt pastoraler Aufsicht (Episkope) zur Bezeugung und zum Schutz der Einheit und Apostolizität der Kirche "nötig ist" (Nr. 15 (9), S. 45), ohne deshalb aber als ein besonderes Amt göttlicher Einsetzung neben dem ordinierten Amt bestimmt zu werden.

Doch wie verhalten sich *Priestertum aller Glaubenden, ordiniertes Amt* und *Episkope* genau zu einander? Hier bleiben viele Fragen offen. Klar ist nur folgendes:

• Das *Priestertum aller Glaubenden gründet in der Taufe*: "Alle Getauften sind berufen, in einer Gemeinschaft des Priestertums zu leben und Gott Lobopfer darzubringen, die gute Nachricht miteinander zu teilen und sich an der Sen-dung und dem Dienst für die Menschheit zu beteiligen" (Nr. 4, S. 37).

- Das *ordinierte Amt ist ein "Amt göttlicher Einsetzung"*, das vom "Amt des ganzen Volkes" unterschieden, diesem aber dienend zugeordnet ist (Nr. 15 (8); Nr. 4, S. 45; 37).

- Am *Priestertum aller Glaubenden* hat jeder durch die Taufe teil, zur Ausübung des *ordinierten Amtes* dagegen bedarf es einer besonderen *Ordination* (vgl. Nr. 17 A (3), S. 47 und 17 B (4), (6) und (7), S. 51-53).

- Während im Blick auf die *Taufe* (und damit die Berufung ins Priestertum aller Glaubenden) Einigkeit besteht (Nr. 15 (4), S. 43), bestehen im Blick auf die *Ordination* (und damit die Berufung in das ordinierte Amt) unausgeräumte Differenzen (Nr. 17 B (6) und (7), S. 51-53).

- Diese Differenzen werden inhaltlich nicht ausgeführt. Der Text der *Gemeinsamen Feststellung* gibt aber verschiedene Hinweise, die sich in drei Anfragen bündeln lassen:

1. Verständnis der Ordination:

Ist die Ordination als eine sakramentale Handlung wie Taufe und Abendmahl zu verstehen? Dafür könnte die Reihung von "Taufe, Herrenmahl und Ordination" an verschiedenen Stellen sprechen (Nr. 17 B (3); Nr. 8, S. 49; 39).[2] Umgekehrt spricht dagegen, daß in Nr. 17 A die Anerkennung der rechten Verwaltung der Sakramente Taufe und Herrenmahl auf der einen deutlich von der Anerkennung der ordinierten Ämter auf der anderen Seite unterschieden wird. Im ersten Fall ist die Anerkennung uneingeschränkt, im zweiten dagegen mit dem Vorbehalt verbunden, daß sich "unsere Kirchen" noch nicht "in vollem Einklang befinden" (Nr. 17 A (3), S. 47). Taufe und Abendmahl sind damit klar dem *gemeinsam Christlichen*, die Ordination dagegen dem *unterschiedlich Kirchlichen* zugeordnet.

Das ist auch sachgemäß. Nach evangelischem Verständnis ist die Ordination als Beauftragung und Bevollmächtigung zum Dienst der öffentlichen Verkündigung und Sakramentsverwaltung kein Sakrament (Heilsmittel), sondern die ordnungsgemäße Berufung in das kirchliche Amt, das als öffentlicher Dienst an Wort und Sakrament auf anderer Ebene steht als diese. Sakramente sind Worthandlungen, durch die Menschen in das Heilsgeschehen in Christus einbezogen und in der Gemeinschaft mit Christus und untereinander erhalten werden. Sie setzen Differenzen zwischen Christen und Nichtchristen, aber niemals zwischen Christen: Einen sakramental begründeten Unterschied zwischen Christen kann es nicht geben. Durch die Sakramente werden vielmehr alle in gleicher Weise dem einen Leib Christi inkorporiert und in ihm erhalten. Sakramente bewirken deshalb niemals Ungleichheit im Leib

Christi, sondern gerade umgekehrt die fundamentale Gleichheit aller Christen, durch die alle natürlichen, gesellschaftlichen, kulturellen, religiösen, wirtschaftlichen, politischen oder sonstigen Differenzen zwischen Juden und Griechen, Knechten und Herren, Männern und Frauen, Reichen und Armen, Mächtigen und Abhängigen in der christlichen Gemeinde theologisch außer Kraft gesetzt werden (vgl. Gal 3,28). Sakramente sind deshalb auch etwas anderes als Charismen: Sie legen den Grund der Gleichheit aller Christen, auf dem sich deren unterschiedliche Begabungen zum Aufbau des Ganzen überhaupt erst entwickeln und entfalten können.

Die Alternative ist also klar:

• Entweder ist die Ordination eine sakramentale Handlung, dann kann sie nur die Gleichheit aller Christen grundlegen, taugt damit nicht zur Beauftragung und Bevollmächtigung für das besondere kirchliche Amt, sondern allenfalls für das Priesteramt aller Getauften, konkurrierte in diesem Fall jedoch mit der Taufe und unterminierte gerade die Unterscheidung zwischen Priestertum aller Getauften und kirchlichem Amt, auf die hin sie doch ausgerichtet ist.

• Oder die Ordination wird als Bevollmächtigung und Verpflichtung zum besonderen Dienst der öffentlichen Verkündigung und Sakramentsverwaltung verstanden, kann dann aber keine sakramentale Handlung sein.

2. Form und Verantwortungsbereich der Ordination:

Ist die Ordination eine kirchliche Handlung, deren Gestaltung in die Regelungskompetenz der Kirchen fällt und die deshalb unterschiedlich geregelt sein kann, oder ist die ordnungsgemäße Berufung in das ordinierte Amt an eine bestimmte Form gebunden, die nicht in die Freiheit der Kirche gestellt ist? Auch zur Beantwortung dieser Frage bietet der Text der *Gemeinsamen Feststellung* nur Andeutungen. Unbestritten ist, daß das ordinierte Amt nicht im Belieben der Kirche steht, sondern als "Gabe Gottes an seine Kirche" (Nr. 15 (8), S. 45) zum Grundbestand und damit zu den beharrlichen Momenten der Kirche gehört; und unbestritten ist auch, daß es in unseren Kirchen jeweils "ordnungsgemäß berufene Geistliche" und damit eine geordnete Berufung in das Amt gibt (Nr. 17 B (4), S. 51).

Unklar ist dagegen, ob die Ordination als Berufung in das öffentliche "Amt des Wortes und Sakramentes" (S. 45, Nr. 15 (8)) die kirchlich geregelte Einweisung in *das* Amt *der* Kirche oder in das *ordinierte Amt* einer *bestimmten* Kirche ist. Kann man in einem Atemzug von der gemeinsamen Teilhabe "an einer Taufe, einem Herrenmahl und einem Amt" sprechen (Nr. 8, S. 39), oder ist - wie evangelischerseits betont werden muß - zu unterscheiden zwischen der aus der Gabe von Gottes Wort resultierenden *Verpflichtung* der Kirche und dem insofern unveränderlichen *Auftrag* an sie, das Predigtamt der öffentlichen Evangeliumsverkündigung in Wort und Sakrament zu ordnen, und der *konkreten Weise,* in der diese Verpflichtung in einer Kirche eingelöst und diesem Auftrag Rechnung getragen wird? Im ersten Fall wäre es nicht sinnvoll, von einem in der anglikanischen (oder römischen oder griechischen usf.) Kirche ordinierten Priester zu verlangen, sich neu ordinieren zu lassen, wenn er das Predigtamt in einer evangelischen Kirche anstrebt - und umgekehrt.[3] Im zweiten Fall wäre das aber durchaus sachgemäß, weil die Ordination stets die Einweisung in das geordnete Predigtamt einer *bestimmten* Kirche und nur so in das Verkündigungsamt *der* Kirche ist.

Die Unterscheidung hat eine Reihe weitreichender Folgen. *Die* Kirche gibt es gar nicht anders als in Gestalt *bestimmter Kirchen:* Sie ist keine Größe neben oder zusätzlich zu den bestimmten Kirchen, sondern der eine Leib Christi, an dem alle Christen *in ihren jeweiligen* Kirchen teilhaben. Mitgliedschaft in einer Kirche ist Gliedschaft am Leib Christi, und Gliedschaft am Leib Christi gibt es für uns in diesem Leben nur aufgrund der - wie distanziert auch immer wahrgenommenen - Mitgliedschaft *in einer bestimmten* Kirche. Anders als die Kirchen kennt der Leib Christi aber keine Ämter, sondern nur das *eine* Amt, das Christus selbst ausübt. Für dieses Amt aber gibt es keine Ordination, und in dieses Amt kann eine Ordination niemanden einweisen. Ordiniert werden kann nur für das *kirchliche* Amt, und das ist immer das Amt bestimmter Kirchen. Dieses nimmt im öffentlichen Vollzug der Gemeinschaft die Aufgaben wahr, zu denen jeder Christ befähigt und verpflichtet ist. Denn jeder nimmt durch die Taufe teil an dem einen Amt Jesu Christi und dessen priesterlicher Unmittelbarkeit zu Gott. Teilhabe an dem einen Amt Christi gibt also die Taufe, nicht die Ordination. Diese bevollmächtigt und verpflichtet nur dazu, die *allen* Christen zuteil gewordene Befähigung und Verpflichtung zur Evangeliumsverkündigung durch Wort und Sakrament *öffentlich* auszuüben. *Öffentlich* aber heißt stets *in der Öffentlichkeit einer bestimmten Kirche,* und deshalb kann die Ordination prinzipiell nur verstanden werden als Bevollmächtigung zum öffentlichen Amt in einer bestimmten Kirche.

Entsprechend muß auch die Einmaligkeit und Nichtwiederholbarkeit der Ordination anders verstanden werden als im Fall der Taufe: In der "Taufe mit Wasser im Namen des Dreieinigen Gottes" werden alle "Getauften mit dem Tod und der Auferstehung Jesu Christi vereint" (Nr. 15 (4), S. 43), in der Ordination dagegen werden einzelne Getaufte "zu der Ausübung der ordinierten Ämter als von Gott gegeben und als Werkzeugen seiner Gnade" (Nr. 12, S. 41) in einer bestimmten Kirche berechtigt. Wer getauft ist, bleibt daher immer getauft und kann nicht noch einmal getauft werden. Wer dagegen ordiniert ist, ist - lebenslang

- in das öffentliche Predigtamt einer bestimmten Kirche berufen und kann in dieses nicht noch einmal berufen werden.[4] Damit ist er aber noch nicht in das öffentliche Predigtamt jeder anderen Kirche berufen. Deshalb ist zwar keine zweite Taufe, wohl aber eine *weitere Ordination* in das Predigtamt einer *anderen Kirche* theologisch denkbar - eine *weitere* Ordination, wohlgemerkt, keine *Reordination*, weil die Berechtigung, Gültigkeit und Wirksamkeit der früheren Ordination dadurch in keiner Weise in Frage gestellt werden muß.

3. Ordiniertes Amt und Episkope:

In welchem Verhältnis stehen das ordinierte Amt und das "Amt pastoraler Aufsicht (Episkope)" (Nr. 15 (9), S. 45)? Auch dazu macht die *Gemeinsame Feststellung* nur indirekte Aussagen. Keine Rede ist davon, daß die Episkope ein Amt göttlicher Einsetzung wäre: das wird nur vom ordinierten Amt gesagt. Die Episkope wird auch nicht als (funktionale) Ausdifferenzierung des ordinierten Amtes beschrieben[5] und damit als eine bestimmte Gestalt oder als ein Teil der besonderen "Gabe Gottes an seine Kirche" (Nr. 15 (8), S. 45) bestimmt. Andererseits wird sie aber auch nicht für beliebig oder verzichtbar gehalten, sondern für notwendig erklärt, "um die Einheit und Apostolizität der Kirche zu bezeugen und zu schützen" (Nr. 15 (9), S. 45). Wie ist diese 'Notwendigkeit' der Episkope dann zu verstehen? Verschiedene Möglichkeiten bieten sich an:

• Ist das - vom ordinierten Verkündigungsamt unterschiedene - Amt pastoraler Aufsicht *funktional notwendig*, um die Einheit und Apostolizität der Kirche in der Vielzahl von Gemeinden zu wahren? Oder ist es *konstitutiv* dafür, daß überhaupt ein ordiniertes Amt in der Kirche da ist bzw. ordnungsgemäß besetzt werden kann? Ist dieses Amt also - mit anderen Worten - *pragmatisch notwendig* (d.h. zur Bewältigung bestimmter Probleme des kirchlichen Lebens hilfreich und nützlich) oder ist es *sachlich konstitutiv* dafür, daß es überhaupt ein kirchliches Leben gibt?

• Ist für dieses Amt eine *bestimmte Gestalt* notwendig, damit es die ihm zugeschriebene Aufgabe erbringen kann, oder kommt es nur darauf an, daß es in personaler, kollegialer und gemeinschaftlicher Weise *ausgeübt* wird, in welcher konkreten Gestalt das auch immer geschieht? Worauf - mit anderen Worten - erstreckt sich die zugestandene Notwendigkeit der Episkope: auf die *Gestalt* oder auf das *Faktum* ihrer Ausübung?

• Ist dieses besondere, vom ordinierten Predigtamt unterschiedene Amt notwendig, um die Kirche zu leiten und insbesondere um eine ordnungsgemäße Berufung in das ordinierte Predigtamt zu gewährleisten? Nach evangelischem Verständnis gehört es nicht zu den spezifischen Aufgaben des ordinierten Amtes, für die *Ordnung* dieses Amtes zu sorgen oder die ordnungsgemäße

Berufung in dieses Amt zu ordnen. Seine Aufgaben sind allein die Evangeliumsverkündigung in Wort und Sakrament. Für eine Ordnung dieses Amtes und der Berufung in dieses Amt zu sorgen, ist Aufgabe der *ganzen* Kirche und damit *aller* Christen, nicht nur der Inhaber des ordinierten Amtes. Denn das ist eine - wenn nicht die - zentrale Aufgabe der *Kirchenleitung*, und die Leitung der Kirche sowie das Ordnen des kirchlichen Lebens obliegt allen Christen, nicht nur den Inhabern des ordinierten Amtes. Eine Kirche kann diese Aufgabe zwar den Inhabern des Predigtamtes übertragen oder ein besonderes Amt dafür schaffen. Aber auch dieses Amt bleibt ein Amt der Gesamtkirche, das prinzipiell allen, also auch zu Leitungsaufgaben befähigten Laien und nicht nur ordinierten Amtsträgern offen stehen muß und deshalb prinzipiell immer auch von der Gesamtkirche ausgeübt werden kann und "im Bedarfsfall auch wieder von ihr ausgeübt werden muß".[6] In diesem Sinn wird das Bischofsamt in vielen evangelischen Landeskirchen ausgeübt. Notwendig ist damit aber nur, daß die Kirche geleitet und das kirchliche Leben geordnet wird, es ist aber nicht notwendig, daß dies durch ein Bischofsamt mit eigenständiger Tradition geschieht.

Daß in all diesen Punkten Unterschiede zwischen anglikanischen und evangelischen Auffassungen bestehen, wird kaum bestritten werden. Sie werden in der *Gemeinsamen Feststellung* aber nicht dargelegt. Ausdrücklich konstatiert wird nur, daß die evangelische Seite "die bischöfliche Sukzession >als ein Zeichen der Apostolizität des Lebens der ganzen Kirche<" zwar würdigt, aber der Überzeugung ist, daß "diese besondere Form der Episkope nicht eine notwendige Bedingung für >volle, sichtbare Einheit< werden sollte", während auf der anderen Seite "[d]as anglikanische Verständnis voller, sichtbarer Einheit ... den historischen Episkopat und volle Austauschbarkeit der Pfarrer" einschließt (Nr. 16, S. 45).

Man muß genau lesen, um die Pointe des damit beschriebenen Unterschieds zu erfassen: Beide Seiten würdigen die bischöfliche Sukzession als Zeichen der Apostolizität der ganzen Kirche oder sind doch zunehmend bereit dazu. Keine Seite aber bezeichnet sie als eine notwendige Bedingung für volle, sichtbare Einheit. Von evangelischer Seite wird sie als solche ausdrücklich abgelehnt. Aber auch den Anglikanern wird diese Auffassung nicht zugeschrieben. Es heißt vielmehr vorsichtiger, ihr Verständnis voller, sichtbarer Einheit schließe den historischen Episkopat und die volle Austauschbarkeit der Pfarrer ein. Offen bleibt dabei nicht nur, was dieses 'einschließen' (include) besagt, sondern auch, welches Verhältnis zwischen bischöflicher Sukzession (episcopal succession) und historischem Episkopat (historic episcopate) über das hinaus besteht, daß die erste in besonderer Weise mit der Apostolizität, der zweite dagegen mit der Einheit der

Kirche in Zusammenhang gebracht wird. Deutlich dagegen ist, daß die notierte Differenz mit einem unterschiedlichen Verständnis dessen zu tun hat, was volle, sichtbare Einheit meint und welche Rolle darin dem historischen Episkopat zugeschrieben wird. Und unübersehbar sind auch die aus dieser Differenz gezogenen Folgerungen:

- eine volle Austauschbarkeit der Geistlichen bzw. Pfarrer wird für unmöglich angesehen (Nr. 16; Nr. 17 A (3), S. 45; 47);

- die "eucharistische Gemeinschaft", zu der ausdrücklich ermutigt wird (Nr. 17 B (5), S. 51), darf nur so praktiziert werden, daß sie "die Gegenwart zweier oder mehrerer Kirchen erkennen" läßt (Nr. 17 B (6), S. 51), d.h. "Konzelebration im Sinne von gemeinsamer Konsekration wird weder durch Worte noch durch Gesten in Betracht gezogen" (S. 51, Anm.); und

- während dazu aufgefordert wird, "eine Einladung zur Teilnahme an einer Ordination in einer anderen Kirche" anzunehmen, wird ausdrücklich eingeschärft, daß bei Ordinationen in evangelischen Kirchen "ein beteiligter Bischof oder Priester" der Kirche von England "nicht durch Handauflegung oder auf andere Weise eine Handlung vornehmen darf, welche als Zeichen der Übertragung des anglikanischen Priesteramtes (Holy Orders) gilt" (Nr. 17 B (7), S. 53).

Vom 'anglikanischen Priesteramt' ist dabei allerdings nur im deutschen Text die Rede. Doch es ist die Frage, ob das gemeint ist und von Ordination hier tatsächlich als einem primär kirchenrechtlich zu verstehenden Akt die Rede ist. Nach anglikanischer Auffassung ist unter dem *conferring of Holy Orders* nicht die Berufung in ein Amt der anglikanischen Kirche (die dadurch faktisch bewirkt wird), sondern die Ordination in das von Gott gestiftete Amt des Wortes und Sakramentes zu verstehen, wie Bischof Stephen Sykes herausgestellt hat.[7] Doch damit wird nicht nur das dreifache Amt von Bischof, Priester und Diakon - denn das meint 'Holy Orders' in diesem Zusammenhang - als das unveränderliche Amt der einen, heiligen, apostolischen und katholischen Kirche ausgegeben, was theologisch kaum zu rechtfertigen sein dürfte. Es ergeben sich auch andere Probleme. Daß das von Gott gestiftete Amt des Wortes und Sakramentes - im Unterschied zu einem 'anglikanischen Priesteramt' in seiner gegliederten Struktur - auch in den evangelischen Kirchen vorhanden ist, wird ja ebenso ausdrücklich anerkannt (Nr. 17 A (3), S. 47) wie die Tatsache, daß es auch hier "die Treue gibt ... zu der Ausübung der ordinierten Ämter als von Gott gegeben und als Werkzeugen seiner Gnade" (Nr. 12, S. 41) und auch hier "ordnungsgemäß berufene Geistliche" (Nr. 17 B (4), S. 51)[8] diese Ämter ausüben. Wenn es aber das ordinierte Amt in beiden Kirchen gibt und auch in beiden Kirchen ordnungsgemäß in dieses Amt berufen wird, worin besteht dann der *theologische*

Unterschied zwischen evangelischer und anglikanischer Ordination, der daran hindert, nicht nur von gegenseitiger Anerkennung (recognition), sondern vom vollen Einklang (reconciliation) der Ämter zu sprechen? Welche *theologische* Qualität besitzt das anglikanische *conferring of Holy Orders*, die der evangelischen Berufung ins ordinierte Amt abginge?

Die Frage bleibt in der *Meissener Gemeinsamen Feststellung* offen. Ihre Antwort hat aber offensichtlich mit zwei Fragen zu tun, nämlich

* welche theologische Bedeutung die anglikanische Seite der Struktur des gegliederten dreifachen Amtes von Bischof, Priester und Diakon für eine angemessene Gestalt des ordinierten Amtes zumißt, und

* welche Rolle sie dem Bischofsamt in Gestalt des historischen Episkopats bei der Ordination zuschreibt.

Nach Lage der Dinge spricht alles dafür, daß es nach anglikanischer Auffassung *ohne das dreifache Amt kein gemeinsames Amt[9], ohne bischöfliche Ordination - also ohne Ordination durch einen Bischof in historischer Sukzession - keine volle Austauschbarkeit der Geistlichen und ohne "a single episcopate" keine "visible unity of the Church"[10]* gibt. In diesem Sinn hieß es schon 1973 bei den Anglican-Lutheran International Conversations (§87): "The Anglican participants cannot forsee full integration of ministries (full communion) apart from the historic episcopate". Und daran hat sich bis zu den jüngsten Verlautbarungen nichts geändert.[11]

Die Grundfrage, mit der wir uns auseinandersetzen müssen, ist also nicht, ob es in unseren Kirchen ein ordiniertes Amt gibt oder ob in ihnen ein "Amt pastoraler Aufsicht (Episkope)" (Nr. 15 (9), S. 45) nötig ist, sondern allein, ob es für die *volle, sichtbare Einheit* unserer Kirchen notwendig ist, daß dieses Amt die Gestalt des *dreifachen Amtes* und des *historischen Episkopats* hat: **Ist ohne dreifaches Amt, historischen Episkopat und bischöfliche Sukzession eine volle, sichtbare Einheit unserer Kirchen möglich oder nicht?** Wenn sie möglich ist, was begründet dann den Vorbehalt, daß wir "ein gemeinsames, in vollem Einklang befindliches Amt" noch nicht haben (Nr. 17 B (7), S. 53; vgl. Nr. 17 A (3), S. 47), samt allen Folgen, die daraus gezogen werden? Ist sie dagegen nicht möglich, wie kann dann anerkannt werden, daß beide Kirchen das ordinierte Amt haben und auch ordnungsgemäß verwalten? Und was ist in diesem Fall mit der gegliederten Gestalt des dreifachen Amtes und der Ausübung der Episkope durch Bischöfe in historischer Sukzession zusätzlich gegeben, was der - unterschiedlich geordneten - Amtsgestalt und Ausübung der Episkope in den evangelischen Kirchen fehlte?

3. Hintergründe des Problems[12]

1. Um das Problem und seine Tragweite richtig einschätzen zu können, ist auf das Basisdokument des anglikanischen Engagements für die Ökumene, das Chicago-Lambeth Quadrilateral von 1888 und seine Vorgeschichte zurückzugehen. Der spezifisch anglikanische Terminus 'historischer Episkopat' wurde von dem amerikanischen Anglikaner William Reed Huntington (1838-1909) 1870 in seinem Buch *The Church Idea. An Essay toward Unity* in die Diskussion eingeführt. Gemeint ist damit die historische Sukzession bischöflicher Ordinationen in das dreifache Amt, durch die die anglikanische Kirche in ungebrochener Kontinuität mit der vorreformatorischen Kirche und über sie mit den apostolischen Anfängen der Kirche zu stehen beansprucht. Dieser Anspruch ist komplex und umfaßt mehrere Momente, die zu unterscheiden sind, nämlich

- den *historischen* und *institutionellen Anspruch*, daß die Kirche von England über die Neuordnungen des 16. Jahrhunderts hinweg in ihrer Lehre und Ordnung in der Tradition der Alten Kirche steht;

- den *theologischen* Anspruch, daß sie damit die apostolische Tradition und Sukzession wahre, i.e. "that the Church of England traces its ecclesiastical formation back to the early Church"[13];

- den *ekklesiologischen Anspruch*, daß sich das exemplarisch in der Struktur ihres ordinierten Amtes zeige. Das dreifache Amt von Bischof, Presbyter und Diakon könne zwar "not claim to be the only one authorized in Scripture", aber es sei doch die maßgebliche Manifestation genuin altkirchlicher Tradition, insofern "the threefold pattern eventually prevailed and was generally adopted by the Church"[14];

- den *soteriologischen Anspruch*, daß die bischöfliche Sukzession das Vorliegen der apostolischen Tradition und damit der gültigen und wirksamen Vermittlung des Heils zwar nicht garantiere (wie heute gesagt wird, aber nicht immer gesagt wurde), aber doch unübersehbar markiere.

2. Zumindest dieser letzte Punkt ist auch innerhalb des Anglikanismus durchaus umstritten, da er einigen zu weit, anderen nicht weit genug geht. "Anglicans have no single, common, official explanation of *why* the historic episcopate is important; but we overwhelmingly concur in the consensus that it is."[15] Dieser Konsens kommt in den vier anglikanischen Grundbedingungen für Kirchenunionen im Chicago-Lambeth Quadrilateral darin zum Ausdruck, daß neben den Schriften des Alten und Neuen Testaments, dem Apostolischen und Nikänischen Glaubensbekenntnis und den Sakramenten der Taufe und des Abendmahls an vierter Stelle ausdrücklich auch der "Historic Episcopate"

genannt wird, "locally adapted in the methods of its administration to the varying needs of the nations and peoples called of God into the Unity of His Church".[16] Von *Sukzession* ist dabei - wie auch bei der Wiederholung dieser Einheitsbedingungen im *Appeal to all Christian People* der Lambeth Conference von 1920[17] - auffälligerweise nicht die Rede.[18] Das ist angesichts der Betonung des Sukzessionsgedankens in der anglokatholischen Oxford-Bewegung zumindest bemerkenswert, obgleich John Henry Newman schon 1840 darauf hingewiesen hatte, die Einheit der Kirche könne nur in einer sichtbaren rechtlichen Organisation der Kirche liegen, nicht aber in der apostolischen Sukzession der Amtsträger, weil die Kirche ja trotz der Behauptung einer solchen ununterbrochenen Herleitung von den Aposteln im Schisma lebe.[19] Garantieren kann der Episkopat in apostolischer Sukzession die Einheit der Kirche nicht. Nicht zuletzt deshalb sah sich Newman 1845 zur Konversion genötigt. Und nicht zuletzt deshalb wird in neueren Dokumenten nicht mehr von einer *Garantie* der Einheit und Apostolizität der Kirche durch den Episkopat in historischer Sukzession gesprochen.

3. Ausdrücklich hervorgehoben wird das Moment der apostolischen Sukzession im Begriff des historischen Episkopats dagegen 1927 in Lausanne durch Bischof Palmer[20], und an diesem Punkt bestand und besteht Einigkeit mit den orthodoxen Kirchen: "The apostolic doctrine and tradition, with the apostolic succession, are the elements in which the apostolicity of the Church con-sists".[21] Gerade deshalb wirkte aber auch die kompromißlose Ablehnung der Gültigkeit anglikanischer Weihen durch Leo XIII. in seiner Enzyklika *Apostolicae curae et caritatis* vom 13. September 1896 bei vielen Anglikanern traumatisch: "auctoritate Nostra, motu proprio, certa scientia pronuntiamus et declaramus, ordinationes ritu Anglicano actas irritas prorsus fuisse et esse omninoque nullas" (DH 3319, S. 903). Damit wurde nichts Neues gesagt, sondern im Blick auf das 1550 in der Kirche von England erstmals eingeführte, nach der Aufhebung durch Mary seit 1559 endgültig geltende Ordinale Edwards VI nur das Urteil wiederholt und unterstrichen, das das Heilige Offizium schon 1685, 1704 und 1875 gefällt hatte.

4. In eine grundlegende Krise gerieten damit aber die anglokatholischen Bemühungen, durch ihre Theorie der Übermittlung der Gnade durch eine Kette ununterbrochener Handauflegungen von den Aposteln bis auf die Gegenwart die volle Gültigkeit des Amtes in der Kirche von England zu erweisen. Noch in der Auseinandersetzung um das ökumenische Experiment eines evangelischen Bistums apostolischer Sukzession in Jerusalem, das Friedrich Wilhelm IV. von Preussen 1841 initiiert und die Kirche von England zum Entsetzen der Traktarianer mitgetragen hatte, hatte Newman gegen diese

"Anerkennung" der "Häresien" von "Luthertum und Calvinismus" protestiert und nicht zuletzt deswegen die Kirche von England verlassen.[22] Gemeinsamkeit konnte es ihm zufolge nur mit Kirchen geben, die den Episkopat in apostolischer Sukzession gewahrt hatten oder sich ihm unter Absage ihrer bisherigen Irrtümer unterstellten. Die traditionelle anglikanische Position war damit in eine Richtung verschärft worden, deren Beibehaltung das ökumenische Engagement im 20. Jahrhundert unmöglich gemacht hätte[23]: Zur sichtbaren Kirche können nur diejenigen gehören, die durch den historischen Episkopat mit den Aposteln verbunden sind. Nur in apostolischer Sukzession ordinierte Priester können gültig die Eucharistie zelebrieren. Der historische Episkopat gehört zum *esse* der Kirche.

5. Das war auf anglikanischer Seite nicht immer so vertreten worden. Die Caroline Divines des 17. Jahrhunderts unterschieden zwischen "the essence of a Church", die auch den reformatorischen Kirchen zugestanden wurde, und "the integrity or perfection of a Church", die es ohne Episkopat nicht geben könne. Auch Kirchen mit sog. presbyterialer Ordination sind wirklich Kirche, ihre Ämter zwar irregulär, aber wirksam[24], so daß protestantische Pfarrer Gemeinden in England übernehmen konnten, ohne reordiniert zu werden[25]. Man ging also davon aus, daß es Kirche auch ohne Episkopat gibt, dieses aber der "God-given focus of unity and seat of authority in the Church" sei[26].

Damit war zunächst nur die bestehende Sachlage in der Kirche von England zum Ausdruck gebracht. Als Heinrich VIII die Kirche von England der päpstlichen Jurisdiktion entzog und der eigenen Oberaufsicht unterstellte, griff er in keiner Weise in die inneren Strukturen der Kirche ein. Die überkommene hierarchische Gestalt des ordinierten Amtes von Bischof, Priester und Diakon wurde ungebrochen fortgesetzt, und auch unter Edward VI und Elisabeth I wurden Bischöfe nach der überkommenen Ordnung konsekriert. Theologisch wurde die Funktion der Bischöfe allerdings in reformatorischem Sinn auf ihre geistlichen und pastoralen Aufgaben konzentriert: Bischöfe sollten nicht weltliche Herrscher, sondern geistliche Führer und Lehrer der Kirche sein. Da dies an der faktischen Rolle der Bischöfe wenig änderte, richtete sich die puritanisch-calvinistische Kritik zunehmend nicht nur gegen den politisch-weltlichen Mißbrauch des Bischofsamtes, sondern gegen dieses selbst. Wurde von der einen Seite betont, "that between a Presbyter and a Bishop the Word of God alloweth not any inequality or difference to be made"[27], so bestand die andere Seite darauf, daß "A Bishop is a Minister of God, unto whom with permanent continuance, there is given not onely power of administring the Word and Sacraments, which power other presbyters have; but also a further power to ordain Ecclesiastical persons, and a power of Chiefty in Government over Presbyters as well as Lay men, a power to be by way of jurisdiction a

Pastor even to Pastors themselves".[28] Der entscheidende Unterschied zwischen Bischöfen und anderen Priestern wurde also im Ordinationsrecht gesehen: Beide sind Priester, aber die Funktion und Autorität von Priestern hängt an ihrer Ordination durch Bischöfe in *apostolischer Sukzession.*[29]

6. Der Begriff der *apostolic succession* wurde im Zusammenhang dieser Auseinandersetzung im 16. Jahrhundert geprägt und von Thomas Bilson in seinem 1593 erschienen und 1842 neu aufgelegten Werk *The Perpetual Government of Christ's Church* in die Diskussion eingeführt. Bilson unterscheidet dort zwischen der "succession of function", der ordnungsgemäßen Weitergabe des apostolischen Auftrags durch Handauflegung, und der "orderly succession of place". Apostolische Sukzession meine Weitergabe der apostolischen Funktion, nicht - wie gegen Rom betont wurde - die Fortführung eines "perpetual chair of succession" oder gar die funktionale Gleichsetzung von Bischof und Apostel. Bischöfe setzen nur einen Teil der komplexen Funktionen des Apostelamtes fort. Als Augenzeugen der Inkarnation und von Christus direkt beauftragte Gründer der Kirche konnten die Apostel keine Nachfolger haben, wie auch Hooker betonte. Als Diener von Gottes Wort und Sakrament werde ihr Amt von den Priestern fortgesetzt. Nur ihre Funktion der Episkope und Jurisdiktion sei an die Bischöfe übergegangen, und nur um die Weitergabe dieser Funktion gehe es auch bei der Sukzession der Bischöfe.[30] Die Apostolizität der Kirche wird also nicht allein im Bischofsamt gesehen. Doch Bischöfe setzen eine für die Kirche wesentliche Teilfunktion des den Aposteln zugeschriebenen Amtes fort und sind gerade so ein sichtbares Zeichen der Kontinuität der Kirche mit ihren apostolischen Ursprüngen.

Hooker ließ offen, ob "the apostles themselves left the bishops invested with power above other pastors" oder ob nach dem Tod der Apostel "Churches did agree amongst themselves ... to make one Presbyter in each city chief over the rest".[31] Diese historische Unsicherheit tat der Gewißeit keinen Abbruch, daß Bischöfe diese besondere Funktion und Autorität in der Kirche faktisch haben. Art. 23 der 39 Artikel spricht zwar nur davon, daß das Amt der öffentlichen Verkündigung und Sakramentsverwaltung allein von Personen ausgeübt werden dürfe, "which be chosen and called to this work by men who have public authority given unto them in the Congregation, to call and send ministers", ohne daß Bischöfe ausdrücklich genannt würden, doch faktisch sind genau sie damit gemeint. Auch wenn sich im Lauf der Zeit immer deutlicher zeigte, daß diese Praxis in ihren historischen Urspüngen dunkel, biblisch nicht eindeutig begründet und auf keine klare Einsetzung durch Christus oder die Apostel zurückzuführen ist, konnte gegen Ende des 17. Jahrhunderts Edward Stillingfleet darauf bestehen, daß "there is as great

Reason to believe, the *Apostolical Succession* to be of *Divine Institution*, as the *Canon of Scripture*, or the *Observation of the Lord's Day*".[32] Die Entwicklung des Kanons, der Bekenntnisse und des Episkopats wurden so theologisch parallelisiert und ihre Stellung und Funktion in der Kirche in analoger Weise legitimiert. Bis in unser Jahrhundert wird so die besondere Position des Episkopats auch angesichts einer fehlenden biblischen Legtimation damit begründet, daß die allmähliche historische Entwicklung des Episkopats in der frühen Kirche "would be no evidence that it lacked divine authority, but rather that the life of the Spirit within the Church had found it to be the most appropriate organ for the functions it discharged".[33]

7. Stillingfleets Argumente waren allerdings nicht nur theologisch motiviert. Durch den *Act of Uniformity* von 1662 war im Zusammenhang der Restauration von Charles II eine folgenreich neue Situation entstanden, insofern eine faktische, aber nicht exklusive Praxis der Kirche von England ohne biblische oder theologische Begründung aus kirchenpolitischen Überlegungen kirchenrechtlich zur theologischen Norm erhoben worden war. Hatte es im Prayer Book von Edward VI geheißen "that no man (not being at this present Bishop, Priest, or Deacon) shall execute any of them [d.h. eines dieser Ämter] except he be called, tried, examined, and admitted, according to the form hereafter following", so wird das nach den Wirren der Bürgerkriegsepoche nun folgendermaßen verschärft: "no man shall be accounted or taken to be a lawful Bishop, Priest, or Deacon in the Church of England, or suffered to execute any of the said Functions, except he be called, tried, examined, and admitted thereunto, according to the Form hereafter following, or hath had formerly Episcopal Consecration, or Ordination".[34]

Diese Regel gilt bis in die Gegenwart. Nur bischöflich ordinierte Priester dürfen seither in der Kirche von England - und den übrigen anglikanischen Kirchen - ein Amt ausüben, und nur das dreifache Amt von Bischof, Priester und Diakon gilt als Amt in der Kirche. Mit diesen Entscheidungen *wurde die Kirche von England zu einer episkopalen Konfessionskirche* und verwirkte damit ihren traditionellen Anspruch, *die christliche Kirche* in England zu sein.[35] Denn während "[t]he Church of England had always been episcopal, it now became episcopalian, that is, what had been a matter of practical policy became the requirement of religious principle".[36] Aus der *Anglicana ecclesia*, der christlichen Kirche in England, wurde damit die *Church of England*, die englische Episkopalkirche; und auch die Ordination wurde damit zu einem kirchenrechtlichen Akt dieser partikularen Kirche. Mit dieser (zunächst gar nicht als solche gesehenen) Transformation in eine partikulare Konfessionskirche neben anderen kam nicht nur die vor 1662 zumindest gelegentlich praktizierte, ohne Reordination vorgenommene Übernahme evangelischer

Pfarrer in Ämter der Kirche von England zum Erliegen, sondern es wurden anders als im 16. Jahrhundert ausdrücklich theologisch-konfessionelle Abgrenzungen vorgenommen. So konnten oder wollten sich viele der reformatorisch-puritanisch gesinnten Geistlichen in England nicht reordinieren lassen und weigerten sich, das katholisierend überarbeitete Common Prayer Book zu akzeptieren oder ihre reformatorischen Überzeugungen aufzugeben. Am 24.8.1662 wurden deshalb über 2000 puritanische Geistliche aus ihren Ämtern vertrieben, und im Gefolge der *Conventicle Acts* (1664/1670), die die Teilnahme an nichtanglikanischen Gottesdiensten verboten, kamen über 8000 Dissenters ins Gefängnis (darunter für 12 Jahre der Baptist John Bunyan) und mehr als 60 000 wurden auf andere Weise bestraft.

8. Mit den Entscheidungen von 1662 wurde eine Entwicklung eingeleitet, die die Kirche von England in mindestens zweifacher Hinsicht grundlegend verändert hat. Auf der einen Seite wurde sie aus politischen Gründen auf Betreiben des Parlaments von einer umfassenden Nationalkirche zu einer privilegierten Staatskirche unter bzw. neben anderen Religionsgemeinschaften in England umgestaltet. Auf der anderen Seite äußerte sich innerkirchlich der Protest gegen den politischen Einfluß des Parlaments auf die Leitung der Kirche darin, daß eine wichtige Minderheit die kirchenrechtliche Festschreibung bischöflicher Ordination im Gefolge von 1662 zu einem theologisch-ekklesiologischen Grundsatzprinzip ausgestaltete.

8.1 Als Charles II 1672 die *Declaration of Indulgence* erließ, die protestantischen Nonkonformisten an bestimmten Orten öffentliche Gottesdienste und den Katholiken immerhin private Messen zugestand, sah das Parlament darin einen versteckten Versuch zur Einführung des Katholizismus und reagierte 1673 mit dem *Test Act*, der die Bekleidung von Staatsämtern von der Zugehörigkeit zur anglikanischen Kirche abhängig machte. Die Folge dieser sich zuspitzenden Auseinandersetzung zwischen königlichen Rekatholisierungsversuchen und parlamentarischem Anglikanismus waren die Revolution von 1688 und die *Toleranzakte* von 1689, die den protestantischen Dissenters (Baptisten, Quäkern usf.) das Recht zur eigenständigen Religionsausübung außerhalb der anglikanischen Staatskirche gab. Ausgeschlossen von der Duldung waren - aus politischen Gründen - die Katholiken und die Sozinianer (Antitrinitarier). Die Kirche von England gab damit ihren Anspruch, eine allumfassende (comprehensive) Staatskirche zu sein, auf und wurde zur *established church*, zur staatlich privilegierten Kirche in England. So blieb die Testakte zwar bis 1828 in Kraft, und auch die Schulen und Universitäten und damit das Bildungssystem blieben in anglikanischer Hand, aber andere Kirchen und Religionsgemeinschaften spielten seit 1689 eine legitime Rolle im religiösen Leben Englands. Im Gefolge der Uniformitätsakte von 1662 war es damit zur staatsrechtlich sanktionierten Trennung zwischen 'Konformisten' und 'Nonkonformisten' und zur Aufgabe der Idee einer umfassend inklusiven Staatskirche gekommen.

8.2 Gegen diese Entwicklung und den Einfluß von Politik und Parlament auf die Leitung der Kirche gab es von Anfang an erheblichen innerkirchlichen Widerstand. Eine nicht unbedeutende Gruppe von Bischöfen hatte sich nach der rechtlich problematischen 'Abdankung' von James II und der parlamentarischen Berufung von William III zum König geweigert, den Treueid auf den neuen und, wie sie es sahen, illegitimen König abzulegen und mußten deshalb ihre Positionen verlassen. Im Kreis dieser sog. *Non-jurors* wurde die kirchenrechtliche Festschreibung bischöflicher Ordination von 1662 hochkirchlich interpretiert als Abweisung alles weltlich-politischen Einflusses auf die Kirchenleitung und deren Begründung allein auf das legitime kirchliche Amt. Die Kirche, so wird betont, sei eine eigenständige Größe mit eigener Legitimation unabhängig von allen gesellschaftlichen Gegebenheiten. Nur sie selbst habe das Recht, Personen in kirchliche Funktionen zu berufen, und sie habe dieses Recht nur insofern, als es in ihr eine ununterbrochene Sukzession autorisierter Personen seit Christus gibt: "If there be no *Uninterrupted Succession*, then there are no Authorised Ministers from Christ; if no such Ministers, then no Chrstian Sacraments; if no Christian Sacraments, then no Christian Covenant, whereof the Sacraments are the Stated and Visible Seals."[37] An diese Auffassung konnten die Tractarianer im 19. Jahrhundert mit ihrer Theorie der ununterbrochenen Kette der Handauflegung als der physischen Gnadenvermittlung und damit einzig maßgeblichen Legitimation der Gültigkeit kirchlicher Ämter unmittelbar anknüpfen. Aus der faktischen Praxis der Kirche von England war so über die kirchenrechtliche Normierung von 1662 ein theologisches Grundprinzip geworden, daß die Identität und das Kirchesein der Kirche von der historischen Sukzession der Amtsträger abhängig machte: Wo es keinen Bischof in apostolischer Sukzession gibt, dort gibt es auch keine Kirche.

9. Das war und ist nur *eine* Ansicht in der Kirche von England, und es ist nicht die gegenwärtig maßgebliche. Aber an ihr wird besonders deutlich, daß mit dem historischen Episkopat nicht nur die Frage der theologischen Legitimität kirchlicher Ämter und die ökumenische Einheit der Kirchen zur Debatte stehen, sondern auch die *Eigenständigkeit der Kirche* und die *Unabhängigkeit der Kirchenleitung von Staat und Gesellschaft*. Zugespitzt könnte man sagen: *Motor der Ausbildung der anglikanischen Episkopaltheologie waren nicht primär oder ausschließlich theologische, sondern immer auch (kirchen)politische Erwägungen.*

4. Theologische Beurteilung

Eine theologische Beurteilung der anglikanischen Betonung des historischen Episkopats wird daher drei Sachlagen unterscheiden müssen, nämlich

- die faktische kirchliche Praxis vor 1662,

- die kirchrechtliche Situation seit 1662, und

- theologische Theorien zur Erklärung und Rechtfertigung dieser kirchenrechtlich sanktionierten Praxis wie die hochkirchlich-anglokatholische Sukzessionstheorie einer Transmission der Amtsgnade durch eine ununterbrochene Kette physischer Handauflegungen (die als theologische Rechtfertigung der Regelung von 1662 zur Wahrung der Eigenständigkeit der Kirche und ihrer Unabhängigkeit von Staat und Gesellschaft verstanden werden kann) oder die Zeichentheologie, die in Porvoo diese Funktion übernimmt und in der neueren anglikanischen Theologie die anglokatholische Theorie abgelöst zu haben scheint.

Daß die Praxis der Kirche von England theologisch legitim ist, ist aus evangelischer Sicht unstrittig. Bischöfe werden in Fortsetzung vorreformatorischer Praxis konsekriert, Priester durch Handauflegung des Bischofs ordiniert, Getaufte vom Bischof konfirmiert. Bischöfe stehen so in der Kontinuität des 'historischen Episkopats', Priester in 'apostolischer Sukzession' und Getaufte werden durch bischöfliche Konfirmation zu vollen Mitgliedern der Kirche von England gemacht. Das ist die faktische Praxis und Ordnung der Kirche von England, die mit der Praxis und Ordnung einiger, aber nicht aller anderen Kirchen übereinstimmt.

Diese Praxis ist infolge der kirchenrechtlichen Regelung von 1662 für die Kirche von England verbindlich, aber deshalb und als solche noch nicht für andere Kirchen.[38] Das könnte sie allenfalls aufgrund ihrer theologischen Begründung sein. Doch worin besteht diese? Darauf werden von anglikanischer Seite unterschiedliche Antworten gegeben:

Die anglokatholische Begründung, die in der ununterbrochenen Kette physischer Handauflegungen seit den Aposteln eine notwendige Bedingung für die Transmission der Gnade und damit das wahre Kirchesein einer Kirche sieht, ist selbst unter Anglikanern umstritten: Sie stützt sich nicht nur auf kaum haltbare historische Thesen über den Ursprung und die ununterbrochene Kontinuität des historischen Episkopats[39], sie ist auch theologisch unzureichend. Zum einen leistet sie nicht, was sie leisten soll, weil es "no support from the Bible" gibt, "that the apostolic succession through the laying on of hands guarantees the church", wie Michael Ramsey schon 1936 betont hat.[40] Zum andern setzt die Vorstellung

der "Transmission der Gnade durch die lineare Kette bischöflicher Handauflegungen ... ein materielles, immanentes, besitzbestimmtes und gleichsam juristisch
an das Amt gebundenes Gnadenverständnis voraus", das die "Apostolische
Sukzession als Extension des inkarnierten und auferstandenen Herrn in Zeit und
Raum hinein" werden läßt.[41] Und schließlich ist sie ökumenisch untauglich, weil
sie nicht-bischöflichen Kirchen das Kirchesein absprechen und die Defizienz
ihrer Ämter behaupten muß. Nicht von ungefähr spricht das Chicago-Lambeth
Quadrilateral daher nicht von apostolischer Sukzession, sondern vom *historic
episcopate*, und nicht von ungefähr betonten die Anglikaner in den ökumenischen
Gesprächen dieses Jahrhunderts von Anfang an, daß ihre Forderung nach
Übernahme des historischen Bischofsamtes nicht mit der Übernahme einer
bestimmten - nämlich der anglokatholischen - Lehre von der apostolischen
Sukzession verwechselt werden dürfe.[42].

Die anglokatholische Sukzessionslehre wird auch inneranglikanisch von der in
unserem Jahrhundert dominierenden theologischen Strömung abgelehnt, ohne
daß man dem historischen Episkopat gegenüber theologisch gleichgültig wäre.
Seine Bedeutung wird aber nicht in seiner Funktion für das Sein, sondern für die
sichtbare Einheit der Kirche gesehen: Das Bischofsamt sei wirksames Zeichen
und Instrument der Einheit der Kirche. Diese Begründung - das ist ihr Vorteil -
ist nicht an fragwürdige historische Thesen über die Entstehung des Bischofsamtes gebunden, sondern eine theologische Aussage über dessen *rechte Funktion*.
Sie ist deshalb auch nicht durch den Hinweis auf das historische Versagen des Bischofsamtes zu widerlegen. Und sie beansprucht auch nicht, daß allein die Sukzession dieses Amtes die Kontinuität der Kirche konstituiere. Wesentlich für die
Kontinuität der Kirche ist vielmehr die Verkündigung durch Wort und Sakrament, das in Sukzession stehende Amt kann diese Kontinuität nur bezeugen und
bewahren.[43] Auch Kirchen, die dieses Zeichen nicht haben, kann so das
Kirchesein nicht abgesprochen werden, ohne daß sie deshalb im Blick auf die
Sichtbarkeit der Einheit der Kirche von England gleichgestellt werden könnten.
In diesem Sinn formulierte die Lambeth Conference von 1948, daß es für Anglikaner gleichermaßen unmöglich sei, "to declare the sacraments of non-episcopal
bodies null and void", und "to treat non-episcopal ministries as identical in status
and authority with the episcopal ministry".[44]

Offen bleibt dabei freilich, worin der mindere Status und die geringere Autorität
nicht-bischöflicher Ämter bestehen soll, wenn die anglokatholische Begründung
für ihre Defizienz hinfällig ist. Was fehlt den Ämtern einer Kirche, die nicht das
historische Bischofsamt und das dreifache Amt besitzt, oder was gewönnen sie
hinzu, wenn die entsprechende Kirche das historische Bischofsamt und die
gegliederte Amtsstruktur übernimmt, wie es in *"Toward Full Communion" and
"Concordat of Agreement"* und im Porvoo Common Statement *Together in*

Mission and Ministry vorgeschlagen bzw. angestrebt wird? Besteht im Blick auf die Vollzüge ordinierter Ämter in beiden Fällen kein grundlegender Unterschied, dann gibt es keinen theologischen (im Unterschied zu einem kirchenrechtlichen) Grund, die Reordination von nicht-bischöflich ordinierten Amtsträgern zu fordern. Mit Recht wird diese Forderung deshalb jetzt in *"Toward Full Communion" and "Concordat of Agreement"* und in *Together in Mission and Ministry* nicht mehr erhoben. Das kann aber nur bedeuten, daß auf die Forderung der Übernahme des historischen Episkopats und der bischöflichen Ordination als *Bedingung und Voraussetzung* für die Aufnahme uneingeschränkter Abendmahlsgemeinschaft mit anderen Kirchen verzichtet wird, wie J.A.T. Robinson und andere anglikanische Theologen schon zu Beginn der 60er Jahre gefordert haben und jetzt praktiziert werden soll.[45] Warum hält man dann aber daran fest, der historische Episkopat und das damit verknüpfte dreifache Amt "in historic succession" müsse das "future pattern of the one ordained ministry of Word and Sacrament" sein[46]? Wird hier nicht doch einem kirchenrechtlichen Sachverhalt der Kirche von England ein ekklesiologisches Gewicht beigemessen, daß ihm theologisch nicht zukommt? Denn auch von anglikanischer Seite wird zugestanden, daß "the historic episcopate or apostolic succession as a condition of a true Church is certainly incompatible with a genuine Reformation ecclesiology, according to which word and sacrament suffice for the full integrity of ecclesial life since through their means Christ has promised to be present with his people".[47] Gilt das dann aber nicht auch von der dahinter stehenden Auffassung von *Kirche*, insofern das Verhältnis zwischen der geglaubten einen, heiligen, apostolischen und katholischen Kirche als dem universalen Leib Christi und der besonderen geschichtlichen Institution der Kirche von England (oder irgendeiner anderen Kirche) nicht klar bestimmt ist? Und müßte dann nicht auch im Verständnis der *Ordination* deutlicher von einer Parallelisierung von Taufe und Ordination Abstand genommen und die Ordination strikter als Beauftragung und Berechtigung zur Ausübung des ordinierten Amtes in einer *bestimmten* Kirche verstanden werden, ohne die konkrete Form, in der diese hier vorgenommen wird, auch für andere verbindlich zu machen? Und kann dann noch einer historisch kontingenten Ausgestaltung des Amtes in einigen Kirchen wie dem dreifachen Amt in historischer Sukzession ein solches theologisches Gewicht beigemessen werden, daß von seiner Auf- und Übernahme die uneingeschränkte sichtbare Kirchengemeinschaft abhängig gemacht wird?

Daß sich aus all dem ökumenische Schwierigkeiten ergeben, ist offensichtlich. Sie zeigen sich kaum, wenn es um die Beziehung anglikanischer Kirchen zu Kirchen wie den Altkatholischen Kirchen der Utrechter Union oder der Kirche von Schweden geht, die den historischen Episkopat haben, oder die ihn, wie die Philippine

Independent Church, bei der Aufnahme voller Gemeinschaft mit den Anglikanern übernahmen. Doch schon im Fall der Church of South India, in der in einer Übergangsperiode neben bischöflich ordinierten auch nicht-bischöflich ordinierte Amtsträger fungierten, gab es Vorbehalte seitens einiger anglikanischer Kirchen.[48] Und in Meissen unterblieb der letzte Schritt zur uneingeschränkten Gemeinschaft, weil die Meinungsverschiedenheiten über die Bedeutung des historischen Episkopats für die sichtbare Einheit der Kirche nicht ausgeräumt werden konnten.

Doch warum besteht die Kirche von England auf dieser Bedingung? Die anglokatholische Position hatte darauf eine klare Antwort, auch wenn diese sich nicht als haltbar erwies. Die inneranglikanische Kritik dieser Antwort verwirft die anglokatholische Begründung, hält aber am Begründeten fest. Sie muß deshalb eine andere Begründung dafür geben, warum es "ein gemeinsames, in vollem Einklang befindliches Amt" (Nr. 17 B (7), S. 53) ohne historischen Episkopat und dreigliedrige Amtsgestalt nicht geben können soll. In der *Gemeinsamen Feststellung* ist dazu nichts gesagt. In *Apostolicity and Succession* dagegen wird eine Begründung angedeutet: Seit den neutestamentlichen Anfängen der Kirche gebe es ein "ministry of oversight", das sich "in the patristic centuries" im Rahmen eines "relatively settled and consistent system of threefold ministry" konsolidiert habe und dessen zentrale Aufgabe es sei, "[to] serve the unity of the community" (§ 44). Da diese Einheit der Kirche heute nicht mehr gegeben sei, wird als eine ökumenische Forderung erhoben, es sei "necessary to bring into being a single ministry of oversight, for only then will the churches renew the ministry of oversight and be able to take common decisions for the whole Church, teach together with conviction and engage in common service and mission" (§ 51).

Doch warum sollten die angeführten Aktivitäten nur unter Voraussetzung eines "single ministry of oversight" möglich sein? Kommt hier nicht unter der Hand ein amtskirchliches Einheitsverständnis ins Spiel, das nicht nur für notwendig erklärt, daß die Aufgabe der Episkope in jeder Kirche geordnet wird, sondern daß sie in allen Kirchen *auf dieselbe Weise* geordnet wird? Kann das ein realistisches Ziel ökumenischer Bemühungen sein? Spricht nicht vielmehr alles dafür, daß es zu gemeinsamen Entscheidungen christlicher Kirchen in ihrer Vielfalt in Lehre, Dienst und Mission nicht kommen wird, wenn dies zur Voraussetzung gemacht wird? Haben nicht gerade die schnell wachsenden christlichen Kirchen weltweit schon längst ganz andere Wege eingeschlagen? Und selbst wenn es zuträfe, daß zum Vollzug der genannten Aktivitäten "the visible unity of the Church served by a single episcopate" notwendig wäre (§69), wäre damit doch noch nichts darüber gesagt, daß dieses "single episcopate" die Gestalt des historischen Bischofsamtes annehmen müßte. Auch wenn man der Überzeugung ist, daß "the continuity with the Church of the apostles finds profound expression in the successive laying on of hands by bishops" (§50), folgt daraus nicht, daß diese Kontinuität so zum Ausdruck gebracht werden müßte oder so besser, sichtbarer, wirkungsvoller oder überzeugender zum Ausdruck gebracht würde als durch die glaubenwirkende Verkündigung des Evangeliums durch Wort und Sakrament in einer Kirche, die ihre Verkündigung immer wieder neu an der apostolischen Norm der Schrift ausrichtet und überprüft.

Das ist nicht der Weg, der in *Apostolicity and Succession, "Toward Full Communion" and "Concordat of Agreement"* oder *The Porvoo Common Statement* eingeschlagen wurde. Im Anschluß und in Fortführung mannigfacher Vorarbeiten anglikanischer Theologen in den vergangenen fünfzig Jahren[49] wird hier vielmehr eine andere Lösung gesucht. Ich beschränke mich auf das, was in Porvoo vorgelegt wurde.

5. Der Lösungsversuch von Porvoo

Die sich in der *Gemeinsamen Feststellung* andeutende differenzierende Behandlung der Fragenkreise *Sukzession, Apostolizität* und *Episkopat* wird in Porvoo so fortgesetzt, daß das Problem des historischen Episkopats nicht direkt, sondern indirekt angegangen wird. Methodisch wird dabei von der *Kirche* über das *Amt* auf das *Bischofsamt* und die *historische Sukzession* hin gedacht. Die darauf aufgebaute Argumentation läßt sich folgendermaßen zusammenfassen:

- Das Kennzeichen der *Apostolizität* kommt primär, grundlegend und umfassend der Kirche als ganzer zu: Die Kirche ist apostolisch, insofern sie in der Gesamtheit ihres gottesdienstlichen, missionarischen und diakonischen Handelns und damit in all ihren Vollzügen der *leitourgia, marturia, koinonia* und *diakonia* ihren apostolischen Auftrag ausführt, Zeichen, Werkzeug und Vorgeschmack des Reiches Gottes zu sein (§§32f; 36-39, S. 17-24).

- Innerhalb dieser "apostolic tradition of the Church as a whole" (§39, S. 23f) hat das - von Christus gestiftete und durch die Apostel weitergegebene - *ordinierte Amt* die besondere Aufgabe, "to assemble and build up the body of Christ by proclaiming and teaching the Word of God, by celebrating the sacraments and by guiding the life of the community in its worship, its mission and its caring ministry" (§41, S. 24).

- Dieses Amt wird einzelnen *Personen* durch Ordination und das Auflegen der Hände auf Lebenszeit übertragen.

- Das *eine* Amt hat *verschiedene Aufgaben,* die in der *Struktur* des ordinierten Amtes ihren Ausdruck finden. Als diese hat sich seit der frühen Kirche allgemein das *dreifache Amt* von Bischöfen, Priestern und Diakonen durchgesetzt, auch wenn dieses im Verlauf der Geschichte beträchtlichen Veränderungen unterzogen wurde und noch immer wird (§41, S. 24).

• Auch im Blick auf das Bischofsamt wird zwischen dem *Amt* (Episkope) und dem *Amtsinhaber* (Bischof) unterschieden. So erfordert die Verschiedenheit und Vielfalt der Gaben Gottes und Aufgaben der Kirche ein "ministry of co-ordination" bzw. "ministry of oversight, *episcope*" (§42, S. 24). Dieses Amt "is the particular responsibility of the bishop" (§43, S. 25) und wird von den Bischöfen personal, kollegial und gemeinschaftlich ausgeübt (§44, S. 25).

• Der Gedanke der *apostolischen Sukzession* ist auf die Kontinuität des *Amtes* und die Folge der *Inhaber des Amtes* bezogen. Primär manifestiert sich diese Sukzession in der apostolischen Tradition der Kirche als ganzer (§39, S. 23f), zu der auch die "continuity of the ministry of oversight" gehört (§46, S. 26).

• Davon zu unterscheiden ist die "[a]postolic succession in the episcopal office", die als "a visible and personal way of focusing the apostolicity of the whole Church" beschrieben wird (§46, S. 26). Das wird bei "the ordination or consecration of a bishop" durch "the laying on of hands by the ordaining bishop" zum Ausdruck gebracht (§47, S. 26).

• Diese Handauflegung bei der Konsekration eines Bischofs ist eine in vier-facher Hinsicht wirksame Zeichenhandlung: Sie bezeugt das Vertrauen der Kirche in Gottes Treue; sie bringt die Absicht der Kirche zum Ausdruck, Gottes Gabe treu zu wahren; sie bringt durch die Mitwirkung anderer Bi-schöfe die Akzeptanz des neuen Bischofs und die Katholizität der Kirche zur Darstellung; und sie überträgt das bischöfliche Leitungsamt und seine Auto-rität "in accordance with God's will and institution" (§48, S. 26).

• Die "Historic Episcopal Succession" ist so insgesamt "as Sign" zu verstehen, und zwar auf drei Ebenen: (1) "The whole Church is a sign of the Kingdom of God"; (2) "the act of ordination is a sign of God's faithfulness to his Church"; und (3) auch die Ordination eines Bischofs "in historic succession (that is, in intended continuity from the apostels themselves)" ist ein Zeichen, und zwar ein Zeichen der Sorge der Kirche "for continuity in the whole of its life and mission" (§50, S. 27).

• "The use of the sign of historic episcopal succession" garantiert als solcher weder "the fidelity of a church to every aspect of the apostolic faith, life and mission" noch "the personal faithfulness of the bishop". Aber die Beibehaltung dieses Zeichens "remains a permanent challenge to fidelity and to unity" und zu einer vollständigeren Verwirklichung der "permanent characteristics of the Church of the apostles" (§51, S. 27).

- Eine Kirche "which has preserved the sign of historic episcopal succession is free to acknowledge an authentic episcopal ministry in a church which has preserved continuity in the episcopal office by an occasional priestly/presbyterial ordination at the time of the Reformation." Und umgekehrt kann eine solche Kirche "enter a relationship of mutual participation in episcopal ordinations with a church which has retained the historical episcopal succession, and ... embrace this sign, without denying its past apostolic continuity" (§52, S. 28). Denn die Wiederaufnahme des "use of the sign of the laying on of hands in the historic succession" impliziert kein negatives Urteil über die Ämter einer Kirche, die dieses Zeichen bislang nicht benutzten, sondern ist "a means of making more visible the unity and continuity of the Church at all times and in all places" (§53, S. 28).

An dieser Argumentation sind eine Reihe *methodischer* und *theologischer Aspekte* besonders bemerkenswert.

- *Methodisch* ist der Versuch hervorzuheben,

- das Problem des historischen Episkopats ekklesiologisch zu 'kontextualisieren' und es nicht isoliert für sich, sondern im Gesamtzusammenhang der Kirche in den Blick zu fassen; und

- deutlich zwischen *kirchlichem Amt* und *Amtsträger* zu unterscheiden[50], damit auch zwischen der *Kontinuität des Amtes* und der *Sukzession der Inhaber eines Amtes*, und zwar sowohl im Blick auf das ordinierte Amt im allgemeinen (§41, S. 24) als auch im Blick auf das Episkopat im besonderen (§§42ff, S. 24ff).

- *Theologisch* bemerkenswert dagegen ist,

- daß das dreifache Amt funktional über die verschiedenen Aufgaben des einen ordinierten Amtes (und nicht als Institution der Apostel oder Jesu Christi) erklärt und nicht theologisch, sondern pragmatisch als Resultat einer historischen Entwicklung legitimiert wird (§41, S. 24);

- daß die *Episkope* als "requirement of the whole Church" (§42, S. 24) vom Amt des Bischofs ("bishop's office" (§43, S. 25) bzw. "episcopal office" (§46, S. 26)) unterschieden wird, so daß - obgleich das nicht geschieht - über andere als bischöfliche Gestaltungen des "ministry of oversight" gesprochen werden könnte und die personale, kollegiale und gemeinschaftliche Ausübung der Episkope nicht nur - wie es faktisch geschieht (§§44f, S. 25f) - als funktionale Dimensionen des Bischofsamtes verstanden werden müßte;

- daß das Bischofsamt (episcopal office) im Unterschied zu dem, was über das dreifache Amt gesagt wurde, *nicht* funktional, pragmatisch oder historisch, sondern *theologisch* begründet wird, indem die Konsekration eines Bischofs als Übertragung des "ministerial office and its authority in accordance with God's will and institution" charakterisiert (§48, S. 26) und damit (das bleibt unklar) entweder direkt auf die Institution des ordinierten Amtes durch Christus (§41, S. 24) oder eine davon unterschiedene Institution Gottes zurückgeführt wird; und schließlich

- daß die Bedeutung, die der apostolischen Sukzession im Bischofsamt und dem historischen Episkopat insgesamt zugeschrieben wird, mit Hilfe einer 'Theologie des Zeichens' zu begründen versucht wird, die ekklesiologisch umfassend angelegt ist.

Es ist unübersehbar, daß die Unklarheiten der theologischen Argumentation mit jedem Schritt zunehmen und in der Zeichentheologie kulminieren:

- Während das ordinierte Amt in der Kirche theologisch als "instituted by our Lord and transmitted through the apostles" begründet wird, wird seine Ausgestaltung zum dreifache Amt funktional-pragmatisch begründet (§41, S. 24).

- Im Fall der Episkope dagegen wird genau umgekehrt argumentiert: Die Notwendigkeit eines "ministry of co-ordination" wird funktional über "this diversity and multiplicity of tasks" im Dienst an der Einheit der Kirche begründet (§42, S. 24), die Konsekration in das episcopal office dagegen theologisch als Amts- und Autoritätsübertragung nach "God's will and institution" (§48, S. 26).

Doch ist die *Existenz* des ordinierten Amtes, aber nicht seine kontingente Gestaltung als *dreifaches Amt* theologisch notwendig, wie kann dann umgekehrt das Bischofsamt im Kontext des dreifachen Amtes theologisch notwendig sein? Müßte das nicht - wenn überhaupt - von der Episkope gesagt werden, deren Notwendigkeit funktional begründet wird? Werden hier nicht Aussagen über das *Amt* (Episkope) und über die historisch kontingente *Ausübung des Amtes* durch Bischöfe in historischer Sukzession vermischt und den Bischöfen damit eine Bedeutung zugeschrieben, die allenfalls dem Amt der Episkope, nicht aber den Amtsinhabern zukommt? Und wird nicht überhaupt erst dadurch die Sukzession der Amtsinhaber zum Zeichen der Kontinuität des Amtes aufgewertet, das doch mit der Kirche gesetzt und mit dieser kontinuierlich gegeben ist, weil es sich funktional aus den Aufgaben des ordinierten Amtes ergibt?

Die Unklarheiten steigern sich, wenn man sich der Zeichentheologie zuwendet, mit deren Hilfe die besondere Bedeutung der Historical Episcopal Succession im Lebensprozeß der Kirche zu begründen gesucht wird. Auf den ersten Blick scheint damit eine erhebliche Zurücknahme des traditionell mit dem historischen Episkopat verbundenen Anspruchs zum Ausdruck gebracht zu werden. Doch der Schein trügt. Es wird ja nicht gesagt, daß die Kirche *nur Zeichen* des Reiches Gottes, der Ordinationsakt *nur Zeichen* der Treue Gottes, die Ordination eines Bischofs in historischer Sukzession *nur ein Zeichen* für die apostolische Kontinuität der Kirche sei (§50, S. 27). Vielmehr *ist* die Kirche Zeichen des Reiches Gottes, der Ordinationsakt *ist* Zeichen der Treue Gottes und die Konsekration in den historischen Episkopat *ist* Zeichen apostolischer Kontinuität. Auf keines dieser Zeichen kann verzichtet werden, ohne auch die damit bezeichnete Sache zu verlieren oder zu verdunkeln. Denn diese Zeichen *bewirken*, was sie bezeichnen, sie sind - wie im Fall der Bischofskonsekration in sakramentaler Sprache gesagt und in vierfacher Hinsicht ausgeführt wird - "effective" (§48, S. 26). Bewirken diese Zeichen aber, was sie bezeichnen, dann heißt, sie nicht oder nicht korrekt zu haben oder zu gebrauchen, daß man sich in einer - zumindest - irregulären Situation befindet. Deshalb sollen Kirchen, die zwar die "continuity in the episcopal office by an occasional priestly/presbyteral ordination", aber nicht "the sign of historic episcopal succession" bewahrt haben (§52, S. 28), dieses Zeichen unbedingt wieder übernehmen, um die Einheit und Kontinuität der universalen Kirche *deutlicher* (more visible) zu machen (§§52f, S. 28). Es scheint also die Möglichkeit zu geben, durch wirkkräftige Zeichen die Sichtbarkeit der Einheit und Kontinuität der Kirche zu *steigern*, und dazu gehört insbesondere der historische Episkopat. Doch die ganze Argumentation gibt keine theologische Begründung für diese Behauptung, sondern sagt nur, *daß* das so sei. Doch ist es so? Ist der historische Episkopat wirkkräftiges Zeichen einer größeren Sichtbarkeit der einen Kirche Jesu Christi? Das wird ausdrücklich behauptet trotz der selbstkritischen Einsicht, daß der Gebrauch dieses Zeichen die ihm zugeschriebene Wirkungen oft nicht erzielt hat und sie auch nicht garantieren kann: Das Zeichen bewirke die Einheit nicht, es zu besitzen garantiere diese auch nicht, aber es sei dennoch "a means of making more visible the unity and continuity of the Church at all times and in all places" (§53, S. 28). Deshalb sei "the retention of the sign" wichtig, denn es stelle zumindest "a permanent challenge to fidelity and to unity" dar (§51, S. 27). Weiter kann die These von der angeblichen Wirkkraft dieses Zeichens zur Sichtbarmachung der Einheit kaum zurückgenommen werden. Dennoch wird an ihr festgehalten.

Das signalisiert das Problem der ganzen Argumentation: Hinter der Zeichentheologie von Porvoo stehen Bruchstücke einer nicht erklärten und nicht ausgeführten *Sakramentstheologie*. Indem die herausragende Bedeutung des "Episcopal Office in the Service of the Apostolic Succession" (C, S. 26) und der "Historic Episcopal Succession as Sign" (D, S. 27) für die volle, sichtbare Einheit der Kirche mit einem sakramentstheologischen Zeichenbegriff begründet wird, wird einer *sakramentalen Auffassung* der *Ordination in das kirchliche Amt* und der *Konsekration ins Bischofsamt* das Wort geredet, ohne daß angesichts der historischen Realitäten daraus die entsprechenden Konsequenzen gezogen werden. Die Argumentation bleibt schillernd, weil der Zeichenbegriff nicht geklärt wird. Die mit ihm operierende Theologie des Zeichens hat damit aber das Gegenteil einer klärenden Funktion: Sie beschreibt etwas Dunkles mit Hilfe von etwas noch Dunklerem und leistet so gerade nicht, was sie soll: die Bedeutung einsichtig zu machen, die dem historischen Episkopat ekklesiologisch und ökumenisch beigemessen wird. Und schon gar nicht stellt sie eine Zurücknahme der traditionellen Behauptung einer unverzichtbaren Notwendigkeit des historischen Episkopats für die Kirche dar, sondern im Gegenteil eine *theologische Steigerung* dieses Anspruchs: Ordination und Amt bzw. Konsekration und Bischofsamt sind sakramental zu verstehen und insofern *als Zeichen* für die sichtbare Einheit der Kirche unverzichtbar.[51] Die anglokatholische These, der historische Episkopat sei für das *Sein* der *Kirche* unverzichtbar, ist so durch die neuanglikanische These ersetzt, er sei für das *Sichtbarsein* der *Einheit* der Kirche unverzichtbar.

Ich halte diese Zeichentheologie mit ihren sakramentalen Unter- und Obertönen für einen Irrweg. Sie operiert mit einem ungeklärten Zeichenbegriff; sie beschreibt nicht präzis, was wofür aus welchen Gründen von wem und für wen als Zeichen gebraucht wird; sie sagt nicht, was der Gebrauch bestimmter Zeichen (etwa "the sign of the laying on of hands in the historic succession" (§53, S. 28)) anderen Zeichen (etwa der Handauflegung ohne historische Sukzession) theologisch voraus hat; sie läßt ungeklärt, was die "whole Church" ist, die als "a sign of the Kingdom of God" bestimmt wird (§50, S. 27); sie oszilliert auf unklare Weise dazwischen, das *Amt* (das Predigtamt oder das Bischofsamt) oder den *Akt der Bestellung zum Amt* (die Ordination bzw. Konsekration) oder die *Träger und Inhaber* des Amtes als Zeichen zu deuten; und sie führt so insgesamt theologisch nicht weiter, sondern in eine Sackgasse. Um den verwendeten Zeichenbegriff zu klären - und das wäre dringend notwendig -, müßte man sich mit Problemen wie der Repräsentationsstruktur, der Wirkkraft, der Bezeichnungs- und Verdeutlichungsfunktion, der Referenz, der Systembezogenheit usf. von Zeichen auseinandersetzen sowie ihrer Auswirkung auf das Verständnis der als Zeichen gedeuteten Sachverhalte Kirche, Amt, Ordination, historischer Episkopat usf. auseinandersetzen. Das öffnet ein weites Feld theologischer Forschungen, dürfte aber kaum dazu beitragen, die in Meissen offen gebliebenen Fragen so zu klären, daß sie einer Lösung zugeführt werden können. Denn man würde sich dann über eine theologische Theorie auseinandersetzen, die nur schwerlich auf allgemeine Zustimmung stoßen dürfte. In Status und Funktion steht die Zeichentheologie von

Porvoo auf derselben Ebene wie die anglokatholische pipe-line Theorie. Nur hat diese jener gegenüber voraus, daß sie klarer ist.

Weiterführend ist m.E. nicht die Zeichentheologie von Porvoo, sondern das dort angewandte *Verfahren*. Hier gibt es Anknüpfungspunkte für eine fruchtbare Weiterführung des Gesprächs. Das sei abschließend angedeutet.

6. Vom Kirchenverständnis zum Verständnis des kirchlichen Amtes

Es ist ein altes und wohlbegründetes Verfahren, dunkle und kontroverse Fragen von den hellen und nicht kontroversen her anzugehen. Es ist deshalb auch methodisch richtig, die kontroverse Frage des historischen Episkopats und des ganzen damit verbundenen Problemkomplexes von dreifachem Amt, Ordination und Konsekration vom nicht-kontroversen Verständnis der Kirche als ganzer her anzugehen. Daß an diesem Punkt im Entscheidenden Übereinstimmung besteht, wird in der *Gemeinsamen Feststellung* (Nr. 15 (7) - (9), S. 45 sowie Nr. 17 A (1) und (2), S. 47) ausdrücklich erklärt. Beide Seiten bestätigen sich, daß sie wahre Kirchen sind, daß sie "an der apostolischen Sendung des ganzen Volkes wahrhaft teilhaben", daß "das Wort Gottes" bei ihnen "authentisch gepredigt wird und die Sakramente der Taufe und des Herrenmahls recht verwaltet werden".

Nimmt man das ernst, dann ergeben sich eine Reihe von Folgerungen:

1. Damit wird zunächst einmal das, was mit der *Apostolizität* der Kirche gemeint ist, in übereinstimmender Weise *inhaltlich bestimmt*: Die Apostolizität der Kirche wird wesentlich in der *Sendung des ganzen Volkes* gesehen, die sich ihrerseits zentral in der *authentischen Evangeliumspredigt* und *rechten Sakramentsverwaltung* manifestiert. Damit wird diese *Sendung*, an der *alle Getauften* (das ganze Volk) in gleicher Weise Anteil haben, durch einen *bestimmten Auftrag* gekennzeichnet, der inhaltlich durch das apostolische, in den kanonischen Schriften bezeugte *Evangelium* bestimmt wird und darin besteht, dieses Evangelium der ganzen Welt in Wort und Tat zu bezeugen. Die apostolische Sendung besteht also in der Beauftragung und Bevollmächtigung zu einem bestimmten *Dienst*: der - umfassend zu verstehenden - diakonia an der Welt.

2. Daß das Kennzeichen der Apostolizität grundlegend und primär für die Kirche als ganze gilt, wird in allen ökumenischen Dialogen der letzten Jahre betont. Damit wird unterstrichen, daß alle Christen durch ihre gemeinsame Taufe in gleicher Weise zur Teilnahme an der apostolischen Sendung der Kirche befähigt und verpflichtet sind. Das ist der reformatorische Grundsatz vom Priestertum aller Gläubigen, der sich aus diesem Verständnis der

Apostolizität ergibt: Weil die Kirche als ganze apostolisch ist, hat jeder Christ in gleicher Weise das Amt, an ihrer Sendung zum Dienst der Versöhnung in der Welt mitzuwirken.

3. Dieser der ganzen Kirche und damit allen Christen gegebene apostolische Auftrag wird durch das besondere ordinierte Amt in keiner Weise eingeschränkt oder aufgehoben, sondern bestätigt und bekräftigt. Denn das ordinierte Amt hat keinen anderen apostolischen Auftrag und keine andere inhaltliche Aufgabe als das Priesteramt aller Getauften, sondern ist dessen funktionale Spezifizierung einiger seiner Aufgaben für einen bestimmten Bereich: den Dienst der *öffentlichen Verkündigung*. So ist das ordinierte Amt - nach reformatorischer Auffassung - nicht sacerdotium, sondern *ministerium*, und zwar genauer *ministerium verbi divini* und als solches "die Ausübung des der ganzen Gemeinde anvertrauten und befohlenen Dienstes"[52]. Seine Besonderheit besteht darin, daß es diesen der ganzen Kirche anvertrauten und befohlenen Dienst zum einen im Hinblick auf bestimmte Funktionen, nämlich die *Evangeliumsverkündigung durch Wort und Sakrament*, und zum andern in bestimmter Weise, nämlich *öffentlich* wahrnimmt, die Verkündigungsaufgaben dieses Dienstes also im Auftrag und im Namen der ganzen Kirche ausübt, um so "dem Amt des ganzen Volkes Gottes zu dienen" (Nr. 15 (8) S. 45). Im Namen der ganzen Kirche kann aber niemand von sich aus sprechen, das Recht und die Vollmacht dazu muß vielmehr von der ganzen Kirche übertragen werden. Deshalb bedarf die Wahrnehmung dieses besonderen Amtes in der Kirche der *Ordination*, der ordnungsgemäßen Beauftragung und Bevollmächtigung zum Dienst der *öffentlichen* Verkündigung.

4. Die öffentliche Ausübung des der ganzen Kirche anvertrauten und befohlenen Dienstes steht nicht in deren Belieben. Sie kann ihn nicht nicht ausüben. Insofern gehört das ordinierte Amt als "eine Gabe Gottes an seine Kirche" (Nr. 15 (8), S. 45) wesentlich zur Kirche als Kirche. Es ist keine Einrichtung der Kirche, die diese haben oder auch nicht haben kann, sondern eine Institution, ohne die sie ihre apostolische Sendung zum Dienst der Versöhnung nicht ausüben könnte. Denn dieser Dienst vollzieht sich wesentlich in der Evangeliumsverkündigung durch Wort und Sakrament, um deretwillen allein es das "ministerium docendi et porrigendi sacramenta" als Einrichtung Gottes in der Kirche gibt (CA V), und beides, Wortverkündigung in der Gemeinde und Feier der Sakramente Taufe und Abendmahl sind ihrem Wesen nach *öffentliche Vorgänge*. Als solche bedürfen sie der Ordnung, und für diese zu sorgen ist eine Aufgabe der Kirche als ganzer, zu der sie aufgrund ihrer apostolischen Sendung berechtigt und verpflichtet ist.

5. Daß das ordinierte Amt keine verzichtbare Einrichtung der Kirche, sondern eine Gabe Gottes an sie ist, heißt nicht, daß es neben Wort und Sakrament zu stehen käme. Es ist vielmehr klar von ihnen unterschieden, indem es ihnen funktional zugeordnet ist. Das Amt ist kein Heilsmittel wie Wort und Sakrament, die den Leib Christi aufbauen und die Kirche konstituieren, sondern es ist der Kirche um der Evangeliumsverkündigung in Wort und Sakrament willen gegeben: Es gehört zur Kirche als Kirche, weil diese nur ist, was sie ist, wenn die Vollzüge, die sie konstituieren, auch vollzogen werden; und das Amt ist diejenige unverzichtbare Konkretionsform der Kirche, in der diese zur Befolgung ihres Auftrags in Gestalt einer institutionellen Selbstverpflichtung dafür sorgt, ihrer Verpflichtung zum öffentlichen Vollzug der sie konstituierenden Grundvollzüge von Wort und Sakrament tatsächlich auch nachzukommen und jederzeit auch nachkommen zu können. Anders als Wort und Sakrament geht das Amt der Kirche also nicht sachlich voraus, sondern ist mit ihr gegeben, aber nicht als eine unter Umständen auch verzichtbare Einrichtung der Kirche, sondern als institutionelles Implikat der ihr aufgetragenen Grundaufgaben und sie konstituierenden Grundvollzügen der Evangeliumsverkündigung.

6. Als institutionelles Implikat der die Kirche konstituierenden Grundvollzüge der Evangeliumsverkündigung in Wort und Sakrament ist das Amt, das dieser Funktion dient, nicht nur Ausdruck der Apostolizität, sondern auch der *Einheit* der Kirche. Die Kirche ist eine, insofern sie "das eine Wort Gottes, das wir zu hören und dem wir im Leben und im Sterben zu vertrauen und zu gehorchen haben" verkündet[53] und damit diejenige Gemeinschaft ist, "in der Jesus Christus in Wort und Sakrament durch den Heiligen Geist als Herr gegenwärtig handelt"[54]. Die Einheit der Kirche ist der eine Herr, der durch sein Handeln die Glieder der Kirche zur Einheit vereint. Dieses einheitsstiftende Handeln vollzieht sich in der Evangeliumsverkündigung durch Wort und Sakrament. Die um Wort und Sakrament versammelte Gemeinde ist daher Kirche im vollen, universalen Sinn des Begriffs. Denn durch die Einigung mit Christus wird sie nicht nur untereinander geeint, sondern in den universalkirchlichen Zusammenhang mit der communio sanctorum aller gestellt, die zu anderen Zeiten und an anderen Orten durch Christus mit diesem und so untereinander geeint werden. Indem es der Evangeliumsverkündigung dient, anhand derer sich das vollzieht, dient das Amt damit zugleich auch der Einheit der Kirche. Als institutionelle Selbstverpflichtung der Kirche zur dieser Verkündigung ist es zugleich die Selbstverpflichtung der Kirche zur Einheit - freilich der Einheit, die allein durch Christus selbst und nicht etwa durch die Kirche hergestellt wird, weil

diese selbst stets Empfängerin dieser Einheit bleibt. Das kirchliche Amt kann diese Einheit weder herstellen noch repräsentieren, sondern nur dadurch sichtbar machen, daß es unmißverständlich von sich weg und auf das hinweist, dem es dient: dem gegenwärtigen Handeln Christi in der Evangeliumsverkündigung durch Wort und Sakrament. Je deutlicher das geschieht, desto besser macht das Amt die Einheit sichtbar, die die Kirche aller Zeiten und Orte auszeichnet.

7. Gerade weil die Kirche nicht für die Einrichtung und Existenz des Amtes verantwortlich ist, hat sie die unabweisbare Verpflichtung, für die *Ordnung dieses Amtes* zu sorgen. Als Resultat kirchlichen Handelns ist die Ordnung des ordinierten Amtes deshalb anders als seine Existenz in der Kirche geschichtlich veränderlich und variabel. Daß das ordinierte Amt "ein Amt göttlicher Einsetzung ist" (Nr. 15 (8), S. 45) besagt nicht, daß dies auch von irgendeiner Ordnung dieses Amtes gesagt werden könnte. Mit Recht sagt die *Gemeinsame Feststellung* nichts davon, daß das ordinierte Amt die Struktur des dreifachen Amtes haben müßte. Denn jede Struktur und Ordnung dieses Amtes ist geschichtliches Resultat kirchlichen Ordungshandelns und als solches allein daran zu messen, ob die Art der Gestaltung, Strukturierung und Ordnung dieses Amtes dazu dient, die unveränderliche *Aufgabe* dieses Amtes, im Dienst der öffentlichen Verkündigung "dem Amt des ganzen Volkes Gottes zu dienen" (Nr. 15 (8), S. 45), unter den jeweiligen geschichtlichen Bedingungen in der bestmöglichen Weise genügt. Es gehört zum apostolischen Auftrag der Kirche, das Amt der öffentlichen Wahrnehmung dieses Auftrags zu ordnen. Apostolisch ist eine Kirche aber nicht durch eine bestimmte Ordnung dieses Amtes, sondern allein dadurch, daß sie dieses Amt ausübt. Zwischen dem *Dasein des ordinierten Amtes in der Kirche* und der *Gestaltung des ordinierten Amtes in einer Kirche* ist daher grundsätzlich zu unterscheiden - eine Einsicht, die in Porvoo erste Früchte getragen hat.

8. Dasselbe gilt auch für die *Episkope*. Auch sie ist keine beliebige oder verzichtbare Ordnungsstruktur der Kirche, aber ebensowenig ist sie in einer vom ordinierten Amt noch einmal unterschiedenen Weise konstitutiv für die Kirche oder Ausdruck einer besonderen sakramentalen Hierarchie geistlicher Kompetenzen in der Kirche: Wo es Kirche gibt, gibt es das kirchliche Amt und damit auch die Episkope. Tritt diese in besonderer Weise institutionell in Erscheinung, dann nur als die funktionale Ausgestaltung eines kirchlichen Aufgabenbereichs, der strikt von den grundlegenden Aufgaben, Rechten und Pflichten der Kirche als ganzer und damit dem Priestertum aller Getauften her zu verstehen ist. Von dort her ist die Episkope aber durch zwei Sachverhalte charakterisiert:

Auf der einen Seite ist sie als "Amt pastoraler Aufsicht" (Nr. 15 (9), S. 45) eine funktionale Spezifizierung des ordinierten Amtes zur Wahrnehmung der Aufgaben, die in Porvoo dem "ministry of co-ordination" zugeschrieben werden (§42, S. 24): Sie markiert ein besonderes pastorales Aufgabenfeld im Rahmen des ordinierten Amtes, ist somit Ausdruck einer Gliederung der Aufgaben, aber nicht der geistlichen Kompetenzen ihrer Inhaber; und zu diesen Aufgaben gehört in der Regel besonders der Auftrag, darauf zu achten, daß sich keine Ortskirche aus dem Zusammenhang mit der communio sanctorum anderer Zeiten und Orte löst und die dem ordinierten Amt obliegende Pflicht zur Beachtung und Wahrnehmung des universalkirchlichen Zusammenhangs auch nachgekommen wird.

Auf der anderen Seite ist sie aber auch eine funktionale Spezifizierung von Aufgaben, die nicht nur dem ordinierten Amt, sondern jedem Christen obliegen: die Aufgaben der Ordnung und Leitung der Kirche. Durch die Taufe ist jeder Christ zur Wahrnehmung aller Aufgaben und Funktionen berechtigt und verpflichtet, die mit der apostolischen Sendung der ganzen Kirche gesetzt sind. Dazu gehört neben Verkündigung durch Wort und Tat auch die Ordnung und Leitung der Kirche. In ihrer öffentlichen Ausübung sind diese Aufgaben kirchlich zu ordnen. Das ordinierte Amt ist die funktionsspezifische Ausgestaltung der Verkündigungsverpflichtung aller für den Bereich der öffentlichen Lehre und Gottesdienstleitung; und daran hat auch die Episkope als ordiniertes Verkündigungsamt anteil. Doch das geordnete Amt ist nicht zugleich das ordnende Amt, es bleibt vielmehr in den Gesamtzusammenhang der Kirche eingebettet. Die Aufgabe der Ordnung und Leitung der Kirche ist und bleibt die Aufgabe aller Christen und nicht nur der ordinierten Amtsträger. Aber auch diese Ordnungs- und Leitungsaufgabe aller Christen bedarf in ihrer öffentlichen Ausübung der Ordnung, und diese ist die zweite Komponente der Episkope. In dieser Hinsicht ist sie aber nie nur Sache von Inhabern des ordinierten Verkündigungsamtes, sondern auch von anderen Christen. Deshalb kann die Wahrnehmung der Episkope nach evangelischer Auffassung *nicht auf ordinierte Geistliche beschränkt werden*, sondern ist in ganz entscheidender Hinsicht Sache der *Gemeinden und Synoden*. Es ist nicht zufällig, sondern sachlich begründet, daß sie "in unseren Kirchen in einer Vielfalt von bischöflichen *und nichtbischöflichen Formen*" (Nr. 17 A (4), S. 49; meine Hervorhebung) ausgeübt wird. Daß die Episkope in personaler, kollegialer und gemeinschaftlicher Weise praktiziert wird (Nr. 15 (9), S. 45), kann nach evangelischem Verständnis daher nicht von vornherein und ausschließlich auf die im Bischofsamt tätigen Geistlichen bezogen werden. Besser wäre es, von einem *synodalen Episkopat* zu sprechen, dessen Autorität sich auf die mit der Taufe verliehene Autorität aller Christen und damit der Kirche als ganzer gründet und nicht auf besondere Traditionslinien der Weitergabe des Bischofsamtes in der Sukzession des historischen Episkopats.

Gerade deshalb ist die in Porvoo angebahnte, aber nicht konsequent durchgehaltene Unterscheidung von *Episkope* und *Bischofsamt* wichtig und weiterführend: *Wird das Amt des Bischofs als Ausdifferenzierung des ordinierten Amtes verstanden, kann es die Aufgaben der Episkope nicht vollständig übernehmen. Soll es die Aufgaben vollständig übernehmen können, muß es ein 'Bischofsamt' sein, das im Prinzip auch Christen offen steht, die nicht für das geistliche Amt ordiniert sind.* Dieser Vorbehalt muß auch dann gemacht werden, wenn die Episkope in einer Kirche faktisch nur von ordinierten Geistlichen ausgeübt wurde, würde oder wird: Die Kontinuität der Episkope in einer Kirche kann nicht mit der Sukzession von ordinierten Geistlichen in der Wahrnehmung dieser Funktion identifiziert oder auf diese reduziert werden. Aber nur für *diese* Sukzession könnte der historische Episkopat als Zeichen fungieren, und deshalb ist er nur dort ein aussagekräftiges Zeichen, in der die Wahrnehmung der Episkope von der ganzen Kirche in die Verantwortung speziell berufener Geistlicher gelegt wird. Für die evangelischen Kirchen kann das nur eine mögliche, keine theologisch verbindliche Regelung sein, weil sie die Aufgabe der Leitung und Ordnung der Kirche in Konsequenz des Priestertums aller Getauften prinzipiell als Aufgabe der ganzen Kirche und nicht nur eines Teils der Kirche verstehen. Auch hier gilt deshalb: Es steht nicht in der Freiheit einer Kirche, *Episkope* zu praktizieren oder nicht zu praktizieren: dazu ist sie aufgrund ihrer apostolischen Sendung verpflichtet. Es steht aber sehr wohl in ihrer Freiheit, die *Ordnung und Wahrnehmung* der Episkope zu gestalten, und diese Gestaltung unterliegt keiner anderen Bedingung als der, daß sie dem Sendungsauftrag der ganzen Kirche nicht widersprechen darf und in ihrem spezifischen Aufgabenbereich der Episkope den Dienst der ganzen Kirche so fördern muß, daß dieser unter den jeweiligen geschichtlichen Bedingungen in der bestmöglichen Weise ausgeübt werden kann.

9. Apostolisch ist damit jede wahre Kirche als ganze, nicht aber durch eine spezifische, rechtlich beschreibbare Ordnung ihrer Ämter. Daß die Kirche von England und die evangelischen Kirchen Deutschlands in diesem Sinn apostolisch sind, bestätigen sie sich in der *Meissener Erklärung* ausdrücklich. Hat aber jede Kirche als ganze in der beschriebenen Weise an "der Einen, Heiligen, Katholischen und Apostolischen Kirche Jesu Christi" teil (Nr. 17 A (1), S. 47) und gehört das ordinierte Amt konstitutiv und wesentlich zur Kirche (Nr. 15 (8), S. 45), dann erstreckt sich diese Teilhabe auch auf das ordinierte Amt der jeweiligen Kirche. Denn gälte es für diese nicht, könnte es

auch nicht für die Kirche als ganze gelten, wenn denn das ordinierte Amt als ein "Amt göttlicher Einsetzung" (Nr. 15 (8), S. 45) für die Kirche als ganze konstitutiv ist. Sind beide Seiten aber wahre Kirchen mit ordiniertem Amt, dann müssen sowohl die ordinierten Ämter der anglikanischen wie die der evangelischen Kirchen ihrem apostolischen Auftrag angemessen sein - und das sind sie auch, wenn sie - was ihre apostolische Pflicht und Aufgabe ist und in Meissen als Tatsache auch wechselseitig bestätigt wird - für die rechte Evangeliumsverkündigung in Wort und Sakrament Sorge tragen. Daraus aber folgt, daß keine der beiden Kirchen in ihren Ämtern der anderen im Blick auf die Ausführung ihres apostolischen Auftrags irgendetwas voraus hat: Beide leisten genau, was sie leisten sollen und müssen. Und beide tun das auf eine Weise und in einer Gestalt, die ihre spezifische Geschichte und die sie prägenden Erfahrungen spiegeln.

10. Ich habe schon darauf hingewiesen, daß die kirchenrechtliche und theologische Betonung des historischen Episkopats auf anglikanischer Seite ganz wesentlich die religiösen und (kirchen)politischen Erfahrungen spiegelt, die die Kirche von England im Verlauf ihrer Geschichte gemacht hat. Dasselbe gilt auch für die evangelischen Kirchen. Die Ordnung ihrer Ämter mag im 16. Jahrhundert als irreguläre Notordnung begonnen haben. Sie nur so zu verstehen, hieße zu übersehen, daß sie von Anfang an und mit guten Gründen auch eine *reformatorische Erneuerungsordnung* war. Sie war es, weil sich die damals reguläre Form der Ordnung des Amtes als unfähig erwiesen hatte, seine verantwortliche Wahrnehmung zu gewährleisten. Bischöfe gaben "durch ihrer Härtigkeit Ursach ... zu Spaltung und Schisma, das sie doch billig sollen verhuten helfen" (CA 28, BSLK, S. 133, 4-7). Sie fragen, so klagte Melanchthon, "gar nichts darnach, wie man lehre oder predige, sie fragen nicht darnach, wie christlicher Brauch der Sakrament erhalten werde, sie ordinieren grobe Esel; damit ist christliche Lehre untergangen, daß die Kirchen nicht mit tüchtigen Predigern bestellt sind".[55] Sie zogen daraus die Konsequenz, daß keine Ordnung des Amtes regulär genannt zu werden verdient, die dazu führt, daß notwendige evangeliumsgemäße Reformen in der Kirche durch die Amtsinhaber verhindert werden können. Deshalb bestanden sie darauf, daß sich Amt und Amtsträger am Evangelium messen lassen müssen und nicht umgekehrt, und daß die Ordnung des Amtes sowie alle übrigen Strukturen und Vollzüge der Kirche im Licht des Evangeliums *semper reformanda* sind und sein müssen. Indem sie sich an dieses Prinzip hielten, blieben sie dem apostolischen Auftrag der ganzen Kirche treu. Und indem sie in der Befolgung dieses Prinzips angesichts des Versagens der bischöflichen Amtsinhaber die Ordination in das öffentliche Predigtamt und

die Erfüllung der notwendigen Aufgaben der Episkope anders regelten und ordneten, setzten sie die apostolische Verpflichtung der Kirche als ganzer, für die rechte Evangeliumsverkündigung, Sakramentsverwaltung und Kirchenleitung zu sorgen, konkret um. Das aber heißt: *Die evangelischen Kirchen sind nicht nur als ganze apostolisch geblieben, sondern auch im Blick auf das ordinierte Amt haben sie die apostolische Sukzession nie verlassen oder aufgegeben, sondern diese gerade umgekehrt gewahrt und zur Geltung gebracht.*

11. Es ist deshalb theologisch falsch, im Blick auf ihre Ämter von einem 'defectus ordinis' zu sprechen (wie es seitens der römisch-katholischen Kirche geschieht), und es ist theologisch problematisch, ihnen zwar die "apostolic continuity" zuzugestehen[56], für eine sichtbare Darstellung der Einheit der Kirche und die Aufnahme voller Kirchengemeinschaft aber auf ihrer Wiedereingliederung in die Sukzession des historischen Episkopats zu bestehen (wie es von anglikanischer Seite geschieht). Plausibel sind beide Ansichten nur, wenn man sie nicht als theologische, sondern kirchenrechtliche Argumente wertet: Das ordinierte Amt in der evangelischen ist nicht dasselbe wie das in der römischen oder anglikanischen Kirche, auch wenn es in der evangelischen Kirche dieselben apostolischen Funktionen erfüllt, die die römischen bzw. anglikanischen Ämter in diesen Kirchen erfüllen. Doch warum sollten die Regelungen des Codex iuris canonici oder des anglikanischen Ordinale von 1662 in den evangelischen Kirchen oder umgekehrt deren Regelungen in der römischen oder anglikanischen Kirche gelten müssen?

12. Das einzige in der Debatte seit Meissen erkennbare Argument ist das der *besseren oder größeren Sichtbarkeit der Einheit der Kirche*: Ohne den "Dienst eines versöhnten, gemeinsamen Amtes"[57] sei die - bestehende und gar nicht bestrittene - Einheit der beiden Kirchen in Jesus Christus und ihre - ausdrücklich bekannte - Einigkeit im Glauben nicht zureichend sichtbar zu machen.[58] Doch was immer das heißt: Es kann nicht die wechselseitige Übernahme kirchenrechtlicher Regelungen bedeuten. Gemeint sein kann nur, daß *beide Seiten auf je ihre Weise* die Einheit und Apostolizität *nicht nur ihrer, sondern auch der anderen Kirche bezeugen.* Und das tun sie durch nichts anderes sichtbarer und überzeugender als dadurch, daß sie dasselbe Evangelium verkünden, dieselben Sakramente feiern, denselben Glauben zum Ausdruck bringen, dieselben aus der Taufe resultierenden Befähigungen und Verpflichtungen eines jeden Christen betonen und anerkennen, derselben Aufgabe zur Ordnung des öffentlichen Amtes in der Kirche nachkommen und sich in derselben Weise bemühen, ihren Auftrag zur *diakonia* an der Welt zu erfüllen.

Nicht gemeint kann damit aber sein, daß sie die ihnen gleiche, wesentliche und ursprüngliche Aufgabe zur Ordnung des Amtes auch in gleicher Weise realisieren müßten, dieselbe Gestaltung des ordinierten Amtes zur vollen, sichtbaren Einheit der Kirche also erforderlich wäre. Ziel der Bewegung auf sichtbare Einheit hin ist ja keine Einheitskirche, sondern "die Kirchen und Ämter ... innerhalb der weiteren Gemeinschaft der universalen Kirche zum vollen Einklang zu bringen"[59]. Die universale Kirche aber ist keine besondere Institution oder Organisation neben den anglikanischen und evangelischen Kirchen, sondern das, was diese jeweils zu Kirchen macht und in ihnen selbst manifest werden muß, wenn sie tatsächlich Kirchen sein und als Kirchen sichtbar und wirksam sein wollen. Die universale Kirche kennt auch keine Ämter, sondern nur das eine Amt Jesu Christi, an dem alle Getauften in gleicher Weise Anteil haben. Ämter gibt es nur im geschichtlichen Leben der Kirche, wo das Amt Jesu Christi in der Evangeliumsverkündigung durch Wort und Sakrament in Raum und Zeit sichtbar, erfahrbar und wirksam zum Zuge kommt und eine bestimmte kirchliche Gemeinschaft bildet. Und diese Ämter gibt es nicht als sichtbare Zeichen, Abbilder oder Repräsentationsgestalten des Amtes Jesu Christi, sondern nur als *ministeria verbi divini*, d.h. als *Dienstämter* an den Vollzügen, in denen und durch die sich das Amt Jesu Christi in geschichtlichen Kirchen vollzieht. Die *Einheit* der Ämter zeigt ich daher allein in der Selbigkeit ihrer Funktion und damit in dem *einen gemeinsamen Dienst*, den sie leisten, nicht in einer identischen Gestalt, historischen Herkunft oder theologischen Legitimation. Entsprechend kann auch die "weitere Gemeinschaft der universalen Kirche", in denen die Ämter "zum vollen Einklang" gebracht werden sollen, nur *in* jeder Kirche gefunden werden, nicht neben oder außerhalb von ihr; und sie kann in ihr nur in dem gefunden werden, was nicht nur sie, sondern eben auch jede andere Kirche zur Kirche macht: die Evangeliumsverkündigung in Wort und Sakrament, der allein das Amt zu dienen hat.

---

[1] Im folgenden wird zitiert nach *Die Meissener Erklärung. Eine Dokumentatio.n* Bearbeitet von K. Kremkau, EKD-Texte Bd. 47, Hannover 1993.

[2] Für eine sakramentale Auffassung der Ordination hat sich in jüngster Zeit auf anglikanischer Seite vor allem L. W. Countryman, *The Language of Ordination. Ministry in an Ecumenical Context*, Philadelphia 1992, Kap. 3 ausgesprochen.

[3] In diesem Fall ist es im übrigen auch nicht sinnvoll, im Fall der "Full Communion" zwischen verschiedenen Kirchen die Transitivität dieses Sachverhalts zu bestreiten oder einzuschränken und wie in *"Toward full Communion" and "Concordat of Agreement". Lutheran-Episcopal Dialogue, Series 3* (hg. von W. A. Norgren /W. G. Busch, Mineapolis/Augsburg 1991) den Vorbehalt zu machen, daß "[t]his Concordat of Agreement with the Evangelical Lutheran Church in America does not imply or inaugurate any automatic communion between the Evangelical Lutheran Church in America and the other provinces of the Anglican Communion or any other churches with whom the Episcopal Church is in full communion" (§ 12, S. 103). Dieser Vorbehalt hat nur Sinn, wenn man von Amt und den Amtshandlungen *bestimmter* Kirchen her denkt, also gerade nicht das *eine* Amt der *einen* Kirche im Blick hat.

[4] Auch von diesem Verständnis her lassen sich die Regelungen von *"Toward Full Communion" and "Concordat of Agreement"* § 7 theologisch nur zum Teil nachvollziehen. Warum sollte aus der lebenslang geltenden Beauftragung in das Amt einer Kirche die Folgerung gezogen werden müssen, daß auch - wie es hier im Fall von Bischöfen gesagt wird - diejenigen, die aus ihrem Amt durch "retirement, resignation, or conclusion of term" (ebd. S. 101)ausgeschieden seien, weiterhin "be regular members of the Conference of Bishops" (ebd. S. 101)? Alle kirchlichen Ämter sind auf Zeit, auch wenn Personen lebenslang zu ihnen beauftragt werden: Ausscheiden aus dem Amt beendet nicht den Auftrag, aber die Teilnahme an dessen Ausübung. Bei Bischöfen scheint diese Regel nicht zu gelten.

[5] Anders als in *Toward Full Communion and Concordat of Agreement* wird nicht ausdrücklich von "the distinct ministry of bishop within the one ministry of Word and Sacrament" (§ 3, vgl. §7,ebd. S. 99; 101) gesprochen.

[6] Vgl. E. Herms, *Stellungnahme zum dritten Teil des Lima-Dokuments 'Amt'*, KuD 31 (1985) S. 65-96, 71f.

[7] S. W. Sykes, *The Laying on of Hands in Succession*, in: H. Meyer (Hg.), *Gemeinsamer Glaube und Strukturen der Gemeinschaft*, Frankfurt/Main, 1991, S. 185-197, 191f. Bischof Palmer hatte in diesem Sinn 1927 in Lausanne erklärt, Kirchen, die "the traditional form of the ministry of Holy Orders" bewahrt hätten, gingen davon aus, daß "In ordination Christ ordains": "It is Christ who consecrates or ordains, and in consecration or ordination He, using the bishop as His mouthpiece, makes a man a bishop, or a priest, or a deacon" (*The Church's Ministry*, in: H.N. Bate (Hg.), *Faith and Order. Proceedings of the World Conference Lausanne, August 3-21, 1927*, London 1927, S. 233-248, 236f.). Und Erzbischof William Temple hat dies 1943 vor der Convocation of Canterbury folgendermaßen bekräftigt: "Wenn ich einen frommen und gelehrten Mann zum Amt und zum Werk eines Bischofs in der Kirche Gottes konsekriere, handle ich nicht als ein Repräsentant der Kirche, sofern darunter die Gesamtzahl der zeitgenössischen Christen verstanden wird; sondern ich handle als das dienende Instrument Christi in Seinem Leibe, der Kirche. [...] Die Autorität, zu konsekrieren und zu ordinieren, ist in sich selbst eine Bezeugung der Kontinuität des Lebens der Kirche in seiner unaufhörlichen Abhängigkeit von ihrem Haupt, Jesus Christus." (Zitiert nach H. Werner, *Die apostolische Sukzession im anglikanischen Amtsbegriff*, LM 4 (1965), S. 593-603, 598).

[8] Was 'ordnungsgemäß' (authorized) genau einschließt, ist freilich die offene Frage. Das *rite vocatus* von CA 14 war in Apologie 14 ausdrücklich als nicht identisch mit der kanonischen Weihe ausgelegt worden: Weil "die Bischöfe die Unsern nicht dulden wollen", müssen wir "die Bischöfe fahren lassen und Gott mehr gehorsam sein", denn wir wissen "daß die christliche Kirche da ist, da Gottes Wort recht gelehret wird" (BSLK, S. 297, 11-20). Als *rite vocatus* wird damit faktisch der bezeichnet, der nach den *Ordnungen der jeweiligen Kirche* berufen ist. In den 13 Artikeln von 1538, die sich eng an die Confessio Augustana

anschlossen, wurde vom Ordinationsrecht dementsprechend ausdrücklich gesagt, es liege bei "those in the church into whose hands the laws and customs of each region, in keeping with the Word of God, have placed the right of calling and admitting people into the ministry" (zitiert nach S. W. Sykes, *The Ministry and the Episcopal Office: An Anglican Approach to the Confessio Augustana*, in: H. Meyer (Hg.), *The Augsburg Confession in Ecumenical Perspective*, Stuttgart 1980, S. 29-59, 45). Diese Wendung wird seit den 42 Artikeln von 1553 fallen gelassen. In Art. 23 der 39 Artikel wird das *rite vocatus* mit *lawfully called (legitime)* übersetzt, und in Art . 36 durch den Verweis auf das Ordinale von Edward VI konkretisiert. Dort wird im *Preface* eine Praxis reklamiert, die auf die Schrift und "ancient Authors" zurückgeführt wird, ohne daß für sie besondere theologische oder gar sakramentale Ansprüche erhoben werden. Erst 1662 wird diese Praxis als "Episcopal Consecration, or Ordination" präzisiert und kirchenrechtlich festgeschrieben. Vgl. zum Problem R. H. Fuller, *Sukzession oder Ordination? Zum anglikanisch-lutherischen Gespräch*, in: K. Fröhlich (Hg.), *Ökumene: Möglichkeiten und Grenzen heute*, Tübingen 1982, S. 24-31; B. M. G. Reardon, *The Thirty-Nine Articles and the Augsburg Confession*, LuthQ 3 (1989) S. 91-106, 102.

[9] Das wird unmißverständlich in §4 von *Toward Full Communion and Concordat of Agreement* formuliert: "the threefold ministry of bishops, presbyters, and deacons in historic succession will be the future pattern of the one ordained ministry of Word and Sacrament in both churches as they begin to live in full communion" (a.a.O. (Anm. 3) S. 99).

[10] Apostolicity and Succession, House of Bishops Occasional Paper, London 1994, § 69, S. 28.

[11] Das Porvoo Common Statement *Together in Mission and Ministry*, London 1993, belegt das ebenso unmißverständlich wie das Dokument *Toward Full Communion and Concordat of Agreement* (a.a.O. (Anm. 3)).

[12] Aus der umfangreichen Literatur erwähne ich: N. Sykes, *Old Priests and New Presbyters*, Cambridge 1956; W. Telfer, *The Office of a Bishop*, London 1962; P. Avis, *The Church in the Theology of the Reformers*, London 1981; ders., *Anglicanism and the Christian Church. Theological Resources in Historical Perspective*, Minneapolis 1989; S. W. Sykes/ J. Booty (Hg.), *The Study of Anglicanism*, London 1988. - Zur neueren ökumenischen Diskussion aus anglikanischer Sicht vgl. R.H. Roberts, *Der Stellenwert des kirchlichen Amtes im ökumenischen Gespräch aus anglikanischer Sicht unter Berücksichtigung der Leuenberger Konkordie und der Lima-Erklärung*, ZThK 83 (1986) S. 370-403.

[13] W.S.F. Pickering, *Sociology of Anglicanism*, in: S.W. Sykes/J. Booty, a.a.O. (Anm. 12) S. 364-375, 367.

[14] God's Reign and Our Unity, §91.

[15] L. W. Countryman, a.a.O. (Anm. 2) S. 10.

[16] Zitiert nach ebd. S. 9.

[17] Vgl. G.K. Bell, *Documents on Christian Unity*, London 1924, S. 1ff.

[18] In Resolution 6 der Lambeth Conference von 1920 ist nicht einmal vom historic episcopate die Rede, sondern von "[a] ministry acknowledged by every part of the Church as possessing not only the inward call

of the Spirit, but also the commission of Christ and the authority of the whole body" (*The Lambeth Conferences 1867-1930*, London 1948, S. 39).

[19] J.H. Newman, *Über die Katholizität der Anglikanischen Kirche* (1840), in: *Critical and historical Essays*, London 1871, Bd. 2, S. 1-75.

[20] The bishop has inherited the authority of the Apostles, and he, like them, speaks for Christ in ordination". Das "involves the apostolic succession", was immer dagegen an historischen Einwänden vorgebracht werden mag, denn die praktische Erfahrung in Missiongebieten lehre, daß dies "is exactly how the authority of the Apostles passed into that of the bishops" (Palmer, in: H. N. Bate, a.a.O. (Anm. 7) S. 237ff.).

[21] Erzbischof Chrisostomus, The Nature of the Church, in: H. N. Bate, a.a.O. (Anm. 7) S. 106-115, 114. Vgl. auch die Vorbehalte, die in Lausanne seitens der orthodoxen Kirchen gegen das Abschlußdokument der Sektion V (The Ministry of the Church) in einem Sondervotum zum Ausdruck gebracht wurden: "The Orthodox Church, regarding the ministry as instituted in the Church by Christ Himself, and as the body which by a special *charisma* is the organ through which the Church spreads its means of grace such as the sacraments, and believing that the ministry in its threefold form of bishops, presbyters and deacons can only be based on the unbroken apostolic succession, regrets that it is unable to come in regard to the ministry into some measure of agreement with many of the Churches represented at this Conference ..." (H. N. Bate, a.a.O. (Anm. 7) S. 470f).

[22] J. H. Newman, *Apologia pro vita sua. Being a History of Religous Opinions*, London, 1948; vgl. E. Benz, *Bischofsamt und apostolische Sukzession im deutschen Protestantismus*, Stuttgart 1953, S. 183ff.

[23] Nicht von ungefähr wird von anglikanischer Seite immer wieder betont, daß - wie in Lausanne formuliert wurde - "the acceptance of any special form of ordination as the regular and orderly method of introduction into the ministry of the Church for the future should not be interpreted to imply the acceptance of anyone particular theory of the origin, character or function of any office in the Church" (H. N. Bates, a.a.O. (Anm. 7) S. 469).

[24] So betonte etwa John Cosin im Anschluß an John Overall, "though we are not to lesson the *jus divinum* of episcopacy, where it is established and may be had, yet we must take heed that we do not, for want of episcopacy where it cannot be had, cry down and destroy all the Reformed churches abroad, both in Germany and France and other places, and say they have neither ministers nor sacraments, but all is void and null that they do" (*Works*, Bd. IV, Oxford 1850, S. 449. zitiert nach S.W. Sykes, The Minisatry and the Episcopal Office, a.a.O. (Anm. 8) S.56).

[25] Vgl. A. J. Mason, *The Church of England and Episcopacy*, Cambridge 1914, S. 223ff.

[26] Zitiert nach H. Werner, a.a.O. (Anm. 7) S. 601.

[27] Richard Hooker, *Of the Laws of Ecclesiastical Polity* (1661), VII, x, 1, hrsg. von P. G. Stanwood (The Folger Library Edition of The Works of Richard Hooker), Cambridge (Massachusetts)/ London 1981, Bd. 3, S. 202.

[28] VII, ii, 3, ebd. S. 152.

[29] *"Toward Full Communion"* and *"Concordat of Agreement"* nimmt faktisch genau diese Regelung auf: In §7 wird davon gesprochen, daß lutherische Bischöfe "like other pastors" ordiniert seien "for life service of the gospel in the pastoral ministry of the historic episcopate", in §8 wird angehalten, dafür Sorge zu tragen, "that only bishops shall ordain all clergy" (a.a.O. (Anm. 3) S. 101).

[30] R. Hooker, VII, iv, 1-4, a.a.O. (Anm. 27), S. 155-158.

[31] VII, xi, 8, ebd. S. 208.

[32] Fifty Sermons, London 1710, S. 374.

[33] So die Lambeth Conference von 1930, a.a.O. (Anm. 18) S. 218. Die Problematik dieser theologischen Überhöhung faktischer historischer Entwicklungen wird deutlich, wenn man sieht, daß damit z.B. auch der universale Primat des Bischofs für Rom als Gottes Wille für seine Kirche akzeptiert werden kann. Vgl. ARCIC I: *The Final Report of the Anglican-Roman Catholic Interntaional Commission*, London 1982, S. 83ff.

[34] The Form and Manner of Making, Ordaining, and Consecrating of Bishops, Priests, and Deacons, according to the Order of the Church of England, The Preface, *The Book of Common Prayer*, Cambridge/London 1992, S. 534-567, 534.

[35] Auchdie Ordination wird damit nicht mehr einfach die Bevollmächtigung für *das* Amt *der* Kirche, sondern die Bevollmächtigung zum Amt *einer Kirche unter anderen.*

[36] H.H. Henson, *The Church of England*, Cambridge 1939, S. 123.

[37] W. Law, *Works, Three Letters to the Bishop of Bangor*, London 1762 (Nachdruck 1892 = Hildesheim/New York 1974), Bd. I, S. 9

[38] Es ist theologisch nicht überzeugend, wenn man meint, es genüge, die anglokatholische Sukzessionstheorie abzulehnen, um sich auf der Basis der kirchenrechtlichen Regelungen von 1662 ökumenisch treffen zu können. Dieser Weg wurde im Fall der Church of South India gegangen. Und das scheint auch der Weg zu sein, der in *Toward Full Communion and Concordat of Agreement* gegangen wird, wenn von einer "temporary suspension" der Regel von 1662 gesprochen wird, um die "full interchangeability and reciprocity of all Evangelical Lutheran Church in America pastors as priests or presbyters and all Evangelical Lutheran Church in America deacons as deacons in the Episcopal Church without any further ordination or re-ordination or supplemental ordination whatsoever" zu ermöglichen (§5, a.a.O. (Anm. 3) S. 100). Künftig soll diese Regel dann für beide Kirchen uneingeschränkt gelten: "the threefold ministry of bishops, presbyters, and deacons in historic succession will be the future pattern of the one ordained ministry of Word and Sacrament in both churches" (§4, ebd. S. 99). Eine theologische Begründung für diese Übernahme der "17th century restriction ... of the Ordinal of 1662" (§5, ebd. S. 100) wird nicht gegeben.

[39] Die Behauptung des Ordinale von 1662 , es sei "evident unto all men diligently reading holy Scripture and ancient Authors, that from the Apostles' time there have been these Orders of Ministers in Christ's Church; Bishops, Priests, and Deacons" (a.a.O. (Anm. 34) S. 534), ist so sicher falsch, stützt sich aber auf keine problematische Sukzessionstheorie. Weder der angebliche historische Sachverhalt noch die für ihn offerierte theologische Theorie läßt sich patristisch begründen. Die Berufung auf Irenäus belegt nur, daß

271

Irenäus eine Bischofsliste kannte und dieser theologische Bedeutung beilegte. Sie belegt nicht, daß die Apostel Bischöfe einsetzten und daß es eine ununterbrochene Kette von Einsetzungen gibt. Daß der (nach Petrus zweite) römische Bischof Linus vermutlich eine Fiktion ist und aus dem Mißverständnis eines griechischen Adjektives entstand, ist wohlbekannt und nur einer der problematischen Fälle. Vgl. R.L. Fox, *Pagans and Christians,* London 1986, S. 498f; zur Sache auch G. Gaßmann, *Apostolische Sukzession und Einheit der Kirche in der anglikanischen Theologie,* KuD 10 (1964), S. 257-283, S. 269f.

[40] *The Gospel and the Catholic Church,* 1936, S. 83; 80 (zitiert nach H. Werner, a.a.O. (Anm. 7) S. 602).

[41] G. Gaßmann, a.a.O. (Anm. 39) S. 269f.

[42] So schon 1922 in 'Church Unity', in: G.K.A. Bell , a.a.O. (Anm. 17) S. 46. Heute muß genau dies auch im Blick auf die im Porvoo Common Statement vorgetragene Zeichentheologie gelten: Die Forderung nach Übernahme des historischen Bischofsamtes kann nicht bedeuten, daß man sie übernehmen muß. Ohne sie gibt es aber keinen theologischen Grund, den historschen Episkopat zu übernehmen.

[43] Vgl. *The Fullness of Christ. The Church's Growth into Catholicity being presented to His Grace the Archbishop of Canterbury,* London 1960, S. 81f.

[44] *The Lambeth Conferences,* 1867-1948, Teil II, S. 50.

[45] J.A.T. Robinson, *On Being the Church in the World,* London 1961, S. 101ff; *Intercommunion - An Open Letter to The Archbishop of Canterbury and The Archbishop of York,* London 1961.

[46] *"Toward Full Communion"* and *"Concordat of Agreement",* §4, a.a.O. (Anm. 3) S.99.

[47] P. Avis, *What is 'Anglicanism'?,* in: Sykes/Booty (a.a.O. Anm. 12) S. 405-424, 419.

[48] Vgl. L. W. Countryman, aaO. (Anm. 2) S. 11. Ähnliche Probleme dürften im Fall der angestrebten Lösungen mit den skandinavischen und amerikanischen Lutheranern zu erwarten sein.

[49] Das wird ausführlich dokumentiert und dargestellt in G. Gaßmann, *Das historische Bischofsamt und die Einheit der Kirche in der neueren anglikanischen Theologie,* Göttingen 1964.

[50] Mit dieser Unterscheidung wird auf eine Schwierigkeit reagiert, die Hermann Sasse schon 1929 bei der Übersetzung der Dokumente von Lausanne in: *Die Weltkonferenz für Glauben und Kirchenverfassung. Deutscher amtlicher Bericht über die Weltkirchenkonferenz zu Lausanne 3.-21. August 1927,* Berlin 1929, S. 297f, Anm. 2 notiert hatte: "Das englische Wort *ministry* hat eine doppelte Bedeutung. Es bedeutet entweder 'das geistliche Amt' oder 'die Gesamtheit seiner Träger, die Geistlichkeit'. ... Wir haben im Deutschen kein Wort, das dem englischen *ministry* genau entspricht. ... Das Wort 'Amt' in seinem vollen Sinne, wie Luther es der Grundbedeutung gemäß für das neutestamentliche diakoniva gebrauchte und wie es schon im Mittelalter zur Übersetzung von ministerium benutzt wurde, ist die einzig mögliche Wiedergabe von *ministry.* Leider müssen wir damit auch das englische *office* übersetzen, soweit es nicht mit 'Stelle' übersetzt werden kann, so daß die Gegenüberstellung von *ministry* und *office* im Deutschen nicht genau wiedergegeben werden kann. Unübersetzbar ist auch das Wort *order.* Wird es betont, so geben wir es mit 'Stand' wieder, während wir sonst von 'den Stufen' oder 'Graden des Amtes' reden, z.B. in einer Wendung wie *the three holy orders of the ministry* (Episkopat, Presbyteriat, Diakonat)."

[51] Daß anglikanische Theologie genau in diese sakramentale Richtung denkt, belegt deutllich L. W. Countryman, a.a.O. (Anm. 2); ders., *The Gospel and the Institutions of the Church With Particular Reference to the Historic Episcopate*, AThR 66 (1984) S. 402-415.

[52] *Theologische Erklärung der Bekenntnissynode von Barmen*, These IV, in: Die Barmer Theologische Erklärung. Einführung und Dokumentation, hrsg. von A. Burgsmüller/R. Werth, Neukirchen-Vluyn ³1984, S. 37.

[53] These I, ebd. S. 34.

[54] These III, ebd. S. 36.

[55] Apologie 28, BSLK 397, S. 23ff.

[56] *Together in Mission and Ministry* § 52, a.a.O. (Anm. 11) S. 28.

[57] *Die Meissener Erklärung* Nr. 8, a.a.O. (Anm. 1) S. 39.

[58] So auch G. Evans, *Episcope and Episcopacy: The Niagara Report*, OiC 25 (1989) S. 281-286, 284ff.

[59] *Die Meissener Erklärung* Nr. 19, a.a.O. (Anm. 1) S. 55.

Die Reformation in Deutschland und das bischöfliche Amt

Dorothea Wendebourg

Die Entwicklung des bischöflichen Amtes in den evangelischen Kirchen Deutschlands[1] ist durch zwei Koordinaten bestimmt: durch die theologischen Vorgaben der Reformation, und zwar vor allem der Wittenberger Reformation, und durch die politischen Verhältnisse im Heiligen Römischen Reich deutscher Nation, wie sie sich im Laufe des Mittelalters herausgebildet hatten und für das Reich bis zu seinem Ende maßgeblich blieben. Beginnen wir mit dem zweiten Punkt!

I. Die Kirche im Heiligen Römischen Reich

In allen Königreichen des mittelalterlichen Abendlandes war die Kirche, waren vor allem die Bischöfe eingebunden in das politische System. Darin schlug sich die Vorstellung von der Einheit der christlichen Gesellschaft in ihrer weltlichen und geistlichen Dimension nieder, wie sie dem Mittelalter bei allen Auseinandersetzungen um die konkrete Zuordnung beider selbstverständlich war. Innerhalb dieses allgemeinen Rahmens zeichnete sich das Heilige Römische Reich deutscher Nation durch eine besondere Rechtskonstruktion, eine gesteigerte Verdichtung der Zusammengehörigkeit des Geistlichen und des Politischen aus: durch die geistlichen Fürstentümer, die um 1500 gut fünfzehn Prozent des Reichsterritoriums ausmachten.[2] Nach dieser Rechtskonstruktion, die ihre Wurzeln[3] in der ottonisch-frühsalischen Reichskirche des 10./11. Jahrhunderts[4] hat, waren Erzbischöfe und Bischöfe - sowie weitere geistliche Würdenträger - zugleich Landesherren neben, ja dem Rang nach vor den weltlichen Fürsten. Als solche waren sie reichsunmittelbare Stände, mit Sitz und Stimme auf dem Reichstag vertreten, in Gestalt dreier der sieben Kurfürsten Wähler des Kaisers und Inhaber der wichtigsten Reichsämter, vor allem des Erzkanzleramtes, das dem Erzbischof und Kurfürsten von Mainz zukam.[5] An Zahl überwogen sie gegenüber den weltlichen Fürsten auf dem Reichstag, im Jahre 1521 etwa standen im Fürstenkollegium fünfzig geistliche Stimmen zwanzig weltlichen gegenüber.[6] Kurz, die Bischöfe waren tragende Säulen des Reiches, ihre politische Rolle als Territorialherren war unverzichtbares Element der Reichsverfassung.

Zugleich galt nun aber auch umgekehrt: Das Reich war der Rahmen der Kirche. Eigene übergreifende Strukturen wie etwa Synoden besaß die Kirche des Reiches nicht, das einzige Gremium, in dem ihre Bischöfe zusammenkamen, war der Reichstag, und hier trafen sie sich eben als Fürsten. Ja mehr noch, auch ihre innerkirchliche Durchsetzungskraft hatte in ihrer fürstlichen Gewalt ihren Grund und ihre Grenze. Das zeigt sich am Schicksal ihrer Diözesen. Diese umfaßten aufgrund der skizzierten verfassungsrechtlichen Lage Gebiete von zweierlei Art: das Territorium, in dem der Bischof zugleich der Landesherr war - das "Hochstift" -, sowie Territorien und Städte, die ihre eigene, meist weltliche Obrigkeit besaßen. Die Möglichkeiten, die bischöfliche Jurisdiktionsgewalt zur Geltung zu bringen, waren hier und dort sehr unterschiedlich. Während sie im Hochstift, ohne konkurrierende landesherrliche Gewalt und selbst mit der politischen Macht gekoppelt, von ihren Inhabern durchgesetzt werden konnte, lag das Kirchenregiment in den weltlichen Territorien und Städten in hohem Maße in der Hand der jeweiligen Obrigkeiten, d.h. der Fürsten und der städtischen Räte; Visitationen, die Besetzung kirchlicher Stellen, Klosterreformen u.a.m. wurden hier weitgehend von diesen Instanzen durchgeführt und nicht oder nur nominell oder im Rahmen landesherrlicher Maßnahmen vom Bischof.[7] Die Kirche des Reiches war faktisch landesherrliche Kirche. Das gilt für die weltlichen Gebiete, das gilt in spezifischer, gewissermaßen gesteigerter Form aber auch in den geistlichen Territorien, insofern die Bischöfe ihre Gewalt hier kraft ihrer Position als Territorialherren zur Geltung brachten.

II. Die Auffassung der Wittenberger Reformatoren vom Bischofsamt

Martin Luthers Auffassung vom Bischofsamt kommt sehr deutlich bereits in der Schrift "An den christlichen Adel deutscher Nation" von 1520 zum Ausdruck. Hier heißt es: "Nach Christi und der Apostel Festsetzung soll jede Stadt einen Pfarrer oder Bischof haben, wie Paulus klar schreibt Tit. 1,.... Denn ein Bischof und ein Pfarrer ist ein und dasselbe bei St. Paul, wie das auch St. Hieronymus beweist. Aber von den Bischöfen, die es jetzt gibt, weiß die Schrift nichts, sondern sie sind durch Anordnung der christlichen Gemeinde eingesetzt, damit einer über viele Pfarrer regiere." Allerdings sollte laut dem Apostel der Pfarrer oder Bischof "neben sich mehrere Priester und Diakone haben ..., die den Haufen und die Gemeinde zu regieren hülfen mit Predigen und Sakramenten".[8]

Dies Zitat enthält und impliziert eine Reihe von Aussagen, die Luther auch weiterhin festhalten wird und die in die Bekenntnisschriften der von Wittenberg her reformierten Kirche Eingang gefunden haben.[9] Danach ist "Bischofsamt" Bezeichnung für das grundlegende, von Christus eingesetzte, apostolische Amt in der Kirche. Aufgabe dieses Amtes ist die für die Kirche konstitutive Tätigkeit der Gemeindeleitung durch Predigt und Sakramentsverwaltung. Wo wird solche Tätigkeit ausgeübt? In der um eine Kanzel, einen Taufstein und einen Tisch versammelten Ortsgemeinde. D.h., das Bischofsamt ist kein anderes als das Amt des Pfarrers. Die Identität von Pfarramt und Bischofsamt im Sinne des grundlegenden, apostolischen Amtes in der Kirche entnimmt Luther den Pastoralbriefen, wonach der επισκοπος der Leiter einer Einzelgemeinde ist; außerdem führt er Hieronymus' Auslegung dieser Briefe an.[10] Und er verweist überhaupt gerne auf die Verhältnisse in der Alten Kirche: "Eine jegliche Stadt hat einen Bischof gehabt, wie sie jetzt Pfarrer haben, und Sanct Augustinus, der von seinem Pfarrer oder Bischof Valerius zum Prediger geweiht oder ordiniert wurde und nach seinem Tode an seiner Statt Bischof wurde, hat keine größere Pfarrei gehabt als unsere Pfarrei zu Wittenberg, wenn sie überhaupt so groß gewesen ist."[11]

Der eigentliche Grund für jene Identifizierung liegt für Luther aber nicht in diesem oder jenem biblischen oder patristischen Zitat, sondern im Wesen des Amtes selbst: eben darin, daß das Amt per definitionem Dienst der Predigt und Sakramentsverwaltung und somit primär im Dienst an der Einzelgemeinde verwirklicht ist. Wie man es bezeichnet, ist demgegenüber zweitrangig.[12] Da Neues Testament und frühe Kirche in diesem Zusammenhang das Wort "Bischof" verwenden, ist es aber angemessen, ihren Sprachgebrauch aufzunehmen und so zugleich den ursprünglichen Sinn des Wortes im christlichen Kontext wieder zur Geltung zu bringen. Ja, es ist sogar zweckmäßig, da dieser terminologische Rückgriff - wie gleich zu zeigen sein wird - die Möglichkeit bietet, auch das Wesen des Amtes gegenüber vielerlei Verdunkelung wieder herauszustellen.

Mit dem allen ist nicht gesagt, daß es in der Kirche keine den Pfarrern übergeordneten Amtsträger gibt, "Bischöfe" in jenem Sinne des Wortes, der sich im Laufe der Kirchengeschichte entwickelt hat, d.h. Leiter ganzer Diözesen. Doch nicht nur dieser Wortgebrauch ist sekundär, sondern auch diese Amtsstufe selbst im Verhältnis zum Pfarramt - entstanden "durch Anordnung der christlichen Gemeinde".[13] Ebensowenig wollen die zitierten Ausführungen verneinen, daß der Pfarrer-Bischof weitere Amtsträger um sich hat, Presbyter - "Priester" - und Diakone, wie sie die Pastoralbriefe kennen. Doch sie sind ihm untergeordnet und in seinen Dienst für die Gemeinde integriert - dazu bestimmt, ihm hierbei zu "helfen".[14]

Wenn Luther nicht ein übergemeindliches Amt, sondern den apostolischen Dienst (ministerium)[15] in der Gemeinde als das von Christus gestiftete grundlegende Amt betrachtet, steht er nicht nur in Kontinuität zur frühen Kirche. Sondern er setzt damit auch die in der mittelalterlichen Amtstheologie vorherrschende Linie fort.[16] Zwar hatte sich längst die gemeindeübergreifende Diözesanstruktur herausgebildet - im außeritalienischen Abendland zudem mit großen Flächenbistümern - und war der Terminus "episcopus" auf diese Ebene "hinaufgewandert". Doch es war nicht der nun "Bischof" genannte Leiter eines viele Gemeinden umfassenden Bezirkes, in dem man das grundlegende, apostolische Amt in der Kirche verwirklicht sah. Das Amt, der Ordo in seiner Fülle war nach Ansicht der meisten mittelalterlichen Theologen vielmehr im Presbyterat gegeben.[17] So schrieb Petrus Lombardus in seinen Sentenzen und prägte damit das weitere amtstheologische Denken des Mittelalters: Nach seinen Quellen gebe es nur zwei heilige Amtsstufen (sacri ordines), den Diakonat und den Presbyterat.[18] Der Episkopat stellt demgemäß keine eigene Amtsstufe dar, er ist nur eine spezifische Würde und Funktion (dignitas et officium).[19]

Diese Entwicklung war konsequent, insofern die Presbyter nach und nach die meisten Aufgaben der Bischöfe in den Gemeinden übernommen hatten und selbst zu Gemeindeleitern geworden waren. Sie ging aber zugleich mit einer inhaltlichen Veränderung von Verständnis und Praxis des Amtes einher: Das Amt wurde mehr und mehr von seiner Funktion für das als Opfer aufgefaßte Abendmahl her bestimmt. D.h., der Presbyter galt in erster Linie als Priester, außerdem als Spender der Absolution. Demgemäß stand im Mittelpunkt seiner Ordination die Übereignung der Opfergewalt mit der Gabe der Opfergeräte (porrectio instrumentorum).[20]

Luthers und der anderen Wittenberger Rückgriff auf den Terminus "episcopus" in seiner neutestamentlich-frühkirchlichen Bedeutung war ein Protest gegen dies Verständnis und eine inhaltliche Neubestimmung des Amtes - oder besser, die Rückgewinnung seines ursprünglichen Sinnes. So sehr er mit den mittelalterlichen Theologen den apostolischen Dienst an der Basis als das grundlegende, volle kirchliche Amt ansah, so wenig bestimmte er dessen Aufgaben vom mittelalterlichen Priesteramt her, sondern er stellte mit Nachdruck fest, daß seine Aufgaben die des Bischofs der Pastoralbriefe und der ersten Jahrhunderte seien:[21] Der Amtsträger hat das Evangelium zu verkündigen, wie es die Briefe an Timotheus und Titus dem επισκοπος vorschreiben, er hat zu predigen und die Sakramente zu verwalten, wie es die Zeugnisse der ersten Jahrhunderte vom Bischofsamt entfalten.[22] So wird der evangeliumsgemäße Sinn des kirchlichen Amtes wiedergewonnen, so wird zugleich aber auch der Begriff "Bischof" wieder mit genuin geistlichem Sinn gefüllt.

Der Rückgriff auf Verständnis und Praxis des Bischofsamtes in neutestamentlich-frühkirchlicher Zeit bei Luther ließe sich nun in den verschiedensten Zusammenhängen zeigen. Ich verweise nur auf zwei: Für die Formula missae, die reformierte Gottesdienstordnung von 1523, ist der Leiter des Gottesdienstes episcopus[23] - nicht anders, als für die Kirchenordnungen und die liturgischen Formulare der Alten Kirche, etwa die Traditio Apostolica, die Didaskalia oder die Apostolischen Konstitutionen. Und das Wittenberger Ordinationsformular von 1535[24] gestaltet die Ordination der Pfarrer deutlich als Bischofsweihe: Die

Lesungen sind 1. Tim. 3,1-7 und Apg. 20,28-31; die darauf folgende Vermahnung spricht die Ordinanden als zukünftige "Bischöfe" an[25]; den rituellen Mittelpunkt bildet, gemäß den Auskünften der Pastoralbriefe zur Ordination des Bischofs und altkirchlichem Brauch, die Handauflegung mit Gebet, eine Darreichung von Geräten gibt es nicht. Als Ordinatoren sollen Pfarrer benachbarter Städte amtieren, d.h. Nachbarbischöfe, wie es can. 4 des Konzils von Nizäa für die Bischofsweihe vorschreibt[26], auf den man sich ausdrücklich bezieht.[27] Die Tatsache, daß in Wittenberg und anderwärts Pfarrer die Ordination durchführten, gehört in diese Traditionslinie: Sie taten es als Inhaber des einen, vollen, bischöflichen Amtes, zu dem - wie schon die Zeugnisse aus der frühen Kirche zeigen - auch die Vollmacht gehört, dies Amt weiterzugeben. Der Neuordinierte trat damit in eine bischöfliche Sukzessionslinie ein.[28] Allerdings war dieser Gedanke in den Überlegungen der Beteiligten ohne Gewicht, so wie die Konzeption der apostolischen Sukzession im Bischofsamt im 16. Jahrhundert überhaupt - auf allen Seiten - nur ganz am Rande eine Rolle spielte.[29] Worauf es den Wittenbergern ankam, das war die Treue in der Weitergabe der evangeliumsgemäßen Verkündigung - die "Lehrsukzession" -, ihr hatte die Ordination von Bischof zu Bischof zu dienen.[30]

Nun ist die Identifikation von Pfarramt und Bischofsamt bei Luther und in der von Wittenberg aus reformierten Kirche nur eine Seite der Medaille. Denn zugleich wird hier durchaus auch der Episkopat im Sinne eines übergemeindlichen Amtes bejaht. Schon das Zitat aus der Schrift "An den christlichen Adel" plädiert nicht für die Abschaffung des Diözesanbischofsamtes, und das tun die Wittenberger auch sonst bei aller Kritik an den vorhandenen Bischöfen nicht. Und bereits in den nächsten Jahren macht Luther mehrfach[31] positive Vorschläge für die Gestaltung eines legitimen, evangeliumsgemäßen übergemeindlichen Bischofsamtes. So rät er in der kleinen Schrift "De instituendis ministris" Ecclesiae von 1523 an die Böhmen[32] den Adressaten, sie sollten sich nicht mit Pfarrern begnügen, sondern über diesen auch kirchenleitende Bischöfe haben, denen die Aufsicht über die Pfarrer obläge; d.h., wenn man der - auch hier festgehaltenen - Identität von Pfarramt und Bischofsamt terminologisch Rechnung trägt, es sollten wie in der Alten Kirche über den Bischöfen in den einzelnen Städten Metropoliten oder Erzbischöfe für ganze Regionen stehen.[33]

Bevor dieser Gedankengang weiter verfolgt wird, ist allerdings zu betonen: Die Bejahung und schließlich auch die bewußte Gestaltung übergemeindlicher episkopaler Strukturen ändert nichts an der prinzipiellen Aussage, daß das apostolische Amt in der Kirche das Pfarramt ist. Ja, die übergreifenden Ämter ruhen ganz und gar auf dem Pfarramt auf. In ihnen sind Funktionen ausgegliedert, die ihrem Wesen nach in den Aufgaben des Pfarrers, in Predigt und Sakramentsverwaltung, mitgegeben sind.[34] Deshalb ist der übergemeindliche Bischof seinem Wesen Pfarrer, Bischof im ursprünglichen Sinne des Wortes - auch seine grundlegende Aufgabe stellt die Verkündigung des Evangeliums dar. Allerdings ist er ein Pfarrer, der bestimmte Funktionen des Amtes eigentümlich wahrnimmt. Daß er das als besonderer, dafür abgeordneter Amtsträger tut, ist - anders als Wesen und Vorhandensein des kirchlichen Amtes selbst[35] - in die Entscheidung der Kirche gestellt[36], es ist nicht iure divino, sondern iure positivo[37], humana autoritate.[38]

Ist es auch in die Entscheidung der Kirche gelegt, ob übergemeindlicher Zusammenhang überhaupt hergestellt und übergemeindliche Aufsicht überhaupt wahrgenommen wird? Luthers Vorrede zu Melanchthons "Unterricht der Visitatorn"[39], der ersten Kirchenordnung in Sachsen, gibt eine klare Antwort auf diese Frage: Die Wahrnehmung des "Besuchsdienstes", wie er die Aufgabe der Visitation oder Episkope hier auf deutsch nennt, ist für die Christenheit "nützlich und notwendig".[40] Wie, in welcher institutionellen Form das geschieht, ist variabel - wobei die Wittenberger sich im allgemeinen personale, nicht synodale Formen vorstellen.[41] Aber daß es geschieht, kann nicht zur Disposition stehen. Denn darin kommt eine Dimension der Kirche zur Geltung, die zu ihrem Wesen gehört: ihre Katholizität, d.h. ihre Einheit in der Wahrheit durch Raum und Zeit. Diese Dimension der Katholizität ist mit dem Evangelium selbst und darum mit dem Amt der Verkündigung in Predigt und Sakrament an sich gegeben. Doch es dient ihrer Bewahrung, wenn eigens dazu abgeordnete Amtsträger sich in geregelter Form ausdrücklich und kontinuierlich dafür einsetzen. Dazu müssen sie in bestimmten Bereichen den Gemeindepfarrern übergeordnet sein: "Damit die Kirche eine und übereinstimmend sei, hat Gott immer dasselbe Evangelium verbreitet, durch die Väter und die Propheten und danach durch Christus und die Apostel, und Christus hat das Amt (ministerium) eingerichtet, das bis ans Ende der Welt bleiben wird. ... Denn er bewahrt das Evangelium und wollte, daß nach den Aposteln in allen Gemeinden Hirten berufen würden, die die Aufgabe der Evangeliumsverkündigung wahrnähmen; diese erweckt er, wie verschieden an Gaben, doch als Inhaber desselben Amtes. Es besteht also die Einheit der Kirche in dieser Verbindung unter einem Haupt durch dasselbe Evangelium und dasselbe Amt... Damit aber alles ordentlich geschieht in der Kirche nach der Regel des Paulus und die Hirten untereinander stärker verbunden seien...und die einen für die anderen Fürsorge übernähmen und Spaltungen oder Schismen vermieden würden, kam die nützliche Ordnung hinzu, daß aus vielen Presbytern ein Bischof erwählt wurde, der die Kirche durch die Lehre des Evangeliums und die Aufrechterhaltung der Disziplin leiten und den Presbytern selbst vorsitzen sollte... Diese Ordnungen sind, wenn die Vorsitzenden ihre Pflicht erfüllen, nützlich zur Erhaltung der Kircheneinheit".[42] Die konkreten Aufgaben der "vorsitzenden" Bischöfe sind Lehre und Beurteilung von Lehre, Ordination einschließlich der

Prüfung der Ordinanden, Visitation, kirchliche Gesetzgebung und Rechtsprechung, gegebenenfalls auch die Einberufung von Synoden.[43] Für all diese Tätigkeiten gilt, was für das Verkündigungsamt, aus dem sie ausgegliedert sind, überhaupt gilt: In ihnen wird das Wort Gottes zur Geltung gebracht, d.h. es sind kirchlich-geistliche Vollzüge. Sie dürfen nicht mit politischen Mitteln durchgesetzt oder mit politischen Zielen verbunden werden.[44] Das bedeutet für die bestehenden kirchenlichen Verhältnisse: Eine Rechtskonstruktion wie die Geistlichen Fürstentümer ist damit im Prinzip nicht vereinbar.[45]

III. Der Versuch einer Entwicklung übergemeindlich-episkopaler Strukturen im Rahmen des mittelalterlichen Diözesanwesens

An und für sich gab es Amtsträger, deren Sache die Wahrnehmung der skizzierten episkopalen Aufgaben war: die Diözesanbischöfe mit ihren festumrissenen Bistümern und ihren traditionellen Bischofssitzen.[46] Nichts lag für die Wittenberger Reformation näher, als an dieser Zuordnung festzuhalten. Voraussetzung dafür war allerdings, daß jene Bischöfe sich tatsächlich als bischöfliche Träger des apostolischen Amtes erwiesen. Eben das sprachen die Reformatoren den amtierenden Bischöfen des Reiches ab. Und zwar mit zwei Argumenten: Sie dienen - zum einen - nicht dem Evangelium, sondern sie vertreten und decken falsche Lehre und Praxis und sind so die Hauptverantwortlichen für den verderblichen Zustand, in dem sich die Kirche befindet[47]; nichts zeigt das deutlicher als die Tatsache, daß sie die Anhänger der Reformation verfolgen.[48] Und sie sind - zum anderen - nur nominell Bischöfe[49], in Wirklichkeit aber Fürsten und in ihren Interessen wie ihrem Verhalten ganz und gar politisch bestimmt.[50] M.a.W., die amtierenden Bischöfe müssen sich bekehren und wirkliche christliche Bischöfe werden.[51] Dann kann sie die Reformation und wird sie sie als Inhaber der Episkope über ihre Gemeinden anerkennen.[52] D.h., sie müssen zur reinen Predigt des Evangeliums und zur rechten Sakramentsverwaltung zurückkehren. Und sie müssen auch wirklich das tun, was die Aufgabe eines Bischofs ist: verkündigen und lehren, visitieren, ordinieren usw.

Ein Bild des bekehrten, reformierten und so von den Gemeinden der Reformation anzuerkennenden Diözesanbischofs skizziert Luther bereits 1522, in jenem Jahr, als sich erstmals die Notwendigkeit einer gewissen institutionellen Festigung der reformatorischen Bewegung zeigte. Die Schrift "Wider den falsch genannten geistlichen Stand des Papstes und der Bischöfe"[53], die - wie schon der Titel deutlich macht - eine schneidende Abrechnung mit den amtierenden Reichsbischöfen darstellt, will zugleich eben diese Bischöfe aufrütteln und zur Besinnung auf das Evangelium und auf den eigentlichen Sinn ihres Amtes bringen.[54] Hätte dieser Weg Erfolg gehabt, würden die deutschen lutherischen - und die meisten unierten - Kirchen heute wohl ähnlich aussehen wie die Skandinaviens. Sie würden die vorreformatorischen Diözesen und Bischofssitze aufweisen mit Bischöfen, die auf eine Kette von Vorgängern bis ins Mittelalter, z.T. sogar bis in die Antike zurückblickten. Diese Bischöfe wären allerdings darauf verpflichtet, das Evangelium nach der Lehre der Wittenberger Reformation zu verkündigen und ihre spezifischen Aufgaben demgemäß wahrzunehmen. Und ihr Amt selbst wäre so bestimmt, wie es dem reformatorischen Verständnis des übergemeindlichen Episkopats entspricht, als besondere Ausprägung des einen - primär im Gemeindepfarramt verwirklichten - Verkündigungsamtes in der Kirche.

So müßig derartige Spekulationen sind, muß doch eingeräumt werden, daß die von Luther geäußerte Hoffnung auf eine Reformation des vorhandenen Episkopats und mit dem vorhandenen Episkopat nicht gänzlich unrealistisch war. Drei Jahre später, 1525, gab es die ersten Fälle: In Preußen, gerade zum evangelischen Herzogtum geworden, schlossen sich zwei Bischöfe der Reformation an, Georg von Polentz (1478 - 1550), seit 1519 Bischof des Samlandes mit Kathedra in Königsberg, und Erhard von Queiß (1490 - 1529), 1523 zum Bischof von Pomesanien gewählt, allerdings noch nicht vom Papst bestätigt und geweiht; ihre Stifter traten sie an den Herzog ab. Luther begleitete diesen Vorgang mit Zustimmung und Ratschlägen.[55]

Preußen gehörte nicht zum Heiligen Römischen Reich. Damit kommt im Kontrast das entscheidende Problem in den Blick, das einen entsprechenden Schritt durch Vertreter des Episkopats im Reich verhinderte: Die preußischen Bischöfe waren keine Reichsfürsten, ihre Stellung ohne die mit den Geistlichen Fürstentümern im Reich gegebene verfassungsrechtliche Relevanz. Wenn sich bei ihnen Veränderungen in Verständnis und Führung ihres Amtes ergaben, war das zwar auch nicht politisch folgenlos, aber von begrenztem Gewicht. Bei den Bischöfen des Reiches dagegen wäre damit ein wesentliches Element des politischen Gesamtgebäudes ins Wanken geraten: Die institutionalisierte Bindung des Reiches und des Kaisers an die römische Kirche durch die Position dieser Männer in Reichstag und Kurfürstenkollegium hätte auf dem Spiel gestanden. Und der Charakter einer großen Zahl von Reichsständen hätte sich grundlegend geändert, wenn wie in Preußen die Konsequenz aus der Forderung der Reformation nach einem genuin kirchlichen Bischofsamt und der Kritik an den Geistlichen Fürstentümern gezogen worden wäre und diese sich in weltliche Teritorien verwandelt hätten.[56]

Die preußischen Vorgänge machten folglich keine Schule im Reich.[57] Um aber doch auch hier Bewegung in die Bischofsfront zu bringen, ließen sich die Wittenberger herbei, auf die Verwirklichung ihrer Idealvorstellungen von einem evangelischen Bischof zu verzichten und Kompromisse vorzuschlagen: Wenn keine Bekehrung der amtierenden Bischöfe zu erwarten sei, sollten sie wenigstens der evangelischen Verkündigung ihren Lauf lassen, deren Anhänger nicht verfolgen und evangelische Pfarrer ordinieren; dann würden die reformatorischen Gemeinden ihre Jurisdiktion anerkennen.[58] Außerdem waren die Wittenberger bereit, auf die Forderung zu verzichten, daß die Geistlichen Fürstentümer abzuschaffen seien. Bei der Anerkennung von Bischöfen, die die Reformation nicht übernehmen, aber sie gewähren lassen würden, war dies Zugeständnis ohnehin eingeschlossen; Voraussetzung mußte freilich sein, daß die geistlichen Fürsten strikt zwischen ihrem kirchlichen und ihrem politischen Amt unterschieden und nicht die Ziele und Mittel des einen und des anderen miteinander vermischten - ein Programm, das der achtundzwanzigste Artikel des Augsburgischen Bekenntnisses dem Kaiser unterbreitete.[59] Doch die Wittenberger waren auch bereit, Bischöfen, die sich der Reformation anschlössen, notfalls ihre fürstliche Herrschaft zu belassen, ein Zugeständnis, das diesen den Anschluß erleichtern sollte und die verfassungsmäßigen Verhältnisse unangetastet ließ.[60] Alle tatsächlich eingeleiteten Versuche, im Reich zu einem evangelischen Episkopat im Rahmen des mittelalterlichen Diözesanwesens zu kommen[61], gingen von diesem Status quo aus. Indessen drohte, auch wenn er respektiert wurde, mit dem Übergang von Fürstbischöfen zur Reformation die schwerwiegende Veränderung, daß die evangelischen Reichsstände im Reichstag und Kurfürstenkollegium zur Mehrheit werden würden. Daß der Kaiser eine solche Verschiebung nicht hinzunehmen gewillt war, machte er jedesmal unter Aufbietung aller Machtmittel deutlich, und das mit Erfolg.[62]

So wurde denn kein Reichsbischof mit seinem Bischofssitz für die Reformation gewonnen. Es gab verschiedentlich Bewegungen in dieser Richtung, etwa in den vierziger Jahren bei dem Erzbischof und Kurfürsten von Köln Hermann von Wied (1477-1552), einem der höchsten geistlichen Fürsten des Reichs, oder bei dem Bischof von Minden, Münster und Osnabrück Franz von Waldeck (1491-1553). Köln wurde vom Kaiser selbst mit militärischen Mitteln bei der Stange gehalten (1547), der Erzbischof mußte abdanken und starb als exkommunizierter Protestant.[63] Sein Osnabrücker Amtsbruder entging einem entsprechenden Schicksal durch Kehrtwendung.[64] Es gab eine Ausnahme, die aber gerade die Regel bestätigt: Der Bischof des Bistums Brandenburg Matthias von Jagow (um 1480-1544), im Amt seit 1516, schloß sich 1539/40 der Reformation an und wirkte für deren Durchsetzung im Kurfürstentum Brandenburg.[65] Sein Hochstift besaß aber keine Reichsunmittelbarkeit mehr.[66] So ergaben sich hier keine reichsrechtlich-politischen Komplikationen, nachhaltige Proteste blieben aus.[67]

Die Kompromißvorschläge führten nicht weiter, Matthias blieb ein Einzelfall. So unternahmen die Wittenberger noch einen anderen Versuch, das Projekt "mittelalterliches Bischofsamt im Einklang mit dem Evangelium" zu verwirklichen. Wenn von seiten der amtierenden Bischöfe nichts zu erwarten war, mußte man Sedisvakanzen ausnützen und von vornherein evangelische Kandidaten auf freie Bischofsthrone setzen. An und für sich standen solchen Versuchen dieselben Schwierigkeiten entgegen wie dem Anschluß eines Reichsbischofs an die Reformation. Deshalb konnten sie, wenn überhaupt, nur gelingen, wo die Reichsstandschaft eines Bischofs eingeschränkt und er von einem evangelischen Landesherrn geschützt - aber auch abhängig war. In den drei Fällen, in denen in der ersten Hälfte des 16. Jahrhunderts evangelische Männer vakante Bischofssitze übernahmen, verhielt es sich so: in den sächsischen Stiftern Naumburg-Zeitz (1542) und Merseburg (1544) und im pommerschen Kammin (1545).

Sehen wir uns die Vorgänge in Naumburg und Merseburg Bischöfe Nikolaus von Amsdorff (1483-1565)[68] und Georg von Anhalt (1507 -1553)[69], kurz an, weil sie für das Verständnis des Bischofsamtes und seiner Übertragung bei den Beteiligten höchst aufschlußreich sind. Die liturgische Ordnung[70] entsprach weitgehend dem Wittenberger Ordinationsformular, hinzu kamen einige, z.T. der Bischofs-weihliturgie nach den mittelalterlichen Pontifikalien entstammende Elemente, die auf die besonderen Aufgaben des neuen Bischofs bezogen waren.[71] Diese Abweichungen sind gering - der liturgische Ausdruck der bereits angesprochenen Überzeugung, daß der nun übertragene regionale Episkopat kein anderes Amt ist als das eine primär im Gemeindepfarramt verwirklichte Verkündigungsamt. Wird dies Amt nun hier zum zweiten Mal übertragen, die Ordination - die die betroffenen Kandidaten sämtlich bereits erhalten hatten - schlicht wiederholt? Auffälligerweise gab es keine Erörterungen dieser Frage. Daß die einmal empfangene Ordination nicht zu wiederholen sei, betrachteten alle Beteiligten als ebenso selbstverständlich wie die wesensmäßige Identität von Pfarramt und Bischofsamt. Offenbar stellte die Bischofseinsetzung für sie eine Aktualisierung der Ordination für die speziellen episkopalen Aufgaben dar.[72]

Die Auswahl der handelnden Personen spricht dieselbe Sprache: Im Fall der sächsischen Stifter war es Luther zusammen mit Superintendenten und Pfarrern aus benachbarten Städten, im Fall Kammins waren es die Superintendenten der Nachbarherzogtümer.[73] Das entsprach der schon für die Ordination ausgesprochenen Bestimmung, daß der Bischof bzw. Pfarrer nach altkirchlichem Brauch möglichst von mehreren Nachbarbischöfen zu ordinieren sei.[74] Bemerkenswert ist, daß der Kandidat für Merseburg, Georg von Anhalt, zunächst versucht hatte, einen Bischof - natürlich einen die Reformation vertretenden Bischof - zu gewinnen. In Frage kamen grundsätzlich der Erzbischof von Köln, einer der preußischen Bischöfe und der Brandenburger Matthias, aus Gründen der Entfernung allerdings konkret nur letzterer; mit ihm trat Georg denn auch in Verhandlungen ein. Matthias sagte zu, starb aber vor der geplanten Reise, so daß sich der ganze Plan zerschlug und Martin Luther die Handauflegung vornahm.[75].

Es wurde vermutet, Georg habe diese Verhandlungen geführt, um über Matthias in die apostolische Sukzession der Bischöfe einzutreten.[76] Das ist nicht unmöglich, aber aus den Quellen geht dergleichen nicht hervor. Zwar wurde in jenen Jahren die Konzeption der apostolischen Sukzession im Bischofsamt, verstanden als Diözesanbischofsamt, in bestimmten Kreisen erstmals wieder diskutiert, nachdem man die Bindung der Ordination und Konsekration an den Bischof jahrhundertelang als feststehende Regel betrachtet, aber nicht zum theologischen Thema gemacht hatte - wir werden darauf zurückkommen. Doch bei Georg gibt es keine Aussage, in der er seinen Wunsch nach bischöflicher Handauflegung so begründete[77], und die Schnelligkeit, mit der er sich nach Bischof Matthias' Tod an Luther wandte[78], spricht eher gegen die Vermutung, ihm sei an einer solchen bischöflichen Handauflegung um einer damit gegebenen apostolischen Sukzession willen gelegen gewesen. Schon gar nicht kann es ihm um eine Weihesukzession gegangen sein, denn Matthias von Brandenburg war ungeweiht.[79] Das Interesse des Merseburger Bischofskandidaten, der für seine konservative, auf die Bewahrung möglichst vieler Traditionen gerichtete Einstellung bekannt war, galt wohl eher der Beibehaltung einer guten Ordnung, ferner der Anerkennung seines Amtes im Reich - die war, wenn überhaupt, nur unter der Bedingung der Einsetzung durch einen Bischof zu erreichen.[80]

Eine fatale Hypothek stellte auch in diesen Fällen das Geistliche Fürstentum dar. Man sollte denken, nun, da der Bischof evangelisch war, habe die Möglichkeit bestanden, das kirchliche Aufsichtsamt von der politischen Position zu lösen, wie es die Reformatoren verfochten hatten. In Merseburg geschah das, anders als in Naumburg und Kammin, auch tatsächlich - aber um den Preis, daß man die letzte Konsequenz aus der Idee des politischen Reichsbischofs ziehen mußte: Der Bischofstitel ging an den Inhaber der politischen Macht, einen - nun evangelischen - Fürsten verloren. Konkret, die fürstlichen und die geistlichen Aufgaben des Bischofs von Merseburg wurden getrennt, erstere übernahm ein sächsischer Herzog, der auf diese Weise ein Territorium gewann[81], letztere eben Georg.[82] Voraussetzung aber war, daß der Bischofstitel mit allen politischen Implikationen am Territorium und seinem - nun ganz weltlichen - Fürsten hing[83]; nur so konnte man sich im reichsrechtlichen Koordinatensystem halten - eine Lösung, die die Entwicklung nach dem Augsburger Religionsfrieden und die Entscheidungen des westfälischen Friedens hinsichtlich der mittel- und norddeutschen Stifter vorwegnahm.[84] Der eigentliche Bischof durfte sich offiziell nur "Coadjutor" nennen.[85]

Georg bemühte sich redlich, gleichwohl alles zu tun, was einem evangelischen Bischof obliegt.[86] Doch auch hier stieß er bald an Grenzen: Als Bischof ohne politischen Herrschaftsbereich besaß er auch kaum finanzielle Mittel, die zur Durchführung seiner episkopalen Aufgaben notwendig waren, da das Hochstift die wichtigste wirtschaftliche Basis eines Bischofs darstellte. So stand er in ökonomischer Abhängigkeit von den sächsischen Herzögen, abgesehen davon, daß seine prekäre rechtliche Lage ihn ohnehin an diese band. M.a.W., ausgerechnet der Versuch, die bischöfliche Macht von der politischen abzukoppeln, machte sie in anderer Weise dieser gegenüber unselbständig. So stand das Merseburger Bischofsexperiment trotz, ja wegen seiner theologischen Sauberkeit auf schwachen Füßen - innerhalb des reichsrechtlichen Rahmens war solche Sauberkeit anders nicht zu haben.

Der Sieg des Kaisers im Schmalkaldischen Krieg machte dem allen ohnehin ein Ende und bildete damit für die Experimente östlich der Elbe ebenso einen Markstein wie für das in Köln am Rhein. In Merseburg erzwang Karl die Aufgabe der Trennung von geistlicher und weltlicher Gewalt, auf seinen Befehl übernahm wieder ein romtreuer, von ihm selbst ausgewählter Bischof die Kathedra, der zugleich Territorialherr und Reichsfürst war.[87] Ein gegenreformatorischer Kandidat kam auch in Naumburg auf den Thron, die Verbindung beider Gewalten und der Reichsfürstenstand des Bischofs wurden bekräftigt,[88] ebenso wie im Fall des neuen, Kaiser wie Papst genehmen Bischofs von Kammin.[89] Doch auch dieser Zustand sollte nicht lange währen. Mit dem Rückgang der kaiserlichen Macht in den fünfziger Jahren schwand der politische Halt der fürstlichen Bischöfe. Und so setzte sich nach dem Augsburgischen Religionsfrieden die Lösung durch, die man in Merseburg bereits ausprobiert hatte: Evangelische Fürsten übernahmen als Administratoren die bischöfliche Position.[90] Coadjutoren für den geistlichen Bereich hatten sie nicht mehr. Dafür gab es mittlerweile andere Instanzen.

Bevor dieser Abschnitt an sein Ende kommt, soll die Frage gestellt werden, warum die Wittenberger Reformatoren sich so nachrücklich um die Beibehaltung des Episkopats in der überkommenen Ordnung bemühten. Denn es ist ja auffällig, mit welcher Hartnäckigkeit, mit wieviel Kompromißbereitschaft auch sie nach Mitteln und Wegen suchten, dies Ziel zu erreichen. Hinter dem Bemühen steckten einerseits zweifellos politische Motive: Man wollte sich nicht außerhalb der Rechtsordnung des Reiches stellen. Doch es fragt sich, ob es nicht noch andere, möglicherweise auch theologische Gründe gab.

Dazu ist zunächst einmal zu sagen, daß die Reformatoren sich um die Beibehaltung des bestehenden Episkopats jedenfalls nicht deshalb bemühten, weil sie ihn für notwendig gehalten hätten, für geboten vom Evangelium her (iure divino). Das ergibt sich aus dem oben Gesagten, das zeigte sich dann aber auch ganz handgreiflich, als sie andere Lösungen entwickeln mußten und diese für theologisch ebenso legitim, ja unter den gegebenen Umständen allein legitim hielten. Auch der Gedanke der apostolischen Sukzession im Sinne der Sukzession im Diözesanbischofsamt konnte für sie keine bindende Kraft haben. Wie bereits angedeutet, spielte dieser Gedanke in den Auseinandersetzungen der Reformationszeit nur am Rande eine Rolle, er hatte es schon im Mittelalter kaum getan. In den Religionsgesprächen zu Worms und zu Regensburg war er, kurz zuvor wiederentdeckt,[91] auf die Tagesordnung gekommen.[92] Die Wittenberger reagierten mit scharfer Ablehnung: Mit der Theorie von der apostolischen Sukzession im Episkopat werde die Kirche von der Abfolge der Bischöfe abhängig gemacht. Denn danach solle die wahre, apostolische Verkündigung durch die Sukzessionskette garantiert und an sie gebunden sein.[93] Eine solche Vorstellung widersprach den Erfahrungen, die man mit den Bischöfen machte. Und sie widersprach der reformatorischen Auffassung vom Evangelium, von der Kirche und von ihrem Amt.

Gleichwohl hätte man den bestehenden Episkopat, wenn möglich, gerne behalten. Und zwar deshalb, weil er eine seit alten Zeiten vorhandene, über lange Strecken auch bewährte, grundsätzlich reformierbare und der Reform würdige Einrichtung sei: "wir haben oft beteuert, daß wir inständigst begehren, die Kirchenverfassung (politia ecclesiastica) und die Stufen in der Kirche zu bewahren, auch wenn sie kraft menschlicher Autorität geschaffen sind. Denn wir wissen, daß die kirchliche Ordnung von den Vätern mit guter und nützlicher Absicht so eingerichtet worden ist, wie sie die Canones beschreiben"[94]. Hier spricht sich die teils gelobte, teils kritisierte konservative Haltung der Wittenberger Reformation aus, die auf Kontinuität auch in Punkten bedacht war, die vom Wort Gottes her nicht festgelegt seien. Man schätzte die mit solcher Kontinuität gegebene Ordnung und Verläßlichkeit und änderte Überliefertes nur, wenn es notwendig war, d. h. wenn die überlieferte Ordnung sich nicht mit dem Gehorsam gegen das Wort Gottes vereinbaren ließ[95] - dann allerdings auch beherzt und mit gutem theologischen Gewissen.

Im Fall des Episkopats kam noch ein besonderer Gesichtspunkt hinzu. Die Wittenberger bemerkten sehr wohl, daß ihre Kritik an den Bischöfen Wasser auf die Mühlen der weltlichen Fürsten war, denen auch aus Gründen ihrer eigenen Interessen an der Entmachtung der Bischöfe lag. Denn die Fürsten sahen in jener Kritik nicht nur die Legitimation, Stifter in ihre Gewalt zu bekommen und so ihre Territorien abzurunden, sondern auch die Rechtfertigung für das Bestreben, ihren Einfluß auf das Leben der Kirche festzuschreiben, ja über das landesherrliche Kirchenregiment vorreformatorischer Zeit hinaus zu erweitern. Die Wittenberger durchschauten das durchaus.[96] Zwar nahmen sie selbst mangels reformationswilliger Adressaten in der kirchlichen Hierarchie die Fürsten in Anspruch und konnten sie den Landesherrn als "Notbischof" bezeichnen, der in der gegebenen Lage das tun müsse, was die eigentlichen Bischöfe versäumten[97]; doch stand der provisorische Charakter dieser Lösung für sie außer Frage, sollte das Kirchenregiment in der reformierten Christenheit so bald wie möglich durch nichtpolitische kirchliche Instanzen wahrgenommen werden, und das hieß für die Wittenberger in erster Linie, durch Bischöfe. Es war unübersehbar, daß es bei den weltlichen Fürsten wenig Interesse an einer solchen Perspektive gab und sie das Provisorium meist[98] als Dauerlösung festhalten wollten. Luther wie Melanchthon sah diese Gefahr, ihr Bemühen um evangelische oder jedenfalls die Reformation zulassende Bischöfe hatte nicht zuletzt das Ziel, ihr einen Riegel vorzuschieben.

Es fragte sich freilich, woher ein evangelischer Bischof die materielle Infrastruktur nehmen sollte, die ihm ein unabhängiges Wirken ermöglichen würde - jenes Problem, das sich in den Amtsjahren Georgs von Merseburg so deutlich zeigte. Diese Infrastruktur hatten den Bischöfen bislang eben vor allem ihre eigenen Territorien geboten; ja mehr noch, auf den Territorien und der damit gegebenen politischen Rolle ruhten in hohem Maße ihre bischöfliche Autorität und Durchsetzungskraft. Weil sie das einsehen mußten, kamen die Wittenberger dazu, die bischöfliche Territorialherrschaft nicht nur als Kompromiß einzuräumen[99], sondern ihr unter den gegebenen Umständen sogar eine positive Funktion zuzugestehen - nur Bischöfe mit solcher Basis würden auf die Dauer den Fürsten Paroli bieten und die Kirche vor deren Machtansprüchen schützen können: "[Es wird] den Kirchen mit der Zeit vonnöten sein..., daß sie durch stattliche Personen visitiert werden. Denn die weltlichen Herren werden auf die Dauer die Kirche auch nicht groß achten... Nun wäre es nützlich, wenn sich etliche Prälaten der Kirche treulich annehmen wollten, da sie doch die Güter haben und die Visitation erhalten könnten, daß sie solches täten".[100]

Diese Feststellung aber bedeutete nichts Geringeres als das Eingeständnis, daß das, was man eigentlich erstrebt hatte, ein genuin kirchlicher Episkopat in der reformierten Christenheit, sich unter den gegebenen Umständen nicht erreichen ließ. Bischöfliche Unabhängigkeit war nicht ohne die Geistlichen Fürstentümer möglich, anders ausgedrückt, sie war nur als ihrerseits politische, landesherrliche und nicht als kirchliche möglich. Als solche hatte sie eine Funktion im Reich, die - wie die skizzierten Ereignisse zeigen und der Augsburger Religionsfriede festschreiben sollte[101] - mit allem politischen und juristischen Nachdruck an die römisch-katholische Kirche gekoppelt wurde. Diese konfessionelle Bindung zu lösen, bedeutet den Verlust der politisch-reichsrechtlich begründeten Selbständigkeit und - da es eine andere nicht gab - der bischöflichen Selbständigkeit selber. D.h., ein evangelischer Episkopat war, da nicht reichsrechtlich verankert, chancenlos, die Übernahme der bischöflichen Gewalt durch die Fürsten auch langfristig unvermeidbar. Die Form des landesherrlichen Kirchenregiments, die sich so in den evangelischen Territorien etablierte, stellte das spiegelverkehrte Gegenstück des politischen Reichsepiskopats dar[102] und reflektierte damit dieselbe Verknüpfung von politischer und kirchlicher Ordnung, die erst nach dem Ende des Reiches zu überwinden war[103].

IV. Das Superintendentenamt als eigener Typ des Episkopats

So weit haben wir uns mit den Bemühungen der Wittenberger Reformatoren beschäftigt, ein übergemeindliches Bischofsamt in Gestalt des - gereinigten - mittelalterlichen Episkopats zu gewinnen. Diese Bemühungen um Kontinuität sind nun aber nicht das Einzige, was sich zum Thema "Reformation und bischöfliches Amt" anführen läßt. Daneben, ja für das tatsächliche kirchliche Leben im Vordergrund stand die Wahrnehmung der Episkope aus eigener Initiative und die Entwicklung eines eigenen episkopalen Amtes, des Superintendentenamtes. Daß es zu einem solchen Neuansatz kam, lag am Versagen der vorhandenen Bischöfe. daß es zu einem Neuansatz kommen konnte, hatte seinen Grund in der reformatorischen Theologie. Daß er gerade so aussah, ergab sich wiederum im Kontext der historischen Lage.

Die Notwendigkeit episkopaler Maßnahmen ohne Rücksicht auf die Diözesanbischöfe erwies sich erstmals und mit alles Weitere bestimmenden Folgen in der zweiten Hälfte der fünfzehnhundertzwanziger Jahre, als unübersehbar wurde, daß die evangelischen Gemeinden der Visitation bedurften[104]. Diejenigen, denen die Visitation von Amts wegen oblag, fielen aber eben aus, weshalb Luther anregte, eigene evangelische Visitatoren aufzustellen. Aufsicht in der Kirche sei notwendig[105], und wenn sie nicht geleistet werde, müsse man Abhilfe schaffen. Dies zu tun, hatte unter den gegebenen Umständen nur der Kurfürst die Mittel und Autorität[106], der denn auch dafür sorgte, daß Kommissionen von Visitatoren gebildet wurden. Es waren ad hoc, jeweils für ein bestimmtes Visitationsvorhaben zusammentretende Gremien aus Theologen und Juristen, keine ständigen Behörden. Doch sie taten genau das, was zu den wichtigsten Vollzügen bischöflichen Handelns gehört: Sie führten Aufsicht über die Gemeindepfarrer, und zwar konkret, indem sie deren theologische Bildung, Verkündigung und Lehre, Amtsführung, Lebenswandel, die Finanzverhältnisse in den Gemeinden usw. prüften und gegebenenfalls Maßnahmen zur Beseitigung von Mißständen ergriffen. Folgerichtig bezeichnete Luther die Visitatoren, darunter zeitweilig auch sich selbst, als "Bischöfe"[107] -Bischöfe, weil und solange sie das taten, was dies Amt ausmacht.

Als langfristige Lösung betrachtete man solche ad hoc angesetzte Wahrnehmung episkopaler Aufgaben gleichwohl nicht. Aufsicht und übergemeindlicher Zusammenhalt sollten dauerhaft und kontinuierlich gewährleistet werden, weshalb man im Rahmen jener Visitationen ein neues bischöfliches Amt einrichtete. Dieses Amt hieß auch Bischofsamt, nur nicht in griechischer, sondern in lateinischer Sprache: Amt des "Superintendenten" oder "Superattendenten"[108] - eine alte Übersetzung von επισκοπος, die schon in patristischer Zeit belegt ist[109]. Als Inhaber des neuen bischöflichen Amtes wurden die Pfarrer der Amtsstädte ausersehen[110]- eine naheliegende Option, die ihre Parallele in der institutionellen Entwicklung der Alten Kirche hat, als den Bischöfen der Provinzhauptstädte eine Vorrangstellung gegenüber ihren Amtsbrüdern zuwuchs. Und wie in altkirchlichen Zeiten gewannen unter diesen evangelischen "Metropoliten" einige noch weiter ausstrahlende, die anderen Superintendenten überragende Bedeutung, i.a. die der Haupstädte eines Gesamtterritoriums, etwa Wittenbergs im Kurfürstentum Sachsen[111]. Ihnen legte man z.T. den Titel "Generalsuperintendent" zu.

Die Superintendenten waren und blieben Gemeindepfarrer, darin allen Amtsbrüdern ihres Bezirkes gleich. So kam konkret zum Ausdruck, daß ihre episkopale Tätigkeit Entfaltung des einen ihnen gemeinsamen kirchlichen Amtes war, eben Entfaltung seiner katholischen Dimension. Sie vollzog sich nicht nur in der Aufsicht über die Pfarrer des Bezirks und verwandten Funktionen wie der Prüfung und Einstellung von Kandidaten; zu den Aufgaben des Superintendenten gehörte vielmehr auch, daß er Seelsorge an den Pfarrern zu üben, ihren Zusammenhalt durch Konvente zu fördern und ihnen durch öffentliche Lehre Grund und Inhalt ihres Wirken immer wieder vor Augen zu stellen hatte[112] - klassische episkopale Tätigkeiten. Und wie stand es mit der Ordination? Da hier die Notwendigkeit eigener Initiative nicht so drängend war wie hinsichtlich der Visitation, konnte man es sich leisten, länger auf eine mögliche Kooperation der Diözesanbischöfe zu warten, ohne - von Einzelfällen abgesehen - eigene Lösungen zu entwickeln. Schließlich wuchs auch diese Aufgabe meist den Superintendenten oder den zentralen Superintendenten zu.[113]

Betrachtet man die Liste der Funktionen, die das Amt des Superintendenten, dann auch des Generalsuperintendenten umfaßt, so kann kein Zweifel sein: Es handelt sich um ein bischöfliches Amt - langfristig gesehen sogar um das wichtigste bischöfliche Amt in der Geschichte der lutherischen Kirche. Und so drängt sich die Frage auf: Warum nannte man die Inhaber dieses Amtes nicht schlicht und einfach "Bischöfe"?[114] Wozu nahm man den Umweg über die lateinische Übersetzung?

Man benutzte den Titel "episcopus" für diese Amtsträger nicht, um ihn freizuhalten, freizuhalten für die Instanzen, die ihn führten, die amtierenden Bischöfe. Und das hieß zugleich, man hielt sich die Möglichkeit offen, die Superintendenturen in die Diözesen zu integrieren, die Superintendenten den Bischöfen zu unterstellen, so sie sich bekehren oder wenigstens die Reformation dulden sollten. Wo es solche Bekehrung oder Duldung gab, wurde tatsächlich so verfahren: Im schlesischen Liegnitz erkannten die evangelischen Superintendenten jahrzehntelang den Bischof von Breslau als ihren Bischof an, der zwar nicht die Reformation übernommen hatte, aber sie gewähren ließ.[115] Und die Superintendenten der sächsischen Diözesen Naumburg und Merseburg erhielten in den schon genannten Bischöfen Nikolaus und Georg sogar evangelische Oberhirten. Gerade hier zeigte sich aber, daß in den Superintendenturen faktisch bereits ein eigenständiger Episkopat herangewachsen war; es kam zu Kompetenzstreitigkeiten, die nicht befriedigend gelöst werden konnten.[116]

Die Selbstbegrenzung, die in der Verwendung des Wortes "Superintendent" statt "episcopus" bzw. "Bischof" lag, hatte aber noch eine andere Dimension: Es war auch eine Begrenzung gegenüber dem Landesherrn. Wie dieser die Visitationskommissionen zusammenstellen ließ und mit Autorität ausstattete, so wurde das neue Amt in seinem Namen verordnet.[117] Der Superintendent hatte renitente Pfarrer seines Sprengels, die er nicht gütlich zur Einsicht bewegen konnte, mit den Mitteln des Staates zur Raison bringen zu lassen[118] und mit den Beamten des Landes in Fragen der Sittenzucht zusammenzuarbeiten.[119] So trat er in vieler Hinsicht selber als Beamter seines Fürsten auf.[120] Auch diese Abhängigkeit, das Eingeordnetsein in den übergreifenden kirchenregimentlichen Zusammenhang des Territoriums drückt sich in dem Verzicht auf den Bischofstitel und der Benutzung des ungeprägten lateinischen Äquivalentes aus.

Am Ende liefen freilich die beiden Dimensionen der Selbstbegrenzung im bischöflichen Amt der Reformation auf dasselbe hinaus. Der "Notepiskopat" der Landesherren wurde zur langfristigen Einrichtung, kirchliche Spitzen in Gestalt kirchlicher Amtsträger und d.h. Bischöfe in diesem Sinne erhielten die evangelischen Territorien nicht. Und die Reichsverfassung, die diese Lösung als Provisorium erzwungen hatte, sanktionierte und integrierte sie im Augsburger Religionsfrieden, negativ wie positiv, auch auf Dauer: Der Friedensschluß schrieb die alten reichskirchlichen Verhältnisse unter den neuen mehrkonfessionellen Bedingungen fest. Er bekräftigte die geistlichen Fürstentümer in der alten Form und reichsrechtlichen Stellung und band sie an die römisch-katholische Konfession.[121] Der Titel "Bischof" blieb an sie gekoppelt und reduzierte sich, da es über die Hochstifter hinausgehende Diözesen in einem Großteil des Reiches nicht mehr gab, noch weiter auf den politischen Aspekt. Offiziell galten die Rechte der Reichsbischöfe in den evangelischen Gebieten als suspendiert[122], was einerseits die Fiktion aufrechterhielt, der Reichsepiskopat sei nach wie vor der Träger des Bischofsamtes im ganzen Reich, und was andererseits der Wahrnehmung der bischöflichen Rechte durch die evangelischen Territorialherren den verfassungsmäßigen Rahmen bot.

So blieb es bis zum Beginn des 19. Jahrhunderts, bis zum Tod des Heiligen Römischen Reiches. Es ist bezeichnend, daß dessen Untergang mit der Beseitigung der geistlichen Territorien im Reichsdeputationshauptschluß (1803) begann.[123] Noch in ihrem Ende bestätigte sich die konstitutive Bedeutung dieser Rechtskonstruktion für das Reich.

Der Zusammenbruch einer tausendjährigen Ordnung, der sich hier zutrug, betraf die Reichskirche, d.h. die römisch-katholische; so wurde er für diese zum Ausgangspunkt einer grundlegenden Neugestaltung des Bischofsamtes als eines kirchlichen Amtes. Auf evangelischer Seite ließ die Entflechtung von fürstlicher und bischöflicher Gewalt noch hundert Jahre auf sich warten, bis zum Untergang der Monarchien nach dem Ersten Weltkrieg, der das landesherrliche Kirchenregiment hinwegfegte. Nun nahmen die evangelischen Kirchen ihre übergemeindliche Organisation und Leitung in die unpolitische Hand.[124] In der Mehrheit führten sie früher oder später den nun nicht mehr politisch besetzten Bischoftitel für den obersten Träger des kirchlichen Amtes ein, der jedoch an der Spitze einer Stufenfolge anderer episkopaler Ämter - Superintendenten, Landessuperintendenten u.ä. - steht, welche in den meisten Fällen für Visitation und Ordination zuständig sind. Die Flexibilität in der konkreten Wahrnehmung der Episkope, wie sie die Reformation verfochten hat, prägt so die Ausgestaltung des bischöflichen Amtes in den evangelischen Kirchen bis zum heutigen Tag.

---

[1] An einschlägigen Beiträgen zu diesem Thema, auf die die folgenden Ausführungen häufig zurückgreifen werden, seien vorweg genannt: P. Brunner, Vom Amt des Bischofs (in: ders., Pro Ecclesia. Gesammelte Aufsätze zur dogmatischen Theologie. Bd. I. Berlin-Hamburg 1962, 235-295); M. Brecht (Hg.), Martin Luther und das Bischofsamt. Stuttgart 1990; G. Kretschmar, Die Wiederentdeckung des Konzeptes der "Apostolischen Sukzession" im Umkreis der Reformation (in: Kirche in der Schule Luthers. FS. J. Heubach. Erlangen 1995, 231-279).

[2] S. dazu J. Ficker, Vom Reichsfürstenstande. Bd. I. Innsbruck 1861, 270-376; A. Hauck, Die Entstehung der geistlichen Territorien. Leipzig 1909 (ASGW.PH 27,18). Zusammenfassend P. Moraw, Art. Fürstentümer, Geistliche I. Mittelalter, TRE 11, 711-715. Moraw, ibd. 711, spricht von "ungefähr ein[em] Sechstel oder Siebtel des engeren Reiches", das diese Gebiete ausgemacht hätten.

[3] Damit ist nicht gesagt, daß sich nicht Entwicklungslinien noch weiter in die Vergangenheit, in die fränkische Zeit, ja in die Spätzeit des alten Römischen Reiches ziehen ließen, doch die entscheidenden Weichenstellungen erfolgten in dieser Epoche.

[4] Vgl. dazu L. Santifaller, Zur Geschichte des ottonisch-salischen Reichskirchensystems. Wien 1964[2] (SB Akad. Wien 229,1); J. Fleckenstein, Grundlagen und Beginn der deutschen Geschichte. Göttingen 1980[2], 148-151; dens., Zum Begriff der ottonisch-salischen Reichskirche (in: E. Hassinger - J.H. Müller - H. Ott, Geschichte - Wirtschaft - Gesellschaft. FS. Cl. Bauer. Berlin 1974, 61-71).

Einen Überblick über die weitere rechtsgeschichtliche Entwicklung im Mittelalter s. bei A. Werminghoff, Geschichte der Kirchenverfassung Deutschlands im Mittelalter. Bd. I. Darmstadt 1969 (Nachdruck der

Ausgabe von 1905), Dritter Abschnitt, bes. § 35f.; dems., Verfassungsgeschichte der deutschen Kirche im Mittelalter. Berlin 1913^2, Dritter Abschnitt, bes. § 26.27.31-34; H. Conrad, Deutsche Rechtsgeschichte. Bd. I, Frühzeit und Mittelalter. Karlsruhe 1962, 287-296.

5   S. R. Aulinger, Das Bild des Reichstages im 16. Jahrhundert. Göttingen 1980, 103. Ein Bild von innen heraus, das zwar schon die mehrkonfessionelle Lage nach dem Westfälischen Frieden spiegelt, aber ansonsten auch für die frühere Situation aussagekräftig ist, bietet J.J. Moser, Grund-Riß der heutigen Staats-Verfassung des Teutschen Reichs. Tübingen 1754 , bes. Buch IV Cap. 5 § 11ff.; Cap. 8 § 1; Cap. 10, § 1.2.4.

6   Aulinger (wie Anm. 5), 104.

7   Vgl. M. Schulze, Fürsten und Reformation. Geistliche Reformpolitik weltlicher Fürsten vor der Reformation. Tübingen 1991; Conrad (wie Anm. 4) 317f.; Einordnung in den weiteren europäischen Rahmen bei J. Hashagen, Staat und Kirche vor der Reformation. Eine Untersuchung der vorreformatorischen Bedeutung des Laieneinflusses in der Kirche. Essen 1931.

8   WA 6,440,21-35 (sprachlich modernisiert); ähnlich WA 10/2,140,9-17.

9   S. den Tractatus de potestate papae, bes. 60f., BSELK 489,30-43.

10   Seit 1519 zieht er Hieronymus' Aussagen über die ursprüngliche Gleichheit des Amtes von Bischof von Presbyter heran (s. WA 2,227,32ff.). Noch 1538 gibt er den Brief des Kirchenvaters an Evangelus/Evagrius (CSEL 56,308-312) mit eigenem Vorwort heraus, der jene Gleichheit betont (WA 50,339-343) (vgl. Brunner [wie Anm. 1] 253f. und zu dem ganzen Komplex H.-M. Stamm, Luthers Berufung auf die Vorstellungen des Hieronymus vom Bischofsamt [In: Brecht <wie Anm. 1> 15-26]). Im übrigen wird Hieronymus' Argument auch von Erasmus in seinem Instrumentum Novum zu 1. Tim. 4 angeführt, das Luther benutzte ("antiquitus nihil intererat inter presbyterum, sacerdotem, et episcopum, ut testatur et divus Hieronymus", Ausgabe Basel 1516, 569). Wie das Zitat aus der Schrift "An den christlichen Adel" (zu Anm. 8) zeigt, kann Luther durchaus auch in diesem Zusammenhang einen Unterschied zwischen Bischof und Presbyter machen, das allerdings - und hier liegt das Entscheidende - gemäß der Lage in den ersten Jahrhunderten auf der Ebene der Einzelgemeinde: der Bischof als deren Leiter und die Presbyter als seine Helfer (vgl. zu Anm. 13).

11   WA 38,237,25-30 (sprachlich modernisiert).

12   So können die Reformatoren auch das Wort "Presbyter" für den Gemeindepfarrer verwenden, wenn sie zugleich vom übergemeindlichen Amtsträger sprechen und gemäß dem mittlerweile üblichen Wortgebrauch diesen "Bischof" nennen; s. etwa u. das Zitat zu Anm. 42.

13   S. Zitat zu Anm. 8.

14   S. ibd.

15   Vgl. Brunner (wie Anm. 1) 236-243.252.

16   S. den Überblick bei L. Ott, Das Weihesakrament. Freiburg/Br.-Basel-Wien 1969 (Handbuch der Dogmengeschichte. Hg. M. Schmaus - A. Grillmeier - L. Scheffczyk, IV,5), Kap. 4 und 15, bes. § 10.15.16 sowie die Ausführungen von M. Landgraf, Die Lehre vom Episkopat als Ordo (in: ders., Dogmengeschichte

der Frühscholastik. Regensburg 1955, III/2, 277-302), und R.P. Stenger, The Episcopacy as an Ordo (Medieval Studies 28, 1967, 67-112).

[17] Vgl. die Zusammenfassung bei Ott (wie Anm. 16) 80f.: "Die überwältigende Mehrzahl der scholastischen Theologen betrachtet den Episkopat ... nicht als Ordo, sondern als eine zum Priestertum hinzukommende Würde und als Amt, z.B. Alexander von Hales, Albert d. Gr., Bonaventura, Thomas von Aquin. Demgemäß betrachten sie die Bischofskonsekration nicht als Sakrament, sondern nur als Sakramentale".

[18] Sent. IV, 24,12,1.

[19] Ibd. 14f.: Sunt et alia quaedam, non ordinum, sed dignitatum vel officiorum nomina. Dignitatis simul et officii nomen est episcopus. Vgl. zum Lombarden Ott (wie Anm. 16) 50. Kretschmar (wie Anm. 1) 234 weist darauf hin, daß die Bischofskonsekration schon im Römisch-deutschen Pontifikale (10. Jh.) "überhaupt nicht mehr bei den klerikalen Ordinationen, sondern bei den Ordnungen zur Segnung des Königs und zur Kaiserkrönung" steht. Landgraf (wie Anm. 15) 301 führt einen Text des 13. Jahrhunderts an, der sie auf eine Stufe mit der Salbung von Königen und Königinnen, der Weihe von Äbten und Ordensfrauen, der Segnung von Bräuten und Wallfahrern stellt.

[20] S. exemplarisch Thomas, S. Th. Suppl. q37 a5; Decretum pro Armenis, DS 1326. Vgl. Ott (wie Anm. 16) 94f.

[21] Diese Anknüpfung der Wittenberger an Verständnis und Praxis des Bischofsamtes in der Frühzeit der Kirche herauszustellen, ist das besondere Anliegen der einschlägigen Beiträge von G. Kretschmar, etwa: Das Bischofsamt als geistlicher Dienst in der Kirche anhand der altkirchlichen und reformatorischen Weihegebete (in: Der bischöfliche Dienst in der Kirche. Eine Dokumentation über die zehnte Begegnung im bilateralen Dialog zwischen der Russ.-Orth. Kirche und der EKD vom 25. - 29. Sept. 1984 in Kiew, Beih. ÖR 53,53-89), und: Die Wiederentdeckung des Konzepts der "Apostolischen Sukzession" im Umkreis der Reformation (wie Anm. 1). Zu Recht beklagt Kretschmar, daß dieser wichtige Aspekt der Ausführungen Luthers über das kirchliche Amt in den neueren Monographien zum Thema nicht herausgestellt wird (Das Bischofsamt als geistlicher Dienst 69, Anm. 45). Das gilt leider auch für das jüngste Buch zum Thema: O. Mittermeier, Evangelische Ordination im 16. Jahrhundert. St. Ottilien 1994, das jenen Sachverhalt zwar berührt (z. B. 65f. 104.138), aber nicht für seine Darlegungen fruchtbar macht.

[22] Z.B. WA 10/2,143,3f. 27f.; 12,194,26f.; 53,253,6-8.

[23] Z.B. WA 12,211,6; 214,4; 215,8.19.27; 216,8; 218,19; 219,13f., gelegentlich - 215,8 - verbunden mit dem Funktionsbegriff minister. Auch der Adressat der Schrift, der Zwickauer Pfarrer Nikolaus Hausmann, wird als episcopus - "Bischof der Gemeinde von Zwickau" (episcopus Cygneae ecclesiae) - angeredet (ibd. 205,3f.). Bezeichnend ist, daß die - jedenfalls dem Druck nach - erste deutsche Übersetzung, die noch 1523 erschienene sog. "Nürnberger" (Die weyse der Meß und geniessung des hochwirdigen Sakraments für die Christliche gemain verteutscht. Wittenberg 1523), das Wort "Pfarrherr" an die Stelle von "Bischof" setzt (s. die Entsprechungen zu den genannten WA-Angaben A4[V]. B2[V]. B3[r]. B3[V]. B4[r]. C[V]. C2[V] und schon die Widmung an Hausmann, der nun "Pfarrherr zu Zwickau" heißt) - offensichtlich, um Mißverständnisse auszuschließen und den im Text gemeinten Sinn gegenüber dem mittlerweile eingebürgerten Verständnis von "Bischof" sicherzustellen. Die Übersetzung von Paul Speratus (Ein weyse Christlich Mess zu halten und zum Tisch Gottes zu gehen. Wittenberg 1524), auf Luthers eigenen Wunsch (ibd. A3[r]) und wohl unter seinen Augen entstanden, schreibt durchweg "Bischof" (s. B2[V]. C[V]. C3[r]. C3[V]. C4[r]. D3[r]. D4[r], auch die

Anrede an Hausmann).Speratus selbst bezeichnet sich in einer vorgesetzten Widmung an die Gemeinde von Iglau, wo er Pfarrer gewesen war, als deren Bischof (A2^V/WA 12,204,29).

[24] WA 38,423-433.

[25] Das gilt für das deutsche Formular (I) in den Relationen F und R und für das lateinische (II); I.D enthält keine Vermahnung nach diesen Lesungen, sondern nur eine Ansprache nach der Kollekte. Zu dieser Ordinationsliturgie s. H. Lieberg, Amt und Ordination bei Luther und Melanchthon. Göttingen 1962, 191-196 und Mittermeier (wie Anm. 21) 102-112. Beide Arbeiten übersehen aber gerade, daß die Ordination hier als Bischofsweihe verstanden und gestaltet wird (bei Mittermeier berührt S. 104, aber ohne Konsequenzen) (vgl. o. Anm. 21).

[26] Hg. Fr. Lauchert, Die Canones der wichtigsten altkirchlichen Konzilien. Freiburg-Leipzig 1896 (Nachdruck Frankfurt/M. 1961), 38.

[27] WA 53,257,19-21 (Berufung auf diesen Canon bei Luther bereits WA 2,238,15-18, aber mit anderer, nämlich antipäpstlicher, Zielrichtung [s.a. 258,17f.; 397,26; vgl. Melanchthons Tractatus de potestate papae 13, BSELK 475,13-15]); WABr 12, Nr.4330,5A,10; Nr.4330,6,17f.; Nr.4330,7,10f.; Nr.4330,8,16f. (Ordinationszeugnisse, "zum mindesten teilweise von Melanchthon verfaßt", ibd. 447).

[28] Es wäre auf dem Hintergrund dieses Amtsverständnisses nicht sachgemäß, die Ordination in den lutherischen Kirchen "Presbyteralordination" zu nennen.

[29] S.u. S.

[30] S. die Vermahnung an die Ordinanden und das ihr entsprechende Gelöbnis, dem die Handauflegung folgt (WA 38,427f.;432,27ff.), und vgl. auch die Tatsache, daß die Kandidaten vor der Ordination eine Lehrprüfung zu durchlaufen haben (s. den Anfang des Wittenberger Ordinationsformulars, WA 38,423,6f., und die Ordinationszeugnisse in WABr 12,451ff. sowie in: B. Moeller, Das Wittenberger Ordinationszeugnis für Bartholomaeus Wolfart vom 27. September 1544 [Lutherjb. 61, 1994, 117-122] 121f.). Diese Zuordnung der Amtsträgersukzession zur Verkündigungssukzession, in deren Dienst jene steht, entspricht ganz dem Interesse der Pastoralbriefe (s. 2. Tim. 2,2).

[31] S. neben der Schrift an die Böhmen die Schrift "Wider den falschgenannten geistlichen Stand des Papstes und der Bischöfe" (s.u.).

[32] Wa 12,169-196.

[33] Ibd. 194,18f.

[34] Vgl. Brunner (wie Anm. 1) 252.

[35] Z.B. WA 6,440,21 (s.o. Zitat zu Anm. 8); ibd. 441,24; CR 4,367 (s.u. Zitat zu Anm. 42).

[36] WA 6,440,29: "vonn Christlicher gemeyn ordnung gesetzt" (s.o. Zitat zu Anm. 8); 2,229,39 und 230,10: (ex) ecclesiae consuetudine; CR 4,368: accessit utilis ordinatio (s.u. Zitat zu Anm. 42).

[37] WA 2,228,36f.; ibd. 229,39-230,2.9-11: nicht dispensationis divinae veritate, sondern ecclesiae consuetudine.

[38] Apologie 14,1, BSELK 296,18; Tractatus de potestate papae 63, ibd. 490,29f.

[39] CR 26,49-96/WA 26,201-240/Ph. Melanchthon, Werke in Auswahl. Hg. R. Stupperich. Gütersloh 1951, Bd. I, 220-271.

[40] CR 26,43-44/WA 26,196,33/Melanchthon, Werke I (wie Anm. 39) 217,32f.

[41] 41S. aber ASm II 4, BSELK 430,7-10, wo Luther, beides verbindend, das Ideal einer durch das Zusammenwirken der Bischöfe zusammengehaltenen Kirche entwirft. Brunner (wie Anm. 1) 264 kennzeichnet die hier zum Ausdruck kommende Auffassung als "synodalen Episkopalismus".

[42] CR4,367f. (von Melanchthon verfaßte Stellungnahme der Wittenberger zum Regensburger Buch, CR 4, Nr. 2254): Ut sit...una Ecclesia et consentiens, semper Deus idem Evangelium propagavit per patres et Prophetas et postea per Christum et Apostolos, et instituit Christus ministerium duraturum usque ad consummationem mundi... Conservat enim Evangelium et voluit post Apostolos vocari pastores in omnibus Ecclesiis, fungentes officio docendi Evangelii, quos excitat, quanquam dissimiles donis, tamen eodem fungentes ministerio. Consistit igitur unitas Ecclesiae in hac consociatione sub uno capite per idem Evangelium et idem ministerium... Ut autem omnia ordine fierent in Ecclesia iuxta Pauli regulam, et ut Pastores inter se magis devincti essent... ac alii aliorum curam susciperent et dissidia seu schismata vitarentur, accessit utilis ordinatio, ut ex multis presbyteris eligeretur Episcopus qui regeret Ecclesiam docendo Evangelio et retinenda disciplina, et praeesset ipsis presbyteris... Hae ordinationes, si hi, qui praesunt, faciant officium suum, utiles sunt ad retinendam unitatem Ecclesiae.

Anders als in den bisher angeführten Zitaten wird hier, wo es um die gemeindeübergreifenden Strukturen geht, der Ortspfarrer "Presbyter" genannt und das Wort "Bischof" für den Amtsträger mit übergemeindlichen Aufgaben gebraucht. Diese Anknüpfung an den üblichen Sprachgebrauch ändert aber nichts daran, daß auch hier das apostolische Amt in der Kirche im Pfarramt gesehen wird.

[43] CR 4,547.368f.; 5,601f. Vgl. Brunner (wie Anm. 1) 271-279.

[44] CA 28,1-9.12-17.20f., BSELK 120,1-122,9.21-123,9.22-124,5.

[45] WA 10/2,154,25-30: Sie widerspricht dem Willen Christi. WABr 3, Nr.756,37: Sie gleicht, weder weltlich noch geistlich, einem Hermaphroditen.

[46] Im folgenden wird dem geläufigen Sprachgebrauch gemäß das Wort "Bischof", wo nicht anders vermerkt, für den Träger der übergemeindlichen Episkope verwendet.

[47] Z.B. WA 10/2,119,29-120,18; 125,8-126,18; 133,14-23; 137,34-138,17; CA 28,70, BSELK 131,40-132,3; Apologie 21,38, BSELK 325,36-42.

[48] Z.B. Apologie 14,2, BSELK 297,1-5; 21,38f., BSELK 325,36-50; ASm III, BSELK 458,5f.; Tractatus de potestate papae 66, BSELK 491,1f.; WA 10/2, 143,10-12; 158,12f.

[49] CR 4,546f.: Nos in Germania titulos habemus Episcoporum, Episcopos qui officium suum faciant, non habemus.

[50] Z.B. WA 10/2,135,6f.; 141,7-9; ASm III, BSELK 458,1-5 (vgl. a. 411,27-412,6); CR 5,599.

[51] WA 10/2,107,19-21; 154,10f.; 158,7f.; 12,240,10-13.

[52] WA 10/2,154,10-22; 158,7-10; ASm III, BSELK 457,7-11; CR 5,599.

[53] WA 10/2,105-158; s. dazu G. Krodel, Luther und das Bischofsamt nach seinem Buch "Wider den falsch genannten geistlichen Stand des Papstes und der Bischöfe" (in: Brecht [wie Anm. 1] 27-65).

[54] WA 10/2,107,19-21; 154,10f. Krodel (wie Anm. 53) 33 faßt die Schrift dahingehend zusammen, daß Luther mit ihr ein negatives und ein positives Anliegen verfolge: die Zertrümmerung des päpstlichen Bischofsamtes und den Aufbau eines echten, evangelischen Bischofsamtes; um letzteres zu erreichen, wolle er zeigen, was ein solches echtes "Bischofsamt ist und wie ein evangelischer Bischof handelt", und die amtierenden Bischöfe zur Umkehr bewegen, so daß mit ihnen das angestrebte evangelische Bischofsamt aufgebaut werden könne.

[55] Vgl. zu diesem Vorgang J. Höß, The Lutheran Church of the Reformation. Problems of its formation and organization in the middle and north German territories (in: The Social History of the Reformation. FS H.J. Grimm. Ed. L.P. Buck - J.W. Zophy. Columbus/Ohio 1972, 317-339), 332-339; dies., Episcopus evangelicus. Versuche mit dem Bischofsamt im deutschen Luthertum des 16. Jahrhunderts (in: E. Iserloh [Hg.], Confessio Augustana und Confutatio. Münster 1980, 499-516), 512-516; P. Gabriel, Fürst Georg von Anhalt als evangelischer Bischof von Merseburg und Thüringen 1544-1548/50 - ein Modell evangelischer Episkope in der Reformationszeit. Diss. theol. Göttingen 1994 (im Druck), 35-43.

[56] WA 12,232,25-32; 18,408,17-20; 410,5-13; WABr 3, Nr. 756,22-45. Dies Auseinandertreten der beiden Dimensionen eines Geistlichen Fürstentums wird an der Reformation Preußens, das selbst ein solches war, anschaulich: Sein Herrscher Albrecht von Brandenburg (1490-1568), Kleriker und geistlicher Fürst, gibt den geistlichen Status auf und behält nur die weltliche Gewalt, indem er sein Territorium in ein säkulares Herzogtum umwandelt und nun als dessen Herzog regiert. Ihm stehen Bischöfe gegenüber, die umgekehrt die politische Gewalt in ihrem Hochstift aufgeben und Albrecht übertragen und sich ganz auf ihre geistlichen Aufgaben konzentrieren (vgl. Bischof Georgs Begründung für die Aufgabe der weltlichen Gewalt: daß es "ime als einem prelaten und bischofe, dem das worth Gottes zu predigen und zu vorkundigen schuldig ist, nicht geburen will, lande und leute zu regiren, auch schlosser, lant und stete zu besetzen" [P. Tschackert, Urkundenbuch zur Reformations-geschichte des Herzogthums Preußen, Bd. II. Leipzig 1890, Nr. 356]). Freilich ist hier - abgesehen von der Lage außerhalb des Reiches - der besondere Fall gegeben, daß der geistliche Fürst an der Spitze des Territoriums nicht selbst Bischof, sondern Ordensritter, Hochmeister des Deutschen Ordens, war.

[57] Luther hatte eben dies gehofft, namentlich im Blick auf den Mainzer Erzbischof und Kurfürsten Albrecht, den Vetter des preußischen Albrecht, der in der Mitte der zwanziger Jahre tatsächlich mit entsprechenden Erwägungen umging (s. WA 18,408,17-20; 410,5-13; vgl. M. Brecht, Martin Luther. Bd. 2. Stuttgart 1986, 188).

[58] CA 28,77, BSELK 132,33-38; Apol. 14,1f., BSELK 296,14-297,7; WA 30/II 342,3-8.

So wenig dieser Vorschlag eine zukunftsträchtige Lösung sein konnte, wurde doch hier und da ein Stück weit entsprechend verfahren. So erkannten die Lutheraner Schlesiens bis in die zweite Hälfte des Jahrhunderts hinein die Jurisdiktion des Bischofs von Breslau an und nahm er jurisdiktionelle Aufgaben für sie wahr. Worin diese im einzelnen bestanden, ist nicht klar, jedenfalls gehörten dazu eherechtliche Entscheidungen, zumindest gelegentliche Visitationen und zwar nicht die Ordination, aber doch möglicherweise die Bestätigung ihm präsentierter evangelischer Pfarrer (s. A. Sabisch, Beiträge zur Geschiche des Breslauer Bischofs Balthasar von Promnitz (1539-1562). I. Teil: Bis zum Regierungsantritt. Breslau 1936, 67-70; dens., Die Bischöfe von Breslau und die Reformation in Schlesien. Münster 1975,85.87-89); vgl. Kretschmar (wie Anm. 1) 245, der auch auf Oberungarn hinweist, wo "Ähnliches...möglich" war.

[59] Vgl. zu diesem Programm W. Maurer, Historischer Kommentar zur Confessio Augustana. Bd. I. Göttingen 1976, §9 - §14.

[60] WA 10/2,154,32f. (vgl. dazu Krodel [wie Anm. 53] 34); CR 5, 599f.

[61] S.u.

[62] S.u. S.

[63] Vgl. A. Franzen, Bischof und Reformation. Erzbischof Hermann von Wied in Köln vor der Entscheidung zwischen Reform und Reformation. Münster 1971[2]; A. Schröer, Die Reformation in Westfalen. Bd. 2. Münster 1983, 72-111.

[64] Vgl. F. Fischer, Die Reformationsversuche des Bischofs Franz von Waldeck im Fürstbistum Münster. Hildesheim 1907; Schröer (wie Anm. 63) 203-235; M. Kißener, Ständemacht und Kirchenreform. Bischöfliche Wahlkapitulationen im Nordwesten des Alten Reiches 1265-1803. Paderborn-München u.a. 1993, 81-83.106-109.126-128; T. Unger, Kirche und Konfession im Niederstift Münster. Der Reformationsversuch von 1543 und seine Folgen bis 1620. Diss. theol. Göttingen 1995 (im Druck).

[65] Vgl. P. Steinmüller, Die Einführung der Reformation in die Kurmark Brandenburg durch Joachim II. Halle 1903; H.-U. Delius, Die Reformation des Kurfürsten Joachim II. von Brandenburg im Jahre 1539 (ThViat 5, 1953/54, 174-193); dens., Die Kirchenpolitik des Kurfürsten Joachim II. von Brandenburg in den Jahren 1535-41 (JBBKG 40, 1965, 86-123).

[66] S. P.-H. Hahn, Kirchenschutz und Landesherrschaft in der Mark Brandenburg im späten 15. und frühen 16. Jahrhundert (JGMOD 28, 1979, 179-220), 194f. 204f. Wie Hahn zeigt, war damit aber durchaus noch keine Landsässigkeit gegeben, wie vielfach behauptet wird.

[67] Zum Übergang des Stiftes zur Reformation s. W. Schößler, Die Reformation im Domstift Brandenburg (in: H.-U. Delius - M.O. Kunzendorf - F. Winter (Hg.), "Dem Wort nicht entgegen...". Aspekte der Reformation in Brandenburg. Berlin 1988, 49-62). Kurzlebige Übergangserscheinungen stellen die Episkopate der Lübecker Bischöfe Detlev Reventlow (1535-1536) und Balthasar Rantzau (1536-1547) dar, die sich der Reformation zuwandten und sie zuließen, ohne sie aber formell einzuführen, und auf die gegenreformatorische Bischöfe folgten. Erst nach dem Augsburgischen Religionsfrieden wurde das Stift unter einem Bischof, der sich der Reformation angeschlossen hatte, Eberhard von Holle (1561-1586), evangelisch und hielt sich als - einziges - evangelisches Geistliches Fürstentum im Reich, allerdings um den Preis, daß seine Herren und Träger des damit verbundenen Bischoftitels nichtgeistliche Fürsten waren und die bischöflichen Funktionen an einen nicht "Bischof" genannten Superintendenten übergingen (s. W.D. Hauschild, Kirchengeschichte Lübecks. Lübeck 1981, 225f.). Ähnliche Übergangsphänomene gab es nach 1555 auch in Verden (s. I. Mager, Die drei evangelischen Bischöfe von Verden [JGNKG 86, 1988,79-91]).

[68] Zu ihm s. P. Brunner, Nikolaus von Amsdorf als Bischof von Naumburg. Eine Untersuchung zur Gestalt des evangelischen Bischofsamtes in der Reformationszeit. Gütersloh 1961; J. Rogge, Art. Amsdorff, Nikolaus von, TRE 2 (487-497).

[69] Zu ihm s. Gabriel (wie Anm. 55); vgl. a. G. Wartenberg, Landesherrschaft und Reformation. Moritz von Sachsen und die albertinische Kirchenpolitik bis 1546. Gütersloh 1988, Kap. 7.

[70] Naumburg: (Anonymus), Bericht über die Wahl und Einführung des Nikolaus von Amsdorff als Bischof von Naumburg (Neue Mitteilungen aus dem Gebiet historisch-antiquarischer Forschungen 2, Halle

1835, 180-185), abgedruckt bei Mittermeier (wie Anm. 21) 119-123, der Wittenberger Ordinationsliturgie gegenübergestellt bei Brunner (wie Anm. 68) 67-69. Merseburg: E. Sehling, Die evangelischen Kirchenordnungen des 16. Jahrhunderts. (Bd. I/1ff. Leipzig 1902ff.) II (1904), 6f., abgedruckt bei Mittermeier 130-136, Zusammenfassung bei Gabriel (wie Anm. 55) 164f.

[71] Naumburg: Akklamation der Gemeinde zur Wahl des neuen Bischofs am Beginn und Inthronisation am Schluß des Gottesdienstes, beides mittelalterlichen Pontifikalien entsprechend, ferner in der Vermahnung des Kandidaten Hinweise auf seine zukünftige Verantwortung für das ganze Stift und Bistum sowie, in sehr allgemeiner Form, auf seine eigentümlichen Aufgaben (vgl. Brunner [wie Anm. 68] 69; Mittermeier [wie Anm. 21] 124-126). Merseburg: Scrutinium zu Beginn, entsprechend mittelalterlichen Pontifikalien, wobei allerdings keine bischofsspezifische Frage gestellt wird und ein solcher Ritus offenbar auch für die Pfarrerordination in Merseburg vorgesehen ist, und ausdrücklicher Hinweis auf die Aufgabe der Ordination in der Verpflichtung des Kandidaten vor der Handauflegung (vgl. Mittermeier 137). Erheblich stärker an liturgischen Traditionen des Mittelalters orientiert war offenbar die Einsetzung des evangelischen Bischofs von Kammin Bartholomäus Suave im Jahre 1545 (s. H. Waterstraat, der Camminer Bistumsstreit im Reformationszeitalter [ZKG 22,1901,586-602; 23,1902,223-262] 228) - dem müßte einmal genauer nachgegangen werden.

[72] Als Bezeichnung für diesen Akt wird sowohl "Ordination" (z.B. WABr 10 Nr.3728,25; Sehling II [wie Anm. 70], 6f.) als auch der mittelalterliche Begriff "Weihe/Konsekration" (WA 53,219 (Titel); 256,19; 257,14.20) gebraucht, manchmal beides zusammen (WA 53,231,5; 232,21); einen Bedeutungsunterschied macht man nicht. Welche Bedeutung tatsächlich mit den Termini verbunden ist, kann nicht ihnen selbst entnommen werden, sondern nur der Sache, auf die sie sich beziehen, und den Reflexionen der Wittenberger darüber. Vgl. Brunner (wie Anm. 68) 69f.

[73] Zu Naumburg s. Brunner, (wie Anm. 68) 71f.; zu Merseburg s. Gabriel (wie Anm. 55) 162f.; zu Kammin s. J. Wächter, Das Verhältnis von Territorialgewalt und Kirche in Pommern nach Einführung der Reformation (1534/35) (JGNKG 86, 1988, 93-107), 96.

[74] Im Blick auf die Naumburger Bischofseinsetzung von Luther ausgesprochen in WA 53,257,13-21.

[75] Gabriel (wie Anm. 55) 150-155.

[76] Ibd. 153-156.159; Kretschmar (wie Anm. 1) 275.

[77] Das zeigen nicht nur die gedruckten, sondern auch die ungedruckten Quellen, die Gabriel (wie Anm. 55) 150-155 erstmals herangezogen hat; umso erstaunlicher ist es, daß er ganz selbstverständlich von einem Interesse Georgs an "apostolischer Sukzession" im Bischofsamt ausgeht. Auch die Zusammenhänge, die Kretschmar (wie Anm. 1) 275 herstellt, führen nicht zu einem solchen Befund - bezeichnenderweise relativiert er seine eigene Folgerung mit dem Wörtchen "offenbar" - "[man] griff... dann offenbar auf das neu vorgestellte Konzept der episcoporum successio zurück" - und spricht in diesem Zusammenhang auch von "Spekulation". Die argumentativen Brücken, die zu diesen Vermutungen führen, sind nicht sehr stabil: Weder ist der Anteil Georgs von Anhalt an der Brandenburgischen Kirchenordnung mit Sicherheit so hoch einzuschätzen, wie Kretschmar es tut (ibd. 270 - vgl. R. Stupperich, Die Eigenart der Reformation in der Mark Brandenburg [in: Delius u.a. <wie Anm. 67> 13-30],20), noch gibt es einen Beleg dafür, daß das Regensburger Buch oder eine unmittelbar damit zusammenhängende Quelle Georg bekannt und für ihn wichtig gewesen wäre.

Reformation in Deutschland

78 Aufschlußreich ist auch, daß er im Blick auf die an ihm vollzogene Handauflegung von "D. Martino Luthero/und andern Pastoribus/und revera Episcopis" spricht (Gabriel [wie Anm. 55] 155), also die "bischöfliche Sukzession" nicht auf der Ebene der Diözesanbischöfe, sondern der Pastoren ansiedelt. Der Satz wurde zwar einige Jahre nach dem Ereignis geschrieben, doch ist die darin ausgedrückte Anschauung die Voraussetzung dafür, daß sich Georg an Luther wandte.

79 Kretschmar (wie Anm. 1) 270: Er war nicht einmal Diakon - "nichts Ungewöhnliches in der damaligen Zeit".

80 Nicht umsonst waren die beteiligten Herzöge sehr an einem möglichst unanstößigen Verfahren interessiert; so rät Herzog August, der die Herrschaft über das Hochstift übernehmen will, Georg ausdrücklich, er möge sich "durch einen evangelischen bischofen weyhen lassen" (Gabriel [wie Anm. 55] 151). Zwar hatte Georg diesen Gedanken schon früher gehabt (ibd. 153) und war darin nicht von dem Herzog abhängig, aber daß auch ihm der Gesichtspunkt der Akzeptanz im Reich wichtig war, ist selbstverständlich.

81 Nämlich Herzog August von Sachsen. Dahinter stand dessen älterer Bruder Herzog Moritz, der auf diese Weise Merseburg, über das er bereits die Schutzherrschaft ausübte, stärker in sein Herzogtum einzubeziehen suchte. Zur Kirchenpolitik Moritz', der gleichwohl eine episkopale Kirchenverfassung in seinem Territorium erhalten wollte, vgl. Wartenberg (wie Anm. 69) und Gabriel (wie Anm. 55), bes. 370-374.

82 S. zu diesen Vorgängen Gabriel ibd. 125-132.

83 Genau genommen nannte der Fürst sich "Administrator" des Stiftes Merseburg, ein Titel, den postulierte, aber noch nicht mit den erforderlichen Weihen versehene Bischöfe bis zum Erhalt dieser Weihen trugen (vgl. P. Hinschius, System des katholischen Kirchenrechts mit besonderer Rücksicht auf Deutschland, Bd. 2. Berlin 1878,254).

Diese Konstruktion hatte schon früher dazu dienen können, Fürsten Bischofssitze zu sichern, die gar nicht beabsichtigten, selbst die geistlichen Funktionen eines Bischofs wahrzunehmen (s. Schulze [wie Anm. 7] 29). Das war auch nach der Reformation in der Reichskirche Deutschlands weiterhin der Fall, s. H.E. Feine, Die Besetzung der Reichsbistümer vom Westfälischen Frieden bis zur Säkularisation. Stuttgart 1921, 34f.

84 Vgl. M. Heckel, Deutschland im konfessionellen Zeitalter. Göttingen 1983, 71f.191f.; J. Heckel, Die evangelischen Dom- und Kollegiatstifter Preußens, insbesondere Brandenburg, Merseburg, Naumburg, Zeitz. Stuttgart 1924.

85 In stifts- und bistumsinternen Dokumenten findet sich auch der dem theologischen Sachverhalt entsprechende Titel "Bischof". S. zur Titelfrage Gabriel (wie Anm. 55) 147-149.

86 Zu seinem bischöflichen Wirken und seinem Verhältnis zu den sächsischen Herzögen s. ibd. Kap. V.

87 Der Kaiser befahl dem Domkapitel, den Titularbischof von Sidon und Weihbischof von Mainz Michael Helding zu postulieren, und verlieh ihm nach der päpstlichen Bestätigung die Regalien, ibd. 410-412. Es ist aufschlußreich für das Selbstverständnis des evangelischen Bischofs Georg, daß er nichts gegen die Übertragung der weltlichen Gewalt an Helding einzuwenden hatte, aber gegen dessen Einsetzung zum geistlichen Leiter der Diözese protestierte, ibd. 414f.

299

[88] Zu Naumburg, wo nun der ursprünglich vom Domkapitel gewählte strikt antireformatorische Julius Pflug zum Zuge kam, s. Brunner (wie Anm. 68) 145-148.152.

[89] Zu den höchst verwickelten, auch die in manchem noch fließenden Übergänge zwischen den Konfessionen spiegelnden Vorgängen in Kammin, wo mit Martin Weiher ein eigentlich evangelischer Kandidat Bischof wurde, der aber seine Bereitschaft erklärte, sich weihen zu lassen, und vom Papst die Bestätigung sowie Zugeständnisse für den Vollzug der Weihen erhielt und den der Kaiser nun als Reichsfürsten behandelte, s. Waterstraat (wie Anm. 71) 230-247.

[90] Brunner (wie Anm. 68) 157f.; Waterstraat (wie Anm. 71) 248-251; J. Heckel (wie Anm. 84) 23.

[91] Das ist die Entdeckung G. Kretschmars und das Thema seines Aufsatzes "Die Wiederentdeckung des Konzeptes der 'Apostolischen Sukzession' im Umkreis der Reformation" (wie Anm. 1), s. 247ff.

[92] Ibd. 251-267. S. das neunzehnte Kapitel des - auf eine in Worms verfaßte Vorlage zurückgehenden - Regensburger Buches (in: ARCEG VI 24-88), 75,1-15.

[93] Melanchthons Kritik an der entsprechenden Passage im Regensburger Buch in CR 4,415: Erant et haec errata in articulo, Episcopos successisse in locum Apostolorum: quo dicto multi errores continentur. Alligatur Ecclesia ad successionem ordinariam, quasi impossibile sit, Episcopos errare, quia Apostolorum locum teneant, aut quasi hi sint Episcopi, qui sic vocantur, et necesse sit, eos tanquam Ecclesiae capita audiri (dt. 423). Vgl. a. CR 3,598f./Melanchthon, Werke I (wie Anm. 39) 330, 16-29.

[94] saepe testati sumus, nos summa voluntate cupere conservare politiam ecclesiasticam et gradus in ecclesia, factos etiam humana auctoritate. Scimus enim bono et utili consilio a patribus ecclesiasticam disciplinam hoc modo, ut veteres canones describunt, constitutam esse. Apol. 14,1, BSELK 296,19-297,1.

[95] Vgl. die Fortsetzung des Apologiezitats von Anm. 94, wo begründet wird, warum man gleichwohl die amtierenden Bischöfe nicht anerkennen könne: Sie zwängen die Anhänger der Reformation, dem evangelischen Bekenntnis abzusagen (Apol. 14,2, BSELK 297,1-7).

[96] Z.B. WABr 10, Nr.3930,13-16: Sathan pergit esse Sathan. Sub papa miscuit ecclesiam politiae, sub nostro tempore vult miscere politiam ecclesiae. Sed nos resistemus deo favente et studebimus pro nostra virili vocationes distinctas servare. WABr 10, Nr. 4011,9-12: "es ist doch mit dem Hofe nichts. Ihr Regiment ist eitel Krebs und Schrecken... Christus optime ecclesiae consuluit, quod aulae non commisit ecclesiarum administrationem". Ähnlich Melanchthon CR 2,334 im Blick auf die Räte der Reichsstädte. S.a. Luthers Kritik an der Umwandlung von bona ecclesiastica in bona politica WATR 5, Nr. 5635b/286,3-5, die ihn anfangs die Merseburger Lösung einer Trennung von Stiftsherrschaft und Bischofsamt ablehnen ließ. Vgl. Brunner (wie Anm. 1) 268f.; K. Holl, Luther und das landesherrliche Kirchenregiment (in: ders., Gesammelte Aufsätze zur Kirchengeschichte. Bd. I. Luther. Tübingen 1927[4], 326-380), bes. 375-377.

[97] WA 53,255,5-8: "Mussen doch unsere weltliche Herrschaften jtzt Not Bischove sein und uns Pfarherr und Prediger (Nach der dem Bapst und sein Rotte nicht dazu, sondern da wider thut) schutzen und helffen, das wir predigen, Kirchen und Schulen dienen konnen. Vgl. J.L. Schaaf, Der Landesherr als Notbischof (in: Brecht [wie Anm. 1] 105-108), der im übrigen zeigt, daß solche Aussagen bei Luther nicht häufig vorkommen.

[98] Anders Moritz von Sachsen, der eine episkopale Kirchenverfassung, allerdings in landeskirchlichem Rahmen, anstrebte. Vgl. o. Anm. 81.

[99] Vgl. o. S.

[100] WABr 9, Nr.3436,480-487 (sprachlich modernisiert). Im folgenden wird diese Lösung als Zugeständnis dargestellt: "Wo nun etliche Bischöfe und Stifter die rechte Lehre und die nötigen Stücke annehmen und der Kirche dienen wollten, wäre nachzugeben, daß sie in ihren Dignitäten blieben...". D.h., die Einstellung auf die politischen Verhältnisse schwankt zwischen einem Realismus, der direkt pragmatisch, und einem solchen, der vom Ideal her gebrochen ist. Pragmatisch auch CR 5,599f.: "Sollen nu Bischöffe seyn, die auf andre ein Aufsehen haben, so müssen sie Güter haben... ...weil die Regiment und Güter nu also geordnet sind, und gottfürchtige Bischöffe konnten sie recht brauchen: so lassen wir diese Ordnung, wie sie ist, und wollen, daß gleichwohl auch diese Bischofstift, Herrschaften und Landschaften zu rechter heilsamer Lehr und Erkenntniß Christi gebracht würden."

[101] S.u. S.

[102] Vollkommen trifft die Spiegelbildlichkeit allerdings nicht zu. Denn während der Geistliche Fürst die gesamte kirchliche und politische Gewalt in seiner Hand hatte, gehörten die geistlichen Funktionen im engeren Sinne wie Predigt, Sakramentsverwaltung oder Ordination nicht zum Kirchenregiment des weltlichen Landesherrn.

[103] Vgl. Kretschmar (wie Anm. 1) 272f.

[104] Vgl. zu diesen Vorgängen im Einzelnen Brecht (wie Anm. 57) 253-266.

[105] S.o.S.

[106] Herangezogen wurde er für diesen Dienst nicht aufgrund seiner politischen Rolle, also nicht als Obrigkeit, sondern als Glied der christlichen Gemeinde, das wie alle Christen, kraft seiner besonderen Stellung aber noch in besonderer Weise zum Liebesdienst gegenüber der Kirche verpflichtet sei (s. Luthers Vorrede zum Unterricht der Visitatorn, WA 26,197,19-29/Melanchthon, Werke I [wie Anm.39] 218,22-34, dazu Holl [wie Anm. 96] 366-375). Zur vorreformatorischen Praxis der Visitation auf landesherrliche Initiative mangels bischöflicher Visitation, an die man hier anknüpfen konnte, vgl. Hashagen (wie Anm. 7) 324-336; Schulze (wie Anm. 7) pas., bes. 136-138.

[107] Z.B. WABr 4, Nr.1347,5f.; Nr.1350,14; 5, Nr.1410,Anrede.20; vgl. Holl (wie Anm. 96) 376.

[108] Zu ihm s. W. Elert, Der bischöfliche Charakter der Superintendentur-Verfassung (Luth. 46, 1935, 353-367). Historisch hat dies Amt eine Wurzel im mittelalterlichen Archipresbyterat (ibd. 353) und wurde auch hier und dort so genannt (ibd. 353, dort auch weitere Bezeichnungen), doch es gewann über diesen hinausgehende episkopale Züge, was sich in der Wahl des Begriffs "Superintendent" niederschlug.

[109] Augustin, De civitate Dei 19,19; vgl. Hieronymus Ep. 146,1.

[110] Kurfürstliche Visitationsinstruktion von 1527 (in: Sehling [wie Anm. 70] I/1,142-148), 146; Melanchthon, Unterricht der Visitatorn (wie Anm. 39), CR 26,89 / WA 26,235,7f. / Werke I 264,20f.

[111] Elert (wie Anm. 108) 365.

[112] Ibd. 360-363.

[113] An erster Stelle ist hier natürlich der oberste Superintendent des sächsischen Kurkreises zu nennen, der Stadtpfarrer von Wittenberg, der ordinierte, seit es in Sachsen eine geregelte evangelische Ordinationspraxis

gab. Wenn der erste Inhaber dieser Position, Johannes Bugenhagen, sogar als Ordinator für Kandidaten aus dem gesamten Ausstrahlungsbereich der Wittenberger Reformation tätig wurde - und neben ihm auch andere Geistliche der Stadt wie etwa Luther -, dann entsprach diese überregionale episkopale Tätigkeit der besonderen Bedeutung Wittenbergs für die von Luther geprägte Reformation. Zur Ordination durch die Superintendenten in anderen Territorien s. z.B.: Braunschweigische Kirchenordnung von 1543 (in: A.L. Richter [Hg.], Die evangelischen Kirchenordnungen des 16. Jahrhunderts. Weimar 1846. Bd. II, 56-64), 60; Württembergische Synodalordnung von 1547 (ibd. 93-97), 94.

[114] Vgl. etwa den Fall Dänemarks, wo die nach der Reformation eingesetzten Superintendenten sehr schnell "Bischof" hießen (P.G. Lindhardt, Skandinavische Kirchengeschichte seit dem 16. Jahrhundert. Göttingen 1982 [KiG M3], 239).

[115] Sehling (wie Anm. 70) III (1909) 391, vgl. Elert (wie Anm. 108) 363 u. vgl. o. Anm. 58.

[116] Brunner (wie Anm. 68) 133-136; Gabriel (wie Anm. 55) Kap. V 8b.

[117] Visitationsinstruktion von 1527 (wie Anm. 110), 146.

[118] Ibd.; Melanchthon, Unterricht der Visitatorn (wie Anm. 39), CR 26,89/WA 26,235,16-25/Werke 264,31-265,7.

[119]Visitationsinstruktion von 1527 (wie Anm. 110), 146.

[120] Das galt desto mehr, je stärker sich das Landesherrliche Kirchenregiment ausbildete, innerhalb dessen der Superintendent dann meist dem zum landesherrlichen Verwaltungsamt entwickelten Konsistorium untergeordnet und so in einen staatlichen Behördenzug eingeordnet war (vgl. Elert [wie Anm. 108] 353f.; E. Sehling, Art. Superintenden, RE^3 XIX (167-172),169). Daß das Superintendentenamt gleichwohl nicht in dieser Dimension aufging, zeigt Elert 355ff.

[121] Augsburger Religionsfriede 6 (K. Brandi [Hg.], Der Augsburger Religonsfriede vom 25. Sept. 1555. München 1896, 23f.)

[122] Ibd. 8 (28f.).

[123] S. dazu kurz K.O. von Aretin, Vom Deutschen Reich zum Deutschen Bund. Göttingen 1980, 90-96.

[124] Zu dieser Neuordnung vgl. A. v. Campenhausen, Entstehung und Funktion des bischöflichen Amtes in den evangelischen Kirchen in Deutschland (in: ders., Gesammelte Schriften. Hg. J.E. Christoph, Chr. Link u.a. Tübingen 1995,8-26) 17-23.

Apostolizität, Episkopé und Sukzession

Jan Rohls

Die lutherische, reformierte und unierte Tradition

Die Gemeinsamkeit der lutherischen und reformierten Tradition hinsichtlich der Fragen der Apostolizität, Episkopé und Sukzession resultiert aus der Abgrenzung gegenüber der römischen Position. Das bedeutet nun allerdings nicht, daß die lutherische und reformierte Position deckungsgleich wären. Zwar scheint es, was die reformatorische Ära und das konfessionelle Zeitalter angeht, zwischen Lutheranern und Reformierten keinen Dissens im Hinblick auf die Apostolizität und Sukzession gegeben zu haben. Ein solcher Dissens trat vielmehr erst auf, als bestimmte Kreise des Neuluthertums im neunzehnten Jahrhundert ein hochkirchliches Amtsverständnis entwickelten, für das sie sich auf die lutherische Reformation meinten berufen zu können. Dagegen bestand von Anfang an ein Unterschied zwischen dem lutherischen und dem reformierten, genauer: dem calvinistischen Verständnis des Amts, und diese Differenz wirkte sich dann auch aus auf die Auffassung der Episkopé. Seit der Unionsbewegung am Anfang des neunzehnten Jahrhunderts übt im übrigen die calvinistische Auffassung der Episkopé einen entscheidenden Einfluß nicht nur in den unierten, sondern auch in den lutherischen Kirchen aus. Und es sind letztlich diese neuen Formen der Episkopé, wie sie sich zu Beginn des neunzehnten Jahrhunderts in den unierten und lutherischen Landeskirchen ausbildeten, denen dann das hochkirchliche Neuluthertum seine eigene Auffassung von Episkopé entgegensetzte. Die seitdem vertieften Differenzen zwischen Lutheranern und Reformierten in der Amtsfrage brechen in regelmäßigen Intervallen wieder auf, und dies zumal dann, wenn unterschiedliche ökumenische Interessen auf dem Spiel stehen. Soviel zur Einleitung, und ich werde nun so verfahren, daß ich die lutherische, reformierte und unierte Auffassung von Apostolizität, Episkopé und Sukzession nacheinander darstelle.

1.

Bei den klassischen Reformatoren begegnet der für die Abgrenzung gegenüber dem römischen Amtsverständnis grundlegende Gedanke des allgemeinen Priestertums nirgends so ausgeprägt wie bei Luther. Mit der Taufe werden ihm zufolge alle Christen zu Priestern geweiht, so daß alle Christen dem geistlichen Stand angehören. Damit sind alle Christen gleichermaßen unmittelbar zu und haben dieselben Rechte und Pflichten vor Gott. Damit ist gemeint die doppelte Vollmacht, die potestas ordinis und die potestas iurisdictionis, die nach römischer Vorstellung dem geweihten Priester vorbehalten ist. So kann Luther in der für die Amtsthematik entscheidenden Schrift „De instituendis ministris ecclesiae" erklären, daß alle getauften Christen die Vollmacht hätten zu predigen, die Taufe und das Abendmahl zu spenden, die Schlüsselgewalt in der Buße auszuüben, Fürbitte zu halten, Dankopfer darzubringen und Lehre zu beurteilen. Das sind aber Funktionen, die nach römischer Auffassung entweder wie die Spendung des Abendmahls an die Konsekrationsvollmacht oder wie die Ausübung der Schlüsselgewalt an die Jurisdiktionsvollmacht des Amtspriesters gebunden sind. Mit dem Gedanken des allgemeinen Priestertums fällt die römische Institution eines besonderen Amtspriestertums weg. Das bedeutet nun aber nicht, daß Luther kein besonderes Amt kennt. Nur ist dieses für ihn aufgrund seiner Kritik des Meßopfers nicht länger das Amt eines Priesters, der allein kraft der Weihe zur Darbringung eines solchen Opfers befähigt ist. Luther bestimmt es vielmehr als das Amt der öffentlichen Wortverkündigung und Sakramentsverwaltung, und das bedeutet, daß das besondere Amt ein öffentliches Amt ist. In seiner Öffentlichkeit aber liegt begründet, daß ein Christ es nur mit Einwilligung der anderen Christen, also der Gemeinde ausüben darf. Seine Ausübung durch eine bestimmte Person setzt mithin deren ordentliche Berufung durch die Gemeinde voraus, und diese Berufung läßt sich durchaus mit der Berufung in weltliche Ämter vergleichen. Wie ein Bürgermeister vor seiner Berufung bereits Bürger ist, das Bürgerrecht besitzt und aufgrund seiner Geeignetheit von der Bürgerschaft in das Amt berufen wird, so ist auch der geistliche Amtsträger bereits vor seiner Berufung Priester, genießt also priesterliche Vollmachten und wird von der Gemeinde gleichfalls wegen seiner Geeignetheit in das besondere Amt berufen. Das Wort Gottes öffentlich zu verkündigen und die Sakramente zu verwalten, hat Luther zufolge aber Gott selbst befohlen, so daß es sich bei dem besonderen Amt, das diese Aufgabe wahrnimmt, um eine Stiftung Gottes handelt. Das ergibt sich nun auch aus der „Confessio Augustana", wenn man denn CA 5 in Verbindung mit CA 14 liest. Dann nämlich ist das von Gott eingesetzte Predigtamt, das in der öffentlichen Predigt des Evangeliums und der Verwaltung der Sakramente besteht, identisch mit jenem besonderen Amt, das von Personen ausgeübt wird, die ordentlich berufen (rite vocatus) sind.

Nach lutherischer Auffassung gibt es also neben dem allgemeinen Priestertum das besondere Amt der öffentlichen Wortverkündigung und Sakramentsverwaltung, dessen Ausübung die Berufung durch die Gemeinde erfordert. Mit der Berufung kommen wir nun aber zu den Fragen der Apostolizität, Episkopé und Sukzession. Denn sie tritt ja an die Stelle der römischen Priesterweihe, der sakramentalen Ordination, die vom Bischof vollzogen wird, der dank seiner Weihe in apostolischer Sukzession steht. Luther und Melanchthon kommen nun aber zu einem neuen Verständnis nicht nur der Ordination, sondern auch des Bischofs und der apostolischen Sukzession. Die Ordination ist für Luther letztlich identisch mit der Berufung, insofern es sich bei ihr um die Übertragung des besonderen Amtes handelt, in das jemand ordentlich berufen wird. Als ideal betrachtet Luther daher auch die Ordination in der konkreten Gemeinde, in die jemand berufen wird. Eine solche Ordination wird auch Luther zufolge von einem Bischof vollzogen, nur daß Luther und Melanchthon in Anlehnung an Hieronymus den Bischof mit dem Presbyter und Pfarrer der lokalen Gemeinde identifizieren. Dies aber ist ihnen möglich, weil sie mit dem Gedanken des einen von Gott gestifteten besonderen Amtes arbeiten. Es mag daher zwar faktisch einen Unterschied zwischen einem örtlichen Gemeindpfarrer und einem regionalen Bischof geben, aber dieser Unterschied läßt sich nicht auf göttliche Stiftung zurückführen. Er besteht nicht iure divino, sondern nur iure humano, und es gibt daher kein von Gott gestiftetes hierarchisches Amt mit dem bischöflichen Amt an der Spitze. Die Legitimität der Ordination hängt daher auch nicht davon ab, daß sie von Bischöfen vollzogen wird, in denen dank der Bischofsweihe die von den Aposteln ihren Helfern durch Handauflegung übertragene geistliche Gabe bis auf uns gekommen ist. Daß nämlich eine derartige apostolische Sukzession im Sinne der historischen Kontinuität der Kette der Handauflegungen von den Aposteln an als solche eine theologische Bedeutung hat, wird von Luther ebenso bestritten wie von Melanchthon. Denn gerade die in ihren Augen offenkundige Tatsache, daß die römischen Bischöfe, die sich ja auf die Apostel zurückführen, die apostolische Lehre nicht bewahrt haben, läßt beide vielmehr umgekehrt an der theologischen Bedeutung der bischöflichen Sukzession und des historischen Episkopats zweifeln. Theologisch relevant für den Gedanken der Apostolizität ist für sie vielmehr nur die Bewahrung der apostolischen Lehre. Die Apostolizität wird somit nicht formal, sondern inhaltlich definiert, und die inhaltliche Kontinuität mit der apostolischen Lehre wird weder garantiert noch ermöglicht durch die apostolische Sukzession im Sinne einer ununterbrochenen Kette bischöflicher Handauflegungen.

Nun liegt ein Grund, weshalb Luther und Melanchthon schließlich zur presbyterialen Ordination schreiten und diese mit der ursprünglichen Identität von Bischof und Ortspfarrer legitimieren, natürlich darin, daß sich in der damaligen deutschen Situation keine Bischöfe zur Ordination evangelischer Pfarrer bereit fanden. Es gehört zu den besonderen Kennzeichen des Lutherthums oder - mehr noch - des Landeskirchentums in Deutschland, daß in ihm seit dem Speyerer Reichstagsabschied das Kirchenregiment, das zuvor von Bischöfen ausgeübt worden war, in die Hände der Landesherren überging. Die Landesherren waren also aufgrund fehlender reformatorisch gesinnter Bischöfe Notbischöfe, die Sorge für die rechte Wort- und Sakramentsverwaltung zu tragen hatten. Das bischöfliche Aufsichtsamt und damit die Episkopé wurde so von weltlichen Fürsten wahrgenommen. Melanchthon konnte dieses landesherrliche Kirchenregiment dann damit begründen, daß der evangelisch gesinnte Landesherr das vornehmste Glied der Kirche (praecipuum ecclesiae membrum) sei, dem zudem die Sorge für die beiden Tafeln der Zehn Gebote (custodia utriusque tabula) obliege. Darin impliziert war die Sorge für den rechten Gottesdienst, auf den die erste Tafel abzielt. Es ist also der an die Stelle des Bischofs getretene Landesherr, der die Episkopé ausübt. Allerdings geschieht dies nicht unmittelbar durch ihn als weltlichen Herrscher oder durch eine von ihm eingesetzte weltliche Kommission, sondern mit Hilfe von geistlichen Amtsträgern, den Superintendenten. Das alte Bischofsamt wird also im deutschen Luthertum von mehreren Instanzen beerbt. Da iure divino kein Unterschied zwischen Bischof und Ortspfarrer besteht, ist der Ortspfarrer selbst Bischof, da es nur ein einziges iure divino bestehendes geistliches Amt der öffentlichen Wortverkündigung und Sakramentsverwaltung gibt. Den Bischof als geistlichen Amtsträger beerbt also der Ortspfarrer. Die kirchenregimentlichen Funktionen, die dem Bischof zufielen, übernimmt hingegen der Landesherr als Notbischof, und ihm als Beamte untergeordnet sind schließlich die Superintendenten. Bei ihnen handelt es sich um dazu eigens beauftragte Pfarrer, die mit der Visitation von Pfarrern einer bestimmten Region betraut sind. Sie sind die eigentlichen Erben des Bischofstitels, insofern der Begriff „superintendens" die lateinische Übersetzung von „episkopos" ist. Faktisch üben die Superintendenten somit als Kirchenbeamte in landesherrlichen Visitationskommissionen und Konsistorien durch Visitationen die Episkopé über Amtsverwaltung und Lebenswandel der Pfarrer des ihnen zugewiesenen Sprengels aus. Die Visitationskommissionen und später die Konsistorien sind dabei als Organe des landesherrlichen Kirchenregiments gemischt aus geistlichen und weltlichen Amtsträgern gebildet. Der Superintendent ist somit immer an die Mitwirkung weltlicher Amtsträger gebunden.

Die Aufgabe des Superintendenten wird erstmals in der sächsischen „Instruktion" für Visitatoren umrissen. Der dabei zugrunde liegenden Auffassung, daß es sich bei den Superintendenten um landesherrliche Beamte handle, versucht bereits Luther dadurch entgegenzuwirken, daß er ihre Aufgabe in der Vorrede zu Melanchthons „Unterricht der Visitatoren" als rein innerkirchliche definiert. Daß Luther an einem genuin reformatorischen Bischofsamt als Visitationsamt, das die Aufgabe der Episkopé wahrnimmt, interessiert war, belegt nicht zuletzt die Einführung von Nikolaus von Amsdorf als Bischof von Naumburg-Zeitz samt der zu diesem Anlaß verfaßten Schrift „Exempel, einen rechten christlichen Bischof zu weihen". Auch plädiert Melanchthon unter der Voraussetzung der Gewährleistung der rechten Evangeliumsverkündigung für die Beibehaltung des episkopalen Aufsichtsamtes. Die Grundvoraussetzung dabei ist allerdings, daß es sich bei diesem Amt nicht um eine iure divino bestehende Stiftung, sondern um eine der Ordnung wegen existierende rein menschliche Einrichtung handelt. Im Rahmen der menschlichen Kirchenordnung ist also der lutherische Bischof als Träger des Aufsichtsamtes dem Ortspfarrer übergeordnet. Das ändert jedoch nichts an der Tatsache, daß das Bischofsamt sich in den lutherischen Landeskirchen Deutschlands nicht durchsetzen konnte. Seine Funktion als Aufsichtsamt übernahm vielmehr das Amt des Superintendenten, also ein Beamter des landesherrlichen Notbischofs. Das landesherrliche Kirchenregiment setzte sich so vollends durch und schob jede institutionelle Alternative zur Wahrnehmung der Episkopé durch den Superintendenten beiseite. Ebenso aber schaltete dieses Modell eine andere, gleichfalls in der lutherischen Reformation angelegte Möglichkeit der Wahrnehmung der Episkopé aus. Wie es die über-kommene bischöfliche Kirchenverfassung nahelegt, die kirchliche Aufgabe der Episkopé einem Bischof zu übertragen, der den Pfarrern seines Sprengels übergeordnet ist, so legt es der spezifisch lutherische Gedanke des allgemeinen Priestertums nahe, die Wahrnehmung der Episkopé der Gemeinde zu übertragen. Denn die Gemeinde hat ja Luther zufolge das Recht und die Pflicht, für die rechte Wortverkündigung und Sakramentsverwaltung zu sorgen, wie sie ja auch das Recht und die Pflicht hat, Pfarrer zu berufen. Doch diese Alternative der gemeindlichen Episkopé kam ebensowenig zum Tragen wie die der bischöflichen Episkopé. Sondern mit dem Sieg des landesherrlichen Kirchenregiments und der Einführung des Amts des Superintendenten teilten sich der geistliche Lehrstand und der weltliche Wehrstand die Aufgabe der Episkopé.

2.

Es ist für das reformierte Amtsverständnis bezeichnend, daß grundsätzliche Überlegungen, die das Verhältnis zwischen allgemeinem Priestertum und besonderem geistlichen Amt betreffen, hier völlig fehlen. Das gilt nicht nur für die einzelnen Bekenntnisse, wo dieser Überlegungen ja auch im Luthertum keinen Raum einnehmen, sondern die reformierte Theologie überhaupt. Bei Bullinger heißt es ebenso wie bei Calvin, daß das Amt der öffentlichen Wortverkündigung und Sakramentsverwaltung von Gott eingesetzt sei, um durch seine Diener die Kirche zu sammeln, zu gründen, zu leiten und zu erhalten. In dieser Funktions-bestimmung des Pfarramtes besteht ebenso wenig eine Differenz zwischen reformiertem und lutherischem Amtsverständnis wie in der Frage der apostoli-schen Sukzession, die natürlich auch im reformierten Bereich als Sukzession in der apostolischen Lehre gefaßt, und der Ordination von Pfarrern durch Pfarrer, die mit der Identität von Bischof und Pfarrer in der alten Kirche begründet wird. Der Unterschied zwischen reformiertem und lutherischem Amtsverständnis beginnt vielmehr damit, daß Calvin auf lokaler Gemeindeebene nicht nur von einem Amt, sondern von drei oder vier Ämtern spricht. Darauf muß hier deshalb näher eingegangen werden, weil sich diese Differenz auch auswirkt auf das Verständnis der Episkopé. Es handelt sich zudem nicht um einen allgemeinen Zug des reformierten Amtsverständnisses, sondern um einen, der in Zürich fehlt, während er für Genf und die von Genf beeinflußten Kirchen entscheidend ist. In Zürich kennt man in der Nachfolge Zwinglis nur das eine besondere geistliche Amt, so daß hier keine Differenz zum Luthertum vorliegt. Die neutestamentlichen Begriffe des Bischofs, des Ältesten, des Hirten und des Lehrers sind nur verschiedene Bezeichnungen für ein und dasselbe Amt der öffentlichen Wortverkündigung und Sakramentsverwaltung. Nun zweifelt zwar auch Calvin nicht an der zentralen Bedeutung der öffentlichen Wortverkündigung und Sakramentsverwaltung für die Kirche, da auch für ihn Kirche nur da existiert, wo die Wortverkündigung recte und die Sakramentsverwaltung rite geschieht. Aber daneben kennt er doch noch andere kirchliche Funktionen, die sich aus den ekklesiologischen Ansätzen des Neuen Testaments ergeben. Daher gelangt Calvin zu der These, daß dem Amt der öffentlichen Wortverkündigung und Sakramentsverwaltung, also dem Pastorenamt, drei weitere Ämter zugeordnet sind, und zwar das Amt des Lehrers, des Diakons und des Ältesten oder Presbyters. Daß dies kein starres Schema ist, zeigt bereits das von Calvin mit entworfene Hugenottische Bekenntnis, das neben dem Pastor nur das Amt des Diakons und das des Ältesten kennt. Die für die calvinistische Ämterlehre grundlegende Unterscheidung ist die zwischen Diakon und Presbyter, wobei dann in vermeintlich korrekter Interpretation des Neuen Testaments zwei Arten von Presbytern voneinander abgehoben werden. Zum einen handelt es sich um die mit der öffentlichen Wortverkündigung und Sakramentsverwaltung betrauten Presbyter, also die Pastoren, und zum andern um die die Kirchenzucht ausübenden Kirchenvorsteher oder Ältesten. Entscheidend ist nun, daß die Leitung der Ortsgemeinde anders als im Luthertum nicht bei der einzelnen Person des Pfarrers, sondern bei dem aus dem Pastor und den Ältesten, teilweise auch den Diakonen gebildeten Konsistorium, also bei einem Kollegium liegt.

Anders als im Luthertum, anders aber auch als im Zwinglianismus untersteht nun die Wahrnehmung der Episkopé im Calvinismus nicht mehr der weltlichen Obrigkeit, die sie dann allenfalls gemeinsam mit Vertretern des geistlichen Amtes ausübt. Vielmehr wird die Episkopé in die Hände des kirchlichen Kollegialorgans gelegt. Denn wenn die Funktion der Episkopé darin besteht, die Reinheit der öffentlichen Wortverkündigung und Korrektheit der Sakramentsverwaltung zu überwachen, so wird sie im Calvinismus auf lokaler Ebene von den Ältesten als im Konsistorium vertretenen Amtsträgern wahrgenommen. Der Bestand der Kirche ist ja da gefährdet, wo die konstitutiven Merkmale der wahren Kirche, rechte Wortverkündigung und Sakramentsverwaltung, durch den Träger des

Amtes der öffentlichen Wortverkündigung und Sakramentsverwaltung, also den Pastor, nicht mehr gewährleistet sind. Die Ältesten sind mit einer eigenen geistlichen Jurisdiktion betraut, die es ihnen nicht nur ermöglicht, sondern sie auch verpflichtet, einen Pastor, der von der rechten Wortverkündigung und Sakramentsverwaltung abweicht, zur Rechenschaft zu ziehen und disziplinarisch zu maßregeln. Das bedeutet, daß die calvinistische Ämterlehre es mit sich bringt, daß bereits auf lokaler Ebene die innerkirchliche Wahrnehmung der Episkopé gewährleistet ist.

Nun hatte es sich allerdings bei dem herkömmlichen Bischofamt um ein regionales Aufsichtsamt gehandelt, während das Konsistorium nur eine lokale Episkopé wahrnimmt. Ein solches regionales Aufsichtsamt ist natürlich in erster Linie in solchen Kirchen erforderlich, die kein lokales Aufsichtsamt kennen, und das ist nicht nur bei den Lutheranern der Fall, sondern auch im Einflußgebiet Zwinglis. Gerade in den reformierten Landeskirchen Deutschlands begegnet das auch bei den Lutheranern vorhandene Amt des Superintendenten. So bezeichnet etwa die Herborner Generalsynode die Superintendenten als Diener am Wort, also als Pfarrer, denen außer der ordentlichen Tätigkeit, nämlich der öffentlichen Wortverkündigung und Sakramentsverwaltung, noch die Tätigkeit der Inspektion übertragen ist und die die Gemeinden visitieren und die Pfarrkonvente und Pfarrer leiten sollen. Der Superintendent übernimmt hier also eine Rolle, die auch Bullinger in der Züricher Kantonskirche kennt. Der Antistes oder Senior übernimmt hier nach dem Vorbild des Petrus in der Jerusalemer Gemeinde den Vorsitz im Kirchensenat. Er trägt unter anderem dafür Sorge, daß keine Unordnung entsteht, ohne daß diese Funktion mit einer größeren geistlichen Vollmacht verbunden wäre. Vielmehr gilt hier wie im Luthertum, daß ein derartiges dem Ortspfarramt übergeordnetes Amt der Episkopé hinsichtlich seiner geistlichen Vollmacht mit dem Ortspfarramt identisch ist. Doch wie gesagt: ein derartiges dem alten Bischofamt nachgebildetes Amt der Episkopé gibt es im Calvinismus nicht. Das bedeutet nicht, daß Calvin es für untragbar gehalten hätte. Denn er selbst ist der Meinung, daß es in der alten Kirche ein solches Amt gegeben habe, und er kann sogar dem König von Polen eine in diesem Sinne episkopale Verfassung vorschlagen. Die Aufgabe des Bischofs besteht danach darin, bei Synoden den Vorsitz zu führen und für die Einigkeit und Ordnung seiner Diözese zu sorgen, und natürlich handelt es sich bei diesem Bischofamt um eine menschliche Einrichtung. Im Calvinismus ist es nun aber nicht nur nicht zur Ausbildung eines derartigen Amtes der Episkopé gekommen, sondern diese Form der Wahrnehmung der Episkopé ist darüber hinaus auch zusehends abgewertet worden. So unterscheidet Beza drei Formen des Episkopats. Die römische Auffassung von der iure divino bestehenden Überordnung des Bischofs über den Pfarrer bezeichnet er als Satanus Episcopatus. Demgegenüber toleriert er zwar die in lutherischen und zwinglianisch beeinflußten Kirchen nur iure humano bestehende Überordnung des Bischofs als Humanus Episcopatus. Aber schriftgemäß und daher wünschenswert ist in seinen Augen nur der Divinus Episcopatus, wie er in den calvinistischen Kirchenordnungen festgeschrieben ist. Danach wird das Amt der Episkopé auf regionaler Ebene wahrgenommen von der Synode. Das zuerst von der hugenottischen Kirchenordnung entwickelte synodale Modell der Episkopé hat dann über die niederländische Kirche und ihre Flüchtlingsgemeinden auch im Westen Deutschlands Fuß gefaßt. Es liegt hier ein eigenständiges Modell der Episkopé vor, daß sich von dem sowohl auf lutherischer als auch reformierter Seite im Rahmen des landesherrlichen Kirchenregiments vertretenen Superintendentenmodell schon dadurch abhebt, daß es nicht personal, sondern kollegial verfaßt ist. Die presbyterial-synodale Kirchenverfassung ist die Gestaltung einer unabhängig vom Schutz der staatlichen Obrigkeit existierenden Kirche. Die Kirche nimmt danach nicht nur auf der lokalen Ebene der Ortsgemeinde das Amt der Episkopé durch Presbyterien oder Konsistorien wahr. Sondern jene Probleme, die das Aufsichtsamt betreffen, die sich aber in den lokalen Presbyterien nicht lösen lassen oder die mehrere Gemeinden bzw. die Gesamtkirche betreffen, müssen den übergeordneten Synoden, den Klassenkonventen, Provinzialsynoden und schließlich der Generalsynode zugeleitet werden. Es entsteht so ein gestaffeltes System der Episkopé vom örtlichen Presbyterium bis zur Generalsynode, in dem das Subsidiaritätsprinzip herrscht. Die Verbindung zwischen den örtlichen Presbyterien und den übergeordneten Synoden ist dabei so geregelt, daß die Synoden sich aus den dazu bestimmten Mitgliedern der Presbyterien zusammensetzen. Auf diese Weise kommt zugleich zum Ausdruck, daß keine Gemeinde einen Vorrang oder eine Herrschaft über eine andere besitzt. Das regionale Amt der Episkopé wird so von den Synodalvertretern der lokalen Presbyterien paritätisch wahrgenommen.

Man muß sich dieses presbyterial-synodale Modell der Episkopé einmal klar vor Augen führen. Die Episkopé wird auf jeder Stufe, von der einzelnen Ortsgemeinde bis hin zur Gesamtkirche eines Landes, von kircheneigenen Institutionen wahrgenommen. Und zwar auf jeder Stufe von Institutionen derselben Stufe. Die Episkopé über die Ortsgemeinde liegt beim Presbyterium, die über die Gesamtkirche bei der Generalsynode. Die Synoden sind anders als die lutherischen Synoden keine reinen Geistlichkeitssynoden. Sie sind vielmehr wie die Presbyterien oder Konsistorien zusammengesetzt aus Pfarrern, Ältesten und Diakonen. Zwischen Presbyterien und Generalsynode existieren meherer Stufen synodaler Gremien, die regelmäßig zusammentreten, so daß eine durchgängige Episkopé der Kirche erfolgt. Dabei ist wichtig zu sehen, daß es sich bei den Synoden ebensowenig wie bei den Presbyterien um eine repräsentative Vertretung der Gemeindeglieder handelt. Vielmehr setzen sich sowohl die Presbyterien als auch die Synoden nur aus Amtsträgern zusammen. Das Entscheidende aber ist, daß es nicht erst auf unterster regionaler Ebene ein kollegiales Organ der Episkopé, nämlich die Klasse als die Synode der Nachbargemeinden gibt. Sondern ein derartiges kollegiales Organ der Episkopé existiert bereits auf der untersten Ebene der Ortsgemeinde in Gestalt des Presbyteriums oder Konsistoriums. Der Unterschied zum Luthertum ist deutlich. Dort hatten sich ja drei Größen das Erbe des alten Bischofsamts geteilt. Die geistliche Vollmacht des Bischofs war auf den Pfarrer übergegangen, das bischöfliche Kirchenregiment auf den Landesherrn und die eigentliche Episkopé auf den Superintendenten als landesherrlichen Beamten. Im Calvinismus hingegen geht zwar auch die geistliche Vollmacht des Bischofs auf den Pfarrer über, was bedeutet, daß die alte iure divino bestehende Überordnung des Bischofs über den Pfarrer wegfällt. Aber das bischöfliche Kirchenregiment geht hier nicht auf den Landesherrn als Notbischof, sondern auf die Synoden über. Und die eigentliche Episkopé schließlich wird von den Kollegialorganen vom Presbyterium bis hin zur Generalsynode ausgeübt.

3.

Wie man die anglikanische Kirche von heute nicht verstehen kann ohne die Veränderungen, die sie im vorigen Jahrhundert durch den Einfluß des Traktarianismus und Ritualismus durchgemacht hat, so kann man auch die deutschen lutherischen und reformierten Kirchen von heute nicht begreifen, wenn man nicht den Einfluß des Synodalwesens in den deutschen Landeskirchen im vorigen Jahrhundert berücksichtigt. Denn durch die Einführung von Synoden auch in lutherischen Landeskirchen ändert sich nicht nur deren bisherige Struktur. Vielmehr kommt es dabei auch zu einer gravierenden Veränderung des calvinistischen Verständnisses der Synode, und ebenso kommt es im Luthertum als Gegenreaktion zur Ausbildung eines spezifisch hochkirchlichen Amtsbegriffs. Das alles bleibt nicht ohne Folgen für das Verständnis der Episkopé. Der Einführung des presbyterial-synodalen Elements in die deutschen Landeskirchen geht voraus die Kritik des altlutherischen Amtsverständnisses, wie sie vor allem im Pietismus geleistet wird. Es ist dies eine Kritik, die wie bereits die Amtskritik des Sozinianismus und Spiritualismus auf Luthers Gedanken des allgemeinen Priestertums zurückgreift. Wie dieser Gedanke von Luther selbst gegen das römische Priestertum so wird er jetzt gegen das lutherische Amt eingesetzt, das in den Augen seiner Kritiker zu einer Entmündigung der Gemeinde führt. Um das Leben der Gemeinde zu aktivieren, konnte man dabei die presbyteriale Kirchenverfassung Calvins als Vorbild hinstellen. Zu einer grundsätzlichen Änderung der Kirchenverfassung in den deutschen Landeskirchen kommt es jedoch erst im Zuge der durch das Auftreten Napoleons bedingten Neuordnung der deutschen Territorien. Dadurch entstehen gemischt konfessionelle Territorien, was dann in manchen Fällen zu Unionen zwischen der lutherischen und der reformierten Kirche führt. Der Unionsbildung kommt sowohl die im Pietismus vollzogene Vergleichgültigung der innerprotestantischen Lehrdifferenzen als auch die Kritik der Aufklärungstheologie am Bekenntniszwang entgegen. Und im Rahmen der landesherrlichen Unionsbestrebungen werden nun auch Überlegungen laut, die eine grundsätzliche Änderung der bisherigen Gestalt des landesherrlichen Kirchenregiments fordern. Entscheidend sind dabei die Vorgänge in Preußen, das durch den Wiener Kongreß um Rheinland-Westfalen erweitert wird. Denn hier hatte ja bereits in der Reformationszeit über die Niederlande die presbyterial-synodale Kirchenordnung in reformierten Regionen Fuß gefaßt. Elemente dieser Kirchenordnung greift nun Schleiermacher in seiner Schrift „Über die für die protestantische Kirche des preußischen Staates einzurichtende Synodal-verfassung" auf. Schleiermacher will damit eine größere Selbständigkeit der Kirche gegenüber dem Staat erreichen. Natürlich kann er das seit der Reformation bestehende landesherrliche Kirchenregiment nicht beseitigen, aber dieses soll sich in seinen Augen beschränken auf die Aufsicht über die Kirchengüter, während die innere Verwaltung der Kirche von unabhängigen kirchlichen Organen durchge-führt werden soll. Zu diesem Zweck plädiert Schleiermacher für die Einrichtung von Presbyterien auf lokaler Gemeindeebene und von Synoden. Anfangs wollte er diese Synoden als reine Geistlichkeitssynoden verstanden wissen, und sie sollten neben den Bischöfen, die der König ernennt, Träger der Kirchenleitung sein. Auf diese Weise hätte die Wahrnehmung der Episkopé bei einem Gremium gelegen, das das alte lutherische personale Amt des Superintendenten, nunmehr zum Bischof gesteigert, mit dem kollegialen Amt der Synode verbindet. Die Gestalt der Synode entspricht allerdings nicht dem alten calvinistischen Modell, weil es sich bei ihr um eine reine Geistlichkeitssynode handelt. Die Einführung eines protestantischen Bischofsamts scheiterte hingegen wie bereits in der Reforma-tionszeit am Widerstand des landesherrlichen Kirchenregiments. Schleiermacher hat seinen ursprünglichen Entwurf dann in der genannten Schrift modifiziert. Er gibt den Gedanken eines protestantischen Bischofsamts ebenso auf wie den reiner Geistlichkeitssynoden. Stattdessen plädiert er für die Ergänzung der Konsistorial-verfassung durch eine Synodalverfassung, und die Synoden sollen dabei außer von geistlichen Amtsträgern auch von Ältesten als weiteren Vertretern der lokalen Presbyterien besucht werden.

Dieses Modell Schleiermachers, das das konsistoriale und presbyterial-synodale Modell der Episkopé miteinander verbindet, wird in Preußen allerdings nur in der Rheinisch-Westfälischen Kirchenordnung realisiert. Da diese Ordnung vorbild-hafte Funktion für die Einrichtung von Synoden auch in anderen deutschen Landeskirchen hatte, soll ihre Beschreibung der Episkopé etwas näher dargestellt werden. Zunächst einmal steht auf unterster lokaler Ebene das Presbyterium, das die Ortsgemeinde in ihren Gemeindeangelegenheiten vertritt und aus gewählten Pfarrern, Ältesten und Diakonen besteht. Bereits auf dieser Ebene nehmen die Ältesten die Funktion der Episkopé gegenüber den Pfarrern wahr. Auf nächst höherer Stufe steht die Kreissynode, die aus den Pfarren des Kreises und je einem Ältesten aus jeder Gemeinde des Kreises gehören. Jeder Kreissynode sitzt ein von der Synode selbst gewähltes Direktorium vor, das aus dem Superintendenten, dem Assessor und dem Scriba besteht. Dem Superintendenten, der in diesem Fall kein landesherrlicher Beamter, sondern ein von der Synode gewählter rein kirchlicher Amtsträger ist, obliegt nun die Wahrnehmung der Episkopé auf der Kreisebene. Er hat in allen kirchlichen Angelegenheiten über Erhaltung und Ausführung der Kirchenordnung und Synodalbeschlüsse zu wachen und die Rechte der Kirche wahrzunehmen. Er führt zudem die Aufsicht über die Presbyterien, über daas Fortstudieren und die Kandidaten des Kreises, über die Amtsverwaltung und den Lebenswandel der Geistlichen sowie der Kirchendiener nach den Grundsätzen der Kirchenordnung. Auf der höchsten Stufe steht schließlich die Provinzialsynode, die aus den Superintendenten der Provinz und je einem von jeder Kreissynode gewählten Pfarrer und Ältesten besteht. Die Provinzialsynode wählt wiederum einen Präses und einen Assessor, und auch ihr kommt auf der Ebene der dem Kreis übergeordneten Provinz die Aufgabe der Episkopé zu. Sie soll nämlich über die Erhaltung der Reinheit der evangelischen Lehre in Kirchen und Schulen sowie der Kirchenordnung wachen. Damit hält nun die alte presbyterial-synodale Kirchenordnung, in der die Aufgabe der Episkopé auf den verschiedenen Ebenen von Presbyterien und Synoden wahrgenommen wird, in der westlichen Provinzen Preußens Einzug. Allerdings bildet das presbyterial-synodale Element nur einen Teil der Verfassung, die außerdem auch noch staatliche Aufsichtsbehörden über die Kirchen kennt. Neben den Konsistorien und Regierungen ist das der General-superintendent. Dieser wird vom Landesherrn ernannt, ist also der alte Superintendent der Reformationszeit im Sinne eines landesherrlichen Beamten. Und ihm obliegt es, nach den ihm vom Ministerium für Geistliche Angelegen-heiten erteilten Instruktionen die einzelnen Superintendenturen der Provinz zu beaufsichtigen. Er nimmt als landesherrlicher Beamter auch an den Provinzial-synoden teil, um die Rechte des Staates wahrzunehmen. Auf diese Weise entsteht, was die Wahrnehmung der Episkopé angeht, ein eigentümliches Zwittergebilde. Auf der einen Seite haben wir gemäß dem landesherrlichen Kirchenregiment das Amt des Generalsuperintendenten, auf der anderen Seite die sich selbst organisierenden Presbyterien und Synoden. Der entscheidende Unterschied zur alten calvinistischen presbyterialen-synodalen Ordnung besteht dabei darin, daß die Synoden in diesem Fall nicht Träger des Kirchenregiments sind, das nach wie vor beim Landesherrn liegt. Vielmehr stehen sie dem landesherrlichen Kirchen-regiment als Vertretung der Kirche gegenüber und üben eine Kontrolle darauf aus, wie denn auch umgekehrt das landesherrliche Kirchenregiment mit Hilfe des

Generalsuperintendenten eine Kontrolle auf die Synoden ausübt. Die Episkopé wird so von beiden Seiten wahrgenommen.

Selbst in deutschen Landeskirchen, die nicht uniert, sondern wie etwa die bayerische genuin lutherisch sind, hat sich das presbyterial-synodale Modell in dieser abgeschwächten Form durchgesetzt. Je stärker nun auf der einen Seite das presbyterial-synodale Modell sich selbst in der lutherischen Kirche durchsetzte, desto mehr wuchs auf der anderen Seite die Kritik des Luthertums daran im Rahmen eines hochkirchlich-episkopalen Modells. Dabei bestand allerdings der Intention nach kein Unterschied zwischen den Verteidigern eines presbyterial-synodalen und eines hochkirchlich-episkopalen Modells. Denn in beiden Fällen ging es zunächst einmal um die Selbständigkeit der Kirche gegenüber dem Staat. Die lutherischen Hochkirchler wollen das Kirchenregiment von dem Landesherrn, an den es aufgrund der Notsituation der Reformation übergegangen war, auf episkopale Amtsträger, die es zuvor innegehabt hatten, zurückübertragen. Und wie die Verteidiger des presbyterial-synodalen Modells so versuchen auch die Apologeten des hochkirchlich-episkopalen Modells nachzuweisen, daß sich ihr Modell bereits bei Luther findet und das landesherrliche Kirchenregiment demgegenüber eine Abweichung darstellt. Die neulutherischen Hochkirchler wie Stahl, Löhe und Vilmar gehen dabei aus von einem anstaltlichen Kirchenbegriff. Die Kirche wird nicht vom allgemeinen Priestertum her gedacht, sondern als Anstalt, in der der Lehrstand der Gemeinde gegenübersteht. Die Glieder des Lehrstandes sind laut Stahl die Nachfolger der Apostel in dem von Christus gestifteten Lehramt. Eben diese Selbständigkeit des Amtes gegenüber der Gemeinde findet nun ihren Ausdruck in der sakramentalen Aufwertung der Ordination. Denn durch die Ordination wird Löhe und Vilmar zufolge eine besondere Amtsgnade verliehen. Sie kann daher auch nur vollzogen werden durch bereits ordinierte Amtsträger und Glieder des geistlichen Standes. Damit soll der Eindruck vermieden werden, als handle es sich bei der Ordination um die Übertragung von Rechten der Gemeinde im Sinne des allgemeinen Priestertums auf die zukünftigen Pfarrer. Der Gedanke der apostolischen Sukzession wird damit nicht mehr nur im Sinne nicht nur der Sukzession in der apostolischen Lehre, sondern auch im Sinne der Sukzession in dem von Christus gestifteten Amt der Apostel verstanden. So kann Vilmar betonen, daß der heilige Geist im Akt der Ordination in kontinuierlichem Fortgang von den Aposteln an durch Gebet und Handauflegung mitgeteilt werde. Nur dadurch wird auch die Erhaltung der reinen Lehre und Sakramentsverwaltung gesichert. Zudem soll das geistliche Amt nicht nur als ein Amt der Lehre und Sakramentsverwaltung, sondern ebenso als ein Hirtenamt verstanden werden, dem allein die Leitung der Gemeinde obliegt. Da aber das Ziel dieser Betonung der Selbständigkeit des geistlichen Amts gegenüber der Gemeinde die Herausstellung der Selbständigkeit der Kirche gegenüber dem Staat ist, muß letztlich wie der Pfarrer die Gemeinde so der Bischof die gesamte Kirche leiten. Das Kirchenregiment liegt somit dem hochkirchlich-episkopalen Modell zufolge beim Bischof. Der Bischof als Inhaber der obersten Kirchengewalt hat danach die Aufsicht über Lehre, Kultus und Disziplin. So kann Löhe ganz im Einklang mit dem anglikanischen Amtsverständnis eine episkopale Kirchenverfassung auch für die lutherische Kirche fordern, wobei er allerdings betont, daß nach lutherischer Auffassung zwischen Bischof und Pfarrer kein iure divino bestehender Unterschied existiere. Die Aufgabe der Episkopé liegt diesem hochkirchlich-episkopalen Modell zufolge allein beim Bischof, der die Aufsicht über die öffentliche Predigt und den öffentlichen Religionsunterricht wahrzunehmen hat. Dieses Modell der Episkopé steht dem presbyterial-synodalen schon deshalb entgegen, weil es die Wahrnehmung der Episkopé ausschließlich in die Hände der geistlichen Amtsträger legt und den Zusammenhang zwischen geistlichen Amtsträgern und Gemeinde zerreißt.

4.

In den meisten deutschen Landeskirchen, seien sie nun lutherisch, reformiert oder uniert, bildeten sich im Verlauf des neunzehnten Jahrhunderts presbyterialsynodale Institutionen aus. Allerdings blieben sie eingebunden in das System des landesherrlichen Kirchenregiments. Insofern bedeutet das Ende des landesherrlichen Kirchenregiments nach dem ersten Weltkrieg auch das Ende der bisherigen Gestalt der Episkopé. Leiter der Landeskirchen werden nun nämlich in den meisten Fällen einzelne Geistliche, die in vielfach den Bischofstitel führen. Sie sind jedoch in keinem Fall Bischöfe im Sinne des soeben skizzierten hochkirchlich-episkopalen Modells, das die völlige Unabhängigkeit des geistlichen Amtes und damit natürlich auch des Bischofsamtes von der Gemeinde betont. Zwar orientiert sich die Form des Bischofsamtes an dem reformatorischen Modell eines lutherischen Bischofs, der nunmehr auch nicht länger als landesherrlicher Beamter fungiert. Aber der Bischof wird von der Synode gewählt und kann gegebenenfalls auch von ihr abberufen werden, so daß er nicht nur den Gemeinden als oberster Hirte gegenübersteht. Es handelt sich mithin um ein synodales Bischofsamt. Dabei unterscheidet sich der Bischof vom Pfarrer nicht nach göttlichem Recht, und ebensowenig steht er in der apostolischen Sukzession, wenn man darunter die ununterbrochene Kette bischöflicher Handauflegungen seit der Zeit der Apostel versteht. Aber er ist nach menschlichem Recht vom Ortspfarrer sowohl durch den Umfang seines Amtsbereichs als auch durch die Besonderheiten seiner Amtsfunktionen unterschieden. Diese Funktionen betreffen nämlich die gesamte Partikularkirche, deren Leitung ihm obliegt, und dienen alle der Wahrnehmung der Episkopé. Dazu zählen vor allem die Ordination von Pfarrern und die Visitation von Gemeinden, wozu dann auch die Verantwortung für die Reinheit der Lehre, öffentlichen Wortverkündigung und Sakraments-verwaltung gehört. Doch werden diese Funktionen auf untergeordneter Ebene auch von Superintendenten, Dekanen und Pröpsten vorgenommen, denen somit wie dem Bischof auf gesamtkirchlicher Ebene die Wahrnehmung der Episkopé zufällt. Anders als im hochkirchlich-episkopalen Modell liegt in den deutschen Landeskirchen die Leitung der Kirche und damit die Wahrnehmung der Episkopé jedenfalls nicht in den Händen des Bischofs allein. Vielmehr handelt es sich bei ihnen um Mischformen zweier verschiedener Gestalten der Episkopé, nämlich derjenigen des lutherischen Bischofsamts der Reformationszeit und derjenigen der calvinistischen presbyterial-synodalen Kirchenordnung. Ein rein hochkirchlich-episkopales Modell hat sich demgegenüber in den deutschen Landeskirchen nach dem Zusammenbruch des landesherrlichen Kirchenregiments ebensowenig durchsetzen können wie ein rein presbyterial-synodales. Grob gesprochen hat man es bei der Gestaltung der Episkopé auf partikularkirchlicher Ebene hier also immer schon mit einer lutherisch-reformierten Mischform zu tun, und zwar selbst in nichtunierten Kirchen.

Die Frage nach der Gestalt der Episkopé hat in der deutschen evangelischen Kirche in diesem Jahrhundert noch einmal eine zentrale Rolle gespielt in der Auseinandersetzung um das sogenannte Führerprinzip in der Kirche. Die Deutschen Christen forderten nämlich eine neue Kirchenverfassung, die die Organe des kirchlichen Lebens nicht länger nach dem demokratischen Wahlsystem bestellt. Vielmehr sollten alle maßgeblichen Entscheidungen von einer geistlichen Spitze der Deutschen Evangelischen Reichskirche, dem Reichs-bischof, persönlich verantwortet werden. Der Reichsbischof sollte somit dem Führer entsprechende Vollmachten in der evangelischen Kirche besitzen. Gegen dieses Führerprinzip wenden sich nun zunächst zwei reformierte Erklärungen und dann die Theologische Erklärung von Barmen, die von Reformierten, Lutheranern und Unierten der Bekennenden Kirche gleichermaßen getragen wurde. Alle diese Erklärungen sind durch das Amtsverständnis Karl Barths mitgeprägt, und die reformierten Erklärungen greifen zudem zurück auf die Ämterlehre Calvins. Die erste dieser Erklärungen, die „Düsseldorfer Thesen", gehen aus von der Königs-herrschaft Christi in der Kirche, die sich durch die Ausrichtung des von Jesus Christus eingesetzten und geordneten Dienstes der Prediger, Lehrer, Ältesten und Diakonen vollzieht. Geistlicher Führer, also das, was der deutschchristliche Reichsbischof zu sein beansprucht, ist danach allein Jesus Christus, und dieser Königsherrschaft Christi entspricht nicht die Herrschaft einer einzelnen Gemeinde über die anderen oder die eines den anderen Ämtern übergeordneten Bischofsamtes, sondern der Dienst, den die einzelnen Gemeinden einander gegenseitig schuldig sind und den sie in der Form von Synoden ihrer berufenen Diener einander zu leisten versuchen. Dem in Analogie zum staatlichen Führerprinzip konzipierten Amt des Reichsbischofs wird so die presbyterial-synodale Kirchenordnung im Sinne einer repräsentativen christlichen Demokratie entgegengehalten. Auch die zweite reformierte „Erklärung über das rechte Verständnis der reformatorischen Bekenntnisse in der Deutschen Evangelischen Kirche der Gegenwart" läßt die vier als Dienste bestimmten Ämter im Auftrag Christi begründet sein. Für ihre sachgerechte Ausübung trägt dabei nicht das Amt eines bischöflichen Führers, sondern tragen die einzelnen Gemeinden selbst die Verantwortung. Gerade auf dem Hintergrund der Diskussion über die Einführung des Führerprinzips in der deutschen evangelischen Kirche und angesichts des von den lutherischen Theologen Elert und Althaus dafür geltend gemachten Arguments, daß die Kirchenordnung nach lutherischem Bekenntnis dem wandelbaren kirchlichen Recht angehöre, insistiert nun die Barmer „Theologische Erklärung" darauf, daß die Kirche die Gestalt ihrer Ordnung nicht ihrem Belieben oder dem Wechsel der jeweils herrschenden weltanschaulichen und politischen Überzeugungen überlassen dürfe. Es ist statt nur von dem einen geordneten geistlichen Amt auch ausdrücklich in Anlehnung an die presbyterial-synodale Tradition von verschiedenen Ämtern in der Kirche die Rede. Entscheidend ist dabei nun aber, daß die presbyterial-synodale Ämterauffassung verbunden wird mit dem Gedanken des allgemeinen Priestertums. Diese Verbindung fehlt in der alten calvinistischen Ämterlehre völlig, während die Verbindung von Amt und allgemeinem Priestertum bei Luther eine entscheidende Rolle spielt. Die Barmer Erklärung betont, daß die verschiedenen Ämter in der Kirche die Ausübung des der ganzen Gemeinde anvertrauten und befohlenen Dienstes darstellen. Abseits von diesem Dienst dürfe es keine besonderen, mit Herrschaftsbefugnissen ausgestatteten Führer geben. Denn dies widerspricht dem von der Erklärung im Rückgriff auf die alten calvinistischen Kirchenordnungen festgehaltenen Tatbestand, daß die verschiedenen Ämter in der Kirche keine Hierarchie in dem Sinne darstellen, daß ein Amt die Herrschaft über die anderen ausübt. Das bedeutet aber, daß auch die Leitung der Kirche und damit die Episkopé als etwas angesehen wird, das als Dienst der ganzen Gemeinde anvertraut und befohlen ist, wenngleich dieser Dienst von bestimmten Ämtern ausgeübt wird. Zudem darf sich mit dem Amt der Episkopé nicht der Anspruch einer Herrschaft über die anderen Ämter verbinden. Es wird somit von einer Gleichursprünglichkeit der verschiedenen Ämter ausgegangen.

Die von der Barmer Erklärung festgestellte Verbindung von Amt und allgemeinem Priestertum hat nun auch Eingang gefunden in die „Tampere-Thesen" und den Beitrag „Die Kirche Jesu Christi" der Leuenberger Kirchengemeinschaft. Die These 3 der „Tampere-Thesen" befaßt sich dabei mit dem Leitungsdienst, also der Episkopé. Die Leitung der Gemeinde wird als Teil des Dienstes am Wort begriffen, der nicht nur dem ordinierten Amt, sondern der ganzen Gemeinde zukommt. Dementsprechend gilt auch für die Leitung der Gemeinde oder die Episkopé sowohl in der einzelnen Ortsgemeinde wie auch auf übergemeindlicher Ebene nicht nur dem ordinierten Amt obliegt, sondern auch durch andere Dienste geschieht. Trotz der Differenz zwischen Lutheranern und Reformierten in der Frage der Gestalt des Amtes der Episkopé sind die an der Leuenberger Konkordie beteiligten deutschen evangelischen Kirchen sich doch darin einig, daß sie erstens den Dienst der Episkopé als einen Dienst des Wortes für die Einheit der Kirche auffassen und daß zweitens in allen Kirchen auch nichtordinierte Glieder der Gemeinde an der Leitung der Kirche teilhaben. Die unterschiedlichen Strukturen der Kirchenleitung in den einzelnen lutherischen, reformierten und unierten Kirchen bilden dabei kein Hindernis für die Kirchengemeinschaft im Sinne einer Abendmahlsgemeinschaft und die gegenseitige Anerkennung von Amt und Ordination. Zudem heißt es, daß keine einzelne, historisch gewachsene Gestalt der Kirchenleitung als Vorbedingung für die Kirchengemeinschaft und die gegenseitige Anerkennung der Kirchen gelten kann. Von daher gesehen kann der Beitrag „Die Kirche Jesu Christi", der die „Tampere-Thesen" aufgreift, sowohl das historische Bischofsamt wie auch das gegliederte Amt in der presbyterial-synodalen Ordnung als Dienst an der Einheit würdigen. In dieser gegenseitigen Anerkennung der unterschiedlichen Gestalten des Leitungsamtes oder in der Gewährung von Kirchengemeinschaft unter Beibehaltung der unterschiedlichen Gestalten des Leitungsamtes besteht die grundsätzliche Differenz zu den Überlegungen, die von der evangelisch-katholischen Kommission „Lehrverurteilungen - kirchentrennend?" vorgetragen werden. Denn diese Überlegungen laufen wie bereits die „Lima-Erklärung" auf eine einseitige Favorisierung des Bischofsamtes und der Einreihung in die historische Sukzession hinaus. Grob gesprochen läßt sich daher sagen, daß in der gegenwärtigen deutschen Diskussion über Apostolizität, Episkopé und Sukzession von den Vertretern der Leuenberger Kirchengemeinschaft die von Schleiermacher über die presbyterial-synodale Tradition bis hin zu Barmen führende Traditionslinie verfolgt wird, während die Vertreter der evangelisch-katholischen Kommission an die hochkirchlich-episkopale Traditionslinie anknüpfen, die von Stahl und Löhe über Vilmar bis hin zu den lutherischen Anhängern der hochkirchlichen liturgischen Bewegung in unserem Jahrhundert führt.

Das Amt des Bischofs in liturgischen Formularen der Kirchen der EKD

Ulrich Kühn

Es ist im folgenden darüber zu berichten, welches Verständnis des Bischofsamtes in den liturgischen Ordnungen der Einführung in dieses Amt in den Kirchen der EKD sichtbar wird. Es sind dies

- die Ordnung zur Einführung eines Bischofs (Landessuperintendent, Kreisdekan, Prälat) aus Agende Bd. IV für evangelisch-lutherische Kirchen und Gemeinden (gültig für die Kirchen der Vereinigten Evangelisch-Lutherischen Kirche Deutschlands), Hannover 1987

- die Ordnung zur Einführung in übergemeindliche Dienste, aus: Einführung. Gottesdienstordnungen für Einführung, Bevollmächtigung und Vorstellung, vorgelegt von der Arnoldshainer Konferenz, Gütersloh 1974 (gültig für die Kirchen der Arnoldshainer Konferenz),

- die Ordnung zur Einführung eines Bischofs, eines Präses oder eines Kirchenpräsidenten aus: Agende für die Evangelische Kirche der Union, Band II: Die kirchlichen Handlungen. Witten 1964 (gültig für die Kirchen der Ev. Kirche der Union).

Bezug zu nehmen ist darüber hinaus auf die Erwähnung des Bischofs in Formularen zu Ordination und Einsegnung.

I

Folgende Beobachtungen sind zunächst im Blick auf das VELKD-Formular (dem neuesten unter den in der EKD geltenden Ordnungen) festzuhalten:

1. Die Einführung eines Bischofs erscheint unter den sog. "Einführungshandlungen", die spezifisch unterschieden sind von den Handlungen der Ordination (zum Pfarramt) und der Einsegnung (zum Amt des Diakons etc.). Es handelt sich also nicht um die Übertragung von geistlichen Aufgaben und Funktionen, sondern um die Zuordnung von bereits in der Ordination übertragenen Aufgaben und Funktionen zu einem konkreten Funktions- und Aufgabenbereich. Die Bischofseinführung entspricht somit z.B. der "Einführung eines Pfarrers", die den Sinn hat, den ihm in der Ordination grundsätzlich übertragenen Dienst nun einer bestimmten konkret Gemeinde zuzuordnen.

2. Das liturgische Formular zur "Einführung eines Bischofs" gilt zugleich für die Einführung eines Landessuperintendenten, eines Kreisdekans und eines Prälaten. Daneben gibt es z.B. ein Formular für die Einführung eines Pfarrers "im kirchlichen Aufsichtsdienst" (Superintendent, Dekan, Propst).

   Das weist auf die Vielfalt der Dienste übergemeindlich-regionaler Episkopé in den lutherischen Kirchen hin.

3. Allerdings ist die Einführung eines Bischofs dadurch herausgehoben, daß als einführende Amtsträger nur Bischöfe (unter ihnen der Leitende Bischof der VELKD) vorgesehen sind, während für die anderen leitenden Dienste neben dem zuständigen Landesbischof an zwei nicht-bischöfliche leitende Pfarrer gedacht ist. Man kann also von so etwas wie einer bischöflichen Sukzession sprechen.

4. Was den textlichen Inhalt des Formulars zur Einführung eines Bischofs betrifft, so sind die hier vorgesehenen Schriftlesungen identisch mit denen, die sowohl zur Einführung eines Pfarrers in eine Gemeinde, wie zur Einführung eines Pfarrers in einen besonderen kirchlichen Dienst wie zur Einführung eines Pfarrers in einen kirchlichen Aufsichtsdienst vorgesehen werden. Es handelt sich jeweils um die Stücke: Lk. 10, 16; Mt.. 18,18; Apg. 20,28; 2. Tim. 2,1-3.5. Damit soll offensichtlich unterstrichen werden, daß der geistliche Auftrag in all diesen Fällen der gleiche ist.

5. Dies zeigt sich auch bei der sog. Einführungsfrage und beim Einführungsgebet. Die Einführungsfrage greift ausdrücklich zurück auf die Ordinationsverpflichtung, die Grundlage und Inhalt des konkreten Dienstes ist, zu dem der Betreffende jetzt eingeführt wird. Dem entspricht die Formulierung des Einführungsgebetes, das als geistliche Dienstobliegenheiten nennt, "daß er/sie dein Wort recht verkündigt und deiner Gemeinde mit den Sakramenten nach deinem Willen dient". Das ist wortgleich mit den Fragen bei den anderen genannten Einführungshandlungen von Ordinierten. Daß es sich um eine spezifische, besondere Ausprägung des Dienstes im ordinierten Amt handelt, wird bei diesen Gebeten nicht erkennbar.

6. Die einzigen beiden Stellen (außer der Dienstbezeichnung als solcher und der Bestimmung über die Einführenden), die die Besonderheit des Dienstes erahnen lassen, in den nun eingeführt wird, sind folgende: (1) die Frage nach der Annahme des Einzuführenden wird "an die Mitglieder der (General)-Synode und die Pfarrer dieser Landeskirche/dieses Sprengels" gerichtet (S. 80); (2) im Unterschied zu den mit den anderen Handlungen Eingeführten gibt es beim Bischof (Landessuperintendent, Kreisdekan, Prälat) die Überreichung eines Amtskreuzes.

7. Was die spezifisch bischöflichen Funktionen betrifft, bekommt man in den liturgischen Formularen weiteren Aufschluß bei den Bestimmungen über die Ordinatoren (Ordinationsformular, Einsegnungsformular) bzw. die Einführenden. Hier findet der Bischof erst bei der Einführung eines Superintendenten bzw. Dekans oder Propstes Erwähnung, dann natürlich bei der Einführung eines anderen Bischofs. So heißt es bei der Ordination, daß sie durch den "Bischof oder einen dazu Beauftragten und zwei Pfarrer" durchgeführt wird (Ord., S. 17), bei der Einsegnung, daß sie vom "Bischof oder einen vom Bischof dazu beauftragten ordinierten Pfarrer" (S. 25) durchzuführen ist. Die Einführung eines Superintendenten wird "vom Bischof oder seinem Beauftragten gehalten". Durch diese Bestimmungen wird deutlich, daß der Bischof der eigentlich Zuständige für Ordination und Einsegnungen ist, was das Formular zur Einführung eines Bischofs selbst nicht erkennen läßt.

II

Vergleichen wir die Handlung der Einführung eines Bischofs, wie sie die Agende der VELKD vorlegt, mit den entsprechenden Ordnungen der EKU und der Arnoldshainer Konferenz, so fällt folgendes auf:

1. Wie bei der VELKD so wird auch in EKU und Arnholdshainer Konferenz die Einführung eines Bischofs als Einführung eines bereits Ordinierten deutlich unterschieden von der Handlung der Ordination oder der Einsegnung.

2. In der EKU-Agende gibt es indessen ein eigenes Formular speziell für die Einführung eines Bischofs, Präses oder Kirchenpräsidenten. In den biblischen Texten, Fragen und Gebeten dieses Formulars kommt das Spezifische des kirchenleitenden Dienstes deutlicher in den Blick als in der VELKD-Agende. So wird - bei den Lesungen - durch ausführlicheres Zitieren von Apg. 20 sowie durch eine Schriftlesung aus 2. Kor. 4 der Gesichtspunkt der Abwehr von Irrlehre als Auftrag des kirchenleitenden Dienstes zum Ausdruck gebracht. Bei der Einführungsfrage wird neben dem Bezug auf die Ordination des Betreffenden ausdrücklich auf die Ordnungen der Kirche verwiesen, nach denen er sein Amt zu führen hat. Dies sind natürlich vor allem die Rechtsordnungen, in denen sein Dienst konkret beschrieben ist. Schließlich verbindet sich das Sendungswort im EKU-Formular mit einer Art "Vorbehalt" wie es auch in den Ordinationsformularen der EKU üblich ist. In diesem Vorbehalt sagt der Einführende: " Ich weise die Gemeinden und alle, die im Dienst der Kirche stehen, an dich und dich an sie und ermahne dich, daß du der dir anvertrauten Kirche in der Furcht Gottes mit Fleiß und Treue vorstehst ...". An diesen Stellen ist erneut deutlicher als im VELKD-Formular, wo nur von Wort und Sakrament die Rede ist, auf den spezifischen Dienst des kirchenleitenden Amtes verwiesen.

3. Die liturgische Einführungsagende der Kirchen der Arnoldshainer Konferenz hat ein gemeinsames Einführungsformular für alle Einführungen von bereits Ordinierten - von der Einführung als Religionslehrer bis zur Einführung als Bischof. Hierdurch wird der bischöfliche Dienst deutlich in die anderen Dienste Ordinierter eingebunden. Es wird darüber hinaus zugleich die Einbindung in den Auftrag aller Christen unterstrichen, und zwar dadurch, daß nach diesem Arnoldshainer Formular bei den Einführenden ein nichtordinierter Assistent mitwirken soll. Bei den Lesungen wird durch Röm. 12 der bischöfliche Dienst ebenfalls in die Vielfalt der Charismen und Gaben hineingenommen, während Apg. 20 und 2. Tim. 2 nicht vorgesehen sind. Als fakultatives Stück ist 1. Petr. 5, 2 ff. angegeben, wo vom Weiden der Herde die Rede ist. In einem spezifischen Gebet für einen einzuführenden Bischof wird in dem Arnholdshainer Formular allerdings deutlich vom "Dienst der Leitung" gesprochen, der mit dieser Einführung übertragen wird.

Man wird also - im Gegenüber von EKU und Arnoldshainer Konferenz zu dem Formular der VELKD - sagen können, daß einmal die Spezifik des Dienstes, zu dem eingeführt wird, deutlicher zum Ausdruck kommt (EKU) und die Einbindung in die Gesamtverantwortung der Kirche stärker unterstrichen wird (Arnoldshain). So haben wir hier Varianten vor uns, in denen unterschiedliche Ausprägungen des evangelischen Amtsverständnisses sich auch in der Liturgie zur Einführung ins Bischofsamt niederschlagen.

III

Das theologische Konzept, das den liturgischen Formularen zur Einführung eines Bishofs in den Kirchen der EKD zugrundeliegt, ist deutlich: Der Bischof ist ein ordinierter Pfarrer mit einem konkreten Verantwortungsbereich. Sein geistlicher Auftag ist kein anderer als der, der ihm durch die Ordination zum Pfarramt übertragen wurde: die Verkündigung des Wortes Gottes und die Verwaltung der Sakramente (besonders ausdrücklich im VELKD-Formular). Das zeigt sich auch in der Gleichheit der vorgesehenen Lesungen bei den verschiedenen Einführungshandlungen und der Parallelität bei den Einführungsfragen in der lutherischen Agende, die dem insgesamt gemeinsamen Einführungsformular der Arnholdshainer Konferenz für die verschiedenen Einführungen von Ordinierten entspricht. Es gibt keinen Unterschied zwischen dem geistlichen Auftrag eines Pfarrers und dem eines Bischofs, ebenso wie anderer Geistlicher im kirchenleitenden Dienst, während es einen solchen Unterschied zwischen dem in der Ordination und dem in den Einsegnungshandlungen mitgeteilten Auftrag gibt (Teil I von Agende Bd. IV, vgl. EKU-Agende). Die liturgischen Formulare weisen kein dreigegliedertes, sondern nur ein zweigegliedertes geistliches Amt aus. Die Gleichheit des geistlichen Auftrags von Pfarrer und Bischof entspricht dabei der im Tractatus de potestate et primatu papae von Melanchthon ausgedrückten reformatorischen Überzeugung, daß diese prinzipielle Gleichheit sich vom neutestamentlichen Zeugnis her ergibt und dann auch noch einmal von Hieronymus unterstrichen wurde (Tract. 60-65).

Das Problem dieser Konzeption dürfte in der Frage liegen, ob sie der konkreten, in unseren Kirchen praktizierten und auch rechtlich umschriebenen Besonderheit und Spezifik des kirchenleitenden (bischöflichen) Dienstes zureichend gerecht zu werden vermag. Diese Besonderheit wird im VELKD-Formular eher indirekt (z. B. durch die Zeremonie mit dem Amtskreuz) angedeutet, in den beiden anderen Formularen, besonders dem der EKU, schon deutlicher benannt. Auch die lutherische Reformation kann das Spezifische des regionalen Bischofsamtes deutlicher ausformen. So ist im Bischofsartikel CA 28 gewiß grundlegend vom Dienst des Wortes und der Sakramente die Rede. Aber dieser ist dann doch deutlich spezifiziert durch Formulierungen wie: "Lehre urteilen und die Lehre, die dem Evangelium entgegen, verwerfen und die Gottlosen, deren gottlos Wesen offenbar ist, aus christlicher Gemein ausschließen, ohn menschliche Gewalt, sondern allein durch Gottes Wort. Und deshalb seind die Pfarrleut und Kirchen schuldig, den Bischöfen gehorsam zu sein ..." (CA 28, 21 f.). Dies ist die Beschreibung dessen, was Bischöfe nach göttlicher Anordnung an Aufgaben haben. Von diesen Aufgaben ist zumindest im VELKD-Formular zur Bischofs-einführung direkt nichts zu lesen. Hier deutet sich die Schwäche einer evangeli-schen Theologie des Bischofsamtes an.

Natürlich steht hinter dem allem die Kontroverse um das, was in diesem Zusam-menhang göttliches und was menschliches Recht ist. Ganz gewiß ist der Unter-schied zwischen Pfarrern und Bischöfen - im heutigen Sinn - ein geschichtlich gewordener. Aber auch die Zuordnung des Auftrags der öffentlichen Wortverkün-digung zusammen mit dem der Sakramentsverwaltung zum ordinierten Amt ist ja das Ergebnis einer nach neutestamentlichen geschichtlichen Entwicklung. Wieso gilt diese Zuordnung nach CA 5 und CA 14 als grundlegendes ius divinum, die weitere Ausdifferenzierung jedoch nicht? Die Diskussion um diese Probleme hat zu der Frage geführt, ob die überkommene Unterscheidung zwischen ius divinum und ius humanum ausreichend ist. Muß nicht auch die Entwicklung zu regionalen kirchenleitenden Ämtern mit ihren besonderen geistlichen Aufträgen als eine Entwicklung angesehen werden, bei der der Geist Gottes seine Hand im Spiel gehabt hat? Entspricht es nicht dem geistlichen Wesen der Kirche, daß es neben dem geistlichen Auftrag am Ort einen geistlichen Auftrag auf regionaler Ebene gibt, dem spezifische geistliche Funktionen zukommen: die besondere Sorge für die apostolische Wahrheit und für die gesamtkirchliche Einheit der Kirche und damit verbunden die Verantwortung für den Vollzug von Ordinationen?

Als Schlußfolgerung ergäbe sich: die evangelischen Kirchen hätten den Bezug ihrer liturgischen Formulare und deren Einleitung zu dem besonderen geistlichen Auftrag zu überprüfen, der die Ämter der regionalen Episkope und insbesondere das Bischofsamt charakterisiert. Die Einordnung der liturgischen Handlung der Übertragung des Bischofsamtes unter die "einführenden Handlungen" stellt sich jedenfalls als ein offenes Problem dar. Theologisch wäre zu fragen, ob zu der Unterscheidung des geistlichen Auftrags aus der Ordination einerseits, aus der Einsegnung andererseits, nicht auch eine solche zwischen dem geistlichen Auftrag aus der Ordination auf Ortsebene und demjenigen auf der Ebene regionaler Episkopé zu treten hätte. Dies wäre dann aber de facto - horribile dictu? - ein Plädoyer, das in die Nähe der ökumenischen Konvergenz im Blick auf ein dreigegliedertes Amt führt. Aber sollten sich die evangelischen Kirchen dieser Konvergenz verschließen?

Die Ausübung und das Verständnis der Episkope im Recht der EKD und ihrer Gliedkirchen

Eilert Herms, Tübingen

1. Grundlage und Wesen des Rechts der EKD und ihrer Gliedkirchen

Über die Grundlage und das Wesen des Rechts der EKD und ihrer Gliedkirchen geben die Grundordnung der EKD sowie die Grundordnungen ihrer Gliedkirchen selbst Auskunft. Diesen Texten zufolge gilt:

1.1.

Die erfahrbare soziale Gestalt der evangelischen Kirchen in Deutschland und die erfahrbare soziale Gestalt ihrer Gemeinschaft in der Evangelischen Kirche in Deutschland sind durch die Grundordnungen der Kirchen und durch die Grundordnung der EKD rechtsförmig verfaßt. Das *Fundament (die Grundlage)* dieser rechtsförmig verfaßten Sozialgebilde ist "das Evangelium von Jesus Christus, wie es uns in der Heiligen Schrift Alten und Neuen Testaments *gegeben*" und in den altkirchlichen Bekenntnissen zusammengefaßt ist[1].

"Für das *Verständnis* der Heiligen Schrift wie auch der altkirchlichen Bekenntnisse sind in den lutherischen, reformierten und unierten Gliedkirchen und Gemeinden die für sie geltenden Bekenntnisse der Reformation maßgebend"[2]. Diese Bekenntnisse sind *Bezeugungen*[3] des in der Reformation gewonnenen Verständnisses des in der Schrift gegebenen Evangeliums. Und zwar Bezeugungen im Medium reflektierter theologischer Lehre. Die Bekenntnisse aus dem Reformationsjahrhundert dienen nicht dem gottesdienstlichen Gebrauch, sondern sind öffentliche Darlegungen desjenigen - im Medium von theologischer Lehre artikulierten - expliziten Konsenses über das Verständnis des Evangeliums, der für alle Entscheidungen maßgeblich ist, die öffentlich im Namen der jeweiligen Kirche getroffen werden.

So unterscheiden die Grundordnungstexte selbst zwischen dem im kanonischen Glaubenszeugnis der heiligen Schrift *gegebenen* Evangelium (a) und seinem *Verständnis* (b) sowie dessen *Bezeugung* in Gestalten theologischer Lehre (c). Diese Unterscheidung trennt die drei Instanzen nicht voneinander und verselbständigt sie nicht gegeneinander. Sie macht nur auf den einheitlichen Lebensprozeß aufmerksam, in dem alle drei Instanzen eine zwar wesentliche, aber je verschiedene Rolle spielen. Diese Unterscheidung der Instanzen und ihr Zusam-

325

menspiel kann natürlich selbst nur im Medium reflektierter Lehre erfaßt werden. Das ändert jedoch nichts daran, daß sich die kirchliche Lehre durch die Erfassung der Unterschiedenheit dieser Instanzen und ihres Zusammenspiels nur selbst an den weiteren Lebenszusammenhang erinnert, von dem sie abhängig bleibt und innerhalb dessen sie allererst ihre spezifische Funktion gewinnt und ausübt. Dieser tragende und umfassende Zusammenhang ist das geistgewirkte Leben der communio sanctorum, dessen schöpferischer und tragender Grund das gegebene Evangelium als Kraft Gottes (Röm 1,16) ist und bleibt. In ihm besitzt die kirchliche Lehre die oben angedeutete nachgeordnete, der Dynamik des geistlichen Lebens der Glaubensgemeinschaft und damit dem geschichtlichen Wandel unterworfene, aber dennoch unverzichtbare (wesentliche) Funktion: Sie fixiert und legt öffentlich dar denjenigen Konsens, der in der Besinnung auf und im Gespräch über das vom Evangelium als Kraft Gottes selbst geschaffene Verständnis des Evangeliums gewonnen wurde und als solcher nun maßgeblich ist für alle Entscheidungen, die öffentlich im Namen der jeweiligen Kirche getroffen werden.

Die erste dieser Entscheidung ist diejenige, die für die erfahrbare Gestalt der Kirche als Sozialgebilde grundlegend ist und sie gesamthaft[4] umfaßt: die Entscheidung über die rechtsförmige Verfassung (Grundordnung) jeder einzelnen Kirche (ecclesia particularis) und über die rechtsförmige Ausgestaltung (Ordnung) ihrer jeweils anerkannten und praktizierten Gemeinschaft mit anderen Kirchen. Solch eine im Medium von Lehre anerkannte und demgemäß ordentlich praktizierte Kirchengemeinschaft ist zwar nicht ipso facto schon die ecclesia universalis, d.h. die als Gemeinschaft *aller* Kirchen verfaßte Einheit der Christenheit auf Erden, sondern kann geringeren Umfang haben (z. B.: den Umfang der Gemeinschaft der evangelischen Kirchen in Deutschland in der EKD oder die Gemeinschaft europäischer Reformationskirchen in der Leuenberger Kirchengemeinschaft etc.), sie steht aber als solche stets im Horizont der faktischen - durch das Evangelium als Kraft Gottes selbst geschaffenen - Einheit der Christenheit auf Erden, die bestenfalls ihre rechtsförmige Sozialgestalt in einer lehrmäßig erklärten und ordentlich praktizierten universalen Gemeinschaft aller christlichen Kirchen besitzt und als solche die ecclesia universalis ist[5].

Insofern gilt also: Fundament der geschichtlichen *Existenz* der communio sanctorum als erfahrbares Sozialgebilde - an jedem Ort und weltweit - ist das gegebene Evangelium, indem es als Kraft Gottes an den Herzen von Menschen wirksam wird. Aber Fundament - nämlich Basis und normativer Horizont - für das *Recht* der Kirche, durch das sie zu rechtsförmiger Ordnung und zur Gestalt eines erfahrbaren Sozialgebildes gelangt, ist der in einer Kirche bzw. in Kirchen und ggf. zwischen Ihnen jeweils durch Gespräch erreichte und jeweils im Medium von Lehre öffentlich fixierte Konsens über das durch das Evangelium selbst geschaffene Verständnis des Evangeliums[6].

Also: *Grundlage für die Existenz* der Kirche - in der innergeschichtlichen Vielzahl von Partikularkirchen *und* in deren ursprünglicher Verbundenheit in der universalen Einheit der Christenheit auf Erden (Universalkirche) - ist das Evangelium und nicht ein Lehrkonsens. Aber *Grundlage für das kirchliche Recht* als Medium der Sozialgestalt von Kirche ist jeweils ein expliziter Lehrkonsens.

Diesen Lehrkonsens schafft zwar das kirchliche Recht nicht, aber es benennt ihn und erklärt seine Gültigkeit; damit benennt es jeweils seine eigene normative Grundlage und erklärt zugleich deren rechtsmäßige Gültigkeit als Norm allen kirchlichen Rechts.

Der innergeschichtlichen Wandelbarkeit, Vorläufigkeit und Partikularität von Lehrkonsensen entspricht die innergeschichtliche Wandelbarkeit, Vorläufigkeit und Partikularität der rechtsförmigen Ordnung von Kirche als Sozialgebilde. Darin drückt sich die fundamentale Angewiesenheit kirchlichen Rechts auf explizite kirchliche Lehre aus.

Angewendet auf die Existenz und die rechtsförmige Ausgestaltung von *Kirchengemeinschaft* heißt das: Auch diese hat den Grund ihrer Realität nicht in einem expliziten Lehrkonsens, sondern im Evangelium als Kraft Gottes selbst, aber die rechtsförmige Erklärung und Ausgestaltung von Kirchengemeinschaft ist nur auf dem Boden, im Horizont und nach Maßgabe eines dafür ausreichenden expliziten Lehrkonsenses möglich[7].

1.2.

Mit dem Fundament der kirchlichen Rechtsordnung ist auch ihr *Wesen* klar: Die Rechtsordnung der Kirchen ist die elementare und umfassende praktische Umsetzung dessen, was der in ihnen gültige Lehrkonsens jeweils an Einsichten über die erfahrbare Gestalt der communio sanctorum als innergeschichtliches Sozialgebilde enthält.

Es liegt in der Natur der Sache, daß diese lehrmäßig fixierten Einsichten in die Anforderungen, die an die als Sozialgebilde erfahrbare Gestalt der Kirche zu stellen sind, ihrerseits jeweils begründet sind im weiteren Horizont der - ebenfalls in der kirchlichen Lehre fiixierten - Einsichten nicht nur über die Gestalt er Kirche, sondern zuvor schon über ihr Wesen, über ihre Bestimmung und über ihren Ursprung und damit zuerst und grundlegend in den Einsichten über die Offenbarung der Gnade Gottes, ihr Wirken und ihr Wesen[8].

Aus - wiederum in der Lehre zur Sprache kommenden - Einsichten des Glaubens selbst in die Bedingungen seiner irdischen Existenz ergibt sich, daß als Medium für die Ordnung der Kirchen als erfahrbarer Sozialgebilde nur das Mittel des Rechts in Betracht kommt. Wobei weiterhin daran festzuhalten ist - aus Gründen der in der Versöhnungslehre festgehaltenen Schöpfungslehre -, daß das kirchliche Recht mit der Rechtsordnung der Gesamtgesellschaft formal kompatibel sein muß, unbeschadet seiner Selbständigkeit in deren Rahmen.

Schon die Lehre der Kirchen ist geschichtlich veränderbar, bedarf ständig der Kritik und Verbesserung. Dasselbe gilt erst recht von der Ausgestaltung der Kirchen als Sozialgebilde durch eine Rechtsordnung, die durch den einschlägigen Einsichten kirchlicher Lehre begründet und normiert ist. Die kirchliche Rechtsordnung versucht in allen ihren Teilen diejenigen prinzipiellen, durch den Ursprung und Auftrag der Kirche selbst gesetzten, Aufgaben für die Gestaltung der Kirchen als Sozialgebilde zu lösen, welche durch die für sie grundlegende und maßgebliche Gestalt kirchlicher Lehre gestellt sind, und zwar so, daß dabei den jeweiligen sozialen Herausforderungen, die in der Geschichte wechseln, Rechnung getragen wird.

Die kirchliche Lehre erfaßt alle diese wesentlichen Ordnungsaufgaben als solche, die im Willen Gottes, wie er dem Glauben offenbar ist, selbst enthalten sind. Die Glaubenden sind daher durch Gott selbst dazu verpflichtet, diese Aufgaben zu lösen. Das ändert aber nichts daran, daß die Ausführung jeder dieser heiligen Pflichten und daher auch jede erreichte Lösung der dem Glauben gestellten Ordnungsaufgaben, also jede wirkliche Gestalt kirchlicher Ordnung, menschliches Werk ist - im besten Fall das im Glaubensgehorsam vollbrachte gute Werk von Menschen.

Allen wesentlichen Momenten kirchlicher Ordnung liegt also ein göttliches Mandat zugrunde. Aber kein Element einer wirklich bestehenden kirchlichen Rechtsordnung ist als solches direkt durch Gott selbst gesetzt. Auch der Christus Jesus hat den Seinen Aufgaben der Ordnung ihres Gemeinschaftslebens gestellt, aber nicht diese Ordnung selbst gegeben.

2. Die drei wesentlichen Regelungsgegenstände des kirchlichen Rechts

Aus der Grundlage und dem Wesen des kirchlichen Rechts ergibt sich, daß es als Medium der Ausgestaltung der Glaubensgemeinschaft als erfahrbares Sozialgebilde drei Regelungsbereiche umfaßt:

- Die Ordnung der Lehre,

- die Ordnung des Gottesdienstes und

- die Organisationsordnung der Kirche.

Man kann zeigen, daß diese drei Bereiche rechtsförmiger Ordnung in der genannten Reihenfolge einen für die erfahrbare Sozialgestalt der Kirche konstitutiven

Zusammenhang bilden, in dem kein Glied verzichtbar ist. Die Grundordnung jeder selbständigen Kirche ordnet für jeden dieser drei Bereiche das Grundsätzliche:

Durch Präambel und/oder Grundartikel und die Ausführungen über das Ordinationsversprechen ist sie selbst das Grunddokument der kirchlichen Lehrordnung, die dann in der Lehrbeanstandungsordnung der einzelnen Kirche[9] jeweils mehr im Detail ausgeführt ist.

Durch die Aussagen über die Ortsgemeinde ist sie jeweils selbst das Grunddokument der Gottesdienstordnung, die dann jeweils in der Agende der Kirchen im Detail ausgeführt wird.

In ihren Bestimmungen über die je spezifischen Aufgaben und das Zusammenwirken der Organe der jeweiligen Kirche ist sie das Grunddokument ihrer Organisationsordnung, die dann durch das in ihr geregelte Gesetzgebungsverfahren der Kirche im Detail ausgeführt wird.

Die Grundordnung der EKD ist nicht die Grundordnung *einer* selbständigen Kirche, sondern die Grundordnung einer *Gemeinschaft* von selbständigen Kirchen. Deshalb zeigt sie formale Unterschiede zu den Grundordnungen der einzelnen selbständigen Kirchen, Unterschiede, die in der Natur der Sache liegen:

Sie enthält keine eigene Lehrordnung, sondern wiederholt nur die Lehrordnungen der einzelnen Kirchen als diejenigen, die für deren gesamtes öffentliches Leben allein entscheidend sind (GO EKD Art. 1 Abs. 1 S. 2: die EKD "achtet die Bekenntnisgrundlagen der Gliedkirchen und Gemeinden und setzt voraus, daß sie ihr Bekenntnis in Lehre, Leben und Ordnung der Kirche wirksam werden lassen."; vgl. auch Art 2 Abs 2 Halbsatz 1: "Die gesamtkirchliche Rechtssetzung darf das Bekenntnis der Gliedkirchen nicht verletzen"). Das schließt die Anerkennung ein, daß darin - also in diesen eigenen Lehrordnungen der einzelnen Kirchen - auch die lehrmäßigen Gründe liegen, die die einzelnen Kirchen jeweils zu ihrer Teilhabe an der rechtlich geordneten Gemeinschaft der einzelnen Kirchen in der EKD ermächtigen und verpflichten.

Die Grundordnung der EKD enthält auch keine Ansätze zu einer eigenen Gottesdienstordnung.

Die Grundordnung der EKD enthält nur die Organisationsordnung - die rechtliche Bestimmung der Aufgaben und des Zusammenspiels der Organe - der rechtlich geordneten Gemeinschaft von selbständigen Kirchen, die sie ist.

3. Die Lehrgrundlagen für das Recht der evangelischen Kirchen in Deutschland und für das Recht der Evangelischen Kirche in Deutschland

Die Texte der Grundordnungen der evangelischen Kirchen in Deutschland und der Grundordnung der Evangelischen Kirche in Deutschland geben auch über die Gestalten kirchlicher Lehre Auskunft, die für sie jeweils grundlegend und maßgeblich sind.

3.1.

Das sind - wie in der Grundordnung der EKD zutreffend festgehalten wird (Art 1 Abs 1 S. 2) - für die einzelnen Kirchen diejenigen Lehrbekenntnisse aus der Reformationszeit oder auch der Zeit des Kirchenkampfes unseres Jh.s (Barmen), die jeweils in der Präambel oder im Grundartikel der Grundordnung der einzelnen Kirche als Formulierung des maßgeblichen Lehrkonsenses über das Verständnis des Evangeliums explizit genannt sind.

3.2.

Darüber hinaus kann die GO der EKD in ihrer jüngsten Fassung von 1991 aber auch dasjenige Element der Lehrordnung jeder an der Gemeinschaft der EKD Teil habenden einzelnen Kirche explizit benennen, das jede dieser Kirchen zur Gemeinschaft mit allen anderen im Rahmen der EKD ermächtigt und verpflichtet:

Seit 1948 (Gründung der EKD) war unterstellt worden, *daß* in den durch die einzelnen Kirchenordnungen als gültig fixierten Lehrkonsensen auch die lehrmäßigen Gründe *de facto* enthalten sind, die es jeder einzelnen Kirche zur Pflicht machen, die rechtlich geordnete Gemeinschaft mit anderen Kirchen in der EKD zu erklären und zu praktizieren. Diese Gründe blieben jedoch unausgesprochen.

Inzwischen aber hat der Prozeß ökumenischer Reflexion und Verständigung zur Besinnung auf diesen Grund der formellen wechselseitigen Erklärung und Praktizierung von Kirchengemeinschaft geführt und dazu, diesen auf Seiten aller beteiligten Kirchen jeweils in ihren eigenen Lehrgrundlagen liegenden Grund explizit zu benennen und in aller Form öffentlich darzustellen. Dieser Grund ist das in den jeweils eigenen rechtsgültigen Lehrkonsensen jeder beteiligten Kirchen anzutreffende "gemeinsame Verständnis des Evangeliums" als der den Glauben, die Glaubensgemeinschaft und die Gemeinschaft der Kirchen schaffenden Kraft Gottes selbst, wie es in der Leuenberger Konkordie von 1973 dargelegt wurde als notwendiger und hinreichender Grund für die Erklärung und Praktizierung von Kirchengemeinschaft, einschließlich der wechselseitigen Anerkennung der Ämter.

Die Leuenberger Konkordie ist von jeder ihrer Unterzeichnerkirchen aufgrund und in Treue zu dem jeweils in ihr gültigen Lehrbekenntnis unterzeichnet worden. Sie stellt also keine Veränderung des Lehrbekenntnisses der Unterzeichnerkirchen dar[10], sondern jede Unterzeichnerkirche zieht durch Beitritt nur eine Konsequenz aus ihrem schon geltenden Lehrbekenntnis im Blick auf das schon geltende Lehrbekenntnis der Partnerkirchen: die Anerkennung, daß das eigene Verständnis des Evangeliums als Kraft Gottes identisch ist mit dem der mitunterzeichnenden Partnerkirchen[11]. Durch Unterzeichnung der Konkordie nimmt also jede Unterzeichnerkirche auf dem Boden ihres geltenden Lehrbekenntnisses eine Explikation ihres Bekenntnisses hinsichtlich desjenigen fundamentalen Momentes vor, das ihr die formelle Erklärung und Praktizierung von Kirchengemeinschaft mit den anderen Kirchen möglich und zur Pflicht macht: hinsichtlich des für das lehrmäßige Verständnis aller einzelnen Momente der Glaubensgewißheit grundlegenden lehrmäßigen Verständnisses des Evangeliums als der den Glauben, die Gemeinschaft der Glaubenden und die Gemeinschaft der Kirchen schaffenden Kraft Gottes selbst.

Als rechtmäßig vollzogener und rechtsgültiger Akt nimmt die Unterzeichnung der Leuenberger Konkordie diesen Text in die Lehrordnung jeder Unterzeichnerkirche auf.

Folglich besitzen auch die Explikationen von wesentlichen Stücken des Inhalts des gemeinsamen Evangeliumsverständnisses, die in Lehrgesprächen erreicht und von der Vollversammlung der Leuenberger Gemeinschaft angenommen worden sind, für die Unterzeichnerkirchen und ihre Lehrordnung großes Gewicht. Denn sie zu verstehen als die Entdeckung und Formulierung von Gemeinsamkeiten im lehrmäßigen Verständnis einzelner Implikationen des grundlegenden Evangeliumsverständnisses Das gilt exemplarisch von der Entfaltung des im gemeinsamen Evangeliumsverständnis der Konkordie steckenden Kirchenverständnisses, wie es detailliert ausgesprochen worden ist in dem Dokument "Die Kirche Jesu Christi. Der reformatorische Beitrag zum ökumenischen Dialog über die kirchliche Einheit"[12], das sich die Vollversammlung der Leuenberger Gemeinschaft am 9. Mai 1994 zu eigen gemacht hat.

Alle in der Gemeinschaft der EKD verbundenen selbständigen Kirchen haben die LK unterzeichnet. Der in ihr ausgesprochene, im Lehrbekenntnis jeder Unterzeichnerkirche liegende Grund für die Erklärung und Praktizierung von Kirchengemeinschaft gilt also auch als Grund für die Gemeinschaft der Kirchen in der EKD. Deshalb hält die neueste Fassung der Grundordnung der EKD fest, daß der ursprünglich nur unterstellte Grund für die Gemeinschaft der Kirchen in der EKD im Lehrbekenntnis jeder einzelnen Kirche nun in der LK explizit gemacht worden ist. Sie fixiert die Gemeinschaft der EKD selbst als Kirchengemeinschaft im Sinne der LK. GO EKD Art. 1 Abs. 2 sagt: "Zwischen den Gliedkirchen besteht Kirchengemenschaft im Sinne der Konkordie reformatorischer Kirchen in Europa (Leuenberger Konkordie). Die Evangelische Kirche in Deutschland fördert darum das Zusammenwachsen ihrer Gliedkirchen in der Gemeinsamkeit des christlichen Zeugnisses und Dienstes gemäß dem Auftrag des Herrn Jesus Christus".

Das heißt nicht, die LK ist die Lehrgrundlage der EKD, sondern nur, die LK spricht den lehrmäßigen Grund aus, den alle Gliedkirchen dafür haben, die Kirchengemeinschaft in der EKD zu erklären, zu ordnen und ordnungsgemäß zu praktizieren, und den Charakter dieser Gemeinschaft.

Damit spricht die GO der EKD auch den lehrmässigen Grund aus, den alle selbständigen Gliedkirchen dafür haben, u. U. Organe der EKD mit der Wahrnehmung ökumenischer Kontakte und dem Treffen ökumenischer Vereinbarungen zu beauftragen, und gleichzeitig auch das Kriterium sowohl für das in solchen Fällen formal zu beobachtende Verfahren[13] als auch für die Akzeptabilität des Inhalts derartiger Vereinbarungen[14].

4. Die Episkope im Recht der einzelnen Kirchen

Den Grundordnungen aller Kirchen liegt der Konsens zugrunde, daß das Amt der Evangeliumsverkündigung und Sakramentsverwaltung als eine Implikation des Gegenübers von Wort und Glaube, Wort und Glaubensgemeinschaft, der Glaubensgemeinschaft von Christus selbst gegeben und zur Ordnung aufgegeben ist. Ferner liegt allen der Lehrkonsens zugrunde, daß die Zuständigkeit für die ursprungs und auftragsgemäße Ordnung des Lebens der Glaubensgemeinschaft, inklusive der ursprungs- und auftragsgemäßen Ordnung des Amtes der Evangeliumsverkündigung und Sakramentsverwaltung, aber darüber hinaus der Ordnung in allen wesentlichen Bereichen des Lebens der Glaubensgemeinschaft als eines erfahrbaren Sozialgebildes in der Geschichte bei der örtlichen Glaubensgemeinschaft[15] als ganzer liegt. Und schließlich liegt allen der Konsens zugrunde, daß für die Ordnung der Kirche als erfahrbares Sozialgebilde insgesamt die Ordnung von Funktionen der Episkope im Sinne der Leitung unabdingbar ist, und zwar der Leitung mit den zwei wesentlichen Funktionen einer Aufsicht, die der Wahrung der bestehenden verpflichtenden Ordnung dient, und einer Entscheidungsgewalt, die der auftragsgemäßen Fortentwicklung, Korrektur und Verbesserung der kirchlichen Ordnung angesichts neuer geschichtlicher Herausforderungen dient.

Dem zweiten dieser Lehrkonsense tragen die Grundordnungen dadurch Rechnung, daß sie nach dem Versagen der reformunwilligen Bischöfe im 16. Jh. und nach dem Ausfall des als Notbehelf eingetretenen Kirchenregiments durch

den Landesfürsten die Synoden als Repräsentanten der regionalen Gesamt-
gemeinde für die Selbstordnung des Lebens der Glaubensgemeinschaft für
zuständig erklären[16]. Das geschah nicht ohne Rückenwind durch die demokratischen Bewegungen des 19. und 20. Jh.s, hat aber seinen sachlichen Grund in
Einsichten reformatorischer Theologie in das Kirchenverständnis der Heiligen
Schrift. Die Gemeinde lebt zwar aus dem Gegenüber zum Wort, kann und muß
aber notfalls auch kraft dieses ihres Gegenübers zum Wort Handlungen eines
ordinierten Dieners des Wortes effektiv korrigieren. Was nicht bedeutet, daß sie
überhaupt ohne den Dienst ordinierter Diener am Wort im Gegenüber zum Wort
verbleiben könnte.

Dem ersten Konsens wird in allen Grundordnungen dadurch Rechnung getragen,
daß sie ordnen:

- die Aufgaben und Pflichten des Pfarramts

- die Übertragung des Pfarramts an einzelne Personen durch Ordination

- die Voraussetzungen für die Ordination (hier sind über die Grundordnungen
  hinaus die Ausbildungsordnungen der einzelnen Kirchen einschlägig).

Dem dritten Konsens wird in allen Grundordnungen dadurch Rechnung getragen,
daß die Leitung der einzelnen Kirchen durch ein in den Ordnungen jeweils
geregeltes Zusammenspiel zwischen mehreren Leitungsorganen erfolgt - jedenfalls Synode, Synodalausschuß, Kirchenamt und einem von zum Dienst am Wort
ordinierten Personen ausgeübten geistlichen Aufsichtsamt. Viele
Grundordnungen kennen auch die besondere Instanz der "Kirchenleitung" mit
oberster Entscheidungsbefugnis zwischen den Sitzungen der Synode[17], in deren
Auftrag und ihr rechenschaftspflichtig. In der Mehrzahl der Fälle ist das
geistliche Aufsichtsamt in diese Instanz der Kirchenleitung eingebunden, häufig
in regelmäßiger Vorsitzposition[18]. Mit all dem stellen die Grundordnungen sicher,
daß das Gegenüber von Wort und Glaubensgemeinschaft nicht nur auf der Ebene
der einzelnen Gemeinden, sondern auch auf der Ebene der Leitung der selbständigen Kirchen institutionell zur Geltung kommt.

Dem entspricht auch in allen Kirchenordnungen die Organisation und inhaltliche
Aufgabenbestimmung dieses von ordinierten Personen innegehabten geistlichen
Aufsichtsamtes, der wir uns jetzt zuwenden:

Seine Ausübung erfolgt überwiegend kollegial. Andere Regelungen sind meist
durch die Kleinheit der Kirche begründet[19]. Die kollegiale Ausübung ist
regelmäßig mit regionalen Zuständigkeiten verbunden. Dabei bleibt es entweder
beim einfachen Nebeneinander[20], oder es kommt zu einer Ebenenhierarchie
zwischen regional begrenzten Aufsichtsämtern, die nebeneinanderstehen, und

einem (oder mehreren) überregionalen gesamtkirchlichen Aufsichtsamt[21]. Beides kann auch gleichzeitig auftreten[22].

Aufgaben im Bereich der Gesetzgebung und Verwaltung werden diesem Aufsichtsamt in allen Grundordnungen so gut wie keine zugeschrieben. Alle Grundordnungen weisen ihm aber das Wachen über der Einhaltung der Lehrordnung der Kirche und über die dem Lehrbekenntnis entsprechende Gestalt der Gottesdienste zu. Damit ist insbesondere verbunden die Pflicht der Ordination von Pfarrerinnen und Pfarrern (u.U. auch das Recht und die Pflicht zur Letztentscheidung über die Eignung von Kandidaten[23]), das Recht der Predigt auf allen Kanzeln sowie das Recht zu Verlautbarungen oder Hirtenbriefen an die gesamtkirchliche Öffentlichkeit. Nun sind aber alle Fragen der kirchlichen Ordnung, also auch alle Fragen der kirchlichen Rechtssetzung und der kirchlichen Verwaltung, letztlich zu entscheiden an Kriterien, die in der kirchlichen Lehre enthalten sind. Deshalb können Verlautbarungen der Inhaber des geistlichen Aufsichtsamtes zur kirchlichen Lehre auch die in dieser liegenden Prinzipien für anstehende Gesetzgebungsakte oder sogar Verwaltungsentscheidungen (etwa: Investitions- oder Sparprogramme) zum Inhalt haben. Dadurch können sie diese Prozesse, die in Synode und kirchlicher Verwaltung zu entscheiden sind, und letztlich sogar den gesamten Prozeß der reformatio ecclesiae continua tiefgreifend mitbeeinflussen[24]. Indem die Grundordnungen das Aufsichtsamt, das durch Ordinierte wahrzunehmen ist, auf die Lehrordnung konzentrieren, beziehen sie es *dadurch* auf das gesamte Leben der Kirche. Sie gestalten es als ein Amt der umfassenden *Leitung von Kirche durch Lehre*, nämlich durch eine explicatio und applicatio doctrinae ecclesiae, die deren unwandelbare Sachintention jeweils auf die Nöte der Zeit bezieht.

Freilich ist diese Zuständigkeit auf das Wachen über der *je schon geltenden* Lehre konzentriert. Eingriffe in die Lehrordnung der Kirche oder auch in ihre Gottesdienstordnung durch Rezeption neuer Lehrtexte oder Verfügung von gottesdienstlichen Ordnungen ermöglichen die Grundordnungen den Inhabern des geistlichen Aufsichtsamts nicht. Diese Entscheidungen liegen vielmehr wieder bei der Synode. Auch sie sind zwar durch die ordinierten "Episkopen" zu überwachen, können auch u. U. - zumindest zeitweilig - durch episkopale Maßnahmen verhindert werden. Aber die Möglichkeit einer dauernden Verhinderung oder Durchsetzung von Entscheidungen über die Lehr- und Gottesdienstordnung gegen den Willen der Synode räumen die Grundordnungen der Kirchen den Inhabern des geistlichen Aufsichtsamtes nicht ein.

Den am weitesten gehenden Einfluß auf die gesamte Leitung der Kirche räumen diejenigen Grundordnungen den ordinierten Inhabern des geistlichen Aufsichtsamtes ein, die ihnen gleichzeitig den Vorsitz in der Synode, im Kirchenamt und in der Kirchenleitung einräumen. Das sind insbesondere die Grundordnungen der EKiR und der EKiW. Die meisten Grundordnungen - insbesondere die lutherischen - wahren aber das Gegenüber von Synode und geistlichem Aufsichtsamt, indem sie dessen Inhaber nicht einmal die Mitgliedschaft in der Synode zugestehen.

Soweit die Schwerpunkte von Aufgaben und Zuständigkeiten des geistlichen Aufsichtsamtes im Recht der selbständigen Kirchen.

Wie steht es nun mit der rechtlichen Regelung von Aufsicht im Recht von kirchlichen Zusammenschlüssen und Gemeinschaften von Kirchen? Hier sind zunächst die konfessionsspezifischen Zusammenschlüsse von Kirchen zu betrachten, dann die Gemeinschaft aller deutschen evangelischen Kirchen in der EKD.

5. Die Episkope im Recht der VELKD und im Recht der EKU

5.1.

Die VELKD versteht sich selbst als eine Kirche, nämlich als durch den Zusammenschluß von konfessionsidentischen lutherischen Kirchen zustande gekommene "*Vereinigte* Evangelisch-Lutherische Kirche Deutschlands". Dementsprechend sieht ihre Verfassung auch eine gewisse Einschränkung der Rezeptionsautonomie ihrer Gliedkirchen vor, die nur durch Austritt wiederhergestellt werden könnte. Und dementsprechend hat in ihr auch eine eigene Ebene von Aufgaben und Zuständigkeiten des geistlichen Aufsichtsamtes rechtliche Gestalt gewonnen, vor allem im Zusammenspiel der Leitungsinstanzen der Vereinigten Kirche; und - teils dadurch vermittelt, teils direkt - auch gegenüber den Gliedkirchen.

Im Zusammenspiel der Leitungsinstanzen der Vereinigten Kirche besitzt das geistliche Aufsichtsamt dadurch eine gegenüber den Verhältnissen in allen Gliedkirchen stärkere Funktion, als die Synode ihre Beschlüsse nur in Übereinstimmung mit der Bischofskonferenz in Geltung setzen kann. Sofern Gesetze der Vereinigten Kirche per se auch für die Gliedkirchen gelten, kommt dadurch der in der Rechtssetzung der Vereinigten Kirche gesteigerte Einfluß des geistlichen Aufsichtsamts indirekt auch gegenüber den Gliedkirchen zur Geltung.

Direkt kommt das geistliche Aufsichtsamt der Vereinigten Kirche gegenüber den Gliedkirchen zur Geltung durch die in der Verfassung der VELKD geregelten Befugnisse der Bischofskonferenz und des leitenden Bischofs. Beide haben das Recht, sich durch Verlautbarungen bzw. Hirtenbriefe an die Gesamtöffentlichkeit der Vereinigten Kirche zu richten. Der leitende Bischof hat Predigtrecht auf jeder Kanzel der Vereinigten Kirche. Die Vereinigte Kirche besitzt ein gemeinsames Pfarrerrecht, ebenso eine gemeinsame Lehrbeanstandungsordnung (auch das gesamte gottesdienstliche Handeln der Pfarrer betreffend). Diese sieht zwar für den leitenden Bischof - kraft seines Vorsitzes in der Kirchenleitung und Bischofskonferenz - eine Schlüsselrolle für die Einleitung und Durchführung des Verfahrens vor, macht aber andererseits wieder deutlich, daß der Schwerpunkt der Zuständigkeiten des geistlichen Aufsichtsamts auf dem Wachen über der *schon geltenden* Lehre liegt, einsame Entscheidungen sieht das Recht auch nicht über die Lehre und das gottesdienstliche Handeln einzelner Pfarrerinnen und Pfarrer vor.

Dieser relativ starke Ausbau eines gemeinsam wahrgenommenen Aufsichtsamts auf der Ebene der Vereinigten Kirche hat seinen Grund darin, daß es überhaupt zu den wesentlichen Aufgaben der Vereinigten Kirche gehört "für die Erhaltung und Vertiefung der lutherischen Lehre und Sakramentsverwaltung durch Pflege lutherischer Theologie und durch Beratung der Gliedkirchen in Fragen der lutherischen Lehre, des Gottesdienstes und des Gemeindelebens Sorge zu tragen und die Heranbildung eines bekenntnisgebundenen Pfarrerstandes zu fördern" (Verf VELKD Art 7 Abs. 2).

5.2.

Nach der Verselbständigung der Kirchenprovinzen der "Evangelischen Kirche der altpreußischen Union" zu Kirchen mit voller Selbstordnungskompetenz lebt die Evangelische Kirche der altpreußischen Union unter dem Namen "Evangelische Kirche der Union" seit 1951 nicht mehr als *eine Kirche*, sondern als "*Gemeinschaft*" (Ordnung der EKU Art.1 Abs. 1) ihrer Gliedkirchen (eben der ehemaligen Kirchenprovinzen der Evangelischen Kirche der altpreußischen Union[25]). Sie dient diesen im wesentlichen zum gemeinsamen Handeln in denjenigen Angelegenheiten und Fällen, in denen die selbständigen Kirchen gemeinsam handeln wollen - unbeschadet ihrer Selbständigkeit (vgl. Ordnung der EKU Art 6-8). Auch die Organe der Gemeinschaft - Synode und Rat - dienen diesem Zweck. Leitungsbefugnisse, die die Selbstordnungskompetenz und Rezeptionsautonomie der einzelnen Mitgliedskirchen beschränken, besitzen sie nicht, sondern lediglich das Recht "Anregungen und Richtlinien" (Art 7 Abs 1) zu geben[26], sowie Vorschläge zu gemeinsamen Gesetzen zu machen (Art 7 Abs 2).

Dementsprechend sieht das Recht der EKU keinerlei Ergänzung der in den Grundordnungen ihrer Mitgliedskirchen festgelegten Aufgaben und Zuständigkeiten des Amts der Aufsicht über die Lehr- und Gottesdienstordnung vor, das von ordinierten Personen wahrzunehmen ist. Es gibt lediglich eine gemeinsame "Ordnung des Verfahrens bei der Beanstandung der Lehre ordinierter Diener am Wort", die dieses Verfahren jedoch als ein innerhalb der Gliedkirchen und von ihnen selbst durchzuführendes regelt.

6. Die Episkope im Recht der EKD

Auch die EKD ist nicht *eine Kirche,* sondern nur die *Gemeinschaft* mehrerer selbständiger Kirchen. Als diese ist sie von den Gliedkirchen aus dem in deren eigener Lehre enthaltenen (und jetzt in der Leuenberger Konkordie öffentlich dargelegten) Grund erklärt und geordnet worden zu dem Zweck, das Handeln der Gliedkirche soweit wie möglich (d.h. soweit nicht deren eigenes Lehrbekenntnis dem entgegensteht) an gemeinsamen "Grundsätzen" auszurichten (Art 6 Abs 2; Art 19 S 2) und die Kirchen gegenüber den "Inhabern der öffentlichen Gewalt" einheitlich zu vertreten (Art. 19 S 1). Darüber hinaus können ihr die Gliedkirchen Angelegenheiten übertragen, Entscheidungen überlassen (Art 13), ebenso u. U. auch gesetzliche Regelungen (Art 10 Buchstabe b). Die Organe der EKD können von sich aus gegenüber den an der Gemeinschaft der EKD Teil habenden Kirchen aus eigenen Stücken nur folgende Initiativen ergreifen:

- Sie können Anregungen geben (Art 8)

- Richtlinien für genau begrenzte Sachgebiete aufstellen (Art 9)

und

- Kundgebungen an die Öffentlichkeit in und außerhalb der Kirchen ausgehen lassen (Art. 20 Abs 1, Art 29 Abs 1 S 3).

Der Eigenart der EKD und ihren Aufgaben entsprechend bietet ihre Grundordnung nicht das Fundament einer eigenen Lehrordnung und Gottesdienstordnung, sondern nur eine Organisationsordnung, welche die Aufgaben und das Zusammenspiel ihrer Organe festlegt.

Sind darin Elemente der Leitung und Aufsicht rechtlich geregelt? Jedenfalls keine, die speziell in den Bereich des von Ordinierten wahrzunehmenden Aufsichtsamtes fallen und die diesbezüglichen Regelungen der Grundordnungen der einzelnen Kirchen und der VELKD ergänzen könnten. Wenn der Gemeinschaft der EKD überhaupt Elemente einer Aufsichts- oder Leitungsfunktion gegenüber den an ihr Teil habenden selbständigen Kirchen rechtlich (durch die GO der EKD) zugesprochen sind, dann sind es solche, die nicht in den spezifischen Zuständigkeitsbereich von Ordinierten fallen, sondern in die Zuständigkeit aller Christen. Elemente einer solchen Aufsichts- und Leitungsfunktion lassen sich dann allerdings im Recht der EKD entdecken:

a) Der Rat der EKD wacht darüber, daß Kirchengesetze und andere Ordnungen mit Gesetzeskraft, die die einzelnen Kirchen erlassen nicht gegen die "gesamtkirchliche Ordnung" - d.h. gegen die Ordnung der Gemeinschaft der Kirchen in der EKD verstoßen (Art 2 Abs 2 Halbsatz 2). Die Gliedkirchen legen ihre "Kirchengesetze und sonstigen Ordnungen" dem Rat vor, und sie (diese Gesetze und Ordnungen) "sind abzuändern, wenn der Rat mitteilt, daß sie gegen gesamtkirchliche Ordnungen verstoßen" (Art 12).

Darin liegt ein außerordentlich weitreichendes Aufsichtsrecht beschlossen, aus folgendem Grund: Zu den gesamtkirchlichen Ordnungen, denen alle Gesetze und Ordnungen der in der Gemeinschaft der EKD stehenden Kirchen und Ordnungen nicht widersprechen dürfen, zählt auch die Grundordnung der EKD selbst. Diese aber besagt in Art 2 Abs. 1: "Das Recht der Evangelischen Kirche in Deutschland und ihrer Gliedkirchen muß auf der im Vorspruch und in Artikel 1 bezeichneten Grundlage beruhen", das sind: das in der Heiligen Schrift gegebene Evangelium als Grundlage des Glaubens, der Glaubensgemeinschaft und der Gemeinschaft der Kirchen, die altkirchlichen Bekenntnisse als Summe der Heiligen Schrift, die Bekenntnisse der Reformationszeit als maßgeblich für das Verständnis des Evangeliums, die maßgeblichen Lehrbekenntnisse der einzelnen in der Gemeinschaft der EKD stehenden Kirchen und die zur Lehrordnung aller dieser Kirchen gehörende Leuenberger Konkordie. *Alle* Gesetze und Ordnungen der an der Gemeinschaft der EKD teilnehmenden Kirchen dürfen also diesen Lehrkonsensen nicht widersprechen. Wenn der Rat feststellt, daß sie es tun, so stellt er damit fest, daß sie einer gesamtkirchlichen Ordnung - nämlich der Grundordnung der EKD - widersprechen. Und wenn er dies der betreffenden Gliedkirche "mitteilt", so "sind sie (die defizitären gliedkirchlichen Gesetze oder Ordnungen) abzuändern" (Art 12). Also: Obwohl die EKD keine eigene Lehrordnung hat, wird der Rat der EKD doch durch die Grundordnung der EKD zum Sachwalter der Lehrordnung der Teilnehmerkirchen diesen selbst gegenüber erklärt.

Einschlägige Fälle könnten beispielsweise sein: wenn eine Kirche in Ihrer Lebensordnung die Zulassung Nichtgetaufter zum Abendmahl erklärt; oder wenn eine Kirche in ihre Lehrordnung Texte mit einem Evangeliumsverständnis aufnehmen will, das mit dem Verständnis der Leuenberger Konkordie vom Evangelium als einzigem Grund der Realität von kirchlicher Einheit nicht kompatibel ist.

b) Die EKD und ihre Organe bemühen sich von sich aus, auf die Vertiefung ihrer Gemeinschaft (Art 6 Abs.1), auf deren "Erhaltung und inneres Wachstum" (Art 23 Abs 1) hinzuwirken.

c) Dazu kann sie die "leitenden Stellen der Gliedkirchen zu Besprechungen versammeln" (Art 20 Abs 1).

d) Dazu kann sie von sich aus Richtlinien erlassen auf den in Art 9 genannten Sachgebieten, die keineswegs nur Vermögensfragen betreffen, sondern auch Fragen der Lehrordnung der Kirchen: nämlich Fragen der "wissenschaftlichen und praktischen Ausbildung der Pfarrer und der übrigen kirchlichen Amtsträger" (Art 9 Buchstabe a).

e) Sie kann durch ihre Organe - Synode und Rat - "Ansprachen und Kundgebungen" ergehen lassen (Art 20 Abs 1; Art 23 Abs 2; Art 29 Abs. 1). Das tut sie in den Denkschriften und anderen Memoranden kontinuierlich. Damit nimmt sie auf ihre Weise am Auftrag der Verkündigung und der Auslegung des Evangeliums teil. Und zwar in einer Weise, die nicht nur in der Öffentlichkeit erhebliche Beachtung erfährt, sondern auch für den Umgang aller ihrer Gliedkirchen mit ihren eigenen Lehrgrundlagen de facto eine große Orientierungskraft gewonnen hat.

7. Mögliche Entwicklung

Die Ökumenische Bewegung erstrebt die öffentliche Erklärung und geordnete Praktizierung von voller sichtbarer Kirchengemeinschaft zwischen Partikularkirchen. Dieses Ziel wird letztlich auf der Ebene der Kirchenordnung, und das heißt des Rechts erreicht. Darum habe ich die Grundsatzüberlegungen in den Ziffern 1 bis 3 der Bestandsaufnahme in den Ziffern 4 bis 6 vorangestellt. An deren Ende fragt sich nun, welche weiteren Entwicklungen auf dieser Ebene - der offiziell erklärten und in rechtlicher Ordnung praktizierten, also auch voll sichtbaren Gemeinschaft der deutschen Landeskirchen in der EKD - denkbar sind. Dazu zwei Grenzbestimmungen:

a) Nicht vorstellbar ist bei Wahrung der jetzigen Rechtslage eine Mutation der in der Grundordnung der EKD rechtlich geordneten *Gemeinschaft* der deutschen evangelischen Kirchen zu *einer Kirche* - etwa analog dem Zusammenschluß lutherischer Kirchen in der VELKD.

b) Sehr wohl vorstellbar ist jedoch, daß die in der Gemeinschaft der EKD stehenden selbständigen in der EKD, wie sie in der Präambel und in Art. 1 der GO der EKD festgestellt sind, sie und ihre Gemeinschaft in der EKD in eine darüber hinausgehende offiziell erklärte und geordnete Gemeinschaft mit anderen Kirchen stellen.

In Übereinstimmung mit den Grundsätzen ihrer Gemeinschaft in der EKD stünde eine solche über sie hinausgehende Gemeinschaft dann, wenn sie als den einzigen Grund der Realität des Glaubens, der Glaubensgemeinschaft und der Gemeinschaft von Kirchen das Evangelium als Kraft Gottes selbst anerkennt und als ausreichenden Grund für die offizielle Erklärung, Praktizierung und rechtliche Ordnung von Kirchengemeinschaft nur das gemeinsame Verständnis des Evangeliums als der Kraft Gottes zur freien (CA V) Selbstvergegenwärtigung seiner Gnade.

Das wird eine Gemeinschaft sein, in der wie in der EKD und wie in der Leuenberger Gemeinschaft, aufgrund und im Horizont des gemeinsamen Verständnisses der freien Selbstvergegenwärtigung Gottes durch das Evangelium andere Differenzen im kirchlich geltenden Lehrbekenntnis oder in der Ämterordnung der Kirche erträglich sind und kein Grund zur Verweigerung der Erklärung und der geordneten Praktizierung von Kirchengemeinschaft.

Verschiedene Kirchen, die in der Gemeinschaft der EKD stehen, haben schon ihre Zustimmung zur Meissen-Erklärung damit begründet, daß sie diese Erklärung und das durch sie in Aussicht genommene Modell von Kirchengemeinschaft als ein solches verstehen und bejahen, das mit den Grundsätzen derjenigen Gemeinschaft übereinstimmt, in der sie mit anderen Kirchen in der EKD und in der Leuenberger Gemeinschaft bereits stehen[27].

Wo Kirchen *just diese Grundsätze* für ihre Erklärung und Praktizierung von Gemeinschaft mit anderen Kirchen maßgeblich sein lassen, da können sie auch für die geschichtliche Kontinuität aller Ordnungen der Leitungs- und Aufsichtsfunktionen im Leben der Glaubensgemeinschaft offen sein: Sie können die geschichtliche Wirklichkeit der geordneten Wahrnehmung von Aufsichts- und Leitungsfunktionen durch Personen, denen das Amt der Verkündigung und Sakramentsverwaltung übertragen war, anerkennen, den Wechsel in der Ausgestaltung der Ordnung dieser Funktionen, aber auch die durch den Wandel nicht aufgelöste, sondern sich gerade in ihm durchhaltende Kontinuität dieser Funktionen selbst. Sie können diese geschichtliche Wirklichkeit der sich im Wandel ihrer Ordnungsgestalten durchhaltenden Kontinuität dieser Funktion unterscheiden von einzelnen sekundär aufgekommenen Theorien über den Ursprung dieser Funktionen und über die Gründe ihrer geschichtlichen Kontinuität. Sie können die auch in ihrer eigenen Ordnung vorgesehenen Funktionen der Aufsicht und Leitung - inklusive ihrer Verteilung auf Ordinierte und Nichtordinierte - in dieser den Wandel einschließenden Kontinuität der Geschichte des Glaubens der Glaubensgemeinschaft und der Gemeinschaft der Kirchen stehen sehen. Und sie können für die Teilhabe der auch in ihrer Ordnung mit Sachnotwendigkeit vorgesehenen   Leitungs- und Aufsichtsfunktionen an dieser geschichtlichen Kontinuität jedes Zeichen wählen, das sie nicht in Widerspruch versetzt zu den Grundsätzen der Gemeinschaft, in der sie tatsächlich stehen. Dafür kommt grundsätzlich jedes Zeichen in Betracht, das nicht - explizit oder implizit - die *Übereinstimmung in einer bestimmte theologischen Theorie* über die Kontinuität der Leitungs- und Aufsichtsfunktionen in der Kirche (also die Übereinstimmung in einer bestimmten theologischen Theorie des Episkopats) *zum Grund der Wirklichkeit von kirchlicher Einheit* macht und deshalb auch zur unverzichtbaren Bedingung für die Erklärung und Praktizierung von sichtbarer Gemeinschaft zwischen den Kirchen.

[1] Wörtlich heißt es in der GO der EKD: „Gemeinsam mit der alten Kirche steht die Evangelische Kirche in Deutschland auf dem Boden der altkirchlichen Bekenntnisse" (Präambel Abs. 2). Diese Formulierung kommt nahe an die Rede von den "Grundlagen" heran. Das ist nur möglich, weil die altkirchlichen Bekenntnisse - auf der Linie der Reformation - eben nur als Summe der Heiligen Schrift verstanden werden.

[2] Diese Formulierungen aus der GO der EKD wiederholen nur ähnliche Formulierungen, wie sie in den Präambeln bzw. Grundartikeln der Grundordnungen aller Gliedkirchen stehen.

[3] Zahlreiche Grundordnungen formulieren daher kürzer, indem sie nur vom in der Schrift *gegebenen* Evangelium und seiner *Bezeugung* in den Lehrbekenntnissen der Reformationszeit sprechen.

[4] Sie betrifft nämlich alle geschichtlich-sozialen Lebensäußerungen der Kirche in Zeugnis und Dienst.

[5] Nicht jede rechtsförmig gestaltete Gemeinschaft einer Partikularkirche mit einer oder mehreren andern ist die rechtsförmige Sozialgestalt der ecclesia universalis. Aber jede derartige (rechtlich) geordnete Gemeinschaft von Kirchen hat - wie auch jede Partikularkirche selbst - Anteil an der Einheit der Christenheit auf Erden, deren Verfassungsgestalt als Gemeinschaft aller Kirchen die ecclesia universalis wäre, und verweist auf diese. Insofern ist auch jede derartige Gemeinschaft von Kirchen - z. B. die Gemeinschaft von Kirchen in der EKD, ihre Gemeinschaft in konfessionellen Weltbünden, aber auch eine Gemeinschaft zwischen Kirchen mit unterschiedlichem Lehrbekenntnis wie die Leuenberger Gemeinschaft oder die aufgrund der Porvoo- und der Meissenerklärung angestrebte Kirchengemeinschaft ein sichtbarer Hinweis auf die innergeschichtliche ecclesia universalis. Soweit die ecclesia universalis innergeschichtlich realisiert wird, wird sie in nichts anderem als in dem rechtsförmig geordneten Gefüge solcher in rechtsförmiger Ordnung praktizierten Kirchengemeinschaft bestehen. In diesem Gefüge besitzen die Partikularkirchen ihre Selbständigkeit (manifest vor allem in ihrer Kompetenz zur Selbstordnung und in ihrer Rezeptionsautonomie gegenüber den Entscheidungen von Organen der geordneten Kirchen-gemeinschaften, an denen sie Teil haben) und bezeugen gleichzeitig ihre Anteilhabe an der vom Geist durch Wort und Sakrament geschaffenen Einheit der Christenheit auf Erden und ihre Angewiesenheit auf die anderen Glieder dieses Ganzen. - Zum ganzen vgl. E. Herms, Was heißt es, im Blick auf die EKD von „Kirche" zu sprechen? Eine Fallstudie zum Verhältnis zwischen Partikularkirche und Universal-kirche im reformatorischen Verständnis, in: MJTh VIII, 84-119.

[6] Diese Genitivkonstruktion muß zunächst als gen. subj. und darf erst danach und aufgrund dessen als gen. obj. verstanden werden.

[7] Das scheint mir für das Verständnis der sowohl im Porvoo-Statement als auch im Meissen-Statement fixierten "Übereinstimmung im Glauben" wichtig zu sein. Was unter diesem Titel geboten wird, ist de facto eine Übersicht über die Übereinstimmungen in der lehrmäßigen Entfaltung des Glaubens (auf der Linie reformatorischer Theologie), und dieser Lehrkonsens wird in beiden Fällen nicht als der Grund der Glaubensgemeinschaft und der Kirchengemeinschaft - dieser Grund ist viel-mehr das Wirken des dreieinigen Gottes selbst (PS 21, MS) -, sondern als notwendige Voraussetzung, (als "Basis") für die Erklärung und rechtsförmige Ausgestaltung von Kirchengemeinschaft behandelt: PS 58, MS.

[8] Ein Lehrkonsens ist erst konkret, wenn er diesen Ursprung der Wirklichkeit von Glaube und Kirche im Geschehen der Offenbarung explizit mitumfaßt. Denn das lehrmäßige Verständnis dieses Ursprungs der Wirklichkeit von Glaube und Kirche enthält jeweils selbst schon in nuce das Ganze aller einzelnen Lehrstücke und bildet folglich jeweils das inhaltliche Prinzip für die Entfaltung aller einzelnen Lehrstücke und die Einheit ihres sachlichen Zusammenhangs.

Ob ein Konsens in einem Lehrstück bloß verbal ist, oder die Sache betrifft, zeigt sich erst, wenn die betreffenden einzelnen Lehrstücke im Horizont des beiderseitigen Lehrverständnisses von Offenbarung verortet und verstanden sind. Auf die Notwendigkeit einer solchen Orientierung an den Konstruktionsprinzipien der kirchlichen Lehre hat völlig zu recht J. Kardinal Ratzinger hingewiesen. Aber leider ist diese Regel nicht in allen ökumenischen Dialogen beachtet worden.

[9] Vgl. W. Härle/ H. Leipold (Hg.), Lehrfreiheit und Lehrbeanstandung, 2 Bde, 1985; Rechts-dokumente in Bd. 2.

[10] Vgl. die ausdrückliche Feststellung der Generalsynode der VELKD vom 24. 10. 1974 "Stellungnamen zu Rechtsfolgen der Leuenberger Konkordie in den Gliedkirchen der Vereinigten Evangelisch-Lutherischen Kirche Deutschlands", in: Lutherisches Kirchenamt Hannover (Hg.), Bericht über die Generalsynode von Rummelsberg 1974, S. 733f.

[11] Das gemeinsame Verständnis des Evangeliums betrifft das Evangelium als Kraft Gottes, also das den Glauben, die Glaubensgemeinschaft und die Gemeinschaft der Kirchen de facto begründende aktuelle, heilswirksame Geschehen des Wortes Gottes oder eben der effektiven Selbstverge-genwärtigung der Offenbarung von Gottes ewiger Gnade, und das heißt, es betrifft denjenigen Sach-verhalt, der alle anderen Einzelstücke der Glaubensgewißheit und deshalb dann auch der kirchlichen Lehre einschließt. Das gemeinsame Verständnis dieses Grundsachverhaltes begründet daher die berechtigte Erwartung, daß Differenzen in der lehrmäßigen Entfaltung der Einzelelemente dieses allum-fassenden Grundsachverhaltes zwar auftreten können, daß aber eine Verständigung über diese Lehrdifferenzen in Lehrgesprächen möglich ist, die diese Unterschiede - eben als Unterschiede bloß auf der Ebene des menschlichen Werkes kirchlicher Lehre - durchsichtig und erträglich macht.

[12] W. Hüffmeier (Hg.), Die Kirche Jesu Christi. Der reformatorische Beitrag zum ökumenischen Dialog über die kirchliche Einheit, Leuenberger Texte Heft 1, 1995.

[13] Die Organe der EKD können nur als Organe der Gemeinschaft handeln, d.h. aufgrund eines Auftrags aller selbständigen Kirchen und unter Wahrung der Rezeptionsautonomie aller beteiligten Kirchen.

[14] Inhaltlicher Maßstab ist das von der Unterzeichnerkirchen der LK anerkannte und praktizierte Modell von Kirchengemeinschaft, die ihren Grund allein im Evangelium als Kraft Gottes hat und formell erklärt, praktiziert und in geeigneter Weise geordnet werden kann aufgrund des gemeinsamen Verständnisses des Evangeliums in dieser seiner den Glauben, die Glaubensgemeinschaft und die Gemeinschaft der Kirchen schaffenden Funktion.

[15] In der Terminologie reformatorischer Theologie: bei der "Gemeinde".

[16] Vgl. KVf der Ev.-Luth Kirche in Bayern Art. 41 Abs. 1, Art. 42 ....

[17] z.B. GO von unierten Kirchen: EKHN, EKiW, EKiR; aber auch lutherische Kirchen: NEK, VELKD.

[18] So alle in der vorigen Anmerkung genannten Kirchen. EKHN, ... Anders vor allem die KO der Pfalz und der Ev. Kirche in Bremen.

[19] z.B. Oldenburg, Lippe, Schaumburg-Lippe, Görlitz

[20] So z.B. in der EKHN (der Kirchenpräsident hat nur den Vorsitz im "leitenden geistlichen Amt", dem Kollegium der Pröpste. Auch in der Pfalz: Kollegium der Dekane.

[21] So z.B. in Bayern (Kreisdekane/Landesbischof), Hannover (Superindenten/Landessuperindenten/Landesbischof), Württemberg (Dekane/Prälaten/Landesbischof), Rheinland (Superintenden/Präses), Westfalen (Superintendenten/Präses).

[22] So z.B. in der NEK: In den Sprengeln: Pröpste/Sprengelbischof. In der Landeskirche: Bischofskollegium.

[23] So in der KKHW.

[24] Jüngstes Musterbeispiel: die Studie des Leitenden Geistlichen Amtes der EKHN: Auftrag und Gestalt. Vom Sparzwang zur Besserung der Kirche. Theologische Leitvorstellungen für Ressourcenkonzentration und Strukturveränderung, 1995.

[25] Dazu kommt neuerdings die der EKU beigetretene Kirche von Anhalt.

[26] Das entspricht in etwa den Rechten der Organe der EKD gegenüber ihren Mitgliedskirchen.

[27] Vgl. EKD-Texte 47 S. 152 (EKKW), 153 (Lippe), 157 (VELKD), 159 (Hannover), 175 (Berlin-Brandenburg), 178 (KKL).

Die öffentliche Rolle eines nordelbischen Bischofs als Repräsentant der Kirche und in Entscheidungsprozessen - eine Beschreibung

Hans Christian Knuth

Liebe Schwestern und Brüder,

"Der Strukturwandel der Öffentlichkeit" (Habermas) bringt es mit sich, daß auch im Bischofsamt - jedenfalls im evangelischen - repräsentative Öffentlichkeit und tatsächlicher Einfluß oft weit auseinanderklaffen. Nur bei einem kleinen Teil der bischöflichen Aufgaben ist die Öffentlichkeit des Amtes mit der Repräsentation von Macht verbunden. Da der Bischof in Kirche, Gesellschaft und Öffentlichkeit zu wirken hat, werde ich mein Thema entsprechend gliedern.

I Funktion des nordelbischen Bischofs in der Kirche

Die meiste Zeit verbringe ich mit der Vorbereitung und dem Halten von Predigten, Vorträgen und Ansprachen. Wahrnehmung geistlicher Leitung, sine vi sed verbo, theologische Existenz und persönliche Vorlieben mischen sich hier zu einem zwar anstrengenden, aber im ganzen erfüllenden Gesamtauftrag. Hier ergänzen sich mein ursprünglicher Berufswunsch, Pastor zu werden, und die bisherigen beruflichen Erfahrungen (Doktorand, Referent der nordelbischen Kirchenleitung, Gemeindepastor, Studienleiter am Predigerseminar, Oberkirchenrat der VELKD für theologische Grundsatzfragen, Pastor und Propst in Eckernförde) und helfen mir zur Bewältigung der beruflichen Aufgaben.

Daneben stehen Ordination und Visitation als klassische, öffentliche bischöfliche Funktionen, die einen hohen Stellenwert besitzen, aber - was die Visitation betrifft - leider sträflich zu kurz kommen. Der Kontakt zu den Gemeinden hat sich von der Visitation verschoben auf Einführungen, Einweihungen, Jubiläen, Feste, auf Besuche in Konfliktfällen, auf regelmäßige Beratung der Pastoren und Pröpste in Konventen und Sitzungen. Dies sind vorwiegend beratende Funktionen, gelegentlich kommt es aber auch hier zu Entscheidungen durch das bischöfliche Amt, vor allem im disziplinären Bereich.

Fragt man nach der unmittelbaren Entscheidungskompetenz des Bischofs, so wären für den Sprengel die Ordination, die Besetzung von Pfarrstellen, Versetzung von Pastoren im Konfliktfall und die Vorgesetzten- und Aufsichtsfunktion gegenüber den Pröpsten zu nennen.

In allen anderen Zusammenhängen sowohl auf Sprengelebene - wir haben davon in unserer Kirche drei - wie auf landeskirchlicher Ebene hat der Bischof nur Stimmrecht in Gremien und keine alleinige Entscheidungsbefugnis. So verbringe ich einen unverhältnismäßig großen Teil meiner Zeit in Gremien, derzeit 38, darunter Kirchenleitung, Synode, Kirchenamt, diverse Ausschüsse, zum Teil als Vorsitzender, Beiräte, Vorstände, Aufsichtsräte, Kommissionen, in denen ich zwar mitbestimmen darf, aber oft genug überstimmt werde, zum Teil nicht einmal eine eigene Stimme habe. Der Bischof soll hier die Gremien vernetzen und bemüht sich um den Konsens nach innen und außen.

Um beispielsweise die Position des Direktors unseres Nordelbischen Missionszentrums zu besetzen, waren folgende Schritte nötig:

a)   Nominierungsausschuß (6 Sitzungen)

b)   Präsentation der Kandidaten im Vorstand des Nordelbischen Missionszentrums

c)   Präsentation des Kandidaten im Nordelbischen Kirchenamt

d)   Präsentation des Kandidaten in der Kirchenleitung

e)   Präsentation des Kandidaten im Vorfeld der Generalversammlung des NMZ

f)   Wahl des Kandidaten in der Generalversammlung des NMZ

Dazu kamen ausführliche Gespräche mit den zukünftigen Kollegen und diversen Einzelinteressengruppen von b - f. Eine ähnlich wichtige Wahl in ein anders Leitungsamt der NEK ist gerade am Widerspruch der Kirchenleitung gescheitert, nachdem zuvor alle anderen Gremien einstimmig votiert hatten.

Im übrigen wird unsere Kirche von der Synode, der Kirchenleitung und dem Bischofskollegium geleitet. Alle drei kirchenleitenden Organe sind sich gegenseitig gleichberechtigt zugeordnet. Es gibt keinen Letztentscheid der Synode gegen die anderen Gremien. Das Bischofskollegium kann allerdings Beschlüsse der Synode, die gegen die Schrift und die Verfassung verstoßen, aufheben, wenn es einvernehmlich votiert.

II: Die gesellschaftliche Funktion

Auch nach außen vertrete ich die nordelbische Kirche als Bischof zumeist durch Reden, am häufigsten durch Grußworte auf Empfängen, zum Beispiel der Bundeswehr, der Handwerkskammer, des Bauernverbandes, der Parteien, der Landfrauen usw., bei Jubiläen und Festen von Vereinen, Verbänden, Schulen usw. Aber auch längere Hauptreden sind hier gefragt, zum Beispiel über die Rolle der Kirche in Rußland bei der Bundeswehr und beim Rotary-Club, über Grundwerte bei der Handwerkerschaft und bei der CDU, auf staatlichen und kommunalen Veranstaltungen zum Volkstrauertag, über die Einheit der Ostseekultur bei der Deutschen Minderheit usw. Zur Eröffnung des neugewählten Landtags werde ich auf Wunsch der Fraktionen den Gottesdienst halten.

Die Kontakte zur Landesregierung, zu Parteien, Fraktionen und Verbänden sind aber genau so wichtig, oft noch wichtiger, wenn nicht öffentliche Reden gehalten werden, sondern gesellschaftliche Verantwortung gemeinsam wahrgenommen werden soll. Öffentliches Aufsehen erregte vor einiger Zeit ein Gespräch mit den Fraktionen des schleswig-holsteinischen Landtages über die Arbeit des Untersuchungsausschusses in der Barschel-Affäre. Solche Gespräche finden laufend statt. Normalerweise wird nicht alles durch gezielte Indiskretion verbreitet, was hier in Kladde gedacht, gesagt, akzeptiert oder auch verworfen wird.

III Die Funktion der Kirche in der Öffentlichkeit

Abgesehen von ihren Reden und Gesprächen mit der Öffentlichkeit nimmt die Kirche aber auch selbst einen Teil der öffentlichen Aufgaben wahr und ist daher nicht nur Partner, sondern Teil der Öffentlichkeit.

Basierend auf der staatlichen Vorgabe der Subsidiarität - das heißt der Bevorzugung nichtstaatlicher Träger für allgemeine Aufgaben der Gesellschaft - einerseits und dem Kirchensteuersystem andrerseits, hat sich die Kirche erheblich im diakonisch-sozialen Bereich engagiert. So gehört zum Beispiel der Vorsitz im Aufsichtsrat (Landesausschuß) der Diakonissenanstalt Flensburg zum Aufgabenbereich des Schleswiger Bischofs. Immerhin ein Werk mit 2.000 Mitarbeitern und ca. 100 Millionen DM Jahresumsatz. Hier ergibt sich naturgemäß eine Fülle von Überschneidungen kirchlicher und öffentlicher Aufgaben, zum Beispiel auch im Bereich der medizinischen Ethik (Transplantation, Abtreibung, Embryoforschung usw.), aber vor allem im Hinblick auf die öffentliche Patientenversorgung und als Arbeitgeber. Alle drei nordelbischen Bischöfe nehmen solche Verantwortung wahr, zum Teil in noch größeren Einrichtungen. Unsere Diakonie hat zusammen mit der Nordelbischen Kirche 31.000 Mitarbeiterinnen und Mitarbeiter. Damit sind wir der zweitgrößte Arbeitgeber nach dem Staat. Die Gewerkschaften sind unsere Partner bei der Tarifgestaltung. Und was wir den Tarifpartnern als Kirche öffentlich empfehlen, müssen wir natürlich als Arbeitgeber selbst erfüllen.

Um darauf hinzuweisen, welche Entscheidungen und Konflikte hier jeweils auch für die Bischöfe entstehen, möchte ich daran erinnern, daß die ehemaligen nordelbischen Bischöfe Dr. Hübner und Dr. Wölber seinerzeit vom Vorsitz der Kirchenleitung zurücktraten, als die nordelbische Kirche Tarifverträge mit den Gewerkschaften abschloß. Sie hielten eine solche Einwirkungsmöglichkeit kirchenfremder Institutionen in die Kirche auf dem Hintergrund ihrer Erfahrungen im Kirchenkampf für unvereinbar mit dem Bekenntnis der Kirche zum alleinigen Gehorsam gegenüber Christus. Die Synode hat trotzdem die Tarifverträge mit den Gewerkschaften abgeschlossen, da die Kirche anderen Unternehmen dies ja auch empfohlen hatte.

Ähnliche Konflikte stehen möglicherweise morgen und übermorgen an, wenn unsere Synode gegen das Votum von zwei nordelbischen Bischöfen die Segnung von Homosexuellen und das Zusammenleben von unverheirateten Paaren im Pfarrhaus billigen sollte.

Zur direkten Konfrontation mit der Regierung ist es über die Abschaffung des Buß und Bettages als arbeitsfreien Feiertag gekommen. Das Land Schleswig-Holstein hatte - einer Empfehlung aus Bonn folgend - den Bußtag als gesetzlichen Feiertag gestrichen, wir wehren uns dagegen mit Hilfe eines Gesetzes zum Volksentscheid.

Die Rolle der Medien in solchen Konflikten ist nicht zu unterschätzen. Zwar helfen die Medien nachhaltig, auch Verkündigungsinhalte zu vermitteln, zum Beispiel wenn sie geistliche Betrachtungen drucken oder senden, wenn in Interviews, Berichten, Bildern über kirchliche Arbeitsfelder informiert wird oder gar ganze Gottesdienste im Rundfunk und im Fernsehen übertragen werden.

Auch Bücher mit Gebeten, Luthertexten oder theologischen Arbeiten wurden mir als Bischof von Verlagen freundlicherweise schon abgenommen. Aber das sind dann eher meine subjektiven Arbeiten.

In der - vor allem überregionalen - Berichterstattung der Medien überwiegen jedoch Beiträge über Skandale und Konflikte. Während die lokalen Medien durchweg freundlich über den Bischof berichten als Repräsentanten der Kirche, wird er überregional eher in seinen politischen oder gesellschaftlichen Äußerungen zitiert und darum auch oft verzeichnet. In der Schubladen-Barschel-affäre wurden wir in der Öffentlichkeit gar nicht verstanden; in Asylfragen, auch in der Auseinandersetzung über Lebensformen werden wir, je nachdem, beim politischen Gegner oder Freund eingeordnet und entsprechend behandelt. Den Kampf um den Bußtag verfolgt die Presse mit wohlwollender Neugier. Im ganzen wird man sagen müssen: Das Bild der Presse von den Bischöfen entspricht so wenig der Wirklichkeit wie das Bild der Kirche insgesamt. Daß ein Bischof predigt, visitiert, Gremien leitet und in ihnen mitwirkt, verwaltet, im Examen prüft, einführt, einweiht, Vorträge hält, Konflikte in den Gemeinden bearbeitet, viele Stunden in Einzelgesprächen seelsorgerlich wirkt, diakonisch, gesamtkirchlich, ökumenisch, wissenschaftlich tätig ist, das interessiert wenig. Wenn er etwas Ausgefallenes sagt oder tut, kann er aber sicher sein, beachtet zu werden.

Lassen Sie mich das am Schluß an einer wahren Anekdote verdeutlichen. Vier Jahre meines Lebens habe ich damit zugebracht, ein dickes Buch zu schreiben über die Auslegungsgeschichte eines Psalms bei den griechischen, lateinischen Kirchenvätern, bei Luther und bis in die Neuzeit. Das Buch hat vielleicht zehn bis zwölf Leser gefunden. Aber einen durchschlagenden Erfolg in der öffentlichen Publizistik hatte ich mit einem Interview zwischen Tür und Angel über die Frage, ob unsere ehemalige Justizministerin, Frau Leutheuser-Schnarrenberg, ihren Dackel Dr. Martin Luther nennen dürfe. Drei Minuten vor Abfahrt zu einer Dienstreise sagte ich nur: Darf ein Dackel denn den Doktortitel tragen - im übrigen wagte ich zu bedenken, ob denn der Name nicht zu lang sei, um den Hund effektiv zu lenken. Denn ehe man ihn zur Ordnung rufen könne, habe er doch längst zugebissen. Dieses Interview wurde von Flensburg bis Konstanz verbreitet. Ob es bischöfliche Qualität hat, möchte ich bezweifeln, jedenfalls hatte es diesen Erfolg als bischöfliches Votum.

Aber Spaß beiseite. Der ursprüngliche öffentliche Auftrag des Bischofs ist ja nach den Lutherischen Bekenntnisschriften das *publice docere*, das öffentliche Eintreten für die Heilige Schrift und das Bekenntnis der Kirche. Das läßt sich in der Regel durch positive Entfaltung des Glaubenszeugnisses in Predigt und Vorträgen erfüllen.

Kommt es aber zum Konflikt, so haben wir im deutschen Luthertum ein Lehrbeanstandungsverfahren, für das ich im Bereich der VELKD im Ernstfall den Vorsitz innehabe. Bisher ist die entsprechende Kammer für Lehrfragen nur einmal nach dem Kriege - im Fall Schulz - zusammengetreten. Lehrverfahren erzeugen in der Regel größere öffentliche Aufmerksamkeit. Kommt es zum Spruch, indem dem Pfarrer Verstoß gegen seine Ordinationsverpflichtung nachgewiesen wird, muß er gerügt, versetzt, suspendiert, schlimmstenfalls entlassen werden.

Abschließend möchte ich auf einen gravierenden Widerspruch hinweisen zwischen den dem Bischof aufgetragenen Aufgaben und den ihm zur Verfügung stehenden Mitteln, um diesem Auftrag gerecht zu werden. Die öffentliche Erwartung entspricht eher dem katholischen Bischofsbild, die innerkirchliche Realisierung entspricht eher dem Bild vom Pastor pastorum, der durch Seelsorge und Beratung, mehr aber noch durch Gebet, Fürbitte und Predigt, Konsens stiftet, Kirche leitet und vertritt.

Zwischen disziplinarischem und geistlichem Handeln klafft oft ein Widerspruch, zumindest ergibt sich dort eine starke Spannung. Aber in dieser Spannung steht ja jeder Christ, da sie auf das Verhältnis von Gesetz und Evangelium zurückzuführen ist. Und dafür gibt es keine endgültige Lösung.

Das bischöfliche Aufsichtsamt in den Deutschen Kirchen, ihr öffentlicher Status, ihre Beteiligung an kirchlichen Entscheidungen in Geschichte und Gegenwart

Axel Freiherr von Campenhausen

I

Der evangelische Bischof ist ein Pfarrer, der in das Amt der Kirchenleitung für den Bereich einer Landeskirche berufen ist. Er teilt das eine kirchliche Amt, das die Kirche stiftungsgemäß kennt (das also iuris divini genannt werden kann), mit allen Pastoren. Das Amt der Aufsicht, Visitation und Ordination, welches eine Institution des menschlichen Kirchenrechts (also iuris humani) ist, teilt er mit weiteren Inhabern bischöflicher Aufsichtsämter, die Superintendent, Landessuperintendent, Dekan, Kreisdekan, Prälat oder Propst heißen. Die Besonderheit des Amtes eines evangelischen Bischofs besteht darin, daß er die bischöflichen Funktionen in der ganzen Landeskirche ausübt, daß er seine Teilkirche nach außen und innen vertritt, daß er mit anderen (verschieden benannten) Leitungsorganen gemeinsam die Landeskirche leitet und insbesondere der Landessynode gegenübersteht.

Die deutschen evangelischen Bischöfe stehen als ordinierte Pfarrer in der Nachfolge des Amtes der Verkündigung. Durch die Ordination stehen sie auch in der Folge der Handauflegungen, welche seit apostolischer Zeit üblich ist. Ob es sich dabei um Handauflegungen durch Bischöfe oder Presbyter oder gar um eine physisch ununterbrochene Kette von Handauflegungen seit den Aposteln handelt, ist ohne prinzipielles Interesse, weil es hierbei allein um die geistliche Identität der Kirche geht[1.]

Dieses Verständnis des evangelischen Bischofsamtes genießt heute allgemein Anerkennung. Das zeigt ein Blick auf die Kirchenverfassungen[2] sowohl wie die kirchenrechtliche Literatur[3]. Der Weg zu diesem Stand, in dem Rechtswissenschaft und Praxis sich treffen, war nicht ohne Hindernisse.

Die Reformatoren haben dazu keinen Anlaß gegeben, wohl aber die von staatlicher Vorherrschaft und Rechtsüberlagerung geprägte Entwicklung des äußeren Kirchenwesens nach dem Augsburgischen Religionsfrieden (1555).

Das bischöfliche Amt fassen Reformatoren und Bekenntnisschriften in Wiederaufnahme biblischen Sprachgebrauchs in doppelter Bedeutung auf. Zunächst ist für das evangelische Verständnis das "Recht Bischoflich und besucheampt" (WA 26, 197, 12 ff.) identisch mit dem Amt der Wortverkündigung und Sakramentsverwaltung. Es gibt nur ein Amt iuris divini. Luther verwendete die Bezeichnung episcopi, ministri seu pastores synonym (WA 12, 194, 1 f.); das Augsburgische Bekenntnis ist ihm hierin gefolgt (CA 28). Daneben ist das bischöfliche Amt ein Amt der menschlichen Kirchenordnung für die Leitung der Kirche. Die Reformation und die Bekenntnisschriften (CA, Schmalkaldische Artikel) suchten das überlieferte Bischofsamt zu bewahren, soweit dies vom Evangelium her vertretbar ist, nämlich als Amt, dem Visitation, Prüfung und Ordination der Pfarrer übertragen ist[4].

In dieser Funktionsbeschränkung waren die Reformatoren bereit, das bischöfliche Regiment als eine nützliche, löbliche, aber doch menschliche Ordnung anzuerkennen und sich ihm um des Friedens willen zu unterwerfen, aber auch deshalb, weil es gefährlich sei, rechtliche Ordnungen willkürlich zu ändern[5].

Kirchengewalt (geistliche Gewalt) ist danach die Gewalt des Wortes. Sie begründet das eine Amt, das die Kirche hat. Die Funktionen dieses Amtes sind die Wortverkündigung einschließlich der Last der Lehrbeurteilung und der Lehrverwerfung, die Verwaltung der Sakramente und das Schlüsselamt. Mit ihnen geschieht Kirchenleitung[6]. Die Besonderheit des reformatorischen Durchbruchs besteht für den vorliegenden Zusammenhang also in zwei Punkten: Erstens verzichtet die Kirchenleitung auf jede Unterstützung durch äußere Gewalt. Sie muß sich durch die ihr innewohnende Autorität, non vi sed verbo durchsetzen. Zweitens ist diese von CA 28 unbefangen jurisdictio genannte Kirchengewalt allen Inhabern des einheitlichen kirchlichen Amtes gleichmäßig anbefohlen. Reformatoren und Bekenntnisschriften verwenden nicht nur die Amtsbezeichnungen episcopus, minister, presbyter und pastor synonym, sie gehen alle von der Einheit des Amtes aus. Das heißt, daß alle Diener der Kirche gleichen Anteil am göttlich-rechtlichen Amt haben.

Gerade die Abtrennung der weltlichen Funktionen vom Bischofsamt zugunsten des Territorialherrn und die Beschränkung auf die geistlichen Funktionen lehnten die Bischöfe der Reformationszeit in Deutschland indessen mit wenigen Ausnahmen ab. Der Verzicht einzelner und die Ordinierung und Einführung einiger evangelischer Bischöfe in Sachsen, Preußen und der Mark Brandenburg waren die Ausnahme. Sie blieben Episode[7].

Die Funktion des früheren bischöflichen Amtes lebte fort in den evangelischen Superintendenten. Hatte Deutschland vor der Reformation dem Titel nach Bischöfe, die die bischöflichen Funktionen nicht oder nicht richtig ausübten[8], so hatte es nach der Reformation zunächst Geistliche gegeben, die die Funktionen des Bischofsamtes ausübten, aber andere Titel führten[9].

Mit dem Wort Superintendent (auch Superattendens) übernahmen die Reformatoren nicht nur eine lateinische Übersetzung des griechischen episkopos; sie hielten auch am Bischofsamt selbst fest[10].

Soweit es vom Evangelium her vertretbar erschien, sollte das überlieferte Bischofsamt erhalten bleiben. Auch unter der Bezeichnung des Superintendenten konnte sich das evangelische Bischofsamt jedoch nicht frei entwickeln. Schon im Unterricht der Visitatoren werden den Superintendenten nicht nur die charakteristischen Aufgaben des kirchlichen Aufsichtsamtes zugewiesen: hier beginnt bereits ihre Inpflichtnahme in den Dienst obrigkeitlicher Sittenzucht[11].

Und je mehr sich das landesherrliche Kirchenregiment mit den charakteristischen konsistorialen Behörden entwickelte, desto mehr wurde der spezifische Ansatz des evangelischen Aufsichtsamtes in dem einheitlichen kirchlichen Amt vom weltlichen Recht überdeckt und seine Entfaltung behindert: Das Problembewußtsein blieb jedoch erhalten; das läßt sich an den theoretischen Versuchen, den Einfluß des Landesherrn auf die geistliche Leitung der Kirche einzudämmen, ablesen[12].

Die entscheidenden Schritte für die Entstehung des selbständigen Bischofsamtes erfolgten im 19. Jahrhundert.

Es war die Gewissenhaftigkeit des preußischen Königs als Summus Episcopus, welche der Entwicklung einen neuen Anstoß gegeben hat, die in der eigenständigen Hervorbringung eines evangelischen Bischofsamtes gipfeln sollte. Die Wurzeln, aus denen es hervorgewachsen ist, waren das Amt des Superintendenten und des Generalsuperintendenten[13].

Im Jahre 1828 wurde das Amt eines Generalsuperintendenten durch Friedrich Wilhelm III. neu geschaffen, ihre besonderen Befugnisse in der für die östlichen Provinzen bestimmten Instruktion vom 14. Mai 1829 aufgezählt. Diese Instruktion wurde mit dem 31. Mai 1836 auf die Westprovinzen übertragen[14].

Nach dieser Instruktion waren die Generalsuperintendenten Geistliche, denen die Aufsicht über mehrere Superintendentursprengel neben den Provinzialkonsistorien übertragen war (1). Sie sollten sich "Kenntniß von der Beschaffenheit des evangelischen Kirchenwesens ... verschaffen, vornehmlich auf dem Wege des persönlichen Verkehrs, wenn auch gleich der Schriftwechsel zur Vervollständigung und Erleichterung dieses persönlichen Einwirkens nicht ganz ausgeschlossen werden soll" (2). Sie sollen "bald anregend, bald nachhelfend, bald vermittelnd auftreten" (5). Im besonderen war ihnen die Aufsicht für die

"Lehrart" der Geistlichen, der Wandel der Kirchenbeamten in Familie und Amt und die Sorge für "Aufrechterhaltung und Wiederherstellung der Reinheit, Ordnung und Würde des öffentlichen Gottesdienstes" übertragen (6). Sie sollten die wissenschaftliche Fortbildung der Pfarrer anregen, nähren und unterstützen (6). An den Prüfungen der letzteren konnten sie als Mitglieder des Konsistoriums teilnehmen, um dadurch "in den Stand gesetzt (zu) werden, sich von der Tiefe und dem Umfange ihrer wissenschaftlichen Bildung und vom dem Charakter ihrer theologischen Richtung eine genaue Kenntnis zu verschaffen" (20). "Zunächst" lag "ihnen das Geschäft der Kirchenvisitation" an den Superintendenturorten ob (7 ff.). Neben diesem regelmäßig wiederkehrenden Visitationsgeschäft, das mit einer Revision der Registratur und des Archivs zu verbinden war, konnten sie an Visitationen der Superintendenten teilnehmen (13) und nicht zuletzt "zuweilen außerordentliche und unvermuthete Untersuchungen an Ort und Stelle ... veranstalten" (14). "Zu ihren Obliegenheiten gehörte die persönliche Einweisung der neuernannten Superintendenten" (15) und "ferner das Ordinationsgeschäft" (22). Sie waren an der Schulaufsicht beteiligt (6, 13) und prüften die "jährlichen Conduitenlisten über Geistliche und Schullehrer", welche die Superintendenten einreichten (23). Als "väterliche Pfleger" (5) sollten die Generalsuperintendenten wirken. Sie bildeten "keine Zwischeninstanz" (3). Bei ihren Amtshandlungen, wie der "Feierlichkeit" der Einführung eines Superintendenten sollten sie "die Bande der brüderlichen Gemeinschaften unter der Diözesan-Geistlichkeit durch Einführung eines neuen Vermittlers fester ... schlingen" (16).

Trotz des bürokratischen Stils dieser Instruktion ist unverkennbar, daß im Amt des Generalsuperintendenten das kirchliche Aufsichts- und Visitationsamt wieder zu Selbständigkeit gelangte.

Tatsächlich wirkte diese Instruktion des preußischen Königs als Summus episcopus beispielhaft für alle deutschen Landeskirchen. Der Aufgabenkatalog der Landesbischöfe in den Kirchenverfassungen des 20. Jahrhunderts ist in wesentlichen Teilen derselbe geblieben[15.]

Merkwürdig ist hierbei, daß den Ansatz zur Bildung des Generalsuperintendentenamtes die Bemühungen des frommen Königs um eine geisterfüllte Verstärkung des landesherrlichen Kirchenregiments bildete. Er hoffte, in den Generalsuperintendenten königliche Vertrauensleute zu finden, die ihrerseits das Vertrauen der Pfarrer genossen.

Freilich trug der Generalsuperintendent die Züge eines hohen königlichen Beamten noch deutlich an sich. Die Entstehung seines Amtes aus königlicher Machtbefugnis zeigte sich auch in der Titulierung als Bischof oder gar Erzbischof, welche als königliche Gnade einem Orden gleich verliehen wurde und

nicht hinderte, daß die Generalsuperintendenten in § 52 b der Rheinisch-
Westfälischen Kirchenordnung noch in der Fassung von 1908 als königliche
Kommissare bezeichnet wurden.

Die andere Wurzel des evangelischen Bischofsamtes war das Amt des Superintendenten. Dieses war nach der Reformation, wie gesagt, bald in das System des
landesherrlichen Kirchenregiments integriert. Der Superintendent war nicht
Inhaber eines staatlichen Aufsichtsamtes, sondern Organ des untersten
("Kreis"-)Synodal-verbandes, in dessen Synode und Synodalvorstand er
präsidierte[16]. Er war also gerade kein staatliches Aufsichtsorgan und gleichzeitig
auch Pfarrer, sondern er war immer ein Pfarrer, der als Superintendent Exponent
und Repräsentant der Kirchenkreissynode war. Mochte der Staat kraft
landesherrlichen Kirchenregiments an der Bestellung eines Pfarrers zum
Superintendenten mitwirken, so war er als Superintendent dennoch Träger eines
geistlichen Amtes, welches sich aus der Synode herleitete, und diese war eine
geistliche Institution[17.]

Damit hat das Superintendentenamt ein Moment in die Entwicklung eingebracht,
das dem Amt des Generalsuperintendenten noch fehlte. Dieses war wahrhaft
bischöflich ausgestattet. Aber der Generalsuperintendent übte es doch kraft
königlichen Willens aus und stand den Synoden, welche kirchliche Organe waren,
kraft seines königlichen Amtes gegenüber. Das Amt des Superintendenten war
demgegenüber nicht bischöflich ausgestattet in dem Sinne, wie Reformatoren und
die heutigen Kirchenverfassungen das Amt des Landesbischofs verstehen. Der
Superintendent ist vielmehr Vorstand und Organ der Synode[18].

II

Äußerer Anlaß für die Wiederherstellung des evangelischen Bischofsamtes war in
Deutschland die Beseitigung des landesherrlichen Summepiskopats 1918. Daß
dieser Übergang in der Kirche nicht mit großen äußeren Erschütterungen einher-
ging, hängt damit zusammen, daß die evangelischen Kirchen im Laufe des 19.
Jahrhunderts bereits eine vollständige Kirchenverfassung mit eigenen kirchlichen
Organen erhalten hatten. Dabei hatte man auf ältere Kirchenrechtstheorien
zurückgegriffen. Danach verkörperte der König zwei Personen, nämlich einerseits
den Herrscher des Staates, andererseits den Notbischof der evangelischen Kirche.
In dieser Eigenschaft hat er im Laufe des 19. Jahrhunderts die Kirchen aus der
unmittelbaren Staatsverwaltung schrittweise ausgegliedert und durch Einrichtung
der Behörde des Evangelischen Oberkirchenrats die unmittelbare Unterstellung
unter staatliche Instanz abgelöst. 1919 ging es deshalb nur noch um die Frage,
wer den freigewordenen Platz, den der Summus Episcopus innegehabt hat,
nunmehr besetzen solle. Die Bischofsfrage wurde alsbald lebhaft erörtert. "In fast
allen deutschen evangelischen Landeskirchen ist gelegentlich der Neugestaltung

ihrer Verfassung die Frage aufgeworfen und erörtert worden, ob neben dem synodalen und dem konsistorialen auch das episkopale Element in den Verfassungsbau einzufügen sei - nicht jedoch in dem Sinne, als ob man daran gedacht hätte, den durch die Staatsumwälzung gefallenen landesherrlichen Summepiskopat in irgendeiner modernisierten Form wiedererstehen zu lassen, sondern in dem, das geistliche Amt in das eigentliche Verfassungsleben einzubeziehen und es in einer seinem Wesen entsprechenden Weise an der Leitung der Kirche zu beteiligen"[19]. Zunächst waren Funktion sowohl als Amtsbezeichnung noch umstritten[20]. Deshalb ist hier zwischen der Einfügung des bischöflichen Amtes in die neuen Kirchenverfassungen und der damit nicht notwendig verbundenen Amtsbezeichnung "Bischof" oder "Landesbischof" zu unterscheiden. Wie wichtig dies ist, zeigt sich schon daran, daß die bayerische Kirchenverfassung, die "das kraftvollste und inhaltsreichste deutsche evangelische Bischofsamt" geschaffen hatte, den Träger dieses Amtes mit dem Titel eines Kirchenpräsidenten ausstattete[21].

Auch in der Altpreußischen Landeskirche wurde die Stellung der Generalsuperintendenten in einer Weise ausgestaltet, daß von Anfang an deutlich war, "das werden Bischöfe sein mit dem Namen Generalsuperintendenten"[22].

Ein Überblick über die Kirchenverfassung nach 1919 ergibt folgende Zuständigkeiten des Bischofs bzw. des Inhabers des bischöflichen Amtes[23].

- Sammlung und Pflege der kirchlichen Kräfte, Förderung und Beobachtung

- Überwachung und Förderung der Vor- und Weiterbildung der Geistlichen

- Seelsorgerliche Beratung der Geistlichen

- Die Leitung der theologischen Prüfungen und die Verantwortung für die Predigerseminare

- Das Recht der Ordination, dieses in der Regel in Konkurrenz mit Inhabern regionaler bischöflicher Ämter

- Vorschlagsrechte für die Besetzung geistlicher Stellen

- Die Einführung der Superintendenten, Pröpste, Dekane, Generalsuperintenden-ten, Kreisdekane

- Regelmäßige Besprechungen mit den Superintendenten, Dekanen, Generalsuperintendenten

- Das Visitationsrecht, z.T. in Konkurrenz mit Superintendenten

- Beobachtung und Förderung der Jugendpflege, Wahrnehmung der kirchlichen Interesse in der Schule, Beobachtung der kirchlichen Vereinstätigkeit, der inne-ren und der äußeren Mission usw.

- Anordnung von Buß-, Festgottesdiensten u.ä.

- Einweihung von Kirchen und gottesdienstlichen Gebäuden

- Das Recht, Ansprachen an die Geistlichen und Gemeinden der Landeskirchen zu richten, welche im öffentlichen Gottesdienst zu verlesen sind und im kirchlichen Gesetz- und Verordnungsblatt bekannt gemacht werden

- Das Recht zur gottesdienstlichen Wortverkündigung in allen Gemeinden

Durchwegs herrscht die Ansicht vor, daß der Bischof in dauernder Verbindung mit der kirchlichen Zentralbehörde stehen muß. In der Regel übt er auch die Funktion der rechtlichen Spitze der Landeskirche aus.

Dazu zählen folgende Zuständigkeiten:

- Die Vertretung der Landeskirche nach außen

- Die Ernennung der Geistlichen und der Kirchenbeamten

- Die Ausfertigung und Verkündung von Gesetzen und Verordnungen

Dazu kommt die Eingliederung in die Zentralbehörden der Kirche, vielfach als Vorsitzender. Mit Rücksicht auf seine seelsorgerlichen Aufgaben kommen dem Inhaber des bischöflichen Amtes disziplinarische Befugnisse nur selten zu. Von der Landessynode ist der Bischof (ebenso wie die übrigen Mitglieder der Leitungs- und Verwaltungsbehörde) regelmäßig ausgeschlossen, hat jedoch das Recht, unter Umständen die Pflicht, an den Sitzungen teilzunehmen und das Wort zu ergreifen[24]. Eine selbständige Stellung gegenüber der Landessynode hat der Bischof vor allem in Bayern (aufschiebendes Einspruchsrecht, Recht zur Auflösung der Landessynode, Art. 36, 37). Der Landesbischof wird auf Lebenszeit berufen, d.h. bis zur normalen Pensionierungsgrenze. Mehrere Landeskirchen sind dazu übergegangen, das Amt des Bischofs zeitlich zu befristen[25].

III

Überall in Deutschland ist der Landesbischof bzw. der leitende Geistliche mit der Vertretung der Kirche nach außen betraut, nicht zuletzt also der Vertreter der Kirche gegenüber dem Staat.

Das Verhältnis von Staat und Kirche hat mit dem Ende der Monarchie eine umfassende Regelung erfahren, welche an jahrhundertealte Regelungen anknüpfen konnte. Abgestreift wurde dabei der christliche Charakter des Staates und die Bevorzugung des christlichen Bekenntnisses im Verhältnis zu anderen. Die Bestimmungen der Reichsverfassung von 1919 sind wörtlich in das Grundgesetz der Bundesrepublik Deutschland von 1949 übernommen worden. Dieses setzt den Rahmen, der von den Ländern ausgefüllt wird, bei denen der Schwerpunkt der für die Kirche relevanten Materien traditionellerweise liegt.

Grundlegend ist die Garantie der Religionsfreiheit (Art. 4 GG). Sie wird unterstrichen durch die organisatorische Trennung von Staat und Kirche, welche mit dem merkwürdigen Satz "Es besteht keine Staatskirche" (Art. 140 GG i.V.m. Art. 137 I WRV) umschrieben wird. Wesentlich ist für Deutschland, daß diese Trennung den Gesetzen der deutschen Verfassung folgt, also nicht mit der nur verbal ganz übereinstimmenden Trennung von Staat und Kirche in den USA, in Frankreich oder im Ostblock verglichen werden kann. Hier ging es nicht darum, die Kirche zu bekämpfen. Sie sollte auch nicht durch staatliche Manipulationen in ihrem äußeren Bestande erschüttert werden. Es ging vor allem darum, das seit Konstantin dem Großen in ganz Europa traditionelle institutionelle Band zwischen Thron und Altar zu lösen. Der Staat streifte seine konfessionelle Bindung ab. Die Kirche verlor ihre Bevorzugung, gewann allerdings erstmals in ihrer Geschichte volle Freiheit und Verantwortung auch für ihre äußere Gestalt. Maßgeblich war also nicht eine Stimmung, wie sie mit dem Schlagwort "Cut the Connection" zum Ausdruck kommt[26]. Der Zweck der Deutschen Verfassung war, die Freiheit für alle Staatsbürger gleichmäßig zu gewährleisten. Für die Kirchen hatte das zur Folge, daß die jahrhundertelange staatliche Kirchenaufsicht aufhörte. Die Beteiligung des Staates an der Ernennung der leitenden Geistlichen verlor die ursprüngliche Bedeutung und wurde allenfalls in der Gestalt eines Verfassungseids der katholischen Bischöfe oder höflichen Anfragen, ob Bedenken bestünden, fortgeführt. Dies ist allerdings Ausdruck der Courtoisie und nicht staatlicher Hoheitsbefugnis.

Da Staat und Kirche die gleichen Menschen zu gliedern haben und auf vielfach gleichen Arbeitsfeldern ihre Tätigkeit entfalten (Schule, Kindergarten, Krankenhaus, Altersheim) und da die Staatsbürger das Recht haben, auch in staatlichen abgeschlossenen Anstalten ihre Religionsfreiheit zu pflegen (Krankenhaus, Armee, Gefängnis), bedarf es der Absprache, damit staatliche und kirchliche Behörden sich nicht in die Quere kommen und der Staat, womöglich ohne es zu wollen, Religions- und Kirchenfreiheit verkürzt. Solange der Staat die Kirchenaufsicht innehatte, konnte mancherlei auf dem inneren Dienstwege geregelt werden. Die rechtliche Selbständigkeit beider Institutionen macht entgegen der Vermutung des ersten Anscheins Absprachen in einem viel höheren Maße erforderlich, als sie es vorher gewesen waren. Das ist der Grund, warum in Deutschland seit 1924 zahlreiche Verträge mit der römisch-katholischen Kirche und den evangelischen Kirchen, später auch mit kleinen Religionsgemeinschaften geschlossen worden sind. Hier geht es nicht zuletzt darum, die Zusammenarbeit auf solchen Gebieten zu regeln, welche für beide Seiten von Interesse sind. Für einige solche Fragen hat die Verfassung selbst die Zusammenarbeit vorgesehen und geregelt. So für den Religionsunterricht, der gemäß Art. 7 GG in allen öffentlichen Schulen (mit bestimmten Ausnahmen) nach den Grundsätzen der respektiven Religionsgemeinschaft als staatlicher Unterricht zu erteilen ist. Für die Theologischen Fakultäten gibt es Regelungen in den Landesverfassungen, vor allem aber in den Kirchenverträgen, wie der Staat die Kirchen bei der Berufung von Theologieprofessoren, welche ja zugleich staatliche und kirchliche Funktionen wahrnehmen, beteiligt. Schließlich gibt es Abmachungen über die Anstaltsseelsorge in Armee, Gefängnissen und Krankenhäusern. Entscheidend ist, daß alle diese Rechte natürlich von den Kirchen, denen ein Großteil der Bevölkerung angehört, insbesondere wahrgenommen werden können, daß rechtlich aber andere Religionsgemeinschaften gleiche Möglichkeiten haben. Daß die Muslime von dem Recht der Kirchensteuererhebung und des Religionsunterrichts bislang keinen Gebrauch gemacht haben, hängt mit ihren internen Problemen zusammen. Sie haben Schwierigkeiten, sich selbst zu organisieren, da sie von Hause aus eine migliedschaftliche Organisationsform nicht kennen, der Staat verständlicherweise aber nicht darauf verzichten kann zu erfahren, wer denn der Religionsgemeinschaft angehört, die Rechte für sich beansprucht.

Das deutsche System ist für unseren Zusammenhang dadurch charakterisiert, daß es die rechtliche Selbständigkeit in optimaler Weise mit der Bereitschaft zur Zusammenarbeit der Institutionen von Staat und Kirche auf vielfältigen Gebieten verbindet, zum Teil regelt. Staat und Kirche gehen dabei davon aus, daß Religionsfreiheit und Trennung von Staat und Kirche gleichermaßen Distanz und Zusammenarbeit erforderlich machen.

In diesen Zusammenhängen treten die Bischöfe wieder in Erscheinung: Sie sind die natürlichen Sprecher der Kirche, und die Autorität des Bischofsamtes ermöglicht manche Kontaktaufnahme, die sonst schwieriger wäre. Innerkirchlich sind Bischöfe nach evangelischem Verständnis allerdings keineswegs Alleinherrscher, sondern stehen in einer Reihe mit anderen landeskirchlichen Leitungsorganen, wie der Synode, einem die Synode vertretenden Hauptausschuß, der kirchlichen Verwaltungsstelle, einem (oft Kirchenleitung genannten) Organ, das die anderen Organe zusammenfaßt. Der Landesbischof spricht für sie alle. Staatskirchenrechtliche Verträge sehen vielfach vor, daß Staat und Kirche etwa auftauchende Probleme gemeinsam in freundschaftlichem Geiste zu lösen bereit sind. Dazu sind regelmäßige Kontakte und Besprechungen vorgesehen, auch Antrittsbesuche neuer Amtsinhaber.

Nicht zuletzt das öffentliche Erscheinungsbild läßt erkennen, daß die Kirchen sich zwar vielfach wie große Verbände verhalten, in dieser Rolle aber nicht aufgehen. Im Unterschied zu Verbänden ist ihre Stellung in der Verfassung selbst geregelt, nicht wie früher im Interesse der christlichen Wahrheit, sondern heute im Interesse der staatsbürgerlichen Freiheit, welche alle Staatsbürger genießen. Für die Kirche ergeben sich in der säkularen Gesellschaft dabei bedeutende Möglichkeiten des Wirkens.

Geblieben ist von den Erschütterungen des Kirchenkampfes vor allem die verbreiterte Anerkennung des Bischofsamtes als eines Faktors evangelischen kirchlichen Lebens und Verfassungsrechts. Sie spiegelt sich in der Annahme des Bischofstitels in Württemberg und Bayern[27] und in der Nachkriegsliteratur zum Bischofsamt wider[28]. Was nun folgte, war - aus kirchenrechtlicher Sicht - im wesentlichen der Ausbau des gewonnenen Rechtszustandes und die systematische Bestimmung des Verhältnisses des Bischofsamtes zu anderen Leitungsämtern.

---

[1] Zum Verständnis der Ordination (oder Weihe) Amsdorfs als Bischof von Naumburg durch Luther vgl. P. Brunner, Nikolaus von Amsdorf als Bischof von Naumburg, S. 60 ff. In diesem Sinne äußerte sich auch Amsdorf selbst: "Denn titel, name vnd ampt thut nichts zur sache, darumb erbet die Kirche nicht auff die nachkomen, es sey denn das diese stimme vnsers lieben Hern vnd hirten Jhesu Christi mit nach folge. Darumb hilfft die opfferpfaffen gar nichts, das sie sich der Aposteln Succession rühmen, dieweil sie Successionem uerbi et doctrinae Christi nicht haben. Wenn sie aber Successionem uerbi rümen kunten, so wollten wir sie gerne für ein stück vnd theil der Christlichen Kirchen halten." So in: Antwort Glaub und Bekenntnis auff das schöne und liebliche INTERIM, Niclasen Amssdorffs des verjagten Bischoffs zur Naumburgk, in: O. Lerche (Hrsg.), Nikolaus von Amsdorff, Ausgewählte Schriften (1938) S. 50.

Die Begründung des geistlichen Amtes und damit der Ordination in der Reformationszeit sind noch nicht erschöpfend erforscht. Verdienstvolle Arbeiten liegen vor: W. Brunotte, Das geistliche Amt bei Luther (1959), E. Kinder, Der evangelische Glaube und die Kirche (2. Aufl. 1960), H. Lieberg, Amt und Ordination bei Luther und Melanchthon (1962), dazu S. Grundmann, Sacerdotium-Ministerium – Ecclesia particularis (1959) und Kirche, allgemeines Priestertum und kirchliches Amt (1962), jetzt in: Abhandlungen zum Kirchenrecht (1959) S. 156 ff. Diese Arbeiten behandeln zwar unser Problem. Sie gehen jedoch von einer überwiegend dogmengeschichtlichen, nicht eigentlich historischen Fragestellung aus. Dazu nunmehr G. Kretschmar, Die Ordination im frühen Christentum (vgl. oben Anm. 3a) und eine weitere angekündigte Arbeit über das Ordinationsverständnis der Reformation.

[2] Vgl. aus den Kirchenverfassungen: Grundordnung der Ev. Landeskirche in Baden, § 120 Abs. 1: "(1) Der Landesbischof ist der zum Dienst an der Kirchenleitung berufene Inhaber des Predigtamtes, der die Gemeinden und die Amtsträger der Landeskirche unter Gottes Wort ruft. Wie die Pfarrer die Ortsgemeinde, so leitet der Landesbischof die Landeskirche durch Gottes Wort. Er kann in allen Gemeinden der Landeskirche Gottesdienste und andere Versammlungen halten."

Verfassung der Ev.-Luth. Kirche in Bayern, Art. 59 Abs. 1: "(1) Der Landesbischof ist ein Pfarrer, der in das kirchenleitende Amt für den Bereich der Evangelisch-Lutherischen Kirche in Bayern berufen ist."

[3] Ich beziehe mich im folgenden auf v. Campenhausen, Entstehung und Funktionen des bischöflichen Amtes in den evangelischen Kirchen in Deutschland (1975) jetzt in: Gesammelte Abhandlungen 1995, S. 8 ff.

[4] "Denn eigentlich heisst ein Bischoff ein auff seher odder visitator und ein Ertzbischoff, der uber dieselbigen auff seher und visitatores ist, darumb das ein iglicher Pfarher seine pfarkinder besuchen, warten und auff sehen sol, wie man da leret und lebet. Und der Ertzbischoff solche bischove besuchen, warten und auff sehen sol, wie die selbigen leren"; (WA 26, 196, 5 ff.); vgl. ferner Tractatus de potestate et primatu papae, § 61 ff., in: Die Bekenntnisschriften der evangelisch-lutherischen Kirche (5. Aufl. 1963), S. 489 ff.; Apol. XIX; Schmalk. Art. 1 Teil III Art. X.

Die Reformation knüpfte hierbei an die frühe Kirche an, wo jede Gemeinde von einem ordinierten Bischof geleitet wurde. Ob der Bischof in der frühen Kirche tatsächlich die Aufgaben des heutigen Gemeindepfarrers wahrnahm, läßt sich nicht einheitlich beantworten. In Gegenden, wo auch kleinere Städte einen Bischof hatten, darf man wohl davon ausgehen. Für Antiochien gilt dies aber schwerlich. H. D ö r r i e s, Erneuerung des kirchlichen Amts im vierten Jahrhundert, in: M o e l l e r - R u h b a c h (Hrsg.), Bleibendes im Wandel der Kirchengeschichte (1973), S. 1 ff., 4.

[5] Alle Argumente in dem von Melanchthon verfaßten Bedenken der Wittenberger Theologen (1530), Corp. Ref. T. II Sp. 280 ff. (283, 284) und in dem gleichzeitigen Gutachten ebenda T. II Sp, 373 ff., 376. Dazu (mit ausführlichen Zitaten) L. R i c h t e r, Geschichte der evangelischen Kirchenverfassung in Deutschland (1851, Neudruck 1970), S. 62 ff., 67 ff.; grundlegend P. B r u n n e r, Vom Amt des Bischofs. Pro Ecclesia, Ges. Aufs. I (1962), S. 235 f., 259 ff.

[6] Wenn die evangelischen Kirchenordnungen des 16. Jahrhunderts diese Bedeutung von Kirchenleitung in das evangelische Kirchenrecht übernehmen, nämlich als Regierung der Kirche allein durch das göttliche Wort, so nehmen sie damit den Sprachgebrauch der vorreformatorischen Kirche wieder auf. Auch dort wurde regere ecclesiam auf die geistliche Gemeindeleitung bezogen. Deshalb auch hieß der Pfarrer ecclesiae rector. Vgl. R i c h t e r - D o v e - K a h l, Lehrbuch des katholischen und evangelischen Kirchenrechts (8. Aufl. 1886), S. 526 Anm. 7 und S. 465 ff.

[7] Vgl. dazu A. N i c o l o v i u s, Die bischöfliche Würde in Preußens evangelischer Kirche (1834); E. B e n z, Bischofsamt und apostolische Sukzession im deutschen Protestantismus (1953); P. B r u n n e r, N i k o l a u s v o n A m s d o r f a l s B i s c h o f v o n N a u m b u r g (1 9 6 1).

[8] Vgl. Melanchthon, De abusibus Ecclesiarum emendandis (1541), Corp. Ref. T. IV Sp. 542 ff. Die entscheidende Stelle ist zitiert bei R i c h t e r, Geschichte der Kirchenverfassung, S. 69.

[9] Den "bischöflichen Charakter" der Supenintendentur-Verfassung hebt E l e r t in dem gleichnamigen Aufsatz in: Luthertum 46 (1935) S. 353 stark hervor.

[10] Die Bischöfe in Schweden, Dänemark, Norwegen und Schleswig führten zeitweilig den Titel eines Superintendenten. P. B r u n n e r, Amsdorf, S. 12, hebt hervor, daß in dem Superintendentenamt die Einheit von pastor und episcopus und damit eine Entsprechung zum altkirchlichen Bischofsamt am stärksten festgehalten worden sei.

[11] WA 26, 235, 21 ff.; S e h l i n g, Bd. 1, S. 149 ff. (171).

[12] Die Vertreter des Episkopalsystems wie die frühen Kollegialisten entwickeln ihre staatskirchenrechtlichen Theorien in der Absicht, den Landesherrn in den Kirchenorganismus einzubinden, seine Kirchenfunktionen kirchlich zu erklären, aber auch sie zu begrenzen.

Martin Heckel, Staat und Kirche nach den Lehren der evangelischen Juristen Deutschlands in der ersten Hälfte des 17. Jahrhunderts (1968); Klaus Schlaich, Kollegialtheorie, Kirche Recht und Staat in der Aufklärung (1969); Ders., Kirchenrecht und Vernunftrecht. Kirche und Staat in der Sicht der Kollegialtheorie, ZevKR 14 (1968/69) S. 1 ff. Speziell zu Johann Gerhard und seiner weiterführenden Abgrenzung der geistlichen Leitung gegenüber der obrigkeitlichen Gewalt vgl. Wilhelm Maurer, Geistliche Leitung und Leitung der Kirche, in: Frör - Maurer, Hirtenamt und mündige Gemeinde (1966), S. 51 ff., 57 ff.; Martin Honecker, Cura religionis Magistratus Christiani. Studien zum Kirchenrecht im Luthertum des 17. Jahrhunderts, insbesondere bei Johann Gerhard (1968).

[13] Zum folgenden neben der o.a. Literatur insbesondere W. Maurer, Das synodale evangelische Bischofsamt, S. 8 ff.

[14] Text bei Hinschius, Das Preußische Kirchenrecht im Gebiete des Allgemeinen Landrechts. Abdruck von Theil II Titel 11 aus der achten Auflage von C.F.- Kochs Kommentar zum Allgemeinen Landrecht (1884), S. 161 ff. Im folgenden geben die in Klammern gesetzten Zahlen die Abschnittsnummern der Instruktion wieder.

[15] Darauf weist W. Maurer, Das synodale evangelische Bischofsamt, S. 8, hin.

[16] P. Schoen, aaO., S. 264

Dies war der Rechtszustand im Westen seit Einführung der Rheinisch-Westfälischen Kirchenordnung 1835, im Osten seit der Kirchengemeinde- und Synodalordnung 1873.

[17] Daß auch die Synode vielfach in Parallele zu weltlichen Parlamenten gesehen wurde, ändert daran nichts. Daß sie weder den landständischen Korporationen noch den Parlamenten vergleichbar, sondern eben kirchliche Organe waren, war von Anfang an deutlich. Das parlamentarische Mißverständnis scheint aber unausrottbar zu sein, wie die moderne Demokratisierungsforderung in den Kirchen zeigt.

Zum Verständnis und Selbstverständnis der Synode vgl. aus der Flut der Literatur S. Grundmann, Abhandlungen zum Kirchenrecht, S. 99 ff., 139 ff., 476 ff.; A. v. Campenhausen, Synoden in der evangelischen Kirche, in: Synode. Amtliche Mitteilungen der Synode der Bistümer in der Bundesrepublik Deutschland Nr. 4 (1971), S. 4 ff.; G. Heinemann, Das Verhältnis von Synode und Parlament, in: E. Lomberg (Bearbeiter), Emder Synode 1571—1971 (1973), S. 285 ff. Dagegen die wiederholte Forderung nach parlamentarisiertem Synodalverständnis bei R. v. Thadden, Kirche ohne Demokratie?, in: Böll - Gollwitzer - Carlo Schmid, Anstoß und Ermutigung. Gustav W. Heinemann, Bundespräsident 1969—1974, (1974), S. 111 ff.

[18] Das ist er in Westfalen und Rheinland bis heute geblieben, und ebenso wird das Amt des Präses dieser Kirchen begründet. "Der Präses der Landessynode ist Vorsitzender der Kirchenleitung und des Landeskirchenamtes", so Art. 200 Kirchenordnung der Ev. Kirche im Rheinland. Abgehoben davon Art. 148 Abs. 1 Kirchenordnung der Ev. Kirche von Westfalen.

[19] P. Schoen, Der deutsche evangelische Bischof nach den neuen evangelischen Kirchenverfassungen, VerwArch 30 (1925) S. 403 ff.

[20] "Die Religion in Geschichte und Gegenwart" spiegelt die kontroverse Situation wider, wenn sie noch 1927 keinen Artikel über das Bischofsamt bringt, sondern nur einen über die "Bischofsfrage". Vgl. RGG (2. Aufl.) Bd. 1 (1927) Sp. 1131.

[21] Darauf wiesen schon hin P. Schoen, Der deutsche evangelische Bischof usw., aaO., S. 406; R. Oeschey, Verfassung der ev.-luth. Kirche in Bayern r.d. Rhs. (1921) S. LV.

[22] So Frhr. von Soden in der ao. Kirchenversammlung zur Feststellung der Verfassung für die Evangelische Landeskirche der älteren Provinzen Preußens. Erster Teil, Sitzungsverhandlungen, Berlin 1923, S. 122 a. E.

Auch die Preußische Kirchenverfassung selbst gab dieser Ansicht recht, wenn sie in einer Beilegung des Bischofsnamens an die Generalsuperintendenten lediglich die Änderung der Amtsbezeichnung sieht, worauf Art. 111 (2) 6 als Möglichkeit hinweist. Zitat nach P. Schoen, aaO., -S. 405.

[23] P. Schoen, aaO., S. 414 ff.; Ders., Das neue Verfassungsrecht der evangelischen Landeskirchen in Preußen (1929), S. 165 ff.; W. Maurer, Das synodale evangelische Bischofsamt seit 1918, S. 17 ff.; Irmtraut Tempel, Bischofsamt und Kirchenleitung (1966).

[24] Nassau, Bayern, Braunschweig und Lübeck kennen eine Auskunftspflicht des Bischofs gegenüber der Synode; in Hannover und Nassau ist der Bischof der Synode gegenüber verantwortlich.

[25] Martin Heckel, Kirchenreformfragen im Verfassungssystem. Zur Befristung von Leitungsämtern in einer lutherischen Landeskirche, ZevKR 40 (1995) S. 180 ff.

[26] Colin Buchanan, Cut the Connection. Disestablishment and the Church of England, London 1994.

[27] Württembergisches Vorläufiges kirchliches Gesetz zur Ermächtigung des Kirchenpräsidenten vom 15.5.1933 (ABl. Bd. 26 S. 54; AKBl. S. 164); Bekanntmachung des Ev. Oberkirchenrats über die Amtsbezeichnung des Kirchenpräsidenten vom 8.7.1933 (ABl. Bd. 26 S. 128).

[28] Vgl. aus der kirchenrechtlich bestimmten Literatur die zum Artikel "Bischof" III und IV (Tröger), TRE Bd. VI (1980), S. 697 angeführten Schriften.

Bibelarbeit zu Markus 10, Verse 32-45

Reinhard Frieling

Den Vorschlag, Mk 10, 32-45 der Bibelarbeit heute zugrunde zu legen, habe ich gern übernommen. Er besteht aus zwei zunächst selbständigen Gesprächen und Ereignissen, die aber bei weiterem Bedenken wesentliche gemeinsame Bezüge haben: die dritte Ankündigung des Leidens und der Auferstehung Jesu, und dann aufgrund der Frage der Zebbedäus-Söhne das Problem von Herrschen und Dienen.

Im Zusammenhang unserer Konferenz über den historischen Episkopat und die Kirchenleitung kann es sich nahelegen, rasch mit unseren Fragen über den Text zu meditieren. Ich halte das prinzipiell für legitim. Doch hilfreich wird der Text erst, wenn wir zunächst durch eine historisch-kritische Exegese diese beiden Perikopen analysieren.

Vers 32

Der Gang nach Jerusalem signalisiert dem Gefolge Jesu, daß bald etwas Entscheidendes geschieht. Die Verkündigung Jesu vom Anbruch des Reiches Gottes kommt in die entscheidende Phase. Die Haltung im Gefolge Jesu wird drastisch geschildert: "sie entsetzten sich" ('έθαμβουντο) und "sie fürchteten sich" ('εφοβουντο). Eine Begründung wird nicht angegeben. War es eine unbestimmte apokalyptische Angst? War es Furcht vor gewaltsamen Auseinandersetzungen, die das eigene Leben bedrohen würden, weil man sich im Gefolge Jesu ja offensichtlich nicht auf Gewalt vorbereitet hatte? Wir wissen es nicht.

Wer waren die 'ακολουθουντες die Nachfolger Jesu? Hier ist wohl von einer größeren Gefolgschaft die Rede, die sowohl Menschen umfaßte, die aus eigenem Antrieb zum bekannten Jesus von Nazareth liefen, als auch Menschen, die Jesus eigens in seine Nachfolge berufen hatte. Von diesen forderte Jesus einigen Verzicht angesichts des unsteten Wanderlebens: z. B. die Aufgabe des bisherigen Berufs, die Lösung von Familie und Besitz. Dabei ging es jedoch nicht um ein klassisches Lehrer-Schüler-Verhältnis, wie es sonst bei den Schriftgelehrten üblich war. Die Rabbinenschüler wurden ausgebildet, um selber einmal selbständig Rabbi zu werden. Die berufenen Nachfolger Jesu blieben hingegen ihr Leben lang Jünger ihres Rabbi. Die Jesusjüngerschaft entsprach wohl eher den prophetisch-charismatischen Bewegungen, die schon im AT eine Rolle spielten (1. Kön 19, 19-21: Elia) und in der Zeit Jesu eine neue Blüte erreichten.

Das Besondere an Jesus und den Jesusnachfolgern war nun, daß Jesus zur Teilnahme an der ihm von Gott anvertrauten Aufgabe berief: zur Buße zu rufen und den Anbruch der Gottesherrschaft zu verkünden. Und jetzt beim Gang nach Jerusalem bedeutete es: Teilhabe an Jesu Weg zum Leiden, Sterben und Auferstehen. Das geht über ein Lehrer-Schüler-Verhältnis weit hinaus.

Vers 33-34

Bevor ich auf die Sonderrolle der Zwölf eingehe, möchte ich zunächst die Leidensankündigung Vers 33 - 34 kurz ansprechen. Es ist nach Mk 8, 27 - 9, 1 und Mk 9, 31-50 die dritte Leidensverkündigung Jesu. Die kleinen unterschiedlichen Akzente brauchen uns jetzt nicht zu interessieren.

Wichtig ist, daß Jesus den Gang nach Jerusalem nicht als Siegeszug einer machtvollen irdischen Gottesherrschaft sieht, sondern als "Auslieferung" an die "Hohepriester" und an "die Völker", die Heiden. Für "ausliefern" steht im griechischen Text παραδώσουσιν Es könnte sich eine Meditation nahelegen, über "paradosis/traditio" und über "Tradition und Sukzession" in diesem tieferen theologischen Sinn nachzudenken. Ich komme später darauf zurück, wenn der Zusammenhang von "Dienen" und "Teilhabe an Jesu Weg zum Kreuz" zur Debatte steht.

Jesus kündigt hier in Vers 33/34 seinen Tod an und deutet ihn als Weg zur Auferstehung. In Vers 45 kommt dann hinzu, daß Jesus selbst seinen Tod als Heil deutet, als λύτρον, (englisch "ransom", deutsch "Lösegeld") für viele. Die Exegeten sind sich einig, daß Vers 45 in dieser Form eine Bildung der späteren christlichen Gemeinde im semitisch-palästinensischen Bereich darstellt. Λύτρον meint die Befreiung eines Gefangenen oder Sklaven, der durch Schuld sein Leben zum Todesurteil verwirkt hat. In diesem Sinne Jesu Tod soteriologisch zu deuten, ist gewiß kein Widerspruch zur Verkündigung Jesu, die das Gesamt von Leiden, Tod und Auferweckung als das eschatologische Ereignis der angebrochenen Gottesherrschaft verstand. Die Anlehnung an Jes 53 mit dem Lied vom leidenden Gottesknecht ist unverkennbar.

Diese Hinweise auf das Geschehen in Jerusalem mögen genügen. Ich muß jetzt noch darauf zurückkommen, daß Jesus diese Leidensverkündigung nach dem Markus-Evangelium nicht groß vor dem ganzen Gefolge erläuterte, sondern nur dem Kreise der Zwölf.

Die Auslegungsgeschichte war großenteils in der römisch-katholischen wie der griechisch-orthodoxen Tradition geneigt, im Zwölferkreis eine rang- und funktionsmäßig aus dem übrigen Kreis der Jesusnachfolger hervortretende Gruppe zu sehen. Tatsächlich hat Jesus hier in der Perikope wie sonst häufig die Zwölf beiseitegenommen und ihnen gesondert etwas erklärt. Auch zum Passahmahl lud

Jesus offensichtlich nur "die Zwölf" ein (Mk 14, 17 ff.) οἱ δώδεκα ohne weiteren Zusatz wie "Jünger" oder "Apostel".

Aber folgt daraus zwingend, daß Jesus mit der Berufung der Zwölf der Kirche ein hierarchisches Amt eingegliedert hat, bei dem ein besonderer Kreis von Christen im Sinne eines Klerus von den übrigen Christen abgehoben wird? Von einer besonderen Weihehandlung Jesu an den Zwölfen ist nicht die Rede; konstitutiv war nur der Ruf Jesu. Also zumindest bei Markus und den übrigen Synoptikern ist von einer besonderen Konsekration nicht die Rede.

Wenn keine Weihestufe anzunehmen ist, so wäre weiter zu fragen: legt Jesus nicht mit der Auswahl der Zwölf eine klare Ordnungsstruktur innerhalb der Jesusbewegung und dann der späteren Kirche fest? Ist hier nicht durch Jesus von vornherein so etwas wie Kirchenleitung und Episkopé vorgesehen?

Die Wahl des Matthias als Nachfolger von Judas Iskariot (Apg 1, 15ff.) könnte es nahelegen, im Zwölferkreis eine bleibende von Jesus Christus gewollte Grundstruktur der Kirche zu sehen. Aber diese Folgerung stößt an ihre Grenze, wenn wir schon in der weiteren Urgemeinde das Zwölfer-Prinzip nicht durchgehalten sehen. Mit dem Märtyrertod des Zebedaiden Jakobus (Apg 12, 2), der für das Jahr 44 angesetzt wird, endet der Zwölferkreis. Eine weitere Nachwahl findet nicht statt. Und Paulus hatte wohl schon bei seinem ersten Jerusalembesuch (ca. 35/37) die Zwölf als Leitungsgremium nicht mehr vorgefunden (Gal 1, 18 f.), während andere Auferstehungszeugen bereits den Titel "Apostel" trugen und neben Petrus vor allem der Bruder Jesu, Jakobus, eine leitende Rolle spielte.

Ich schließe mich darum der allgemeinen mir vorliegenden protestantischen Exegese an, daß die Berufung der Zwölf eine die Verkündigung Jesu für Israel veranschaulichende Zeichenhandlung bedeutete. Die Zwölferzahl ist das Symbol für die Ganzheit des Gottesvolkes der zwölf Stämme, und für Jesus war die Wahl der Zwölf Symbol für die endzeitliche Restitution des Gottesvolkes. In dem Maße, wie die Urgemeinde später zur jüdischen Häresie wurde und unter Absonderung von Tempel und Synagoge eigene Lebensformen entwickelte, brauchte sie eine eigene Organisationsstruktur, für die das Zwölfer-Symbol nicht mehr konstitutiv war.

Neben diesen Beobachtungen zur Sonderstellung der Zwölf im gesamten neutestamentlichen Zeugnis gibt gerade unsere Perikope Mk 10 noch einen besonderen Akzent. Ich formuliere zugespitzt: Neu oder bleibend konstitutiv an Jesu Organisationsprinzip war nicht eine bestimmte Organisationsform - sei sie hierarchisch oder an eine Weihe gebunden oder etwa nur Männern vorbehalten. Nein, neu und bleibend konstitutiv ist das Prinzip des Dienens!

Vers 35-45

Die Perikope Mk 10, 35-45 macht das anschaulich und eindringlich. Der Skopus ist eindeutig Vers 43: Irdische Herrschaftsstrukturen sind nicht adäquat und erst recht nicht konstitutiv für die Kirche. Wer "groß" (μέγα) sein will, soll ein Diener sein, διάκονος, und wer "erster" sein will, πρῶτος, soll δοῦλος aller sein, Diener. Knecht oder Sklave ist dafür im Deutschen die angemessene Übersetzung; "slave" steht in der englischen Bibel.

Das sind in Jesu Mund stärkere Worte als beispielsweise "minister", was ja ursprünglich auch "Diener" heißt, im politischen Bereich aber ein Titel für die staatliche Machtausübung und im angelsächsischen Sprachgebrauch terminus technicus für das geistliche Amt ist. Diese Sprache macht deutlich, wie zweideutig es ist, wenn immer wieder in Gesellschaft und Kirche im Namen des Dienens Macht ausgeübt wird, und wenn umgekehrt - sicher guten Gewissens - Machthaber betonen, daß sie nur dienen. Wieviele Könige und absolute Herrscher haben sich gern "erste Diener des Staates" genannt und im Namen des Dienens für die Staatsräson die Untertanen beherrscht und unterdrückt - also genau das getan, was Jesus Vers 42 im Blick hat!

Im kirchlichen Bereich müssen wir uns genau dieser Frage stellen. Der schöne Titel "servus servorum dei" wurde rhetorisch geschickt von Papst Gregor dem Großen als päpstlicher Hoheitstitel gewählt, um dem Patriarchen von Konstantinopel entgegenzutreten, der sich den Titel "ökumenischer Patriarch" zugelegt hatte. Mit Bezug auf Mk 10, 43 stellte der Papst sich als Diener aller vor - und somit eben gerade als der "Erste". Ich halte diese Wortspiele für eine fatale Wirkungsgeschichte unserer Perikope.

Wir müssen nun wieder in Mk 10 an den ersten Teil mit der Leidensankündigung anknüpfen und Jesu Antwort an Jakobus und Johannes bedenken. "Dienen" heißt im geistlichen und theologischen Sinn: Teilhabe an Jesu Dienst, wie er sich im Gang zu Leiden, Sterben und Auferweckung vollzieht.

Vers 38: "Könnt ihr den Kelch trinken, den ich trinke?" fragt Jesus, und Jakobus und Johannes sagen: "Ja, das können wir" (Vers 39). Gemeint ist der Märtyrertod, der von Jakobus bezeugt ist (Apg 12, 2), von Johannes nicht.

Ποτήριον ist schon im AT (in der Septuaginta) der Kelch, den Gott reicht und der mit Zorneswein gefüllt ist. Er bedeutet Unheil, Leiden und Tod. Später wurde wie in Mk 10 ποτήριον ein Bild für Leiden und Tod eines Märtyrers.

Das parallele Bild von der Taufe ist hier gleichbedeutend mit "Kelch" und Märtyrertod. Sonst begegnet diese Taufbedeutung im NT nicht. In Röm 6 verbindet Paulus die Taufe mit dem Tod Jesu, aber das hat doch einen anderen

Sinn als das leibliche Martyrium: es ist die Taufe als Tod des Alten Adam durch Untertauchen und Reinigen von allen Sünden. Gemeinsamer Bezugspunkt von "Kelch" und "Taufe" ist die Teilhabe am Gang Jesu durch den Tod hindurch zur Auferstehung.

Etliche Ausleger sagen, in der Urgemeinde habe es also zwei Weisen der bevorzugten Teilhabe an Jesu Weg gegeben: zum einen das Martyrium von Christen und zum andern die sakramentale Gemeinschaft in der Taufe und im Abendmahl durch den Kelch und das Brot.

Eine besondere Pointe unserer Perikope lautet nun, daß selbst der Märtyrertod nicht besondere Rangstufen im Reiche Christi beschert (in der "Herrlichkeit Jesu", heißt es Vers 37). Wem es vergönnt ist, zur Rechten oder zur Linken Jesu zu sitzen, bleibt in Vers 40 völlig offen.

Die verärgerte Rückfrage der übrigen zehn Jünger wird von Jesus dann mit dem radikalen Dienen beantwortet. Vers 45 bringt inhaltlich zum Ausdruck, worum es geht: Dienen wie Jesus, das heißt radikal für andere da zu sein, bis zur Preisgabe des eigenen Lebens. Wie etwa der Sklave die Gäste bei Tisch bedient und nichts für sich selbst nimmt, sondern ganz für die Gäste da ist, so soll der handeln, der der "Erste" oder der "Größte" sein will oder sein soll in der Kirche als der Christusgemeinschaft.

Nach diesen exegetischen Bemerkungen komme ich auf die Eingangsfrage zurück, ob diese Perikope etwas zu unserem Tagungsthema "Episkopé und Kirchenleitung" beiträgt. Ich meine "nein" und "ja".

1. "Nein", sofern wir fragen, ob die Berufung der zwölf Jünger und ob ihre Sonderstellung in der Nähe Jesu etwas bleibend Gültiges für unsere Kirchenverfassungen und Amtsstrukturen hergibt. Das Priesteramt oder das Bischofsamt lassen sich als notwendige Struktur nicht unmittelbar aus der Wahl der Zwölf ableiten. Wenn wir Pfarrer und Episkopen für wichtig oder unerläßlich halten, müssen wir sie anders begründen.

   Aus unserer Perikope ist auch nicht zu begründen, daß Menschen, die in besonderer Weise an der Sendung Jesu teilhaben, hierfür eine sakramentale Konsekration brauchen und dann so etwas wie einen besonderen ontologischen Status haben, wie er beispielsweise in der Rede von einem besonderen Amtscharisma und einem character indelebilis zum Ausdruck kommt, die durch den Akt der Ordination zuteil werden. Eine Theologie, die das lehrt, findet das jedenfalls nicht synoptisch begründet. Wie es sonst in Schrift und Tradition begründet sein mag, kann ich jetzt nicht erörtern. Ich deute nur an, daß ich persönlich mit der reformatorischen Tradition in der Urkirche das Amt der Verkündigung und Kirchenleitung nur funktional als Teilhabe an der Sendung

Jesu Christi begründet sehe, nicht ontologisch durch besondere Weihen, welche die Person des Amtsträgers neu qualifizieren.

2. "Ja" sage ich zur Bedeutung unserer Perikope für die Ausübung jedes Amtes in der Kirche, wie immer es begründet oder strukturiert ist. Die Dimension des Dienens, wie sie hier von Jesus gefordert wird, bezieht sich freilich nicht nur auf die ordinierten Amtsträger in der Kirche, sondern ist eine Grundkategorie der christlichen Existenz.

Diese darf und soll freilich bei den Repräsentanten der Nachfolger Jesu Christi in besonderer Weise spürbar und erkennbar sein. Hier liegt die Anfrage unserer Perikope an all unsere Ämter und Dienste in der Kirche.

Wem dienen wir, wenn wir in der Ökumene uns oft weniger mit dem Kampf gegen Schuld und Sünde befassen als mit Fragen der Kirchenverfassung und der vollen gegenseitigen Anerkennung und Versöhnung? Der beste Dienst, den ich mir aufgrund von Mk 10 von dieser Konferenz erhoffe, besteht darin, daß wir alle als anglikanische und protestantische Christen, als Pfarrer und als Bischöfe sowie als Kirche insgesamt uns als διάκονοι und δοῦλοι Christi verstehen, "acknowleged and reconciled" durch Christus und untereinander als Kirchen.